Savage Money

Studies in Anthropology and History

Studies in Anthropology and History is a series which develops new theoretical perspectives, and combines comparative and ethnographic studies with historical research.

Edited by James G. Carrier, University of Durham, UK

Associate editors: Nicholas Thomas, The Australian National University, Canberra and Emiko Ohnuki-Tierney, University of Wisconsin, USA.

This book is part of a series. The publisher will accept continuation orders which may be cancelled at any time and which provide for automatic billing and shipping of each title in the series upon publication. Please write for details.

C. A. Gregory

Savage Money

The Anthropology and Politics of Commodity Exchange

h● harwood academic publishers
ap
Australia • Canada • France • Germany • India • Japan • Luxembourg
Malaysia • The Netherlands • Russia • Singapore • Switzerland

OPA (Overseas Publishers Association) N.V. Published by license under the Harwood Academic Publishers imprint, part of The Gordon and Breach Publishing Group.

First published 1997
Second printing 2000

Amsteldijk 166
1st Floor
1079 LH Amsterdam
The Netherlands

BRITISH LIBRARY CATALOGUING IN PUBLICATION DATA
Gregory, C. A.
Savage Money:
the anthropology and politics of commodity exchange. –
(Studies in anthropology and history; v. 21)
1. Money 2. Economics – Sociological aspects
I. Title
332.4

ISBN 90-5702-092-0

To

Judy, Polly and Melanie

Contents

List of Figures

List of Tables

List of Maps

Preface

This book has been a long time in the making and I have incurred many debts. They begin with Alfred and Simeran Gell who introduced me to Bastar District, India. I first went there in 1981 for a few weeks and returned a year later for an extended fieldtrip as part of Alfred's project on rural marketing in Bastar. This research was funded by the then SSRC (Social Science Research Council) of the UK. This funding gave me a two year (1982–83) research fellowship in the Department of Anthropology at the London School of Economics (LSE) and enabled me to spend 13 months in India learning Hindi and conducting field research. I am very grateful to these institutions for their support, to Alfred and Simeran for their friendship and generosity, and to my former colleagues at LSE for providing such a lively intellectual climate in which to work.

Prior to taking up the LSE fellowship I was a research fellow at Clare Hall, Cambridge, where my colleagues helped me in many ways. I am particularly grateful to Polly Hill who has taught me much about agrarian relations in the areas of India and Africa where she has worked. John Harvey suggested that *Savage Money* would be a good title for a book many years ago; however, it was only after I had written the first draft of this book that I recalled his suggestion and realised that *Savage Money* would be a fitting title.

In India I was based in the small market town of Kondagaon where I met countless people who were extremely generous with their time and assistance. I am indebted to our Dewangan, Dureja and other neighbours in Sargipalpara, the Muslim, Gujerati, Punjabi and Marwari shopkeepers in the main street, and the many merchants both big and small in the weekly markets who fed me, talked to me, and travelled with me to the many markets in the local area. I am particularly indebted to Mali Guruji who taught me about village life in the Bare Dongar area. Particular mention must also be made of Jaidev Baghel, the founder of the *Paramparik Bastar Shilpi Parivar* (The Bastar Aboriginal Artisans Association) of Bhelwapadapara, Kondagaon. He was my host on a return visit to Bastar in the long vacation of 1989–90. Jaidev's thoughts and practices have enabled me to appreciate, in a concrete way, some of the merits and problems of the Subaltern Studies approach to Indian studies. In Delhi Sunanda Sen, Ravi Chopra and Jo McGowan looked after me and my family, providing us with much material as well as intellectual sustenance.

In 1984 I took up a position as lecturer in Anthropology at the Australian National University (ANU). The Faculties Research Fund financed two short trips to India in the long vacations of 1985–86 (when I went to Rajasthan to follow up some family connections of Bastar-based merchants) and 1989–90 when I was finally able to return to Bastar. The pressures of teaching a range of new courses meant that my manuscript on the Bastar marketing system had to be confined to the bottom drawer. It stayed there for some time as I struggled to come to terms with the ethnographic literature on Indian society and the theoretical implications of the *Subaltern Studies* approach, the first volume of which came out in 1982. My thinking on this matter has been influenced by my colleague Ranajit Guha, the founder of the school. Ranajit and I have spent many hours discussing Indian society and culture and I have learned a great deal from him. I have also benefited from comments made by my colleagues at ANU who have given me much to think about as I presented various sections of this book at seminars over the years. Don Gardner and Leslie Devereaux have provided useful comments on some of the chapters. Nic Thomas read the whole manuscript through twice; his perceptive comments, and his thought-provoking writings, have enabled me to sharpen my argument.

A visiting fellowship at the Wissenschaftskolleg zu Berlin in 1994–95 enabled me to complete the final draft of this book. I am very grateful to the Rektor and his staff for the excellent working conditions provided and to colleagues Ram Guha, Hans Medick and Amit Bhaduri for comments on some of the chapters. I am also indebted to Georg Elwert, Professor of Anthropology at the Free University of Berlin, for his assistance and encouragement. He read some of the chapters and supplied me with much valuable material on the shell money of the slave trade in West Africa.

Chapters VI and VIII are reworked versions of previously published papers (Gregory, 1988 and 1989); a version of Chapter VII has recently been published (Gregory, 1996).

CHAPTER I

The Value Question

THE ARGUMENT

Although this book reports fieldwork in 'Tribal' India (Bastar District) and includes a comparative analysis of shell money use in India, readers expecting to find a conventional anthropological study of 'primitive money' will be disappointed. I have chosen the title *Savage Money* to describe the period since 15 August 1971 when President Nixon was forced to shut the gold window in order to pay for the Vietnam war. This event, which broke the 38 year-old U.S. government pledge to foreigners to convert foreign U.S. dollar holdings into gold at the fixed rate of 35:1, is one of the many that contributed to what Lash and Urry (1987) call the *End of Organized Capitalism*. Savage money, then, is my way of talking about the beginnings of disorganised capitalism. Nixon's wild dollar is the key symbol of this era. It signifies a decline in the power of the State to tame the forces of the market and a growing distrust among citizens of the world in the capacity of the State to act morally.

The U.S. government was the principal organiser of the post-war era of organised capitalism, a role it took over from the British government. The sign of any imperial organiser is the domestication of special commodities, such as gold bullion, silver bullion, or cowrie-shells, and the creation of a national standard of value that is convertible into gold at a fixed rate; in other words, the creation of token money that is as good as gold. This applies as much to world powers such as the U.S. as to regional powers such as the eighteenth century Dahomey slave state. World standards of value are, of course, the standards of the dominant imperial power and when this political power begins to wane so too does the standard. One economic consequence of the Vietnam war, the most expensive in world history, was that gold quite literally escaped from Fort Knox. The U.S.

government lost its power to domesticate gold and the so-called 'invisible hand' of the world market took control. Nixon's action on the 15 August 1971, a highly symbolic one to be sure, marked the beginning of an era of monetary history that has few parallels in recent world history. Rarely has the value of gold, the supreme commodity from the beginning of commercial time, been able to vary freely on the world market for so long. For example, the value of the pound sterling was pegged to gold at a rate of £3.89 per ounce from the beginning of the eighteenth century to the First World War. The price then went wild for a brief time in the aftermath of the War. The price of gold rose to a height of £5.68 in 1920 but was eventually domesticated at £4.25 in 1925 by a state that had lost the power to maintain it at this rate. The subsequent rise in the U.K. price of gold—£7.10 in 1935, £8.60 in 1945, £12.55 in 1955, £14.60 in 1971—can be read as an index of the decline of the political power of the British Empire[1] just as the fixity of the U.S. dollar price of gold over the same period can be read as an index of the relative strength of U.S. imperial power.

Gold, then, has escaped the domesticating forces of imperial powers for the longest period of time in hundreds of years—since 1497 to be precise[2]—and has resumed its free commodity form. The world money markets have, as a result, gone wild. They have become casinos where the big players gamble billions. Free market anarchism,[3] with its one-dollar, one-vote democracy, is in the ascendancy; its enemy, statism, is in the decline as evidence of the tyranny and corruption of the modern nation-state accumulates. The values of the free market are celebrated as never before. They have become the standard by which all others are analysed and judged. These values have not only permeated every nook and cranny of the globe, they are also dissolving the institutions of the old welfare state as water, sewerage, electricity, health, education, and the like are privatised. Not even the academy has escaped this commodification process. In Australia and England, for example, the language of the market has swept throughout universities bringing about many changes in the daily life of academics. The social and economic policies of President Reagan, Prime Minister Thatcher and President Yelstin, implemented in the name of democracy and freedom, are the basis of this trend and these free market anarchist values are being enthusiastically embraced by political leaders in nations the world over.

The decline in the relative power of the state has coincided with a rapid rise in ethnic violence as minority groups struggle for power and recognition. The violence and terror between ethnic groups has reached such a level of intensity in the world today that some commentators argue it 'is beginning to rival the spread of nuclear weapons as the most serious threat to world peace that the world faces' (Maynes, 1993: 5). The various calls to nationalism and ethnicity are idioms created in a larger realm of political actions. 'Politicians in the Balkans and in other nations of the former Soviet Union,' the anthropologists Desjarlais and Kleinman (1994: 9) argue, 'have cynically and murderously manipulated the ideas of ethnic dispute and nationalist threat in order to provide a new charter for old systems of power.' Nagengast (1994: 11), in his review of anthropological responses to these developments, has identified the paradox at the heart of the matter.

> Since the Berlin Wall fell in 1989, twenty-two new global communities have been created, fifteen from the remains of the Soviet Union alone. There are over fifty ethnic conflicts now taking place, mostly within the confines of diverse nation-states—a veritable explosion of violence with the state lending the force of arms to one side or the other... At the same time there is an apparently contradictory trend, namely the globalization of capitalist economy and culture. These two trends—the fragmenting of illusory nation-states and the simultaneous homogenisation of culture—may only appear contradictory; the latter may be driving the former.

The era of savage money, then, is not only marked by the victory of the values of free market anarchism over statism, but also by the simultaneous emergence of divided cultures from the fragmented remains of once unified societies. These changes are mirrored in the academy where the language of *culture* and *identity* has replaced that of *society* and the *individual* as the key terms in a new post-modern debate.[4] The rise of American cultural anthropology at the expense of British social anthropology has not just shifted the focus of attention away from the explanation of the functioning of society to the interpretation of cultural diversity, it has transformed the nature of anthropological inquiry itself. 'The 1960s at Chicago,' notes Geertz, (1995: 114) 'redefined anthropology by placing the systematic study of meaning, the vehicles of meaning, and the understanding of meaning at the very center of research and analysis: to make anthropology, or anyway cultural anthropology, a hermeneutical discipline.' 'What looked once to be a matter of finding out whether savages could distinguish fact from fancy,' he noted elsewhere (Geertz, 1983: 151), 'now looks to be a matter of finding out how others, across the sea or down the corridor, organize their significative world.' This culturalist approach has been energetically developed by a younger generation of American anthropologists in the 1980s who see the *commodity* as a universal cultural form that has a social life and a biography.[5] Society, then, is no longer conceived of as an institutional form but as a reified attribute of things; the problem is no longer one of constructing social types but that of deconstructing cultural collages. Some critics of this post-modern trend in anthropology have noticed that this new approach has flourished in the conservative era of Thatcherism and Reaganism; but they also note that there is no reason why these new modes of thought should necessarily be seen as conservative (Keesing, 1994: 307). Is this new definition of anthropology a creative response to the era of savage money or an expression of it? Questions like this have no simple answer but they must be continually raised and debated if the critical humanist tradition of anthropological thought is to survive and develop.

An anthropological inquiry must begin with unity, not difference. Furthermore, this unity must be an historically informed anthropological argument, not a psychological assumption about the 'psychic unity of mankind'[6] or an argument from biological anthropology about the distinguishing characteristics of human beings.[7] The forgoing argument about savage money is my premise. Historico-anthropological premises of this kind are, of course, questionable. As such, any conclusions drawn from them are also doubtful. This doubt is of the pre-Cartesian humanist kind rather than of the Cartesian mathematical variety. The former arises from dialectical questioning of a type that may lead to rival cognitions and unresolvable antagonisms. Cartesian doubt, by way of contrast, is eliminated by the assumption of an ahistorical axiom. Historico-anthropological premises have a planned obsolescence because they require constant revision in the light of new historical conditions.

While such premises are useless for a mathematician, they are the essence of anthropology. Mathematics, the study of dead forms, must begin with axioms; anthropology, the study of living human beings, must begin with history.

The economic polity of the world today is of such complexity that it lies beyond the comprehension of any scholar; so too for that matter is the economic polity of a village or even a household, as Paul Radin reminds us.[8] However, it is not only possible to gain some understanding of the values that people invent to make sense of the world, it is imperative that we do so. Values describe and prescribe. Our parents and grandparents created the values which we live by, while we, as parents, create the values we expect our children to live by. People, then, are both subjects and makers of the values that guide human actions and influence human destiny. The value problem arises because people have different values and those of the dominant usually, but not always, triumph at the end of the day. For any given historical period and region, then, a limited range of values are in the ascendancy. These values give a time and a place its recognisable cultural unity.

The values of the free market anarchists are in the ascendancy in the world today. Their reach is global even if they are not everywhere accepted. As such the cultural unity they give rise to is historically specific rather than universal. These values are seen as good by those in power whereas statism is increasingly seen as bad. Thus, in the realm of economic policy, it is the Friedmanites who have the ear of the minister today, not the Keynesians. The institution of the Market, not the State, is the favoured means of achieving freedom, liberty and equality at the end of the twentieth century. It has not always been this way. When the word 'state' first appeared in sixteenth century Europe its value was positive because it offered a way to organise populations in secular, non-pluralist terms. But four centuries and many abuses later, Desjarlais and Kleinman, (1994: 9) note, 'many now tend to think of the state as something innately repressive and evil.' If the U.S. dime has two sides, with 'heads' symbolising the power of the state that makes *tokens* and 'tails' the market that converts money into a *commodity* with a price,[9] then the savage dime has a bias that makes tails the better bet today. Moreover, the coin is not only being spun at Wall Street and other major financial centres but also in the towns and villages of the world. Even the Trobriand Islands, which anthropologists like to represent as a money-free zone, has its spinners. The university educated Trobriander of today has not given up the values of *kula* exchange but has acquired those of the international businessman. *Kula* is now done at the weekends in Port Moresby with the aid of Mercedes Benz cars; during the week deals are struck with European and Asian businessmen for the sale of gold, timber and other natural treasures of Papua New Guinea. On the island itself villagers, as we shall see in the next chapter, make sharp distinctions between gift values and commodity values, have developed rituals and ideologies to express these differences, and constantly switch between them according to pragmatic needs.

My subject is *standards of value* rather than money as such. Books that begin with a definition of money eliminate the most interesting question the subject poses, that of how different people define money to suit the pragmatic needs of the specific situations they find themselves in.[10] The various definitions of money that emerge from these different situations all raise the general question of value because to define money in one way or other is always to adopt a standard of value of some sort. But how many standards of value are there? How are they related? What are the political implications of rival conceptions? My aim is to approach these questions concretely by means of an analysis of the way certain people value certain material objects in an era of savage money. The objects I consider are farmland, rice, Indian rupees (Rs), U.S. dollars ($), cowries, silver, and gold. Even though I report fieldwork done in central India, this book is not an ethnography in the conventional sense of the term. The data I present is partial rather than holistic, multi-sited rather than village-based, multi-timed rather than ethnographically present, compared, contrasted and generalised rather than specified, particularised and differentiated.[11] In other words, I present my case material in the form of exemplars using an historically informed comparative method to elucidate a general argument. This, as I see it, is the essence of historical anthropology. As a method it differs from that of anthropological history[12] which is concerned with an in-depth temporal study of one local area. I make no claim for the superiority of the method I have adopted because, in my opinion, the choice of a method is governed by the problem in hand.

Approaching the question of value in this way has its problems but these are not those in which the old debates have been framed: 'tribe' versus 'peasant', 'peasant' versus 'capitalist', 'class' versus 'caste', and so on. The value perspective enables one to dissolve, rather than resolve, the problems posed by these categories. It does this by posing new problems in a different theoretical language. Values involve both the *is* and the *ought*, the fact and the norm. Values determine the question posed, the mode of description, the evaluation of that description, and the normative judgements that follow. Values are often equated with *ought*, the norm or moral, and separated from *is*, the fact. I do not see it this way. For me fact and norm are parts of a dialectical unity mediated by value, something I will elaborate on in the next section of this chapter.

My antithesis is free market anarchist values. I question the explanatory adequacy of anarchist theories and their tendency to subordinate *is* to *ought* in the advocacy of their case.[13] While I provide some evidence to back up these assertions, my main concern is to be positive rather than negative, to argue my own thesis rather than counter someone else's.

My thesis has *alternate* values as its thematic content. I am not concerned to defend statism as against anarchism but, rather, to *affirm* the coevalness of rival value systems and to ponder the implications of this for an anthropologically informed theory of value. Anthropology's great contribution to the history of value theory has been to record, and to a certain extent celebrate, the existence of alternate value systems. If the values analysed by the statists and the anarchists can be said to those associated with the institution of the Market and the State, then the alternate values described in the ethnographic archive are those associated with the House. If political economy has been concerned to analyse the implications of the general principle that to make a profit one must buy cheap and sell dear, then anthropologists have been concerned with the implications of what Nelson (1969) calls the 'Deuteronomic double standard', the idea that you *Take profits from the Other*[14] *not thy Brother*. The notion of the House, like that of the State and the Market, is an abstraction from a wide variety of historical and geographical forms; but what differentiates the values associated with the institution of the House is that they spring from *reciprocally recognised* relations of consanguinity, affinity, and contiguity. The content of such values is a matter for historical and anthropological investigation, as are the rival cognitions that result from *asymmetrical recognition*.

I am not concerned to celebrate the alternate values associated with the House but, rather, to subject them to critical analysis. These values divide, in the first instance, into *superalternate* and *subalternate* values. The former are those of the master, the landlord, the husband, and the parent; the latter the values of the slave, the tenant, the wife, and the child. Because a parent is necessarily also a child of another and contingently the master or slave of yet others, these binary concepts do not define an unambiguous ethnographic classification. Nor do they define a 'continuum', the favoured image of the anthropologist opposed to binary thought of the kind I will use, and defend, in this book. A person is never 'half' a slave, although it is possible for a relatively well off slave to be the master of another as the history of Mali illustrates.[15]

People create multiple value systems for themselves and are constantly *switching*[16] between them according to the dictates of the moment. Sometimes these dictates are principled, sometimes unprincipled. Human beings are never trapped in a single set of values and this applies as much to a Rockefeller as it does to an Ongka in the highlands of Papua New Guinea. The latter is able to distinguish between money-values and gift-values as well as the former, but it is one thing to know that profits are made by buying cheap and selling dear but quite another to put these values into practice. Switching, then, has its limits. You have to choose your ancestors carefully if you want to make money and to give gifts like a Rockefeller.

To affirm the coevality of rival value systems is to assert the primacy of *commonplace contradiction*.[17] This contradiction may be antagonistic or non-antagonistic. In Indian logic the opposition between the mongoose and the cobra is the image used to illustrate antagonistic contradiction (Stcherbatsky, 1962: 407). These two animals are natural enemies and when one strays onto the territory of the latter a deadly battle invariably ensues in which the mongoose usually, but not always, wins.[18] Contradiction of this kind holds generally rather than universally, that is, within historical and geographical bounds rather than eternally and everywhere. Commonplace contradiction of this kind lies at the heart of Guha's (1983a) theory of peasant insurgency where the 'mongoose' takes the three-headed form of *sarkar, sahukar* and *zamindar*, government, money-lender, and landlord. An example of a non-antagonistic commonplace contradiction is the opposition between the eaglehawk and the crow found in Australian Aboriginal thought (Radcliffe-Brown, 1958). Non-antagonistic contradiction is much discussed in anthropological circles, antagonistic contradiction hardly at all. Dumont's (1980a) theory of caste, for example, has non-antagonistic contradiction as its centrepiece. He contrasts this with *axiomatic contradiction*—the idea that nothing is both, say, a snake and a not-snake—which he claims is at the heart of 'Western' thought. The fact is that *commonplace contradiction* and *axiomatic contradiction* are coeval both in 'Western' thought and in 'non-Western' thought; thinkers like Dumont deny this coevality. Fabian's (1983) critique of this style of anthropological thinking issues a challenge that must be confronted. According to him (1983: 29–30),

> the idea of Physical Time is part of a system of ideas which includes space, bodies, and motion. In the hands of ideologues such a time concept is easily transformed into a kind of political physics. After all, it is not difficult to transpose from physics to politics one of the most ancient rules which states that it is impossible for two bodies to occupy the same space at the same time. When in the course of colonial expansion a Western body politic came to occupy, literally, the space of an autochthonous body, several alternatives were conceived to deal with that violation of the rule. The simplest one, if we think of North America and Australia, was of course to move or remove the other body. Another one is to pretend that space is being divided and allocated to separate bodies. South Africa's rulers cling to that solution. Most often the preferred strategy has been simply to manipulate the other variable—Time. With the help of various devices of sequencing and distancing one assigns to the conquered populations a different Time.

To affirm coevalness is to oppose those who deny it. If Fabian (1983) is right, then my position places me at odds with many people in the profession. It gives me comfort to observe that many Fabian-type critiques of anthropology appeared simultaneously in the 1980s and 1990s. The turn to history in the works of scholars such as Wolf

(1982), Mintz (1985), Thomas (1991) and many others has established a tradition of thought with which one can identify. My own book, *Gifts and Commodities* (1982) was also part of this movement even though I did not use the language of coevality. The fact that my book was based on 'coeval' ethnographies such as Marilyn Strathern's important, but neglected, *No Money on our Skins* (1975) is further evidence that not all ethnographers deny coevality. Nevertheless, Fabian has identified a dominant theoretical value in anthropological discourse that continues to this day.[19]

Gifts and Commodities was, as the title suggests, an attempt to affirm the coexistence of gifts and commodities in colonial Papua New Guinea but, much to my astonishment, has been read by some as an attempt to do precisely the opposite. *Savage Money* attempts to develop the arguments in *Gifts and Commodities*. I reply to my critics and extend the argument by moving the ethnographic focus from Papua New Guinea to India, the conceptual focus from *gifts* and *commodities* to *commodities* and *goods*, and the methodological focus from the library to the field. I have also revised my thinking in the light of theoretical developments in the eighties. In my opinion Ranajit Guha's *Subaltern Studies* approach to Indian studies, the first volume of which appeared in 1982, is the most significant theoretical event of that decade. His work is, of course, particularly salient to someone who has carried out fieldwork in India. While Guha's thought has inspired me in the writing of *Savage Money* I have not felt obliged to follow the post-modernist direction of recent work in the Subaltern Studies school.[20] I argue for a rehabilitation of the radical humanist tradition of thought and I read the historical work of Guha, and the anthropological work of Das[21] and DaMatta,[22] as steps that lead in this direction. I am not concerned with what Guha 'really meant' and nor do I think that this is an interesting question. There are many implications of his work and these should all be pursued. He has quite literally changed the terms of debate in Indian studies and his approach to the question of value has implications that go far beyond India. Guha has replaced Dumont as the *bête noire* of Indian studies and, like it or not, he is now the *Rahu*[23] with whom anthropologists must do battle.

What, then, are the generic characteristics of those who deny coevality? From the radical humanist's perspective, they are not only the old schools of anthropological thought Fabian identified but also, somewhat paradoxically, the new 'cultural collage'[24] school who strives to affirm coevality using the language of 'cultural construction'. These culturalists speak of disjunctures and differences in the global cultural economy rather than the paramountcy of free market anarchism, of diverse cultures rather than contradictory values, of shared meanings rather than rival cognitions, of juxtaposed fragments rather than commonplace contradiction, and of the social life of things rather than human relations between people. The radical humanist does not deny the existence of shared meanings but affirms the coexistence of the rival cognitions. For example, 'Waterloo', as James (1907: 118) notes, spells a 'victory' for an Englishman but 'defeat' for a Frenchman; a peasant rebellion, notes Guha (1983a: 89) quoting Mao Tse-tung, is judged 'terrible' by the landlord class and 'fine' by the peasants. Thus affirmation of coevality, to pursue Mao's example, involves a move from the *meaning* of values such as the 'It's terrible' of the landlords to the *question* 'Is it terrible?' The analyst notes that the *answer* 'It's fine!' belongs to the peasants and that the *commonplace contradiction* between the two rival cognitions leads to *equivocation* rather than shared meaning. The next step is *evaluation* of the contradiction and, finally, to *action*, be it with pen[25] or sword. Commonplace contradiction does not imply incommensurability. To get the measure of the human values behind these contradictions one must move from an analysis of the dominant culture to the analysis of the power relations between valuers. These can only be revealed if the premises of one's analysis are concrete, that is, if the premises are anchored historically, geographically and anthropologically in pre-Cartesian doubt. General theoretical conceptions are needed for this analysis but these must not be confused with ahistorical abstractions on the one hand and ethnographic classifications on the other. Concepts are the instruments of any thought and all thinkers need them if their thought is to be clear. Post-modern anthropology has done much to rehabilitate pre-Cartesian rhetoric but the tools of pre-Cartesian *commonplace* logic are in more urgent need of rehabilitation. Just because the world we study is full of muddles and contradictions it does not mean that our theories about it should be. The muddles we are confronted with today demand the skilful use of binary logic (of the humanist kind), not its abandonment as the culturalist argues.

Notwithstanding these differences, then, the radical humanist recognises the culturalist as a worthy adversary, as one from whom it is possible to learn a great deal about the human condition and, above all, as one with whom it is necessary to debate. Indeed, of all the schools of thought that contend in the discipline of anthropology today, the culturalists of the collage school are the most deserving of critique because they have done more than most to confront the *fin-de-siècle* problems of the savage money era. The culturalist is to be distinguished from the free market anarchist. The latter has little knowledge of cultural difference and certainly no tolerance for it. They use their own unexamined values to construct a problematic notion of culture that is used as a standard by which others are judged—always negatively of course. They are so ignorant of alternative values that they do not know how ignorant they are. Nor have they any tolerance for debate. They have a universal theory of what ought to be which is very attractive to the person who likes simple solutions to the world's problems. The anarchist is unable to see that simple solutions are part of the problem. If the culturalist is the humanist's adversary on some issues, then both are united in their opposition to the free market anarchist.

Having outlined my argument in very general terms, and having signalled my intention to argue from the perspective of value theory rather than culture theory, it remains for me to define the term *value* in a little more detail as a prelude to outlining the scope and limits of this book.

WHAT IS VALUE?

Values are those invisible chains that link relations between things to relations between people. They are invisible in the sense that they are, first and foremost, forms of human consciousness that describe what is and prescribe what should be. As descriptions they clarify the relations between the reproduction of things and people in specific historical, geographical and social settings; as prescriptions they guide the actions taken to transform a found chaos into a desired order, or, what amounts to much the same thing, to reform an existing state. For a value system to operate effectively there must be a generally accepted standard of value because valuation is essentially a comparative process by which two unlike entities—be they commodities in the market, gifts in the *kula* ring, or castes in India—are compared and judged to be the same or different with reference to this standard. Standards of value are generally accepted but never universally so. This is because people are endowed with a potential, not always realised, to question the reasonableness of authoritative judgements. For the humanist, the essence of the value creation process is human consciousness. This refers to the reciprocally recognised relations between people in concrete historical, geographical, and anthropological settings. Human valuers are the means by which values exist. Material objects of use to people, such as land, rice, rupees, dollars, cowries, silver, and gold, are transformed into marked social forms such as *gifts, commodities,* and *goods,* and the process through which they acquire these values are institutions such as the Market, the House, and the State.

The House, following Rodgers (1985: 55), can be defined as a corporate body who owns an estate consisting of land, tools and livestock, and intangibles such as family stories, names, titles, religious powers, and character. This definition, an extension of Lévi-Strauss's (1984: 151-52) notion of the House to southeast Asia, applies equally to India and possibly many other places as well. What characterises the House in India is the overlap between House and Market. The bookkeeper of the Indian merchant family, for example, mixes the cost of religious rituals, dowries, and jewellery with business accounts, 'as if they were one and the same thing' (Cottam Ellis, 1991: 104). But this does not mean that these families are unable to distinguish between the valued objects that pass through their hands. A material object such as silver is now a *commodity,* now a *gift,* now a *good* depending upon the specific context of a transaction. If *commodities* are those values that arise as things pass from House to Market, then *gifts* are those values that pass between Houses and *goods* the inalienable keepsakes that are stored within a single House. 'House relics,' notes Rodgers (1985: 55), 'are crucial in this type of culture for they condense a great deal of feeling about the family's ancestry, social position, and future prospects into an observable and subjectively quite beautiful form.'

A *commodity* purchased on the Market for money acquires new values as it is stored, hidden, praised and ritually manipulated within the House where it becomes a *good.*

The distinguishing feature of the State is the token money it creates. These tokens are created by marking *commodities* such as gold, silver, copper, or paper with a sign such as $, £, ¥, Rs and recognising the product so created as legal tender within a clearly defined territory. Thus the Australian dollar only has currency in Australia, the rupee in India, and so on; but imperial monies can acquire wider currency through a combination of coercive state policy and free choice on the part of households. The aim of the State is to create a single uniform standard of value but this objective quantitative standard often does not hold in the House where state tokens may be re-marked in a multitude of visible and invisible ways as they become subject to the laws of the House. A paradox in the monetary history of the U.S., revealed by Zelizer (1994: 17), illustrates this point. She shows that while the state and the law worked to obtain a single national currency over the period 1870 to 1930, people actively created all sorts of monetary distinctions. As money entered the household its use became the subject of domestic standards of value and it was re-marked in various ways. This process converted a generalised quantitative standard into multiple specialised qualitative standards. In one case quoted by Zelizer (1994: 39) a housewife used eight tins that were labelled groceries, carfare, gas, laundry, rent, tithe, savings, and miscellaneous. Another example (1994: 71) comes from the 1909 issue of *The Ladies' Home Journal* where women are given instructions on how to disguise money given as a gift so that it would not seem like a commercial transaction. This domestic 'earmarking' of money, as Zelizer calls it, was fuelled on the one side by the consumer revolution and rising disposable incomes, and on the other by changing gender relations within the household as women struggled to gain control of the household income. As one observer put it in 1928: 'more quarrels between husband and wife have been started by the mention of money than by chorus girls, blond waitresses, dancing men with sleek hair, or traveling men' (Zelizer, 1994: 37).

To affirm the coevality of multiple standards of value, then, is to recognise the paradox of diversity within uniformity and this applies as much to the House in the U.S. as it does to the House in the colonies. The value question can be approached in one of four ways: the power *by which, from which, through which,* and *on account of which* value exists. Theories of value, themselves meta-values, can also be classified in this way. Symbolists focus on marks and their meanings, institutionalists on the formal processes of valuation, materialists on the ecology and technology of production, and radical humanists on the relations of reciprocal recognition between the valuers. Humanists do not deny the importance of the other approaches but they do see them as secondary. But they are not the only theorists who recognise the primary importance of the human valuer: the free market anarchist, the Marxist and the humanist all agree on this point. Wherein, then, lies the difference between these three approaches?

Psychology, rather than history or anthropology, is the starting point for the free market anarchist. They give primacy to the problems of choice faced by the pusher of the supermarket trolley. The focus, then, is on *individual cognition* rather than on human relations. The distinguishing feature of the classical Marxist is the focus on *class consciousness* and, in particular, on the proletarian consciousness of the factory worker. The humanist does not deny the relevance of individual cognition or class consciousness but notes the limitations of an approach to value that views the world from the perspective of the supermarket or the factory floor. The humanist anthropologist focuses on *reciprocal recognition* and, in particular, on reciprocally recognised relations of consanguinity, affinity, and contiguity. This focus of kinship, marriage, and household politics is as much an artefact of the fieldwork method as it is a philosophical standpoint. Historically speaking, anthropologists have tended to work with rural dwellers rather than urban industrial workers with the result that the site of most of their observations of human life has been the hearth rather than the supermarket or the factory floor. My own fieldwork is no exception to this general rule. Many anthropologists, Wolf (1982: 12ff) has noted, have tended to transform this methodological imperative into high philosophical principle. It is important, then, not to give a spurious primacy to the House; equally, it is important not to be fooled by the claims of the anarchists and Marxists that their perspective is somehow privileged. Anthropologists have made an important contribution to the theory of value but this can only be appreciated if the methodological limitations of the fieldwork method are seen for what they are. In what follows I will attempt to outline the distinguishing features of the anthropological approach as a prelude to developing a constructive critique of it.

The ascendancy of free market anarchism is an expression of the fact that the Market has emerged as the most politically significant institution of valuation in the world today. The State and the House are still important but less so. If the world market has colonised the globe and become transnational, then the various national states have divided and occupied every square inch of land on it. The territoriality of the House, by contrast, is local and subject to the laws of a state. Theories of value that limit themselves to a consideration of the Market and the State are, not surprisingly, the most influential theories of value today. Thus most of the debates about value usually centre on notions of *class consciousness* or *individual cognition* rather than on *reciprocal recognition*. I begin, therefore, with a discussion of the former two.

The logic of market valuation is quantitative and mathematical and it goes as follows. Suppose that one Rupee (Rs 1) can buy 1 kg of rice or 6 glass bangles. This fact can be represented as two equations of the following kind:

$$1 \text{ kg rice} \quad = \quad \text{Rs } 1 \tag{1}$$
$$\text{Rs } 1 \quad = \quad 6 \text{ bangles} \tag{2}$$

These two equations can be viewed as the premises of a syllogism that implies a quantitative exchange-ratio between the heterogenous objects of the form:

$$1 \text{ kg rice} \quad = \quad 6 \text{ bangles} \tag{3}$$

This quantitative relationship between things poses the question of the relationship of the things to the people who value them. An answer to a question of this kind is a theory of value that describes the functioning of the invisible hand of the market and prescribes what people should be doing about it.

For Marx values of the kind in equation (3) arise only when things become *commodities*. Exchange-values of this kind are the fetishised form of relations between wage-labourers and capitalists in the sphere of factory production. The invisible hand of the market belongs to the capitalist who expropriates the surplus-labour of the worker. The workers, for their part, are proletarians who are obliged to sell their own labour on the market in order to survive; these people are not free individuals, but, as the term proletarian suggests, unfree members of a propertyless class. This labour becomes embodied in *commodities* during the production process and it is the abstract form of this labour, which reduces all differences in quality to one of quantity, that enables two heterogenous things to be compared and valued.

The hidden logic of the equations above, then, is a labour valuation system that equates the hours of abstract labour required to produce the 1 kg of rice with the hours of abstract labour required to produce six glass bangles. If this amount of labour time is, say, six hours, then the heterogenous mix in equation (3) is made possible by an homogenous equality of the following kind:

$$\text{6 hours labour embodied in rice} = \text{6 hours labour embodied in bangles} \tag{4}$$

This particular form of the labour theory of value, which has its eighteenth century origins in the work of Adam Smith (1776) and its twentieth century destination in the work of Sraffa (1960), not only explains *prices*, it also explains *wages* and *profits* in terms of the historically specific mode of exploitation that is capitalism. The implication of this for Marx was not so much that surplus-labour be abolished but that its control be placed in the hands of those whose labour it was. That is, the expropriators should be expropriated and the ownership of the means of production placed in the hands of the producers.

This theory of value, then, has *class consciousness* as it ideological basis and versions of it have informed the official theory of the various nations of the Second World in the twentieth century. In the First World, by way of contrast, official theory has been informed by a radically different theory of value that rose to dominance in the 1870s at the expense of the labour theory of value. This theory has *individual cognition* as its ideological basis and its basic tenets are exemplified by the work of Milton Friedman who draws political conclusions from the theory that are as conservative as Marx's are radical.

For Friedman a relation between things, such as equation (3) above, is conceptualised using the language of *goods* rather than *commodities*. This language is highly significant because it is the mark of a radically different theory of value. It means that the market and everything associated with it, such as 'use-value', 'prices', 'wages', 'profit', are conceived of in a completely new way which reflects the move from *class consciousness* to *individual cognition*. Take the notion of 'utility' for example. This is the foundation of the whole theory for it is the balancing of marginal utilities that gives rise to exchange-ratios of the '1 kg rice = 6 glass bangles' kind. Individuals, Friedman holds, are confronted with an economic problem when their wants, which tend to be unlimited, exceed their limited means. Faced with hundreds of kilos of rice, thousands of bangles, and many other things, how does a buyer choose between the competing ends? Is the decision purely random and haphazard, in strict conformity with some customary, habitual mode of behaviour, or a deliberative act of choice? The latter, says the economist. Utility is the common something that enables two heterogenous things to be compared and valued so that a choice can be made. The act of deliberative choice means that individuals seek to maximise utility and it is the marginal utility of one good relative to another that determines how good a good really is. Should I buy half a kg of rice and 9 bangles or some other budget-constrained option consisting of more rice and fewer bangles or less rice and more bangles? The balance of marginal utilities lies at the basis of the choice because the more one has of something the smaller the marginal utility becomes. The aggregate of these choices constitutes the market signals that serve to optimise efficiency of the market system as a whole. Thus private greed leads to public good and the magic of the market brings about the transformation.

The essence of this approach is best seen in terms of the ancient paradox: Why are diamonds so much more expensive than water when water is much more useful? The classical writers such as Smith and Ricardo rejected the utility theory of value in favour of a labour theory because use-value could not explain this paradox. Friedman (1962: 39) copes with the problem by distinguishing between *marginal* utility and *total* utility: 'the marginal utility of diamonds can be very high (because diamonds are very scarce) relative to the marginal utility of water (because water is very abundant) and, in consequence, the price of diamonds can be high relative to the price of water; and yet the total utility of water can be much greater than the total utility of diamonds.' *Total utility* is what the classical economists called *use-value*, a notion whose meaning is, in this example at least, the opposite of the *marginal utility* notion that underlies the theory of goods. To discover the use-value of something is the work of history. To discover marginal utility, on the other hand, one must study the individual preferences of a consumer and the natural scarcity of the objects from which the individual has to choose; this is the work of psychology.

Thus for Friedman, the common something that lies behind the valuation process in equation (3) is marginal utility; this standard of value is based on equalities of the form

$$\text{marginal utility of rice } = \text{ marginal utility of bangles} \qquad (5)$$

An important distinction of market valuation theory is that between *money* prices and *real* prices. Equations (1) and (2) above are examples of the former, and equation (3) an example of the latter. The distinguishing feature of Friedman's approach is the missionary zeal with which he advocates the quantity theory of money approach to money price determination. The elements of this theory are extremely simple and it has won over many adherents who have been seduced by its apparent obviousness. For Friedman (1962: 245) the stock of money is one of the three main categories of capital in a place like the USA, the others being material capital, such as buildings and machines, and human beings. (Note that this positivistic conception of capital conceives of workers as a species of capital in their capacity as individual human beings and that it has nothing in common with Marx's conception of capital as a social relation between classes.) The stock, or quantity, of money is the determinant of money prices for Friedman. His argument goes as follows: 'Consider two societies which are alike except that in one there are twice as many pieces of paper, each labelled one dollar, as in the other. The only effect will be that nominal prices are twice as high in the first as in the second society. The total stream of services from the stock of money is the same in the two societies' (Friedman, 1962: 245). The policy implication for Friedman is that social welfare is maximised when the market is given an unfettered run. Governments should not intervene in the market except to ensure that the stock of money which comes off their printing presses is just sufficient to meet the growing demands of new trade. Marginal utility theory has also been used to develop more statist policy conclusions of a Keynesian type but Friedman, the guru of free market anarchism, has assumed Keynes's crown and Chicago has replaced Cambridge as the seat of the new reign.

This brief discussion of the theories of value of Marx and Friedman is sufficient to establish that what is sometimes loosely called 'Western ideology' has, at the very least, two radically different meanings. It is not a matter of materialism versus idealism but a battle of ideas that has its political expression in the wars, Cold and otherwise, that have dominated world politics for most of this century. There is, of course, the world of difference between the theory of value of a thinker and the official theory of a nation; but the fact remains that First World Nations have found Friedmanite-type theories compatible with their goals whilst Second World nations adopted some form or other of Marxism. The collapse of communism has thrown Marxist theory into crisis and unleashed a further rapid expansion of free market ideology. Not only is it rapidly conquering the former Second World, whose policy makers naively see it as the panacea to all their ills, but it is also intensifying its grip in the First World where public services such as electricity, water, sewerage, communications, and even education have been sacrificed to the ideology of the free market. Free market economists see the collapse of communism as a vindication of their advocacy of the market as the most efficient allocater of resources. Choice theory is now applied to anything and everything: family life, child rearing, dying, sex, suicide, crime, politics, ecology,—you name it, nothing is excluded. Chicago school theorists even argue for a free market in babies to overcome the problems of irregularity in adoption procedures, dismal foster care, scarcity of white babies and surplus of black babies, and excessive abortion (Wolfe, 1989: 37). This has prompted many critics to label them 'imperialists',[26] an apt term for what is at stake here is the expansion of a theory that mirrors the history of the all conquering market. The Friedmanites are free market missionaries who have a moral answer to give rather than a theoretical question to pose. Wolfe (1989) brings this out very clearly in his insightful analytical review of modern economic thought. Choice theory, he rightly notes, is based on the notion of optimality. The balance of marginal utilities in equation (5), for example, is the optimal result that comes from maximising utility subject to the constraint of a budget. 'If the notion of optimality makes little sense scientifically,' notes Wolfe (1989: 34), 'it makes a great deal of sense morally.' By upholding an ideal standard against which actual behaviour can be found wanting, the notion of optimality asserts the primacy of what ought to be over what is.

Wolfe charges Marxism with the same moral crime, arguing that the notion of 'false consciousness' does the same work as that of 'optimality'. Whatever the merits of this critique it is clear that, from an anthropological perspective, the consciousness of some Marxists is questionable. This becomes glaringly obvious when they write about the so-called 'peasantry'. Consider the words of Hobsbawn, England's greatest Marxist historian who, in his latest book, refers to the rural population of the U.S.S.R. in the 1920s as 'a collection of peasant and animal herding peoples mentally living in the Western equivalent of the eleventh century' (1994: 390). He adds:

> The only persuasive policy for the Bolsheviks, was to transform it from a backward into an advanced economy and society as soon as possible. The most obvious known way to do this was to combine and all-out offensive against the cultural backwardness of the notoriously 'dark', ignorant, illiterate and superstitious masses with an all-out drive for technological modernisation and industrial revolution (1994:376).

This passage reveals an anthropological understanding of the human condition that takes us back to the days of J. G. Frazer. It also reveals the persistence of a naive nineteenth century belief in evolutionary progress and in the ability of industry and science to deliver it. Sentiments of this kind are an expression of a consciousness informed by a labour theory of value, a theory whose vision of humanity is seen through the eyes of a factory worker in nineteenth century England. This vision is limited rather than wrong.

The same can be said of the marginal utility theorist whose image of the decision maker 'is one of a home-maker going down the aisle in the supermarket, or an investor calling a broker: both are isolated individuals acting on their own' (Etzioni, 1991: 6). The history of the theoretical journey from Marx to Friedman, then, is one from factory floor to shopping centre. If Marx's theory centres on the *proletarian* who is chained to the factory floor and from whom *commodities* are alienated, then Friedman's *individuals* are free to wander around the supermarket to buy whatever *goods* they like within the limits of their budget. The problem with both theories is that they both unjustifiably claim a privileged perspective and they both try to explain too much from that perspective; as a result, they have both expanded beyond the level of their explanatory competence. But where are the boundaries of these theories and what lies beyond them? What contribution have anthropologists made to the theory of value?

Marx's theory of value is part of a labour theory paradigm that rose to dominance in England with the publication of Adam Smith's *Wealth of Nations* (1776) and declined with the publication of Jevon's *Theory of Political Economy* (1871). The latter, in turn, marks the beginning of the rise to dominance of the utility theory, the paradigm that is still dominant today. The labour theory paradigm, more accurately termed the English factory worker's theory of value, rose to dominance at the expense of a French landlord's theory of value, Physiocracy as it is called (Schumpeter, 1954: 209ff). The latter, in turn, rose in opposition to a mercantilist theory of value which saw precious metals as the source of wealth. Thus the location of the imagined source of value has moved from the hoarder's treasury, to the landlord's estate, then to the factory floor and finally to the supermarket. These paradigm shifts are correlated with changes in technology and society. Friedman's theory is to the consumer revolution of the twentieth century as Marx's was to the industrial revolution of the nineteenth. If Friedman celebrates the individual's freedom and equality in the market place by denying the existence of inequality and power relations, then Marx riles against the authoritarian hierarchy of the industrial workplace by dismissing the freedom of the market as an illusion.

But what about the values of farmers in the colonised countries? What about those domains of human endeavour that lie outside that covered by the estate of the landlord, the factory floor of the industrialist and the shopping area owned by the limited liability company? What about the values that spring from hearth and home for example? What about the House and the relations of consanguinity, affinity and contiguity?

Enter the anthropologist.

Anthropologists have no generally accepted theory, such as 'labour' or 'utility', that epitomises their approach; but a general orientation, centred on the House, can be readily identified. The form of consciousness associated with the values of the House is not the *class consciousness* of the factory worker or the *individual cognition* of the pusher of a supermarket trolley but the *reciprocal recognition* of people concerned with the reproduction of a House. This form of consciousness creates the relations of consanguinity, affinity and contiguity that link the dead with the unborn by means of the possessions and passions of the living. When someone says 'I am your son' the speaker only becomes a relative when the addressee replies 'I am your father'. Acts of reciprocal recognition of this kind, which are always the subject of the contingencies of time, place and person, mean that parenthood is, for the anthropologist, always a cultural fact rather than a biological one. Sex is not the same as marriage, notwithstanding the correspondence that may sometimes exist between the two. Furthermore, parenthood is first and foremost the product of reciprocal recognition. A man is not a son until another man reciprocates the acknowledgement. This can be done orally by means of kinship terms but, because of the property implications in a world of *commodities*, it is now often done in writing with the State as the third party. For some people the quest for reciprocal recognition can be a life long quest as Connolly and Anderson's (1988) film *Joe Leahy's Neighbours* illustrates. Joe, the son of an Australian miner and a Papua New Guinean woman, was not recognised by his biological father. He acquired the status of son after his father died by getting his father's brother to recognise him, in writing, as an uncle.

As an exemplar of the anthropological approach to the question of value, I will now consider the work of Dumont and one of his recent critics, Veena Das. This discussion will enable me to set the scene for the argument that I want to develop.

Dumont divides the world neatly between 'us', the moderns in the First World, and 'them', the traditionals of India. 'With us modern Westerners,' says Dumont in his *Affinity as a Value* (1983: vii),

> affinity is subordinated to consanguinity, for my brother-in-law, an affine, becomes an uncle, a consanguineal relative, for my children. In other words, affinity is ephemeral, it merges into consanguinity for the next generation. As values are by definition conceived as permanent, durable, I may say that affinity is inferior to consanguinity, or *undervalued in relation to it*. Now my thesis is that the specificity of the South Indian kinship system lies in the fact that affinity there is transmitted from generation to generation, is thus permanent or durable, and so has *equal status* with consanguinity, or a value equal to it (his emphasis).

Associated with this is a Western ideology that has egalitarianism as the paramount value and an Eastern ideology where hierarchy is supreme. Underlying this opposition is another of more general application: The West values the individual, considered as a free, equal, independent, autonomous, non-social moral being, over holism where the differences between people are recognised and united into a complex whole. In the 'traditional' societies of the latter kind 'relations between men are more important, more highly valued, than the relations between men and things' (1977: 5). Thus we do not need a theory of value to reveal the relations between people that lie hidden behind the relations between things in equation (3) above because the former are laid bare for all to see.

What are these values in a 'traditional' society like India? Dumont's *Homo Hierarchicus* is devoted to answering this question. His conviction is that 'caste has something to teach us about ourselves' (1980a: 1). Caste, he shows, is a unique configuration of the relations of consanguinity, affinity, and contiguity based ultimately on the reciprocal awareness of different castes of their relative purity and impurity. This standard describes and prescribes the division of labour, the rules of marriage, and the exchange of raw and cooked food. These rules define in-groups and out-groups and value them according to the standard of Brahmanic purity; the labour of these groups, and the products of this labour, are similarly valued.

Dumont's theory, the product of intensive fieldwork and meticulous comparative research, is one of the best anthropological accounts of Brahmanic household polity that has ever been produced. His theory would not have been controversial if this was the only claim that he made for it; but, in the grand tradition of all leading value theorists, he has pushed his theory beyond the limits of its explanatory competency and drawn too many problematic political lessons from it. Brahmanic values are important values in India but they are not the only values and nor are they the paramount values. Dumont not only denies the importance of other religious values such as auspiciousness and sacredness, he also denies the importance of the non-religious values of the other castes in the classic four-caste theory of Indian society that he employs. The four-caste theory ranks priests, kings, merchants and farmers in that order and Dumont takes the pure values of the priests to be the values of the totality. True, there is reciprocal recognition of Brahmanic values by these castes but there is also asymmetric recognition and some indifference to them. The merchant castes are intimately familiar with the principles of 'modern' market valuation and so too are the people from other castes they trade with, be they Brahmans or Untouchables. The principle of profit and loss is as much a part of 'traditional' Indian values as are those of purity and pollution. These market values are sometimes more important than Brahmanic values, sometimes less, but always coeval, contrary to what Dumont supposes. Indeed, given the almost complete neglect of market studies by caste-obsessed anthropologists in India, a reader of the anthropological literature on India could be forgiven for believing that Dumont was right about the absence of commodity exchange.[27]

Thus, just as Marx saw the values of the factory worker in nineteenth-century England as being the key to understanding nineteenth-century capitalism and Friedman sees the values of the supermarket shopper as the key to understanding the twentieth-century global market economy, so Dumont sees Brahmanic values as the key to understanding Indian society. Moreover, by seeing egalitarian values as the characteristic values in the 'West', Dumont denies the coevalness of rival cognitions and implicitly accepts a Friedmanite view of the 'Western' world. The decision making structure of the modern organisation, Wolfe (1989: 122) notes, is not egalitarian. Hierarchical authority, the direct opposite of the presumed voluntarism in the external market, is necessary so that the managers can manage its internal relations efficiently. As Wolfe puts it: 'Organisations can be free only if individuals live in chains'. In other words, theorists like Friedman and Dumont affirm equality in the 'modern' world by denying the pervasive co-existence of unfree, hierarchical values.

Critics often dismiss Dumont's theory of caste as a conservative defence of social stratification and social inequality. Dumont disputes this charge but admits to an 'irenic preference' for hierarchy over conflict (1980b: 239). Dumont argues for an ordered holistic conception of society that recognises difference by uniting opposites; he is against an individualism that flattens the integral whole to create an aggregation that must, in his opinion, lead, as a matter of logical necessity, to totalitarianism and other sorts of violence. He adheres to Aquinas's dictum that 'order is seen to consist mainly in inequality' (1980b: 238), a statement, he believes, which contradicts our stereotypes and prejudices. From his position, then, it is the so-called radicals who are the real conservatives. In their calls for equality—with which he has no theoretical problem in so far as it is a matter of enfranchisement in general—they fail to perceive the slip from equality to identity through the non-recognition, insubordination, or neglect of difference with the result that values get set that are impossible to attain. Against those advocates of difference who claim 'separate but equal', his counter-claim is that this is impossible as the transition from slavery to racism in America illustrates.

Dumont's theory of value is a classic illustration of Fabian's denial of coevality thesis. Dumont's opposition between the hierarchical East and the egalitarian West consigns India to another time, another place and another mode of being human in the world. Not only does he deny the coevality of these 'modern' and 'traditional' modes of consciousness, he also denies the coevality of 'traditional' mercantile and agrarian values in India, and the coevality of conflicting class and individualist forms of 'modern' consciousness in Europe. Dumont is a formidable opponent because his denial of coevality is a conscious, radical one. He is aware of the history of imperialism but simply denies its importance; he is aware of the existence of alternative values in India but he simply asserts the predominance of Brahmanic values. For him values are 'by definition conceived of as permanent, durable' (1983: vii). They can stand apart from power and can even be above it. This is the message of India for the West and those Westerners who fail to grasp this point, argues Dumont, are so entrapped by egalitarian values that they are unable to see hierarchy for what it is. Dumont tries to insulate himself from criticism by means of this circular rhetoric. But his argument contains one fatal flaw. It is one thing to deny the coevality of the Other by assigning her to another place and another time but quite another to stop her from affirming the contrary. It is not surprising, then, that the most telling criticism of Dumont's theory of value has come from an Indian anthropologist, Veena Das.

Das (1994a) tells us that she used to have a consuming interest in relocating Sanskrit texts in modern knowledge systems and that Dumont's work fascinated her. Slowly she learnt to engage the problems of her immediate environment. Since 1984, the year of the Delhi riots following the assassination of Mrs Gandhi, she has been engaged in a study of violence and the way moral communities are created through suffering. Her work with the female riot victims caused her to rethink some of her positions. Furthermore, she read the newly launched *Subaltern Studies* project as 'an invitation to think anew the relations between history and anthropology from a point of view that displaces the central position of the European anthropologist or historian as the subject of discourse and Indian society as its object' (1989a: 310). Anthropologists, she noted, 'are interested in seeing how order is created out of chaos… not how it is violated to create structures of power within the family'. Her recent work develops some of the implications of the subaltern approach. For her the subaltern is not a morphological category, but a perspective. She adopts this perspective in her article 'Moral Orientations to Suffering' (1994b) where she draws a distinction between 'negative responsibility' and 'positive irresponsibility'.

'Negative responsibility' refers to the tragic consequences that can arise when a powerless person uncritically accepts the values of the dominant in their attempts to make sense of an inexplicable world full of capricious gods, contingent events, and accidents of life. The powerful create meaning out of this chaos by means of values expressed in political theologies that give meaning and order to life. Only the powerful have the luxury of assuming that life has meaning, writes Das (1994b: 149), because only they can exercise the kind of control over events that makes the personal, social and political life of people seem logical. These are the values of 'positive responsibility', the values that make for a culture.

From this perspective the values that spring from the institution of the House in India lose their specificity and become recognisable variations on a general theme found anywhere. The relations of consanguinity, affinity and contiguity acquire a value whose essence is captured by the word *patriarchy*. Das's understanding of this notion contrasts sharply with Dumont's notion of 'affinity as a value' and it is useful to pursue the idea for it lies at the heart of my analysis as well.

Abstractly considered, the values of patriarchy define *con-sanguinity* as a patriline where sons are more highly valued than daughters, where male honour is paramount, and where male ancestors are worshipped in expensive and time consuming rituals; it defines *affinity* as an unequal relationship between low status wife-givers and high-status wife-receivers that creates obligations on the former to make periodic, prestige-maintaining gifts; and it defines *contiguity* as a form of patrilocal residence where wives are obliged to live with, and to serve, their husband's family. The net effect of this is to create a situation where women are 'in between' as Marilyn Strathern (1972) so aptly put it in her ethnographic analysis of the Melpa women of highlands Papua New Guinea.[28] Figure I.1 illustrates this. As a daughter, ego is separated from her mother by relations of contiguity; as a mother, she is required to value her sons more highly than her daughters because of the relations of consanguinity; and, as a sister's daughter, she is distanced from her mother's brother by the relations of affinity.

The values of the patriarchal House overlap with those associated with the State and the Market. The relations between these values are often *inexplicable*. But meaning has to be constructed if order is to be maintained. This paradox may have tragic consequences for the 'woman-in-between' raised to accept, uncritically, patriarchal values. The moving case study reported by Das illustrates this.

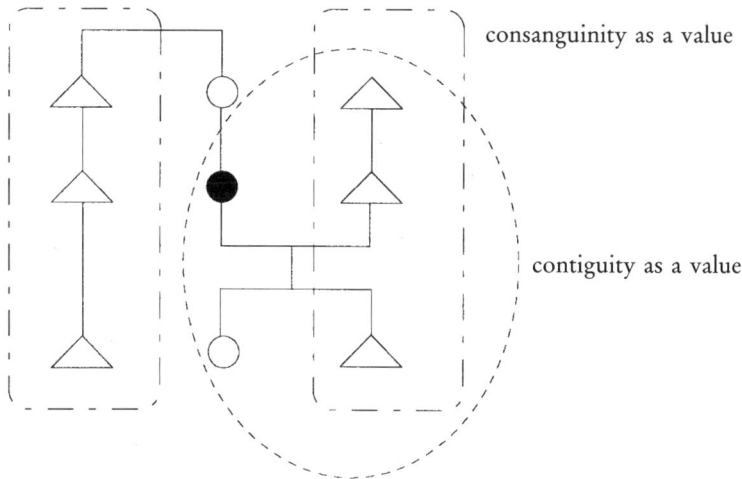

consanguinity as a value

contiguity as a value

FIGURE I.1   *The woman in between*

During her work with some of the survivors of the anti-Sikh riots, Das got to know a Sikh woman called Shanti whose husband and three sons were burnt alive by a mob as they hid in an abandoned house. An informer told the mob of the whereabouts of the man and his sons and, after hurling abuse at the hidden men, the house was doused with kerosene and set alight. Shanti and her two surviving daughters witnessed the event from the terrace of the house in which they were hiding. Shanti was eventually given Rs 40,000 compensation by the government for the loss of her family but this did not alleviate her suffering. She took the pain as evidence of her guilt and eventually took her own life. An unanswerable question tormented Shanti: 'What did we have to do with the assassination of Indira Gandhi?' This was resolved in the courtroom of her mind. She found herself guilty of the crime and administered her own justice.

Das's analysis of the facts of this tragic case stresses the inexplicability of the decidedly human logic that connects national events with personal lives. 'Reflecting on Shanti's case,' she notes (1994b: 149), 'we see events that may seem remote and distant to a family in a slum, such as the assassination of a national leader, can lead to calamity in their personal lives, but so absurd are the connections through which this happens they can only testify to the chaotic nature of the world in which they inhabit.' As such, Das does not try to explain or interpret the events; her aim is to reveal the contradictory human values that inform existential dilemmas of this kind.

First, the values of the killers. For them, Das (1994b: 142) notes, 'there seems to have been an implicit contract that the death of Indira Gandhi was to be avenged by a kind of ritual killing of adult men'. This value establishes a logical equation between the death of a Hindu prime minister and the death of numerous adult Sikh men. The standard of value that informs this logical equation is a particular Indian form of the general principle that Otherhood (Sikhs in this case) is the negation of the Brotherhood (Hindus). This value presupposes that Brothers reciprocally recognise one another and that they constitute an exclusive integral whole. Thus injury to a part of the Brotherhood is injury to the whole and compensation must be exacted when it occurs. This is what Radcliffe-Brown (1957) calls the Principle of Justice and rightly characterises it as a fundamental principle of human society.

Consider now the values of the victims. The tragedy in Shanti's case is that she was an unjust victim of the Principle of Justice that operated during the riots because she was the only woman to have lost a young child to the murderous crowd. 'Every woman knew children were not being killed,' Shanti told Das (1994b: 144). 'Only I was stupid. Only I lost a child.' Shanti did not question the values informing the Hindu Brotherhood but other women did. 'If they had wanted to take revenge,' they told Das, 'they should have killed those guards who were the assassins. What had we done that such devastation was wrought upon us?'

Shanti was also the victim of betrayal in that her mother's brother was an informer. 'He revealed the hiding places of the Siglikar Sikhs to the leaders of the mob,' Shanti told Das (1994b: 143). 'He bartered their lives for his own protection'. The value behind this barter not only equates one person's life with another's death, it also equates the continuity of a wife-giving lineage with the extinguishment of a wife-receiving lineage. The significance of this fact lies in the local evaluation of such behaviour. Given the relatively low status of wife-giving groups, an act of affinal betrayal of this kind is unlikely to arouse the moral outrage that consanguineal betrayal would. Das does not explicitly deal with this matter but she does implicitly when she notes (1994b: 148) that the consanguines of the dead began talking of martyrdom, of the long tradition of martyrdom in Sikh history, and the obligation to remember dead family members. Shanti expressed these values when she criticised her husband's refusal to sacrifice his own life to save that of his sons:

> They hurled challenges upon my husband to come out. If he had been brave he would have come out and then my little child would have been spared. But he remained mute. The crowd burnt the house (Das, 1994b:143).

Shanti compared her husband's actions to those of another man who did face the crowd and whose child was saved because the killers were honour-bound to do so.

Shanti had so internalised the patriarchal discourse of the family, writes Das (1994b: 144), that to her all sense of worth came from being the mother of sons. In failing to protect her son, she had failed as a woman. 'The greatest duty of a woman,' Shanti repeatedly told Das, 'was to ensure the continuity of men.' So great was her commitment to her son that she devalued her daughters calling them 'counterfeit children' (*nakli bacche*). Her mother, sisters and other women contested this value: 'Are they not born of your womb, the same as your sons?' Her five year old daughter even tried to assure her that she would not marry, that she would stay with her, and that she would be 'like a son'.

Patriarchal values of this kind also govern the mode of distribution of money coming into the household. Shanti's husband's father felt that the Rs 40,000 compensation money Shanti received rightly belonged to him as the only surviving male member of the lineage. When Shanti's mother came to live with her to comfort her in her suffering, the patriarch insinuated, through various subtle forms of innuendo, that she wanted to grab the money. He appealed to the norm of contiguity:

> Circumstances have compelled her to stay, otherwise, which woman can stay on in her married daughter's house like this? If nothing else the world would say "What a shameless woman!" (Das, 1994b: 146).

The mother found it impossible to stay and returned home leaving Shanti to inhabitant the valued male space herself.

On another occasion the patriarch wanted to hold an expensive ritual to ensure peace for his dead son and grandson. Shanti questioned the values underlying this request by raising the issue of the future of her daughters and of the need to have money for their marriages. The old man construed this as a betrayal of the male line: patriarchy values the memory of a dead son more highly than the marriage of a living daughter.

What this case illustrates is that values have valuers and that the ruling values are the values of the dominant. These values are never universal because power is never absolute. Furthermore, the co-existence of many different value systems, such as those that link the House with the State, are often connected by an inexplicable logic. The unmeaning of this logic can send people mad as they struggle to find meaning. Sometimes the paradox can only be resolved by rejecting the values one is brought up to believe are 'natural'. Shanti's values can be seen as 'false consciousness', as can the values of people like her who find the answer to problems like this in the work of the gods rather than the values of men. Das is not prepared to make this value judgement. For her Shanti's death 'must forever remain elusive... a testimony to the unequal dialectic between the norm giving, powerful male society and the attempts to resist those norms by the constant reconstruction and kaleidoscopic organisation of memory in the inner lives of the individual' (1994b: 150). However, unlike Dumont who has an irenic preference for hierarchy over conflict, Das is prepared to accept that irresponsibility may be positive, or, to use my terms, that asymmetrical recognition may be a good thing.

Just as Das is unwilling to pass a judgement on Shanti, the reader must reserve judgement on her husband's father. While it is possible to judge him from the perspective of the values of the House, these values are not the only ones he is caught up in. From the point of view of the Hindu Brotherhood he is a Sikh, an anti-Hindu, someone without humanity who deserved to be eliminated. From another point of view, he is a member of a low-status ironsmith community. People like him switch between these different values systems and one value system is usually in the ascendancy at any particular time. But the choice of the switch is not always free as this case suggests. Thus while contradictory values can be sharply distinguished at the conceptual level the implication is that, at the ethnographic level, unambiguous classification becomes impossible.

In the second part of her article Das (1994b) moves from a consideration of the values of the House to those of the State. She examines the process through which the Indian courts arrived at the figure of 470 million dollars as compensation for the 300,000 victims of the Bhopal disaster, the worst industrial accident in human history when between 30 to 40 tons of methyl isocyanate escaped from huge storage tanks at the Union Carbide factory on the night of December 2–3, 1984. She shows how the Indian government stepped in between the company and the victims and reached a settlement without the consultation of the latter thereby rendering them into double victims. She quotes a moving speech of an illiterate women victim protesting the judgement which says it all: 'We ask the judges only one thing— please come here and count us' (Das, 1994b: 161).

What unites Das's approach with that of Marx's is the argument that value is an expression of an antagonistic power relation between people located historically, geographically and anthropologically. This argument distinguishes Das and Marx from Friedman and Dumont. The latter, for example, argues that value 'encompasses' power rather than the other way around. Such an approach reifies values and contradicts the humanist's position that political relations between people are 'the measure of all things'.

SCOPE AND LIMITS OF MY STUDY

Having outlined three approaches to the question of value it remains for me to specify the scope and limits of the perspective I am adopting.

This book is an anthropological inquiry in that it takes a field-work-informed, comparative approach to the analysis of those values that spring from reciprocally recognised relations of affinity, consanguinity and contiguity. It does not deny the importance of values associated with class consciousness or with individual cognition. However, while it complements the relational class approach it contradicts the individualist approach in that the analysis of historically constituted relations between people are given primacy over the psychological states of individuals. Psychology, then, is relegated to a position of secondary importance. This is a philosophical stance and my concern is to examine its implications rather than to justify it because this would require a book of a very different nature.

In terms of the 'four-varna' theory of Indian society—the theory of the 'pen', the 'sword', the 'purse' and the 'plough' as it is sometimes called—my analysis concentrates on the purse and the plough, the merchant family and the farm household. I do not deny the importance of the pen (religious values) and the sword (the State). To the contrary, I regard them as very important. However, I focus on the values associated with the purse and the plough to redress an imbalance. Anthropological studies in India have concentrated almost exclusively on Brahmanic values. The reason is not hard to find. Brahmanic values are unique to India. These values, as norms, are codified in ancient texts and talked about on a daily basis in village India; they are also acted upon and the outsider cannot help observing their visual form—the cow, the *sadhu*, the eating rituals, the washing rituals—even if he or she does not understand them fully. The values of the purse and plough are equally visible but these are much more familiar to the outsider. The values found in the markets and farms of India are minor variations on those found in Asia, Africa, Latin America and even Europe. The 'profane' values that inform the actions of farmers and merchants are not the subject of lengthy exegesis. They coexist with religious values and it is important to affirm this coevality. This obvious point must be stressed because many anthropologists implicitly deny it by asserting not only the primacy of religious values over all others but also, in the case of anthropologists like Dumont, the primacy of one religious value, purity, over all others such as auspiciousness, sacredness, and so on While I assert the primacy of free market anarchism as a historically specific global value, and while I believe that we are all victims of this value to a certain extent, I do not see it as a universal value, as something that is eternal and immutable. It coexists with many other values and people switch, and are switched, between these different values in a way that can only be understood by means of the concrete analysis of concrete conditions. Most of the households I have data on are located in the logical space defined by the intersection of the values of the pen, sword, purse and plough. For example, one Brahman household is both landlord and merchant; a low-caste farming household contains a priest, a teacher and shopkeeper, and so on. Values, then, are not classifications; any one household possesses a variety of values such that now this, now that value is dominant at any given time.[29] However, their relative importance varies according to the contingencies of history. Guha (1983a), for example, analyses those values that are dominant in times of insurgency. In this book, by way of contrast, I concentrate on those less spectacular everyday farming and mercantile values associated with 'business as usual'.

In terms of the theory of kinship, I am concerned with the politics of valued relations rather than the logic of kinship structures. Thus I begin not with Lévi-Strauss's 'atom of kinship' but with Das's 'visible hand of patriarchy'. But whereas Das is concerned primarily with gender relations within the family, I take such relations as given and concentrate on inter-family relationships. Further, whereas she is concerned with the pain and suffering that follows inexplicable eruptions of violence, I am mainly concerned with the non-violent interactions between people that I was fortunate to experience during my fieldwork.

In terms of the theory of symbolism, my focus is money, the symbol of all symbols. Nixon's closing of the gold window was a symbolic act that cultural anthropology has not even posed as a problem let alone decoded. This is doubly surprising because not only is money the supreme symbol in the world today, it is also the origin of the term *symbol* itself. The word comes from the Greek *symbolon*, a metal object that was broken in half as a sign of a pledge between two parties, each of whom would retain a part as evidence of their pledge. Thus, to decode a symbol one located the two material components in order to deduce the non-material idea that united them. In the case of the U.S. dollar, one part of the *symbolon* was the stamped paper circulating above the ground while the other part was the gold stored underground at Fort Knox. To decode this symbol we must ask, first, what was the thinking behind the 1934 pledge to convert every dollar into 1/35th ounce of gold, and, second, why was Nixon forced to break this pledge in 1971? The questions are part of a general theory of taboo because gold has been an untouchable substance in U.S. for almost half of the twentieth century. An edict in 1934 required all privately held gold to be surrendered to the U.S. Treasury and this lasted until 31 December 1973. Taboo, as I see it, is a matter of power and value.

In terms of the theory of commodities, Marx's analysis of the various forms of exchange—C-C, C-M-C, M-C-M', M-M'—provides the structure for this book. Chapter II develops the analytical distinction between *commodities, goods* and *gifts* that I will be using. This builds on my previous work in Papua New Guinea but my focus here is on *goods* and *commodities* that I analyse in terms of a theory of value based on reciprocal recognition rather than class consciousness or individual cognition. Thus the substance of my analysis of *commodities* differs from that of Marx's. Furthermore, my theory of *goods* only has a nominal connection to the neoclassical notion of *goods*. I have thought of marking this distinction but decided against because the context makes the meaning clear. Most words in the English language have more than one meaning and the word 'goods' is no exception. In Chapter III, I argue that land is the supreme *good* and that this notion is as important for understanding the rise of capitalism in England as it is for understanding agrarian relations in places like India today. I distinguish between elite *goods*—inalienable keepsakes of the landed aristocracy—and subaltern *goods,* the inalienable keepsakes of the relatively less well off. In Chapter IV, I argue that the distinguishing feature of market relations in Bastar is not their 'tribal' or 'peasant' nature but that it constitutes a classic example of Marx's C-M-C formula, selling commodities (C) for money (M) in order to buy other commodities (C). But the producers of such values, I argue, produce these on land that is a *good*. The coexistence of these two value systems (*goods* and *commodities*) creates contradictions that enable people to switch in ways that will always confound the theorist, be they Marxists or neoclassicals, who strive to understand agrarian relations exclusively in terms of one theory of value or the other. In Chapter V, I look at M-C-M', buying cheap *here* in order to sell dear *there*. This commercial value, which is as old as *Homo sapiens* ourselves, is also coeval with other values and my concern here is to reveal the relations of consanguinity, affinity, and contiguity that stratify mercantile capital by examining the role of *territoriality* as a

value. Chapter VI has M-M' as its theme, the borrowing of money
today and the ideal return of a larger sum *tomorrow*. Again, my concern
is to reveal how the coevality of different value systems can confound
our understanding of the mathematical logic of the interest rate formula
that is supposed to connect a small sum of money today with a larger
one tomorrow. I do this by means of a discussion of *temporality* as a
value. Chapters VII and VIII look at money, M, as a creation of the
imperial state. The fact of power means that there is always at least two
ways of valuing money, the standards of the elite and the standards of
the subalterns, and these chapters present a comparative and historical
analysis of these standards by looking at the experience of India, Africa
and Papua New Guinea. It is important to note that by using these
formulae I am in no way endorsing the logical and historical primacy
Marx gives to C-C (barter) over M-M'. To the contrary, as the
equations (1) to (3) above illustrate, C-C can just as readily be seen as
the logical consequent of money as its antecedent. Furthermore, barter,
as many anthropologists have stressed (Hart, 1987), and my analysis
confirms, coexists today with money. It is best, therefore, to see C-C
as a form of direct exchange of commodities that consists of three
logical types: simultaneous in time and place, same place different time,
and same time different place. In other words, it is necessary to affirm
the coevality of the different forms that Marx differentiated as stages
in an evolutionary process.

NOTES

[1] See Feaveryear (1963) who surveys the history of the pound sterling from
the middle ages to the present day. Chapter VIII, below, contains an analysis
of Nixon's actions.

[2] Imperial monetary policy provides an excellent Piercean *index* of imperial
power. In 1497 the Spanish government issued an ordinance at Medino del
Campo which abrogated all previous existing systems of money and the
Spanish dollar began its reign as the supreme world money. The goodness
of the Spanish coins exalted them above the prevailing rates in Europe and
they were eagerly sought in consequence. The basis of their goodness was
conquistadorial rather than mercantile imperialism. The mines at Potosi
supplied the kings of Spain with their wealth and the extravagant spending
of the kings supplied the world with a much needed instrument of commerce.

(See Shaw, 1895: 106ff, 319ff.) Potosi is now a tin mine and Nash's (1979) important ethnography brings the story up to date. The year 1825 marks the beginning of the rise of the British pound as supreme currency and the fall of the Spanish dollar. In this year the Home Government made its attempt to introduce British silver (backed by gold in the first instance and the mercantile power of British imperialism in the second). 'The real justification of the measures of 1825', notes Chalmers (1893: 24), 'was one which was only vaguely felt at the time... the Spanish dollar, the universal coin of three centuries, had lost its supremacy, and... its universal dominion was in process of disintegration.'

[3] I elaborate on this in Chapter VIII below.

[4] The title of a new journal, *Social Identities*, first launched in 1995, suggests that the debate might be moving in new directions. See, in particular, the article by Martin (1995). He argues that narratives of identity are produced in order to create and mobilise groups towards particular goals, that these are based on 'liberating amnesia' and careful selection, and that they cannot be understood as representations of immutable realities.

[5] I refer here to the work of Appadurai (1986). Ferguson's review (1988) not only celebrates Appadurai's work as a 'milestone in the development of a new, culturally informed economic anthropology', he makes a point of defending Appadurai's 'fetishistic thinking'. Marcus (1990) sees Appadurai's work as the most stimulating culturally oriented response within economic anthropology to the postmodern conditions of disorganised capitalism. Miller's (1995) recent review of the literature on commodities and consumption echoes these opinions. I question this new orthodoxy. I develop a specific critique of Appadurai in Chapter II and general critique of the culturalist approach in Chapter IX.

[6] The only thing that links Freud, Piaget, von Neuman, and Chomsky (to say nothing of Jung and B. F. Skinner),' argues Geertz (1983: 150), 'is the conviction that the mechanics of human thinking is invariable across time, space, culture, and circumstance, and they know what that is.' Geertz also notes that the assumption of psychic unity 'has remained a background article of faith among even the most thoroughgoing of them, anxious as they were to do away with any notion of primitive minds or cultural racism.' See Spiro (1992) for a recent defence of the assumption of psychic unity.

[7] American culturalists begin here. Sahlins (1976: vii), for example, takes 'as the distinctive quality of man not that he must live in a material world, a circumstance he shares with all organisms, but that he does so according to a meaningful scheme of his own devising, in which capacity mankind is unique.'

[8] 'Manifestly to overcome the difficulties confronting an ethnological investigation, it would require the cooperation of a group of supermen' (Radin, 1933: 103).

⁹ I borrow this image from Hart (1986).

¹⁰ The latter approach is taken by Zelizer (1994) in her fascinating analysis of the social meaning of money in the U.S. over the period 1870–1930.

¹¹ 'Anthropology,' Kottak and Colson (1994: 396) argue, 'needs, and is developing, models of its subject matter that reflect the structure of today's world. Various recent multilevel, multisite, multitime research projects illustrate this development. Such projects are one indication of a shift towards the study of process, of an engagement with history, and of an anthropology that takes care to consider the role of political and economic power'. This argument owes much to people like Wolf (1982: 13) who note that 'the very success of the [fieldwork] method lulled its users into a false confidence. It became easy for them to convert merely heuristic considerations of method into theoretical postulates about society and culture.'

¹² Two excellent anthropological histories of Bastar have been written: Sundar (1994) focuses on relations between the villagers and the state; Anderson and Huber (1988) on forest policy.

¹³ Wolfe (1989: 34) makes this point in his enlightening analysis of the disciplines of economics, politics and sociology.

¹⁴ This notion of the Other refers to the Otherhood of the Market, that is alienation, and should not be confused with the notion of the Other as used in recent anthropological discourse.

¹⁵ Mamadou Diawara (personal communication, 1995) tells me that slavery in Mali was based on this principle.

¹⁶ See Guha (1983a: 93ff) on code switching. Elwert (1995) has independently developed this idea in his attempt to understand the phenomenon of ethnic identity.

¹⁷ I take this term from John Milton's (1982 [1672]) humanist logic. See Chapter IX below.

¹⁸ The battle is the stuff of myth. See: Emeneau (1940), Kipling (1959), Schmitt (1983), Williams (1930).

¹⁹ See Keesing (1994).

²⁰ See, for example, Prakash (1994) and Chakrabarty (1995).

²¹ Das (1989a) was one of the first anthropologists to appreciate the implications of Guha's work for anthropology. See also Das (1990, 1994a, 1994b).

²² See DaMatta (1994) where he argues for recuperation of anthropology's humanist project. He is opposed to 'interpretivism' and claims that the interpretivist's notion of 'ethnographic distance' enables them to avoid 'radical political questioning' (1994: 125).

²³ Rahu is an eclipse deity. The myths of the elite portray him as an anti-god, those of the subalterns as a god. These are analysed in Guha (1985).

²⁴ Anthropology, notes Geertz (1994:454) 'has found itself faced with something new: the possibility that the variety is rapidly softening into a

paler, and narrower, spectrum'. He likens the present historical conjuncture to a 'cultural collage' and contrasts it with the old 'still life' (1994:464). Spiro (1992) makes the same distinction in a rather different way and defends the latter.

[25] Compare Das (1994a:164): 'the victims of these disasters continue to bear the burdens of modern Indian society and as their scribe I struggle with the hopeless inadequacy of my conceptual tools to give them voice.'

[26] See Harcourt (1982) and Swedberg (1991).

[27] 'The relationship between a hierarchical order of castes, with its focus on the superior position of the Brahman, on the one hand, and a conception of sovereignty which focuses on the Hindu king or the royal functions of the dominant caste at the level of the village, on the other, has been a central reverberating issue in the anthropological and historical study of South Asian society, so much so that it has been called "the central conundrum of Indian social ideology". Virtually all the major contributions to the anthropological, Indological, and historical study of Hindu South Asia have been concerned in some fashion with this relationship, and have seen it to be constitutive of fundamental aspects of social life, polity, and religion' (Raheja, 1988b).

[28] In a recent article on value theory she extends my analysis (Gregory, 1982) to an area that I hesitated 'to apply the word, namely the "equation" set up between things and persons, such as bride and bridewealth' (Strathern, 1992:177). My analysis here continues our long running dialogue on the value question. I accept her extension of the term value to this domain and try, in turn, to extend her analysis beyond Melanesia.

[29] This was made clear to me at an annual fair I attended in Bastar. For the merchants (many of whom are also farmers) these fairs are money making opportunities and the values of profit and loss predominate. For other farmers, the fair is a religious event and the values of purity, sacredness and auspiciousness predominate. In both cases these values are switched on and off at different periods of time. For example, clan gods are carried to the market on wooden constructions called *anga*. During this time the construction is deemed to be highly sacred and must not be touched by anyone except the four people carrying it who themselves become possessed by the spirit temporally resident in it. The guardians of the *anga* get very angry if anyone touches it, as I found when I naively touched one. A ritual is performed at the village temple on the morning of the fair to transfer the spirit of the ancestral god to the *anga* and the reverse ritual is performed at the end of the day. Having just witnessed the latter, I was observing the 'undressing' of the *anga* and gingerly approached to assist. 'Don't worry *sahib*', one of the men called out laughing, 'it is just wood now. You can touch it.' This 'just wood' value was reciprocally recognised by other people around just as its previous sacred value was so recognised. My lack of understanding of these values evoked anger on one occasion and mirth on the other.

CHAPTER II

Beyond Gifts and Commodities

GIFTS AND COMMODITIES: A DEFENCE

The analysis of value in an era of savage money presents the anthropologist with a theoretical dilemma. On the one hand, the object of study is full of contradictions and fuzzy boundaries; on the other, one's instruments of analysis must be free of contradiction and one's concepts clearly distinguished. This dilemma is difficult to negotiate. I struggled with it in *Gifts and Commodities* (Gregory, 1982), a book that has attracted a measure of critical comment. In this chapter I respond to some of this criticism by examining how two of my critics have coped with the dilemma. My aim is to set the theoretical and ethnographic agenda for the subsequent chapters. In this chapter, then, I move from a consideration of gifts and commodities in Papua New Guinea to the problems of analysing commodities and goods in central India. I defend the use of a binary logic as an indispensable instrument of anthropological thought and re-affirm the importance of fieldwork, and of an historically informed comparative method, as the material grounds for the development of anthropological knowledge.

Gifts and Commodities was my attempt to make sense of the world that I lived in for three years from 1973 to 1975 as a lecturer in economics at the University of Papua New Guinea (PNG). From an expatriate academic's perspective this academic world was made up of three rival paradigms: first there were the neoclassical economists who apprehended the world in terms of a theory of *goods* that led them to focus on marginal utilities of consumption; next came the neomarxist political economists who saw everything in terms of a theory of *commodities* and class relations of production; and finally, there were the anthropologists whose theory of *gifts* led them to focus on the big-men and their prestige in the sphere of exchange. My response to this was to forge a theoretical alliance between the political economists and anthropologists against the neoclassical economists. Thus my book was intended as a constructive critique of the theory of *commodities* and *gifts* and a destructive critique of the marginal utility theory of *goods*. The result was, of course, yet another outsider's view but one that struggled to adopt a critical stance towards Australian economic and political imperialism in the country.

Responses to my book fall into the three classes: some, mainly anthropologists,[1] have critically accepted the basic distinction and have sought to develop the theory in their own way; others, again mainly anthropologists, have rejected it outright; and the rest, which includes the economists and political economists to whom it was addressed, have simply ignored the book altogether. While there is much in *Gifts and Commodities* that I would change today, the basic distinction at the heart of the book is not one of them. It is this distinction that I want to defend here. As such, I will restrict the following discussion to those critics whose reject binary thought in favour of a 'cultural perspective' that stresses conceptual continuity over conceptual discreteness. From this culturalist perspective my book is yet another exercise in binary thinking with all the problems that this approach is supposed to entail. I find some aspects of this critique challenging and thought-provoking but in many other aspects I find it muddled in the sense that the distinction between the object of study and the instruments of study is sometimes muddled. I consider the approach of two prominent theorist—Appadurai and Parry—to highlight the strength and weakness of this critique.

Appadurai's culturalist approach to the analysis of commodities has been celebrated by Marcus (1990) as the way ahead for an anthropology concerned to confront the challenge of the post modern world of disorganised capitalism. Appadurai's long essay, now recognised as a turning point in the theory of commodities (Miller, 1995), has been modified and developed by the Comaroffs (1990) and many others. I concentrate here on Appadurai's work because the problems in his theory are reproduced by his followers.

According to Appadurai (1986: 11, 54) I am among those who 'overstate' the contrast between gifts and commodities. Appadurai does not elaborate this claim and nor is he concerned with the many theoretical differences that differentiate the work of 'overstaters' such as Taussig, Sahlins, and myself. Instead, he gets on with the task of presenting his new 'cultural perspective'. But what does this perspective entail? In Appadurai's case it is, first of all, a position that denies the problem that I am trying to cope with, namely, the paradox of the efflorescence of gift exchange in a commodity world economy. For example, he describes the *kula* as 'the best-documented example of a non-Western, preindustrial, nonmonetised, translocal exchange system' (1986: 18). This proposition, which anthropologists repeat *ad nauseam* in the literature, is a classic example in the 'denial of coevality' tradition of anthropology. The fact is that the Milne Bay area of PNG was one of the first regions colonised at the end of the last century. Gold miners, planters and missionaries poured into the area and, over the years, thousands of migrant labourers and students have flowed in and out. *Kula* is to a large extent an artefact of this history; like many other indigenous exchange systems in PNG it flourished when the colonial state suppressed clan warfare. Not only is *kula* 'Western', and 'monetised', it is also 'national' in the sense that *kula* paths now wend their way through Port Moresby via the houses of top Trobriand Island public servants.[2] Here Mercedes Benz cars and their horns substitute for the boats and conch shells of the Islands.

The second defining feature of Appadurai's 'cultural perspective' is that it denies the logical principle of specific difference by affirming the universality of the commodity form. '[I]n trying to make sense of what is distinctive about commodity exchange,' he argues (1986: 13), 'it does not make sense to distinguish it sharply either from barter on the one hand, or from the exchange of gifts on the other.' According to him we must look for 'the *commodity potential of all things* rather than searching fruitlessly for the magic distinction between commodities and other sorts of things' (emphasis added).

Thus for him everything is a commodity and only with this proposition uppermost in mind can one navigate the contradictions that riddle his account. Consider the following:

> Though an interesting range of *goods* is discussed in these essays, the list of *commodities* not discussed would be quite long, and there

> is a tilt towards specialised or luxury *goods* rather than 'primary'
> or 'bulk' *commodities* (Appadurai, 1986: 6, emphasis added).

Note the implicit equation of *commodities* with *goods* here and the
use of equivocal adjectives ('specialised or luxury', 'primary or bulk')
to distinguish the different types of 'commodity potential'. *Gifts* are
equated with commodities and goods by means of the following argument:

> Of course there are many differences between the kula and
> commodity futures in scale, instrumentalities, context, and goals.
> But the similarities are real... The trade in relics, the market in
> commodity futures, the kula, the potlatch are all examples of
> 'tournaments of value' (Appadurai, 1986: 50).

Thus for Appadurai the equation *commodity = gift = good* is 'real',
the differences exist but are apparent. The result is a contradictory
theory of commodity-as-everything and commodity-as-something:
the *commodity* is both *genus* and *species*. The only way he is able to
differentiate his concepts is by employing a diverse group of adjectives in a totally *ad hoc* way: 'primary' commodity, 'specialised'
commodity, 'bulk' commodity, 'enclaved' commodity, etc. Wherein
lies the difference between these categories? My argument is that if
exchange is taken as the genus then a conceptual distinction can be
made between gifts and commodities; furthermore, I argue that the
distinction must be made if the ethnographic reality is to be grasped.

The third defining characteristic of Appadurai's approach is the
most curious of all for it is tantamount to the denial that anthropology is, first and foremost, the study of people. He argues (1986: 3)
that 'exchange creates value' rather than people, and that 'commodities, like persons, have social lives'. This is a quite conscious attempt
to elevate 'commodity fetishism'—the process by which relations
between people assume the fantastic form of a relation between things
(Marx, 1867: Ch. 1.4)—to a methodological principle. From this reified 'cultural perspective' what becomes important is the 'commodity potential' of a thing. This universalisation and reification of the
commodity form bewilders me. For a humanist, the commodity is
an historically specific form whose value is created by relations between people. If this position is an example of the 'tendency to

excessively sociologize transactions in things' that Appadurai (1986:5) seeks to correct, then I refuse to be corrected.

Appadurai would no doubt protest that this is not what he 're-ally' meant. If the 'cultural biography of thing' approach he endorses does not mean this then it means nothing at all except the totally un-controversial proposition that the objects of exchange, be they people or things, have a history that can be charted. This history would show that, say, some of the gold at Fort Knox was once ore in the ground in South Africa, that it was then smelted, formed into jewellery and sold as a commodity, kept as an heirloom for many years, sold as a com-modity to a mint, circulated as a gold coin, and, finally, taken out of circulation and remoulded into a bar of gold along with other old coins. So what is new? Who has ever denied that objects have many differ-ent social forms depending on the context? Certainly not me. But the various species of value must be sharply distinguished when writing histories of this type. This is just what Appadurai does not do: as I have argued above, he elevates a specific value, the commodity form, to the status of a genus and makes no clear distinction between this form of value and others such as gifts and goods.

Appadurai's claim that the politics of value 'has its source in the fact that not all parties share the same *interests* in any specific regime of value' (1986: 57) is one that I can identify with. However, I am unable to see how he reconciles this proposition with his advocacy of fetishism as a methodological principle. In short, I find his thinking muddled. On the one hand he advocates a cultural theory based on the logic of diversity, on the other he seems to be advocating a value theory based on the logic of commonplace contradiction. The former tendency is the dominant one. Milton ([1672]1982: 223) comments on the logical status of the argument from *diversity* are relevant here:

> Arguments of disagreement which are diverse are those which disagree only in relation to something. This name seems most suitable for designating this very slight sort of disagreement, for by this expression are signified those things which, though they have a certain agreement among themselves and can by themselves and by their nature belong simultaneously to the same subject, are nevertheless not identical nor do they belong to the subject in relations to which they are said to disagree.

In other words, *diversity*, as a logical construct, is midway between *unity* (agreement) and *difference* (disagreement). Thus the cultural constructionists find their sameness and opposition within diversity. Spiro (1992: 126ff) calls this position 'epistemological relativism' and notes that the magnitude of cultural diversity it leads to is limitless. He argues that this unsatisfactory position comes about because relativists reject the notion of the psychic unity of mankind and hold that any notion of the unity of humanity can only be vacuous if true. One does not have to accept Spiro's defence of the principle of 'psychic unity' to see the merits of his critique. Anthropology must begin with unity and my argument is that the historical unity created by the dominance of free market anarchist values is a real one.

Parry's critique of *Gifts and Commodities* is from the point of view of what I call 'continuum theory'. From a logical point of view it shares all the problems of Appadurai's approach. Like Appadurai, Parry too finds my distinction 'greatly over-drawn':

> It might, I recognize, be objected that by emphasising the continuity between incremental exchange systems of the moka variety and Marx's general formula of capital accumulation, I am ignoring a fundamental contrast which emerges from Gregory's (1982) synthetic view of Melanesian exchange systems: the contrast between gift exchange systems of this kind in which the objective is to maximise net outgoings (to out-give), and commodity exchange in which the objective is to maximise net receipts or profit (to out-take). This contrast, however, is greatly over-drawn for if — as Gell (1992: 146) points out — it were literally true the Big Man would tend to seek out 'rubbish men' as exchange partners, and ply them with gifts in the confident expectation that they would never be repaid... Moreover, in many traditional Melanesian societies commodity exchange in the form of barter relations with trade partners on the periphery of one's social universe does not seem to possess a radically different character from many gift exchange relations firmly within that universe. In both cases (and again I am indebted to Gell) an enduring bond is established, and in both the objects exchanged seem to be definitively alienated. Gregory's neat opposition... does scant justice to these very real continuities (Parry 1989: 86-87, emphasis added).

My first reply is to note, yet again, that this critique denies the problem I was trying to explain, the coevality of different value systems in colonial Melanesia. The systems of exchange in so-called 'old' Melanesia are, I believe, best left to the archaeologist. Could it be that the 'denial of coevality' thesis has such a pervasive hold over anthropological thought that it influences the way people read texts as well as write them?

Secondly, Parry's suggestion that the logical implication of my theory is that the big man would seek out rubbish men to ply them with gifts is a complete distortion of my actual argument. I state, for example, that the 'aim of an inter-clan gift transactor is not simply to maximise the number of gifts of a given rank he gives away, but to give away a gift of the highest rank'. I add that 'these usually circulate amongst a small group of big-men' (Gregory, 1982: 52). I then give ethnographic evidence from Rossel Island and the Highlands. I also qualify my argument by noting that in those areas where 'leadership is in the hands of elders rather than big-men, balanced rather than incremental giving is practiced'. I quote evidence from the Sepik where exchange partners 'receive exactly the same in return'. In other words, the logical implications Parry (and Gell) draw from my analysis are false.

Thirdly, Parry's counter-argument conflates *ethnographic classification* with *logical conceptualisation*. This conflation is found in most 'continuity theorists' and it is based on a very simple confusion. When Lévi-Strauss divides the world into 'hot' societies and 'cold' societies, for example, he is *classifying* societies by means of the *concepts* 'hot' and 'cold'. Thus it is one thing to criticise him for the adequacy of his classification but quite another to criticise him for using the concepts 'hot' and 'cold'. I reject his classification but am quite happy to accept the idea that 'hot' is the opposite of 'cold'. In other words, it is one thing to make a conceptual distinction but quite another to use this distinction to classify societies. The problematic deployment of concepts does not mean that the concepts themselves are problematic.

I have never used the distinction between gifts and commodities to classify societies and nor have I ever suggested that 'we' are to commodities as 'they' are to gifts. Such an approach is anathema to me. My problem in *Gifts and Commodities* was to explain the paradox, brought about by colonisation, of the efflorescence of gift exchange in a world dominated by commodity production and exchange. I characterised Papua New Guinea as 'an "ambiguous" economy where things are now gifts, now commodities, depending on the social context' (1982: 117). Thus I developed the logical opposition between gifts and commodities in order to try to understand the ambiguity of the historically specific situation of colonial Papua New Guinea.

Just as the bricklayer needs raw materials, proper instruments, and an imaginative plan to build a house, so too does the writer. For the anthropological artisan the skill lies in collecting data by means of the fieldwork method and the analysis of it using an historically-informed comparative method. A key instrument in this process is a logically coherent conceptual framework. The end may be an ethnographic classification of a Lévi-Straussian hot and cold kind; but to confuse *concepts* with *classification* is to confuse instrument with end, the tools with the product. It follows, then, that one can reject the product without rejecting the tools. Consider the analogy of the painter. The logic of the colour cube, which every good artist understands very well, is based firstly on the opposition of black to white and, secondly, on the opposition of the primaries (red, yellow and blue) to the secondaries (green, violet and orange). This is sufficient to generate an infinite variety of discrete hues and artists use this logic to create works of art of great complexity. Guha (1983a) uses this analogy, unconsciously it seems, to organise his thoughts. The primary opposition that informs his notion of power is one between domination and subordination. This can be likened to that between black and white. A secondary opposition is drawn between insurgency and peace. Insurgency, in turn, opposes coercion to resistance as green is to red. Peace opposes persuasion to collaboration as blue is to yellow. The qualitative logic of these oppositions defines many other hues and contrasts such as the greeny blues within the relations of dominance and the shades of orange within the contingent relations of subordination. This logic is used to paint an overall picture of peasant insurgency in colonial India of great clarity. Consider the following extract from the conclusion of his work.

> We had set out to describe the *figure* of insurgency in its common form and in terms of its general ideas. These, the reader will have noticed, have been made to emerge out of a welter of individual

instances not all of them of the same *hue* or arranged in quite the same way. *Visualized as a pattern*, that form may indeed to said to be made up not only of elements and tendencies which are in *agreement but also those which clash and contrast.* Altogether, it stands for a generality in which ideas, mentalities, notions, beliefs, attitudes, etc., of many different kinds come together to constitute a whole. However, it is not a generality which is 'something external to, or something in addition to' other features or abstract qualities of insurgency discovered by reflection. On the contrary, 'it is what permeates and includes in it everything particular'—a pervasive theoretical consciousness which gives insurgency its categorical unity and helps to sort out its specific and separate moments (Guha, 1982: 333-34, my emphasis).

Marx, as I have already mentioned, is another example of someone who manages to great a theoretical work of great complexity from a basic dichotomy. The list goes on. I do not claim for one minute that *Gifts and Commodities* is in the same category as these classic works but I have no qualms about appealing to the authority of these writers as exemplars in rejecting the claims of those thinkers who believe that we can dispense with logical distinctions of a dichotomous kind. The fact is that conceptual distinctions are tools of thought that we cannot do without.

Ethnographic classification, then, is quite distinct from conceptual division by the logical principle of dichotomy. The latter is an instrument of intellectual labour, the former, ethnographic classification, one possible product of it. These divisions have no life of their own but can be useful when working on the raw material—which, for the anthropologist, consists of data collected during fieldwork, archival data, library materials, and so on—to produce an argument, the end cause of the intellectual's labour. Of course, the adequacy of a conceptual opposition can be questioned on logical and empirical grounds. While I can now see the need to revise some aspects of my analysis of PNG history, I have read nothing that convinces me that the logic of my fundamental conceptual opposition between gifts and commodities is in need of revision.

This brings me to the second confusion I see in the writings of my opponents: the meaning of 'binary' opposition. I have used the word 'dichotomy' or 'conceptual division by the logical principle of dichotomy' rather than 'binary' in the preceding discussion. This is because a distinction must be made between binary logic of the axiomatic type associated with George Boole (1854) and the logic of the 'commonplace' or 'topical' type. The latter flourished in Europe from the time of Aristotle to that of Milton in the seventeenth century but thereafter fell into desuetude. As mentioned in the previous chapter, the axiomatic opposite of a *snake* is a *not-snake;* the commonplace opposite is, to use an example from Indian logic, a *mongoose*. A mongoose is a 'not-snake' but the two concepts are not identical. My critics do not recognise this. Instead, the word 'binary' is used to cover both types of opposition.

Lévi-Strauss's binary logic is in the Aristotle-Milton tradition, although he shows no awareness of this fact. Guha's logic, I would argue, is also in this tradition. This can be seen if we pursue the sense in which a mongoose can be said to be the opposite of a snake. The opposition is one of killer to killed. The Indian logicians used this image because the animals, which live in India, are natural enemies. The mongoose normally wins when the battle is against a cobra, a fact that has inspired the imagination of story tellers in India from time immemorial. This commonplace opposition is obviously of great generality and it appears in different societies in different forms. Commonplace opposition is either antagonistic or non-antagonistic. Anthropological thought has tended towards the former type of opposition. Take Lévi-Strauss for example. He finds order in the chaos of the ethnographic record by means of a cultural geography that establishes equivalence between, say, the drought-affected mythical thought of this tribe with the flood-affected thought of that. This theoretical operation, perfectly legitimate in its own terms, is premised on the denial of the chaos brought about by imperialism. This structuralist form of opposition is very close to Radcliffe-Brown's (1958: 123) 'union of opposites' which operates within societies to ensure their smooth functioning. Another variation can be found in Dumont's (1980a: 222) notion of 'hierarchical opposition', the idea that purity encompasses impurity in much the same way the human body encompasses its parts. Dumont's theory denies the antagonistic coexistence of rival cognitions. Countless other examples of this type of denial can be found in the history of anthropology as Fabian's thought provoking *Time and the Other* (1983) illustrates. Fabian draws attention to a fundamental contradiction in anthropological practice:

> On the one hand we dogmatically insist that anthropology rests on ethnographic research involving personal, prolonged interaction with the Other. But then we pronounce upon the knowledge gained from such research a discourse which construes the Other in terms of distance, spatial and temporal (1983: xi).

With the benefit of hindsight, I can now see that it was precisely this that I was reacting to when struggling to come to terms with the ethnographic record on PNG. While I greatly admired the work of the Melanesian ethnographers, it was as if colonisation never happened for most of them. There were some significant exceptions of course, and things have changed much over the past twenty years. However, books in the allochronic mode continue to be produced.

Gifts and Commodities was an attempt to grapple with the commonplace contradiction brought about by colonisation: the power struggles between the powerful mongoose, represented by the unholy trinity of the Australian colonial state, capital (both mining and plantation), and the missionary, and the snake in the form of the bewildering complexity that is the economy, society and culture of village PNG. The affirmation of the existence of commonplace contradiction is, of course, an affirmation of the coevalness because a common-time contradiction (coevalness) is also a common-place contradiction.

As an attempt to come to terms with the specific contradictions of colonial PNG, the second part of *Gifts and Commodities* is already dated both because time has moved on and because new studies, such as the Carriers (1989), have emerged which highlight weaknesses in my account. What survives, though, is the general thrust of the conceptual argument presented in the first part of my book, although this, I can now see in the light of my fieldwork in India and the reading I have done since 1982, is in need of some modification.

Concept construction involves abstraction from specific historical, geographical, and anthropological situations and the formulation of logically coherent schema. On the logical side there is a need, as Fabian (1983: 117) reminds us, for greater understanding of the commonplace logical tradition that informs anthropological discourse in so many unconscious ways. Unlike Fabian who uncritically accepts Ong's negative representation of this tradition, I believe that its re-habilitation is essential if coevality is to be affirmed. Given the na-ture of this book all I can do here is to make the assertion and to demonstrate it implicitly under the cover of more substantive issues.

GIFTS AND COMMODITIES:
A RESTATEMENT

Let me begin by restating the logic of the fundamental oppo-sition that informs *Gifts and Commodities* in terms of the following tree diagram:

This schema is a synthesis of the work of Marx, Lévi-Strauss and Sahlins (among others). A logical opposition between gifts

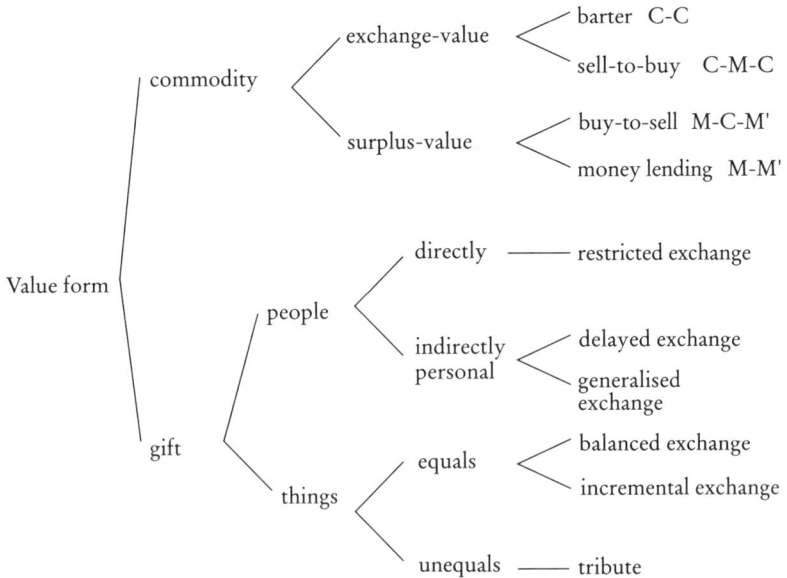

FIGURE II.1   *The conceptual opposition between gifts and commodities*

(relations between non-aliens by means of inalienable things) and commodities (relations between aliens by means of alienable things) is the primary distinction. Continuous application of this principle of dichotomous opposition yields a finely graded set of ten categories. These do not form a continuum, the favoured linear image of those who prefer fuzziness to dichotomies, but rather a multi-dimensional semantic space analogous to that used by Roget in his original thesaurus.[3]

It is one thing to construct a conceptual apparatus but quite another to use it to reveal the commonplace contradictions found in concrete situations, especially in comparative work when one's raw material is the allochronic ethnography of others. Ethnographic film offers one way around this because the immediacy of this medium allows the commonplace contradictions of daily life to peep through even in the most tightly edited film concerned to establish the contrary. In what follows I offer a brief analysis of how villagers draw the boundaries between gifts and commodities in contemporary PNG using the film *The Trobriand Islanders*. I then contrast this with the situation I found in India in order to introduce the themes that I want to develop in this book. To anticipate, I will argue that the framework above needs to be extended to include an anthropological conception of *goods,* a theoretical notion that is invariably confused with *commodities* in the work of my critics.[4] I will also argue that Marx's formulas of commodity exchange acquire new meaning when located concretely in the context of relations of consanguinity, affinity, and contiguity.

GIFTS AND COMMODITIES: 'TRIBAL' INDIA AND 'TRIBAL' PNG COMPARED

In the film *The Trobriand Islanders*, which lasts for 51 minutes, one sees an astonishing number of exchanges involving a large variety of things including yams, cooked taro, uncooked taro, tobacco, money, specially prepared banana leaves (hereafter bundles), grass skirts, manufactured cloth, betel nut, pigs, and many other things besides. The images flash by at a rate that makes it impossible for the

commentary, when supplied, to do little more than give a one sentence description of a complex situation. For example, a voice-over
during a 35 second sequence showing people sitting around a boiling cauldron at night says: 'Men work into the night, boiling taro
pudding for their sisters'. This verbal description is clearly inadequate
in itself but the nature of the film medium is such that it matters little. For the anthropologically informed viewer the sequence is
strangely familiar. It brings to life what one has read about in the
ethnographic literature and one cannot help but locate the event
comparatively from one's own field experience. Thus the 35 second
sequence, which delivers 875 frames of visual information, evokes
many other images in the mind of the viewer and sets one thinking
but not always in the way that the anthropologist and film-maker
want you to. Ethnographic film, then, can be treated in much the same
way as the historian's archive and, as such, even the worst film can
teach us something and be used for something other than that intended. I am not, then, concerned with the merits or demerits of *The
Trobriand Islanders* as a film but, rather, as evidence to prove that
Appadurai's image of the Trobriands as a 'a non-Western, preindustrial, nonmonetised, translocal exchange system' is wide of the mark
and also to show that my distinction between gifts and commodities
is not overstated. The film is a visual representation of the paradox
that I was concerned with in *Gifts and Commodities*: the efflorescence
of gift exchange in a world dominated by the values of the commodity. The film reveals how the Trobriand Islanders cope with the paradox both in their actions and in their verbalised thoughts.

First of all, the film re-affirms the general configuration of
exchanges that the ethnographies have described. Every kinship relationship in Trobriand society seems to be marked by its own product. For example, cooked taro marks the relationship between brother
and sister, uncooked small yams the relationship between wife's
brother and sister's husband, and banana leaves and skirts the relationship between women of different matrilines. The status of chiefs
is marked by the familiar storehouses full of yams. But what about
the exchanges involving money and commodities? How do the Trobriand Islanders handle the commonplace contradiction of gifts and
commodities? On this question the film is very revealing.

As one might expect, the chiefs have appropriated the symbols of commodity status and wealth. The traditional yam house remains a symbol of his authority but also of importance today are the things that money can buy such as Benson and Hedges cigarettes, watches, cement for the graves of deceased chiefs, Toyota four-wheel drive vehicles, and so on. The borrowing and lending of money among chiefs has introduced a new element into their power game. As the commentator informs us at the film's 34th minute:

> In Omarakana village Paramount Chief Puliasi has a problem. As a new chief he had to spend most of his wealth mourning his predecessor. Now he had to find cement to put on the grave. And cement costs money. Another chief, richer and older than Puliasi, has offered cash to get the job done. It is an act that undermines the Paramount Chief's power.

Commoditisation has also affected relations between women but they have developed an ingenious means of overcoming the contradictions. In one sequence, which begins at 22 minutes and 45 seconds into the film (hereafter 22:45) a woman called Bomapota is filmed bartering stick tobacco, which she bought in the trade store for cash, for bundles of banana leaves she needs to give away in a *sagali* because of the death of her 'aunt'. We are informed later (42:10) that her husband, like many other men in the Trobriands, supports his wife's need for bundles by selling his carvings to tourists for cash. The trade store, one of the few in the Trobriands, is owned by Sarah Kalubaku, a University graduate and relative of Chief Nalibutau.

It is clear from this sequence that the Trobrianders make a number of important distinctions between different forms of exchange. The following figure, which shows the path of the transactions, helps us to see the general point behind the specifics.

carvings (C) → cash (M) → tobacco (C) → bundles (C) → bundles (G)

The four products assume three social forms—commodities (C), money (M), and gifts (G)—and describe three distinct circuits. The first is C-M-C, selling in order to buy, which converts carvings into tobacco. The second is C-C, barter, which converts the purchased tobacco into bundles. The third is the transformation of the bundles into a gift (C-G). At each stage the social form of a product undergoes a transformation but the crucial transformation is the final one of bundles into gift.. This particular strategy of gift creation is akin to what Andrew Strathern (1969) has called the 'finance' as opposed to the 'production' strategy. This roundabout way of acquiring a gift keeps the alien world of commodities at bay, not by erecting a *cordon sanitaire* around the island, but by providing a means by which commodities can become domesticated and transformed into gifts. From the point of view of human relations this ideology is really a means to prevent Trobrianders from becoming strangers in their own island. The film in effect argues this point. It finishes (48:45) with the following revealing sequence where Bomapota and her son give verbal expression to the values that inform the actions previously shown.

> *Bomapota*: I want my son, Joseph, if he works for money to return here. And when he comes back and people come to see him, he has to help them with money. Not just a little bit. I want a large amount because if he gives people a little bit of money, people will say: 'His father and mother stopped him from giving a lot of money'. So when Joseph goes to school and goes to work, I will advise him that when people go to him he must give them big presents.
>
> *Joseph:* Only some of us go to school. Some parents hold their children back in the village. I'm going to do training in whatever I can, and then I'm going to help my parents in the village. Yes, when I earn cash I will bank the money so that when I come back I can help my parents. We are all one group.

This 'one group' ideology finds its social expression in the four clan division of Trobriand society that functions to relate one to all by means of a complicated set of rules relating to sub-clans, land tenure, residential patterns and so on. We see the force of this ideology today in a sequence (40:30) involving Rose Acaripa. She owns a supermarket on the mainland and has returned to pay people at a *sagali*. In this sequence village women place the traditional banana leaf bundles and grass skirts in a pile on the ground. When it comes to Rose's turn she places generous amounts of cloth and paper money on the pile instead of the traditional bundles. (The money is quickly appropriated by some men and the viewer is left wondering who they are and by what right they take the money.) Rose explains her actions in the following way:

Rose: I have a name on the island now I have a big business. I have to show that I am a woman and I can do it. So I had to do it on my own and I just have to spend how much I could spend... What I did was because I worked in the town. I have to put money in material, or clothes or whatever.

The forgoing is far from being an adequate analysis of the film but it illustrates my general point that the commonplace contradiction between gifts and commodities is a very real concern for the people on the Trobriand Islands. The six categories of gift exchange I have distinguished above in Figure II.1 are adequate for general comparative analysis but if one is concerned with the specificities of the situation in different parts of the Trobriand Islands then further distinctions are needed. But the problem I want to address in this book leads me in the opposite direction because my fieldwork in India has highlighted, for me a least, a more general problem with this conceptual framework.

In 1982 I carried out fieldwork on a rural marketing system in Bastar District, India, and have been back a couple of times since. Bastar District is to India what the Trobriands is to PNG in that it lies in a remote out of the way place, albeit in the centre of India. The region is one of the last economic frontiers in India in that it is still relatively heavily forested and one of the few areas of India without rail. A prominent anthropologist (von Fürer-Haimendorf, 1982: 201) once described it, rather inaccurately I was to find out, as an 'unblemished tribal haven'. Fresh from my work on gifts and commodities in PNG, I set off to the field expecting to find many similarities with PNG, but how wrong I was.

Before I arrived in the field I paid an obligatory visit to the Commissioner of Tribal Welfare in Bhopal to inform him of my work. It was then that I heard the first of many versions of what I call the 'Tribal exploitation hypothesis'. 'The Tribal people of Bastar know nothing of modern ways,' he told me, 'and are ruthlessly exploited by shrewd merchants from Rajasthan.' There is, of course, an element of truth in this. Who can deny that merchants try to buy at the cheapest price and sell at the dearest? Nevertheless, the idea that the village people are innocent, passive victims of the commercial world is a stereotype image of the kind that I found was wide of the mark. What struck me was how thoroughly commercial the people of Bastar were in their dealings with each other. It was as if commodity exchanges structured the lives of villagers in Bastar in the way that gift exchanges did in PNG. Not only did a commercial morality pervade everyday relations between people, I also found it in their rituals and myths.

Bastar District is thoroughly integrated into the national economy through a flourishing system of periodic markets. This means that any one village in the district is no more than a few hours walk away from some market or other every day of the week. Women specialise in the marketing of village produce and many go to the market every day taking with them a few kilos of rice or home-grown vegetables to sell in order to buy the imported commodities they need like kerosene, cooking oil, clothes, jewellery, and so on. Itinerant traders are forever wandering around the villages with things to sell; small stores can be found everywhere. Relations between households within a village are highly commercialised too. Take Mr. P. Gardener of Minipur village for example. I could never understand how he managed to survive because he and his sons had insufficient rice land to support their big family. However, Mr Gardener spent most of the day sitting around playing his flute and looking relatively prosperous. The riddle was solved one day when I saw a neighbour climb his palm tree, extract the wine, and pay him for it in both cash and kind. Mr Gardener, it transpired, had one of the few palm trees in the village and he extracted a monopoly rent from it. His caste, it should be noted, smoke marijuana but do not drink and the wine is sold to a caste that drink but do not smoke.

These observations led me to pose some questions. Where are the boundaries of commodity exchange in Bastar? Is there no domain that is free from the alienating influences of commodity exchange? One can understand why Trobriand ethnographers have concentrated on the gift to the exclusion of the commodity but why are there almost no studies of commodities and markets in India? Market studies abound in Indonesia, in Mexico and in other places but why not in India? Why have Indianist anthropologists been so fixated on purity and pollution and caste? It seemed to me that mercantile profit and loss, rather than purity and pollution, was the central opposition in the Indian society I was observing.

As I delved into the myths and rituals of the people I found more evidence for the ideological significance of a commercial morality. The boundary of the world of commodities is marked by a ritual called *haat nikarani,* literally the 'coming-out market'. This ritual is performed ten days after the death of a relative to lift the taboos that follow death. The family members concerned set up a symbolic market at cross-roads in their village where they pretend to buy and sell. They are free to attend the weekly market when the ritual is over. This ritual has been around for at least fifty years and possibly much longer. Elwin (1947: 157) describes a 'mock bazaar' that is held some distance from the market. In these rituals old clothes, bits of wood, seeds and beans are laid out for sale on the ground as if in a real market. For money broken pieces of an earthen pot are used. He also describes a situation where the villagers go to the nearest market to buy parched rice, gram and liquor. They walk around the shops scattering rice and gram; they then visit the grave of the dead man, offer him a drink, and ask him to return home with them.

The following myth told by Mr. Jaidev Baghel, an aboriginal artisan from Kondagaon, provides further insights into attitudes towards markets in India.

> It is said that in the olden days there was a market under a banyan tree. A cyclone came as it was being held. A pregnant woman had come to the market to sell vegetables. When the cyclone hit people ran for cover in all directions but the pregnant lady was unable to move due to the onset of labour pains. The woman gave birth to a baby girl under the banyan tree but, because of the unbearable pain of childbirth, she died. After the death of her mother the baby started to cry out in hunger. Having heard her cries, the banyan tree took pity on her. One of the hanging fibrous roots of the banyan tree then came into the mouth of the baby. The baby, thinking that it was her mother's nipple, started sucking. As she sucked, juice from the tree flowed into her mouth. Many days passed in this way with the baby obtaining her sustenance from the juice of the tree. One day a woman saw the girl. It is said that the woman was barren. Upon seeing the girl the woman thought, 'O Bhagwan, how kind you have been to me.' Having thought this she felt very happy and, having lifted the girl up, took her home. Her husband was also very pleased to see the baby. But they thought that if they told people how

they got the baby then the mother would come and take her back. The woman then made a bundle of cloth, placed it on her stomach, and started to tell people she was pregnant. After four to six months she said that she had given birth and showed the baby to the villagers. The girl grew day by day. Right from childhood, the girl liked to eat good food, to wear fine clothes, ornaments and make-up. The village children used to play with her too. She loved everybody and used to teach them about religious and moral matters. Even though only young, she used to talk like a mature experienced person. News of her teachings spread throughout the region. People came to see her. They used to listen to her teachings and follow them. In this way she was able to form an army from her followers and began to punish amoral people. She was very helpful to moral people. The king of that region was very amoral. The king, on hearing of this woman's boldness, started a war with her. The woman's army had insufficient weapons. The king defeated them and took them prisoner. After some days he released them. After their release, they again prepared for war with the king. Another war then started. The king was defeated in this war. To celebrate their win, they organised a burnt offering under a big banyan tree. At that very moment the king and soldiers suddenly appeared and started to beat them. Then they told the girl to surrender or they would kill everybody. The people were unarmed at this time. The girl said, 'Kill me but let the children go.' 'No! No!' shouted her comrades, 'You have helped us like a mother.' 'Even though you are younger than us you have loved us like a mother,' they added. 'We will never let you surrender to the king.' 'I am one person and if my death saves the lives of many others then I will be very happy,' she said. 'But,' she added, 'be careful and don't forget my teachings.' On saying this, she jumped into the fire pit and died. Then they said, 'Look, see how much she has loved us throughout her life and today she has sacrificed herself to save us.' From this day people began to call her 'Maybali'. From this word 'Maybali' (Lit. mother-sacrifice) the name 'Mabali' and then 'Mavli' was derived. And from this day Mavli Mata worship began in the Bastar region. A special fair called Mavli Fair was started in her memory and is still going.

It would take some time to unpack the messages of this myth but it suffices to note here that a banyan tree is found in almost every large market. The market, symbolised by the banyan tree, does not have negative associations; indeed, it seems to have a positive maternal association. Negative feelings are reserved for the divine king whose family has been ruling Bastar for many centuries. The people of Bastar, then, are not one big family as in the Trobriands. For someone like Jaidev who identifies himself as an Aborigine, the King is an alien, a Hindu outsider whose family colonised the region some 20 generations ago; but for many natives of Bastar whose origin myths identify them as Hindus, the king is looked upon as a father.

For Jaidev 'family' means, first and foremost, his immediate family. The terms used are *ghar, kutumb, bus, thok,* and *jat*; these may be glossed as household, family, clan, lineage, and endogamous group respectively. These groups serve to define the Other as a non-*jat* and because artisans are landless these groups cannot be mapped onto a piece of territory as they can in the Trobriands. But territoriality remains an important concept: it exists as a form of *consciousness* that binds people together around the notion of a homeland. Temples in various locations mark the religious centres of the *ghar, kutumb, bus,* etc.; the distribution of the *jat* members throughout the district creates a sense that Bastar District as a whole is their aboriginal homeland.

For Jaidev 'family' also means the various *jat* that make up the *Paramparik Bastar Shilpi Pariwar,* the Traditional Artisan Families of Bastar. This group has official institutional status today and Jaidev is its Chairman. Its aim is to fight for the right of artisans to land, education and the general well being of the community against the many foreigners who have colonised the District such as government officials, land-seeking migrants from neighbouring districts, and the wealthy merchants from Rajasthan. For people like Jaidev, all these people are foreigners. But the latter do not see things in this way.

Take the government officials. They say that the Rajasthani merchant is the 'real' foreigner because they exploit the Tribal people whereas the government is there to help them. As always, there is some truth in this claim but this must be seen in the light of the distinctions merchants draw between themselves and the government officials. The merchants say that the officials use them as scapegoats to divert attention from the fact that many civil servants engage in invisible transactions of dubious propriety with timber dealers and other transactors of commodity wealth. Of course, not all civil servants are corrupt but one thing is clear: the relations that bind civil servant and timber dealer have little in common with the kinship relations that bind market traders together.

Mercantile capitalists observe a simple principle: they must buy cheap and sell dear. However, it is not the percentage difference between buying and selling price that is important but the *absolute value* of commodities sold. It is one thing to buy something for Rs 1 and to sell it for Rs 6 to make a 500% profit of Rs 5 but quite another to buy something for Rs 10,000 and to sell it for Rs 10,200 to make a 2% profit of Rs 200. Anti-merchant stories are full of figures of dazzling profit rates but these stories miss the crucial point that it is the amount of trading capital that is all important. One way to acquire the trading capital is by means of credit, but who is going to advance it? The Rajasthani merchants have solved this problem. They have a long history of migration and they operate in markets all over India. However, they maintain their kinship links with each other and with their homeland. Hereditary Bards record these connections in books that trace genealogies back over hundreds of years. Life-cycle rituals performed in the birthplace of ancestors serve to renew the living relationship between widely scattered kinsmen. These links create a consciousness of territoriality which extends over the whole of India and the patrilineal and patriarchal groups so defined are reproduced by the endogamous exchange of three crucial prestige items: language, women, and credit:

> Language: Marwari is the mother tongue and the basis of the coded commercial script used in ledgers.
> Women: marriages are carefully planned and alliances are only made with those families recorded in the books of the genealogist.
> Credit: herein lies the secret of the wealthy merchants' success for mercantile credit is the supreme gift in a mercantile family.

Mercantile kinship, then, gives the landless Marwaris the sense that all-India is their aboriginal homeland and the currency of mercantile credit defines Brothers and Others. The former are those to whom trading credit is given, the latter those to whom consumer credit is advanced. For consumers like Jaidev, consumer credit is the bitter-sweet milk of the banyan tree; it is the basis of the ambivalent relationship that makes the customer dependent upon the merchant.

Consumer credit therefore enables the merchant to travel to places in Bastar today where many a corrupt forest guard fears to tread. The recent history of violence in Bastar suggests that they have good grounds for these fears. It also suggests that villagers make a clear distinction between clan brothers, mercantile traders, and the hated Others who plunder their forests for profit.

Poor aboriginal artisans like Jaidev and rich immigrant merchants like the Marwaris are landless. However the bulk of the population in Bastar consists of small landed families who produce commodities for sale on the weekly markets. Families own small holdings of land that consist of scattered plots that have tended to get smaller and smaller as population has increased and land has become scarce. Here is what I believe to be the crucial difference between the political economy of PNG and that of central India. Land tenure in PNG is, for the most part, in the hands of the clan and assumes a variety of local forms throughout the country. Perhaps the only generalisation possible is that land boundaries are extremely fluid and subject to endless dispute, especially in those areas where the population density is high. In India, by way of contrast, the land tenure system is a variation on a general pattern found in many parts of Asia, Europe and America. In the language of Marx (1894: xlvii, v) the farmers of Bastar are 'peasant proprietors of land parcels' but this term, and the theory that informs it, needs to be revised as we shall see in the next chapter.

THE 'INDIAN' GIFT AND THE NEED FOR A THEORY OF GOODS

My observations on commodity exchange in India are consistent with some of Parry's. He argues that commodity exchange in India is not only morally neutral but morally obligatory for certain castes. Parry, who conducted ethnographic fieldwork among some Brahman funeral priests of Benares, also reports that 'dire moral peril' attaches to certain kinds of gifts (dan). Funeral priests receive gifts from the family of the deceased that transfer sin (pap) from the giver to the receiver. Raheja's (1988a) research, based on a village study in north India, suggests that gifts of this kind, previously unnoticed by other ethnographers, may be of widespread distribution in India. Raheja shows that the dominant caste transfer inauspiciousness to Brahmans by means of *dan*. In one of her many case studies she describes the ritual the parents of a young boy had to perform to ensure his well being and to prevent his early death. The ritual was necessary because the eclipse demon, Rahu, occupied one of the houses of his horoscope and *dan* had to be given to a Brahman from a distant village to remove the faults *(dos)* and afflictions *(kast)* engendered by the presence of Rahu at his birth. A mediator, a local Brahman, transferred the inauspiciousness from the boy to the *dan*, which took the material form of black cloth, black shoes, a black clay model of a water buffalo, a small amount of gold, and other sundry items, using the principles of contagious magic. The recipient, an outside Brahman, picked up the *dan* and left. The moral neutrality of commercial transactions in India, then, contrasts sharply with the negative valuation placed on the giving of *dan* to Brahmans, an evaluation, Parry (1989) notes, which inverts the evaluations made by people in Melanesia and elsewhere.

This case, as Parry (1986: 463) argues, poses a number of difficulties for our general theory of exchange. It consciously repudiates Gouldner's (1960) universal 'moral norm of reciprocity'. *Dan*, Parry stresses (1986: 462), '*must* be alienated, should *never* return, and should endlessly be handed on.' In other words, *dan* is something for which there is no obligation to return. Given that reciprocity, inalienation and the obligation to return are the central defining characteristics of the gift, what is at stake here is the very notion of the gift itself. Parry's theoretical response is somewhat contradictory. In an early article (1980) he argued that *dan* only has the appearance of contradicting Mauss's theory that every gift creates an obligation to return. Nothing is returned, he says, because *dan* is '*its own counter-prestation*' (1980: 105, emphasis in the original). In a later article (1986) his response was to say that the contradiction is real, that there is no obligation to return *dan*-type gifts, and that *dan* is an example of a 'pure gift', by which he means an unreciprocated gift with Maussian 'spirit'. 'Where we have spirit,' he argues (1986: 463), 'reciprocity is denied; where there is reciprocity there is not much evidence of "spirit"'.

The notion of an 'unreciprocated' gift is a contradiction in terms because reciprocity, along with the inalienation and the obligation to return it implies, is the defining characteristic of a gift. If *dan* is unreciprocated then the very notion of the gift is at stake. Parry's opposing theories on the matter give him an each way bet; however his ethnographical description is a model of clarity and it allows for more than one interpretation.

From a humanist perspective, the 'norm of reciprocity' is a value that has *reciprocal recognition* between people as its basis and power as its means of reproduction. Sanctions, such as the threat of witchcraft, are behind the obligation to repay as Firth pointed out long ago. But what happens if there is no reciprocal recognition? There are two logical possibilities, asymmetrical recognition and indifference, and it is the former that provides the basis of a subalternate interpretation of *dan*.

Reciprocal recognition presupposes agreement as to the meaning of a transaction. This agreement is more likely to occur among *insiders* who, because of relations of contiguity, have been able to develop it over time and who are more likely to have a mutual interest in maintaining their relationship into the future. As Raheja (1988a) reports, transactions involving dangerous *dan* must be with *outsiders*. But what she does not note is that a relation between an insider and an outsider creates the possibility for disagreement as to the meaning of a transaction. In other words, asymmetrical recognition is possible when aliens are involved.

Consider Parry's data on the rituals of death in Benares. Two priests are employed to handle the soul of the deceased as it changes its form from ghost (*pret*) to ancestor (*pitr*). Mahabrahman funeral priests, who enjoy the anomalous status of impure and highly inauspicious Brahmans, perform the dangerous rituals involving *pret* that last for eleven days after death. A household priest, or hereditary pilgrimage priest if he is not available, perform the rituals involving *pitr*. The Mahabrahman accepts highly dangerous gifts in the name of the deceased person's ghost and the hereditary priest accepts much safer gifts in the name of the ancestor. The relationship of a lineage and their household priest is, by definition, an ongoing one; their relationship with the Mahabrahman, by contrast, is once off. The givers of *dan*, for their part, have no desire to sustain a long-term relationship with the funeral priest who has accepted sin-infested gifts; the recipients, for their part, have a system for the allocation of funeral rights based on time of the year rather than a fixed clientele which 'helps to maintain the anonymity of the specialist' (1980: 96).

This alienated relationship between the priest and his client allows for asymmetrical recognition of the significance of the event. In other words, rival cognitions of the transaction become possible. The givers of *dan* identify the Mahabrahman with the ghost of the deceased; they give him *sajja dan* that should consist of the standard requirements of daily life such as a year's supply of grain, cooking utensils, bedding, clothes, and so on. 'The idea,' Parry notes (1980: 96), 'is that the offerings are received by the deceased in the next world.' In other words, the recipient, from the givers' point of view, is the deceased; the priest is a mere *mediator* and the material form of the *dan* the mere *vehicle* that the non-material sin attaches itself to. The Brahmans, for their part, have an ideology that reciprocally recognises this interpretation of the event. Thus, ideally, the receiver rids himself of any sins by giving away with increment the *dan* he has received to other Brahmans and/or by 'turning away' from them and assigning them to various deities (Parry, 1980: 103; Heesterman, 1985: 37); the correct and meticulous performance of daily rituals and the repeated recitation of various sacred formulae are also essential, and Hindu law forbids any commercial-like negotiation over the size and material form of the *dan*.

The family of the deceased have an obvious emotional investment in a religious interpretation of the event, an interpretation that derives its meaning from their bereavement, their religious beliefs about malevolent spirits, and their anxieties about their own future well-being among other things. The funeral priests, by way of contrast, have little emotional investment in a religious interpretation of the event. The limited tenure of their rights to cremation sites oblige them to view the matter in economic terms. This fact, combined with the poor family circumstances of many of the funeral priests and their ignorance of Sanskrit formulae and ritual, means that an economic interpretation of the transaction becomes an issue. As a result, the size and content of the *gift* offered by the bereaved to the deceased becomes, for the priest, a *commodity* with a negotiable price. The mourners, aware of the priest's reputation for avarice, may offer substantially less than custom demands; the priest protests and marketplace-type acrimony follows (Parry, 1980: 96).

Rival cognitions of this kind create contradictions: the transaction is now a gift, now a commodity according to the play of reciprocal and asymmetrical recognition. These vary as much between the transactors as they do within them over time. Priests, like all human beings, are not simple-minded economic men; they are complex human beings motivated by many conflicting passions and thoughts. As such, their avarice has its ideological costs. Many liken themselves to a sewer through which the moral filth of their patrons is passed, a sewer which becomes a cess-pit from which one may contact leprosy and die. As an *economic* occupation, then, the work is *religiously* very dangerous and concerns about the latter may outweigh the profits of the former and different employment sought.

The dilemma facing the *dan*-receiving Benares funeral priest arises because of a contradiction between Brahmanic values and the values of a coeval Indian mercantile world. These contradictions do not arise for all receivers of *dan*. The marginalised, poverty stricken, low status people thoughout India have developed a subalternate value system that reconciles the contradictions facing the receiver of *dan*. Their theological economy redefines the 'unreciprocated gift' as a 'partial repayment of commodity debt'. Guha (1985) develops this argument in his analysis of the myths of Rahu, a deity who appears as a demon in the Brahmanic value system and as a god in the subalternate value system of some Untouchables. The following is a very brief account of the essence of these subalternate values.

During an eclipse low caste people demand *dan* from members of the higher castes. In Gujarat, for example, as soon as the skies begin to darken the Untouchable Bhangis go about shouting *Garhandan, Vastradan, Rupadan,* 'gifts for the eclipse, gifts of clothes, gifts of silver' (quoted in Guha, 1985: 16). Brahmanic myths of Rahu, some of which have been reproduced by O'Flaherty (1973), suggest that, from the standpoint of the elite castes, 'these gifts can only be regarded as a price they have to pay for the return of peace in the heavens and purity on earth' (Guha, 1985: 16). These myths tell the tale of the battle between the gods and demons over the Elixir, of how the gods stole it from the demons, and how Rahu, in his disguise as a god, was decapitated when he was discovered drinking the Elixir at their celebrations. But from the standpoint of the outcaste recipient a different interpretation of *dan* is construed as the following myth suggests:

> The sun and the moon were brothers. A hungry worshipper came to them, saying, 'I am poor and hungry. Give me something to eat.' The brothers went to a sweeper-woman and said, 'Give this man grain'. She had a bin in which were all kinds of grain. She agreed to give grain to the beggar for a year. She was directed by the brothers to take the grain out of the bin from below, and they agreed to fill it by putting grain in from the top. During the year the sun and moon were unable to fill the bin, and when the year was up, the woman said, 'Now pay me, for the bin is not full.' They were unable to pay her and hid themselves. Now, when eclipses occur, the worshippers of the sun and moon collect various kinds of grain, mix them, and distribute them to beggars, and thus deliver the sun and moon from shame (Briggs, 1953: 545; reproduced in Guha 1985: 18).

This myth, and its variants, have widespread currency among low status communities. Crooke (1926: 41), in his survey of 'popular' religion, noted that ideas like this 'may be at the root of the common belief about Rahu' and Guha's essay convincingly demonstrates that this is the case. The implication of this material is that the obligation to repay is conspicuously present[5] from the receivers' point of view: what the elite conceptualise as an obligation to give a *gift*, the subalterns see as unpaid *commodity* debt. As Guha (1985) notes, the myths and rituals of Rahu are an expression of an unresolved antagonism between the dominant and the subordinate. If one ritual action contains three actors of different rank then it is logically possible for the giver to have one interpretation of events, the receiver another, and the mediator a third. Logical possibilities of this kind are realised when there is no reciprocal recognition between the parties and this, I suggest, is precisely the situation that characterises the alienated relations between those who accept Brahmanic values and those who do not. Thus while the notion of an 'unreciprocated gift' is a contradiction in terms, the notion of 'unreciprocated *dan*' is not when *dan* is defined, from a disputatious subalternate standpoint, as a form of commodity exchange.

The fine grained ethnographic research of Parry and Raheja raises the general question of the transfer of *bads,* the generic word I will use to describe the transfer of impurities, inauspiciousness, sin, and the like. Bads inflict the rich as well as the poor, high status people as well as the low; gift exchange is but one means among many by which it is transferred.

In Bastar District, for example, bads are exorcised from a village by ritually dumping them, in the wet-season month of *bhadon* (August-September), on the northern-most border of a village at a *ponhcani* post. The northern recipients of these bads transfer them from the south of their village to the north and so it goes on, according to my informant (Mr. M.S. Mali), until all the accumulated bads reach Keshkal ghat, a mountain pass at the northern extremity of the district. Here they are ritually dumped over the edge of the cliff. The repository of this evil is the goddess Bhangaram whose main temple is at Keshkal and whose distinguishing sign is a black flag. Bastar District has very few Brahmans and this ritual, when placed in the comparative context of the material reported by Parry and Raheja from Brahman-intensive north India, can be seen as their means of coping with the problem of bads.

Of course, a *bad* presupposes a *good,* an opposition that takes on agreed meanings when there is reciprocal recognition, and discrepant meanings when there is not. Thus, from the standpoint of Brahmanic values, an eclipse is a bad whose evil influences must be transferred with *dan* while, from the standpoint of the worshippers of the Rahu, it brings goods, commodities or money.

This brief discussion raises the general question of the theory of goods. As seen in the last chapter, neoclassical economists have dominated thinking about this matter over the past century. Their marginal utility theory of value is from the perspective of the Market and individual cognition. The perspective of the House, based as it is on reciprocal and asymmetrical recognition, suggests that there is room for an alternative theory of goods. In *Gifts and Commodities* my opposition to neoclassical theory was such that I conflated a particular theory of goods with the notion in general. I can now see that neoclassical economists have no monopoly on the term, that the history of thinking about the subject goes back thousands of years,[6] and that a new anthropologically informed theory of goods is needed. The basis of such a theory already exists, if in a somewhat embryonic form, in the anthropological literature. This issue will be addressed in the next chapter.

NOTES

[1]   See, for example, Strathern (1988), Werbner (1990), Thomas (1991), Taylor (1992), and Carrier (1995).

[2]   A top public servant I visited in 1978 had a large *mwali* (armshell) hanging on his wall that he received through a Port Moresby *kula* exchange.

[3]   Note that this involved 1000 lower level classes, grouped into six secondary philosophical categories and arrayed according to the principle of antithesis. The logic of Roget's system is like that of the colour cube but most modern-day versions use the alphabet as the sole logical principle of construction.

[4]   The very title of the Comaroffs' (1990) article 'Goodly beasts, beastly goods: cattle and commodities in a South African context' illustrates this. Here goods = cattle and bads = commodities which is much the same argument made by Taussig (1980), a person the Comaroffs accuse of employing 'facile dichotomies'. Appadurai's theory, as we have seen, makes similar equations. Taylor (1992: 9) has noted this contradiction in the thought of the Comaroffs and opts for the gift/commodity distinction because it 'approximates the indigenous discrimination'.

[5]   Raheja (1988) reproduces this conventional orthodoxy in her extraordinarily rich ethnographic analysis of gift exchange in a north Indian village. I questioned this orthodoxy in my review (Gregory, 1992) of her book. Judging from her response to my comments (see Raheja, 1993) it seems that she has misunderstood the issue I was trying to problematise. I hope that the forgoing analysis clarifies what I see to be the theoretical implications of Guha's work for anthropological theory.

[6]   See, for example, von Wright (1963).

Chapter III

Land as the Supreme Good

Of goods ill got
The third heir joyeth not
(Seventeenth century English proverb)

WHAT IS A GOOD?

There comes a time in the life of an anthropologist, often towards the end of their fieldwork, when informants reveal the existence of certain highly valued possessions. From an outsider's perspective these objects often have little intrinsic value; but, from the insider's perspective, they are very highly valued and this is manifested in the reverential way the objects are handled and the strong emotional reactions they evoke. I shall call these objects *goods* and introduce my discussion of this form of value by means of a few concrete examples in order to clarify the problem that I want to address.

On the 8th February 1990, Mr. M.S. Mali, a member of the Gardener caste and resident of Bastar whom I first met in 1983, was showing me the many gods that he worshipped. We spent over a week touring the village and its surroundings taking photographs of the various icons and talking about the stories behind them. When our work was over at the end of this long, tiring week, we were sitting in his house relaxing when he said that he still had some more icons to show me. We went into a small room of his house where two clay pots were strung above a small altar in the corner of the room. Before we touched anything he got some *ganga pani* (Ganges water) from a brass pot and washed the altar to purify it. He then carefully removed four small metallic objects from the clay pot, the iconic forms of his family gods (*kuldev*), and put them on the altar. One of these objects, an old silver rupee coin, was Dulha Deo, a god who was there 'from the very beginning'. Another, a postage stamp sized piece of silver with an image of the Hindu goddess Durga stamped on it, was Rat Mai 'whose power is greater than Bhagwan when she assumes the form of Durga'. The remaining two pieces of postage stamp sized metal, one gold the other one silver, represented the Seven Sisters, (*sat bahin*).

> There should be seven of these [Mali noted] but we only have two. When these seven *sakti* make one, that *sakti* is called *adisakti* (original female power). The *adisakti* made the earth, Ram, Krishna, Vishnu, etc. Rat Mai and the Seven Sisters are mother goddesses and they, along with Dulha Deo, gave birth to our family. They are the family deities for all the Naik clan (*thok*) but they are kept here in my house because I am from the *pujari* branch (priestly lineage) of the clan. They came here when my elder brother died and his son will look after them when he grows up. These gold and silver images are not mine. They belong to the Naik clan. They should be kept in our family temple but I keep them here so that they don't get stolen.

Compare Sahlins (1994: 392):

> Not far from Suva, in the village of Cautata, Poate Matairavula a few years ago showed me a small wooden chest, set in the furthest corner of the rear right-hand bedroom of his 'European-style' house. The space was the modern equivalent of the most tabu part of the old Fijian house (the *loqi*), where the head of the family slept with his wife and reproductive forms of wealth were stored, including seed yams and the weapons that procured cannibal victims. The wooden chest, Matairavula explained, was the 'basket of the clan' (*kata ni mataqali*), holding the collective treasure in whale teeth. Passing with the leadership of the clan, the chest was a palladium, a sacred safeguard of the group. So long as it was intact, Matairavula said, the *vanua*—the land, including the people—will be preserved.

Another case comes from Papua New Guinea where Libi Gnecchi-Ruscone was working in a village that had been converted to Christianity over four generations before. She was talking to a member of the village about their old beliefs when he asked if she would like to see the ancestral relics of his family. As the man got up to remove the relics from the roof of his house he was completely overcome with emotion, so much so that he had to call the interview off and made no attempt to touch the relics again (Gnecchi-Ruscone, pers. comm.). Yet another case comes from the elite families of Texas studied by Marcus (1985: 237) who observed that certain objects are transformed into 'sacred property' with a high 'domestic exchange value'. These include both objects with a high commodity value, such as a paintings, houses, and land, and trivial inexpensive items such as pocket knives, combs, and lucky charms. By 'domestic exchange value' he means the 'powerfully sentimental meanings that an object acquires by its possession and transference and in the memories that it evokes among descendants'.

In rural areas land tends to be the special subject of affective valuation of this kind. Consider the recent statement by Hopi Religious Leaders:

> Hopi land is held in trust in a spiritual way for the Great Spirit Massau'u... The land is sacred and if the land is abused, the sacredness of Hopi life will disappear and all other life as well... The Great Spirit has told the Hopi Leaders that the great wealth and resources beneath the lands at Black Mesa must not be disturbed or taken out until after purification when mankind will know how to live in harmony among themselves and with nature. The Hopi were given special guidance in caring for our sacred land so as not to disrupt the fragile harmony that hold things together... To us it is unthinkable to give up control over our sacred lands to non-Hopis. We have no way to express exchange of sacred land for money. It is alien to our ways. The Hopis never gave authority to anyone to dispose of our lands and heritage and religion for any price. We received these lands from the Great Spirit and we must hold them for him, as a steward, a caretaker, until he returns (Knudston and Suzuki, 1992: 137).

Examples like this can be drawn from all over the world and from all times. Annette Weiner has drawn some of these together in her *Inalienable Possessions* (1992: 38):

> Landed property is another category of inalienable possessions as the examples from the Middle Ages show. [Simmel (1982:240)

considered that landed property was valued above any utility it might have because men had 'a relation of sovereign power over the soil'.] But even centuries later, Veblen (1899: 38) ... recognized how land acts as the primary 'standard of wealth,' with estates acquired from ancestors even more honorific that those gotten through one's own acquisition. Throughout American society, land is still used as a measure of a family's history and prestige. During the 1970s, while doing fieldwork in a small Texas town, a few of my wealthy informants impressed upon me that among the elite, the accumulation of money could never substitute for extensive land holdings even if the land itself was economically unproductive. Nonprofitable acres were often bought so that a person's heirs would be unable to sell off or subdivide the property. Today, almost one-third of the land mass of Britain is owned by titled families. As Ilse Hayden (1987) points, the aristocracy remains wealthy today, despite the public's impression that they are on the verge of ruin. An important measure of that wealth is in landownership. These attitudes towards land would come as no surprise to ancient Athenians who believed that the sale of land was not only an offence against their children's inheritance but against their ancestors because the dead were buried on such land. [Similar beliefs occur among the Wape of Papua New Guinea whose ancestors' ghosts reside within the lineage land to ensure the fertility of its resources (Mitchell, 1987).] Furthermore, loss of land inevitably led to the loss of aristocratic status because, as Smith was to warn the aristocracy centuries later, without land, one was forced to become a trader, artisan or laborer—all degrading occupations and, for the ancient Greeks, prohibiting them the right to vote.

These examples signal the argument I want to develop here which is that, in an agrarian economy, land is the supreme good; that the transformation of things into goods involves the creation of a culturally specific notion of scarcity; that, ideally, a good is a priceless non-commodity whose value as a good is to be explained with reference to historically specific relations of consanguinity; and that when goods become commodities the price they fetch may be higher or lower than that which market valuation theories would predict. A central defining characteristic of *goods*, then, is *scarcity* and the question arises as to how the scarcity is culturally created and maintained. It is not sufficient to merely assert, as culturalists are want to do, that scarcity is a 'cultural construction' and to leave it at that. Cultural constructions have human builders and the radical humanist's task is to reveal the identity of these builders, to describe the tools they use, to define the form of their construction, and to critique their ends. Culturalists and humanists agree on one thing though, the idea that scarcity is not a natural phenomenon even though it may have a natural basis. Scarcity, for an anthropologist, is defined with reference to historically specific human relationships of inclusion and exclusion whose borders are marked by the creation of inalienable possessions, ie. *goods,* under the control of trusted guardians. Silver rupee coins are in abundant supply but the one chosen by Mr. Mali's ancestors to represent their family god is unique so far as Mr. Mali is concerned.

ANTHROPOLOGICAL APPROACHES TO THE THEORY OF GOODS

Anthropological approaches to the theory of goods are still very much in their infancy. Indeed, the terms of the debate have not even been agreed upon: some people talk of *goods,* others of *inalienable possessions,* and yet others of *valuables.* Nevertheless some progress has been made. An antithesis—the neoclassical rational choice approach to goods—has been more or less clearly defined and a thesis is beginning to take shape. The intention of this chapter is to make a modest contribution to the ongoing process of shaping this alternative theory by presenting some theoretical speculations and illustrating these with selected ethnographic evidence. My discussion makes no claims to be a comprehensive synthesis; it does little more than clarify the terms of the debate.

The anthropological literature on the topic is a complete terminological, conceptual and theoretical muddle where terms such as 'gifts', 'commodities', 'goods' and 'money' are used interchangeably. Culturalists, we have seen in the last chapter, see this as a theoretical virtue. Even a sophisticated value theorists like Dumont, who would be the last to see any merit in fuzzy thinking, is prone to conceptual confusion on this point. Consider the following:

> [E]conomists speak of *'goods and services'* as one overarching category comprising, on the one hand, *commodities* and on the

> other, something quite different from *commodities* but assimi-
> lated to them, namely *services*. This is incidentally an example of
> relations between men (services) being subordinated to relations
> to things (*goods*), and if we were to study, say, a Melanesian
> system of exchanges, it would come nearer to the mark to reverse
> the priority and speak of '*prestations and goods*', I mean '*presta-
> tions*' (relations between men) including things or encompassing
> their contrary, *things* (Dumont, 1980b: 225, emphasis added).

This argument establishes an equation between *commodities*, *goods* and
things on the one hand and between *prestations* and *services* on the
other. The fact is that a service can be a commodity and things can be
gifts. The confusion is overcome by distinguishing the general form
of the relations between things and people from the specific cultural
form that the relations between things and people can assume in
contingent historical settings. Without these conceptual distinctions
the valuation process, and the switching strategies that valuers adopt,
becomes impossible to understand.

The conceptual muddle is not complete however and a sympathetic reading of the literature can uncover some important insights.
Foster's (1965) controversial theory of the limited good notes the
important association between goods and scarcity. Gell (1986), building
on the work of Douglas and Isherwood (1980), takes us well beyond
the neoclassical conception of consumption by noting that what

> distinguishes consumption from exchange is not that consump-
> tion has a physiological dimension that exchange lacks, but that
> consumption involves the incorporation of the consumed item
> into the personal and social identity of the consumer (1986: 112).

Consumption is a pivotal process in the history of a good because it is
the means by which things, be they gifts, commodities or use-values,
become goods. On this point, Weiner makes the important observation
that

> food is the most ineffectual inalienable possession [read *good*]
> because its biological function is to release energy rather
> than store it. Therefore, in its use to humans, food changes, de-
> teriorates, or perishes. So significant is this loss to those without
> extensive durable things that, in some cases, attempts are made
> to transform food into more permanent words or things. Among

the Wamira of the Papuan coast, the genealogical histories of taro plants are sacred inalienable knowledge, whereas on Goodenough, one of the Massim Islands, strings tied around long yams presented in competitive exchanges are kept hidden for many years, publicly revealed only in sudden political confrontations so as to prompt memories about past events (1992: 38).

But a critical reading of this literature is also needed if the theory is to be developed. I focus here on the contributions of Gell and Weiner: Gell because his essay deals with Bastar District and is of direct ethnographic relevance; Weiner because her book, *Inalienable Possessions,* is the most recent general account of the problem.

Weiner never uses the word *good* in her book but it appears as a zero sign in the subtitle which reads *The Paradox of Keeping-While-Giving.* In my terms, her book deals with the politics of switching from *goods* (keeping) to *gifts* (giving) but in a context which, for the most part, denies the coevality of the imperial *commodity.* The only mention of the word *commodity* is a footnote reference to a debate an article of mine (Gregory, 1980) provoked. 'The underlying problem with this debate,' she asserts (1992: 191), 'is its grounding in a simple opposition between gift and commodity.' The nature of the 'underlying problem' is not made clear and given that her own approach is grounded in an opposition between alienable and inalienable possessions, notions that lie at the basis of my distinction between gifts and commodities, the reader is left feeling somewhat bemused.

My use of the concept 'alienation' in *Gifts and Commodities* has provoked the most vigorous and telling criticisms of my book. The notion is a problematic one but the task is to refine and develop it rather than to drop it as many of my critics want to do. Inalienation is the centrepiece of Mauss's theory of the gift. I personally reject Mauss's mystical notion of the 'spirit' in the gift but the idea that there is an 'indissoluble bond' of some form or other between giver and gift is difficult to dismiss. The power of this idea was brought home to me once when I was putting my (then) five-year old daughter to bed. I found an envelope under her pillow with the words 'To Polly with love from Nerida' on the front and a few strands of hair inside. Polly, I noticed, had a gap missing in her hair and the detached hair, she told me, was given to her friend Nerida. This example illustrates the need to distinguish between three quite distinct relations: (1) that between Polly's body and the hair that grows on her head; (2) that between Polly and the hair she gave Nerida; and (3) that between Polly and the hair that drops to the hairdresser's floor. The first, (1), is a relation of part to integral whole; (2) an inalienable relation of a gift exchange kind that has ongoing significance for her relationship with Nerida; and (3) an alienable relation of a commodity kind that has no ongoing significance for her relationship with the hairdresser (which does not rule out the possibility of her establishing an ongoing relationship with the hairdresser because, say, she likes the way the hairdresser talks to her). Considered abstractly, the cultural significance of these three relations can and will vary with the particular historical context of the transaction being considered. An Australian Aboriginal man having his hair cut in Aurukun, for example, will ensure that no hair is left lying around for fear of sorcery (David Martin, pers. com.). With respect to (2) it is important to note that Polly loses *possession* of her hair but maintains a meaningful relationship to it. Her hair, in other words, is *detached* but *not alienated.* In (3), by way of contrast, no *significant* relation is maintained and the bond between Polly and her hair is one of unmeaning. This important distinction has been missed by my critics.

Consider Gell (1992). He objects to my distinction between gifts and commodities for the following reason:

> Objects are *alienated* in gift exchanges. In making a prestation, the donor loses access to the exchange-object, which passes to another, and with it the power to donate that object to a different recipient, whereas the recipient gains both of these. In making a prestation, an object of value is 'sacrificed', and the prestige, power, etc. conferred by the act of giving are proportional to the consensual evaluation of the onerousness of the sacrifice involved. What is *not 'alienated'* in gift-giving is not the gift-object itself, but that which *cannot* be alienated, namely the social identity of the donor, which still attaches to the object after it has been given away. But there would be no increment of glory to the 'name' which clings to the object after it has been given away, unless the giving-away of the object were a genuine sacrifice or 'loss' to the giver expressible as a series of opportunity costs incurred in not

holding onto the object (for consumption or for disposition in some alternative, and possibly more advantageous way) (Gell, 1992: 145, emphasis added).

Gell's distinction between *alienated* and *not 'alienated'* (with quotes) corresponds to my distinction between *detached* and *not alienated*. I reject the idea that there has to be a genuine 'loss' in the *detachment* before there is an 'increment of glory' to the name. What 'sacrifice' has Polly made in giving Nerida a few strands of hair? What 'opportunity cost' does a Trobriand chief suffer when he gives away a decorated armshell that has no use-value? If there was genuine loss in an exchange then the *detachment* would become an *alienation* of the type that occurs when Marx's proletarian walks home without his surplus-value after a hard day's work in the factory.

Let me now come to the problems I have with Weiner's notion of *inalienable possessions*. What makes a possession inalienable for her is 'its exclusive and cumulative identity with a particular series of owners through time' (1992: 33). This notion is derived from her thinking of *kula* objects, objects which must be *given* not *kept*. There is a tension here between giving and keeping but it is resolved always in favour of the former. As such, *kula* objects contrast sharply with the sacred objects of the type under the guardianship of Mr. Mali of the Naik clan. These objects must be *kept* not *given*; they are *goods* not *gifts*. This important distinction is missing from Weiner's work with the result that she confuses *inalienable keepsakes* (goods) with *inalienable detachables* (gifts). The former are valued because, among other things, they store memory of ancestors; the latter are valued because they are the sign of contemporary alliances such as those created between men of renown. Furthermore, we must speak of *guardians* rather than *donors* or *owners* when talking of *goods*. Donors may acquire status and prestige when they give whereas guardians may be punished if the keepsakes in their possession are not successfully guarded. A guardian's status is ascribed rather than achieved; on the death of one guardian another *succeeds* him. One cannot speak of transfer here because, again ideally, the good does not move. Alienation is not an eternal property that attaches to a thing; it is a cultural classification whose duration is dependent on contingent historical, geographical and anthropological factors. Just as the word 'book' can be now a noun, now a verb depending on the grammatical context, so a thing can be now a good, now a commodity, now something else depending upon the social context. The task of the analyst is to look behind the valued thing to the *political* relations between the valuers.

TOWARD A THEORY OF THE HOUSEHOLD PROPRIETORSHIP OF GOODS

Land tenure in Bastar is a classic example of what Marx (1894) called 'peasant proprietorship of land parcels', an extremely widespread form of land tenure that is found throughout Asia and in many places in Europe and other parts of the world. This form of tenure stands opposed to household proprietorship of consolidated land and the two are species of *household proprietorship of inalienable farmland*. There are other forms of inalienable land but these two are, without doubt, the most politically significant forms both globally and historically.

Without doubt? This is a large claim and I make it in opposition to those who see Europe as the homeland of private property, the market, the state. These values are just as much part of India's heritage as is caste. If the uniqueness of India is to be found in its high status Brahmanic household polity, the uniqueness of England is its high status landed household polity, the proprietors of inalienable *consolidated* land. This powerful household polity owes its existence to the form of the capitalist state that developed in England around the time of the industrial revolution. This state was founded on a paradox that has gone largely unnoticed. On the one hand the laws of the English state facilitated the growth and development of a form of capitalism where buyers and sellers could transact *commodities* of the purest *alienable* form ever created; on the other, the development was underwritten by laws which saw the emergence of one of the purest form of *inalienable* property ever created, the farmlands of the elite landed households. If the English state could be said to have adopted a laissez faire approach to the Market, it did precisely the opposite to the institution of the House. The laws, which prevented land from becoming a generalised commodity, created the necessary (but not sufficient) conditions for capitalist agriculture to flourish. The commodity-centric approach of Political Economy has blinded its practitioners to the significance of this fact. Marx, for example, completely abstracts from the politics of the House. His analysis of capitalist ground rent and 'peasant proprietorship' is from the perspective of the *producers* of marketable products and not from the perspective of the *guardians* of land. The result is that he, like all subsequent theorists in this tradition, have not been able to develop a satisfactory theory of the value of scarce things, and the notable absence of the word *goods* in the Political Economy literature is the outward sign of this fact. As such their approach to the 'laws of motion' of capitalist transformation of agriculture is problematic. They see this process as a necessary movement from 'peasant proprietorship' to 'capitalism' brought about by a process of differentiation among the peasantry. The word 'peasant' here is a shorthand for 'pre-capitalist' and the word 'capitalist' is based on the unexamined assumption that land is a *commodity*. But the fact is that farming based on household proprietorship of land parcels actually flourishes in a market economy; furthermore, the historical success which households in Europe and Asia have had in maintaining land as a *good* reveals that the two types of good—parcelised and consolidated—can coexist without any necessity for the former to turn into the latter because of the 'laws of motion of capitalism'. Commodity-centric theorists who have failed to see the paradoxical role of goods in the development of capitalism are invariably led to assert that the process of differentiation is 'blocked' by the 'ideological' structures of caste and kinship (Harriss, 1982: 9). The 'blockage', as usual, is in the theory not the reality it tries to describe. Theories of this kind have informed official theory in the former U.S.S.R. with tragic consequences; equally tragic, too, is the tendency for the Marxist historians of the U.S.S.R., such as Hobsbawn, to blame the peasantry for the shortcomings of their own theories. Hobsbawn's (1994: 390) description of Russian villagers as 'a collection of peasant and animal herding peoples mentally living in the Western equivalent of the eleventh century' is an illustration of what I mean.

To understand the generality of the Bastar case, then, it is necessary to begin with a brief description of the specificity of the

English case. This comparison will reveal the human politics behind the creation of scarcity and the means by which the value of inalienable keepsakes (*goods*) are reproduced.

English farming is unique in the sense that farmlands have traditionally been controlled by elite families who needed to keep land off the market in order to reproduce themselves. The development of capitalist agriculture in England owes much to the barriers to the free trade in land that these families set up. These barriers are the product of a unique form of elite household economy that evolved over time, one where the law of the state played a crucial role. The essence of the system was an arrangement involving primogeniture and legal entailments which rendered the land inalienable and reduced the status of a guardian to that of mediator between the dead and the unborn. The arrangements, notes Habakkuk (1950:15), conformed to a standard pattern.

> In its essentials the marriage settlement first secured that the family estate should in each generation descend to the eldest son. It did this by limiting the interest in the estate of the father of the husband and, after him, of the husband himself, to that of life-tenant, and entailing the estate on the eldest son to be born of the marriage. Secondly, the marriage settlement empowered both the father and husband to raise jointures [ie., money revenue] for their respective wives and portions, ie., capital sums, for their daughters and younger sons when they came of age.

Thus the eldest son received the farmlands, the wives money revenue, and the other children money capital. The eldest son also inherited the problem of finding the money for the jointures and portions. The prudent course, as Habakkuk noted, would have been to save, but the normal practice was to borrow.

Figure III.1 depicts these relationships in a slightly simplified form.

This was the basic building block of a system whose dialectical complexity becomes apparent when it is realised, for example, that one man's wife is another man's daughter and that she gets money revenue from one and money capital from the other.

The role of the state was crucial in that it provided the legal framework for this particular system of household economy to work.

Indeed, the development of this common pattern in the eighteenth century was to a considerable extent the result of technical changes in the land law (Habakkuk, 1950: 16). Demography, too, played a crucial role for it is obvious that the system presupposes that the male line reproduces itself.

From the perspective of market economy this system is a barrier to the free trade in land, a barrier that has its basis in the principles of household economy. Such a system is implicit in Sraffa's (1960) theory of rent. It is also implicit in Ricardo's theory but the evidence is that he understood it much better as suggested by his oblique reference to a seller of land being 'almost always under the necessity

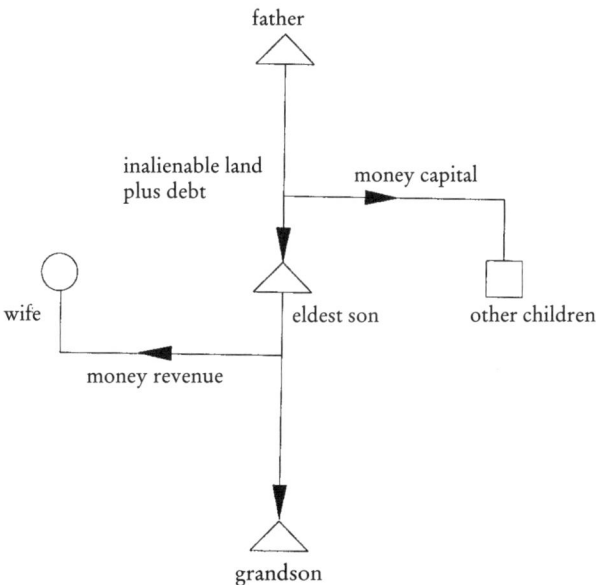

FIGURE III.1   *General form of the marriage settlement among eighteenth century English landlords*

of selling' (1817: 154). This 'necessity' has its basis in demographic failure of the male line and the historical evidence suggests that this was the most important factor in bringing land onto the market (Clay, 1968: 510, 517). For example, the period 1680-1750 saw many land sales because the male reproduction rate in elite families fell below 100% throughout this entire period.

Elite families were not the only kind of landed family found in nineteenth century England but they were, it seems, the predominant one. As Marx noted: 'John Bright's assertion that 150 landlords own half of England, and 12, half the Scotch soil, has never been refuted' (1867: 322, fn 2). A brief history of primogeniture in England since 1500 has been written by Thirsk (1984), who notes it was common among the nobility in the sixteenth century

> and seems to have been deemed by common consent the most acceptable practice for family and state reasons. It reduced strife among brothers when the eldest automatically took the leading position; it maintained the status of the family; and it preserved a class of rulers in society. In general it did not cause excessive hardship to younger sons because the nobility had the means to provide adequately for all. The hardships were felt most keenly among the gentry because their means were not sufficient to provide decently for younger sons (Thirsk, 1984: 368).

She adds (1984: 372) that

> in the eighteenth century the aspirations of the gentry filtered down to the next class below, and produced yeomen who followed the rule of primogeniture and, in order to make the assurance doubly sure, settled their estates. Primogeniture gained ground among the middle classes and provoked another controversy, centring upon that class, in the nineteenth century.

The legal history of primogeniture and entailments provides additional insight into the difference between the two types of household polity I have distinguished. The household proprietorship of consolidated land owes its existence to the state and, in particular, to the development of a legal form, the legacy, that enables the testator to deny the living guardian the right to alienate it. Where goods take the form of land parcels the household polity exists despite the state; here succession is 'universal', as the lawyers say, and the new guardian assumes the legal personality of the old along with all the filial duties that involves. Compare Hunter (1900: 149-50):

> The earliest notions of succession to deceased persons are connected with duties rather than with rights, with sacrifices than with property. In the Hindoo Law, the heir or successor is the person bound to offer the funeral rights required for the comfort

of the deceased's soul; and even in the Roman Law there are wanting indications of the same fact. The property of the deceased was the natural fund to provide the expenses, in some systems of religion by no means inconsiderable, of the necessary religious ceremonies. In Roman Law... the heir was considered to stand in relation to third parties as more than a representative of the deceased, as actually continuing his legal personality. The heir succeeded to all the rights and liabilities *(in universum jus)* of the deceased... the heir was bound to pay all the debts of the deceased, even if he obtained no property from him whatever. An insolvent inheritance was thus a veritable *damnosa hereditas.*

The establishment of the republican state, from which the ideology of egalitarianism springs, emphasised the separation of law from religion. Political economy becomes separated from political theology and a highly prestigious secular *good* is born where its *bads* are equated with the debts of the deceased rather than his or her ghost. In those families that have kept the state at bay—those whose reproduction does not require the intervention of the state—*bads* retain a theological as well as an economic meaning and guardians, as we have seen in the last chapter, have to perform rituals to protect the value of the *goods* under their control. But theological values of this kind also have a political aspect and it is these political relations that are the key to understanding the value of smallholder parcels. What is at stake here, then, is *political* theology not simply religion.

The comparative work done on smallholder farming enables us to assert that household proprietorship of land parcels is usually associated with production for a rural periodic market using family labour and animal-drawn ploughs. 'Family labour' is an elastic term that includes those people reciprocally recognised as family members be they close kin or those adopted into the family by whatever means. Parcelisation, the main concern of this chapter, shows an astonishing uniformity across time and place. Map III.1 illustrates the classic form of parcelisation. This map shows the division of land in the village of Novoselok in North Russia in the nineteenth century. It can be seen that the land consists of a mixture of arable land, meadows, forests, lakes and bog-land divided into a number of strips. Each household has a portfolio of these strips that gives them access to land of various quality in terms of soil type, topography and distance from the

MAP III.
THE VILLAGE NOVOSELOK
IN THE GOVERNMENT OF
P SKOW
(NORTH RUSSIA)
The black strips indicate the land
allotted to one peasant

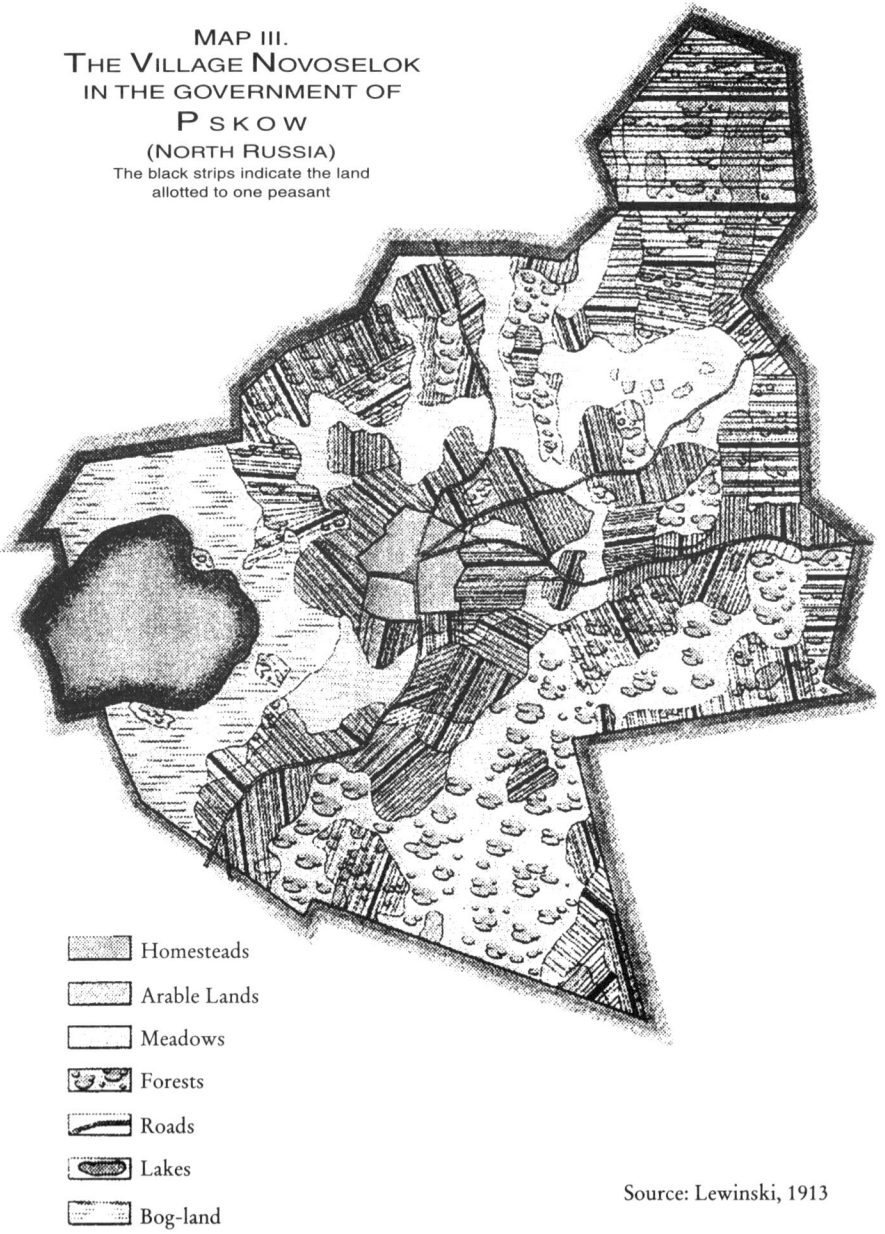

Homesteads

Arable Lands

Meadows

Forests

Roads

Lakes

Bog-land

Source: Lewinski, 1913

MAP III.1   *Parcelisation of land in a Russian village*

homesteads and roads. In this case, some fifty five parcels—shown by the black strips—makes up the holding of one household. In areas where the land is of a more uniform quality and of higher fertility the number of parcels, argues Lewinski (1913: 50-51), will be much less. (He illustrates this with a map of the village of Pavlovka in the fertile South where arable land, which accounts for almost all the village land, is divided into only eight strips.)

Lewinski notes that parcelisation of this kind existed in Germany, England, Scotland, Wales, Russia, Java, India and elsewhere. Why, he asks (1913: 49), is arable farmland divided into small scattered plots rather than consolidated into one large plot?

> The principal cause of this system's origin lies in the fact that the soil is very unequal in quality. Already the first settler, taking possession of unoccupied land, has his fields scattered because it is difficult to find one continuous piece of land which would satisfy all the requirement of cultivation, which would give equally a good crop of oats, of spring corn, of wheat and of rye. Again, with the good land are usually found patches of bad land which is not worth cultivating. Finally the concentration of one man's land into one plot exposes it uniformly to the climatic peculiarities of the locality.

The implication of this argument, which has been put by many others as well, is that the problem to be explained is the relatively unusual English-style consolidation rather than the more widespread parcelisation. But, as the brief discussion of the English case above suggested, the underlying value problem is one of understanding the historical, geographical, and anthropological specificity of the relations of consanguinity, affinity and contiguity of the place in question. Wherein, then, lies the specificity of the value of parcelised plots?

According to Baden-Powell (1892: 223) the valuation process of land parcels is based on two principles:

> (1) the right—held by any class—consequent on first clearing and reclaiming the waste;
> (2) the right claimed by the military and superior caste or ruling races, in virtue of birthright or inheritance, which really meant that the land had been obtained by conquest, grant, or some form of superior might, and that the descendants who inherited it regarded it as their 'birthright'.

The process by which land acquires value as a good by means of labour of the first clearer is different for meadows, forests, and arable lands. Land necessarily degrades with use and labour must be expended to maintain its value. Grazing cattle, for example, can damage a meadow if unrestricted access to ever increasing numbers of cattle are allowed. It can be protected by the erection of fences. The act transforms the meadow from being a natural good into a household good and the household that expends the labour will assert the property right. The creation of arable land, too, requires the expenditure of labour: meadows and forests must be cleared, drained, levelled, manured and fenced before they can be used productively. Such labour is a form of capital investment and is only an option for those households who are not 'too poor to farm' (Hill, 1982: 69). Such once-off *appropriative* labour improves the value of land but subsequent annual *exploitative* labour—ploughing, sowing—degrades it and must be countered by natural and artificial means of fertility renewal.

With the intensification of agriculture a given plot of forest land undergoes a series of transformations. At first it is a natural good unused by people. Common usage gives way to temporary private possession and, finally, to permanent possession through the expenditure of appropriative labour which creates the 'right of the first clearer'. The latter form of labour has long been recognised as the crucial determinant of the value of a good. In old Russia they used to say that land was property 'as far as the axe, the scythe and the plough go'; in India the ancient laws of Manu declare a field to belong to the person who first cleared it; evidence for similar sentiments can be found from many different parts of the world (Lewinski, 1913: 13). This ancestral labour principle not only gives the household permanent use-rights and the power to bequeath land (the path of *goods*) it also gives it disposal rights to sell (the path of *commodities*).

The ancestral labour principle, in turn, leads to two standards of value both of which have their origins in scarcity. Compare Lewinski (1913: 39–40)

> When scarcity begins to be felt the original proprietors cling more
> closely to the land they possess. But with the continuous growth
> of population and the consequent increase of the dissatisfied

members, the struggle between the opposed interests becomes more and more acute. For the poor, the only means of improving their condition is to claim part of the land of the rich. They base their claim on the communistic principle, on the 'theory' that the soil is a gift of God, that it is no man's land, that it is common property, and that, in consequence, all those performing equal duties have the right to equal shares.

The rich, on the other hand, advocate the right of every one to own the occupied soil, and try to justify it by the principle of labour and of first occupation. 'Our lands have been tilled by our grandfathers and great-grandfathers; is it our fault that the parent of others lived in idleness?'

The struggle is not always merely verbal. Those who have not sufficient land sometimes try to take it from the rich by force; as, for instance, among the Cossacks, it sometimes happened that the poor with their ploughs invaded the land of the rich with the intention of appropriating them. These attempts usually ended in a fight which resulted in broken ploughs and pierced heads.

Among the Russian peasants of Europe the passage to a division of land was accompanied by arson, by disputes in which knives and clubs were used, and sometimes even by murder.

Population growth, then, is accompanied by an assertion of ancestral rights over a *good* that denies other people a right of access. A *good*, then, needs a guardian to defend those rights, a guardian whose job it is to give access to those who reciprocally recognise his right to act on their behalf. Culturally constructed scarcity of this kind can arise both when land is 'naturally' abundant relative to a given population and when it is in short supply, as we shall see in the following case study of Bastar.

A BASTAR CASE STUDY[1]

Bastar is one of the richest forest regions of India with over 65% of its 39,060 sq. kms. officially classified as forest. Bastar is also one of India's most sparsely settled districts with a population density of 39 people per sq. km. The population numbered just over two million in 1991, 96% of whom live in rural areas. Almost all rural dwellers practice settled rice cultivation and live land that has been cleared for cultivation, some 20% of the total land area. However, the forest plays a vital role in supplying a multiplicity of products to supplement the diet and income of rural dwellers.

Population has grown rapidly in Bastar as a result of population growth and the immigration of land-hungry settlers from neighbouring regions. This has led to a demand for cultivated land, a demand that has been met by encroaching onto forest areas. In the past encroachers have been given legal title to their newly cleared land by the government on payment of a small fine. The government is now concerned to stop this practice. Not only is it concerned with the ecological consequences of the process but also with the loss of revenue foregone from exploiting the area as a state forest. Government attempts to stop the trend have rendered cultivable rice land scarce in many areas of Bastar. The conflict between the government and the people of Bastar over land use has a long history, but the problem has become particularly acute in recent years.

Consider now the cultivators' perspective. The dilemma facing them is presented statistically in Table III.1 which shows the relationship between the rural population and land use in Bastar from 1931 to 1991.

During this period the population trebled while the area under cultivation increased by only 80%. The period from 1931 to 1951 was a period of relative land surplus. As the population increased, the forest land was encroached upon. The period from 1951, by way of contrast,

TABLE III.1   LAND USE AND POPULATION IN BASTAR, 1931–1991

Year	Rural population	Area under cultivation (acres)	Total area (acres)	Percentage cultivated	Cultivated land per head
	(A)	(B)	(C)	(B/C)	(B/A)
1931	660,822	1,091,153	9,652,116	.113	1.65
1951	895,020	1,593,330	9,652,116	.165	1.79
1971	1,450,321	1,972,221	9,652,116	.204	1.35
1981	1,656,404	1,983,115	9,652,116	.205	1.19
1991	2,109,268	1,988,335	9,652,116	.206	0.95

Source: Census of India

was one of relative land scarcity. Encroachable forest land became scarcer and the farm holdings per household became smaller as more people were forced to live on the same area of land.

Production methods and techniques do not seem to have changed over the past 60 years. Only 1% of all land is irrigated and this on consolidated plots owned by recent migrants from the Punjab and elsewhere. Rice is the main crop of the villagers and this is grown once a year on rainfed land that is ploughed by bullocks or cows using a simple wooden plough. The seed is broadcast by hand, and manure is used as fertiliser if a farmer can afford it. The transplantion method of sowing is growing in popularity. This brings better yields but at the cost of more labour time, which is always in short supply around sowing time. The unchanged technology, coupled with population growth has contributed to the problem of land scarcity. This squeeze on land has led to an intensification of marketing activity and economic diversification rather than an intensification of production. This process is best understood by means of a case study of two contrasting villages, Minipur and Latipur.

Table III.2 shows the land use trends for Minipur village for the period 1921 to 1981. This village is an interior village some 46 kms from Kondagaon, the central market town in the region where I worked.

The general trends discussed above are very much in evidence here. In 1921/22 only 184 acres, representing 25% of all village land, was cultivated. As population increased due to higher birth rates and

TABLE III.2   MINIPUR VILLAGE: LAND USE, 1921–1981

Type of Land	1921/22 acres	%	1954/55 acres	%	1980/81 acres	%
Private property	184	25	300	41	371	51
Public property	4	–	11	1	11	1
Forest	543	75	163	22	92	13
Govt teak plantation			257	35	257	35
TOTAL	731	100	731	100	731	100

Source: The data for this table, and all subsequent tables in this chapter, comes from village land records and my fieldwork

intra-Bastar migration, the cultivable area increased to 300 acres by 1954/55 and 371 acres by 1980/81. Officially only 92 acres were still under forest in 1981/82 but, in reality, no village forest land is left because the 92 acres have already been appropriated and converted into paddy fields. The encroachers will, in the course of time, get the land registered in their names. They will pay the small fine required by law, and the bribe demanded by the land records keeper (*patwari*), and get official title to the land. It should be noted that the land frontier in this village was reached much sooner than it otherwise would have been because of the government's forest policy. Prior to 1951 the village land totalled 731 acres, but the appropriation of 257 acres of this for a reserved forest teak plantation reduced the total area to 474 acres. Land is now very scarce in Minipur and the consequences of this will be examined in detail below.

Consider now Table III.3, which shows comparable data for Latipur village, a small village on the national highway near the market town of Kondagaon. In the thirty two year period to 1954/55 some 121 acres of forest land was encroached upon, which meant that the land under cultivation more than doubled. However, in the period to 1980/81 only 36 acres of forest land was encroached upon. Forest land has declined accordingly from 86% of total village area in 1922 to 65% in 1981. Land is now scarce in this village because the remaining forest land has been declared a reserved forest and, like all reserved forest areas of Bastar, is policed by forest guards to prevent further encroachment.

In order to understand the underlying political implications of these macro level changes in Minipur and Latipur it is necessary to delve a little deeper into the class and caste structure of the two villages.

TABLE III.3 LATIPUR VILLAGE: LAND USE, 1921–1981

| Type of Land | 1921/22 | | 1954/55 | | 1980/81 | |
	acres	%	acres	%	acres	%
Private property	92	12	213	28	249	33
Public property	11	2	11	2	11	2
Forest	641	86	520	70	484	65
TOTAL	744	100	744	100	744	100

Table III.4 classifies the households by size of holdings and by the official caste or tribe classification. The first notable contrast is that Minipur has a relatively egalitarian distribution of land while in Latipur it is very unequal. In Minipur most households have holdings of less than 10 acres, and no one has a holding of greater than 25 acres. In Latipur, by way of contrast, 14 of the 23 households are landless, and one household has over 25 acres of land (66 acres to be precise). The second notable contrast is that in Minipur the land is divided relatively equally between Bastar Hindus and Bastar Tribals, with a slight bias in favour of the latter, while in Latipur almost all the land is owned by Hindus, all of whom, as we shall see (Table III.5), are immigrants.

TABLE III.4   HOUSEHOLD OWNERSHIP OF LAND BY
SIZE OF HOLDING : TWO VILLAGES COMPARED

Size of land holdding (acres)	Minipur village Hindu (number of households)	Tribal	Total	Latipur village Hindu (number of households)	Tribal	Total
0	4	1	5	0	14	14
0 > 5	22	5	27	0	0	0
5 > 10	7	8	15	0	1	1
10 > 15	2	2	4	3	3	6
15 > 20	2	3	5	0	0	0
20 > 25	1	0	1	1	0	1
25 >	0	0	0	1	0	1
	38	19	57	5	18	23

These figures are further disaggregated in Table III.5 which gives details of the land/population ratios by caste for each village. The dominant group in Latipur are Brahmans and they possess over 6 acres of land for every member of their caste. The subordinate group are the Bastar Tribals, the majority of whom are landless. This group used to work as bonded labourers for the biggest Brahman land-owning family, but they were freed under Mrs. Gandhi's 20-point programme. Nowadays a few members of this group continue to work as daily

TABLE III.5   HOUSEHOLD OWNERSHIP OF LAND BY CASTE AND ORIGIN: TWO VILLAGES COMPARED

| Caste | Minipur village | | Latipur village | |
	Land (acres)	Land per head	Land (acres)	Land per head
Immigrants				
Brahmans	–	–	118	6.21
Christians	–	–	14	3.50
Other	5	1.00	–	–
Bastarians				
Maraars	176	1.00	–	–
Tribals	163	1.29	41	0.49
Other	10	0.34	–	–
TOTAL RESIDENT	354	1.05	173	1.63
Non-residents	17	0	77	0

labourers for the Brahman landlord, but the majority earn their living by selling firewood and cut grass (for cow feed) in Kondagaon. In Minipur there is no dominant group. The Maraars (Gardener caste) own approximately the same amount of land as the people officially classified as Tribals. The Maraars have origin myths which identify them as immigrants but, from an anthropological point of view, there is little to distinguish them from those officially classified as Tribal. The genealogies I have collected show continuous residence in Bastar for upwards of ten generations, they speak the local languages, and worship many of the same gods as the so-called Tribals. There are, of course, many differences between the various Bastar groups but when the Bastarians are compared to the immigrant Hindus, most of whom have only lived in Bastar for two or three generations at the most, the cultural differences between the Bastar groups pale into insignificance. In other words, the significant economic and cultural distinction in Bastar is not the official one between Tribal and Hindu but the anthropological one between Bastarian and Immigrant.

While Minipur and Latipur were both established at the same time in the late nineteenth century, Minipur is more representative of the 'typical' Bastar village as Simeran Gell's (1992: Ch 4) work confirms. Most of the cultivators of Bastar are smallholders of this type. In other words, land tenure in Bastar is a classic example of what Marx called 'peasant proprietorship of land parcels'. Latipur is representative of the new villages that are being established near the major towns in Bastar. Both villages were established as a result of migration. But in the case of Minipur it was intra-Bastar migration whereas for Latipur it was inter-Bastar immigration. Intra-Bastar migration between villages was very common during the land surplus period, but it is rare nowadays. Inter-Bastar immigration, by way of contrast, was rare in the pre-1947 period but is very important today.

Towards the end of the last century, the Raja of Bastar encouraged Brahmans to settle in Bastar by giving them land grants. He also had a new road built over the Keskhal *ghat*, which considerably shortened the distance to Raipur. This also led to some immigration which included the father of the major land-owning family at Latipur. Some merchants who arrived in the post-1947 wave of immigration, and who now live in Kondagaon, have also purchased land at Latipur. The landless residents of Latipur are migrants from other areas of Bastar. They left their own villages for a variety of reasons, including family quarrels and landlessness.

A question arises as to why landless people in Bastar have not managed to encroach onto the forest land and become farmers themselves. There are many reasons for this. Firstly, many of them are too poor to farm, a paradox that is, as Polly Hill (1982) has repeatedly pointed out, common in many smallholder farming communities. Land is useless for farming purposes unless one has the basic capital of bullocks and seed. These items are simply beyond the reach of many people. Farmers usually have the necessary skills to make wooden ploughs and other implements. They may also have a plentiful supply of family labour to draw on. But seed and bullocks must be purchased and finding the cash or credit to do this is the stumbling block. A second reason why landless people have not encroached on land is because the conversion of forest land to bunded paddy fields requires an enormous investment of labour. First the trees have to be felled and burnt, then the stumps cleared, then the ground levelled. Every day is a struggle for survival for landless people and they haven't the time for labour of the kind that gives no immediate return.

The government has a policy of granting 5 to 10 acres of deteriorated forest land plus Rs 500 cash to landless people in Bastar and many people have benefited from this policy. Those Tribals with land in Latipur acquired their land in this way. However, the policy does not apply to urban areas. When Kondagaon was upgraded in status to an urban area in the mid-1970s, all villages within administrative control were also upgraded. This included Latipur, and hence a generation of young landless Tribals became ineligible for this land grant by administrative fiat. This then is a third factor accounting for landlessness in the particular case of Latipur.

Given this background we can now proceed to a more detailed analysis of the means by which different households in these two villages create and reproduce land as a valued inalienable keepsake.

Table III.6 provides data on the types of land transactions carried out in Minipur over the period 1921–1981. Encroachment onto forest area was the most important type of transaction during the period 1921–1954, accounting for 40% of all transactions. These encroachments effected a transfer of land from the government to villagers. Another important type of transaction during the first period was the appropriation of abandoned land. This was a feature of the land surplus days when intra-Bastar migration was high. With the development of land scarcity this mode of transfer has ceased to exist. Intra-village migration is very much attenuated nowadays, too. Emigration is usually restricted

TABLE III.6   LAND TRANSACTIONS IN MINIPUR
                    VILLAGE, 1921–1981

Type of transaction	1921–1954			1955–1981		
	No.	Land area (acres)	(%)	No.	Land area (acres)	(%)
Inheritance	5	94.24	31	22	217.38	59
Appropriation of abandoned land	5	57.09	19	–	–	0
Encroachment onto forests	21	119.90	40	5	70.80	19
Sales	–	–	–	6	9.52	1
No transfer	–	29.01	10	–	73.51	21
TOTAL	31	300.24	100	33	371.21	100

to those without land. Members of landed households enagage in migration of a seasonal nature with the cultivator returning to his land during the sowing and harvesting season.

With the development of land scarcity in Minipur, inheritance has emerged as the most important mode of transferring land, accounting for 59% of all transactions in 1955-1981. Sales, by way of contrast, only accounted for a minuscule 1% of land transactions in the second period. In the land surplus period to 1954 no sales were recorded.

Similar trends are apparent in the data for Latipur shown in Table III.7. Inheritance and encroachment are the main modes of land transfer, in terms of land area, in the land surplus era. The category 'no transfer', which accounted for 64% of all land transactions in 1955–1981, represents land that will ultimately be inherited. The figure is unusually high, because the principal land owner in this village (who first arrived in Latipur in the late nineteenth century), was still alive

TABLE III.7   LAND TRANSACTIONS IN LATIPUR
VILLAGE, 1921–1981

Type of transaction	1921–1954			1955–1981		
	No.	Land area (acres)	(%)	No.	Land area (acres)	(%)
Inheritance	3	44	20	3	17	7
Appropriation of abandoned land	2	10	5	–	–	–
Encroachment onto forests	19	123	58	9	46	18
Sales	2	9	4	3	28	11
No transfer	–	27	13	–	158	64
TOTAL	26	213	100	15	249	100

in 1982 and still had land registered in his name. More land has been sold in this village compared to Minipur which can be explained by its proximity to Kondagaon. Nevertheless the amount of land involved, only 28 acres in the period 1955-1981, is still small both in absolute and relative terms.

The consequences of the growing land scarcity are dramatically illustrated by the data on inheritance patterns from Minipur. Figure III.2 shows the transmission of land down three generations of the dominant landholding family at Minipur. The original holding in 1921 was 51.93. This was increased by 26.18 acres through encroachment onto forest lands and reduced by 8.52 acres through sales, giving a balance in 1981 of 66.59. However, whereas the original holding was the joint property of three brothers, the expanded land holding is now the private property of 13 of their male descendants. Thus the landholding per male land owner has fallen from 17.35 acres in 1921 to 5.40 acres in 1981. Had it not been for the build up of the holding through encroachment there would have been only 3.99 acres per head in 1981.

The division of this land has not been equal because of accidents of birth and migration. The original holding of 51.93 acres, together with an additional 5.4 acres acquired by encroachment, was registered in the name of Bisram, the youngest of three brothers and the only surviving brother in 1921 when the land was surveyed. On his death, the land was divided 20% for the descendants of the first brother Biju, 50% for the descendants of the second brother Tiju, and 30% for the descendants of Bisram. It is interesting to note that Gopi, a descendant of the brother who got the smallest share, is now one of the biggest landowners in the village. The reason for this is that Gopi's father, Lakhmu, was able to double the size of his share by encroachment and was able to pass the whole 21.97 acre share down to Gopi without division. Gopi's three uncles were entitled to a share of this estate but forfeited it when they migrated to Aamgaon, a neighbouring village, where they were able to encroach on good forest land. Gopi's brother was also entitled to a share, but he died childless. Thus, it was this fortuitous combination of circumstances that has left Gopi one of the biggest landowners in the village. Had his father's brothers not migrated his inheritance would have been a mere 4.38 acres and would have left his three sons virtually landless with a shares 1.46 acres each.

Gopi's cousins have not had his good fortune; most of them are now virtually landless. Tiju's three sons divided his share in the proportion 20%, 20% and 60%, with the youngest son, Indal, getting the lion's share. However, Indal had seven sons (from three wives), with the result that his 17 acres was subsequently divided into small

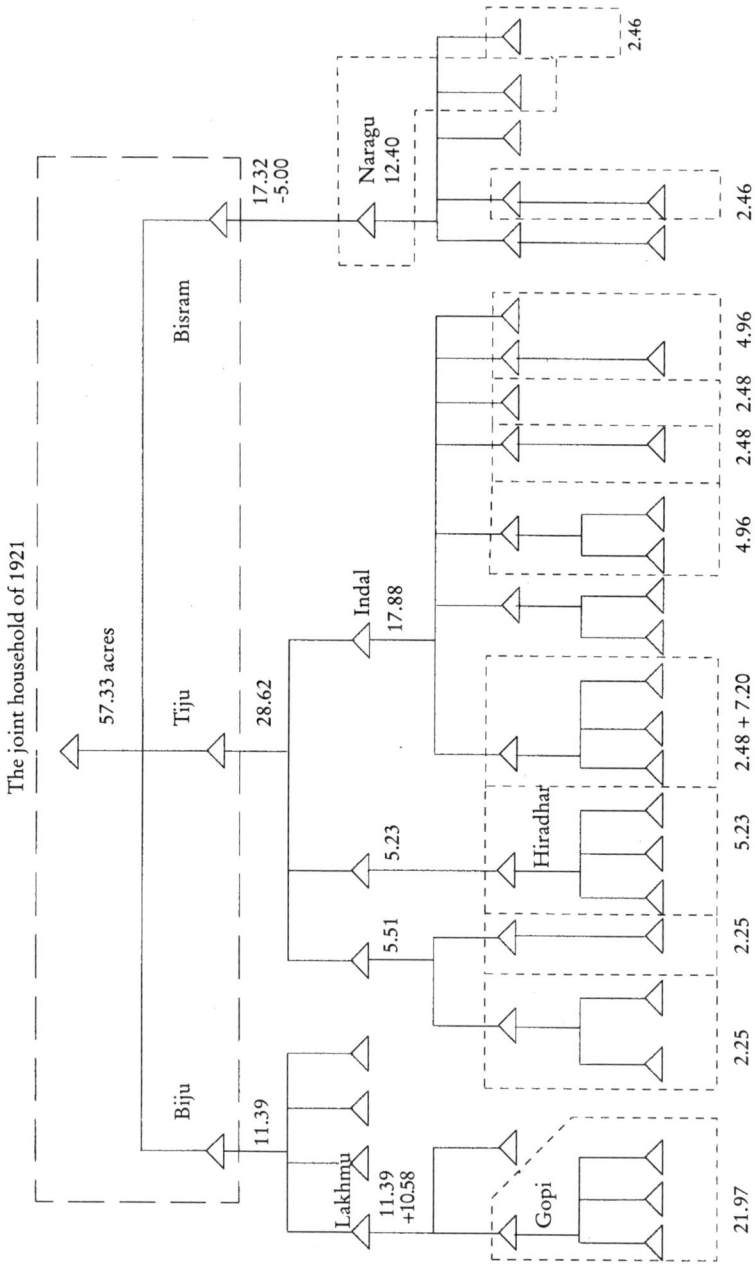

FIGURE III.2   *Division of a farming household in Bastar*

plots of 2.5 acres each. Naragu's 12 acres has been similarly divided amongst his five sons. Hiradhar has benefited most out of this lot for the simple reason that he was an only son. Five acres is sufficient to support a family with difficulty; on two acres it is impossible. Land scarcity is now a reality for the descendants of Tiju and Bisram. There is no longer any forest land to encroach upon.

The actual legal transfer of land is shown in Figure III.3. Prior to 1958 the family lived in one house and the land was owned jointly. Today, there are twelve houses, and the land is owned individually. This break down of the joint family, coupled with the fact that brothers do not die in the order they are born, accounts for the pattern of the actual legal transfers. The head of the joint family in 1921 was Bisram, and all land was registered in his name. On his death most of it was registered in his son's name (Naragu) who subsequently redistributed legal title to his cousins (Indal and Phaganu) and his cousin's son (Hiradhar). Use-rights in land are usually distributed long before the actual legal transfer takes place. Thus, the amount of land a man has legal right to often bears no relation to the land he actually

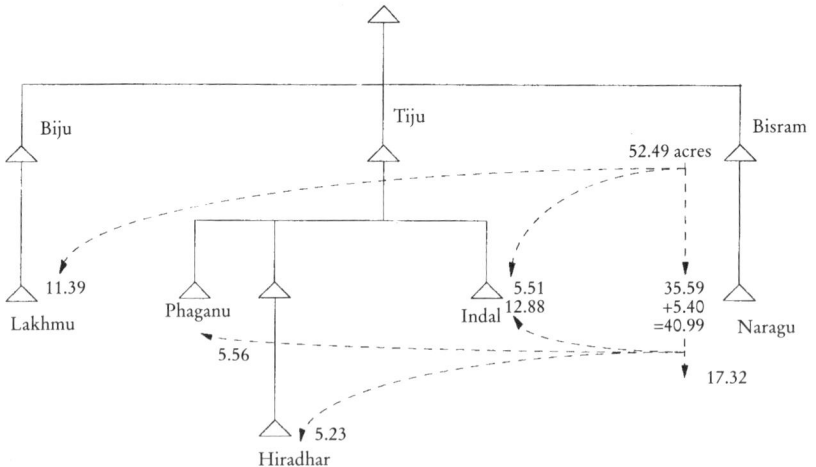

FIGURE III.3   *Registered land transfers of a farming household in Bastar*

cultivates, as was the case with Naragu in 1954. The land records are therefore useless for analytical purposes unless many hundreds of hours of painstaking research is carried out with them in order to construct the real picture using genealogies and land maps.

The break down of the joint family was due to population pressure in the process of transformation from a land surplus to a land shortage situation, or, what amounts to the same thing, from a labour shortage to a labour surplus economy. Had land remained abundant and labour scarce perhaps two or three new joint families would have been formed. However, given the scarcity of land and increasing economic diversification, the *raison d'être* of the joint rural family as a mobiliser of labour was lost and twelve households, each owning tiny scattered plots of land, were created.

Maps III.2a and III.2b show the effect of this transformation on the division of the family's 57 acres of land. In 1922 there was one holding of 7 plots. By 1982 this had become five holdings of 32 plots. This pattern of land holding is a classic example of household proprietorship of land parcels.

One's wealth in terms of land is, as we have seen, largely determined by accidents of birth: the more brothers one has, the less one is likely to inherit. However, brothers do not inherit equally. Many factors conspire to bring this about. For example, a gap of 30 years or more may separate the eldest brother of a family from the youngest. Another factor is that the order of death of brothers has little to do with the order of their birth. As a result, the brother who has been around the longest is usually the one who gets the largest share. From Figure III.3 it can be seen that Indal inherited 17.88, while his brothers only received a little over five acres each. This was because he outlived his brothers by many years, was a prominent and respected elder in the village, and had the political clout to influence the distribution of land.

As the economic condition of this family has progressively deteriorated they have had to diversify their economic activities in order to survive. The forest has cushioned their fall and its existence has prevented the emergence in Bastar of the abject poverty to be found in the rural areas of North India. The collection of minor forest produce which can be sold at the weekly markets is an important source of income for many households. So too is daily labour from

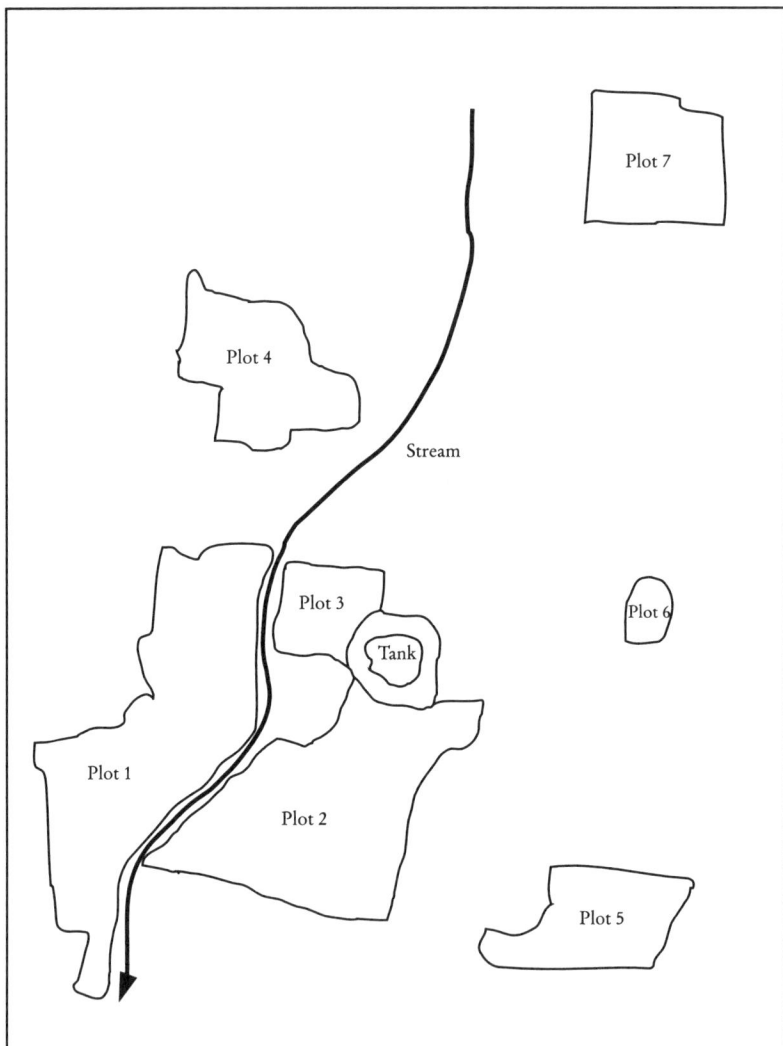

MAP III.2a   *Bisram's parcelised holding in 1922*
                    (57 acres = 1 holding = 7 plots)

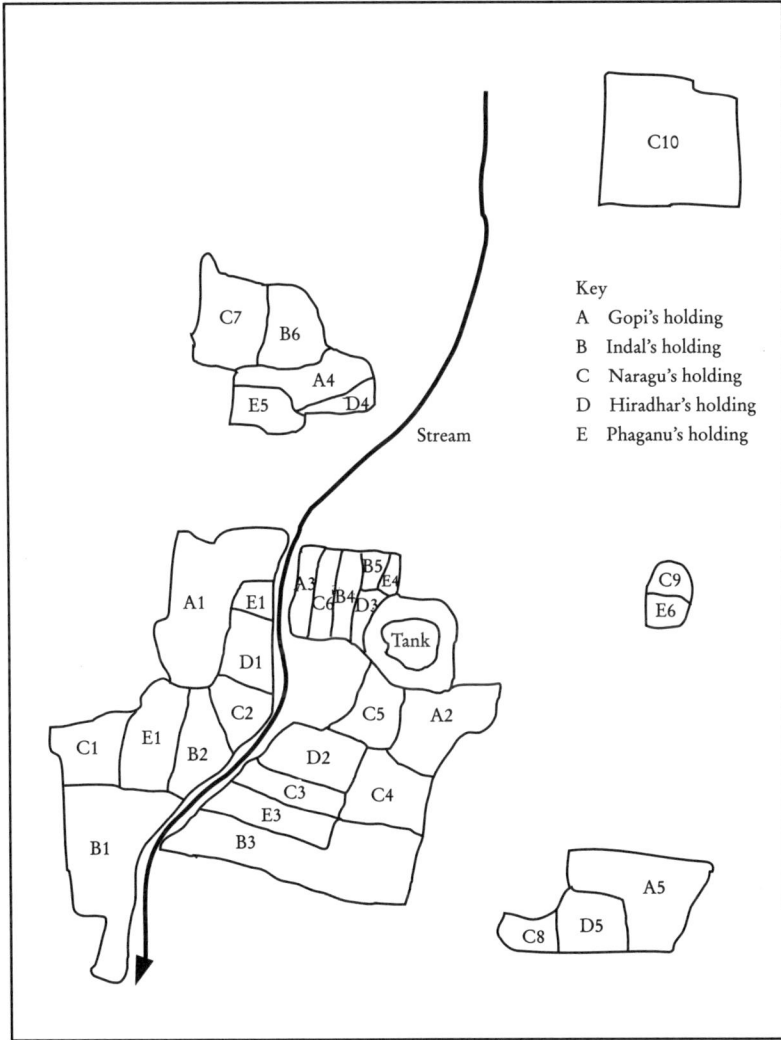

Key
A   Gopi's holding
B   Indal's holding
C   Naragu's holding
D   Hiradhar's holding
E   Phaganu's holding

Stream

MAP III.2b   *Division of Bisram's holding by 1982*
(57 acres = 5 holdings = 32 plots)

the Forest Department (and other government departments). There is a constant demand for labour for felling trees and general maintenance work on Reserved Forests. This work is usually done by young men who camp out on the work site for short periods of up to two weeks. Permanent migration to land surplus areas within Bastar has ceased to be an option for the people of Minipur, and it seems that permanent migration to the towns for work may be the next step.

The pattern of land inheritance among the rich immigrant landowning Brahman family of Latipur provides an interesting contrast to the Maraar family case of Minipur. This is shown in Figure III.4.

The first significant difference to be noted is that only three male descendants have been produced after four generations. Chandra only had one son, Lachmi, who in turn only had one son. These accidents of birth have therefore served to preserve the unity of the original landholding. Had Chandra produced twenty male descendants after three generations, as was the case in Minipur, then the wealth of this family would have been very different today.

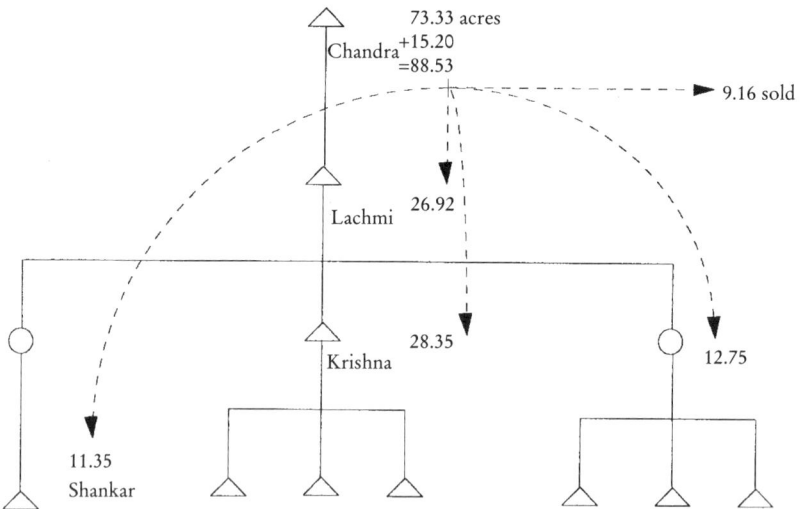

FIGURE III.4   *Registered land transfers of a landlord household in Bastar*

The second significant difference is that many of the transfers shown here are legal fictions to dodge the land ceilings regulations. No one landholding here exceeds 30 acres as required by law. However, the actual size of the land worked by Krishna is 66.62 acres. This has all come from his father Lachmi who originally owned 73.33 acres. He sold 9.16 acres to newcomers to the village, gave 12.75 acres to his daughter's husband, but accumulated an additional 15.20 acres by encroaching onto forest land, giving a net holding of 66.62 which Krishna now works. This is registered in three names to avoid the land ceiling: Lachmi 26.92 acres, Krishna 28.35 acres, and Shankar (who lives 300 kms away at Raipur) 11.35 acres.

The potential division of the 66.62 acres owned by Krishna is into three smaller holdings each of 22 acres for his three sons. However, it is unlikely that this potential division will actually take place. This is because his sons are being educated at University and have ambitions of non-farming careers. Here, then, is a third significant difference between immigrant Brahman families of this type and local Bastar families of the Maraar type. Brahman families have a tradition of pursuing higher education, and this opens up many opportunities for the sons of farmers to pursue careers in business and the civil service. Bastar farming families have no such tradition. The school in Minipur has been open for only a decade and the few children who attend usually leave after a few years of schooling. Thus the option for the children of Minipur farmers to pursue lucrative non-farming occupations is almost non-existent.

It is interesting to note in passing that Lachmi of Latipur was a *malguljar* prior to 1947. North Bastar, unlike South Bastar, did not have the Zamindari System. The collection of revenue from the villages was in the hands of *malguljars* who were given a contract by the Raja of Bastar to collect the revenue from a number of villages on a commission basis. The office carried with it some power and prestige but given the abundance of land at that time the revenue was small and difficult to collect. Many farmers simply abandoned their land after harvest. In Latipur in 1921, for example, there were eight registered landowners of small holdings apart from Lachmi. By the time of the next settlement report in 1955–56 all of these land owners had abandoned their land. After 1947 the office of *malguljar* was replaced by that of *patel*. This office carries no power. Every village has a *patel* who is elected by the villagers. He simply collects the revenue from the village in exchange for a small fee from the government. Lachmi's son Krishna is now the *patel* for Latipur village.

Land sales, as was noted in the discussion of the data in Tables III.6 and III.7, account for only a very small proportion of all land transacted: 1% (9.52 acres) in the case of Minipur in the period 1955–1981, and 11% (28 acres) in the case of Latipur. The market for land is therefore extremely sluggish. As the number of cases is small, it is useful to examine them all in order to understand the process by which the *supreme good* becomes a *commodity*.

Case 1: Mr. S.R. Bihari of Minipur. Mr. Bihari is the only outsider living in Minipur. His birth place was Bihar. Before he settled in Minipur, he worked in Bare Dongar as a salesman for a local liquor licence holder. When the liquor laws changed, and the production and distribution of local liquor passed from the hands of the urban-based licensed monopoly holders to the village-based Tribals, he found himself flush with money but without a means of livelihood. Through the good grace of Indal Singh, the most influential elder in the Minipur, he was allowed to settle in the village and to buy land. Indal Singh sold him 1.72 acres of good rice land. This included a small plot (0.20 acres), on which he was able to set up house with the divorced daughter of a prominent villager of the Maraar caste. His wife became an outcaste as a result of this inter-caste marriage, but harmonious social relations are maintained with her ex-caste relations. He, too, is excluded from caste-based social activities such as marriages but he is fully integrated into the social life of the village in other respects. In addition to the land he acquired from Indal, he purchased 0.80 acres from a man of the Herdsman caste. His last purchase was 2 acres of rice land on 29 April 1981, which he bought for Rs 2300. He acquired this from a young boy from a neighbouring village, who inherited it upon his father's death and who was forced to sell because he had neither the capital nor the experience to farm the land. All in all, then, he acquired 4.52 acres of rice land.

Case 2: Mr. S.C. Gardener of Minipur. S.C. is a member of the Gardener caste, and his family have been living in Minipur for over 40 years. When his grandfather Somaru first came to Minipur, he worked as a labourer for the joint family headed by Bisram. Bisram's family were of the same caste but different patrilineage, and were one of the earliest, as well as one of the richest, families in the village. Somaru's daughter (ie. S.C.'s mother) was married into Bisram's patrilineage and Somaru was lent 7 acres of Bisram's land to work as his own. Over the years 5 acres of this gradually was returned to Bisram's rapidly expanding patrilineage. The remaining two acres has been worked by S.C. for the past 20 years, and it was generally agreed that he had *de-facto* ownership of it. This was made *de jure* on 27 February 1983 when Bisram's son, Naragu, formally sold him the plot for a consideration of Rs 2,000, a price which was considered to be below the real value of the land. S.C. had to pay R 100 bribe to the village land records keeper (*patwari*) to get the land registered in his name.

Case 3: Two brothers of Minipur. Suradu and Sadhu are brothers of the Gardener caste. Their father, Kawanchi, came to Minipur to do *lamsena* for Bisram. This is a form of marriage-labour contract entered into by a prospective son-in-law with the prospective father-in-law when the former does not have the finance to pay for the wedding. After an agreed number of years of labour, the father-in-law conducts the wedding and pays all the expenses. In this case Bisram also lent Kawanchi some land to work (about 5 acres). Saradu and Sadhu have been working this land for over 20 years and it will be eventually be sold to them by Bisram's son, Naragu, in whose name it is currently registered.

Case 4: Mr G. Brahman of Kondagaon. Mr. R. Brahman acquired 10.50 acres of forest land in Latipur from the government in the 1950s which he did not cultivate. In 1981 he sold it to Mr. G. Brahman for Rs 20,000. Mr. G. Brahman is a successful Gujarati merchant. His father originally came to Kondagaon in the 1940s and was one of the first to set up as a grain merchant. When he died, his wealth passed onto his two sons who set up separate businesses. G took over his father's grain business, but subsequently gave this up and moved into glass bangle merchandising and farming. He first purchased good rice land at Masora (a few miles north of Kondagaon) and spent quite a considerable sum of money establishing an electric pump irrigation system. After three years' operation he gave up rice growing—'Too many headaches with labour'—and converted his farm into a cashew plantation. These were planted from seeds, and it will be five years until he gets any yield. However, once production starts he expects to gross Rs 4000 per acre from cashews compared to Rs 1000 from paddy.

The land at Latipur was purchased with the aim of establishing a cashew plantation. Partial clearing of the land has been carried out and seeds planted. In 1982 he was granted government permission to clear the big trees from his land. The land has been fenced. He employs a young caretaker to water the trees and to keep stray cattle out.

Case 5: Mr. S. Punjabi of Kondagaon. Mr. Punjabi purchased 12 acres from the grandson of the biggest landowner in Latipur. Mr. Punjabi is from one of Kondagaon's most prosperous joint families. The family consists of seven brothers and they arrived in Kondagaon in 1951 as penniless refugees from the Punjab. They were assisted in the setting up of their business by a wealthy Punjabi Muslim who first arrived in Kondagaon in the 1930s. The seven brothers have developed an extensive grocery wholesaling and transport business. This purchase of land marks their first entry into agriculture and they have spent large amounts of money in clearing and levelling the land in preparation for grain cultivation. They have also spent Rs 20,000 digging a well for irrigation purposes.

Discussion of the cases. Cases 4 and 5 are examples of the movement of merchant capital into agriculture. These cases are typical of the many other casual observations I made of merchants investing in land in Bastar. This movement of capital is the only source of capitalist development in agriculture. As capitalist farms they differ from smallholders in three important respects. Firstly, they are run using wage-labour rather than family labour. Secondly, large amounts of capital are invested in them to improve their productivity. Thirdly, the farm-holding consists of one large plot rather than a number of small scattered plots.

The 'differentiation of the peasantry' thesis, which holds that capitalist development comes about by internal developments within the peasantry as the rich get richer and the poor get poorer, does not apply to the Bastar case, where, as we have seen, most of the local farmers have become absolutely worse off through inheritance. In

Bastar it has been developments *external* to the farming sector that have provided the impetus to capitalist development, namely the accumulation of capital by the merchants. Merchants are urban based, and prefer to buy in places like Latipur, which is close to a town and on a main road rather than at interior, difficult to get to places such as Minipur.

One of the greatest problems facing any would-be buyer is finding a seller. In smallholder villages such as Minipur, where the average landholding per household is only 3 acres, no one has any excess land to sell. To sell land usually means to become landless and, given this fact, the sluggishness of the land market becomes perfectly comprehensible. Unusable inherited land is the only potential source of supply in such villages as case 1 illustrates. S.R. Bihari was fortunate enough in being able to buy two acres from a young boy who inherited. It was only through the good grace of Indal Singh, who wanted to assist him, that he got a contiguous plot also of two acres. Cases 2 and 3 do not represent real land sales. The cash transfer in these cases was a notional amount to formally acknowledge transfers effectively made years before. It is possible that more land will come onto the market in Minipur as the children of the present generation adjust themselves to the acute land shortage that they will face. If the experience elsewhere is any indication, those with uneconomic, small holdings will sell up and migrate. Consider Bailey's (1957: 48) report from neighbouring Orissa:

> In Bisipara land came, and still comes, into the market because estates of less than a certain size cannot survive the normal contingencies of their owner's lifetime... The most important single cause bringing estates down to this danger-level is the system of inheritance—partition of the estate between all sons at the death of the holder.

Bailey also notes that the ability of farmers to earn non-farm income prevents land from coming onto the market. This is true for Minipur too where economic diversification has intensified with the diminution of land holdings.

The land purchased by the merchants in cases 4 and 5 was, it should be noted, owned by immigrant Brahmans prior to the sale. The land was not, and never had been, owned by Bastar Tribals. The amount of land sold by Tribals to immigrant Hindus has been very small indeed. From 1966 to 1970 only 3,138 acres of the private property of Tribals in Bastar District has been legally sold to outsiders (Baijal & Deo, 1977: 103).

Part of the reason for this is the legal restriction on the transfer of Tribal lands. Under Section 165(6) of the Madhya Pradesh Land Revenue Code of 1959, it is provided that

> the right of a Bhumiswami belonging to a tribe, which has been declared to be an aboriginal tribal by the State Government ... shall not be transferred to a person not belonging to such a tribe without the permission of a Revenue officer not below the rank of collector.

Legislation such as this cannot prevent illegal transfers of land from Tribals to non-Tribals. Such statistics are difficult to obtain. However, a recent survey of 41 villages in 6 tahsils suggests that 3.6% of Tribal holdings are illegally cultivated by non-Tribals. It also showed that for Dantewara tahsil, the site of the Bailadila Iron Ore Project, the rate was 12% (Baijal & Deo, 1977: 103). It seems that here, and in the Tribal areas of Andhra Pradesh studied by Fürer Haimendorf, there has been some 'conquistador imperialism', as immigrants have brutally and forcibly ejected locals from their lands. This has not happened in North Bastar as yet, however.

The usual reason given for the alienation of Tribal lands is not so much the illegal appropriations of conquistador imperialists, but the alleged innocence of the Tribals in the face of dishonest and scheming merchants who get Tribals into their debt and force them to sell. This argument has been criticised by Bailey on the basis of a study of a village subject to much more exposure to outside commercial influences than those in Bastar. The village he studied was completely owned by the original inhabitants in 1885, but by 1953 they owned 28% of the land. He showed that land does not come onto the market for these reasons. The merchant's 'character and his chicanery are an aggravating and marginal factor in a process which has a more fundamental prime cause... the system of inheritance' (1957: 48).

The merits of Bailey's particular argument aside, the search for a single causal theory of the processes by which a good such as land becomes a commodity is a forlorn one. Farm households are creative political units that are always developing new ways to cope with the dilemmas of daily life. True, an increasing population on a given area of land does create problems but the behaviour of households is not governed by rules of inheritance, or any rules for that matter. This is because land, as we shall see in subsequent chapters, is never the only source of income for a village household wherever it may be. As a good, the supreme value of land lies in the prestige and sense of belonging it gives to its guardians and, as the evidence above shows, this makes them very reluctant to sell. Land tenure is first and foremost a political relation and it is important to remember, as Simeran Gell reminds us in her discussion of Bastar village politics, that in making political alliances householders 'exploit the multi-strandedness and historicity of their relations with others' (Gell, 1992:87).

LAND AS A VILLAGE COMMUNITY GOOD

Farm households in Bastar and elsewhere are invariably part of a wider village community and the general question arises as to the relationship between household guardianship of goods and village guardianship. This issue has been hotly debated in those parts of the world where household proprietorship of land parcels, combined with high rates of population growth, are to be found. In India it begins with Maine and Baden-Powell towards the end of last century and has been continued in the twentieth century by Wiser and Dumont among others. In Indonesia Geertz's (1963) notion of 'shared poverty' has provoked an enormous literature and the debate continues to this day (Schrauwers, 1995). The value question lies at the heart of this debate. The concern is not so much a householder's valuation of a parcel of arable land as the community's valuation of the whole of arable land in relation to common rights to meadows, forest, water, and the like. The village community is the guardian of this good which raises the factual question of the role it actually does play and the normative question of the role it should play.

Lewinski's theory gets to the heart of the matter. 'The formation of the village community,' he argues (1913: 33), 'is due to the same element as caused the origin of private property—a growth of population.' 'The function of the community,' he continues, 'is to prevent destruction and to equalize the land. The preventive policy applies exclusively to the non-appropriated lands, because only with regard to them is it necessary. When a man owns his own land, his personal interest is usually a sufficient guarantee against his destroying it.' The equalisation strategy applies to arable land and Lewinski surveys the attempts of village communities in nineteenth century Russia to do this, noting that the more labour a proprietor has expended on the soil, the more they cling to it, and the more strongly they protest against any intervention of the community.

This neglected study of Lewinski's identifies the fundamental contradiction at the heart of the politics of the village community and suggests why the *preventive* strategy is more likely to succeed than the *equalisation* strategy. The data presented in this chapter provides no support for the existence of any equalisation strategy with respect to arable land in Bastar. However, the village community in Bastar does have a preventive strategy.

This is brought out clearly by Simeran Gell in her defence of the village as a unit of study in Bastar. 'The village,' she notes (1992: 67–68),

> is the corporate political group… and the village is administered by its council (*bhumkal*) whose decisions are binding on all. Every village is also a religious congregation with its own specific responsibilities in the cult of the gods, including the so called 'clan' gods who are never worshipped by congregations exclusively drawn from one particular clan. The relationship of people to the soil…is heavily emphasized in the religious system of the Muria and indeed is the basis of the moral bond between people and divinities: it is because the village congregations share 'substance' in that they all draw sustenance from the village earth that they are obliged to contribute to the ritual tributes paid to the gods by the village collectively. The village in practice is not a simple whole, and the unity of the village is often obscured by the competition and rivalry between families within it.

This rivalry takes the form of jealousy of the relative economic wealth of some families and is the cause of sorcery attacks. Her analysis suggests, *pace* Alfred Gell, that envy and jealousy are behind the collectivist consumption ethos of the Muria, and that this is the reason the rich are obliged to consume as if they were poor.

With respect to land alienation, she draws an important distinction between a householders' legal right to alienate land and their obligations as members of a moral community. 'It is unthinkable,' she notes (1992: 76), 'that any person would risk his standing in the village by using his legal ownership to dispose of land at will.' Immigrants, for their part, are not members of the moral community until they are able to buy land which gives them the right to participate in rituals on the same basis as the rest of the villagers. To get the right to buy immigrants must go through a transition stage of getting affiliated with a local family. When land does come up for sale, and this has only happened when emigrants have sold up, they have to compete with other prospective buyers from within the village. More often than not the people buying the land regard it as a political venture rather than an economic investment. The person who is accepted as a buyer scores a victory over his rivals, fortifies his position in the village, and acquires land that he is often unable to farm because of the shortage of labour.

The most valuable land in the village studied by Simeran Gell are *vedang*, levelled rice fields with a water-retaining bank. Other categories include *kotum, dipa,* and *bhat. Kotum* is government-controlled forest areas within the village boundaries which the government exploits for commercial purposes but which the villagers see as belonging to them. *Dipa*, swidden fields, are the former forest areas located between the present forest and the rice fields whose expansion the government controls very tightly. *Bhat* are the infertile former swidden fields now useful only for grazing cattle.

This typology reflects the particular ecological conditions of the village Gell studied but the general point the case illustrates is the intrusive role of the state in the control over village common forest lands. This is the basis of much conflict between villagers and the state in Bastar. This conflict has a long history and has assumed the form of outright rebellion led by so-called Naxalites. It is impossible for an anthropologist to research this topic in Bastar today because the Government will not issue research permits to foreigners. All one can do is report gossip one hears. Gossip is important not because it necessarily reflects the truth of the situation but because it reflects what some people *believe* to be the truth and beliefs, as we know, have a force all of their own.

When I first went to Bastar in 1982 I was told of Naxalite activity in South Bastar on the border on Andhra Pradesh some hundreds of kilometres away. However, when I returned in 1989–90 the activity had spread to the Kondagaon area. An acquaintance in the Forest Department warned me not to go to Minipur because the Naxalites had recently beaten up a forest guard and relieved him of Rs 11,000. This had the desired effect of spreading fear throughout the ranks of the forest guards many of whom refused to perform duties in the interior regions for fear of their lives. The villagers I spoke to, on the other hand, said that I was in no danger. They welcome the Naxalite activity because, from their perspective, the forest guards are corrupt officials who plunder, rather than protect, the forest by selling trees to illegal timber merchants. They are reminded of the forest guard's corruption on a daily basis because they know that the cost of the petrol for the motor bikes the guards ride around on exceeds the income they get from the Forest Department. The Naxalites identify themselves with a *lal salaam* (red greeting) or a *johar dada* (hello brother) and give out medicine. In return they are given food and informed about the behaviour of the forest guards. The villagers also told me about two Naxalites who were killed in 1989. The government buried them at Keshkal ghat, a highly symbolic political act because, as explained in the previous chapter, this is the location of the God Bhangaram, the recipient of the evil exorcised from villages in an annual purification ritual. In an equally symbolic counter act, sympathisers dug up the bodies and cremated them in a ceremony of their own.

LAND AS A NATIONAL AND GLOBAL GOOD

Just as the household is part of a village community, the village community is part of a state, and the state is part of the international community. At each level of this institutional hierarchy the notion of guardian acquires a meaning that encompasses the previous one. Ultimately land is the supreme good of humanity at large. The self-evident logic of this judgement is contained in the Statement of Hopi

Religious Leaders quoted at the beginning of this chapter: 'The land is sacred and if the land is abused, the sacredness of Hopi life will disappear and other forms of life as well'.

The supremacy of land as a good presupposes that its human guardians can protect it from human abuse and human degradation. This is precisely what people everywhere have been unable to achieve with the result that, globally speaking, land degradation is a serious and growing concern. The value question is at the heart of this debate because it revolves around the question of what *is* happening and what *ought* to be done. There are no simple answers to these questions; indeed simple answers are part of the problem not the solution.

One simple answer finds the problem in 'Western civilisation' where land is said to be a *profane* commodity and the solution in the beliefs of Aboriginal people for whom land is *sacred*. The implication of this position is that Westerners must rehabilitate mother earth as the supreme goddess. The proponents of this position range from New Age romantics at one extreme to hard-headed scientists like Loveluck and Suzuki at the other. The normative part of this theory of value— that land must be protected—is beyond question but not so the strategies for protection and the explanatory adequacy of the theories that inform these strategies. The problem with many of these theories is not so much their misunderstanding of Aboriginal societies but their misunderstandings of land tenure in 'Western' society. Consider Knudston and Suzuki for example:

> In the spiritually detached Western view of nature, land is lifeless. It is inert, a two-dimensional physical surface (if we exclude a third dimension, which grants rights of access to urban high-rises above or to mineral or water rights below)—to be surveyed, subdivided, and zoned. It is a commodity—valuable but no more 'sacred' than a stake of cedar logs, a heap of coal, or any other economic resource. It is a financial investment—to be bought, 'developed', and resold (hopefully at a handsome profit) by shuffling official titles and deeds (1992: 121, emphasis added.)

While no one would deny that land is often transacted as a commodity, the paradox remains, as demonstrated above, that capitalist agriculture developed first in a country where land was a *good*, an inalienable keepsake of elite families who kept their land off the market in the name of God, King, and Country. The fundamental issue is not one of profanity versus sacredness, but of the politics of affirmation and denial within a belief system that values land. The landed affirm their rights to guardianship of a given territory by denying others the right of occupation. The fact that this affirmation is done in the name of some superhuman being does not obviate the political character of the implied denial. This is not to say that beliefs about divinely appointed guardians are necessarily insincere but it does highlight the fact that competing beliefs, however sincere, always have a political manifestation. In Bastar, for example, the upward looking political theology of the divine king contradicts the downward looking political theology of the Aborigines. Like royal families everywhere, the Bastar kings claim descent from a transcendental god and justify their claims to guardianship of a given territory by means of mythological charters. Bastar's kings were 'little kings' who emulated the 'big kings' in Delhi in their quest for prestige; by analogy, households in Bastar, such as Mr. Mali's whose family goods were described at the beginning of this chapter, emulated the royal household in their quest for prestige. But emulation, unquestioning agreement, is defined by its opposite, questioning disagreement, and the grounds for subalternate political theologies become defined. Aboriginal households find their deities in the ground that they plough and in the flora and fauna of the countryside they inhabit. Thus a Mr. Baghel (literally 'Tigerman') claims his descent from, and worships, the tiger that used to roam in the jungles of Bastar; the lion (Singh) that the king's deity rides is unmeaning for him because, among other things, this is an animal whose natural habitat was the open plains of north India and Africa. The replacement of a divine kingdom by a secular state—a bloody affair in Bastar that resulted in the death of the king under a hail of police bullets in 1966—has not altered Aboriginal political theology. It has merely given it a new political antithesis, but one that now has a more global orientation. The political theologies of the Bastar Tribals, the Hopi Indians and the Australian Aborigines differ greatly but they also have a new found unity today as multinational corporations, in cohort with many a secular nation state, seek to transform their land first into a commodity with a limited life span.

Pseudo geographical categories such as 'the profane West' versus 'the sacred Other' obscure rather than clarify the commonplace contradictions which lie at the core of the notion of land as a good. The fundamental political issue is a struggle for prestige. Land degradation, as Blaike and Brookfield (1978) have correctly identified, is a *human* problem. The fact that this problem is often expressed in the language of god, as in the Hopi Statement, should not blind us to the truism of humanist thought that informs it: if land is abused Hopi life will disappear and all other life as well. From a humanist standpoint the Great Spirit, Massau'u, is not some abstract transcendental being but, rather, a concrete political manifestation of the relations of human reproduction. In earthly terms humanity is still only very young—a mere 100,000 years or so according to the archaeologists—and its greatest hope for survival is the capacity of its living members to question the values of the elite.

NOTE

[1] The names of villagers and people in this section have been changed to protect the identity of my informants.

CHAPTER IV

Production of Commodities by Means of Goods

THE AGRARIAN QUESTION AND THE PROBLEM OF VALUE

The agrarian question is as old as capitalism itself. The general issues François Quesnay (Groenewegen, 1983) raised in 1757 concerning agrarian relations in the France of his time are still hotly debated today but the locus of the debate has moved to Asia, South America and Africa. Two fundamental questions are at stake: What *is* happening to agrarian relations as the market expands? What *should* happen? These questions are usually posed in terms of a distinction between *peasant* farming and *capitalist* farming: Is capitalist farming replacing peasant farming? Should it be? A theory of value is needed to answer these questions and, not surprisingly, there are as many answers as there are theories of value. Furthermore, the theory of value chosen determines the language used to pose the question. In the post-Marxist world of today the language used is that of *smallholders, largeholders, adaptation,* and *culture.*

For the classical Marxist the issue is one of *class exploitation.* Peasant proprietors are conceived of as capitalists who are also workers. The contradiction, which intensifies as the market grows, leads to differentiation: rich peasants get richer and become capitalists, the poor peasants get poorer and become proletarians. This theory has its origins in Marx's discussion of 'Metayage and Peasant Proprietorship of Land Parcels' (1894: 802–814). Lenin (1899) developed the idea in his influential theory of 'The Differentiation of the Peasantry'. For Lenin peasant farming was an inefficient pre-capitalist form that was destined to disappear in the competitive struggle with capitalist farmers in the same way that the large mechanised factory replaced the small artisan. In other words, capitalism would conquer the farmer's field in the same way that it conquered the factory floor.

For marginal utility theorists such as Chayanov (1966) the issue is one of *self-exploitation*. He questioned the alleged superiority of large scale farmers and argued that differentiation was not taking place. He laid stress on the cyclical mobility of the household as it moved through the various stages of its demographic structure and noted that the consumer/worker ratio varied according to the life-cycle of a family. Thus a newly wed couple with young children have a higher consumer/worker ratio than a family with adult children and have to work harder to balance the household budget. Chayanov also argued that smallholders are sometimes more efficient. The Organisation and Production School to which he belonged believed that agrarian transition to capitalism was neither inevitable nor desirable. This position placed him at odds with the Marxists and, when Stalin came to power, he paid for it with his life.

This debate has set the parameters for most twentieth century discussions of the agrarian question, a debate that included contributions from economists, historians, sociologists, geographers and anthropologists. The anthropological contribution to the debate has focussed on the relations of reproduction of 'peasant' households and, in particular, the role of culture and kinship. Geertz's (1963) theory of 'shared poverty', developed to explain the history of agrarian relations in Indonesia, is perhaps the best known. This work was in the tradition of the American school of 'cultural ecology'. 'Adaptation' is the central analytical concept of this school of thought and Netting (1993) its leading exponent. His recent book, an ambitious survey of the agrarian question today that is informed by his own intensive fieldwork in Africa and Europe, is the latest defence of the 'smallholder'. The merits of this particular theory aside, the general consensus among anthropologists seems to be that the smallholders are here to stay and the 'persistence' of this particular form of farming is what needs to be explained. Even neomarxists recognise this much. Harris (1982), for example, poses this question in his *Capitalism and Peasant Farming* where he argues that the process of differentiation of the peasantry is 'blocked' both because of the 'intermediate' capitalist character of the economy and because of 'the ideological structures of caste and kinship which reinforce existing relations of production and the power structure' (1992: 9). Taussig's (1978: 66) revisionist thesis abandons the evolutionary biases of classical Marxism completely and stresses the fact that quantitative comparisons must be made where the two types of farming '*coexist* in one and the same area and ecozone' (emphasis added). Taussig, too, finds that smallholders are more efficient. He argues, on the basis of his study of the green revolution in the Cauca Valley of Columbia, that capitalist development 'does not so much displace peasant and other forms of non-capitalist production, but rather incorporates their very real economic efficiencies so as to balance the costs of capital investment which are otherwise largely supplied by international financing' (1978: 87–88).

Taussig's paper gets to the theoretical heart of one aspect of the debate: the *quantitative* value problem posed by the *co-existence* of two types of farming practices. There is no general solution to this problem and this can be seen by examining the nature of the value question involved.

From a scientific point of view farming is a process of transforming seed into crops by means of land, labour and other means of production such as tools, machines, fertilisers and the like. The key inputs, then, are land, labour and capital (seed, tools, cattle) all of which can be quantified in terms of some standard weight or measure such as area, time, or volume. If these inputs are considered in relation to a given level of output and in relation to each other six primary ratios can be defined: labour/land, capital/land, output/land, capital/labour, output/labour, output/capital. Other ratios can be defined by inverting these ratios or by forming secondary composite ratios of various kinds such as surplus/output where surplus is defined in some way or other (eg. grain output minus seed input). The complications are endless but whatever ratio is defined one fundamental problem underlies them all, the value question of how to reduce heterogenous quantities to a common measure. This presupposes a standard of value such as money prices, labour-time, or energy flow. The use of these standards poses difficult theoretical and practical problems. For example, if money prices are chosen then which prices? Current replacement prices? Historical cost prices? If historical cost prices are used then this merely substitutes one value problem with another if the things in question were purchased at different times. If current prices are used then how does one value old equipment? Replacement cost or current disposable values? Then there is the problem of valuing unpaid family labour. Having resolved these accounting problems, one is then faced with the question of the interpretation of the results because the use of different standards will tell different stories.

Taussig, who is acutely aware of these problems, found that, at 1971 prices, capitalist farmers had higher ratios for capital/land, output/land, capital/labour, and output/labour but that peasant farmers had higher labour/land and output/capital ratios. The higher labour/land ratio, he argues, reflects the greater labour intensity of peasant farming and the higher output/capital ratio its greater 'capital efficiency'. He also calculated energy expenditures and found, pace Lenin, wage-labour on plantations to be an enormous drain on energy compared to peasant farming and that were it not for their 'non-capitalist modes of sustenance wage labourers and their families would be literally burnt out — consumed by the fire of their own labour' (1978: 86). Thus the labour efficiency of capitalist farming as measured by 1971 prices turns out to be highly 'inefficient' *for the worker* using a kilocalorie standard. Taussig's analysis, then, raises the question of efficiency for whom. Where power relations are involved there will always be at least two answers to this question.

It is not my intention to carry out yet another quantitative value analysis here. Rather, I seek to advance Taussig's revisionist approach to the theory of value by affirming the coexistence of different value forms. My concern is to investigate the commonplace contradictions that arise from the coexistence of *goods* and *commodities*.

The limitations of Marx's approach is that he sees everything from the perspective of the worker on the factory floor. This is the perspective of someone whose labour-power is a *commodity* that is used to produce other *commodities*. Sraffa's (1960) *Production of Commodities by Means of Commodities* captures the essence of this theoretical perspective. The problem with this approach is not so much that it is wrong but that it abstracts from household economy and is unable to handle the problem posed by the existence of *goods,* those inalienable keepsakes under the guardianship of the family. Thus Sraffa has a theory of the rent of land but no theory of the price of land. His theory of rent implicitly assumes that land is a *non- commodity*. Given that the theory of rent he develops has its origins in the particular conditions of English agriculture, this is a perfectly reasonable assumption. The elite landed families of England, as we saw in the last chapter, kept land off the market by maintaining it as a *good*, as an inalienable keepsake that brought them not only power and prestige but also rent. English agrarian capitalism, then, was a system of the *production of commodities by means of goods*. But while classical political economy has a highly developed labour theory of *commodities*, it has no theory of *goods* as evidenced by the fact that the word itself is rarely, if ever, used. Neoclassical economics, by way of contrast, has a utility theory of *goods* but no theory of the *commodity*. What is required is not a synthesis of these two theories of value, but a new theory that gives the words *goods* and *commodities* new meaning by locating them in the concrete agrarian relations of consanguinity, affinity and contiguity created by reciprocal recognition. This is not to deny the importance of an analysis tied to the factory floor and nor does it argue that one should tie one's theory to the hearth and home. My simple point is that when it comes to the analysis of agrarian relations the factory floor is not the best vantage point.

Much of what is called 'peasant' farming falls under the generic label of the *production of commodities by means of goods*. When the agrarian question is framed in these terms the nature of the question changes completely because the grand opposition between capitalists and peasants is dissolved. The issue now becomes one of understanding the commonplace contradiction posed by the 'goodness' of commodities and the 'commodityness' of goods. To put it another way, how do reciprocally recognised relations of consanguinity, affinity, and contiguity influence the principles governing the production, consumption, distribution and exchange of commodities? Conversely, how do inalienable keepsakes acquire market values? These questions shift the focus from an analysis of quantitative *values* to qualitative relations between *valuers*, from land, capital and labour to *guardians*, *owners* and *producers*.

The guardian of land, the owner of the means of production and the producer may be the same person or three different people. In Minipur village, Bastar, where household proprietorship of land parcels is the norm, the valuers are, in most cases, the same person. A similar situation holds in the Murrumbidgee Irrigation Area of Australia where one family typically possesses a large consolidated plot of 500 acres, has purchased all the machinery used to work the land, and does almost all the annual labour themselves. In Latipur village, Bastar, the guardian of land parcels and the owner of the means of production are the same but the producers are different. Formerly they were bonded labourers, today they are day labourers. In nineteenth century England the three valuers assumed the classic form of the landlord, the capitalist and the farm worker. Today, with increasing mechanisation, the number of farm workers has dropped dramatically in England and many capitalist tenants do their own labouring or some of it anyway. The following matrix summarises the logical possibilities.

Guardians of land	Owners of means of production	Producers of commodities	Examples
same	same	same	India, Australia
same	same	different	India
different	different	different	England
different	same	same	England

This perspective enables different questions to be posed. For example, what values influence the household politics of the family that is guardian, owner and producer? What values are dominant? The prestige that comes from land ownership or the profits? Are households prepared to alienate the land and if so at what price? Conversely, if the inalienability of land is highly valued, what implication does this have for the valuation of the products of the land? Are they rendered inalienable too?

The technological aspect of the distinction between peasants and capitalists does not get lost in this perspective but it is de-emphasised. A distinction can be made between householders who farm land parcels using wooden ploughs and those who farm large consolidated plots of land using machines and questions posed concerning the economics of technology. However, my focus is on *politics of prestige* and on the process by which households use the values of land guardianship, capital ownership and household labour to create a distinction between households based on goodness. Household polities create their own conceptions of territoriality and temporality that bear little relation to the positivist conceptions of land and time employed by the theorists of farm household economy. Elite mercantile households in India, for example, have a conception of territory that is centred on the land parcels in their Rajasthani homeland but covers the whole of India because of the links created by 'inalienable' migrants. The migrant families, in turn, have created localised mercantile territories that they protect and nurture for the benefit of their family members. As a prelude to reporting my fieldwork in Bastar, it is necessary to define the specificity of commodity marketing in Bastar and to show how, in general terms, the role of goods fits into a system such a this.

COMMODITIES AND GOODS IN BASTAR

Selling in order to buy

The marketing of farm produce in Bastar is done at periodic rural markets by those who are obliged to sell in order to buy. As such, it is a classic example of the C-M-C type of exchange distinguished by Marx where a commodity (C) is sold for money(M) in order to buy another commodity (C). Or, to put it another way, a farmer sells (C-M) in order to buy (M-C). In Bastar a member of a farm household—usually a woman—will carry a few kilos of grain to the market in a basket, sell it to the grain dealer who waits outside the market, and then proceed to buy the manufactured commodities the household needs, such as clothing, kerosene, oil, matches, and so on. This happens throughout the year on an almost daily basis in some cases. Of course, the grain sales tend to be highest after the harvest when the bigger purchases are made (pots, clothing, jewellery) and accumulated debts have to be paid off. While C-M-C marketing is of a recognisable generic type, it is by no means general throughout India. A brief comparative study of the market system in Saharanpur District north of Delhi brought this home to me. Here most farm householders come to the periodic markets with money to buy commodities having sold their farm produce at other more specialised markets. In other words, in North India selling (C–M) is done at one market, buying (M–C) at another.

From the perspective of merchants (some of whom may also be farmers) periodic marketing is a matter of buying cheap here (M–C) and selling dear there (C–M′), which describes the circuit of mercantile capital M–C–M′ also formulated by Marx. Marx saw C–M–C type marketing as one step up in the evolutionary scale from barter (C–C) and one below buying/selling (M–C–M′). This evolutionary argument is contradicted by the fact that all three forms co-exist in the rural markets of Bastar. Barter, it is true, only accounts for a very small percentage of the trade but it coexists nevertheless. The question is why C–M–C predominates in Bastar and M-C-M′ in rural areas in the Delhi region. The answer is embedded in the question and it has to do with the multitude of ecological, sociological and historical factors that make the intensity of commercial activity higher in one area than another. This difference in intensity is one of quantity and not quality. In other words, the difference is to be measured by the distance from cities, the density of population, the methods of production, and so on and not in so-called 'cultural' factors such as the notion of a 'backward tribal area'.

But where do *goods* fit into this scheme? C–M–C is an exchange circuit and if production (P) is included the circuit becomes

$$\text{C–M–C} \ldots \text{P} \ldots \text{C–M–C}$$

which is a market—production—re-market circuit. This circuit raises the question of the ancient distinction between use-value and exchange-value. Rice, for example, has a number of use-values be it food for a consumer or seed for a producer; its exchange-value, by contrast, is the price it fetches on the market. This distinction has been used to differentiate between those households who consume their own produce and those who sell it on the market. 'Peasant' households, some say, typically produce for use whilst capitalists produce for exchange.

I question this distinction on both theoretical and empirical grounds. As we shall see, in Bastar it is the poor farmers who are obliged to sell in order to buy whilst the rich are able to withhold produce from the market. Furthermore, it is not surpluses the poor farmers are obliged to sell but deficits. Household proprietorship of land parcels, I assert, has always and everywhere been associated with the production of exchange-values. It is the valuation of things as *goods* that keeps them off the market, be these things land or the products of land. Furthermore, it is the richer, high prestige, politically powerful families that are able to assert this value and to thereby make themselves good.

The role of goods in the commodity circuit C–M–C can be formalised by substituting goods (G) for production (P) into the formula to give

$$C–M–C \dots G \dots C–M–C$$

It is not only farm households that value things as goods; merchant households too value things in this way. The values of the household intervene in the spatial gap between the commodities that are purchased cheap here (M–C) and the commodities that are sold dear there (C–M′) to give

$$M–C \dots G \dots C–M′$$

This formula is encompassed by the previous one. This is fitting because no clear distinction can be made between farming and merchant households in Bastar when the perspective of the *household polity* is taken. Some Bastar farm households are small merchants who buy in one market (or village) and sell in another; some big Marwari merchant families have farms in Rajasthan that members operate. The analytical task, then, is not to begin with an abstract definition of a household but to end with an understanding of how the politics of goodness defines it concretely in a world where money, power, and prestige are part of a complex ever-changing totality.

Grain production and the obligation to sell

Paddy is the most important crop grown in Kondagaon Tahsil. It is grown in bunded level fields with rainfed irrigation. Other products grown include cereals such as *kosra* (Panicum milliaceam) and *mandia* (Elusion coracane) and maize. Kosra is ideally suited for hill areas and is widely grown in the neighbouring Narainpur Tahsil where shifting agriculture is practised. Next to cereals, come pulses as the most important foodcrop in Bastar. These include *kulthi* (horse gram), *urd* (black gram) and *mung* (green gram). Cash crops are also grown and the most important of these are oil seeds like *sarson* (mustard), *ramtilli* (nigerseed) and *tilli* (linseed).

Paddy accounts for 69% of all marketed produce in Kondagaon with sarson, the oil seed cash crop, next in importance at 11%. In Narainpur Tahsil, by way of contrast, cash crops (sarson, ramtilli, and tilli) account for 60% of all marketed produce and paddy, the foodcrop, for only 31%. Given that Narainpur has been described by one prominent anthropologist as an 'unblemished tribal haven', can these facts be explained with reference to Narainpur's location on the so-called tribe-caste continuum? The evidence suggests not. Consider Table IV.1.

Population density in Kondagaon is one and a half times that of Narainpur but the ratio of marketed produce per acre is almost twelve to one in favour of Kondagaon. The minor differences in the

TABLE IV.1   BASTAR DISTRICT: TWO SUBDISTRICTS
(TAHSILS) COMPARED

	Kondagaon Tahsil	Narainpur Tahsil
Total cropped area (acres)	260,398	149,136
Marketed produce (Rs)	10,013,000	493,000
Marketed produce (Rs/acres)	38	3
Population density	1.05	0.64
Tribal population (%)	74	64

Source: Government Offices, Kondagaon

percentages of people classified as Tribal in the two areas cannot account for this difference. Narainpur Tahsil includes the Abujhmar hills where shifting cultivation predominates and millet is the main crop. But in the foothills of this region paddy is the main crop and it is grown on arable land that is relatively abundant; the major problem facing most households in this region is a labour shortage. In Kondagaon Tahsil, by way of contrast, arable land is scarce in the sense that encroachment onto forest land is no longer an option for a land poor family; here a shortage of land is the main problem facing households. In the land-rich, labour-poor Narainpur Tahsil, then, the general level of household wealth is higher than the land-poor, labour-rich Kondagaon district. This suggests that, at this macro level of analysis, the richer families in Narainpur market cash crops and with-hold foodcrops for their own consumption, whilst the poorer families of Kondagaon Tahsil are obliged to market foodcrops. In other words, relative poverty is at the basis of the intensification of marketing activity in Kondagaon Tahsil.

Another significant factor here is the relative prices of the principal food and cash crops. In 1982 monthly prices for oil seed fluctuated around Rs 400 per quintal while that for paddy was in the region of Rs 125 per quintal. In a market economy where farm house-holds sell in order to buy (C–M–C), this means that a householder selling paddy has to carry four times the weight of a seller of oilseed to receive the same income. This fact is significant because women, who do most of the marketing, carry their produce to market on their head on journeys that can take up to four hours one way.

The annual cycle

The annual cycle of household activity in Bastar has three clearly defined phases of roughly four months each. First comes that of production when householders are busy in their fields planting and tending the growth of rice. This lasts from July to October. Then comes the phase of marketing during which time the annual fairs are held. This is also a time of great religious activity for the annual fairs are not only times when new households acquire their durable means of consumption (eg. brassware) and old households renew worn out means of production (eg. cattle) but also times when the deities of the clan and the village meet to play and to test the faith of their followers who engage in public acts of self-flagellation. This phase last from November to March with most of the annual fairs being held in the latter months. The third phase, the summer months from March to June, is the marriage season. During this phase the brassware purchased by parents and relatives at the annual fairs is given to newly weds to enable them to set up house. At these rituals, which can last for days, consanguines and affines, whose definition defies precise distinction because of a history of cross-cousin marriage, gather to eat, drink and be merry at the expense of the bride's parents.

This cycle is underwritten by the pattern of rainfall as the following chart shows.

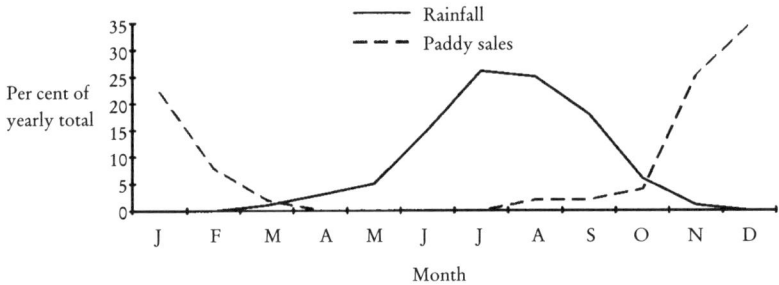

FIGURE IV.1   *The annual cycle in Bastar*

From the perspective of the household, the phases of production, marketing/ritual, and marriage become ones of indebtedness, income, and expenditure respectively. If the economy was in a self-replacing state the debt would be cancelled and renewed each year; but the vagaries of rainfall consign the concept of the self-replacing state to the realms of theoretical fantasy. Indebtedness, then, is the norm but nature is not the only cause because cultural factors, such as marriage expenses, are also important. On the other hand, householders have access to many non-farm sources of income to balance their budgets.

FARMERS AND THE HOUSEHOLD
POLITICS OF SELLING

Classifying households

The regional level finding about the obligation of the relatively poor to sell paddy is reproduced at the household level where we find that it is the rice-deficit households, rather than the rice-surplus producing households, who are obliged to market their produce. However, before the reasons for this are investigated, it is necessary to define what is meant by a 'rice-surplus' and a 'rice-deficit' household.

Many highly-sophisticated techniques have been developed for measuring surplus and deficit households (Harriss, 1982: App. I). However, these techniques have the danger of giving spurious accuracy to the measurement of a phenomenon that can never be precisely quantified. Household production falls within a range that depends, among other things, upon annual rainfall. An average figure for production over a number of years is therefore needed. However, once time is introduced into the measurement of production, other problems arise. For example, the demographic structure of a household can change quite dramatically in the space of a few years through birth, marriage and death. Any quantitative measure of 'surplus' or 'deficit', then, necessarily involves a great deal of approximation. A simple rule-of-thumb measure considered in the light of indigenous conceptions of the relative wealth of a household is, therefore, just as good, if not better than, a highly complex statistical measure.

The simple rule-of-thumb measure I have adopted is the ratio of rice land to household size (hereafter, the 'surplus' ratio). Households with a surplus ratio above 1.00 are classified as rice-surplus households, those with a ratio below 0.60 as rice-deficit households, and those with a surplus ratio between 0.60 and 1.00 as intermediate households. A surplus ratio of 0.80 is the break-even ratio, and the assumptions behind this figure are as follows. It is assumed that each acre of rice land produces 15 *khundi* (450 kg) of paddy per year and that one person consumes 12 *khundi* (360 kg) per year. It follows from this that one person needs 12/15 = 0.80 acres of rice land to balance production and consumption. The surplus ratio, on the basis of these assumptions is therefore a ratio of rice production to rice consumption. It follows that households with a surplus ratio of between 0.40 and 0.80 are without rice for up to six months per year, those with a ratio between 0.00 and 0.40 are without rice for between six and twelve months, while those with a ratio in excess of 1.60 have more than double their requirements. This ratio measures the degree to which a village dweller is a rice farmer. It says nothing about the balance of income and expenditure of a household but enables the question of 'How do rice-deficit households survive?' to be posed. It is, therefore, a way of tackling the question of economic diversification.

Table IV.2 classifies the 55 households of Minipur village. More than half of the households are persistent rice-deficit households, slightly less then one third (31%) are sometimes in deficit, and only 13% of households are persistent rice-surplus producers. These statistics are consistent with the findings of researchers from many different parts of the world (Malinowski & de la Fuente, 1957: 202; McFarlane, 1976: 315; Beals, 1975: 57; Hill, 1982: 142–43; Taussig 1978: 75).

As might be expected, this classification of households is consistent with a number of other indices of wealth. For example, surplus householders own 16 head of cattle on average compared to 4 for intermediate households and 2 for deficit households. This suggests that richer farmers convert their surplus product into capital in the form of cattle. They are unable to invest their surplus in more

TABLE IV.2   MINIPUR VILLAGE: CLASSIFICATION OF
HOUSEHOLDS BY SIZE OF RICE-SURPLUS (DEFICIT)

Type of household	Number	Total land (acres)	Rice land (acres)	Population	Population density	Surplus ratio	Cattle per h.hold
		(A)	(B)	(C)	(C/A)	(B/C)	
Surplus	7	116	80	63	0.54	1.27	16
Intermediate	17	137	81	98	0.72	0.83	4
Deficit	31	101	58	175	1.74	0.33	2
TOTAL	55	354	219	336	0.95	0.65	4

Source: The data for this table, and all subsequent tables in this section, comes from village land records and field work. The data was collected in 1982-83

land because almost no land comes onto the market. Surplus farmers have more land per head than other poorer farmers but this is largely an accident of birth. Gold and silver is another way of investing surplus. I was unable to collect data on this, but I did observe that the male household heads of the surplus families were the only ones who wore gold earrings and necklaces. Apart from cattle and gold there is little else a rice-surplus producing farmer can invest in. Given the existing socio-economic structure of production, it is difficult to see how their surplus could be used to intensify production. There is little scope for improving the instruments of production. For example, ploughs are made by the farmers themselves and cost virtually nothing, save for the farmer's labour, time and the small payment to the blacksmith for fitting the metal tip. Investment in a superior-quality plough would be a waste of money because it would not affect yields. Mechanisation in the form of tractors is simply out of the question. That would require an outlay that would be equivalent to more than ten lifetime's earnings of the richest farmers in Minipur. In any case, a tractor would be useless under the present scattered plot system of land tenure. There is no scope for intensifying grain production either. For example, double cropping could be introduced and more rice planted using the transplanting method. Intensification of production along these lines has little to do with availability of an investable surplus, however. Double cropping means working through the traditional festive season when important religious events are held and marriages take place. Villagers have many family and social obligations to discharge during this period, and a conflict of values— household reproduction versus profit making—would arise if this strategy were followed. Investment in irrigation pumps and/or fertilisers is a real option available to surplus farmers. But the advantages of such an investment are not always outweighed by the disadvantages. Diesel or electric pumps require fuel and maintenance, neither of which are readily available to the farmer living more than four hours walk to the nearest town. These barriers to a productive consumption of a surplus are well nigh insurmountable for farmers of this type.

Large scale capitalist farming on consolidated plots does not have its origins in a process of the 'differentiation of the peasantry'.

Downward mobility is the usual path for commodity farming on parcelised holdings; upward mobility does occur, but it is almost impossible for farmers who produce *commodities* by means of *goods* to convert scattered plots into consolidated holdings. This is because *goods* are inalienable and the supreme good, land, has proved itself to be highly resistant to the corrosive forces of the market. In any case, the annual surplus of a family farm with 20 acres of land is minuscule compared with the mercantile profits realised by the merchants they deal with on a daily basis. Merchants face no obstacles to the accumulation of capital. Any profit can be reinvested in working capital in order to make bigger profits. Merchants who wish to diversify can move into mechanised farming on consolidated plots by buying up land near the urban centres. The few mechanised farms that exist in Bastar have originated in this way and the comparative historical evidence from England (Habakkuk, 1939–40) suggests the general hypothesis that agrarian capital accumulation may have its origins in the mercantile profit rather than the differentiation of the peasantry.

Rice-surplus households

Table IV.3 disaggregates the data on rice-surplus producing households. Statistically speaking, Paklu's household (#7) is the richest with a surplus ratio of 2.50. However, this is because he has no children. His wife is Suku's (#3) sister. When he first came to Minipur he worked for his wife's father and married on a *lamsena* basis. Under this arrangement the bride's father pays for all the wedding expenses in exchange for so many years free labour from the son-in-law to be. Suku's father owned 27.79 acres. When he died he gave 7.49 to Paklu and the balance to Suku, his only son. Suku is the richest man in the sense that he controls more land, labour and cattle than any other household head. He is a follower of Bihari Das, a Hindu missionary who has converted large numbers of Bastarians to his brand of Sankritised Hinduism, which does not permit meat eating, drinking or smoking. Suku has two sons, one of whom has embraced the Bihari Das religion and lives with him; the other hasn't and lives separately.

TABLE IV.3   MINIPUR VILLAGE: RICE-SURPLUS HOUSEHOLDS

Name of household head	Caste	Total Land (acres) (A)	Rice-Land (acres) (B)	Popu-lation (C)	Population density (C/A)	Surplus ratio (B/C)	Cattle
1 Aasman	Maraar	17.77	10	5	0.28	2.00	19
2 Gopi	Maraar	21.97	20	12	0.55	1.67	16
3 Suku	Gond	20.30	16	18	0.89	0.89	25
4 Boti	Gond	16.33	9	9	0.55	1.00	21
5 Pisaru	Gond	17.77	8	6	0.34	1.33	14
6 Duwaru	Gond	14.30	12	11	0.78	1.09	5
7 Paklu	Gond	7.49	5	2	0.27	2.50	11
TOTAL		115.93	80	63	0.54	1.27	111
Average		16.56	11	9	0.54	1.27	16

However, they all work together. In addition, there are another five young men who live in Suku's house and work for him under a variety of labour contracts. Three men are 'just like sons' and are treated as such. One of these sons has been living with Suku since birth but it is unclear at this stage how much land, if any, he or the other two will inherit. Of the other two men, one is working for Suku on a *kamivaal* basis, an indigenous form of short-term labour contract, and the other works for Suku on a *kabari* 'bonded labour' basis. In this particular case Suku gave the man's father a bullock in exchange for the labour of his son. Until such time as the bullock is returned, the man will live and work for Suku. Suku has large stocks of paddy in his granaries which he never sells. He uses this grain to pay the casual labour that he employs in the wet season and to feed the 18 members of his household. His marketing activity is restricted to the sale of his oil seed cash crops.

Joint families of Suku's type were quite common in days gone by, when land was abundant and labour relatively scarce. However, with the reversal of the land/labour availability relationship, the *raison d'etre* for the joint family has gone and with it the institution of the rural joint family. Joint families, as we shall see in the next chapter, are still important institutions in the urban areas though.

After Suku, the next wealthiest household belongs to Gopi (#2) of the Maraar (Gardener) caste. His household consists of his three sons and their families. Like Suku, Gopi does not sell paddy.

Household consumption is between 150–180 *khundi* (2250–2700 kg) per year, while production grosses about 200 *khundi* (3000 kg). Of this 20 *khundi* (300 kg) is paid out in wages for weeding and 15 *khundi* (225 kg) is kept as seed. On these figures this household has a surplus of 15 *khundi* or a deficit of the same amount depending upon which consumption figure is used. In other words, the household is able to more or less break even in terms of paddy production. However, they never buy rice. Gopi's granaries have sufficient stocks to get them over bad years. Also, in summer their rice consumption is less. They mix rice with a cereal called *madia* to make a watery mixture called *pej*. This is carried around in a gourd and both quenches the thirst and provides nourishment in the hot summer months. Even though Gopi's paddy consumption roughly balances his production, he nevertheless manages to realise a cash surplus. This comes form his sales of non-rice crops such as *urad, sarson, madia, kulthi, tilli* and vegetables—nions, aubergine, tomato, bean, lady finger—which are carried to the market and sold by the female members of the household. The price they get for these vegetables is determined by the distance from the market in question to the main highway. In remote markets vegetables are purchased by local villagers and petty merchants from nearby urban centres. In the markets near the main road, the purchasing is done by big merchants from the city areas such as Raipur. They purchase in bulk; when a large, quick sale is needed, the women from Minipur carry their vegetables on their heads to Farasgaon, four hours' walk away. Income from the sale of vegetables is a major income earner for Gopi, as he has one of the largest market gardens (*atars*) in Minipur. This requires a big investment of labour time, as the vegetables have to be tended intensively on a daily basis.

Rice-deficit households

Consider now the rice-deficit households. These households are more integrated into the wider commercial economy because they are unable to produce their basic staple in sufficient quantity to meet their own demand. They are therefore forced to do wage-labour work for the forest department or road work for the public works department in order to obtain money to buy the rice they need to see them over the deficit period. The income from wage labour provides them with the ready cash to purchase rice from the market place. Given the periodicity of the markets, sometimes they are forced to purchase from within the village from the granaries of a rice-surplus producer. This price is usually higher than the market price, and the availability of this intra-village demand is an additional reason why surplus-rice producers do not market their surplus. Apart from the labour market, the weekly market place provides many opportunities for deficit producers to make ends meet. They can sell their cash crops, minor forest produce, and other products there. Some deficit producers survive by becoming petty merchants for three or four days per week; some set up tea shops, others become commission agents for grain merchants.

The key to understanding deficit-household behaviour, however, is to remember that their rice deficit is only for a part of the year. After harvest all rice producers have a surplus above immediate requirements that must be stored. These granaries are like banks and are used as such. They represent ready cash which can be drawn upon when necessary. If a householder has no vegetables, for example, a few kilograms will be withdrawn from the granary and sold to the grain merchant at the market. Poorer households are more likely to do this because they have a shortage of everything. A rich household, such as Gopi's, by way of contrast, is more likely to sell non-rice forms of food at the market rather than to buy it. Money is also needed to buy non-food commodities, such as clothing, glass bangles, matches, and kerosene. If the item is urgently required and no cash is available, the poor householders are forced to deplete their granary. This running down of the granary increases the number of days per year that a deficit household will be without rice. The people are aware of this, of course, and the economic strategies they adopt are geared to minimising this.

It is useful now to consider some of the strategies adopted by some of the poorer households as an illustration of some of these general points.

All deficit households have one or more members who are away for some part of the year wage labouring. Forest and road work for government departments is the most popular. This involves

TABLE IV.4   MINIPUR VILLAGE: RICE-DEFICIT HOUSEHOLDS

Size of deficit (months without rice)	Name of household head	Caste	Total land (acres)	Rice land (acres)	Popu-lation	Popu-lation density	Surplus ratio	Cattle
			(A)	(B)	(C)	(C/A)	(B/C)	
0–6	1 Hiradhar	Maraar	5.23	4.00	7	1.34	0.57	6
0–6	2 Murli	Maraar	2.46	2.50	3	1.22	0.83	2
0–6	3 Aasman Bisaru	Maraar	3.00	2.00	3	1.00	0.67	–
0–6	4 Sukhchand	Maraar	4.89	6.50	14	2.86	0.46	13
0–6	5 Devi	Maraar	3.50	2.50	4	1.14	0.63	–
0–6	6 Phaganu	Maraar	2.36	2.50	5	2.12	0.50	2
0–6	7 Sampat	Maraar	4.00	2.50	4	1.00	0.62	4
0–6	8 Batuku	Gond	5.80	2.50	4	0.69	0.62	3
0–6	9 Karathi	Halba	3.00	3.00	5	1.67	0.60	3
0–6	TOTAL		34.24	28.00	49	1.43	0.57	33
	Average		3.80	3.11	5	1.43	0.57	4
6–11	1 Ganasu	Maraar	2.48	1.00	3	1.21	0.33	–
6–11	2 Pasu	Maraar	2.48	1.00	4	1.61	0.25	4
6–11	3 Ghunshyam	Maraar	4.96	2.00	6	1.21	0.33	–
6–11	4 Panka	Maraar	9.68	3.00	12	1.24	0.25	6
6–11	5 Baratu	Maraar	4.96	1.00	5	1.00	0.20	–
6–11	6 Shanker	Maraar	2.25	2.00	5	2.22	0.40	2
6–11	7 Nathlu	Maraar	2.25	2.00	5	2.22	0.40	3
6–11	8 Radhe	Maraar	2.46	1.00	3	1.22	0.33	–
6–11	9 Lacchan	Maraar	3.00	3.00	7	2.33	0.43	–
6–11	10 Lachmu	Maraar	3.00	2.00	4	1.33	0.50	–
6–11	11 Lachminath	Maraar	3.00	2.00	5	1.67	0.40	–
6–11	12 Bhikari	Maraar	2.50	1.50	6	2.40	0.25	8
6–11	13 Ramji	Maraar	5.50	2.00	10	1.81	0.20	3
6–11	14 Shiva	Maraar	5.05	1.50	5	0.99	0.30	4
6–11	15 Sadhu	Maraar	2.50	2.00	7	2.80	0.29	4
6–11	16 Ghassu	Rawat	5.93	2.00	4	0.67	0.50	–
6–11	17 Chamra	Rawat	4.50	1.00	10	2.22	0.10	–
	TOTAL		66.50	30.00	101	1.52	0.29	34
	Average		3.91	1.76	6	1.52	0.29	2
12	1 Lachmu	Rawat	0	0	6	–	0.0	–
12	2 Dol	Lohar	0	0	2	–	0.0	–
12	3 Somaru	Lohar	0	0	8	–	0.0	–
12	4 Chamar	Ganda	0	0	4	–	0.0	–
12	5 Raju	Gond	0	0	5	–	0.0	–
	TOTAL							
	GRAND TOTAL		100.74	58.00	175			67
	Average		3.24	1.87	5.6	1.74	0.33	2

absences from the village for periods of up to ten days. Sometimes young unmarried women go to do this work. For example, labour contractors often recruit all the female members of the Gond's village dormitory (*ghotul*) *en masse* for road work. Seasonal and longer term migration to urban centres is just beginning to be seen as another option. For example, Aasman Bisaru, who has only three acres of land and no cattle (see Table IV.4), has found seasonal employment with a cloth merchant. He drives a bullock cart containing the merchant's stock to the circuit of markets the merchant attends. From the end of the rains of one year to the beginning of the rains the next year, he is continually on the move. His round takes him from Kondagaon on Sunday, to Sampur on Monday, Makdi on Tuesday, Randhna on Wednesday, Bare Dongar on Friday, Lanjoda on Saturday, returning to Kondagaon on Sunday. He travels all night and sleeps during the day at the market. Because Bare Dongar is close to his village, he is able to spend one night per week at home. In 1982 he earned Rs 80 per month clear after food and other expenses. Another deficit householder in this group, Devi, is now much better off, because his son found work as an office boy (*peon*) in Kondagaon. If a migrant can secure a relatively well paid job, the family fortunes can improve as is the case with Padmu. This household is now in the 'intermediate' category. They own 11.85 acres of land and 10 head of cattle. Padmu is the eldest of a joint family of three brothers, the youngest of whom is in the Home Guard at Kondagaon. He earns Rs 275 per month and sends a regular amount home to the village. This is a statement that he is not alienated from the village and that he wishes to share in the division of the family land, when it is made.

Another form of migration is where sons of poor farmers go off to work for a rich relative for an indefinite period of time. If they get on well with the relative, the stay may become permanent because, being a relative, the migrant can expect a share in the land for all the unpaid kinship labour supplied. Aasman Bisaru's extended family is a case in point. His father had three wives and six sons: one, Lacchu, from the first; three sons, Lacchan, Lachman and Aasman, from the second; and two sons, Lacchmi and Lacchmu, from the third. Lacchu inherited one-third of his father's land, including some highly fertile land at Bare Dongar, where he now lives. Lacchu, now an important elder in the Naik patrilineage, has not been able to produce a son in spite of marrying four times. He is unable to work his land by himself, so Aasman's two sons, as well as brother Lacchmi, have moved from Minipur to go and live and work with him. Lacchu's land will almost certainly be divided up among these relations.

All deficit households have at least one female member who attends two or more markets per week. These women both sell grain and oil seeds to merchants as well as set up shop on a small, crowded patch of land next to other women from their village. For example, at the Bare Dongar market I attended on 18 December 1982, I saw the wife of Ganasu (a deficit farmer in the 6–11 months category) selling vegetables from her own garden together with onions and *haldi* which she purchased from a store keeper and was trying to sell at a profit. She was sitting next to the wife of her husband's brother, Ghunshyam, another deficit farmer. Ghunshyam's wife was selling cooked sweet potato, which she prepared at home, and vegetables. These two women go to two markets per week and earn between Rs 2 and Rs 10 per market. Another ten women from Minipur were sitting with them. They were also selling cooked sweet potato and vegetables. Only one of these women was a Gond. The Tribals from Minipur, I was told, prefer to sell grain to a merchant rather than set up shop. Petty marketing of this kind is regarded as women's work.

Men mainly attend the market to purchase, to gossip, or to gamble at the cock fights in season. The latter can bring a large windfall gain, but it can also bring equally large losses. Fighting cocks can cost anything up to Rs 150, and if such a cock loses its first fight then all this is lost. The losing cock, which is either dead or close to it, is taken by the winner's owner and eaten in a celebratory dinner. The winner also collects money, which varies according to the bets he has laid. The market offers other income earning opportunities for men apart from gambling. Some get jobs as commission agents *(kochiya)* for grain merchants—to be discussed below—and others set up businesses, such as tea shops. Budram, a member of the Rawat caste, is one such example. His elder brother Chamra farms their 4.50 acres, and his younger brother Sudram does the traditional caste work of grazing the village cows. They work as a joint family and assist each other when they are not busy with their own work. Budram, for example, attends three markets—Bare Dongar, Uranda Beda and Godma—and helps his brothers on the other four days. His tea shop business required a small amount of capital (about Rs 75) in the way of tea pots and glasses but business is brisk on market days, and the net return he gets is good (Rs 5–Rs 30 net profit per market in 1982–83).

Apart from this economic activity outside the village, money-making opportunities within the village are also exploited. Seven of the wives of deficit household heads are small shopkeepers. They keep a small stock of general goods, such as matches, kerosene, coconuts, and other similar commodities. Customers from the village visit the store, but the women also go on selling trips (*raps*) to nearby villages.

Minipur had five completely landless households in 1982–83, and the question of their means of survival remains to be answered. Four of these households perform traditional caste occupations. The two Lohar (blacksmith) households are kept extremely busy making a wide range of new farm tools and repairing old ones. Nowadays, they buy their iron in bars from the market, but up until as recently as the 1960s they used to smelt their own. They used to collect the ore from a nearby range and smelt it in a small mud blast furnace of simple design. The government has declared this illegal, but it is still done in many areas. Blacksmiths never get cash for their work. Payment is always in kind such paddy, vegetables, and other farm products. It is said that the Minipur blacksmith would be a wealthy man, were it not for the fact that he drinks so much. The *ganda* (weaver) household is a poor one, being a victim of competition from imported machine cloth. The head can weave a sari in one day and sell it at the market for Rs 10 (1982 prices). However, raw materials cost Rs 9 and he therefore makes only Rs 1 profit. Drumming at wedding ceremonies is another traditional occupation of this caste, and this brings additional income in the months January to May. Most of his income comes from the sale of minor forest produce and daily labouring for the government. The *rawat* (herder) household arrived in Minipur in 1977. He grazes over 60 head of cattle, for which he is paid in kind. The remaining household is a Gond widow with four young children. She manages to survive by help received from her late husband's relatives.

MERCHANTS AND THE HOUSEHOLD POLITICS OF BUYING

Commission agents

The first dealer a villager meets as he or she approaches the market place is the *kochiya*, the commission agent for the grain merchant. After harvest a medium-sized market place is ringed with literally hundreds of these agents. They squat down beside the tracks leading into the market and try to cajole the passers-by into selling their grain to them. They squat on bags behind a set of steel-arm scales slung from an overhanging tree branch or from a triangular arrangement of sturdy poles. On one side of them lies the pile of small change advanced to them by a big merchant, on the other heaps of grains and oil seeds of various types. The *kochiyas* are the first dealers in the market place to set up business; their work is over by mid-day or soon after, which is the time when the seller-merchants are just beginning their work. The competition between *kochiya* is fierce. They haggle with their women customers over prices and sometimes even try to grab the basket of grain from their heads. This is all done in a good-humoured, jocular fashion and the 'game' is enjoyed by all. The *kochiya* all come from nearby villages, and both customer and dealer are well known to each other. During the season they will probably see each other at up to three or four different markets per week. Each customer brings on average 2–3 kg of grain, for which, in 1982, they were paid Rs 2–4, depending on the produce. At the end of the day the *kochiya* gives the grain to the merchant who has advanced him the money and receives a commission of around Rs 3–4 per quintal of grain purchased. During the season this can earn him up to Rs 30 per market. Competition between *kochiya* is not so much one of price but one of quantity. Prices are virtually fixed, and the struggle between *kochiya* is over the quantitative share of the market they can appropriate.

In the Kondagaon marketing area, there were 352 *kochiya* in 1983, all of whom are men. The caste and place of origin of these *kochiya* is shown in Table IV.5. Sixty percent of these agents are Bastarians who live mainly in the rural areas and are rice-deficit

TABLE IV.5   CASTE OF COMMISSION AGENTS
(KOCHIYAS)

Origin and caste	Number	%
Bastarians		
Tribals	70	20
Kalar	39	11
Dewangan	29	8
Harijan	18	5
Maraar	7	2
Santnami	19	5
Katiya	16	5
Other	15	4
TOTAL	213	60
Immigrants		
Sahu	18	5
Rajput	16	5
Muslim	24	7
Jain	10	3
Brahman	8	2
Others	63	18
TOTAL	139	40
GRAND TOTAL	352	100

farmers of the type discussed above. They attend the markets in the vicinity of their village, which on average consists of one or two big markets where competition from other *kochiya* is fierce, and three or four small markets where they compete with only a few others. Of the 213 Bastarian *kochiya* only 70 were Tribals. Of the Hindus, the Kalar and Dewangan castes are predominant. The traditional occupations of these castes was wine making and silk weaving, respectively; however nowadays they are cultivators. The immigrant *kochiya* live in the main urban centres—Kondagaon, Lanjoda, Farasgaon, Dahikonga—and travel by cycle and/or bus to the markets surrounding these towns. These men are usually landless, but not necessarily poor, because being a *kochiya* is just one of many occupations they pursue.

Ganda is an example of a *kochiya* from the Bastarian group. He lives in Banyagaon, where he has a small holding of 5 acres. This is not sufficient to maintain his family, and he travels to four markets each week—Kondagaon (Sunday), Kanera (Tuesday), Banyagaon (Thursday), and Mardapal (Saturday)—to work as a *kochiya*. He does this all year round and gets to the markets on his hired cycle. His traditional caste occupation is weaving, but he gave this up in 1975 and started *kochiya* work because of the competition from machine cloth. The weavers like him who live close to the big urban centres were the first to suffer the effects of this competition; weavers in remote areas still manage to struggle on, because the transport costs of getting machine-made cloth to these areas raise the price of cloth by a margin that is just big enough to ensure their survival. Another example of the Bastarian *kochiya* is Ghini and Ghasu, two brothers of the Gond Tribe from a village near Hirapur. They work together at three markets—Hirapur (Thursday), Amraoti (Friday) and Chhinari (Saturday)—during the season. They walk to Amraoti on Thursday evening, sleep at the market, and then walk to Chhinari the next evening, where they again stay overnight. They farm their land with their father under a joint family arrangement. Their household is 'intermediate' in terms of rice production and consumption, and the *kochiya* work they do gives them valuable extra ready cash. Yet another example of a Bastarian *kochiya* is Singh, of the Kalar caste from Lubha village. He attends only two markets—Makdi (Tuesday) and Randhna (Wednesday)—during the season. His village is situated mid-way between these markets, and he walks to them from home each day. Like the two brothers above, his competition comes from village-based *kochiya* in the neighbourhood of these markets. These 'Orissa side'-markets, as they are called, are too far from Kondagaon and the main highway to be serviced by the urban-based *kochiya*.

Hari Singh is a relatively prosperous immigrant *kochiya*. He is a retired army sergeant and purchased 22 acres of land at Bijapur when he first settled in Bastar. This is worked by his sons, and he spends all year attending seven markets per week doing *kochiya* work. He attends all the Orissa side markets—Umrakote (Monday), Makdi (Tuesday), Erla (Wednesday), Hirapur (Thursday), Amrawati (Friday) and Chhinari (Saturday)—as well as the big Kondagaon market on Sunday. These markets are the biggest in the region, and he does good business. In August 1982, when he was interviewed, he was purchasing two quintals per day on average, giving him a profit of between Rs 10–15 per market in the off-season. His earnings during the season are probably double or treble this. Vishnu Charan is another relatively well-off immigrant *kochiya*. His father migrated from Maharastra and the family is Harijan-turned-Buddhist, like many other Maharastrians in the area. His father, with whom he worked, has five acres of land and is also a *kochiya*. They attend all the markets in the Kondagaon area—Sampur (Monday), Kanera (Tuesday), Kondagaon (Wednesday), Bamhni (Thursday), Dahikonga (Friday), and Mardapal (Saturday), and Kondagaon (Sunday). He earns Rs 400–500 per month in the off-season and Rs 1000 per month during the season, which is roughly the same as Hari Singh.

Kochiya have a reputation for cheating and avarice. They are often blamed for 'exploiting the Tribals'. This proposition is part of popular mythology and has little basis in fact. While it is no doubt true that the seller of grain is cheated now and again in a transaction, it is certainly not the case that *kochiya* systematically cheat their customers. Firstly, *kochiya* are part of the farming community, not a class apart from it. They are dealing with friends and relations, and their profits depend upon establishing and maintaining good relations with people, not by exploiting them. Secondly, the range of prices a *kochiya* bargains within is so small to render prices virtually fixed. It is not from buying cheap and selling dear that his profits come; rather it comes from the absolute quantity that he can purchase, because commission received depends upon this. Thirdly, whilst it is true that *kochiya* can sometimes understate the weight of grain received from an illiterate customer, these amounts are very small per customer. For example, a woman usually only extracts a *pailli* or two of paddy from the granary in order to make a particular purchase. Whilst she does not know the *weight* of this rice, or the price per kilogram, she does have a very good idea of the price per *volume* of rice and knows approximately how much she can expect in money terms for the *volume* of rice she has taken to the market. Finally, competition between *kochiya* is fierce; the market is closer to the pure competitive ideal type rather than the monopolistic type.

Grain merchants

The food grain and oil seed marketing in the Kondagaon area is controlled by eight merchants. These merchants have divided up the markets between themselves in order to minimise competition. This can be seen in Table IV.6, which shows the relative importance of the different merchants and the division of markets between.

Consider first of all the markets. The relevant data from Table IV.6 has been reproduced on Map IV.1. This map shows very clearly a phenomenon mentioned at the beginning of this chapter, namely, as one moves from east to west towards the Narainpur Tahsil, the

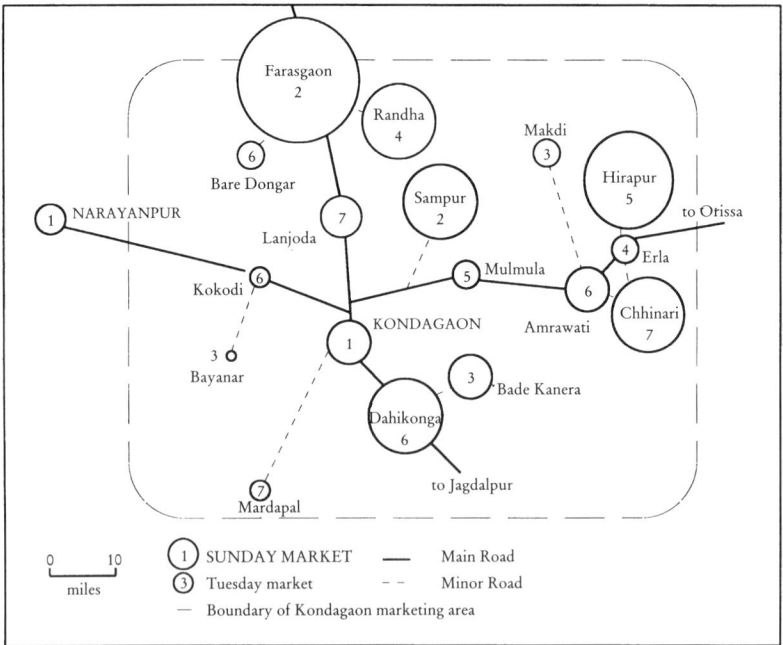

MAP IV.1   *Relative importance of periodic markets in terms of grain purchased by merchants*

TABLE IV. 6 GRAIN MERCHANTS: MARKET PURCHASES OF PADDY OCTOBER 1982 TO JANUARY 1983 (QUINTALS)

Market	(day)	TMK Jain from Rajasthan	JRKC Jain from Rajasthan	Hiralal Jain from Rajasthan	R.J. Buddhist Maharashtra	Khan Muslim from UP	Jethu Tribal from Bastar	Mansuk Hindu from Bastar	Harish from Gujarat	Govt. agencies	Other agents	Total (qtls)	%
Farasgaon	(M)			1829	873					450	1745	4897	16
Hirapur	(Th)	2526				768				134	173	3601	11
Chhinari	(S)	2408				185				142		2735	9
Randhna	(W)			1005	1231					482		2718	8
Sampur	(Tu)		1466			317		509		133	251	2676	9
Dahikonga	(F)		1809							614		2423	8
Kondagaon	(Su)	214	387						48	448	780	1877	6
Amrawati	(F)	1352				139				257		1748	6
Kanera	(Tu)		1475							178	81	1734	6
Lanjoda	(Sa)			719	567					226		1512	5
Bade Dongar	(F)			629	388					188		1205	4
Makdi	(Tu)						900			94		994	3
Erla	(W)	547				259				51		857	3
Mulmula	(Th)		685							69		754	2
Kokodi	(F)							101	125	165		391	1
Mardapal	(Sa)		154						36	187		377	1
Urandabeda	(W)										339	339	1
Mungapadar	(Tu)										301	301	
Bamhni	(Th)										101	101	
Bhongal	(Su)										66	66	
Chignor	(Th)										65	65	
Girola	(Th)										46	46	
Banyagaon	(Th)										27	27	
Bayanar	(Tu)								14			14	
TOTAL		7047	5976	4182	3059	1668	900	610	223	3818	3975	31458	
%		22	19	13	10	5	3	2	1	12	13	100	100

quantity of marketed paddy declines sharply. Farasgaon and Hirapur are the major centres of marketed paddy, with Kondagaon, ranked seventh. This calls for some explanation, because Kondagaon's Sunday market is universally regarded the most important market in the area. Furthermore, Hirapur's Thursday market is regarded as being only of average size and importance by the locals.

The Hirapur—Amrawati—Chhinari market area is physically isolated from the other markets in the Kondagaon area by the presence of large areas of reserved forest. However, it also borders Orissa, which was until the 1960s, an under-populated forest area. The resettlement of Bangladeshi refugees in the area has transformed the local economy. Large areas of forest have been cut down and the land turned into bunded fields producing paddy and other crops. Because of the relative isolation of the area and the underdevelopment of marketing facilities, farmers there have found that they can get a much better price for their paddy in the Bastar markets. Hirapur and Chhinari, being the nearest, are the markets they go to. They deliver their produce by the bullock cart load-full and these markets are the only ones in the study area where this is done. The usual method of bringing paddy to the market in Bastar is in small amounts carried on the head (women) or on the shoulder (men). The Orissa-side method of marketing paddy, then, is an exception to the proposition advanced above that only deficit-households tend to market their rice as, and when, they need cash.

The relatively small arrivals of paddy at the Kondagaon Sunday market does not reflect the general importance of this market for a number of reasons. Firstly, marketing in the immediate area of this town is more decentralised compared to Farasgaon. The markets Sampur, Bade Kanera and Dahikonga take away some of the business that otherwise would have gone to Kondagaon. Secondly, being the main urban centre of the district, there are alternative ways to dispose of ones's produce. These range from pretty traders in grain to small millers. However, these factors do not alter the fact that Farasgaon and surrounding district is the biggest area of marketed paddy. The Farasgaon rural area is more densely settled than those of Kondagaon. Kondagaon borders Narainpur Tahsil, and the factors that work to keep paddy from the market there also operate, if in somewhat weaker fashion, in the rural areas surrounding Kondagaon.

If the data in Table IV.6 is examined once again, it can be seen that most important markets have been divided up between three merchants who purchase over 54% of all marketed paddy. These merchants are all Jains from Jodphur District in Rajasthan, and they, along with their relatives, are the single most powerful force in the marketing system of Bastar today. They are involved in the merchandising of almost every commodity that enters and leaves Bastar. These 'Marwaris', as they are called, have kinship-cum-trading links that cover all India, and the Bastar Marwaris are part of this all-India elite.

The territory is controlled by the different merchants are shown in Map IV.2. The Orissa-side markets, is controlled by TMK Company, the biggest Marwari firm. Khan, a Muslim merchant, also has a small share in these markets. The markets in the immediate vicinity of Kondagaon are virtually monopolised by JRKC. Hiralal

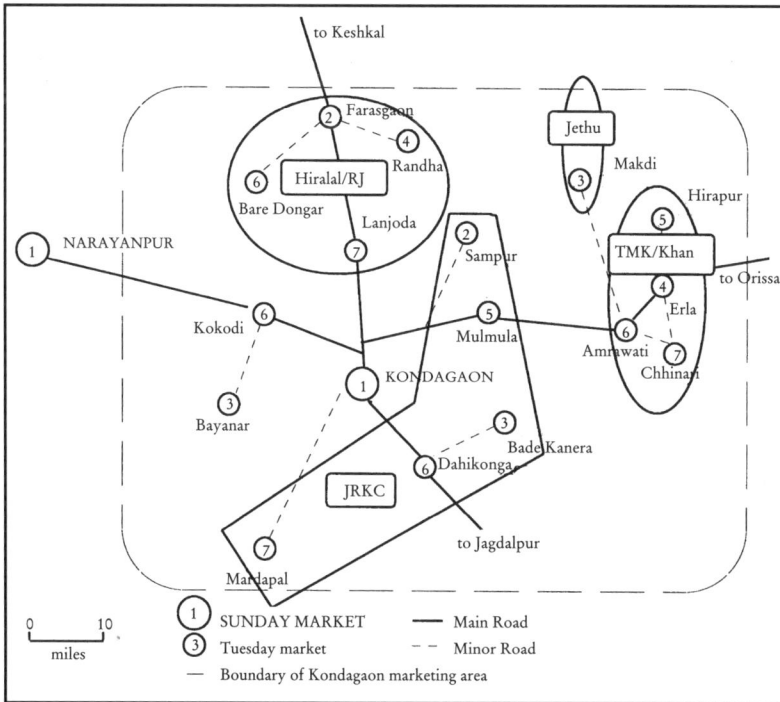

MAP IV.2   *Market areas of grain merchants*

and R.J. Trading work the markets to the north of Kondagaon whilst Jethu Ram controls the remaining area consisting of just two markets. The minor markets to the west of Kondagaon are controlled by a number of small merchants/big *kochiya* who buy and re-sell to one of the big merchants.

The Marwari families are extremely wealthy, and they make no attempt to hide the fact. The firms are joint family business concerns, and the members of the families live together in mansions in Kondagaon (TMK and JRKC) and Lanjoda (Hiralal). Large numbers of motor vehicles of various kinds—the most obvious symbol of wealth in Bastar—are usually parked outside these houses. The wealth of these merchants is legendary, and most people who live in Kondagaon can give a very accurate account of their tangible assets. For example, it is well known that TMK has 6 trucks, 2 jeeps, 1 car, 1 Bullet motor bike, 1 Rajdoot motor bike, 1 scooter, a rice and flour mill worth Rs 100,000, a 20-acre farm at Bijapur, and a cloth shop. Hiralal and Co. of Lanjoda, who are not as wealthy, only have 2 trucks, 1 tractor, 1 Rajdoot motor bike, 1 jeep, and a farm.

Like most Marwari families in Kondagaon, these families are very large. TMK, for example, consists of seven brothers and six sisters. The eldest surviving brother has eight children, the second eldest six so far, and the other brothers are yet to produce. A high population growth-rate with a large proportion of males is essential for the continued prosperity of a merchant family. This is the only source of managerial labour for running their various businesses. Large sums of money have to be handled, and relatives are the only people who can be trusted.

The wealth of these merchants has been accumulated since the 1950s, when the migration of Marwaris to Bastar began. Some brothers elected to go it alone on first arrival in Bastar, others formed partnerships. The present structure of big firms in Bastar reflects these initial decisions rather than inherited wealth. Take the JRKC firm, for example. The founders of this firm were two brothers. They had four and five sons respectively, the eldest of whom are now working for the firm (the younger ones were still at school in 1983). As the two founding brothers are still in their fifties, the problem of eventual division of this estate is unlikely to arise for some time. The most likely outcome will be the creation of two new joint families around the two groups of brothers. It hardly needs to be said that the consequences of this division will have little or no affect on the potential profitability of the firm. Population growth and inheritance does not affect rich merchants in the same way it affects farmers. The division of one million rupees in merchant capital into two parts is not the same as the division of 10 acres of land into two equal shares. The founding brothers of the JRKC firm had three other brothers. They all started their own independent cloth businesses, and all have ended up extremely wealthy, as well. They started off both retailing and wholesaling cloth and grew in wealth as marketing activity intensified.

While the Marwaris compete with one another in the lucrative cloth trade, a notable feature of grain and oil seed marketing is the absence of any direct competition from other Marwaris in the territories they have carved out for themselves. The competition has come from other castes.

Competition between purchasing merchants is primarily of the non-price type. This is because there is little room for price manipulation. In the paddy market, for example, a floor price is fixed by the government—Rs 122 per quintal in 1982–83—and the ceiling price is fixed by market forces outside Bastar. When there is a good harvest, paddy market prices tend to fall below the government floor price. In such circumstances all paddy is traded at the floor price and there is no price competition. When the rain fails and the harvest is not as good as usual—as it was in 1982–83—the market price prevails. This gives merchants some room for price competition, but not very much. Competition among merchants in Bastar, then, is more concerned with quantity rather than price. The aim of the merchant is to capture the largest share of the market and his ability to do this depends on his capital. Merchants must advance cash to their *kochiya* before the market begins, and the more *kochiya* he can employ to purchase grain and oil seed for him, the greater his share of the market is likely to be.

Table IV.7, which shows the prices and quantities of paddy purchased at Hirapur market over the period 11 November 1982 to 27 January 1983, illustrates these points. Hirapur market is in the territory controlled by the TMK firm, the biggest Marwari merchant.

TABLE IV.7   PADDY: PRICES AND QUANTITIES OF
PADDY PURCHASED BY MERCHANTS AT
THE HIRAPUR THURSDAY MARKET, 1982-83

Date	TMK quintals price (Rs)		Khan quintals price (Rs)		Lamps quintals price (Rs)		Govt.rice mill quintals price (Rs)	
Nov 11	150	123	75	122	7	122		
Nov. 18	305	124	38	122	7	122		
Nov. 25	316	122						
Dec. 2	190	122	70	122	21	122		
Dec. 9	145	122	75	122	28	122		
Dec. 16	160	122	75	122	62	122		
Dec. 23	160	122					100	125
Dec. 30	193	125	88	122			11	125
Jan. 6	250	125	185	125			62	127
Jan. 13	252	126	70	126				
Jan. 20	181	126	96	125				
Jan. 27	179	128	64	125				
Average capital advanced per market	Rs 25,631		Rs 9,330					

Khan, a small Muslim merchant, has encroached onto his territory.
Khan attended this market eight times during this period. In five out
of these eight times, TMK was able to offer a slightly higher price.
This, however, is not the main reason TMK captured the lion's share
of the market. TMK, being a much bigger concern, is able to bring
much more working capital to the market. This averaged Rs 25,631
for the three months in question, compared to Rs 9,330 for Khan. It
is clear that if Khan is only able to bring say Rs 10,000 in cash to the
market, then there is a ceiling to the absolute amount of grain that he
is able to buy.

Purchasing merchants work on a gross profit margin of around
5%. From this, expenses such as storage, transport, agents' fees, must
be deducted. Their net profit margin then is very small. Big absolute
profits can only be achieved through high turnover. This is a further
reason why quantity rather than price competition is the arena of conflict.

The government purchasing agency representatives — called
'lamps' — are present at every market. They offer to buy rice at the
floor price and their intervention in the market prevents the price from
dropping below this. As Table IV.7 shows, they intervened in the

Hirapur market in November and December, when it was not clear what the harvest was going to be like. However, by the end of December paddy prices began to rise, and they ceased purchasing — or, to be more precise, farmers stopped selling to them, because they continued to offer to buy at Rs 122. *Lamps* officials set up business at every market during the season and offer the same price every week. They have nothing to do when the market price is high, as most sellers are well informed on the latest price. However, if a farmer makes a mistake and offers grain for sale to them, they are just as likely to buy it, rather than tell him or her that a better price can be had elsewhere. Such occurrences are rare, but they do highlight some of the problems that arise through bureaucratic intervention in the market.

Another occasional purchaser at the markets is the Government co-operative rice mill. It occasionally 'raids' a market and appropriates the share it wants by paying the best prices, as can be seen from its intervention in the Hirapur market in December 1982. The role of this mill is considered further below.

It is clear that the Marwaris have the grain merchant business well and truly under control. They have carved up the territory and their businesses have grown with the growth in marketing activity. They got in 'on the ground floor', as the saying goes. Locals have no hope of making inroads into this business.

Jethu Ram's case is worth considering here, because he was the only Bastarian Tribal who has been able to break into the grain merchant business. He is extremely wealthy by local standards. He has a large *pakka* house, a Rajdoot motor cycle and has recently purchased a tractor and trailer for carting grain. However, his wealth pales in significance compared with the Marwari firms. He buys only 2% of total paddy marketed compared with 22% for TMK. Jethu Ram lives at Makdi and is the sole purchaser at this market and Gamhari, a neighbouring market. His father was the *patel* of Makdi and was a man of some means. He began to work as the grain merchant for Makdi, when the previous merchant—a Gujarati Brahman—decided to move into a sedentary business in Kondagaon. The Brahman gave him a loan of the crucial finance that he needed, and his business has not looked back since. However, the small territory he controls, coupled with the limited business opportunities in a remote village such as his, limits the growth potential of a firm such as his. But the opportunities Jethu Ram had to get started are no longer open to Bastarians. Immigrants have cornered the market and will continue to control it for a long time to come.

Agricultural Produce Marketing Committee (*Mandi*)

In 1973 The Agricultural Produce Marketing Committee (*Krishi Upaj Mandi Adhiyam*) was set up. Its aim was to 'provide for the better regulation of buying and selling of agricultural produce and the establishment of proper administration of markets for agricultural produce in the state of Madhya Pradesh'. The *Mandi* regulations cover a wide range of fibres, cereals, pulses, oil seeds, narcotics, sugar cane and gur, fruits, vegetables, condiments and forest products. So far the Kondagaon *Mandi* has restricted its activities mainly to paddy, maize, sarson, harra, mahua, ramtilli, and tilli.

Its income comes from a 0.5% tax levied on the purchases of traders. As the turnover of merchants is regularly in excess of Rs 20 mill., this brings in large sums of money, as can be seen from Table IV.8. This money has been used to build imposing new premises on about 5 acres of land near the Kondagaon market. The complex includes an office block, godown, covered market place, and special rest houses for traders, farmers and bureaucrats.

TABLE IV.8   AGRICULTURAL PRODUCE MARKETING
COMMITTEE (MANDI): NET INCOME

Year	Merchants' turnover	Income (Rs.000s)	Expenditure (Rs.000s)	Net Income (Rs.000s)
1976–77	20,600	103	45	58
1977–78	22,600	113	74	39
1978–79	21,600	108	60	48
1979–80	20,600	103	53	50
1980–81	30,600	151	123	28
1981–82	36,200	181	142	39

The Mandi is governed by an elected body of 7 people, 5 agriculturists and 2 merchants. The agriculturists elect the president. There are about 270 such boards in Madhya Pradesh and these, in turn, are presided over by an MP State Marketing Board.

An auction is held on market day every Sunday at Kondagaon. Middlemen bring their produce here after 3.00 pm and it is auctioned off to wholesalers and rice millers. Plans have been set in motion to have Mandi premises built at all the major centres in the Kondagaon range—Bade Dongar, Makdi, Hirapur, Chhinari, Mardapal, Farasgaon, Dahikonga, Amrawati and Sampur—and to establish similar weekly auctions at these places. This will send small commission agents out of business in these places and, it is believed, will raise the price received by the farmer.

At present Mandi staff visit every market to check that merchants and their agents are not cheating the farmers: they check scales and weights and make sure that all buyers are licensed. They also collect data on purchases, so that tax returns can be checked. Formerly, they used to collect the taxes as well, but the system was changed after it was discovered that one of the tax collectors was misappropriating funds.

It is too early to assess the success or failure of the Mandi at this stage. As it poses no threat to the profits of the big merchants, its continued existence seems assured. In return for their tax contribution they are getting an institution which centralises marketing activity and hence makes their job that much easier. The commission agents (*kochiya*) are the ones most likely to suffer. But, as they have no power, nothing will come of this opposition. If commission agents do suffer, then small farmers, to the extent that they are also commission agents, will suffer.

The rice mills

Having purchased paddy from the various market places in the region, merchants bring it to Kondagaon for resale to the local rice mills or, in the case of the biggest merchant, re-sell to merchants outside Bastar. The rice mills are required by law to sell a fixed percentage (60% in 1982) of their milled rice production to the government-run Food Corporation of India. They are free to dispose of the balance as they wish; in 1982–83 this balance went to private dealers in Orissa and Kerala.

There are ten rice mills in North Bastar, seven of which are privately run and three government owned. The latter are located in the three biggest urban centres—Jagdalpur, Kondagaon and Kanker. Jagdalpur, the administrative capital, has five private mills; Kondagaon has two.

In Kondagaon—the only town for which I have data—the two private mills are highly profitable operations, while the government-run mill is facing serious financial problems.

The government mill—the Kisan Rice Mill—was established in 1969 and was the first rice mill in Kondagaon. It is a co-operative and had 1381 members in 1982. The majority (1340) are small farmers, who have paid between Rs 25 and Rs 100 for a share; the remaining members are nominated officials and government institutions.

The paddy purchases and rice production figures for the Kisan Rice Mill for the period 1960–1982 are shown in Table IV.9. Of particular note are the purchasing and production figures for 1980-82. Paddy purchases for 1981–82 declined accordingly.

TABLE IV.9   KISAN RICE MILL: PADDY PURCHASES
                 AND RICE PRODUCTION

Year	Paddy purchased (quintals)	Rice milled (quintals)
1969–70	26,136	9,395
1970–71	14,125	10,416
1971–72	8,273	7,879
1972–73	6,246	4,560
1973–74	10,263	6,661
1974–75	22,066	13,227
1975–76	33,067	17,433
1976–77	27,805	19,103
1977–78	21,391	12,176
1978–79	17,252	14,329
1979–80	28,062	15,586
1980–81	10,104	3,150
1981–82	2,481	1,194

These figures must be seen in the light of the data in Table IV.10, which gives relevant financial data, as well as rainfall statistics. The price of paddy has more than doubled over the period of 1969–82, reflecting the general inflationary trend throughout India. The selling price of milled rice has shown a similar trend, increasing from Rs 0.80/kg in 1969–70 to Rs 1.94/kg in 1981–82. The gross profit margin—the difference between buying and selling prices—averaged 75% over the period, with a peak of 128% in 1974–75. This was the only year that the mill succeeded in making a profit of any size. It was also a drought year as the rainfall statistics show. Only 1247 mm of rainfall fell in 1974-75. This was the lowest rainfall for the entire period and some 275 mm below the average rainfall of 1522 mm. The inescapable conclusion, then, is that the Kisan Rice Mill can only function profitably in abnormal situations, ie. that it is not a going concern. The mill has ceased operations.

In 1973, the first, and biggest, private rice mill was established in Kondagaon. This is owned by the Chitaliya Brothers, Bania caste migrants from Gujarat. The eldest of this family of four brothers arrived in Dhamtari in 1948 and set up a service station business there. He was joined by his second brother in 1955, a third in 1958, and the fourth in 1961. The latter is university educated and runs the rice mill very efficiently and profitably. The family, which is now one of the richest in Kondagaon, has *harra*, tamarind and oil seed exporting businesses in addition to their rice mills and petrol stations.

TABLE IV.10   KISAN RICE MILL: PROFITS AND LOSSES

Year	Purchase price of paddy (Rs/kg)	Selling price of rice (Rs/kg)	Gross profit margin (%)	Profit (+)/ Loss (–) (Rs 000s)	Rainfall (mm)
1969–70	0.54	0.80	48	n.a.	n.a.
1970–71	0.52	0.90	73	–203	1593
1971–72	0.54	0.90	67	–107	1448
1972–73	0.66	0.92	40	– 88	1453
1973–74	0.79	1.40	77	+ 9	1447
1974–75	0.97	2.21	128	+667	1247
1975–76	0.85	1.38	62	+ 82	2112
1976–77	0.83	1.62	95	+ 33	1678
1977–78	0.88	1.59	81	+ 3	1556
1978–79	0.86	1.47	71	+ 3	1546
1979–80	1.07	1.93	80	–220	1590
1980–81	1.07	2.02	89	+ 33	1304
1981–82	1.16	1.94	67	– 70	1297

The other private mill was established in 1979. This is owned by a Punjabi family. The head of this family is a Hindu refugee from Pakistan. He and a number of his relatives fled Pakistan in 1947 and settled temporarily in Hardwar, U.P. They then moved to Bastar in the early 1950s and are now all very successful businessmen.

The private mills have the same gross profit margin as the Kisan rice mill. In January 1983, for example, the Punjabi mill was buying paddy from merchants at Rs 1.30 per kg and selling rice to the Food Corporation of India at the fixed price of Rs 1.68 and on the private market for Rs 2.50. This represents a gross profit margin of 52% and 92% respectively, or around 70% on average. The private mill owners blame the failure of the government mill on the bureaucracy: 'Government mills never run efficiently. The managers are not allowed to make decisions without reference to a higher authority. A decision that takes me five minutes to make takes them five days.'

The private mills get all their paddy from the eight merchants. They do not compete for the merchants' paddy. Merchants have standing business arrangements with one or other of the mills and sell all their paddy to it on a regular basis. For example, Chitaliya Brothers buy from TMK, JRKC, Hiralal, R.J Traders and Harish Kumar, while the Punjabi mill deals with Khan, Jethu and Mansuk.

The merchants Chitaliya Brothers dealt with are by far the biggest. They purchased 20,000 kgs of all market arrivals in 1982–83 compared with the 3000 kgs purchased by the merchants who supply the Punjabi mill. However, the Punjabi mill is smaller than the other private mill and works at full capacity during the season. Furthermore, as the closure of the government mill means extra business for the private mills, peaceful co-existence, rather than competition, will continue to be the basis of future relationships between these mills.

CONSUMPTION OF GOODS BY MEANS OF COMMODITIES

The discussion so far has concentrated on the *production of commodities by means of goods*. I finish with a brief discussion of its converse, the *consumption of goods by means of commodities*.

To recapitulate briefly, the Bastar political economy is a classic example of Marx's selling-in-order-to-buy which he represents as C–M–C. But Marx's argument denies the coevality of goods and with it the reality of the relations of consanguinity, affinity and contiguity. If this coevality is affirmed the formula has to be expanded to include goods which gives M–C ... G ... C–M′ where G represent *goods*. The formula could just as well be written as G ... C–M–C...G. The only difference lies in the interpretative emphasis. The former has the Market encompassing the House, the latter gives the values of the House primacy. Marx takes the Market perspective and ignores the existence of the House.

The discussion to date has concentrated on G ... C–M, the *production of commodities for money by means of goods*. The evidence has shown, among other things, that the 'tribal' economy of Bastar is a variation on a very general pattern and that there are is nothing in the notion of 'tribe' that gives it any cultural specificity. The notion is an administrative category not a cultural one. Furthermore, any idea that Bastar is a 'subsistence' or 'use-value' economy is simply nonsense.

The *consumption of goods by means of commodities* can be represented by the formula M–C ... G, the return journey from the market as it were and the two parts considered together give G ... C–M–C ... G. It is important to note that the G at the beginning of the formula is not the same G as at the end. The former consists, for the most part, of farm land, the supreme good; the latter consists of subordinate goods purchased on the market for non-commercial purposes. This raises the question of the theory of consumption on which there is now a burgeoning literature (Miller, 1995). I restrict myself here to an analysis of Alfred Gell's (1986) 'Newcomers to the World of Goods: Consumption Among the Muria Gonds' because this is an attempt to apply cultural theory to the case of Bastar.

Gell (1986) is concerned to understand what he calls the 'collectivist consumption ethos' of the Muria Gonds of Bastar. This ethos, he claims, obliges the rich to consume as if they were poor with the result that they still become richer. He argues (1986: 123) that the collectivist ethos 'has its roots in a phase of the tribe-caste conversion process in which interhousehold economic differences was minimal and inequalities in wealth between households would be at most temporary, owing to the absence of media of capital accumulation.' This tribe to caste movement is from nature to culture, from forest to farmland. 'As I understand it,' argues Gell, 'during the period of Hindu expansion in north Bastar during the last century, Muria moved into the forest, pushing out from Hindu enclaves, felling trees and clearing fields, which then proved attractive to incoming Hindus. The Hindus took over the land, expanding their enclaves, and the displaced Muria moved on to repeat the process elsewhere. The Muria did not simply give way to force majeure; the land was ceded amicably against payment in animals, grain, liquor, and small quantities of gold and silver that would be quickly be reconverted into food or, more likely drink. Hindus we spoke to claimed that in the good old days it was possible to obtain large areas of land from the Muria in exchange for a single gold earring or some other token payment. These Hindus attributed the Muria's fecklessness about land to their uncontrollable desire for intoxicating liquor' (1986: 117). Gell acknowledges the great political, social and economic changes that have occurred this century and that this 'old easy come, easy go' attitude to land has vanished with the introduction of permanent fields 'whose construction and upkeep represent years and years of accumulated labor' (1986: 124).

The general thrust of Gell's argument, then, is that even though the Muria have partially succeeded in turning themselves into castes of a farming kind, their values derive from a nineteenth century era of tribal harmony and equality when they welcomed the liquor-bearing conquerors with open arms. This version of a tribal paradise lost may reflect a certain 'native point of view' of Bastar history but it is not one that should be accepted uncritically. I concede that the 'tribe/caste continuum' thesis has had a profound influence on anthropological thought in India and that most anthropologists accept some version of it. In my opinion, though, it is a barrier to understanding because the categories 'tribe' and 'caste' are part of the problem, not the answer. These notions are extremely important political categories in India today and their significance cannot be understood without reference to the official policies of the state and the official theory that informs those policies. Millions of people are classified as belonging to one category or the other and these classifications have important economic and political implications. The anthropologist who uses these categories is also getting involved in a process of ethnographic classification. To distinguish between tribes and castes, and to place these categories at the endpoints of a 'continuum', presupposes a generally agreed set of objective criteria for locating a given group of people somewhere along the slippery slope. But whose values do these 'generally agreed' measures express?

Consider Gell:

> Among the items of tribal art for which Bastar is famous, the most prominent are the gunmetal figurines made by the lost-wax process. Like all Muria material culture with 'tribal' associations, these sculptures are not actually made by Tribals at all, but by the local bronze-working caste (Ghassiya). These objects are placed in temples, and they are avidly collected by tourists (1986: 135) ... The Kondagaon lost-wax sculpture establishment ... produces mainly for tourists. Significantly the leading craftsman is an educated adivasi [tribal], not a member of the low-ranking (Hindu) Ghassiya caste traditionally occupied with this work (1986: 137).

The fact of the matter is that, contrary to popular belief, the leading craftsman in question, a person with whom I have worked closely, has had *no* formal education and *is* a member of the Ghassiya group. The idea that the Ghassiya are low-caste Hindus is official government theory; it is also a generally accepted fact in Bastar, a value that has been uncritically reproduced in the anthropological literature first by Elwin (1947: 13) and now Gell. The Ghassiya and other artisans of Bastar do not accept this classification and are engaged in a dispute with the government over it. They point to the contradiction between the generally agreed idea that their products are classified as *Tribal* whilst they, the producers, are classified as *Hindus*. They claim that they are the Aborigines of Bastar and that the Gonds, whose 'Tribal' status is uncritically accepted, are the immigrants. This claim is not as outrageous as it sounds. For example, their mother tongue, Halbi, is the local dialect, their long genealogies reveal no evidence of migration, and their myths establish Bastar as their origin place. Gond myths of origin, by way of contrast, all tell a tale of migration into Bastar (Elwin, 1947). The thesis that all Bastar Hindus, including the royal family, are Aborigines is also one that must be taken seriously. All commentators on Bastar, for example, uncritically accept Royal myths of origin and migration as historical truth. It may be that the Bastar kings have genealogical links with the ancient centre of power at Delhi but it is also equally possible that these genealogical tales are the product of a royal tribal imagination.

My simple point here is not that Gell is wrong and I am right but that the status of the Ghassiya is in dispute and that there is an irreconcilable contradiction between the generally accepted 'native point of view' and the point of view of the Ghassiya. Gell uncritically reproduces the generally accepted ideology. 'Continuum' theory needs this generally accepted ideology because if the definition of its end points are thrown into question the 'continuum' that is supposed to connect them loses all meaning.

I also question Gell's claim that the roots of a value system are to be found in the values of long dead ancestors and that they somehow leapfrog a century of genealogical history to bear down on the minds of the living. The values of goods, I assert, establishes a link between the dead and the unborn by means of the living, and, furthermore, it is the struggle for prestige among the living that determines what standard of value reigns supreme. The Ghassiya are losing this battle but they are not down and out: two standards exist, not one.

CHAPTER V

Mercantile Kinship

Shylock. I will buy with you, sell with you,
talk with you, walk with you, and so following;
but I will not eat with you, drink with you, nor pray with you.
Merchant of Venice

TERRITORIALITY AS A VALUE

Merchants buy cheap and sell dear. This principle
of merchant capital accumulation, a general one which has been
discovered by many people from many places in many times, has the
objective form Money-Commodity-more Money, or M-C-M' to use
Marx's celebrated formula. Thus buying cheap (M-C) and selling dear
(C-M') ensures a profit amounting to the difference between M' and
M. Marx's labour theory of value enabled him to expose the 'secret'
of this form. According to him, commodities exchange at a ratio that
is in proportion to the labour embodied in them. Exchange, then, is
a sphere of equalised labour-values and any divergence from this
equality is a zero sum game of distribution. The factory floor, by way
of contrast, is the sphere of inequality and the origin of profit; it is
here that the capitalist relieves the worker of his surplus-labour.
Guided by this theory, then, Marx quickly moves the focus of his
analytical attention from the market place to the factory floor. Given
the nature of the nineteenth century English society he was looking
at, this was a reasonable move. But for someone concerned with the
analysis of agrarian relations in the twentieth century Asian countryside the labour theory of value is doubly misleading. Apart from the

163

empirical fact that a place like Bastar has no industry to speak of, the labour theory of value abstracts from a very important *territorial* fact of merchant capitalism: the idea that mercantile profits are made by buying cheap *here* and selling dear *there*. Human relations mediate this space, but what is the nature of this relationship? What links the *here* of M-C with the *there* of C-M'?

History and ethnography reveal that specific forms of 'joint-ness' have been established for this purpose: the ancient joint family and the relatively new joint stock company. The joint stock company is without doubt the most important institution in the world today. The faceless men who run these companies control ever-growing amounts of money which gives them great power and influence in the political arena. The rise of the joint stock company has been specta-cular. In many cases this has been at the expense of the joint family company but not always for the relationship between the two types of organisation can sometimes be very close. Consider the following account of Chinese merchant families in the Philippines for example:

> [T]he Chinese kin group has several important features like those of stock corporations, with perhaps the greatest difference being that kinship limits participation. The resemblance is so strong that it has been explicitly recognized, and some families have actually issued 'stock' shares (informally, without a charter) to their members. In one case, for example, thirteen shareholders divided profits at the end of each year. Further-more, after the death of two of the original shareholders, rather than reapportion the deceased relatives' shares, income accruing to them has been set aside to finance education for the sons of family members (Davis, 1973).

The merchant family thrives in rural areas where land is a parcelised good, markets are periodic, merchants mobile, and where non-indus-trial methods of agricultural production such as ox-drawn wooden ploughs constrain profits and mercantile capital accumulation. For a given merchant this profit varies with the particular mode of distribu-tion of periodic markets in an area and the mode of transport owned, be it shoes, bicycle, private vehicle or public transport. The joint stock company, by contrast, has no such limitations. Industrial production and global distribution offer seemingly unlimited scope for the accumulation of capital for a legal entity of this kind. The local and limited nature of the merchant family, then, is what gives it its specificity and its human importance for it serves as the buffer between the village and the world at large.

The principles governing the jointness of stock companies are enshrined in the laws of the nation state, in company law, contract law, taxation law and so on. But what principles govern the reproduction of the merchant family? This is an empirical question that can only be answered by fieldwork, comparative ethnographic analysis and theoretical reflection. In this chapter I offer my theoretical reflections on these questions in the light of ethnographic research done in Central India. Central to my theoretical argument is the notion of *territoriality* as a value. I begin with a brief discussion of this concept to set the stage for the ethnographic material that follows.

Territoriality is a form of consciousness that binds people together. It is made up, Guha notes (1983a: 279), 'of a sense of belonging to a common lineage as well as a common habitat'. Territoriality, then, is the union of consanguinity with contiguity that defines an *ethnic space*, a domain that is much larger than the physical boundaries defined by the *supreme good,* the inalienable farmland under the guardianship of a particular branch of a family. The term *territoriality* is Guha's but the idea behind it, as Guha acknowledges, comes from Lowie (1962: 73) who noted that if 'we inquire into the bond of consanguinity we find lurking in the background a spatial determinant of the sentiments underlying it. Abstractly separated by a chasm, the two types of union are in reality intertwined.'

From the perspective of value, territoriality is like the shade cast by a big tree. It has the same materiality as a shadow but, like an actual shadow, it can bring real advantages to those under its cover and disadvantages to those outside it. If in times of war it describes the limits beyond which insurgency cannot carry (Guha, 1983a: Ch 7), then it times of peace it describes the limits of capital accumulation of a specific mercantilist kind. The ethnic space defined by the latter manifests itself as a nested hierarchy of heterogenous regions of various sizes rather than as a single flat ethnically homogenous domain. Each ethnic space is defined by a notion of *home*, by rules of *endogamy*, and by forms of commodity *specialisation*.

Home. The notion of place at the heart of territoriality is defined by the link between homeland and tradeland. The homeland, the birthplace of ancestors, the location of family *goods,* is the ground upon which prestige is cultivated; the tradeland, which is usually described by those periodic market places within travelling distance of the current residence of a merchant, is the domain of profit.

Endogamy. The boundaries of this ethnic space are described by rules of endogamy. This includes not only the rules of marriage, which describe the innermost circle of territoriality, and the shared language, which describes the outer circle, but, most important of all, the principles governing the transmission of mercantile credit within these circles and over time.

Specialisation. Territoriality is associated with commodity specialisation of a mercantile kind. Thus we find that high prestige, high profit commodities such as gold and silver tend to be in the hands of wealthy traders, while low prestige, low quality commodities are associated with poor, low status traders. Not too much must be made of this latter principle however. Commodity specialisation is an observed tendency rather than an ideological principle.

Territoriality is to merchant household polity what purity is to Brahmanic household polity. Within the mercantile household polity of India the Marwari territoriality is the most extensive. The Marwaris are to India what the Chinese are to southeast Asia and the Jews were to Europe. Marwar was the name of the former princely state now know as Jodhpur District; the term Marwari is used today as a generic label for people who come from this area and its surroundings. It includes a heterogenous collection of people from different castes and tribes but the Marwari dialect they speak sets them apart at this very general level of classification. Within the Marwaris the Jains are the undisputed mercantile elite. Jainism is an ancient religion in India that has its origins in anti-Brahman protest. Jains denied the sanctity of the Vedas. They questioned the ideology that Brahmans were the indispensable intermediaries with the gods. They protested the hereditary power of the Brahmans and their costly animal sacrifices. In its place, they developed a doctrine of non-violence and vegetarianism of an extraordinary and uncompromising kind. 'Jains,' as Carrithers and Humphrey note (1991:1), 'are to avoid harm to even the smallest living thing, to purify themselves strenuously through self-mortification, and to conduct lives of strict moral rectitude.' Jains are also known for their mobility: every major city and every market town of any importance in India has a resident Jain community. These communities, and the broader Marwari grouping of which they are part, often control most of the mercantile activity in any given market town. One estimate has it that Marwaris control over 60% of the assets of Indian industry (quoted in Timberg, 1978:11). Such an estimate is mere guesswork but, as an order of magnitude, it is one that few people familiar with the workings of the Indian economy would bother to question.

Marwari merchant 'migration' has been the subject of a study by Timberg (1978) who highlights the importance of 'communal credit networks' (1978:6). 'The genius of a trading community,' he argues (1978:29), 'lies in its manipulation of credit.'[1] He notes that the origin of much of the present day 'migration' has its origins in the 1870s when the growth of the Bombay and Calcutta ports caused a decline in traditional trade routes through Rajputana and Cutch. I have placed the word 'migration' in quotes because, as Timberg himself notes (1978:91), the notion as it is generally understood does not apply to the Marwari case. Place of birth tables, he notes (1978:87), would show most Marwaris as 'born in Rajasthan' because wives either stayed at home or returned to their home towns in Rajasthan to give birth. What is at stake here, I assert, is an *expansion of territoriality* rather than migration. This is best illustrated by considering a specific example such as the patrilineage shown in Figure V.1.

The leader of this clan, PP Jain, was born in Lohawat, Rajasthan six generations ago. When he was around five years old his *mundan* was performed half here and half in the village of Erlaya a short distance away in Bikaner District. During this ritual, which is performed throughout India by many different castes, a boy's head is shaved and the hair offered to the family gods. This ritual is, therefore, crucially important for establishing a sense of connectedness with home and relatives. PP lived in Lohawat after he was married and had seven sons and an unrecorded number of daughters. Four of the sons have produced lineages and their descendants are spread out along the track shown in Map V.1.

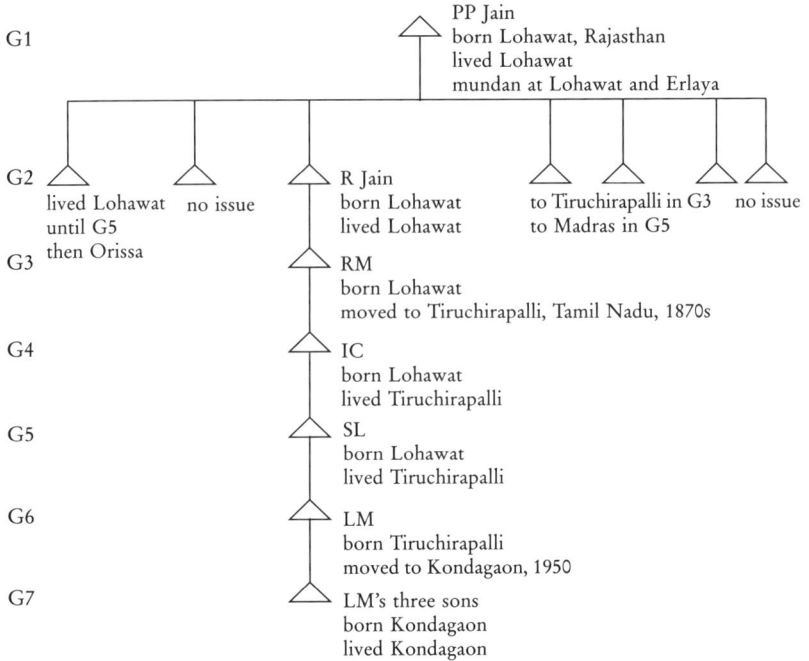

FIGURE V.1   *Birthplace and residence in a Jain lineage*

The sixth and seventh generation descendants of the third son of PP Jain have settled in Kondagaon. The place of birth, work, and *mundan* for this lineage reveals a pattern that is reproduced in the other branches of the family. The third generation moved to south India after they were born and had performed their *mundan* ritual. Their wives, it seems, stayed behind in Rajasthan where they gave birth to the next generation of sons who lived and worked with their fathers. The fourth generation copied their father's practice but the fifth generation brought their wives with them and moved further north to work. The sixth and seventh generation have established a new pattern and their only link with Rajasthan is the *mundan* ritual. The expansion of territoriality, then, has weakened the physical links with the homeland but not the ideological links. Indeed, territoriality as a form of reciprocally recognised consanguineal consciousness has probably strengthened as the descendants have moved to keep on the edge of India's commercial frontier. Affinal and contiguous relations, as we shall see below, are also extremely important for the reproduction of territoriality as a value.

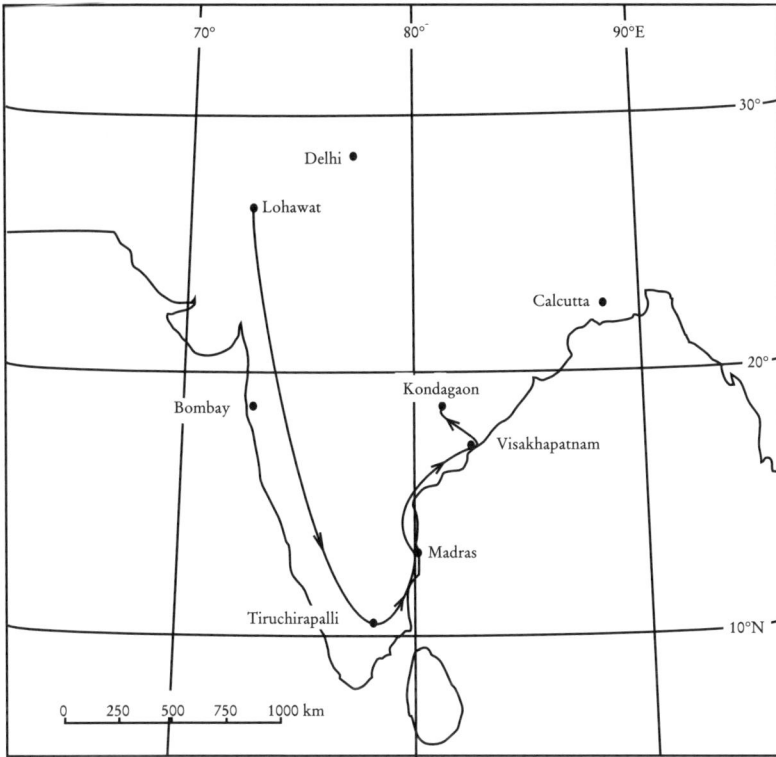

MAP V.1   *Territorial expansion of a Jain lineage*

The following matrix, which summarises the above argument, shows the changing quality of territoriality very clearly.

Generation	Mundan at home in Rajasthan?	Born at home in Rajasthan?	Lived at home in Rajasthan?
1	+	+	+
2	+	+	+
3	+	+	-
4	+	+	-
5	+	+	-
6	+	-	-
7	+	-	-

The physical consequences of this changing territoriality can be seen in Lohawat and surrounding market centres such as Tiwari. Tiwari was a major trading centre as is apparent from the old market town area that is now falling into ruin. It is an eerie experience to wander through the deserted narrow streets between the tumble-down stone buildings of an old market town in a place like India where such places are typically teeming with people. The grandeur of old Tiwari is heightened by the contrast with modern day Tiwari. The green revolution has given the town a new lease of life, but one premised on production rather than exchange. No attempt has been made to restore the beautiful old stone shops in the market area. Instead, tin shacks and sheds have sprung up along the main road in classic frontier-town style.

In Lohawat, a residential village for Jain families, a history of change can be read from the buildings here too. The village consists of row upon row of beautiful three- and four-story stone mansions. These are crowded together along winding streets like the houses in an overpopulated city which makes the contrasts with the open desert land upon which the village is built very dramatic. While most of the houses are still inhabitable and more or less maintained, the place is for the most part deserted. Like Tiwari, this village too has a new section. But here new residential mansions are being built which look just like the old. These houses belong to new branches of the family who assert their prestige by establishing a physical presence in the village by means of a mansion that is rarely lived in. This is not *potlatch* in the sense that property is not destroyed but it is of that genre of prestige-seeking activity. It is certainly not a profit making investment.

The ascetic lifestyle of the Jains gives them few means to assert their identity in the battle of prestige both among themselves and with the rest of the world. Their religious beliefs and practices make them the purest of the pure but for those who do not share these values such beliefs bring negative comment. This is especially so in Rajasthan where meat eating is prestigious. Here the Jains are called misers (*kanjus*), fly-suckers (*makkijus*) and rice-lentil eaters (*dhal battis*) because of their 'poverty stricken' diet and concern for small living things in their food (Cottam Ellis, 1991: 91). Lavish spending on housing and temples is one of the few means they have for disposing of their revenue. They not only build mansions in their places of origin, they also build them in their places of residence. Kondagaon in Bastar District has experienced something of a building boom over the past decade or so as the Marwaris, and the Marwari Jains in particular, have begun to establish their domestic presence there. Each new Jain mansion that is built is opened with great ceremony. Every notable in town is invited along with hundreds of other guests (including anthropologists) who are dined at great expense, but not wined. The new house is opened and guests are free to wander through in a way that will henceforth be impossible for non-family members.

Marwari territoriality, then, has its physical markers of origin and destination. It also has it own invisible boundaries which are which made very clear to those ousted from the in-group. The case shown in Figure V.2 illustrates what I mean. SL, the son of IC and the father of B and LM, died when his two sons were only young. They accompanied their mother who went to live in her father's house. The effect of this was to break the link that should have been maintained between B and LM and their father's father. As they did not live with him they had no opportunity to 'serve' (*sewa*) under him and he did not recognise them as descendants. In other words, the relations of contiguity did not allow a relationship of consanguinity to be established through reciprocal recognition. IC was very wealthy but with his only son dead he had the problem of what to do with his wealth. He made of huge gift (*dan*) of some Rs 40,000 towards the construction of a temple and gave the rest to his brother's son whom he adopted as his own. The father of B's wife got very upset about this because he expected to benefit from the marriage of his daughter to a Jain. However, the fact that he was from the Rajput caste was part of the problem: B not only failed to serve his father's father, he also married out of the Jain community. B's actions, then, led to his out-casting. LM, his younger brother, asserts his Jain identity very strongly. He proudly showed me a map of his lineage but it seems that his claims are not reciprocated. The protector and preserver of the official lineage knowledge is a trusted member of a hereditary caste of genealogists who spends months each year travelling on trains throughout India to maintain his records. He only enters the names of people who it is generally agreed should be entered. He is the

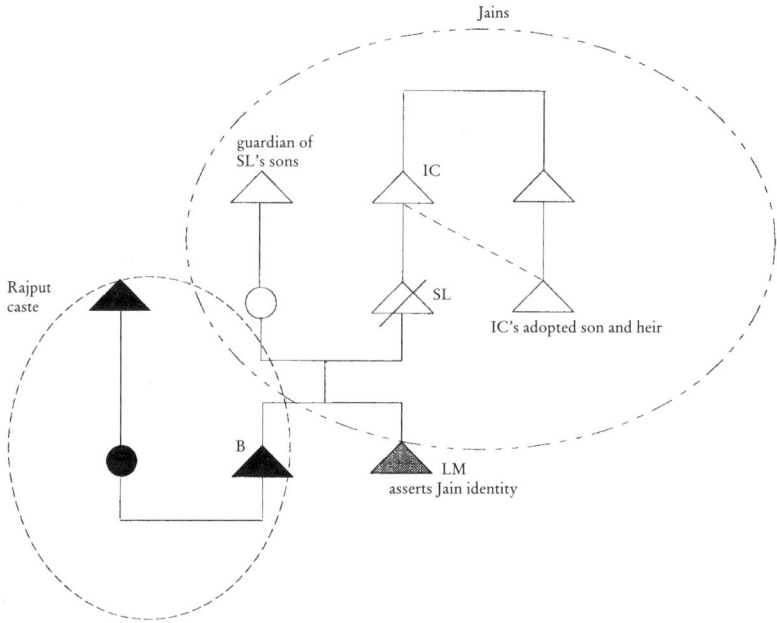

FIGURE V.2   *The boundary lines of a Jain lineage*

boundary rider, the faithful servant of the living elite whose job it is to maintain the goodness of the links between the dead and the unborn. When I attempted to interview him in Tiwari in 1986 he gave me the classic run around for which members of his caste are famous in anthropological circles (Shal, 1959). He never kept appointments and when I eventually did get to talk to him he would not let me see his genealogical records and would tell me nothing about the people whose lineages he kept. Significantly, the only exception was the story of LM Jain and his brother which I have repeated here.

Territoriality of this kind exists for the subalterns too but the latter is not a simple inversion of the former. But nor does the relationship between the elite and the subalterns form a continuum either. Instead we find a *strata* of discrete groups. As we descend the steps the spread of a group's territoriality tends to decline and so too does its money wealth as expressed both it mercantile wealth and domestic *goods* such as housing. We also find that different groups tend to be associated with different commodities. In what follows I illustrate this argument concretely with evidence on the marketing of 'downwardly mobile' manufactured commodities in central India, an argument that was anticipated in my discussion of the marketing of 'upwardly mobile' agricultural commodities in the last chapter. The tinge of *goodness* that clings to agricultural products grown by households using the supreme good is, of course, totally absent from the products that emerge from the factory floor; but, as we shall see, merchants get caught up in the politics of prestige albeit of a somewhat different kind.

THE MARKETING OF DOWNWARDLY MOBILE COMMODITIES IN BASTAR

The principal imports into Bastar are Indian-made manu-factured products. These 'downwardly mobile commodities', as Skinner[2] (1964) calls them, can be divided into three broad categories: ornaments, clothing and groceries. The category 'ornaments' includes jewellery made from gold, silver, bronze, brass and glass as well as other 'fancy goods' (*manihari*) such as combs, mirrors, pins, red powder, and snow cream; 'clothing' includes saris, dhotis, cloth, blankets, blouses, shirts, under shorts and handloom cloth; while 'groceries' (*kirana*) includes such things as tea, biscuits, boiled sweets, incense, matches, and batteries.

These divisions and subdivisions of the imported commodities are the basis of a differentiation amongst retailer-merchants. There is a hierarchy of commodities that correlates roughly with a hierarchy among retailer-merchants: rich merchants control the trade in clothing, gold and silver while poor merchants specialise in the low-value, low prestige commodities. This division is reinforced by caste and kinship factors. Rich merchants tend to be long distance immigrants from Rajasthan or the Punjab consisting of a limited number of castes who rigidly adhere to caste rules about kinship and marriage. Poor mer-chants, on the other hand, tend to be short-distance immigrants or locals from a large number of castes, many of whom intermarry with Tribals. Within the categories of rich and poor we also find further differentiation between rich and very rich, and poor and very poor.

Cutting across this distinction between rich and poor retailer-merchants is a distinction between wholesaler-merchants and retailer-merchants. Wholesalers are, in general, much better off financially than the retailers. A wholesaler is required to maintain large stocks and very few traders have the necessary capital to even contemplate this form of trading. Wholesalers, therefore, form an elite within each commodity classification. Many wholesalers also engage in retail trade.

The aim of this chapter is to describe this process of differentiation amongst the merchants. It examines how merchant capital is acquired, reproduced, and accumulated, and analyses the role of caste and kinship in this process. It also examines the incentives and barriers to social mobility.

THE MARKETING OF CLOTH

The cloth trader is perhaps the hardest working of all merchants. He carries his stock to the market in heavy bundles of 75 kg or more. These bundles contain neatly folded stock, which are wrapped up in plastic and hessian and bound tightly by heavy rope. The trader's day starts early in the morning around 6 or 7 am. He unwraps his pack and replenishes it with new stock if the previous day's sales were heavy. If he is a small trader he then straps his 75 kg load onto the back of his bicycle and begins the ride to the market of that day, a distance that can be up to 18 miles. If it is Tuesday the big merchants in Kondagaon place their load in a jeep trailer and set off at 8 am on the 40 mile drive to the Makdi market. The jeeps are always crammed with people and baggage. A jeep owner carries his regular customers plus extras who have their own reasons for attending the market of the day. Upon arrival at the market—usually around 10 am—the long process of preparing their stall begins. All cloth merchants sit under thatched roofed shelters. They begin by covering the ground with a tarpaulin which is then covered by mats for their customers to sit on. Ropes are then tied in rows 18 inches apart around the posts at the back and sides of the shelter. The slow process of partially unfolding saris and other cloth and draping them neatly over the ropes then begins. By 12.30 or 1 pm this job is finished, and the crowds are beginning to gather. The cloth trader is one of the busiest people in the market. He is usually hidden behind the crowds that inspect his wares. He conducts business with as many as four people at once. While he is collecting money from one person, he will grab yet another bundle of saris to throw at a vacillating buyer, ask a third, a credit customer, her father's name, caste and village, and argue with the fourth over the price of an item. By 3.30 pm most of the customers have gone, and the reverse process begins. Much work is involved in the packing process, because in the act of selling, as anyone who has dealt with an Indian cloth merchant knows, they unfold countless items with great flourish in order to show off their wares to prospective customers. At around 5.30 pm, other merchants who travel by the same jeep as the cloth merchant and who, up until now, have been playing cards, may give some assistance to the cloth merchant if it seems that their trip home will be delayed longer than usual. At 6 pm the long trip home starts. A 15 minute stop is always made to conduct *puja* at the Amrawati temple. Two or three traders will make their way to the temple armed with coconuts, and return later to share the white meat of the coconuts with their fellow travellers. Jeeps usually arrive in Kondagaon by 7 or 8 pm, which is also the time the cyclists arrive. Many traders keep up this exhausting routine seven days per week. Sunday and Wednesday provide some respite from the travelling because markets are held at Kondagaon, the regional centre where the rich merchants live, on these days.

The cloth traders are of three basic types. One group sells unstitched cloth such as saris, dhotis, scarves, plain cloth, and blankets; a second group sells stitched cloth such as blouses, petticoats, under shorts, and shirts; while the third group sells hand-loom cloth. The first two groups have market stalls which are stocked with material with a 1983 value anywhere from Rs 3000 to over Rs 30,000, the real value of which is best grasped by considering each rupee as the equivalent of one kg of paddy. The sellers of stitched cloth invariably belong to a Tailor (*Darzi*) caste of Marwaris and do the stitching themselves at home at night after the markets. The sales of these first two groups account for over 99% of all cloth sales. Their intrusion into the district has been at the expense of the indigenous hand-loom cloth sellers. These people wander around the market with two or three lengths of cloth to sell. Because of the competition, handloom-cloth traders are forced to sell at a rate which returns them a pittance for the work involved in weaving the cloth. Needless to say, the number of people engaged in this activity has declined quite dramatically over the years. The hand-loom cloth is reckoned to be of inferior quality by the consumers and only the very poor, and those regarded as 'jungly', buy it.

The purchase of cloth is seasonal, with most purchases being made after the harvest in November-January. However, this seasonal purchasing pattern is off-set to the extent that merchants are prepared to give credit during the rainy season. In the case of the big merchants, credit sales are a significant portion of total sales, with some merchants having upwards of Rs 50,000 outstanding by the end of the wet season.

The large number of cloth merchants at each market makes for a competitive system which brings about a rough equalisation of rates of gross profit. Buyers are very knowledgeable. Some go to as many as five markets each week all year around. They can tell good quality cloth from poor and know what a reasonable price is. Before buying, they will carefully examine the cloth for flaws and check the accuracy of the merchant's measuring rod by counting out the cloth's length in 'hands', which is the distance from elbow to the fingertip.

The actual price is set after going through a ritual bargaining procedure. For example, a woman, having decided on the sari she desires, will ask the merchant for his price. He will say Rs 33 (1983 prices), if it is an average quality sari. The buyer will then bid Rs 25 and this price is usually agreed by the seller because the cost price of average quality saris is Rs 23, giving a gross mark-up on cost of around 10%, the rate cloth sellers expect. They will not take less than this and will, of course, take more if they ever find an inexperienced buyer. Such people do exist, of course, but they are a minority. By and large, buyers are not stupid. Gross profit rates, then, vary between 10–40%. When the item sold is small and cheap, the profit rate tends to the upper extreme; conversely, for expensive items the profit rate tends to the lower extreme. For example, one transaction I observed in 1982 involved a child's shirt. The cost price of this to the seller was Rs 1.75, and he sold it for Rs 2.50, giving the trader a profit of Rs 0.75 or 43%.

For small traders it is the absolute amount of profit rather than the profit rate that is important. For them, net takings must be sufficient to cover daily needs, and if those cannot be met, then the trader will go out of business. Some are forced to do this when they find themselves having to spend gross takings on food. Their working capital gets smaller and smaller as a consequence. Others simply give up and take up daily wage labouring when this becomes a more profitable investment of labour time. In the cloth industry the handloom sellers are the only people in this category. An elderly weaver I met in the weavers' quarter at Alor village in 1982, for example, labours 6 to 7 hours to produce 9 hands of cloth, which he sold in the market for Rs 14. The cotton used in making this cloth had to be purchased in the market for Rs 12, giving him a profit of Rs 2 or 14%. Looked at from another perspective this 'profit' was equivalent to a daily wage of Rs 2.00. This was well below the Rs 8.25 daily labourers could get from the Forest Department or the Public Works Department at that time. It is not surprising, then, that most weavers have abandoned the craft. The effect of competition, then, has been to drive the handloom sellers out of business and to effect a rough equalisation of the rate of gross profit and prices amongst machine cloth sellers.

Wholesale cloth merchants have a mark-up of between 3% to 5%. This is less than the mark-up of 10% made by retailers, but it is consistent with a uniform rate of profit. In order to grasp this point, a clear distinction must be made between the rate of mark-up, the rate of profits, and the rate of stock turnover. The mark-up rate is the percentage mark-up on costs, the profit rate is the ratio of profit to capital stock, and the rate of stock turnover is the number of times trading capital has to be replaced each year. A retailer has a relatively high mark-up compared to a wholesaler, but the wholesaler has a high rate of stock turnover, and this may bring about an equalisation of profit rates. For example, a retailer with a mark-up of 10% and a rate of stock turnover of 3 has a rate of profit of 30%, while the wholesaler who has a mark-up of 5% but a stock turnover rate of 6 also has a profit rate of 30%. This does not mean that absolute levels of profit are equal of course. These provide a quantitative measure of the stratification among merchants and are directly related to the absolute levels of trading capital. Thus the bigger the absolute size of trading capital the bigger the absolute level of profit.

According to the economics textbooks, a competitive market of this type should be characterised by the existence of many atomistic sellers of the same size. But what we have in Bastar is a situation where merchants are stratified. In order to explain this divergence between economic theory and social practice, it is necessary now to examine the social relations involved in the production and reproduction of merchant capital in Bastar.

Among the cloth traders, the trading capital is controlled by the Marwaris, the Marwari-speaking migrants from Rajasthan. Within this group Jains dominate. They control the wholesale distribution of cloth and many of the retail outlets. They are among the most prosperous people in the district. Another important caste within the Marwaris are the Tailors. They control the trade in stitched cloth and own many of the tailoring shops in Kondagaon. It is common to find a family where one brother works in Kondagaon sewing, while another brother visits the daily markets selling stitched cloth. The remaining Marwari cloth merchants are Brahmans and Sonis (Goldsmiths) who do not follow their traditional caste occupation.

Most of the Marwari cloth merchants carry a stock of upward of Rs 30,000 (1983 prices) and are easily distinguished from the non-Marwari cloth merchants, who carry a stock of not more than Rs 5,000. These small merchants are an assorted, unrelated group, from several castes and places. Here, then, is the beginnings of an answer to the question posed above. The economic theory — be it Marxist or neoclassical — does not consider *territoriality* and it is this that sets up barriers to entry of outsiders into the cloth trade.

An examination of some of the problems faced by non-Marwari traders can serve to illustrate these points.

Take the case of JL Sindhi, who, in 1982, had been living in Kondagaon for one year. People of the Sindhi caste are renowned for their trading prowess, but there are very few members of this caste living in Kondagaon. JL's father and three brothers all live in Umerakote, Orissa State, some 70 miles away. JL migrated to Kondagaon with his wife and young family, and set up business as a tailor. He earned very little from that, so he decided to go into business selling biscuits at the Kondagaon bus stand. This, too, yielded him little income, but he did manage to accumulate Rs 350. He invested this in trading stock for a cloth business and was helped by a Jain wholesaler who advanced him an additional Rs 350 stock on credit. He asked for more but was refused. He complained to me that the Jains only give large amounts of trade credit to other Marwaris. With his Rs 700, he was able to buy 32 saris to take on his market round. He goes to Kondagaon on Sunday, Sampur on Monday (transport cost Rs 6), Kanera on Tuesday (transport cost Rs 6), Kondagaon on Wednesday, Banyagaon on Thursday (Rs 1.50), Dahikonga on Friday (Rs 1.50), and Lanjoda on Saturday (Rs 2.00). These markets are the closest set of markets to Kondagaon, and his weekly transport costs amount to Rs 17. This works out at Rs 2.50 per day on average, which is the profit from the sale of one sari. Thus, the profit of the first sari he sells each day goes on transport. The profit on the next three pays for basic food requirements. It is only after he sells his fourth or fifth sari that profit can begin to accumulate. Rarely does he sell more than five saris though. His stock looks pathetic along side the big merchants who carry upward of 1000 saris plus other items. He finds it very difficult to attract customers; they prefer to shop at the big stalls where there is a great variety to choose from and where, also, credit purchases can be made.

JL Sindhi is one of the poorest cloth traders, but his predicament tells us much — in mirror image, as it were — about the factors underlying the success of the rich Marwari traders. For a Marwari trader, the vital original capital is usually inherited rather than earned. Those who don't have rich fathers can obtain their capital, or at least a significant portion of it, on credit from a fellow Marwari. Thus, they can start business with a capital of around Rs 15–20,000 or more. With their larger stock, they can attract more customers and hence increase sales and the *absolute* level of profit. A higher absolute level of profit means more money available for transport, and hence a chance to visit the profitable Orissa-side markets, which are at some distance form Kondagaon. A higher absolute level of profit also means that a greater surplus over necessary consumption is available for reinvestment in additional trading capital.

Consider now the case of RJ Bengali, a non-Marwari merchant whose wealth lies between that of Sindhi and the Marwaris. RJ Bengali has a capital of Rs 5000 (1983 prices). His family were resettled in Bastar under the Bengali refugee scheme. He goes to Kondagaon market on Sunday and Wednesday, Mulmula on Thursday, Dahikonga on Friday and Lanjoda on Saturday. He rides a hired cycle to the latter three markets carrying his 75 kg load on the back of the cycle. The Thursday market at Mulmula involves a round trip of 26 miles, the Friday market 20 miles, and the Saturday market 22 miles. This trip is done in the company of small merchants. One such merchant is ST Bengali, who has a slightly smaller capital of Rs 3000. ST works seven days per week, including one day at Chhinari. He goes to this market by jeep, for which he pays Rs 8. Another example of the traders in this class is CR Dewangan, a Bastarian Hindu whose father owns a small farm in Kondagaon. He has a capital of Rs 5000, which was advanced by his father. He cycles to three markets—Sampur, Mulmula and Dahikonga—and also attends the Sunday Kondagaon market. He sends his stock to the Mulmula and Sampur markets on bullock cart, which costs him Rs 5.00. On the three days he has off from trading, he works on his father's farm.

These examples are fairly typical cases of the non-Marwari merchants. Their economic condition is secure, unlike the case of JL Sindhi described above. However, the members of this group have not as yet been able to accumulate enough capital to break into the 'big merchant' class monopolised by the Marwaris. Among other things, they cannot afford to advance credit to their customers, and this places a limit on the absolute level sales and hence disposable surplus.

The Jains are the largest sub-group of Marwaris in Kondagaon. The community consists of approximately sixty households. These people come from one small area of the Jodhpur District in Rajasthan and are all related. An illustration of the family structure of ten of the most prosperous households is given in Figure V.3.

These ten households belong to two clans (*gottra*), Surana and Sancheti. These households have kinship links with other households, but these are not shown in order to avoid undue complication. Most of the senior men were born in either Kettu or Jethaniya in Jodhpur District and came to Bastar in 1950. All of their children were born in Bastar, with the exception of G, son of M, who stayed in Rajasthan. A notable feature of the Jains of Kondagaon is the unusually large number of children they have. The four sons of P, for example, had 13, 5, 6 and 8 children respectively which included 9, 4, 3 and 2 sons

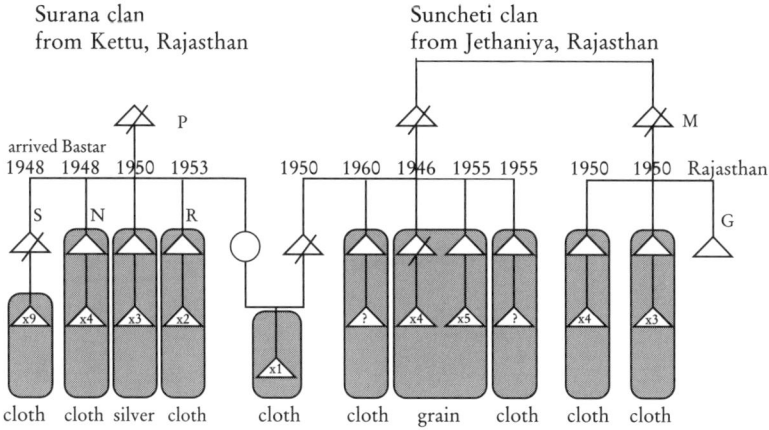

FIGURE V.3 *Kinship relations between ten Jain joint family merchants*

respectively. From the point of view of a rapidly expanding family business, population growth of this kind assists in the creation of wealth rather than the opposite. Most Jains run a cloth store in Kondagaon, as well as maintaining a number of market rounds. These businesses require trusted employees to manage them and *sons* are in great demand for this purpose. If sons are not available, commission agents are contracted to run stalls on a 4% commission. Such arrangements are not very common, however.

Once established, their ever-growing commercial capital passes from father to son without diminution. All property is divided among sons. Take P's sons, for example. They were originally a joint family, but with the coming of age of their sons the inevitable split occurred creating four new joint families in their place. P's eldest son, S, moved from Rajasthan to the Durg District, where he ran a grocery business. When he died, his 9 sons and unmarried daughters moved to Kondagaon to share in the division of the property and to start a cloth business. Three brothers do the market rounds, one is in transport, and the remainder were still at school when the fieldwork was done in 1983. N, the second son of P, and one of the first to arrive in Kondagaon, has a cloth shop. His two eldest sons help out here at night and do the market rounds during the week. The two youngest sons are still at school. R, P's fourth son, has one adult son. He helps in the running of R's large and successful cloth store. When his next son leaves school, he will be set up as a market trader.

Jain market traders are the elite among the cloth traders. In 1982 fathers typically set sons up with a trading capital in excess of Rs 60,000 rupees. They also able to advance credit to customers and as this credit given is often in excess of Rs 60,000 at any one time, the effective working capital of a trader is over Rs 100,000 (10 tonnes of rice in real terms). They travel to markets in a jeep. The jeeps pull trailers that carry the stock. Some merchants store a supply of stock at the more distant markets and use it from week to week to avoid the problem of transportation.

Figure V.3 illustrates another feature of Jain merchant capitalism, and that is diversification. Not only does this group of families dominate the cloth trade from wholesaling through retail store ownership to market trading, they also are engaged in grain trading, forest contracting, medical store ownership, jewellery, and transport. It should be noted that all these activities, with the exception of the latter, involve profit making by buying cheap and selling dear, ie., merchant capitalism rather than productive capitalism. Some Marwaris, it is true, have purchased land and introduced capitalist farming techniques. Nevertheless, it is merchant capitalism in which they specialise.

The Tailor caste are the smallest sub-group of Marwaris, but second in importance to the Jains in the cloth trade. There were 14 households in 1982 and these belonged to six *gottra*: Dehiya (6 households), Dabbi (2), Pawar (2), Solenki (1) and Chawda (1). The householders, as has already been mentioned above, specialise in the trade of stitched cloth as well as running tailoring shops in Kondagaon. The stitched cloth they sell is all produced by themselves. Most of the householders arrived in Kondagaon after the 1960s. This was later than most Jains and it is reflected in the size of their trading capital. While they are obviously better off than the non-Marwaris who carry a stock of around Rs 5000, they do not compare with the Jain merchants with their capital of Rs 100,000. The correlation between date of arrival in Kondagaon and the size of capital accumulated applies not only between castes but between households of the same caste, as will be seen below, when the case of the Sonis is examined.

The type of profit the Tailors receive must be sharply distinguished from the type of profit the Jains receive. The Tailors buy cloth and sell stitched cloth, adding value to the product through the contribution of their own labour. It is, therefore, of a different order to the purely merchant profit received by Jains. Tailors do not hire labour for this purpose: it is all done by *male* members of the household. The Tailors, then, are a group of producer-sellers rather than pure merchants (buyer-sellers).

A feature of all Marwari economic activity, and this is a fact that distinguishes them from other regional groups, is the complete lack of the direct involvement of women in selling. The domain of women is the kitchen, and they are kept there under a form of *purdah* system, not unlike the one that applies to Muslim women. When they venture out of the house, they cover their heads and faces with their saris. Women play a vital indirect role in their husbands' businesses, of course. Indeed, the businesses would collapse without their domestic labour input. They raise the children, clean the house and cook the meals (with the aid of servants in the case of the wealthy). They prepare the *tiffen* of food traders take with them on their mid-day meal and are always on call to prepare tea for customers who call at the shops in Kondagaon.

THE MARKETING OF JEWELLERY

The general arguments about the importance of *territoriality* for the understanding of cloth merchants applies also to jewellery merchants. The wealthy jewellers all belong to the same social group — Marwari — and they are internally differentiated. Relatively poor merchants trade in brass and nickel jewellery but, if they are from Marwar, the possibility of moving into the more profitable, and more prestigious, gold and silver trade is open to them. The merchants who sell gold and silver are the 'kings' of the market. Their stalls are invariably located in the centre of the market, and they serve as a gathering place for local village leaders (Gell, 1982). They squat down next to the jeweller and gossip for hours on end; the jeweller, for his part, orders them cups of tea and supplies them with *bedis* to smoke in between negotiating with customers who spend relatively large amounts of money replacing worn out jewellery and buying new pieces.

The jeweller's wares are displayed on a deep red cloth, which serves to enhance the quality of his sparkling, freshly-cleaned silver. The large items, such as solid silver necklaces and belts—which weigh in excess of 400 grams and valued at over Rs 1000—are draped over a vertical display panel at the back; smaller items, such as ankle bracelets, armlets, old silver rupee coin necklaces, and hairclips, are displayed on a small box in front of the panel, while the small relatively cheap gold and silver noserings and earrings are scattered on the ground in front. The big jewellers also carry a small stock of imitation gold and silver trinkets made from brass and nickel, but trade in these is the specialist preserve of a group of poorer traders. They sell cheap imitations of all items the silver merchant stocks, from large bulky 'nickel' necklaces to small brass earrings. These items look like their gold and silver counterparts and close inspection is needed to see that they are imitations. They even display their wares on pieces of deep red cloth just like silver merchants. However, whereas silver merchants are few in number and located in the centre of the market, imitation jewellers are numerous and very much on the periphery. They squat in the sun and dust along the sides of the market's throughways and are barely noticed, except by the occasional customer, who stops briefly to make a purchase. Most of the customers at the jewellers are women and young girls. They come in twos and threes to admire the jewellery, and few walk away without having purchased something.

While the bargain for cheap trinkets is quickly struck, transactions in the medium and higher-priced commodities involve prolonged negotiations. A woman wishing to trade her old ankle bracelets for new ones, for example, must first strike a bargain on the rate for the old bracelets. Ankle bracelets are moulded sheets of silver and the jeweller first of all rips them open with pliers to clean out the mud which gets trapped inside. The decision to buy new bracelets is now irreversible, because they can only be cleaned by destroying them. If the customer is not satisfied with the rate offered, she will try another jeweller. Having negotiated the rate for the old silver, the customer selects her new bracelets and begins negotiations for the price of them. Often both old and new rates are struck simultaneously by placing the old bracelets on one side of the scales, the new on the other side, and negotiating the difference to be paid. Transactions involving the big expensive ornaments are family affairs, and the bargaining is done by the woman's husband or father. The price is usually paid partly in cash and partly on credit. Customers are unable to tell if a particular necklace has 70% silver content or 97% and take the jeweller's word that it is the latter. This requires trust and jewellers work hard to acquire a reputation for honesty. This takes time, and the successful jewellers are ones who have been around for a long time. If a new jeweller were to set up business in an old established market he would find it very difficult to get customers for his high priced ornaments. While the jewellers no doubt do manage to cheat some of their customers by debasing the silver and by short changing on the weight/ price calculation, the need to develop a reputation for honesty acts as a check on this. Their aim is to secure a good long term return on capital from a loyal clientele rather than a large short term, but non-reproducible, profit from extortion. Avarice, then, has its own morality.

In days gone by gold, rather than silver, was the principal item traded by the jewellers. The substitution of gold by silver is a direct result of the international price movements in these metals which I consider in Chapter VIII below.

Jewellers are differentiated by the type of product sold and caste. Silver merchants are either Jains or Sonis (Goldsmiths) from Rajasthan, with the former the most successful traders. The relationship between these two groups is very similar to the one already noted between Jain cloth merchants and the Tailor caste. The Jains are pure merchants who earn profits solely from buying and selling while the Sonis are producer-traders like the Tailors who work up their finished product from raw material. Within the Soni group there is a further differentiation between rich silver traders and poor imitation jewellery traders.

There were seven big firms of silver traders in Kondagaon in 1982, four of these are Jains and three are Sonis by caste. The markets they visit are shown in Map V.2.

Two points are to be noticed here. Firstly the Jains have captured the territory to the north, south and west of Kondagaon while the Sonis moved into the territory to the east of Kondagaon. The Jains arrived before the Sonis and took over the supply of gold and silver to these established markets. The Soni moved into the then small Orissa-side markets when they arrived and have prospered as these markets flourished with the establishment of the DNK refugee

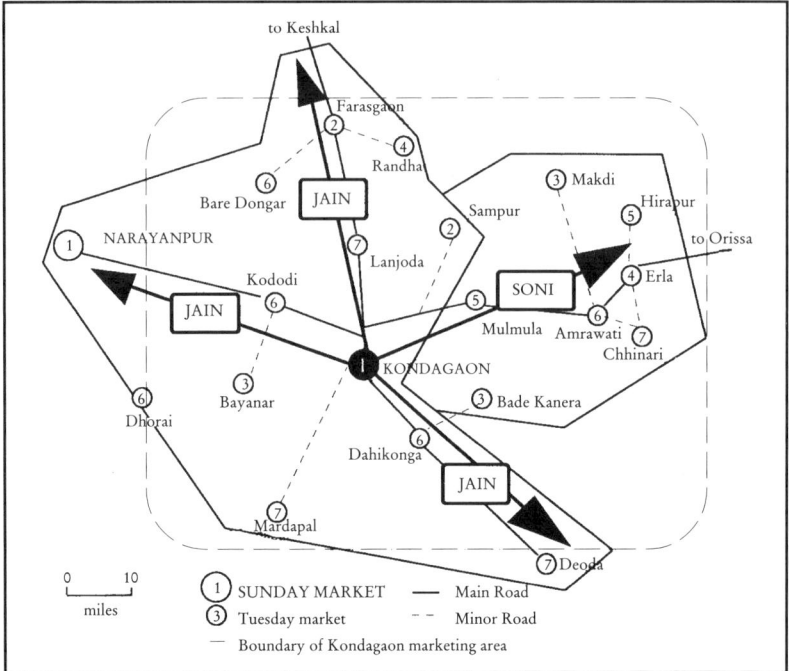

MAP V. 2   *Market areas of silver merchants who travel by jeep*

resettlement project. Secondly, traders capture a cluster of neighbouring markets. This means that they can see their customers more
than once a week at different places and hence become very well
known in a particular area. For example villagers near Erla visit
Hirapur, Amrawati and Chhinari markets and see the same silver
traders at every market.

The biggest gold and silver trader is Jasraj and Company, a
Marwari Jain partnership of cousins and brothers. They sell gold to the
rich Hindus of Kondagaon and silver to the poor of the surrounding
countryside. They have a reputation for being scrupulously honest and
many of their customers have sung their praises to me. My dealings
with this firm have borne this out. I purchased some large intricately
made earrings and had they not volunteered the information that they
were only 70% silver they could have easily extracted another 30% in
Rupees from me. I offer this anecdote not as naive apology for
mercantile capitalism but to counter the naive assumption that all
mercantile capitalism in 'tribal' areas is plunder. The fact is that outright

plunder is not profitable in the long run. Money making of a mercantile kind, then, must have its own morality if it is to survive.[3] This morality is closely tied up with the prestige of the family and the need to maintain appearances. This may involve contradictions of course but this dialectic is not a one-sided story of plunder.

Jasraj is also a government licensed moneylender. Here again they have a reputation for fair dealing. They charge the Government recommended rate of Rs 5 per Rs 100 borrowed per month, ie. 60% per annum. A piece of jewellery double the value of the loan has to be left as security. These rates are to be contrasted with those offered by the illegal dealers. They charge anything up to 300% and are intensely disliked by all. They have a reputation for avarice and cheating.

Like all big trading firms Jasraj and Company have diversified their activities. They have invested their money in 20 acres of farming land and also work as government contractors. This side of the business is run by two younger members of the family.

Jasraj and Company are obviously extremely wealthy and do not try to hide it. To the contrary, they have recently built the biggest and most luxurious mansion in Kondagaon. Just before the house was opened *puja* was performed and over 1000 people from Kondagaon were served food at the house in the celebrations that followed. This celebration was an exercise in prestige building and all the prominent families of Kondagaon engage in activities of this kind. (The celebration of a wedding is another favourite time to display one's wealth.)

While this family has a reputation for honesty they, and the Marwaris generally, also have a reputation for being the most money-minded people in Kondagaon. As a Brahman informant reported: 'Money making is their sole object in life. All their dealings with people are mediated by money. They will not lend money to friends free of interest and are always ready to sell you something. They have no interest in politics or in any social work outside their families.'

A reputation for honesty is also enjoyed by the two other Marwari Jains jewellery merchants but the fourth firm, an Uttar Pradesh Jain family, do not have such a reputation. When I first arrived in Bastar on a preliminary visit in 1981 a group of Kondagaon women were holding a hunger strike in protest against the moneylending activities of this family. The women had borrowed money and left their gold and silver ornaments as security. When they repaid what they considered to be the agreed interest plus capital their jewellery wasn't returned. They complained to the Collector (as the senior Government official in Bastar is called) who told them that as the contracts they entered into were illegal there was no way that they could be legally enforced. Some months later a brave young sub-divisional officer decided to take action against the firm. He had the family head arrested and put on police trial. However, the young officer is now himself on trial for defamation of character as it seems the police officer who arrested the family head committed a minor technical legal error in the process. I have been unable to collect the official version of this story but the truth-value of a story is often less important than its rumour-value. This rumoured version of events does not seem to have adversely affected their business but it is interesting to note that the markets this family visits are the ones at greatest distance from Kondagaon. It is possible, then, that news of their activities in Kondagaon has not reached these distant markets.

The three Soni traders shown in Map V.2 who work the eastern area are rich in comparison with the other Sonis who trade in imitation gold and silver (ie. brass and nickel). It is useful to examine these cases so that further light may be thrown on the processes of merchant capital accumulation and the social mobility of merchants.

RC Soni is the second of five brothers. He was born in Dewartoo, Jodhpur District, Rajasthan and migrated to Kondagaon in 1962. He worked as an assistant for other merchants initially and eventually accumulated sufficient capital to begin a market round on the then small Orissa-side markets. He began initially by selling brass and nickel and eventually moved into silver as his business expanded. His younger brother PR arrived in 1972 to assist him in his business. They opened up a shop on Kondagaon and PR ran this as well as making imitation jewellery. He married the daughter of B Soni, RC's competitor on the Orissa-side market. As their business continued to grow, they invested in a motor bike to get to the markets as well as additional stock for the shop in Kondagaon. In addition to gold and silver jewellery, they now have a large stock of metal pots and pans.

In 1982, RC's third and youngest brother arrived from Jodhpur. He assists in the shop and is able to make silver and imitation jewellery. Like all Marwaris, RC Soni maintains close ties with his home village where his family owns farm land and where his mother and brother still live. He sends money back and they have used it to buy more land and to build a new house. To mark his status he has also funded the building of a shelter for travellers on the outskirts of the village. This includes a small tube well from which they can draw drinking water.

The history of B Soni is similar. He has a joint family business with his son. The son only attends one market (Makdi) and spends the rest of the time in Kondagaon making jewellery, while B attends four markets.

The case of G Soni provides an interesting contrast. He is the youngest of three brothers who have split. G arrived in Kondagaon in 1972. By 1982 he was a successful silver merchant with a large house and a number of cows. His next eldest brother, M, is a cloth merchant. M likewise is very successful, having been in Kondagaon for 16 years. He has invested his money in a motor bike, and a bullock cart which takes his stock from market to market. He employs two servants, one to drive the bullock cart and one to help him with his cloth business. The eldest brother, J, has only been in Kondagaon for three years and is a struggling imitation jeweller producer-seller. J's 15 year-old son is also in the business and they share the work of jewellery making and trading. J finds that the competition from the other imitation jewellers is too fierce these days and he is barely able to make ends meet. He wants to move into cloth trading and is negotiating with his brothers to advance him the necessary capital.

What these cases illustrate is that the longer one has been in Kondagaon the more capital one is likely to have accumulated. The first traders to arrive have been able to appropriate for themselves some territory and have prospered as the market grew in importance. The markets for jewellery are now spoken for and latecomers have little hope of breaking into the trade. The market for brass and nickel jewellery can absorb traders. Only a capital of a few hundred rupees is needed to set up business. Sales are on a cash basis and goodwill is not necessary to attract customers. The barriers to entry to the imitation jewellery trade, unlike the gold and silver trade, are therefore low. However, the trade is highly competitive and the absolute level of profit one can expect is very low.

Apart from Marwari latecomers such as J, discussed above, this group contains a number of poor people of the Soni caste from neighbouring states. These people have no social interaction with the Marwari Sonis because the Marwaris look down upon them as 'primitive tribals'.

There is an intermediate group between the successful silver merchants and the poor brass and nickel merchants. A typical representative of this group is B Soni, one of the few Marwari Sonis of a high ranking sub-caste. He arrived in Kondagaon 1974 as a teacher with no money. He started selling imitation jewellery and now specialises in selling gold plated earrings. These are imported from outside Bastar and are marketed in a little plastic package which makes them look distinctive. He buys these for Rs 5 each and sells them for Rs 7, a profit of 20%. He has also built up a small stock of silver jewellery (Rs 5000 approx) which was acquired by buying up old silver and remaking it himself. He visits four markets in the territory occupied by the Jains (Kondagaon, Mungapadar, Dahikonga and Benur) and is slowly developing a clientele. One of these markets, Mungapadar, he has to himself. This is a new small market and, because it is in a fairly remote area, can reasonably be expected to experience some growth in the future. In the other markets he has direct competition from the Jains and therefore the rate at which he accumulates capital will be checked by this.

The market trade in silver imitation jewellery is monopolised by immigrants. However there is a group of members of the Soni caste who are indigenous to Bastar and who carry out their traditional occupation in their traditional way. Instead of selling jewellery at markets they go on expeditions visiting villages. A group of twenty households of these people live in Kondagaon. They are all related but tend to operate as individuals or in pairs. Every so often a small group of men will set out on a tour lasting 4 to 6 weeks. They walk from village to village with their tools asking for work. They remake old gold and silver ornaments and also sell silver, nickel and brass jewellery.

The Bastar Sonis have a reputation in Kondagaon, and especially among the Marwari Sonis, as dishonest rogues. They freely admitted to me that they dilute a customer's silver in the proportion of fifty parts of silver to 5 parts of nickel. Thus, when they re-fashion someone's silver they receive their labour charge plus this bonus. They also mark-up the silver they sell by between 50% and 70%. Their yearly income, however, is not very high. They can earn as much as Rs 1000 per month (1982 prices) and as little as Rs 10. It all depends upon the luck they have finding work.

While these people have kinship links with other Bastar Soni in the district their *territoriality* bears no comparison to that of the Marwari Sonis. Bastar Sonis are capital-less artisans rather than merchant capitalists; they have no control whatsoever over the national trade in precious metals. When they buy silver for resale, they are forced to buy at the retail market price from Kondagaon-based Marwaris. This fact means that they are precluded from competing with the Marwari-market traders even if they wanted to.

THE MARKETING OF GLASS BANGLES

The economic condition of glass bangle merchants is similar to that of the poorer sellers of brass and nickel jewellery with the difference that it is almost impossible for glass bangle merchants to improve their economic and social condition. They barely earn enough to survive, and are usually in debt to a wholesaler. The best they can hope for is to simply reproduce their situation. If they are able to accumulate some capital the only avenue open for them is wholesaling glass bangles. This, as we shall see, is a highly risky business and means almost guaranteed bankruptcy. So whereas the Marwari imitation jeweller is confronted with a ladder that is possible for him to climb, the glass bangle seller is confronted with a greasy pole. The reasons for this are due partly to the economic structure of glass bangle marketing and partly to socio-cultural factors such as caste and gender; in other words, in the particular form of *territoriality* characteristic of glass bangle marketing.

The demand for glass bangles in India is similar to the demand for rice in that, like rice, they are necessities. The difference, of course, is that whereas food is a natural necessity for survival, glass bangles are a cultural necessity. Glass bangles are the symbol of marriage for almost all castes and are a must for married women. Six or more bangles are worn on each wrist and are only broken off when the husband dies. In Bastar the breaking of a widow's bangles is an important ritual of death. On the procession to the funeral pyre the corpse is laid on the ground and the face uncovered. The widow is then dragged screaming and struggling to the corpse and her bangles broken over the dead man's body. For most women this is the first time in their life that they will be without bangles. Small bangles (usually plastic nowadays) are placed on small baby girls soon after they are born. These are replaced regularly but always in such a way that the arm is never bare. For example if a woman decides to replace her bangles because of wear or because she wants to wear a different colour, the seller will break all but one, fit the new ones, and finally break the last remaining old one. Bangles fit snugly around the wrist and are fitted by the sellers. The hand is squeezed and manipulated to get the bangle on and customers grimace in pain as this done. Many bangles are broken in this process, a cost that is borne by the seller. If a women accidentally happens to break all her bangles in a fall, for example, it is considered inauspicious. She can not go outside her house nor serve food and a glass bangle seller has to be called to refit new ones.

The fact that half the population of India wears a dozen glass bangles that are replaced at least once each year, means that upwards of 6,000 million bangles are produced in India each year. Given that the retail price was six for Rs 1 in 1982, some Rs 1,000 million is spent on them annually. This is big business and big profits are made by the manufacturers and the big wholesalers at the top of the selling pyramid. For those at the bottom of the selling pyramid, however, it is a different story.

Retailers in 1983 bought their bangles at Rs 3 for 24 and sold them at Rs 4 for 24, a gross profit rate of 25%. This is to cover breakages as well as their other costs such as transport. Table V.1 gives some idea of the daily net profit a glass bangle retailer could expect to make in 1982. The data comes from the books of a wholesale merchant and are therefore accurate. I was able spend some time perusing the books of the wholesaler but he was unhappy about my taking notes. I was able to establish, though, that there was no seasonal variation in sales and that these figures are typical of the daily sales of a retail merchant. They also correspond with my direct observations and inquiries made of merchants. Sellers average Rs 37 per day in sales and after cost of sales, transport and breakages they realise a net profit of around Rs 6 per day, or 16%. This compares with a minimum wage of Rs 8 per day.

TABLE V.1   GLASS BANGLE RETAIL MERCHANTS: AVERAGE DAILY SALES AND PROFITS, FEBRUARY 1983

Market	Average daily sales (Rs)	Average net profit* (Rs)
Sunday (Kondagaon)	52	11
Monday (Sampur)	34	5
Tuesday (Bade Kanera)	32	4
Wednesday (Kondagaon)	16	5
Thursday (Mulmula)	19	2
Friday (Amrawati)	31	4
Saturday (Mardapal)	73	8
Overall average	37	6

Note: * After transport costs and breakages

Source: Books of wholesaler, February 1983.

A feature of any trader's income is its variability and a glass bangle trader's income is no exception. As sellers of cultural necessities their income is not subject to seasonal fluctuations. Rather, it depends upon the particular daily market visited and the market's 'hotness' or 'coldness', which is a random factor. Table V.1 shows that the Sunday market at Kondagaon yields the high average daily net profit. This is the biggest market in the region and attracts the highest number of sellers. It is the home market for many sellers, which means of course that transport costs are zero. The Wednesday market at Kondagaon is a very minor affair and is one of the low points of the week for both sellers and buyers. The Mardapal market has the highest average daily sales of any market but this market is 25 miles from Kondagaon and transport costs absorb a significant portion of the gross profit.

As the markets run 'hot' and 'cold', visiting distant markets such as Mardapal involves a certain amount of risk. If the market happens to be 'cold' then a loss is possible. Small merchants must absorb such losses by either reducing their consumption or running down their capital. It is for this reason that glass bangle merchants concentrate on the markets nearest to their home to minimise travelling costs. We find then that they are decentralised relative to the rich Marwari traders. Whereas most of the latter live in Kondagaon the glass bangle sellers live in the four main towns, Kondagaon, Narainpur, Banyagaon and Lanjoda, and work the markets nearest to these towns. This defines four of the overlapping territories as shown in Map V.3. Some Kondagaon-based sellers travel to the distant Orissa markets, Erla, Hirapur, Amrawati. These markets are on consecutive days and traders minimise their transport costs by sleeping in the markets at night. This defines the fifth market area.

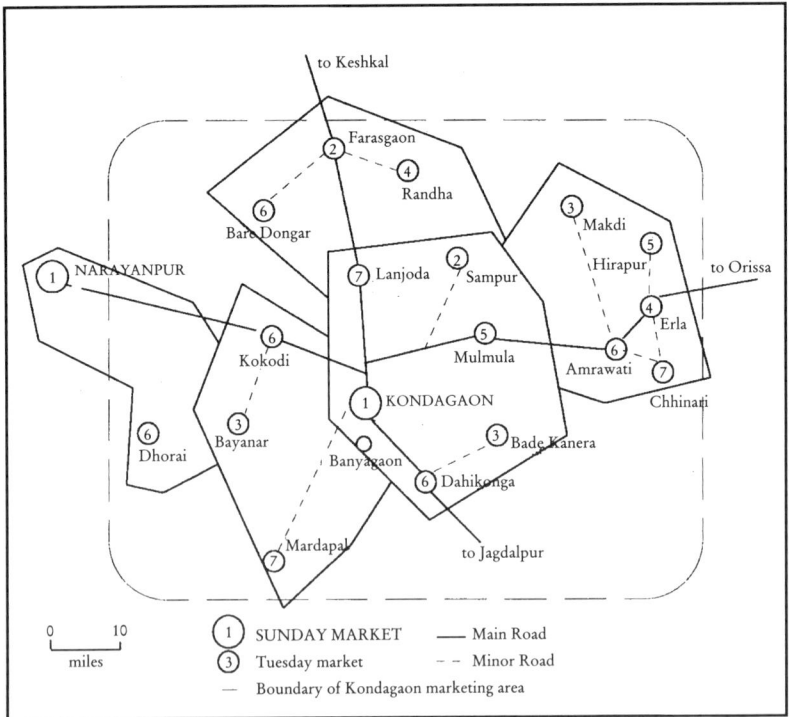

MAP V.3   *Market areas of some glass bangle merchants who travel by public transport*

While the demand for bangles is more or less constant throughout the year, traders do good business on religious holidays, such as *diwali* and *dashera*, and during the *mela* (fair) season which is held during the months of March and April. Every large market place has a *mela* once a year and on these occasions a trader can expect sales in excess of Rs 100. For example, at the Amrawati *mela* a trader had sales of Rs 130, while at the Mardapal *mela* she had sales of Rs 481, giving gross profits of Rs 33 and Rs 120 respectively. Profits of this magnitude are probably only enjoyed by the glass bangle trader a few times each year and represent super profit to her. The Marwari trader, on the other hand, enjoys profit of this magnitude or better most of the year round.

In 1982 glass bangle traders carried a trading stock of between Rs 100 and Rs 1,000, with an average of around Rs 500. All traders aim to carry a large stock of bangles of different size and colours. This is because carefully laid out multicoloured stock attracts customers and hence profits. This is just another way of saying that money makes money and it is a principle that one can observe working in the market every day. At the Bade Kanera market on Monday 18 October 1982, to take one illustrative example, Brij Kumari was sitting next to Shanti Bai. Brij's capital was down to only Rs 300 and consisted of bangles of only three qualities and five colours. These were laid out in front of her in five short columns. Shanti's capital, on the other hand, was worth over Rs 1,000 and consisted of bangles of many qualities and colours. These were laid out in over twenty long columns and made Brij's stock look feeble. The market was 'cold' that day and Brij was anxious to attract more customers. As a potential customer walked past she would attract their attention and harangue them in an attempt to coerce them into buying her stock. Their eyes would quickly pass over Brij's wares and onto Shanti's from whom they usually purchased. Shanti never engaged in verbal battle with Brij. She would, upon catching the eye of a customer, merely raise an eyebrow and draw attention to her larger stock by straightening up the bangles on display. This, along with her attractive stock, was usually enough to seduce the customer.

The operation of this 'money makes money' principle has the effect of reproducing inequalities between traders by making it harder for the poor to improve their position and easier for the better off to improve theirs. The principle also has the effect of reproducing the differentiation between sellers. However a trader's fortunes are not determined solely by market relations. Family, kinship and caste relations play an important role and it is to these that we now turn.

Glass bangle retailing is usually done by women of the Pathari or Muslim caste both of whom are landless. Table V.2. classifies the 29 traders who attend the Kondagaon market by caste and gender. Women account for 73% of the traders. Muslims constitute the largest caste group with 48% of traders belonging to this group. Next comes the Patharis (34%) and the Gonds (18%). Many of the female traders are widows while most of the males are married and work in partnership with their wives. The Muslims are a heterogeneous group whose male ancestors came from different parts of India and married local women. The Patharis are an interrelated group of Tribals from the neighbouring Chhatisgarh region for whom glass bangle selling is an hereditary occupation. The Gonds are landless members of the Bastar Tribal community.

TABLE V.2   GLASS BANGLE RETAIL MERCHANTS:
             NUMBERS BY CASTE AND GENDER

Caste	Male %	Female %	Total %
Pathari	3	7	10
Muslim	3	11	14
Gond	2	3	5
TOTAL	8	21	29

Consider now the case of the Muslim traders. While this group contains a number of people who are related, they have no unity as a group, no territoriality in the sense defined above. The Kondagaon Muslims are from different parts of the country—Punjab, Nagpur, Bihar, Kutch—and many have been in Kondagaon for a number of generations. The original immigrants were usually poor men who came in search of work, married local women and settled. With two or three exceptions, the descendants now belong to the poorer classes of Bastar society. Not being a close knit group there is no pressure on women to observe the purdah regulations demanded by their religion. The principal pressures on women are economic and it is this pressure that has forced many Muslim widows to become bangle traders. When their husbands died they found themselves without means of support for their families. Bangle trading is one of the few avenues of employment open to women.

The Pathari bangle merchants, by way of contrast, are more unified as a group. Consider the case of the three sisters, Brij, Kumla and Kaccheri who were born in Bhanpuri (40 kms from Kondagaon) where, in 1982, their mother and other relations lived and worked as bangle merchants. Brij, of whom mention has already been made above, is the poorest of the three sisters. In 1982 she lived with her husband, five children and daughter-in-law in a small two-roomed rented mud hut in Kondagaon and worked seven days per week. When she attended markets away from Kondagaon, she left home around 8-9 am and returned around 6-8 pm. Her work yielded her around Rs 150–250 per month. Her two rickshaw pulling sons earned about Rs 200–300 per month each, giving a gross family income of around Rs 550–850. Her family ate about 5 *paillis* (9 kg) of rice per day, all of which has to be purchased at a rate of Rs 5 per *pailli*. The monthly rice bill was therefore around Rs 700 which was sometimes in excess of the household income, sometimes below. Both Brij and her sons had irregular incomes and their precarious situation prevented her from accumulating capital. On an average day Brij would bring home Rs 40 from her sales for that day. Of this Rs 30 should have been spent replacing sold stock leaving a gross profit of Rs 10 and a net profit of Rs 6 after transport expenses and breakages, which is sufficient to buy about 1.25 *paillis* of rice. When her sons did not earn enough to purchase the remaining 3.75 *paillis*, she was forced to spend the Rs 30 set a side for stock replacement. This reduced some of her working capital and also her future income for reasons discussed above. This could be offset by buying stock on credit from the wholesaler, which created a debt that had to be repaid. When sales continued to be 'cold' this debt had a tendency to build up as further capital was eaten and more credit capital sought.

A continual run of good sales is needed to eliminate to the debt
and to provide sufficient funds from net profits to build up equity
stock. Such runs are rare and many wholesalers have gone bankrupt
lending to traders such as Brij. Borderline traders like Brij rarely go
out of business because they have nothing to lose. Furthermore, from
their perspective the bankruptcy of a wholesaler is a good thing
because it wipes out their bad debt. Shrewd wholesalers only advance
small funds to traders like Brij and this is one of the reasons why her
capital is so small today. Another source of credit for Brij is her sisters.
Her youngest sister, Kaccheri, is one of the most successful bangle
traders in Kondagaon. This is due, in part, to the fact that her husband
is an educated contractor and earns good money. They have over Rs
2000 of their own money invested in bangles. Their son helps with
the selling on a full-time basis and the husband assists when he has
no contract work. Their relative wealth is obvious from their appearance: the men wear tailored clothes and the women wear relatively
expensive ornaments. Nevertheless, they are still poor relative to the
Marwari traders. Differences in domestic capital, the marker of the
prestige of a family, is an obvious sign of this. Kaccheri, like Brij, lives
in a small mud hut while the Marwari's have invested considerable
sums in brick houses, furniture, milking cows, and the like.

The economic status of the middle sister, Kumla, was mid-way
between Brij and Kaccheri in the early 1980s. She and her husband
earned around Rs 300 per month from bangle selling which gave them
a surplus of around Rs 60 per month after rice purchases. With careful
budgeting, they could usually manage to break even after the purchase
of other necessities. Like Brij they sometimes need credit. They had
a debt of Rs 2,000 to a previous wholesaler who still lives in
Kondagaon. They will never be able to repay this though and it will
probably be written off in the course of time.

Comparing the case histories of these three sisters, then, it is
clear that the nature of one's marriage and the number of sons one
has can affect one's relative status. Kaccheri's educated contractor
husband liberates the household from complete dependence on glass
bangle selling and their policy of educating their children opens up
possibilities that are closed to the illiterate children of the other two
sisters. Sons are something of a double bind: if they can find

employment they boost household income and if not they are a drain on its resources.

The Marwari kinship web is nation-wide and they exercise considerable control over the cloth and jewellery trading network. The Pathari kinship web is only Bastar-wide and they exercise no control over the national trade in glass bangles. They merely specialise in marketing at the very bottom of the selling pyramid. Their kinship network is not simultaneously also a commercial network as it is for the Marwaris. Thus whereas Marwari territoriality offers scope for economic mobility, Pathari territoriality functions to reproduce their relatively disadvantaged position. The Muslims of Bastar who have neither kinship webs nor commercial networks, have even less hope of improving their position. The absence of wide mercantile kinship networks is not to say that individual households have no hope of social mobility, but it does make it exceptionally difficult.

One further factor which makes it difficult for a glass bangle trader to be upwardly mobile is the nature of the product they sell. Glass bangles are the cheapest per unit of all ornaments and the most labour intensive to sell. A silver merchant can sell Rs 1,000 worth of jewellery in less then five minutes but a glass bangle seller would have to work non-stop for hours to sell the equivalent in bangles. In 1982 a single bangle cost Rs 0.16 and, given that it takes between 18 and 20 seconds to fit, the theoretical maximum a seller can earn is around Rs 200–300 per hour. Thus the labour-intensive nature of bangle retailing places a ceiling on potential profit.

Wholesaling glass bangles to retailers is not a very profitable venture either. Bangle traders, as we have seen, are impecunious and prefer to buy from a wholesaler who supplies credit. Competition among wholesalers has sent many wholesalers bankrupt as they overextended credit to capture a larger share of the market. In 1982 the north Bastar market was supplied by two wholesalers. One firm was a long established merchant family with diversified economic interests, the other a young man with a little capital who was trying to establish himself. The latter moved into bangle wholesaling when the established firm, concerned about the large number of outstanding debts, stopped advancing credit to the retail merchants. By offering credit the young man was able to capture the wholesale market. This is shown in Table V.3 which shows the sales figures of the established firm before and after the change in selling policy.

TABLE V.3   GLASS BANGLE WHOLESALER: EFFECT OF
             CREDIT ON SALES

| | Average weekly sales | |
	when credit was given	after credit was stopped
Cash	544	27
Credit	65	–
TOTAL	609	27

Source: Wholesaler's books

Sales dropped from Rs 609 to Rs 27 when credit was refused. Credit sales only amounted to 10% of total sales but as most of these were bad debts the firm was only breaking even because a wholesaler's profit is also around 10%. The new wholesaler had been operating for one year in 1982 and had not as yet gone bankrupt when my main fieldwork was done, but when I returned for a brief visit in 1990 I noticed that he had gone out of business.

THE MARKETING OF 'FANCY GOODS'

The socio-economic structure of the market trade in 'fancy goods' (*manihari*) is similar to that of glass bangle trading. The 'fancy goods' merchant stocks cheap imitation jewellery; items for self-beautification such as cheap powders, creams, combs and mirrors; items for repairing clothes such as pins, needles, cotton and buttons; and other items such as fishing lines, and hooks. Their presence in the market is advertised by the brightly coloured ribbons they have hanging on lines in front of their stalls.

Traders carry a stock valued in 1982 at between Rs 200 to Rs 2000, sales averaged around Rs 40 per day and the mark-up on cost was 33% as it was for glass bangle sellers. The territorial organisation of selling is identical to bangle merchants, being decentralised and divided up into small areas surrounding the major towns. Again like bangle merchants, most 'fancy good' traders come from the neighbouring Chhatisgarh region after the Second World War. There are a few significant differences however. 'Fancy goods' merchants tend to be members of either the Kosaria or Chhatri castes. Members of the former group are predominantly female, while the letter are predominantly males, some of whom own some land.

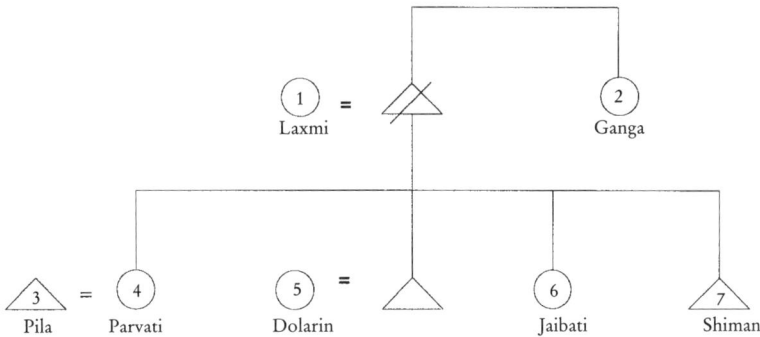

FIGURE V.4   *Kinship relations of seven Kosaria 'fancy goods' merchants*

'Fancy goods' merchants sit together in the market and it is usual to find a line of merchants to be related in some way. Figure V.4 shows the family relations between seven of the merchants at the Bade Dongar market in 1982.

These people all lived at Farasgaon and were all born at Bishrampuri, near Keshkal in Bastar. They belong to a Chhatisgarhi caste called Kosaria. They all visit the same markets but work separately except, of course, for Pila and Parvati, the husband and wife team. They are landless traders and their economic position is similar to the bangle trader cases discussed above. It seems that this caste has specialised in the 'fancy goods' trade because another large group of them live in Orissa and work the markets on that side such as Makdi, Hirapur, and Amrawati.

Pratab Singh and his brother are typical examples of better off traders from the all-male Chhatri group of 'fancy goods' merchants. Their father was born in Raipur and migrated to Kondagaon in the 1950s where Pratab and his brother were born. They have seven acres of land which they work early in the morning before going to the market and in the evening after returning. On occasion, when there is much work to be done on the farm, his wife stands in for him at the Sunday market at Kondagaon. Farmer-traders of these type are quite common among the sellers of groceries and other household items (*kirana*) as we shall see below.

The Chhatris have migrated to Bastar to escape poverty and landlessness in Chhatisgarh. Budh Ram's case (Figure V.5) illustrates this. He and his brother arrived in Kondagaon in 1972 a few years after his uncle Gita and cousin Kamal.

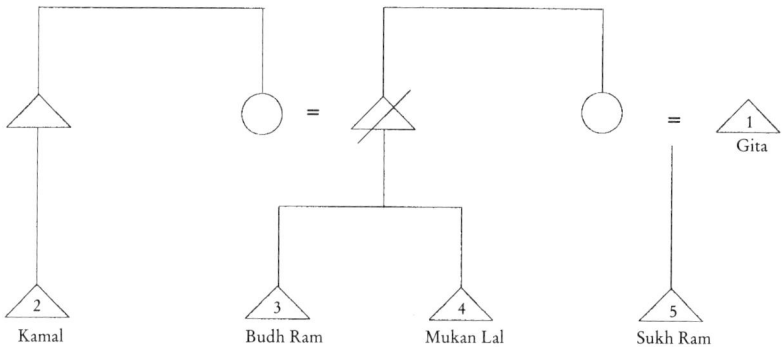

FIGURE V.5   *Kinship relations of five Chhatri 'fancy goods' merchants*

Their father had only seven acres of land in Raipur which was insufficient to support them. They live in Kondagaon with their relations and, in 1982, cycled to Sampur, Mungapadar, Golawand, Bamhni, Dahikonga and Mardapal. Another case is Sukhpal whose family were rendered landless with the development of an irrigation scheme near Dhamtri. Their lands were in the path of a canal and they received no compensation for their fields when they were destroyed. They migrated to Bastar and settled at Dahikonga where they encroached onto some government land. They make ends meet by selling 'fancy goods' at the daily markets.

A number of landless Bastar Tribals have moved into 'fancy goods' retailing. These people are among the poorest of all merchants. One example is Thanwari Bai, a widow. She has two grown-up daughters who are also extremely poor. She lives alone in order not to burden her daughters and survives by selling 'fancy goods'. Her stock, in 1982, was worth only Rs 150-200. From this she earned a monthly income of between Rs 75–100 on which she had to live. She could afford to attend only a few markets. Three of these—Mungapadar, Banyagaon, Dahikonga—are near to her home village and she walked to them. The fourth, the main Sunday market at Kondagaon, had to be reached by bus at a cost of Rs 1.10.

THE MARKETING OF GROCERIES

The third main category of commodities imported into Bastar is groceries *(kirana).* This includes a large heterogeneous collection of household items such as potatoes, onions, turmeric, salt, biscuits, soap, incense, batteries, oils of various kinds, chillis, matches, sugar, tobacco, and betel nut.

The wholesaling of these products is controlled primarily by two immigrant Punjabi families and the retailing is in the hands of a heterogeneous group of people from many different castes. It is difficult to generalise about these market retailers, suffice to say that many are poor farmers who have been forced to diversify their economic activities in order to survive. The wholesaling families provide an interesting contrast because one is wealthy and joint, the other is disjointed and of mixed economic status.

The Punjabi wholesalers—whose joint family relationships are shown in Figure V.6.—are political refuges, who arrived in Bastar penniless in 1950 after Partition. They established businesses in Kondagaon and are now one of the most prosperous families in the town. They have interests in rice mills, land, transport, medical stores and government contracting in addition to their grocery interests. The two main clans *(gottra)* are linked by marriage and the original joint families have been split up and replaced by those shown. The Hanraj family, with seven married brothers, is the largest. Five of the brothers live together in a huge mansion which looks like, and seems to functions like, a hotel. The other two brothers live in Raipur. The eldest brother has supreme authority. Most of the groceries they import come from Raipur and the two brothers live there to handle

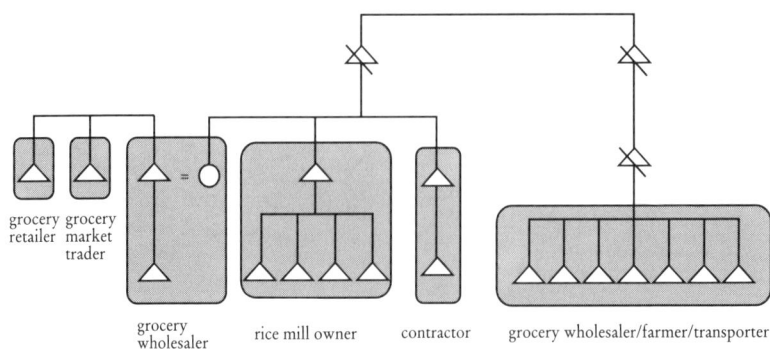

grocery grocery
retailer market
        trader

grocery
wholesaler   rice mill owner   contractor   grocery wholesaler/farmer/transporter

FIGURE V.6   *Kinship relations between some Punjabi business houses of Kondagaon*

this side of the business as well their trucking business. Hanraj and Company do not have a market round. They sell direct from their store in Kondagaon.

The distant markets are all supplied by three brothers from the disjoint Lal family. The age range of the brothers compares with that of the Hansraj family but the price the younger brothers pay for their freedom is high and unequal. Kasturi is the oldest and most successful. He and his sons have a jeep and trailer and visit Farasgaon, Keshkal, Erla, Hirapur and Amrawati where they sell groceries and buy mahua, the flower from which liquor is made. The mahua is subsequently resold at a profit in Kondagaon. His youngest brother, who is not so well off, has a well stocked store in Kondagaon which he closes three days per week to attend the markets. The middle brother just manages to make ends meet by selling oil on the Orissa side markets.

The *territoriality* of the people who sell groceries on the daily markets is very different from that of the cloth and silver traders discussed above. Grocery merchants are usually poor farmers who set up stalls in the market for a couple of days per week in order to make some extra money. They carry capital valued from a few rupees to Rs 1,000 and only go to those markets within walking distance of their villages.

Some of these farmer-traders make relatively good profits. Take, for example, Saligram of the Sahu (oil presser) caste from Badgaon village who sells cooking oil. He farms three days per week (Wednesday, Thursday, Friday), attends three markets on other days during the week (Makdi, Sampur, Katagaon), and visits Kondagaon on Sunday in order to purchase oil. His capital is around Rs 2000 and his sales average Rs 400–500 per market. These are all in cash. His profit rate is 20% giving a gross profit per market of Rs 80-100. On 12 October 1982, for example, his sales were Rs 587, giving a profit of Rs 117. This was just after the wet season and before the harvest. It confirmed his point that oil, being a necessity, is not subject to seasonal variation in demand. Saligram owns a bicycle which he uses to transport his oil from market to market.

Perhaps a more typical example is Sita Ram, a Gond from Aloor. He has eight acres of land, which his son works, plus a trading stock of Rs 500, consisting of biscuits, soaps and assorted sweets. These are packed into a tea-chest which he carries on his back to the six markets in the neighbourhood of his village (see Map V.4). If he is lucky he can earn between Rs 10-50 per market. This is because four of the six markets he visits are very small. Any village in the district has at least two or three daily markets within walking distance. A farmer-trader of his kind who wants to visit only big markets has to become a travelling salesman. This option is not possible for individual farmers such as Sita Ram. However it is possible for groups, as the case of Jala Ram illustrates.

Jala Ram is the senior member of a family group of 10-15 Harijan chilli and garlic sellers who move from one market to another on the Orissa side (see Map V.4). When the big Kondagaon Sunday market is finished, they stock up with enough chillis and garlic to last them a week and head off early on Monday morning to walk to the Sampur Monday market. They carry the loads—anything up to 60 kg—in two big bags suspended from a bamboo stick carried over the shoulder. They sleep at a relative's house near Sampur on Monday night and head off early Tuesday morning for Makdi. On Wednesday morning they go to Erla where they have a base. They walk to the Hirapur, Amrawati and Chhinari markets from here. Early on Sunday morning they return by foot to Kondagaon. In one week, then, they cover 100 miles by foot.

The group are all related to one another and everybody is ranked according to a kinship hierarchy. The numbers in the group

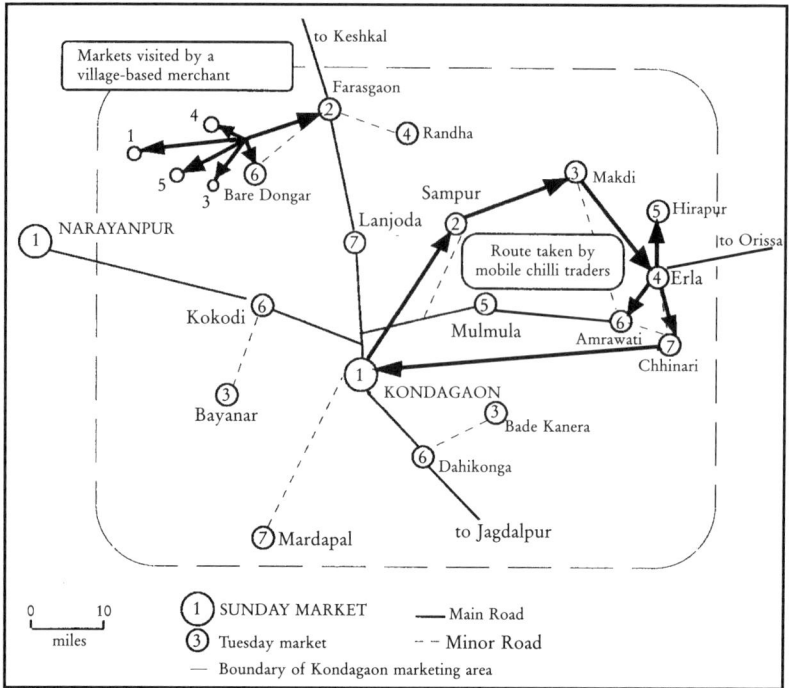

MAP V.4   *Market areas of two merchants who travel by foot*

fluctuate between 10 and 15, depending upon the length of time they have been on the road and the amount of work that needs to be done on their land in neighbouring Raipur District. Each individual spends about nine months per year on the road. There is never a time when they are all at home; their market round is therefore perpetual.

The profitability of this trade is similar to trade in glass bangles and 'fancy goods' discussed above. Chillis are purchased at Rs 3 per kilo and sold at Rs 4–5 per kilo a gross profit mark-up of 30–50%. Sales range from Rs 10–40 per day, giving a gross profit of Rs 5–20 per day per seller. All the profit is given to the senior member of the group who does all the buying and controls the distribution of the money.

The group all sit together in a line at the market and sell their chillies in 'four anna' (Rs 0.25) lots. There is no bargaining but a 'sweetener' is always thrown in as a matter of course. They have no competition from other groups except at Kondagaon where they compete with a group of Bengali traders. The Bengalis are based at Jugani about 12 miles from Kondagaon on the national highway. They are the young sons of refugees who have not been able to make a success of farming. They work the markets up and down the highway which they get to by bus. They also walk to a few interior villages near their home town.

Another important socio-economic group in the market that must be distinguished are the very small scale women traders in groceries. These women travel to two to three markets per week near their village. They spend Rs 20-30 on onions, potatoes, or turmeric and set up shop wherever they can find a spare piece of ground to sit on. They usually travel in family groups and obviously enjoy their day out in the market even though they only make a rupee or two profit. While some of these women are from very poor homes and need the money, the economic motive is not sufficient to explain the existence of this group of traders. It must be remembered that the weekly market is not simply an economic institution, it also has important social functions. For example, because of the patrilocal marriage, sisters tend to be distributed over a much greater territory than brothers. The market therefore provides women with an opportunity to meet on a regular basis. A visit to the market also provides women with a chance to escape from the tedium of the daily domestic labour routine.

Some of these women are contracted to sell salt on a commission basis. Bhadri Bai, a Banjara who lives near Bade Kanera, does this one day per week. Her husband owns three acres of land and the few rupees she earns enables her to buy some provisions at the market. Another woman, whose husband is engaged in his traditional craft occupation of weaving, walks to the three markets nearest her village— Dahikonga, Kanera and Kondagaon—to sell salt. The only barter transactions we witnessed were carried out by these salt sellers. They exchanged 1 *pailli* of rice for 1 *pailli* of *kosra* (akin to rice bubbles). A *pailli* is a unit volume (one litre approx) and all transactions of these small women traders are conducted with this measure.

Not all the items listed as 'groceries' are controlled by the Punjabi wholesalers but the foregoing gives a general picture of the socio-economic structure of the marketing of this diverse category of commodities.

TERRITORIALITY IN COMPARATIVE PERSPECTIVE

Territoriality as a mercantile kinship value is a widespread phenomenon. Its general form is much the same everywhere but local histories give it a particular colour.

Dewey got to the heart of the matter in her pioneering study of rural marketing in Java. She did not use the expression 'territoriality as a value' but her article, 'Trade and Control in Java' (1962b), which was an anthropologically informed critique of the old debate about religion and enterpreneurship, raises all the pertinent theoretical issues. In the Java of the 1950s that she observed mercantile capital had three distinct strata. At the bottom were the Javanese villagers who engaged in small scale trade; next came the Chinese, and to a lesser extent the Arabs and Indians, who dominated the large scale inter-market trade and the import of downwardly mobile manufactures; and at the top were the Europeans who ran the really large economic enterprises. Mercantile stratification of this kind, she noted, is found in parts of Africa and Latin America and people had been apt to explain it in terms of 'primordial cultural patterns'. The key to the relative success of the Chinese, she noted, was the difference in their relationships to the wider world and the quality of their internal relationships. Credit defined the essence of intra Chinese relations, the absence of credit and long term contracts the essence of intra Javanese relations. A Javanese trader working with a minimum of capital and only his own labour, she notes (1962b: 182), cannot compete with the Chinese: 'He cannot borrow money or get credit. He cannot count on the honesty of any other partners he may bring in to augment his capital and labour resources. The Chinese on the other hand can borrow the capital from another Chinese if he does not have it himself.' To understand how something like this comes about, she argues, one must go back into the external and internal history of Chinese settlement in Java. The external history is one of dislike and discrimination: the Indonesian government, for example, has been trying to break their monopoly for years and, in 1959, resorted to ejecting them bodily from the villages and small towns of Java. The internal history is one of boundary maintenance; it tells the story of men who were excluded from community activities because of 'bad' business behaviour.

More recent work on Javanese traders by Alexander[4] (1987) confirms the importance of credit as a marker of mercantile stratification. 'The difference between successful and poor cloth traders,' she argues (1987: 3), 'owes little to marketing skills, shrewdness or tenacity: it is a product of their access to credit, which in turn reflects their class position.' Davis's[5] work in the Philippines (1973) also stresses the importance of credit, of inheritance as a source of trading capital, and of the need to study the history of the social relations of traders.

It would be tedious to cite more examples to illustrate the wisdom that informs Shakespeare's insight into the nature of mercantile capital of the joint family kind. Merchants make a sharp distinction between the values associated with buying, selling, talking and walking and those values that link eating, drinking and praying. The mercantile values—buying cheap and selling dear, creating good customers[6] with talk[7] and sales-credit—are quite distinct from those of territoriality but united as a form of mercantile kinship it creates a very powerful force. But this strength is also mercantile kinship's greatest weakness. The alienating exclusiveness of territoriality breeds resentment of a kind that nationalist political leaders like to exploit for their own advantage. Successful mercantile communities, then, become scapegoats as the history of the Jews in Europe and the Chinese in Southeast Asia reveals. The Marwaris of India have not suffered this fate as yet although their wealth breeds jealousy and malicious gossip.

NOTES

[1] Hazlehurst (1968: 289) makes a distinction between legal credit and social credit. Legal credit is that which is extended to certain citizens of the state because of their status (eg. refugee). Social credit is insider credit. In an open market, for example, the insider will pay less than the publicly agreed price and get his wares on credit while the outsider pays cash at the market price.

[2] Skinner uses central place theory to inform his analysis of rural markets in China. It should be obvious that my notion of territoriality as a value is quite distinct from the market areas of central place theory. Territoriality as a value is a form of consciousness; market areas, by way of contrast, are objectively defined spaces that can be mapped (as illustrated in the maps below).

[3] Alexander (1987: 19) notes that the Chinese in Java 'have a reputation for honesty and straight-dealing' even though the relative wealth of the Chinese raises resentment among the Javanese. Compare Dewey (1962a: 44).

[4] Alexander, following Geertz (1979), is primarily concerned to analyse the market as an institution that structures the flow of information: 'The level of ignorance about everything from product, quality and going prices to market possibilities and production costs,' notes Geertz (1979: 124) 'is very high, and a great deal of the way in which the bazaar is organized and functions (and within it, the ways its various sorts of participants behave) can be interpreted as either an attempt to reduce such ignorance for someone, increase it for someone, or defend someone against it.'

[5] Davis's work addresses the old formalist versus substantivist debate; he interprets social relations of the market in terms of the theory of balanced reciprocity.

[6] A *pratik*, Mintz (1961: 57) notes, is defined as a 'good customer'. 'It means,' an informant told him, 'that you are selling. I come to buy from you each day. I need credit; you sell to me [on credit]; the money is "content" that you sell to me. I always buy from your hand; I pay you well. That means *pratik*.' In the Philippines this is called *suki*: 'But for you says the seller to his *suki*, "the price is only ..." (Davis 1973: 221). The same concept exists in Bastar but if there is a term for it then I missed it. A Hindi-speaking friend from North India was unable to recall a Hindi term for a 'good customer'.

[7] 'My Baniya informants,' writes Fox (1967: 309), 'said that one of the most important if not the most important aspect of good salesmanship is to always "speak sweetly and softly" to the customer, never try to bully him, always attempt to cajole him, and in general make one's own feelings and personality as unobtrusive as possible.'

CHAPTER VI

Usury, Interest and Usance

Shylock. Fair sir, you spet on me wednesday last; you spurned me such a day; another time you call'd me dog; and for these courtesies I'll lend you thus much money?

Antonio. I am as like to call thee so again, to spet on thee again, to spurn thee too. If thou wilt lend this money, lend it not as to thy friends,—for when did friendship take a breed for barren metal of his friend?—but lend it rather to thine enemy; who if he break, thou mayst with better face exact the penalty.

Merchant of Venice

TEMPORALITY AS A VALUE

If territoriality is the value that mediates the buying cheap here and selling dear there of mercantile capitalism, then temporality is the human value that links the money of today (M) with the larger amount it begets tomorrow (M'). The difference between M' and M is the hated offspring of money, the 'bastard child'[1] whose begetter has aroused moral indignation since time immemorial.[2] The 'usurer is most rightly hated,' says Aristotle (quoted in Marx, 1867: 162), 'because money itself is the source of gain, and is not used for the purposes for which it was invented. For it originated in the exchange of commodities, but interest makes money out of money, more money. Hence its name *tokos* (interest and offspring). For the begotten are like those who beget them. But interest is the money of money, so that of all the modes of living, this is the most contrary to Nature.' The Indian Laws of Manu define usury as money lending above a stipulated rate which was two parts in the hundred per month if the borrower was a Brahman, three parts in the hundred per month for a member of the warrior caste, four for a merchant and five for a Sudra. Usury is a sin on a par with defiling a damsel, breaking a vow, selling a tank, a garden, one's wife, or child; loss of caste is the punishment (Mueller, 1979: XI, 62). Usury, says Marx (1894: 595), 'attaches itself like a parasite' to a rural society and makes it wretched: 'it sucks out its blood, enervates it and compels reproduction to proceed under ever more pitiable conditions'.

Values of this kind inform much current thinking about rural money lending in places like India. A distinction is made between 'modern' urban based systems of bank lending where the market forces keep interest rates low and a 'backward', isolated, rural based system where 'personal values' rule to keep interest rates high and collateral undervalued. The latter, which is defined as usury, is seen as bad. Usury is seen as highly exploitative because the function of the ruinously high interest rates is to enable the usurer to accumulate assets via the transfer of undervalued collateral brought about by large scale default (Bhaduri, 1993: 16). Bank lending at competitive rates of interest, by way of contrast, is seen as progressive because it can alleviate poverty by financing the development of the productive forces. Aristotle, Manu, Marx and Friedman all seem to agree on this much; so too do twentieth century Marxists and World Bank economists.

This argument is a powerful one. It occupies the high moral ground and has the backing of authorities from the left and the right. However, morality and authority do not necessarily make good anthropology, especially when the theories of moral authorities are accepted uncritically. Money lenders are notoriously secretive in their dealings and detailed ethnographic studies of village money lending practices are rare.[3] In the absence of reliable data, abstract theories that bear no correspondence to reality have multiplied to fill the vacuum. Village-based money lenders do have power and wealth but this is never absolute. Borrowers may suffer in their hands but they are not passive victims. Furthermore, bank lending at low rates of interest can, as we shall see, also bring about the transfer of highly valued collateral and impoverish the poor.

But the major problem with this generally accepted theory is its quantitative approach to the notion of temporality. The problem to be explained is posed in quantitative-value terms and this begs an answer that must be given in like terms. For example, the question 'Why are interest *rates* on money in rural areas so *high*?' presupposes that rural money lending involves quantifiable *rates* and that these are *high* relative to urban rates. However, if one looks carefully at actual cases of village money lending it is clear that they divide into three broad categories: those that make *explicit* reference to an interest rate, those that contain *implicit* reference to an interest rate, and those for which the notion of an interest rate is *unmeaning*. For the third kind of money lending, then, it makes no sense to talk about a *high* rate of interest because the notion of *rate of interest* is just not there to be found. As it happens, this is the most important form of money lending in Bastar because it involves borrowing against land. This is not a 'tribal' form of money lending that can be explained away with reference to the culturally specific conditions found in Bastar; it is a general form that has been unnoticed by observers who tend to reduce these three forms to the first. I will call the third form of money lending by the ancient term *usance*[4] and argue that it needs to be distinguished from *usury* and *interest*.

Lending at exceptionally high interest rates (*usury*) does exist in Bastar but it is relatively unimportant in that it never involves land so far as I am aware. For example, there is a particularly shady character in Kondagaon who fits all the stereotypes of a usurer. He is an outsider to the district. In 1983 he had advanced Rs 120,000 in loans at three different rates. The first, expressed as Rs 3 per Rs 100 per month, an implicit *simple* interest rate of 36%, is given to anyone prepared to deposit gold or silver jewellery as collateral. This rate is within the legal limit even though the lender himself is not licensed. The second, at a cost of Rs 10 per month (120%) is extended to those in public service employment who do not have collateral. The third, Rs 20 per month (240%), is extended to card players and other gamblers. While many farmers would be willing to borrow from this man at 36% using silver as collateral, not one farmer has taken out a loan at 240% using land as collateral. Even if the lender was asked for money against a loan of this kind it is highly unlikely that he would extend credit to a farmer against a parcel of land in a village miles from a market town. What would the farmer do with it when he got it? How would he farm it? Most farmland has little value as a *commodity* and no value as a *good* to a person like him.

Lenders and borrowers in rural areas understand the household politics of lending against silver, labour and land very well. The challenge for the observer is to suspend one's sense of moral outrage, to listen carefully to the stories that lenders and borrowers tell, and to pose anew the question of temporality as a value. I will do this by means of a comparative analysis of the lending practices of the World Bank and the village money lenders in Bastar. Given the complexity of the subject, I limit myself, in the main, to an analysis of those loans involving arable land. My aim, as usual, is to develop some generalisations by examining this particular case in comparative perspective.

WORLD BANK LENDING IN BASTAR

The World Bank has played a major role in the promotion of capitalist development in Asia in the past two decades. In the agricultural sector it has been active since 1966 in extending medium term and long term loans to small farmers. The aim of this strategy has been to ensure the success of the green revolution by strengthening the rural banking system. This has involved, among other things, the extension of massive credit assistance at favourable rates of interest to small farmers. The rationale for this policy is to enable them to adopt new production techniques that will increase their efficiency and help them escape the clutches of the traditional village money lender.

An important World Bank project implemented in Bastar in the mid 1970s was the Land Mortgage Bank (LMB). This is an all-India wide institution set up to provide long term loans (7–15 years) for farmers to purchase expensive capital equipment such as tubewells, tractors, diesel and electric pumps. Its function was seen to be distinct from the central co-operative bank which provides short term loans (maximum 5 years) for less expensive items such as fertilisers, seeds, repairs to fields, and so on. An assumption behind the LMB loans was that they would allow farmers to increase productivity and hence provide them with a surplus to repay the loan. To assist poor farmers, and especially those of Tribal or Harijan background, a subsidy is given in the form of a direct grant from the government towards the initial cost of the item purchased. In the case of Tribals and Harijans with less than 30 acres of land the grant is 80% of the initial cost; non-Tribals with less than 5 acres, 50%; those with between 5–10 acres, 33%; while farmers with more than 10 acres receive no subsidy.

In spite of these rather generous subsidies the project has been a failure. In the Kondagaon Tahsil, 499 loans were granted over the period 1976–1981. Only 23 of these have been closed through repayment of the loan. Eighteen accounts were closed by sale of mortgaged land. Of the 458 accounts outstanding, 195 (45%) are in default. Fifty four of these defaulters have their land mortgaged and will almost certainly lose it; the remainder will lose essential moveable property (eg. cattle) making it virtually impossible for them to farm.

The Land Mortgage Bank, then, had consequences precisely the opposite to those intended. Instead of abolishing poverty the institution has become the single most important cause of landlessness in Bastar and has been responsible for an upsurge of village-based money lending.

The Bastar experience is not an isolated case. An anthropologist working in a village in Andhra Pradesh gave the following account of the operation of the Land Mortgage Bank in that district.

> In 1975–76, funds for irrigation projects for scheduled tribals were released through a credit institution called the Land Mortgage Bank (LMB) ... Under this scheme thirteen cultivators in the village of Ginnedhari were persuaded to take loans varying from Rs 1,500 to Rs 6,000 (this compares with an estimated income from an average land holding of eleven acres of Rs 3,000 in a good year). All the thirteen had to pay the junior officials of the Land Mortgage Bank between Rs 100 and Rs 200 to have their applications processed. Finally the loans were sanctioned and, without supervision, each person was given the money. Two of the applicants had bad harvests that year and used all the money for household expenses. Eight of them started work on

digging wells. In two cases they ran out of cash before reaching water. In five cases they reached water but failed to line the well, either due to lack of funds or due to an inability to get cement, so that in the next monsoon season the well caved in. Only in one case was the well successful, but even then it was not deep enough to store sufficient water to actually irrigate a crop, though the well has subsequently been deepened and is operating. One person built a small dam across a stream to irrigate a small garden, but he had mixed the mortar incorrectly, and the dam was swept away in the rains. Another built a small earthen barrage dam to irrigate one acre of paddy, but the barrage overflowed, was destroyed, and swept the soil off the levelled paddy fields. The last two applicants purchased diesel engines to lift water from perennial streams, but one was delivered incomplete and unusable, while the other broke down after three week's work, and the owner was unable to repair it. Due to lack of supervision and to expecting people to adopt a technology of which they had no previous experience, all but one of the projects failed, and the other was successful only because the cultivator put considerable personal investment into it. However, the tragedy was that next year the LMB officials came to collect the first instalments on the repayment. All the cultivators understood that the government would take their land until they repaid their debt. Here there appears to have been a lack of communication. As a result of this, the applicant who had made a success began his repayment, one applicant sold two acres of paddy land and paid off his debts in full, and four others mortgaged their land to moneylenders at vastly inflated interest rates and paid off the loans in full. The two with pumps had rusting remains confiscated for auction and were told that the outstanding debt would be collected next year, and the next absconded temporarily but subsequently had all his household brassware confiscated until he attended the bank to settle the claim. Basically, twelve out of the thirteen were harmed by the development loans granted to them. The government target for distribution of loans was reached, but subsequently all the unpaid loans were annihilated by the government, and no increase of irrigated land was achieved at all. The scheme was thus considered a failure by the development office (Yorke, 1982: 232).

These findings have been quoted at length because they illustrate in a very concrete way a number of features about the operation of the World Bank, which, I would hypothesise, are common throughout rural[5] areas of the Third World:

1. Poor farmers are unable to increase their productivity with the new capital. As a result they are unable to generate the extra income needed to meet their repayments.
2. In order to raise the money needed to repay their loans they must borrow from a village money lender or face the prospect of having their mortgaged property confiscated.
3. The inability of the farmer to repay their loans is not seen as the fault of the World Bank or of the theories that inform their actions. In some cases nature is at fault for not supplying enough rain at the critical times. In other cases it is the petty bureaucrats who jeopardise the projects through corruption and inadequate supervision. The inability of farmers to learn how to use the new technology is yet another factor.

The theoretical basis for the World Bank model has been developed by economists such as T. W. Schultz, a Nobel prize winner and follower of Milton Friedman. In his influential book *Transforming Traditional Agriculture* Schultz advances a very simple technical explanation for poverty:

> Thus, in sum and substance, the man who is bound by traditional agriculture cannot produce much food no matter how rich the land. Thrift and work are not enough to overcome the niggardliness of this type of agriculture. To produce an abundance of farm products requires that the farmer has access to and has the skill and knowledge to use what science knows about soils, plants, animals and machines. To command farmers to increase production is doomed to failure even though they have access to knowledge. Instead an approach that provides incentives and rewards to farmers is required. The knowledge that makes the transformation possible is a form of capital, which entails investment—investment not only in material inputs in which a part of this knowledge is embedded but importantly also investment in farm people (Schultz, 1964: 206–207).

Thus for Schultz and for the World Bank strategists poverty is due to a lack of capital, both material and human, and the prescription for the alleviation of poverty is free market capitalism's rewards and incentives. In particular, the development of free competitive money markets in rural areas will give 'traditional' farmers access to that capital they need to help them escape from poverty.

The paradox is that the World Bank could just as readily have used Marx's or Lenin's theory of agrarian transition to justify their policies because both Marx and Lenin saw the development of capitalism in agriculture as 'progressive' (Lenin, 1899: 595).

VILLAGE MONEY LENDING IN BASTAR

Money lending is neither good nor bad; theories of value judge it so. For some people debt has been the source of great wealth and prosperity while for others it has been the source of great poverty and misery. What is crucial for understanding the social consequences of indebtedness is the nature of the power relationship between the borrower and lender. If the power relationship is unequal then obviously the potential for the exploitative use of the debt relationship is much greater than if the transactors are from the same class. Other relevant factors to consider in a comparative analysis of money lending are the social forces that motivate lender and borrower, the nature of the security offered and the sanctions available to the lender.

Jewellery, labour and land are the main forms of collateral offered in rural areas and the principles governing the lending and borrowing of money vary accordingly. In the so-called 'semi-feudal' states like Bihar where landlordism is predominant, labour is the only collateral many borrowers can offer. This creates the phenomenon of 'bonded labour'. In regions like Bastar, where smallholder proprietorship of land parcels predominates, village money lending of this type is rare. As there is no economically dominant household, lending tends to be done by a variety of people and land, rather than labour, is used as security for the loans.[6]

Notwithstanding these important differences, the social forces that motivate borrowers to seek loans are similar in both cases. Village households need to reproduce themselves and this requires people to spend large sums of money on life cycle rituals such as marriages and

funerals, and the problem of finding money for these purposes is a
central preoccupation. For example a quantitative study from Bihar
on debt bondage showed that marriage and funeral expenses
accounted for 51% of loans, consumption 17%, and illness and
medical treatment 12% (Mundle, 1979: 108). My own data from
Bastar is consistent with these findings.

From the perspective of the World Bank this type of borrowing and lending is unproductive. Their agents such as the Land
Mortgage Bank will only give loans for the purchase of material inputs
into the production process. However, as we have seen, there is little
demand for this type of loan among villagers. The small scattered plots
of land they farm require few material inputs apart from seed, ploughs
and working cattle and most farmers manage to get access to these
inputs without having to rely on money lenders. We have a paradox,
then: World Bank institutions have ample supplies of money for
purposes for which there is little demand. They are therefore faced
with the problem of creating a demand for the commodity they have
for sale. Enter the development bureaucrat whose job it is to act as
salesman for the World Bank. They persuade villagers to take loans
by creating unrealistic expectations about the benefits to be had from
an investment in new productive capital. For villagers with very small
holdings there is the added attraction that a significant proportion of
the loan is an outright grant. Those who take the bait more often than
not find themselves caught in a trap from which there is no escape
except to landlessness and poverty. But my data shows that this does
not happen with village money lending even though land is used as
security. This fact seems to deny western economic logic. How is it
that loans for non-productive purposes are able to be repaid while
loans for productive capital are not? The reason is that village money
lending is not subject to the laws of interest bearing capital and the
state; village money lending is based on quite different principles and
these are best grasped by considering an actual example.

> Ghasu, a member of the Herdsman caste, lives with his wife and
> two unmarried sons. He has 5.93 acres of land consisting of three
> scattered plots: plot A measures 3.30 acres; plot B 1.88 acres; and
> plot C 0.75 acres. This land is insufficient to support his family
> and they rely on seasonal day-labouring to balance the house-

hold budget. Ghasu was forced to take out two loans. The first was a consumption loan for Rs 200 cash and use-rights in half of plot C (0.30 acres) was surrendered to the lender for eight years in exchange. At the end of this period the loan was deemed to be repaid. Ghasu's second loan was for Rs 1,000 to finance his eldest son's wedding. Use-rights to plot B was surrendered for five years in exchange. The lender in this case was Lalu, of the Gond Tribe, who owns 33 acres of land which he works on a joint household basis with his three younger brothers.

This example illustrates a number of general points about money lending amongst smallholders. Firstly there is no rigid class difference between borrower and lender. Nevertheless the lender in this case is better off than the borrower. Lalu's joint household is able to produce just enough rice to meet its consumption needs whereas Ghasu's household has a rice deficit for about three months of the year. In land ownership terms there are important differences too. But Lalu's joint household will eventually divide when his younger brothers marry and have children. When the inevitable division takes place what is now a 'rich' household of 33 acres will become four 'poor' households each with 8 acres of land. Secondly, the borrower needed the money for consumption purposes to cover the costs of his son's wedding, the usual purposes for which loans are sought by villagers. Thirdly, the contract involves an exchange of money for land rather than money for money. Time is involved in the exchange but the deal is expressed in terms of rent on land rather than interest on money. In other words village money lending contracts of this type involve no interest. Fourthly, the borrower loses temporary use-rights to the mortgaged property for the duration of the contract.[7] This differs from bank lending where the borrower loses absolute property but only in the event of default in repayments.

The latter two points are related and are the central defining characteristics of village money lending among household proprietors of land parcels. From the perspective of the lender the contract can be analysed as a tenancy agreement. He gets land for which he pays all his rent in advance. The money borrower is therefore acting as a landlord and the money lender as a tenant. In money lending contracts of this type then, the borrower *receives rent* in advance; he does not *pay interest*. The cost to the borrower is the loss of the use of a productive asset for the duration of the contract. Money lending contracts in class-based villages are similar in that the principle of interest does not apply. However, as borrowers have no property they are forced to mortgage their labour in exchange for money. From the perspective of the lender—usually the landlord—the contract can be analysed as a wage-labour contract with the difference that all wages are paid in advance. Thus the borrower *receives wages* in advance, as it were; he does not *pay interest*. The cost to the borrower is the surrender of his (or her) freedom to the landlord for the duration of the contract; the wage rate struck may also be to the borrower's disadvantage.

Bank money lending is radically different from village money lending in that it is governed by the principles of interest bearing capital which means that unpaid debt grows at a compound rate. For capitalist farmers whose average rate of profit typically exceeds the rate of interest, repaying institutional loans presents few problems. (But a prolonged drought can bankrupt them as the Australian experience shows.) A capitalist farmer will not take out a loan for productive capital unless the expected profit from the capital is in excess of the interest. For the farmer with a small holding of scattered plots, whose profit rate is zero or negative, exposure to the laws of interest bearing capital is a disaster. Consider the following example.

> Budhu was persuaded by a development official to borrow Rs 2,500 in 1973 at 9% interest to build a well. It was repayable at a rate of Rs 389 per year for ten years with a 3% penalty rate of interest. His land—ten acres consisting of five plots—was mortgaged. He was unable to make any payments in 1974 and 1975 due to poor rainfall in those years. In 1976, following a good harvest, he repaid Rs 1,013 in 1977, Rs 855 in 1978, Rs 242 nothing in 1979, and Rs 295 in 1980. The Bank was unhappy with his irregular repayments and auctioned off his land for Rs 3,220 to a wealthy merchant. Despite having paid off Rs 2,405 he still owed Rs 1,479 of his principal. This along with Rs 345 in penalty interest and fees, was deducted from the receipts of Rs 3,220, leaving him with Rs 1,396 cash in hand but landless.

With village money lending the contract is a social relation and an obviously exploitative one when labour is the security. But with institutional money lending the relationship between people is mediated by the mystical form of the compound interest formula, $M' = (1 + r)^n M$, where r is the rate of interest, n the number of years, M the size of the money borrowed today, and M' the size of the money to be repaid. Thus money appears to breed money without the need for one class of people to exploit another. Unpaid debt breeds in this expanded way too. If the debits and credits of a borrower's account get too far out of balance the rules of the institution are enforced by petty bureaucrats who are just as much the victims of this commodity fetishism as are the borrowers. This was brought home to me whilst I was conducting an interview with a Land Mortgage Bank official in his office in Kondagaon. Our interview was interrupted by the appearance of a client, a middle-aged village woman. Her husband had borrowed Rs 5,000 against seven acres of land some seven years previously. No repayments were made and the debt now stood in excess of Rs 10,000. The woman had come to the office because her husband had run away and she had been served notice that her land, which provided minimal subsistence for her and her children, was to be auctioned to repay the debt. The woman wanted to renegotiate the loan but was unable to offer any collateral. The bank officer, who was not unsympathetic to her case, patiently explained that there was nothing he could do except enforce the order. After some thirty minutes of heated discussion she was escorted from the office sobbing and in a state of great emotional distress.

Behind the fetishism of interest bearing capital is the awesome power of capital which, in this particular case, assumes the form of the Indian state and the World Bank. They enforce the market discipline and redistribute the property of the poor farmer to the rich. In the case of Budhu they did this by forcing him to sell his land on the market. It should be noted that in the state of Madhya Pradesh a law exists preventing the transfer of land from a person of Tribal status to a non-Tribal person. This restriction does not apply to institutions like the Land Mortgage Bank who are able to sell mortgaged land to recover dues. Thus the Land Mortgage Bank provides the only legal avenue for merchants and capitalist farmers to acquire land from the 'scheduled tribes' of Bastar.

The only option facing the villager who borrows from institutions when he runs into trouble is to reschedule the debt by borrowing from a village money lender. The following is an example of a farmer who adopted this strategy.

> Garanju is a member of the Gond Tribe and farms seven acres of land with his three unmarried sons. In 1980 he purchased two ploughing buffaloes for Rs 1,000. He paid Rs 400 deposit and borrowed the remaining Rs 600 from the State Bank of India. The buffaloes died not long after he purchased them and he was forced to hire buffaloes from his neighbour to plough his fields. He found himself unable to repay his loan and after three years his debt grew to Rs 755. He borrowed Rs 800 from Haroon Khan in exchange for eight years' use of two acres of land.

By renegotiating his loan in this way Garanju has traded the permanent loss of some of his land for the temporary loss of it to a neighbour. This option is only open to people who borrow modest amounts. With big loans worth several years purchase of annual income no one would be in a position to take on the debt.

The conclusion that emerges from this comparison is that while village money lending may reproduce economic inequalities it does not, in general, create landlessness.[8] By giving loans for marriages and consumption it also facilitates the social reproduction of village households. In the case of landless labourers village money lending creates and recreates exploitative bonded labour relations; with poor farmers it converts borrowers into temporary landlords. The money borrowers receive can be likened either to wages or rent in advance; the compound interest formula does not enter into the calculations of the amount of money to be given and received. World Bank lending, on the other hand, usually converts poor farmers into landless labourers. It does this by giving loans only for purposes of capital investment. Borrowers of these loans are charged a market rate of interest which requires the farmers to earn a rate of profit in excess of this if they are to repay their loans. In other words, the logic of interest bearing capital is imposed on poor farmers whose profit rate is zero or negative, which means that they are rarely able to repay their loans. Many lose their land as a consequence, but fortunately only a small number of villagers have taken out Bank loans of this kind. Village money lending is still the most popular form. It is unlikely that this kind of lending will ever be eliminated while ever the system of household proprietorship of land parcels continues to exists. This is because village money lending for the purposes of household reproduction complements, rather than contradicts, bank lending for the purposes of productive investment.

BASTAR MONEY LENDING IN COMPARATIVE PERSPECTIVE

Village money lending in Bastar is not a culturally specific aberration. All the forms of lending identified by Jain in his *Indigenous Banking in India* (1929: 55ff) are to be found here. However, when one is generalising care must be made to compare the concrete practices rather than the language. This is because the one term can have two quite different meanings in different parts of the country. For example, Jain defines *girwin* as the lending of money against gold and silver ornaments (1929: 66). In Bastar the cognate term *girwi* is used to describe something quite different, the lending of money against land of the type discussed above. Jain also discusses this form of lending which he calls *rahan*. He notes that *rahan* is a common method of lending and that it consists of two types. The first is where land is mortgaged but possession is not given to the mortgagee. The second he calls *usufructuary mortgage* where 'the borrower makes over a part of his property, which is occupied by the creditor, who receives the profits therefrom as interest, so land as the principal is not repaid.' Borrowing of this type is called *sudbharna* in Bihar (Rajesh Raj, pers. comm.). The land pledged literally 'stands in' (*bharna*) for interest (*sud*). In some cases, Raj adds, the 'interest' referred to can be for a different loan altogether. This happens in Bastar too as the case of Garanju above illustrates. The land can also stand in for the total amount of the loan as the cases from Bastar illustrate. Pledge taking of this kind is very common. Bailey (1957: 283) reports its existence in Orissa and notes that when 'A pledges a field to B, A receives a sum of money and B has the use of the land for at least one harvest and for all subsequent years until A repays the money.' 'The debt,' he adds, 'may last through generations.' Jacobson (1976: 169) reports that villagers in Madhya

Pradesh have been engaging in pledges of this kind in order to obtain funds for investment in stone quarries noting that 'it may jeapardize the income of the landowner for a year or two but does not itself involve the risk of losing the land'. It also can be found it places outside India. Hill (1982: 214ff) finds similarity between the systems that operate in South India and Nigeria, noting that village-generated credit is often cheaper and far less exploitative than the urban-based kind. 'According to medieval custom and law,' notes Jones (1989: 68), 'a mortgage could be used to raise money, but it meant that the lender took possession of the property mortgaged, promising to return it to the borrower if the loan was repaid. For the lender this was highly advantageous, since he was left in possession of the property, enjoying its fruits without the bother of collecting illegal interest.'

Jain's 'usufructuary mortgage' is an apt term because it suggests that *usance* rather than *interest rate* is the essence of loans of this type. *Usance* is an archaic term but is one, I believe, that needs to be rehabilitated if village money lending is to be understood. *Usance* is not *interest* although the difference is a fine one. Land, for example, has immediate use-in-exchange for money from the lender's perspective; from the borrower's perspective it is the other way around. There is no *interest* involved here because heterogenous commodities are involved and the temporal nature of this exchange makes it impossible to reduce them to a common measure. One could translate the land use into a money equivalent but money does not have an invariable value over time as we shall see in the following chapters.

The notion of *usance* enables us to grasp the essence of the many forms of village money lending. Take loans in kind for example. A farmer who needs grain for consumption or seed takes it as a loan from a village money lender contracting to repay it up to twice over at harvest time. Thus he is getting the use of grain today in exchange for the non-use of some of tomorrow's production. The lender, for his part, exchanges the non-use of some grain today for the use of a larger amount tomorrow. The lender receives a mutually agreed *gain* which has both an absolute qualitative value (so much grain) and a relative quantitative value (two for one). In this case the *rate of usance* (two for one after harvest) implies a *rate of interest;* its calculation requires the specification of an exact *time period* before it becomes meaningful. One cannot assume that time is a *quantifiable* variable in village money transactions. For example the rate of usance is often the same for a loan given six months before harvest as it is for one given six days before harvest. As Polly Hill (1986: 88) notes, it is 'very often inappropriate for outsiders to think in terms of interest *rates*, both because borrowing is apt to be timeless (interest rates are never computed) and again, because of the attitude to default. From the creditor's angle the important question is not how long the debt has been outstanding but the prospects of repayment; as for the debtor, his usual concern is to repay as slowly as possible without incurring his creditor's final displeasure, and maybe to borrow more when his debt has diminished sufficiently'.

The notion of *usance*, then, raises the question of the politics of temporal relations between people, ie. of *temporality* as a value. Formally, the problem can be stated as follows: the borrower exchanges the use of X today for the non-use of Y tomorrow while the lender exchanges the non-use of X today for the use of Y tomorrow. *Temporality* is the value that gives X and Y their qualitative and quantitative form. As such it is a value that has its origins in the historically contingent relationship between the lender and the borrower. Temporality, as a reciprocally recognised relationship between lender and borrower, determines the language used to describe the transaction—use? interest? usury?—and values it as good or bad.

Temporality is a human value that has assumed a limited number of historical forms. Conceptually it is *territoriality* turned inside out. If rich merchants maintain their internal cohesion by a form of solidarity that binds consanguinity to contiguity by means of the endogamous exchange of mercantile credit, they simultaneously exclude others by means of the extension of credit, be it in the form of credit-sales or money lending at interest. From the perspective of the receiver of the latter, the lender is always an outsider and, more often than not, a hated one who has to be tolerated.

The stereotype of the greedy money lender is as much due to the discontent of elite borrower as it is the subaltern borrower. Shylock, we must not forget, tried to extract his pound of flesh from a rich merchant of Venice. Ben Jonson echoed the common opinion of the time that usurers were 'base rogues that undo young gentlemen', a sentiment immortalised in the proverb that 'Usurers live by the fall of heirs, as swine by the dropping of acorns' (Jones, 1989: 45). Consider the case of Lord Dudley. He succeeded to his title in 1586 when he was twenty years old. He proceeded to buy velvet, silk and other wares appropriate to someone of his station. The mercer sold them on credit at interest against a bond. Later Dudley purchased more wares from the mercer on the same terms. When he was unable to meet the payment the mercer extended further credit but with better assurance. The original debt of £500 now stood at £1000. When he was unable to pay this the mercer took him to court where Dudley was able to escape impoverishment because he was able to show that he was not of age when he entered the contract (Jones, 1989: 69).

The idea that money lending is 'bad' while banking credit is 'good' is a value that must be situated in the context of the development of capitalism in England in the sixteenth and seventeenth centuries and the relationship between theology, law and economy. Jones's fascinating study of this question shows that a revolution in values occurred between the 1571 *Act Against Usury* and the acts that were introduced between then and 1624. Sin was internalised by theologians who were invited to stay out of politics and deal only with individuals, not communities. 'A result,' argues Jones (1989: 204), 'was the birth of economics as a distinct system of thought and the establishment of secular criteria for the management of the nation's economy. It also meant that theology was no longer expected to pronounce on the morality of the communal economy.' Another result of this emerging value system was the arrival, some 350 years later, of the World Bank in Bastar.

There is no evidence that World Bank type lending is positively valued by the subalterns in Bastar, certainly not by those who have been impoverished by it. Their attitude to non-professional village money lenders, on the other hand, is sometimes positive. To understand this paradox it is necessary to look a little more closely at the status of village money lenders.

In all the examples I have collected, the lender is invariably a relatively wealthy person and often an outsider. The biggest money

lender in Minipur village, for example, is a Muslim money lender
called Khan who took up residence in a neighbouring village in 1977.
He purchased three acres of land and is a small time grain merchant.
He ingratiated himself to the village headman of Minipur by lending
him Rs 275 so that he could met some marriage expenses of his son.
The headman pledged 1/2 acre of arable for four years as payment
of the loan. He has also lent money on contracts like this to other
members of the village. Khan's aim is to become a farmer and to settle
in the area. He is eager to obtain community acceptance and the
usance quality of his money deals work to the mutual advantage of
all concerned. Sita Ram is the next biggest money lender in the village.
Like Khan, he is an outsider who is slowly working his way into the
village community. He was given permission to purchase some land
in the village and to marry a village women from the Gardener caste.
While this marriage gave him a measure of access to the Minipur
village community it did not give him access to the much bigger inter-
village Gardener caste community, to the contrary, his wife was
outcasted for having married him. He has financed a number of other
weddings against the security of land which have been judged 'fair'
by all concerned. I also have cases of money lending between different
castes in the village but none between members of the same caste. No
doubt some instances could be found of 'unfair' lending of this type
but I found none. Furthermore, the uncertain value of the future
produce from pledged farmland can never assure the lender of a
certain gain. Indeed, the system works because fine grained economic
calculation is impossible and obvious gains and losses only apparent
in the extreme cases.

The Marwaris, whose wealth makes that of lenders like Khan
and Ram seem totally insignificant, never engage in lending of this
money-for-land kind. They advance money today in exchange for
more money tomorrow against the security of gold and silver
jewellery; they also sell on credit to regular customers. Land may be
the *supreme good* for the farmer but not for the merchant. Jewellery
is the ideal security because, from the merchant's perspective, it is the
supreme commodity. Indian Jewellery is renowned for the purity of
the gold and silver from which it is made. Furthermore, the Bombay
prices of these precious metals, as we will see in Chapter VIII, climb

steadily at a rate that is independent of world market forces. As such, they constitute the supreme standard of value for a merchant, for no other standard, be it a commodity or paper money, has such an outstanding track record. For the householder, on the other hand, gold and silver jewellery is a valued *good* not a *commodity* and is the most valued keepsake after land. (Merchant households value their own jewellery this way too; it is only the keepsakes of others in their possession that is seen as the supreme commodity.) Jewellery is to women as land is to men in India and the distinction between these two goods tells us much about gender relations within the family as Jacobson (1976) has demonstrated. It suffices to reaffirm Jacobson's observation that 'the ornamented woman symbolises auspiciousness and prosperity, while a woman naked of jewelry represents poverty and sorrow' (1976: 133). To surrender a keepsake of this kind to a money lender is to place its goodness in jeopardy because it gives the money lender potential rights of alienation in the event of default. This does not happen when land is ceded on a temporary basis to a village money lender. Goods, as we have seen, have an emotive value and the temporary conversion of goods into money on the part of a borrower always involves shame of some kind. It is this, rather than the absolute size of an implicit rate of interest, that excites the passions of borrowers. What is at stake then is more the politics of prestige than the economics of monetary calculation, although the primacy of the former does not rule out the significance of the latter.

My observations on this type of lending are consistent, in general terms, with the picture given by Jones (1991). He managed to obtain access to the books of two Jain shopkeeper-money lenders in a small town in Rajasthan. He found that credit was only advanced to local customers who were regulars at this store; money lending against silver jewellery, by way of contrast, was mainly made to people from villagers outside the town. 'It is noticeable,' he notes (1991: 127), that no Jains and no Brahmans within Chandrapur have borrowed money on this basis. To do so would involve 'loss of face' for the families in these two communities.' Customers who want money of this kind can borrow up to 30% of the scrap value of the silver left as security. A rate of Rs 3 per month per Rs 100 is charged. Most of the loans are small short term loans for consumption purposes such as marriage costs, hospital costs, etc. Bad debt on credit sales is a big problem for these shopkeepers. Again, the bad debts are for small amounts but the large number of them add up to a substantial amount of money. The shopkeepers like to lend additional money against jewellery to these people so that they have some power over them. Thus, when a loan is paid off the shopkeeper will refuse to return the security until the customer's sales account is cleared.

Strategies like this are followed by rich Marwari merchants/money lenders all over India and this, along with their aloofness and obvious wealth, does not endear them to the locals who make a distinction between the calculating strategies of the Marwaris with their *usance rates* and the friendly practices of 'insiders' such as Khan who provide *usance* without the rates. The elite lenders and the subaltern borrowers are not indifferent to one another; to the contrary, they reciprocally recognise the alienated nature of their relationship by means of mutually agreed contracts. Silent recognition is also made of the imbalance in prestige the relation implies: the quantitative gain enjoyed by the lender is matched by a qualitative loss for the borrower who receives cash in exchange for shame. As mutually recognised aliens they develop a pragmatic tolerance for each other that may last for generations without major problems. However, in times of insurgency a different reckoning is made and the Marwaris are often singled out for special treatment. As the Deccan Riots Commission observed: 'where ... Brahmans and other castes shared the money lending business with the Marwaris it was usual to find that the latter only were molested' (quoted in Guha, 1983a: 304). Thus in times like this the contradiction between the *goods* of the subaltern householder and the *money* of the merchant explodes and *temporality*, as a value, assumes the 'supreme' physical form of a pound of the money lender's flesh. The rebellious Santals, for example (Guha, 1983a: 164), settled their accounts by chopping off the offending limb of a landlord or money lender ('With those offending fingers you counted your interest and ill-gotten wealth'). Given that corrupt forest guards in Bastar have already felt the force of this logic, one seems justified in predicting that officials in the World Bank's Land Mortgage Bank will feel it too if their lending policies continue to create landlessness. The World Bank's money-lending practices may be labelled *interest* and judged 'good' by economists but from the borrowers point of view it is *usury*. This subaltern valuation corresponds to an ancient definition of usury which held that it 'occurred only when the lender was guaranteed a profit without regard to the borrower's risk' (Jones, 1989: 4).

NOTES

1   The Bishop of Bangor used this expression when preaching about the sin of covetousness in 1610. See Jones (1989: 153).

2   The equivocation in Deuteronomy (23: 19-20), which holds that one can lend to an Other but not a Brother, has been the subject of debate for centuries. See Nelson (1969).

3   Vatuk & Vatuk (1971) describe a secret, no-interest women's system of private banking. They argue that it is common but that there are few references to it. They also note that the rationale for systems of this type run counter to the explicit ideology of the joint family.

4   'But whatsoever the matter is, the more that men have been in love with the thing it self, the more have they purposely declined and avoided this name. They will not call it *usurie* lest the word should be offensive, or make the thing odious. But it shall be termed *use* or *usance in exchange*, which are smooth words as oil, never a biting letter in them. Or it shall be called *interest*, or *consideration*, which are civil and mannerly terms, though by that they mean nothing else but plain *usurie*' (Fenton, 1611: 4).

5   Poor people in urban areas who borrow from banks suffer in the same way too it seems. A study of bank loans to poor women in Bombay found that programs targeted for self employed poor women 'may actually benefit various intermediaries as much (or more than) they benefit the women themselves' (Everett and Savara, 1984: 290).

6   I have restricted myself to a consideration of loans that use land and labour as collateral. Loans involving paddy and jewellery are also very important in agrarian societies (see Jacobson, 1976; Harriss, 1982: 188ff). These different kinds of loans, Bailey (1964: 113) has noted, are governed by different kinds of behaviour.

7   Transactions of this type have been described by Jacobson (1976: 169, fn. 17) and Bailey (1964). The latter argues that the creditor's 'use of the land represents the interest on the sum borrowed' (1964: 111). However, as the computation of interest necessarily involves the transaction of like-for-like over time,—eg., grain for grain or money for money—it seems to me that use of this concept to describe an unlike-for-unlike transaction is inappropriate. Polly Hill argues that it is 'very often inappropriate for

outsiders to think in terms of interest rates, both because borrowing is apt to be timeless (interest rates are never computed) and, again, because of the attitude to default' (1986: 88).

8 Compare Hill: 'It is mistaken to assume that such borrowing and lending as takes place within a village community necessarily enhances inequality (it may indeed reduce it), or is bound to be "bad" for some other reason' (1986: 83).

CHAPTER VII

Domesticated Money

In the beginning of the world we had the forge and we forged things, we had weaving-looms and we wove our clothes, we had oracle huts where we consulted the oracle, and we had boats from which we caught fish. We had no guns. We had no cowrie money *(akwá)*. If you went to the market you took beans in order to exchange them for sweet potatoes. You exchanged something specific for something else. Then the king brought the cowrie money. What did the king do in order to bring the cowrie money? He caught people and broke their legs and their arms. Then he built a hut in a banana plantation, put the people in it, and fed them bananas until they became big and fat. The king killed the people and he gave orders to his servants to attach strings to their bodies and to throw them into the sea where the cowrie-shells *(akwá)* lived. When the cowrie-shells started to eat the corpses they pulled them in, collected the shells, and put the live cowries in hot water to kill them. That is how cowrie money came to exist. This cowrie money was white like our maize and we called it 'white-corn-money' *(akwé-kún-wéé)* in order to distinguish it from other forms of money. The French came to break this country before they came to bring their metal-money *(gàn-kwé)*. The other money of the French is called paper-money *(biyéé)*.

Klikpo Cece, Ayou Hannya, Benin[1].

COWRIE-SHELL MONEY AND COLONIAL CONQUEST: THE PROBLEM

If the problem of understanding the process by which a commodity acquires value is difficult enough, then the question of the process by which money acquires value is a degree of

233

magnitude more so; and when the money in question is in the form of cowrie-shells, one of the few forms of money that quite literally grows, the problem acquires yet another twist.

But what, precisely, is the problem? It is most emphatically not the hoary old definitional question of whether or not cowries can function as money. This problem has been laid to rest by the meticulous historical work of Hogendorn and Johnson (1986) in their *The Shell Money of the Slave Trade*. Not only used by the slave traders to buy slaves, cowries were also used by the villagers of West Africa as a medium of exchange in their periodic markets. Comparative historical and ethnographic evidence from India and Papua New Guinea[2] suggests that the story that Hogendorn and Johnson tell is not restricted to the particular case of West Africa. This evidence also confirms another important observation by Hogendorn and Johnson: cowries can also be used in bridewealth exchanges, as jewelry, as decorations for clothes, as counters in games, as gifts, and so on.

The problem to be addressed—and here credit must be given to Hogendorn and Johnson for posing it so clearly—is that of explaining the cowrie-shell bubble that occurred in the early stages of the direct colonial conquest of Africa. Put simply the question is this: What is the relationship between the massive import of shells into Africa and the subsequent hyper-inflation and demonetisation of the cowrie? This question, I will show, is a general one. The same phenomenon occurred in India and Papua New Guinea (among other places) in the early phases of colonisation. Although Hogendorn and Johnson do not concern themselves with the general problem, their answer is in very general terms. Like many others who have tackled this issue, they have found the seductive explanatory power of the quantity theory of money too hard to resist. This theory, whose chief exponent these days is the Nobel-prize winning economist, Milton Friedman (1987), not only has academic authority on its side, it seems to be self-evidently true in the case of the cowrie-shell bubbles. In all three cases hyper-inflation followed a massive increase in the quantity of shells. The evidence for their case seems to be watertight, as I hope to show in the first part of this chapter.

As the myth by Klikpo Cece above suggests, villagers in West Africa have their own story to tell. The central message of this myth is plain and clear: The elders of Ayou Hannya village, as if aware that anthropologists have a tendency to over-interpret myth and thereby to miss its simple message, made a point of telling Elwert (1989: 25) that the kings of Dahomey were not their beloved rulers and that the reason for the violence and cruelty of these rulers was their sheer quest for wealth. Elwert notes that behind the symbolic language of Cece's myth is a very realistic interpretation of the economic history of the kingdom of Dahomey and a treatise on money which differs from that of the king's; the myth has many other meanings too, argues Elwert, because the thriftiness of mythical language means that myth can work more efficiently than handbooks and dictionaries as a means of storing information and as a means of evoking emotion.

Stories such as Cece's myth, then, are full of thought-provoking wisdom rather than truth, containing overtones of meaning that resonate sympathetically in the ears of the initiated listener. Although they are not in the form of clearly articulated theories that can be objectively tested, these resonances are not completely esoteric either because the thoughts of an outsider can be stimulated by stories of this kind. When they are situated anthropologically, historically, and geographically, stories like this can be read as archives on the human condition that give figurative expression to unresolved antagonisms.[3] I see in the thoughts of Cece and other people like him the elements of a general criticism of the quantity theory of money. It suggests to me that money is a standard of value created by a state (be it a divine kingship as in Dahomey or an imperial nation-state like France), that it also an instrument of the power of a king over his subjects and an instrument of the power of the imperial state. The theoretical problem that cowrie money poses, then, involves understanding the contradictions among the money-value systems of the imperial state (symbolised in Cece's myth by the metal and paper money of the French), the money value system of the indigenous elite (symbolised by the cowrie money 'caught' by the king through the sacrifice of his subjects), and the values of the subalterns for whom the things produced and exchanged by the labour of farmers and artisans is valued more highly than the inhuman mercantile dealings of a brutal king and his trading partners from over the seas. This perspective raises the question of the *quality* of money and throws the self-evident truths of the quantity theory of money into doubt as will be seen in the second half of this paper. My starting point is the economic history of the shell money of the West African slave trade.

THE SHELL MONEY OF THE SLAVE TRADE[4]

The trade in shell money began in the fourteenth century and was finished by the 1880s. The structure and volume of trade changed greatly over this period, but its efflorescence was in the era of European mercantile imperialism: the end of the trade coincided with the emergence of capitalist imperialism and the scramble for the territories of Africa, Asia and the Pacific. The Maldives, a 475-mile-long stretch of nineteen atolls some 400 miles due west of Colombo in the Indian Ocean, were the basis of the whole system. Here cowrie shells (*Cypraea moneta*), in the form of small live gastropods, are prolific breeders. These shells were harvested and traded to every corner of the globe. West Africa, where the gastropods did not breed, was the ultimate destination for many of the shells, although India, and especially Bengal and Orissa, was another major user of them.

Ecology and economy motivated the commerce in shells. The Maldivians traded shells for rice and other commodities with the Bengalis, who used the shells as currency for petty transactions and other purposes. European merchants, in turn, purchased them from Indian merchants and carried them back to Europe, where they were sold at a profit. Those purchasing the shells in Europe were slave traders who carried them to West Africa as capital to buy slaves. There the shells were absorbed into the West African economies and used for a variety of purposes, the most important of which was as a medium of exchange for small transactions.

The eighteenth century was a prosperous one for the cowrie trade because this was when the Atlantic slave trade was at its peak. The Dutch dominated the cowrie trade until 1750. Thereafter, the proportion of shells traded by the Dutch dropped steadily, falling to zero in 1796 when the Great European War ruined Dutch commerce. The English controlled the trade until 1807, when the abolition of the legitimate slave trade rendered the system unprofitable. Statistics collated by Hogendorn and Johnson (1986: 58) reveal that during the period between 1700 and 1790 some 11,436 metric tonnes of shells were shipped to West Africa by the Dutch and English, equivalent to the staggering figure of 10 billion individual shells.

The nineteenth century was one of boom and bust for the international cowrie trade; it was also one of privatisation and fierce competition because the East India Company lost its monopoly in 1813. The abolition of the slave trade caused a temporary slump in the legs of the cowrie trade going between India and Europe and between Europe and Africa. Its revival was brought about by the growth of palm oil exports from West Africa. Great quantities of cowrie shells were needed to buy the palm oil, which was used in Europe as a lubricant to grease the wheels of the emerging capitalist industrial enterprises and as the chief ingredient of soap to clean the grime of newly invented machines from the bodies and clothes of the working classes. The cowrie trade entered an unprecedented expansion in the 1840s. Records were repeatedly broken, and the high levels of production led to concerns about overfishing. In 1840, for example, the British exported some 205 metric tonnes of cowries to West Africa; in 1845 an all-time high of 569 metric tonnes was exported.

The final phase of the shell trade was the period between 1851 and 1869, when five private German and French companies captured the trade and shipped over 35,000 tonnes (14 billion shells) directly to West Africa. This frenzied trade exploded the cowrie bubble, dropping the price of shells dramatically, making trade unprofitable, and stopping shipments. The beginning of this final phase saw the end of the Maldivian cowrie (*C. moneta*) and the temporary rise of the Zanzibar cowrie (*C. annulus*), a slightly larger cowrie that yielded a merchant's profit of 1,100 percent compared to a meagre 100 percent for the Maldivian cowrie.

The end of the international trade in cowries also marked the virtual end of their domestic circulation in West Africa, although it took some fifty years before they disappeared from circulation completely (Ofonagoro, 1979). Many shells, it seems, were buried underground in hoards, ready to be used again when their value recovered. The Nupe must have thought this day had come when their ethnographer, S. F. Nadel, arrived. He asked to be shown some cowries and was told that they were no longer in use and not available; when he said that he was prepared to pay for them, large baskets full suddenly turned up and he had to do his best not be inundated with them (Nadel, 1942: 310).

Two theoretical questions are posed from this narrative: What principles govern the emergence and explosion of shell bubbles? What are the implications of this for the theory of value in general and the theory of money and the gift in particular? Hogendorn and Johnson have a very definite point of view on both of these questions and it is worth quoting them at length for their position raises a number of general issues:

> The cowrie could very well serve as an object lesson in a money and banking class today. Dramatically and convincingly, near the end of its life as a working money it suffered a hyperinflation that demonstrates nicely the wide application of both the Quantity Theory of Money and Gresham's Law. The Quantity Theory of Irving Fisher states that the stock of money (M) multiplied by the number of times that money is spent each year (velocity, V) must equal the annual value of all transactions, PQ, where Q is the number of transactions and P is the average price level. $MV = PQ$. When an economy is growing, Q rises and therefore, with V relatively constant, the stock of money M can also rise without affecting the level of prices. But should M expand much more rapidly than Q, the theory predicts the likelihood of rises in P, i.e. inflation. The cowrie currency conforms to the prediction of this theory remarkably well. As long as the small shells from the atolls of the Maldives were the only ones imported to West Africa (true for half a millenium at least), the limited growth rate in M did not significantly outrun the growth of the domestic economy, so that the value of the cowrie remained relatively stable. But when the East African variety of the cowrie suddenly was poured into West Africa by European traders in the years after 1845... it generated hyper-inflation that ultimately destroyed the usefulness of the shell money standard (which by that time was mainly associated with palm-oil trade, and not with slaving). At the same time, Gresham's Law—'bad money drives out the good'—was in full operation. The East African shells were much cheaper than the smaller variety produced in the Maldives; wherever they proved acceptable, they were paid out by the importing merchants to the

point that the shells from the atolls virtually disappeared in some areas.

The great cowrie inflation was not the only example of a 'primitive' money badly depreciated by oversupply; the copper and brass currencies of Africa were much eroded by improved manufacturing techniques in Europe, and similar advances in the fabrication of wampum beads ruined that famous American Indian currency. But the cowrie inflation is best documented, and demonstrates clearly how Fisher's rule and Gresham's Law both apply in a world far removed from the coins, paper, and bank deposits for which they were formulated (Hogendorn and Johnson, 1986: 3–4).

The implications of this argument for the theory of gift exchange are spelt out in a lengthy footnote in which the West Africans are described as 'intensely commercial':

> The substantivist school of anthropologists has sometimes written of the cowrie as a 'special purpose money,' governed by principles of reciprocity, redistribution, and ritual. It is true that very late in the life of the cowrie currency it did survive for a few more years as a means of making ritual payment. For most of its life, however, any argument that the shells were a traditional special purpose money is untenable (Hogendorn and Johnson, 1986: 1,fn.2).

The analysis of Hogendorn and Johnson is one of many studies that have used Fisher's Rule and Gresham's Law to explain the end of cowrie currencies in Africa, India, Papua New Guinea (PNG), and other places.[5] But what sets this analysis apart from all others is the fact that it is by far the best documented and most convincing treatment of the subject. Hogendorn and Johnson have introduced the skills of the professional historian into the debate and have combed the archives for data in a way that few others have done.

It is also important to note that Hogendorn and Johnson have identified an important general problem—the phenomenon of the shell bubble in early colonial history—that needs to be explained. Anthropologists have a tendency to problematise difference rather than similarity and are reluctant to accept, for example, that the economic history of PNG has anything in common with West Africa. It is true that there are a great many differences between the early

colonial period of the PNG highlands (1930–60) and the slave trade
of West Africa, but these differences are defined only by the remarkable similarities between the two cases. The meticulous archival
and fieldwork research of Hughes (1977, 1978) establishes beyond any
doubt that a shell money bubble developed and exploded in PNG
during the period between 1930 and 1960.

Hughes shows, for example, that cowries, both *C. moneta* and
C. annulus, were traded up into the highlands where they were used
extensively for a variety of purposes, including that of a medium of
exchange. Other shells traded into the region included the dog whelk
(*Nassa*), the goldlip pearl oyster (*Pinctada maxima*), the baler (*Mela
aethiopicus*), the green snail (*Turbo marmoratus*), the egg 'cowrie'
(*Ovula ovum*), the Leopard cone (*Conus Leopardus*), and five others
of lesser significance. In the period just prior to colonisation, cowries
and dog-whelk shells were the most numerous and widely spread of
the eight main kinds of shells and, as a consequence, had the lowest
relative value. From the archaeological evidence it is known that shells
have been used in the area for at least 6,000 years and possibly longer.
Trade in shells in the highlands, then, is of great antiquity; but we know
little about it, save that shells were bartered up to the highlands from
the north and south coasts without the intervention of professional
traders, merchants, or itinerant peddlers. Most of the supplies of
common shells came from the north coast, reflecting, in part, the
natural distribution of the species. However, there were apparently no
specialist centres of the Maldivian-type. Australian gold miners first
visiting the area in the 1930s discovered that they could use the shells
to hire workers and buy food. These transactions brought about many
radical changes to the volume and structure of the indigenous exchange
system, introducing a merchant capital component into the system
because the miners bought shells cheap on the coast, brought them to
the highlands by air freight, and sold them dear in exchange for the
commodities they wanted. The miners used cowries to purchase
vegetable foods, sex, and daily labour and purchased bigger items with
the more valuable shells where they were current. Needless to say, the
trade in shells boomed, and the quantity of shells available in the
highlands multiplied at a geometric rate. Between the establishment
of the Mount Hagen base in 1933 and 1940 up to ten million shells

were imported into the highlands. The war interrupted the flow of shells, but after the war they were flown in in even greater numbers. Complete statistics are not available but some idea of the magnitude of the trade can be gleaned from the fact that in the six month period September 1952 and February 1953 some 20 million dog-whelk shells were distributed from the Goroka base. This shell bubble, like the one in Africa, burst at different rates in different places and with differing local implications. They ceased to be used by the white colonisers after the 1960s to buy food and labour but today, like the African and Indian cowries, can still be found in some places. The evidence from India, which I shall make no attempt to summarise here, is yet a third variation on this general theme. The examples can be multiplied, and credit must be given to Hogendorn and Johnson for identifying this important general theme in the history of the use of shell money.

Another important point that Hogendorn and Johnson establish is that anthropologists are amateurs when it comes to the craft of history. By and large, the theories of the anthropologists who have tried to explain the historical relationship between metallic monies and shell monies in terms of novel anthropological theories have not performed well. These theories are logically satisfactory but historically unsatisfactory. Consider the case of Bohannan (1959), whose influential 'spheres of exchange' theory, has been the subject of a telling critique by the historian, D. C. Dorward (1976).

Bohannan (1959: 124) notes that if 'we take no more than three major money uses—payment, standard and means of exchange—we find that in many primitive societies as well as in some ancient empires, one object may serve one money use while another object serves another money use'. Bohannan characterises these economies as 'multi-centric' and the 'modern' European one as 'uni-centric'; these economies, he argues, use 'special-purpose money' and 'general-purpose money' respectively. The Tiv economy of West Africa, argues Bohannan, contained three spheres. The first sphere was associated with subsistence and was governed by the 'morality of the free and uncontrolled market' (1959:125). The second sphere was a prestige sphere in no way associated with markets. Only certain ritual objects—slaves, cattle, *tugudu* cloth, brass rods—circulated within this sphere. The third sphere was supreme and contained only one item: rights in human beings other than slaves, particularly women. Its values were expressed in terms of kinship and marriage. With the spread of the world market and the introduction of general-purpose money, argues Bohannan, the multi-centric economy of the Tiv was flattened and transformed into a uni-centric one. Another almost identical version of this theory, I was surprised to discover recently, was independently invented by Keynes (1982) in the late 1920s but not published until 1982. Keynes developed his theory from a study of the ancient Greek empire and expressed his theory in the language of multiple 'standards of value' rather than multiple 'spheres of exchange'.

The substance of Dorward's critique of Bohannan is that he did not have access to, or was unaware of, the relevant documentation and that he relied too heavily on oral evidence. Dorward proceeds to present a wealth of new evidence that is damaging to Bohannan's case. He shows, for example, that *tugudu* cloth was a general-purpose, not a special-purpose, form of money and that, because of his preoccupation with the subsistence economy, Bohannan failed to grasp the significance of the craft industry and the web of commerce in which the Tiv were caught up. Dorward's alternative explanation is a particular illustration of the general theme developed by Hogendorn and Johnson: When the colonial government began to demand payment of taxes in their own metallic currencies Gresham's Law came into operation, and bad money (European coinage) began driving out good money (Tiv cloth currency) (Dorward, 1976: 590).

The answer to the question posed above—what was the impact of European coinage on non-European economies using cowries?— seems to be obvious in the light of the latest historical evidence: Cowries disappeared due to the operation of Fisher's Rule (the quantity theory of money) and Gresham's Law. This conclusion would not surprise Milton Friedman, who has won a Nobel prize for his theoretical contributions to the quantity theory of money. Given the superlative academic prestige of this theory and the overwhelming weight of the supporting historical evidence, it seems ridiculous to suggest that this theory is obviously wrong. However, as I suggested in the introduction above, there is a subalternate point of view which is also obviously right. Before I can present this opposing view, a brief theoretical interlude on the question of power is necessary.

INTERLUDE: THE LOGIC OF POWER

The thought of people such as Klipko Cece, whose version of the cowrie-shell trade in West Africa heads this chapter, is a particular illustration what of Guha (1983a) calls the 'logic of a subaltern consciousness'. This is a form of *political* consciousness, a rival cognition that questions the violence and cruelty of unloved rulers. When Cece's story is read as a *political* tale of monetary conquest and as one that views this history from below, it poses the question of the political status of the quantity theory of money. Is this a theory which describes and interprets events from above, from below, or from afar? The evidence would seem to favour the latter view. The quantity theory has all the attributes of an objective scientific theory. Hogendorn and Johnson's approach, for example, is that of disinterested social scientists. They offer a compelling general explanation for the West African cowrie-shell bubble that applies to the case of India and PNG, and this explanation cannot be linked in any simple-minded way with the interests of the slave traders and the colonial state. Nevertheless, the fact that conquest involves the exercise of raw power does raise the question of the explanatory adequacy of a theory of monetary conquest that abstracts from power relations and makes no attempt to give the native point of view.[6]

Getting access to the native point of view poses special problems for the historian because such things are not the stuff of which archives are made. But Guha's method of inferring the voice of the Indian peasant from the language of the elite opens up new avenues of research for the historian and anthropologist, and his myth-as-archive thesis is an invitation for anthropologists to look anew at the content of many a myth. This is what I have tried to do with the myth by Cece, a member of the Ayizo people, who were at one time sold as slaves and who were, in another period, forced to serve without compensation in the king's slave-raiding army. This story acquires a new saliency when seen in the light of some evidence from Melanesia. Here, European conquest is a relatively recent event, and ethnographers have been able to record the memories of the people involved. These data are fragmentary and, by themselves, of limited use. However, if this evidence from PNG is seen in the comparative light of Cece's tale and located in the context of a theory of power that identifies and inverts the central assumptions of the quantity theory, then a subalternate theory can be constructed by teasing out the generalisations that dwell in every specific instance. Such an exercise must, of necessity, be based on inference; and the conclusions, questionable. However, my aim is not to produce a theory that replaces the quantity theory but, rather, to produce an argument that can stand beside it and raise doubts about its objectivity and explanatory adequacy.

My starting point is the theory of power developed by Guha (1989: 229ff). Power, notes Guha, is a general relation of domination (D) and subordination (S). In its most brutal form, power is a relation of killer to killed, as Cece's myth illustrates. The logic of power is such that, once one side of the relation is identified, the other follows as a logical consequence. This oppositional logic is that of privation rather than axiomatic contradiction: black versus white rather than black versus non-black, to use the analogous logic of colour. This logic is perfectly general, but the actual history of conquest is the outcome of an interplay between the D/S relation and its constituent elements—coercion, persuasion, collaboration, and resistance—which imply each other contingently. It follows, therefore, that the black-and-white contrast between D and S defines a grey area whose limits are set by the antagonistic contradiction between coercion and resistance at one extreme and the non-antagonistic contradiction between persuasion and collaboration at the other. The history of conquest, to pursue the colour metaphor further, gives this general conception of power its unique coloration. Here the primary colours correspond to the political culture of the conquerors and are opposed to the secondaries, representing the culture of the colonised. These primary colours create contrasting hues which complement and harmonise beautifully here and clash and contrast in an ugly way there. Every colonial encounter is a unique creation of these constituent elements. In colonial India, for example, British liberal political culture was expressed in an idiom defined by the terms Order, Improvement, Obedience, and Rightful Dissent corresponding to Coercion, Persuasion, Collaboration, and Resistance respectively. The Indian idiom, derived from its pre-colonial, semi-feudal culture, was expressed in the language of Danda,

Dharma, Bhakti, and Dharmic Protest. Thus, the conquest of India must be understood not as a simple opposition of D to S but in terms of a matrix of constituent elements of the following kind.

Power in general	Constituent elements of power in general	British paradigm of power	Indian paradigm of power
Domination	Coercion	Order	Danda
	Persuasion	Improvement	Dharma
Subordination	Collaboration	Obedience	Bhakti
	Resistance	Rightful Dissent	Dharmic Protest

Guha, the historian, uses this matrix in much the same way that the artist uses the logic of the colour cube to think about paint when mixing and applying them to the canvas.[7] Just as the logic of the colour cube reveals the elementary oppositions behind the complex phenomenon of colour, this matrix helps one grasp the phenomenon of the British conquest of India in all its simple complexity. But just as knowledge of the logic of the colour cube does not make one an artist, knowledge of this theory of power does not make an historian. Thus, Guha's theory of power is not a model that can be mechanically applied. Rather, it serves to focus one's attention on the contradictions and paradoxes of colonialism and to pose questions that are derived from the D/S relation. To give some examples noted by Guha (1989: 272): Why was a democratic Britain happy to preside over a state without citizenship? Why was a vision of Improvement on capitalist lines implemented by means of a neo-feudal system of property? Why, on the side of the indigenous elite, was the leadership of the bourgeoisie resolute in its defence of landlordism? Why, on the side of the subaltern, was the peasant rebel's vision of God a white man who writes like a court clerk? For Guha these questions are the offspring of one central paradox, the coexistence of two paradigms as the determinants of political culture; for him 'the question that calls for an answer is: why two paradigms and not just one?' (1989: 272).

A SUBALTERNATE QUALITY THEORY OF MONEY

The implication of Guha's theory of power is that, whatever the merits the quantity theory of money has in explaining the impact of coins on economies using cowries, another perspective exists. As a starting point it is necessary to adopt the temporary working hypothesis that the quantity theory of money is yet another form of bourgeois knowledge, that it is elitist in Guha's sense of the term. The legitimacy of associating the quantity theory of money with a superaltern imperial idiom can then be tested by inverting the central tenets of the theory and by grounding the resultant propositions historically and comparatively.

The existence of a superalternate quantity theory of money, MV = PQ, in which money prices are held to be determined by the supply of money when velocity is constant, presupposes the existence of a subalternate quality theory of money where money prices are determined by the demand for money when velocity is constant. The basic idea here is extremely simple; the only difficulty lies in the habits of thought that govern everyday thinking about money, one of the most used and least understood symbols ever invented by *Homo sapiens*. A simple example can clarify the point I want to make. Suppose a consumer buys bread to the value of $10 from a baker and that the baker uses the same $10 note to buy flour from a miller. In this case, the quantity of money is ten dollars (M = $10), the velocity of money is two (V = 2) and the total value[8] of transactions is $20 (PQ = $20). Substituting these values in the quantity equation, MV = PQ, gives $10 × 2 = $20. The next step is to conceive of money (M) as a commodity with its own price (quality) and quantity. In this case we have:

$$M = \text{price of money} \times \text{quantity of money}.$$

But what meaning can we give to a notion like 'the price of money'. In this example the price of money must be equal to one (1). This is because money conceived of as a commodity is $10 and the quantity of money is also $10 which means that the price of money must be one (M = 10 = 1 × 10). The price of money, then, is another way of talking about what is called the standard of value. For money to perform this function efficiently the standard must be kept constant. But whose standard is to do the measuring, how is it to be kept constant, and what are the implications of all of this? An analysis of the following truncated version of Cece's myth can help us answer this question.

> We had no cowrie money. If you went to the market you took beans in order to exchange them for sweet potatoes. You exchanged something specific for something else. Then the king brought the cowrie money [by selling slaves to overseas merchants]... The French came to break this country before they came to bring their metal-money.

We had no cowrie money. If you went to the market you took beans in order to exchange them for sweet potatoes. You exchanged something specific for something else. Prior to the existence of cowrie money there was no money standard: One commodity (C), such as beans, was exchanged for another commodity (C), such as sweet potatoes, and indigenous standards of weights and measures provided the means by which the exchange-value of one commodity was measured in terms of the other. Marx (1867: Ch. 1) called this exchange of one commodity for another the 'the relative form of value' and gave it the general symbolic form C-C. Suppose, for the sake of exposition, the standard was weight and the unit was kilograms. In this case prices would assume the form of, say, 1 kg rice equals 5 kgs sweet potatoes. The ethnographic reality was no doubt more complicated. If my fieldwork experience in India is anything to go by, it probably involved mixed standards of volume such as, one tin of rice of this size equals one basket of sweet potatoes of that size, in which the sizes of the 'standard' tin and the basket varied from market to market and over time. Exchange-values of the C-C form are implicit in any market and are revealed by lifting away the 'veil' of money.[9] The process by which these relative values are established is the most controversial subject in the history of political economy, but, as the full version of Cece's myth suggests, labour and technology must obviously be central to any explanation. Neither the quantity of money nor its quality has a role to play in the determination of the exchange values of commodities.[10]

Then the king brought the cowrie money. Money, as Cece quite rightly suggests, is the creation of kings; it is their standard of value. Marx (1867: Ch. 3), by contrast, assumes 'for the sake of simplicity, gold as the money commodity'. This counterfactual assumption has given birth to the idea that there is such a thing as a commodity money that can exist independently of the state. The historical fact is, however, that kings created money by fixing the prices of special commodities such as gold, silver and cowrie shells, or by placing a stamp on a piece of metal or paper. This act of state power creates a new standard of money value which the agents of the state are employed to maintain. The result in Dahomey was prices in the form of, say, one tin of rice = 3 *kan* (string) of cowries, in which the *kan* was the standard required by a law of the king to contain 40 cowries on a threaded string. In Whydah, the official whose responsibility it was to ensure that this and other regulations were kept was called the 'Captain of the Market' (Law 1991:51). Formally, this standard has the following value form:

$$kan = \text{price of cowries x quantity of cowries} = 1 \times 40.$$

This standard was also the basis for higher groupings: five *kan* made one *afo* ('foot') and twenty made one *degba* (basket). Standards like this are the sign that money is an instrument of state power because they provide a fixed standard for measuring the value of all commodities and a means of levying of taxes. The money veil that is thrown over commodities, then, is a form of state power that varies from place to place and time to time: Despite the positions of quantity theorists, money is *never* neutral. In this particular case the veil of cowrie money masked a brutal mercantile power that profited from the purchase and sale of human beings. The imperial monies of this time, such as the pound sterling, did much the same thing but on a much grander scale. The link between the two was established by means of such international standards as in 16,000 cowries equals one ounce gold equals four pounds sterling which the Dahomey state struggled to maintain throughout the eighteenth century.

The French came to break this country before they came to bring their metal-money. Subordinate states are always subjected to the will of the dominant state; and, when the mercantile imperialism of the European states gave way to capitalist imperialism, the money standards changed as a consequence. First comes the imperialist conquest of the kingdom, which breaks the power of the king in an act of brute military force. New monetary standards follow. Prices now are required to assume the form, say, one kg rice equals two French francs and taxes are required to be paid in this new standard. The price of the French franc is now set at unity in those countries colonised by the French; and cowries are demonetized, which is another way of saying that the price of cowrie money falls to zero. But the demonetisation of the cowrie does not happen over night. Rival standards of value are at stake. This is a political struggle between the citizens of the old state, who have their wealth stored in the form of cowrie money,[11] and the new rulers. The citizens who hold their wealth in the form of cowrie money have much to lose and fight it out. As the imperial state gradually assumes control the demand for cowrie money falls because it is no longer legal tender. As this happens, sellers of commodities begin to demand payment in the new standard of value; buyers of these commodities who only have supplies of the old standard will be forced to offer increased quantities of the old standard if they are to persuade the sellers to accept it as a means of payment. This brings about a rise in prices in terms of the old standard of value (that is, cowrie money). Thus, it is this fall in the *demand* for cowrie money, and not an increase in their *quantity*, as the quantity theory of money would have it, that is responsible for the rise in the absolute level of cowrie money prices.

This, in brief, is the *political* economy of the subalternate quality theory of money. Formally speaking, it means that the old quantity equation needs to be rewritten in a new qualitative form as $SMV = PQ$ where S, the standard of value of the ruling state, is equal to one. The establishment of standards of significant value is the result of a struggle for prestige, and the raising of a new standard, like the raising of a new flag, is an expression of the political significance of the victor. In other words, the equation $S = 1$ is a symbol of order; while the existence of multiple standards of subordinated quality represents disorder, or, to be more precise, a challenge to the order imposed by the ruling state. As this exposition of my myth-inspired political approach to the symbolism of money is terse and somewhat unconventional, I will now restate it in the more familiar academic language of semiotics in an attempt to persuade the sceptical reader of its obviousness as against the obviousness of the quantity theory.

The expression 'quality of money' refers to the value of money as a signifier, and to understand what this means, it is necessary to consider the iconic, indexical, and symbolic meaning of money. This is a vast topic, and I shall limit myself to a brief consideration of the symbolic and indexical issues which are pertinent to my discussion. 'The word symbol', a high school textbook on poetry reminds us, 'is related to the Greek word *symbolon*, which was a half-coin carried away by each of the two parties to an agreement as a pledge of their good faith. A symbol, therefore, is like half a coin—it is an object; the other half of the coin is the idea it represents. When a person understands the symbol the two parts come together and the meaning is passed on' (Boagey, 1977: 40). This simple formulation of the notion of a symbol enables an equally simple question to be posed: If metallic coins are one-half of a material object, then what is the other half and what is the nature of the invisible chain that binds them? The answer to the first part of the question is cowrie shells and bullion. As for the second part, the invisible chain that has bound these objects together in different times and places has been the power of various states to maintain fixed rates of exchange between these objects for long periods of time. This is because gold, silver and cowries historically have defined the standard of value by which state-issued money is measured. In other words, the price of money has historically been defined in terms of gold, silver and cowries. Further, the spatio-temporal dimensions of the fixed rate of exchange of metallic money is an index of the coercive power of the state. Herein lies the indexical significance of money.

Consider the facts. As Law (1991: 176) notes:

> The prime cost of cowries in Europe varied considerably, but on the Slave Coast they had a fixed local or 'trade' value: ... the grand cabess of 4,000 cowries was at first valued at 25s. 'trade', but in the mid-1720s this valuation was lowered to £1 'trade'. The 'ounce trade', equivalent to £4 'trade', was therefore valued at 4 grand cabess, or 16,000 cowries.

Given the fixed price of gold established by the British of approximately four pounds per ounce[12], this gives the international standard mentioned above of 16,000 cowries equals one ounce of gold equals four pounds sterling. Polanyi (1968), who seems to have mis-interpreted the data on this rate and exaggerated the success the state had in maintaining its fixity over a long period,[13] makes the important observation that the 'stability of gold in terms of cowries became the absolute requirement of Dahomey's overlordship'. To extend his argument, one can note that the stability of gold in terms of the Pound sterling was an absolute requirement of Britain's imperial over-lordship. In other words, the fixing of the London price of gold at £3.17. 10½d was an index of the imperial power of the British state. The price of gold was set at this rate by Isaac Newton when he was director of the Mint in the 1690s and continued unchanged, save for a few hiccups during the Napoleonic war period, to the First World War. Britain was the only country that maintained a fixed price of money in terms of gold for this period. This fact must be seen in the light of another: From 1934 to 1971 the price of United States (U.S.) money was fixed at $35 per ounce of gold; the United States was the only country in the world able to maintain a constant price of money in terms of gold for this period. This index is a measure of U.S. imperial power just as the declining value of the dollar relative to gold after 1971 is an index of the decline in U.S. imperial power.[14]

States maintain their control over money by forbidding their citizens to handle gold, the supreme standard. Thus, the U.S. government made it illegal for its citizens to hold gold for most of the period when the price of gold was fixed; likewise, in Dahomey, 'gold trade was also a royal monopoly, the purchase of gold by anyone other than the king being a capital offence' (Law, 1991: 308). It is possible to debate the significance of the particular dates defined above, but the general point that a constant price (or quality) of money is an index of the dominance of an imperialist state is a difficult proposition to deny. The quality of money, then, is like the mercury in a doctor's thermometer: If the reading is constant at 98.4 degrees Fahrenheit then the body is in good order; but if it starts to rise over the 100 mark, then it indicates trouble, the monetary equivalent of which is debasement of the currency, an index of declining state power. Some ultra-right wing economists have failed to grasp the significance of this and mistakenly believe that a return to the gold standard will enable the U.S. to recover some of its lost power.[15] The medical equivalent of this is the doctor who believes that the temperature of a patient can be brought down by plunging the thermometer into a glass of cold water.

Monetary standards of value, then, are political standards of value: They express the values of the dominant powers. In this respect they differ from standards of weight and measure. Today, for example, the true or invariable metre is defined as 'a length equal to 1,650,763.73 wavelengths of the orange light emitted by the Krypton atom of mass 86 in vacuo' (Kula, 1986: 81). This definition, introduced in 1961, involved a complete break with the past in that a scientific idea was substituted for a physical object located in a carefully controlled environment. In the European middle ages, for example, standards were cut in stone or cast in heavy metal and displayed in public places; over time, with the need for ever greater precision in the definition of these standards, the objects were stored away in ever more artificially controlled environments until, in 1961, they disappeared altogether. Monetary standards have had a similar history: Gold has replaced silver, copper, cowries, and a host of other standards; but attempts to replace gold with a theoretical idea have been a signal failure. The result is that today gold and the U.S. dollar remain the principal standards of value for world commerce despite the best attempts of economists to emulate the physicists. The fact is, of course, that we will never succeed in eliminating material standards of money. This is because monetary standards are signifiers of political relations between people, whereas standards of weight and measure signify physical relations between objects. Thus, for as long as there is coercion, there will always be resistance, and the subordinated will never trust the motives of the elite. 'The attachment to gold,' as Rist (1938: 103) has noted, 'is one aspect of the eternal struggle between individuals and the state, the former anxious to protect himself against the hazards of the future, the latter anxious to use money as an instrument of its power to keep for itself the monopoly thereof.'

Consider, now, the explanatory adequacy of this subalternate quality theory of money. The first point is that the quality theory of money equation SMV = PQ has the advantage that it combines Fisher's Rule and Gresham's Law into one new quality of money equation. In other words, it is superior to the quantity theory under the Ockham's

Razor principle of explanatory parsimony. The second point is that the equation has to be modified to take account of the particular situation found in colonised countries such as West Africa, India, and Melanesia. What we had in these countries in the early colonial period was a situation of monetary and political disorder brought about by imperialist conquest, or, to be more precise, a transition from one system of political order to another. For quantity theorists like Hogendorn and Johnson and others, these political factors are regarded as being of no significance. (This is rightly called Economics and not Political Economy.[16]) The quality theory, on the other hand, raises the possibility that the new order being established might be of negative significance to, say, the West Africans who were being enslaved. Could it be that the particular standard adopted by the King of Dahomey (16,000 cowries equals one ounce of gold equals four pounds sterling) signified an order that the slaves wanted to disrupt? Could it be that some of the subordinated peoples struggled to get other standards accepted?

Expressed in this way the problem is not one of explaining, say, how bad money drives out good, a theory which is concerned with quantitative changes to a standard which is qualitatively the same, but how one standard drives out another of a completely different quality. This requires a further change to the quality of money equation $SMV = PQ$: The variable S must now be given a subscript according to its position on the power tetrad. Thus, S_d signifies the dominant standard, and S_s the subordinate standard. The latter term acquires additional superscripts according to the multiplicity of standards in existence. These matters are empirical questions, but, at a minimum, it will include two distinct subordinated standards: those of the indigenous elite and those of the subalterns.

With these modifications to the formula it is clear that the question of standards of value is a struggle for prestige, a question of politics. In other words, it is yet another variation on the general theme of resistance that Guha (1983a) has proposed. In order to illustrate this point[17] the following lengthy quote from the autobiography of a Solomon Islander about a tax collection episode is justified:

> When the tax was collected, Basiana had given four shillings to
> Mr. Bell instead of five. Mr. Bell had said, 'No, you have to pay

five shillings—that is the law!' Basiana had said 'Five shillings are impossible for me. I'm a man from the bush and I haven't gone to a plantation—where could I earn a fifth shilling? I'll give you an important valuable instead of the five shillings.' Mr. Bell refused: 'No. You go back this afternoon and look around for a fifth shilling. Then you bring it back. You have to pay the tax tomorrow'. So Basiana climbed the hill, thinking to himself. He went all the way up to the bush, to his own place, high in the mountains at Gounaile.

When he got there, he went to his men's house and got his crescent pearl shell: a sacred chest pendant inherited from his ancestors, and consecrated to them. At first he thought he might trade that *dafi* for someone's shilling. But then his mind turned another way. He was really angry. He took that *dafi*, consecrated to his ancestor, and smashed it to pieces. He took one of the pieces from the smashed pearl shell and began to grind it down. All night long, into the next day, he ground and ground and ground it down, until at dawn it was the same size and shape as a shilling piece. So he had those four shillings, four pieces of money, and his fifth was that piece of *dafi*. At dawn he went down to Gee'abe, where Mr. Bell had had the tax house built. He went to Mr. Bell and put the four shillings and the piece of shell down on the table in front of him. 'Mr. Bell, that one shilling was impossible for me. But this is my own shilling, one I ground down. You want money with the head of your king on it. But this shilling I ground for you is consecrated to my ancestor; my shilling has been passed down from my ancient ancestor. You have to accept it! You can't refuse it!'

Mr. Bell couldn't believe it. 'Oh, you bastard. Don't you do that again! I want five real shillings. Not a piece of seashell like this.' 'This isn't just an ordinary shell. It's just the same size and shape as those of yours. But yours have your king on them, and mine has my ancestor on it. This is my fifth shilling!'

'It's all right for this time, but don't you do that again. Next time, I'll put you in jail.' Basiana was very angry about that. 'I've broken up that important *dafi* passed down by my ancestors, and Mr. Bell doesn't even think it's worth anything' (Fifi'i, 1989: 7).

From the quantity theorist's perspective, the substitution of one standard of value for another in the colonial context appears as the workings of objective economic laws; but from the subjective perspective of someone like Basiana such a theory is manifest nonsense.

The other claim of the quantity theorists—that the cowrie shells were driven out because of excess supply—is also questionable from a quality of money perspective. Pax Britannica imposed its coinage in Africa, India, and Melanesia by the coercive act of demanding that taxes be paid in terms of coins of the realm instead of cowries.[18] This, not surprisingly, led to an excess supply of cowries as the result of the fall in the demand for them.

Dorward (1976: 590) noted that the colonial governments in West Africa demanded payment of tax in their own metallic money but argued that this set Gresham's Law into operation because 'bad money (European coinage) began driving out good money (Tiv cloth currency)'. But Dorward has failed to understand this law because good money and bad money are relative valuations of the same standard of value, not comparisons of different standards. Thus if a good silver coin was one in which the face value of the coin and its instrinsic metal content were in agreement, a bad silver coin was one in which the metallic content fell below the face value. For example if one silver coin marked one pound contained an ounce of silver and another contained only half an ounce, then the former was called good money and the latter bad money. If this law operated in West Africa, it would have to be shown, for example, that a *kan* consisting of a regulation 40 cowrie shells was ousted by a *kan* consisting of a number of shells less than 40. There is no evidence to show that this is what happened in West Africa (or India or PNG).

One Indian historian who has understood the politics of the demise of cowries is De, who notes that 'the abnormal depreciation in the value of the cowries in the nineteenth century was mainly due to the fact that under the British rule the cowries were not accepted for payment of revenue; consequently the demand for it in the market grew less, and there was a proportionate fall in its price' (De, 1952a: 10). In other words, an imperial standard was imposed by force, meaning that the subordinated standard, cowries in this case, lost its value. The British action was unique in the history of imperialist conquest of India: Previous Imperial powers had, it seems, accepted cowries as legal tender. This fact caused great hardship for all those who used cowries in India at the time. The policy was vigorously opposed by moneyed men and landlords who profited greatly from the traffic in cowries. In Orissa the Oriya Paiks, soldiers of the Raja of Khurda, rose in open rebellion against the British government in March 1817, about fourteen years after the British conquest. This rebellion was brutally suppressed by the British by October of the same year (De, 1952b). This fact is sufficient to belie the claim that the cowrie is a humble currency, the coinage of the masses.[19] The cowrie can be, and has been, a standard of significant value to landlords, moneylenders, slave traders, and merchant capitalists throughout history. The fact is that cowries, dollars, gold, and so forth are mere objects; their natural properties provide no clue as to their iconic, indexical, or symbolic significance. What must be comprehended are the invisible chains that bind these objects together: If they are comprehended, then the symbolic meaning is revealed; if not, they remain mere objects. Many historians and economists have failed to understand the symbolism of money, with the result that their theories become apolitical and objectivist.

Anthropologists, on the other hand, ever alert to the importance of the iconic and symbolic significance of money, sometimes make the most elementary mistakes and fail to realise that cowries can be money symbols. For example, in the 1940s a great debate waged in the pages of *Man* concerning the iconic significance of the cowrie. On the one side were the 'horizontalists' who argued that the cowrie was 'obviously' a charm against the evil eye; on the other side were the 'verticalists' who maintained that the cowrie represented the human vulva and was used as a fertility charm. According to my Bengali informant (Ranajit Guha) some of the people who actually used them saw things differently: Parents put cowries around the necks of their new-born children rather than gold, so that the evil spirits would be fooled into thinking that the children had a low value. In other words, the iconic value of cowries to Bengalis was derived from their use as money symbols and not as objects which conjure up, in the anthropological imagination, likeness to various parts of the body. Thus, whereas some economists have failed to realise that money is a symbol, some anthropologists have failed to realise that cowries, as a money symbol, can have iconographic significance.[20]

The subalternate quality theory of money calls for a re-assessment of Bohannan's theory of spheres of exchange and Keynes's theory of multiple standards of value. These theories, it was seen above, were found wanting by Hogendorn and Johnson and by Dorward. But the theories of Bohannan and Keynes are significant contributions to the literature and a great improvement on the quantity theory approach. Indeed, aspects of Keynes's theory of multiple standards are consistent with the quality theory approach developed here. The problem with Bohannan's and Keynes's approach is that it abstracts from power. Keynes' (1982: 259) idea that one standard is replaced by another through 'the normal progress of adaeration' is to give objects a life of their own. There is no natural tendency for metallic standards to oust others (or for general purpose monies to oust special purpose monies), rather, there is a cultural tendency for those with power to impose their standards of value on others with different standards. It is a matter of the cultural logic of power rather than of the natural power of logic.

CREDIT MONEY AND CONQUEST

In order to limit the scope of this book I have arbitrarily excluded so-called 'credit money' from my discussion. However a brief discussion of this topic is necessary because the question arises as to the applicability of the forgoing argument to 'credit money'.

Credit money, or 'negotiable instrument' as it is more correctly termed, comes in a variety of forms but they all originate in debt, are all means of delayed payment. The different forms are distinguished by asking 'Who?' 'What?' and 'When?' The answer to the 'Who?' question gives the parties to the contract, the answer to 'What?' gives the quantity and quality of money involved, and the answer to 'When?' gives the duration of the instrument. A discussion of three basic forms—promissory notes, bills of exchange, and cheques—is sufficient to illustrate these general points.

In a *promissory note* the maker is the debtor who promises to another person, the payee, a certain sum of money at some future time. Here is an actual example from nineteenth century colonial Australia (Butlin, 1953: 64):

Sydney, September 1, 1812.

Ann Marsh

I Promise to Pay the Bearer the sum of Two shillings and Six pence, sterling, on demand, 2s. 6d.

(signed Ann Marsh)

In this case the debtor is Ann Marsh and the payee is an unidentified bearer. The money involved here is 2s. 6d. sterling. The 'sterling' specifies the quality of money. This fact, as we shall see below, is highly significant because the word 'sterling' had a very special meaning in early nineteenth century Australia. This note has unlimited duration because no future time is specified. Promissory notes like this can pass from hand to hand until such time as the bearer presents it to Ann Marsh to collect the 2s.6d sterling.

In a *bill of exchange* the debtor is the drawee who accepts the drawer's (creditor's) demand to pay a third person a certain sum of money at some future time. In India these are called *hundi* and the following is an example (from Jain, 1929: 77):

> To the pleasant and prosperous town Bombay the abode of merit therein to brother Mann Lal Karodi Mal written from Bombay by Ram Prasad Uttam Chand whose greetings you may be pleased to read. Further a *hundi* for R. 500, in words five hundred, twice of rupees two hundred and fifty, is drawn upon you in favour of Mool Chand Kesari Mal on *Chait Sudi* 12. Sixty-one days after date you will please pay the amount thereof in current coin to the presenter after ascertaining his respectability, title and address.
> *Hundi* written on *Chait Sudi* 12, *Samvat* 1983.

Here the drawer, Ram Prasad Uttam Chand, requests his debtor, Mann Kal Karodi Mal, to pay Mool Chand Kesari Mal. The bill has a duration of 61 days, the quantity of money involved is Rs 500 (twice Rs 250) and the quality is 'current coin'.

A *cheque* is a bill of exchange where the debtor is a drawer who asks his bank to pay someone a certain sum of money on demand. No example is necessary because negotiable instruments of this kind are still in use today but maybe not for much longer given the competition from electronic forms of negotiable instrument.

In a promissory note, then, the debtor is the maker of the instrument and there are only two parties to the contract; in a bill of exchange the debtor is the drawee who accepts to pay the bill, and in a cheque the debtor is the drawer who signs it.

Two quite different questions are posed by negotiable instruments. The first concerns the technical relations of exchange, the second the social relations of exchange. The technical questions concern the processes by which certain forms of credit money arise and pass away. This is a problem in the history of institutions. The social questions concern the politics of two distinct standards of value: that of the status of the debtor and that relating to the quality of the money specified in the instrument. These two standards are often conflated but they are quite distinct.

In India the social status of the drawee of a *hundi* has provided the basis for many a legendary tale. One has it that the magnificent Jain temples of Dilwara on Mt Abu were built with the money drawn on a city banker of Ahmadabad. In another the credit of a drawee by the name of Bukhan stood so high that the bearer of one his *hundis* who needed the money tied it to the branches of a tree. A merchant who was passing by saw that it was the bill of the great banker and cashed it on the spot.

In colonial Australia promissory notes functioned as the principal means of exchange from first English settlement in 1788 to the 1830s. Their worth depended on the genuineness of the drawer and was often accepted only at discount. Private notes were referred to as 'base Colonial currency' or 'currency' for short. Bills of exchange drawn on the British Treasury, countersigned by the governor, were referred to as 'sterling' and valued highly relative to 'currency', the 'dirty, scribbled promissory note of a convict'. In 1809, for example, a shopkeeper would give a 4s. in the pound discount to those who would pay 'sterling' (Butlin, 1953: 66). This distinction was, by analogical extension, used to rank the settlers: the native-born children of white settlers were called 'currency' lads and lasses and seen as inferior to the British-born who were 'sterling' characters.

This process of debtor evaluation is unique to negotiable instruments and is related to the 'Who?' question that these instruments pose. But they also raise the 'What?' question concerning the quantity and quality of money and the problems at stake here are those we have been considering above. In other words, the questions of standards of money value are encompassed by questions of the standard of the debtor in a negotiable instrument. The distinction between 'currency' and 'sterling', then, applied both to the valuer and the objects valued.

In the early days of the colonisation of Australia, money was in short supply and a variety of different physical forms of money arose. The distinction between 'sterling' and 'currency' served to divide these monies into 'good' and 'bad' categories, the membership of which changed over time. 'Sterling' always included the bills of the government and the paymaster. It also included the receipts the government store gave in payment for produce received. As Mrs Macarthur wrote in 1795:

> In payment for [grain] the Commissary issues a receipt, approved of by the Government; and these receipts pass current here as coin and are taken by masters of ships and adventurers who come to these parts with merchandise for sale. When any number of these have been accumulated in the hands of individuals they are returned to the Commissary, who gives a bill on the Treasury in England for them... Pigs are bought upon the same system, as would also sheep and cattle if their numbers would admit of their being killed (Butlin, 1953: 32).

The Spanish dollar, 'the universal coin of three centuries' (Chalmers 1893: 24), was classified as 'sterling' during this period. 'Currency', as a material form, included copper coins, wheat, and the like. The familiar logic of 'buy cheap here sell dear there' brought these forms of money into existence as Thomas Muir explains in a letter he wrote to a friend in London in 1794:

> When money is transmitted, cause a considerable part of it to be laid out at the Cape, or at Rio Janeiro, in rum, tobacco, sugar, etc. etc., which are invaluable, and the only medium of exchange. We bought some rum at Oris for 18d. the gallon, and can sell it for 30 shillings. In a country like this, *where money is really of no value*, and rum everything, you must perceive the necessity of my having a supply by every vessel. For a goat I should pay in money £10 sterling; now, for less than eight gallons of spirits, at 18d. the

gallon, I can make the same purchase. Tobacco at Rio sells for 3d.
per pound, here at 3s. 6d. That too is an article to be considered.

(Butlin, 1953: 24, emphasis added.)

This is yet another native point of view on the definition of
money. 'Money', in the sense of tokens of the English state, had little
value in colonial Australia where relatively large numbers of the basic
unit (£1) had to be given in exchange for basic commodities; the flip
side of this proposition is that basic commodities had a relatively high
value. In other words, says Muir, take the perspective of C-M in
Australia, not M-C.

Thus a bill made by someone like Ann Marsh above could be
written using 'sterling' or 'currency' as the standard of value. We know
of nothing of Marsh's status as a debtor but while the 'sterling' or
'currency' status of a debtor was often correlated with the 'sterling'
or 'currency' quality of the money denominated in a bill it was not
always so. One of the three promissory notes of Ann Marsh
reproduced in Butlin (1953: 64), for example, specifies copper coins
rather than 'sterling'.

Governor after Governor in the first forty years of settlement
decried the 'base Colonial currency' and tried to eliminate it. However,
promissory notes and bills of exchange cannot be legislated out of
existence. Commercial instruments are mere tools and like tools they
exist for as long as they have a useful function. What a state can influence,
though, is the *quality* of the monetary standard specified in a commercial
instrument. This is precisely what British imperial policy decreed late
in 1825.[21] It pegged the Australian pound to gold via the pound sterling
and made this the only legal tender. Similar things happened in the other
colonies. This drove Spanish dollars and other foreign coins from
circulation.[22] The year 1825, then, marks the beginning of a new era of
domesticated world money. The silver standard of the Spanish lost its
300 year supremacy[23] and the gold standard of the British empire
emerged triumphant. This was, of course, merely an expression of
underlying changes in the balance of imperial power. While this brought
an end to the division between 'currency' and 'sterling' money in
Australia, the social classifications within the population lived on. The
'sterling' classes ruled over the 'currency' lads and lasses and the
Aborigines until the 1960s when both 'sterling' and 'currency'

recognised the worth of Aborigines and gave them the right to vote. Meanwhile the reign of the U.S. dollar-gold standard, which commenced officially in 1934, was about to end and the era of savage money to begin.

NOTES

[1] Translated from Ayizo by G. Elwert (1989: 23) who notes that this was first published in the Ayizo language in *Gankpanvi* (Vol. 1, 1979), the first issue of a journal that was established as a result of the Ayou literacy movement. I am extremely grateful to Georg Elwert for patiently taking me through a word-for-word translation of the original myth. My argument has benefited immeasurably from the long discussions I have had with him about Benin and the slave trade.

[2] See De (1952a, 1952b); Hughes (1978).

[3] Compare Guha (1985): 'Religion is the oldest of archives ...'(p. 1); 'once the syncretic wrapping is taken off, the content of many a myth can be identified as what it really is—that is, as a figure of some ancient and unresolved antagonism' (p. 2).

[4] The following is a much abbreviated account of the story of the shell money of the slave trade as told by Hogendorn and Johnson (1986). I focus on this book because it provides me with a convenient rhetorical means of raising my general comparative questions. My concern is not to develop a critique of Hogendorn and Johnson's economic history but to raise general questions about the quantity theory of money by means of the expression it gets in their book.

[5] Dubbeldam (1964) and Connell (1977) are among those who have applied Fisher's Rule and Gresham's Law to the PNG case. Perlin (1987) contains an exhaustive bibliography on cowries in India.

[6] Law's (1991: 5) 'scepticism about the potential value of oral tradition' for research of this kind reflects, perhaps, a more general view among historians of a non-anthropological bent. It seems to me that when an oral tradition such as Cece's story about the cowrie-shell trade is written down it becomes an archive like any other. One must take a sceptical approach to all archives; their *relative* value is not an objective property of the document but is determined by the theoretical approach of the historian as Guha's (1983b) essay on the prose of counter-insurgency suggests.

[7] Guha, a sometime painter, makes extensive use of this image throughout *Elementary Aspects* (1983a) and his other writings. This, Guha informs me, was not done consciously. Guha's unconscious use of the logic of colour to structure his thoughts invites comparision with Lévi-Strauss's conscious use of musical logic.

[8] I omit, for ease of exposition, details of the prices (P) and quantities (Q) sold.

[9] If, for example, 1 kg of rice cost $10 from this trader and 5 kgs of sweet potatoes cost $10 from that trader, then the implicit exchange value of the commodities in the market is 1 kg rice = 5 kgs sweet potatoes. Thus the C-M-C form of money exchange reduces to the C-C of commodity exchange which implies that barter forms of exchange are implicit in any market economy. Theories of values such as Sraffa's (1960) are premissed on this fact.

[10] This much should be obvious from the formula C-C. I stress this point because the relative commodity form of value (C-C) and the absolute money form (M-C) are often confused.

[11] Law (1991: 67) quotes a French source which says that the rich had great treasures in cowries, beads, gold dust, women and land.

[12] The actual figure was £3.17.10 d which, if rounded up to £4, gives the standard rate of 16,000 cowries per ounce. There is some disagreement among the authorities on the interpretation of the data relating to the standard rate. Compare Polanyi (1966: 92, 159, 168); Hogendorn and Johnson (1986: 124, 132–35); Law (1991: 51–58, 176).

[13] See Law (1991: 52).

[14] See Gregory (1989) and Chapter VIII for a detailed exposition of this argument.

[15] See the minority report to the Gold Commission (1982).

[16] See Gregory (1982: 10-29) for an elaboration of this point.

[17] See Vansina (1962) for another example from the Congo.

[18] The situation in PNG is slightly different in that the gold-lip shell, *Pinctada Maxima*, was permitted in place of legal tender until 1964 under the New Guinea Coinage and Tokens Ordinance. Its exchange rate was fixed at twelve shillings a pair. It is also interesting to note that in 1920, following the ousting of the Germans from New Guinea after the First World War, the use of German currency was prohibited; yet another illustration of the obvious fact that standards of value are the expression of political dominance. See Phillips (1972) for further elaboration of these details.

[19] This term was first used by Perlin (1987) and seems to have been accepted uncritically by other economic historians of India. See, for example, Richards (1987: 5).

[20] The debate was opened with a letter to *Man* by Murray (1939). One of the best contributions was made by Elwin (1942) in an article dealing with cowrie use in Bastar District India (where, I did fieldwork). A recent monograph has been published by Safer and Gill (1982) that deals exclusively with the iconography of shells; this contains useful surveys of the literature. The iconography of coins and notes is a curiously neglected topic. Hocart's (1952) short but interesting essay is one of the few anthropological contributions to this topic that I have been able to find.

21 A Treasury Minute of 11 February 1825 argued that such a policy would bring about 'a better mode of paying the Army abroad' (Chalmers, 1893: 418). The British government saved money by paying in silver tokens instead of actual silver. If the economic rationale behind the decision was clear, the politics that informed it was less so (see below).

22 It took time, of course. The legislation overvalued gold coins in circulation relative to that of silver which caused big problems in the West Indian colonies. The complex technical matters involved here are discussed in two classic studies in comparative economic history, Pennington (1848) and Chalmers (1893).

23 'The real justification of the measures of 1825 was one which was only vaguely felt at the time, and which required the subsequent experience of half a century to demonstrate and define. That justification is to be found in the fact that the Spanish dollar, the universal coin of three centuries, had lost its supremacy, and that its universal dominion was in a process of disintegration into rival "currency areas," chief among which was destined to be the area dominated by British sterling' (Chalmers, 1893: 24).

CHAPTER VIII

Savage Money

The era of American supremacy in international finance that began in World War II is finished. The monetary and trading system that provided the basis for the postwar era has collapsed. There is no point kidding ourselves about it, that it is just shaky, that we will reconstruct it. It's gone.

> Former U.S. Treasury Secretary, John Connally
> (quoted in Rolfe and Burtle, 1973: 104)

Democracy does not require elected or appointed intermediaries; pure democracy in fact requires that there not be suchlike. Democracy does exist, it does function (greatly hampered by the state). Its common name is the free market. The free market, to the extent that it is free, is an economic democracy; each bid to purchase is a vote for the product or service wanted, a vote that is weighted by the money amount offered and accepted, to register precisely the transaction price level that will yield a profit for the seller and the buyer. The unencumbered market, overall, operates like a societal guidance system that constantly makes multitudinous minute corrections through changing relative prices to direct and coordinate individual human actions towards the maximisation of the total prosperity, the total well being, the total happiness in a society.

> Jerome F. Smith (1974: 66)

THE RISE OF GOLD AND THE FALL OF AN IMPERIAL STATE

From 1934 to 1971 the U.S. dollar was as good as gold because of a U.S. government pledge. During this period the U.S.

government promised foreigners[1] that it would it convert their dollars into gold at the fixed rate of U.S.$35 per ounce if they so wanted. President Nixon's decision on 15 August 1971 to suspend the convertibility of the dollar into gold broke this pledge and set in train a series of events the impact of which are still being felt some 25 years later. The immediate impact was the creation of a 'wild' U.S. dollar and, what amounts to the same thing, a market for gold free of the domesticating power of the U.S. government. The price of gold began to rise at a dramatic rate in its newly freed market. It hit a peak of over U.S.$600 in 1980, dropped back to U.S.$300 by 1985, and has fluctuated around $400 in the decade since then. The only function of the official U.S. dollar price of gold after 1971 was to value monetary gold held in the form of foreign reserves.[2] Gold accounted for only 8% of total foreign reserves in 1985 using this standard of value. However, with the rise in the market price of gold, many governments began to adopt more realistic methods of valuing their gold stocks. The result was that, by 1979, forty of the 103 IMF member countries had abandoned the official price valuation of gold reserves and were using prices ranging from U.S.$57 to the then free market price of U.S.$415 (Brodsky and Sampson 1980a: 178). If 1985 market prices are used to value all monetary gold stocks then gold accounts for 42% of total reserves. This increases the value of total reserves by a staggering $249 billion U.S. dollars, bringing massive windfall gains to gold-holding countries of whom the U.S. is the largest. On the other hand, the value of the dollar has also fallen and those countries who have preferred to keep foreign reserves in this form have lost out. As it was the developing countries who were obliged to hold U.S. dollar reserves, one of the aftermaths of Nixon's decision to suspend convertibility was to redistribute billions of dollars of wealth from the dollar-holding developing countries to the U.S.. This redistribution of wealth, the biggest in world history, has gone by largely unnoticed.[3]

In this chapter I will argue that Nixon's decision was related to U.S. military expenditure overseas—the Vietnam War in particular—and that the effect of the de facto revaluation of gold reserves has been to transfer the cost of the war to the dollar-holding developing countries.[4]

My argument can be summarised briefly as follows. International financial history is a notoriously complicated subject. However, if we think of the U.S. dollar as analogous to a gold coin of yesteryear then the fundamental principles informing the circulation of state money become clear. During the period 1934 to 1971, when the U.S. price of gold was fixed at U.S.$35 per ounce, foreign governments had the option of exchanging their dollars for gold with the U.S. government at this rate. The dollar was, therefore, just like a gold coin. The only difference was that, instead of putting a stamp on a piece of gold of a certain weight and fineness, the U.S. Government put a stamp on a piece of paper that gave its possessor rights to gold of a certain weight and fineness. Until the 1960s, no one exercised this right because it was obvious to all that the U.S. could meet the obligation. By the end of World War II the U.S. was the world's foremost industrial and political power. In addition, it held 75% of the world's monetary stock of gold, most of which was acquired in the 1920s from war-torn European countries who used gold to pay for U.S. commodities. The acquisition of these gold stocks was a phenomenon of U.S. industrial expansion, not its cause. The growth of Fort Knox gold holdings in the 1930s and 1940s was a measure of the U.S.'s rise to power in much the same way as the contraction of gold stocks in the 1950s and 1960s was to be an index of its decline. Gold stocks began to fall in the early 1950s when the cost of the Korean war led to a balance-of-payments deficit. This deficit persisted and by the end of the 1950s foreign governments began to lose confidence that the U.S. could honour its obligation to convert dollars into gold. By this time the dollar was generally accepted as world money and the number of dollars circulating around the world had grown dramatically. Before 1959 the gold value of the dollar, measured by the ratio of gold assets to foreign dollar liabilities, was above 100%. In 1960 it dropped below 100% and declined steadily over the next decade. In other words, if all foreign governments holding dollars presented them for exchange into gold there wouldn't have been enough gold available at Fort Knox to meet the demand. This created a crisis of confidence in the dollar and the U.S. government adopted a variety of stop-gap measures to retain the dollar's value in terms of gold. These complicated financial strategies, which included the establishment of a gold pool, a two-tier gold market, and Special Drawing Rights (SDRs), broke down in the face of a persistent U.S. balance-of-payments deficit which flooded the world with dollars. The escalation of the Vietnam War after 1965 exacerbated the problem and Nixon had no option but to suspend the convertibility of dollars into gold as the ratio of Fort Knox gold to dollars fell to 19%. Thus if all foreign holders of dollars presented them to the U.S. government for exchange into gold they would get only 19% of the promised 1/35 ounce of gold. In the days of gold coinage a rise in the price of gold was inversely related to a fall in its gold content. This is the case with the U.S. dollar. Since 1971 the market has determined the gold content of the dollar. This has averaged around 1/350 of an ounce in the 1980s and 1990s, a tenth of its official value during 1934–1971. In the past, kings often deliberately debased the coinage as a means of financing wars. The effect was to transfer wealth from the citizenry to the state by inflating the economy. It was a strategy of last resort because it was very costly in terms of the political disruption it caused and the havoc it wrought on the organisation of production and distribution of goods and services (among other things). The gold-coin analogy suggests that Nixon was the king, that Vietnam was the war to be financed, and the dollar-holding developing countries the citizens of the world imposed upon to pay.

WHY NIXON WAS FORCED TO BREAK THE GOLD PLEDGE

The postwar period to 1971 divides into a number of critical phases defined roughly by the respective presidential administrations. A brief review of the political and economic history of these periods is necessary if Nixon's decision is to be understood.

The early years of the Truman administration (1945–1950) were characterised by U.S. balance of payment surpluses and general shortages in international reserves. In 1948 total world reserves stood at U.S.$46.6 billion, with gold accounting for U.S.$32.7 billion and foreign exchange U.S.$12.7 billion. Eighty seven per cent of the latter was in the form of debased U.K. pounds sterling. Prior to the war these pounds had a gold backing of 103% but by 1948 this backing had fallen to 13%. The 1948 U.S. dollar, which had a gold backing of almost 300%, were readily accepted as substitutes for sterling (and gold) as the U.S. played a key role in post-war reconstruction. Dollar holdings in the form of foreign exchange assets grew from U.S.$1,850 million to U.S.$4,450 million and accounted for 33% of all foreign exchange in 1950. This growth in the popularity of the U.S. dollar was all at the expense of the British pound sterling.

The turnaround came in the second phase of the Truman administration (1950–1953). Foreign exchange reserves grew to U.S.$15,250 million of which 46% were U.S. dollars. Persistent balance of payments deficits, the first of which appeared in 1951, fuelled this growth. In turn, U.S. military aid to Korea over the period 1950–53 and the development of a global military strategy[5] to translate the United States's technological and economic power into mastery of ever-changing political realities were the basis of the post-1951 balance of payments deficits.

Subsequent administrations have had to operate within the broad politico-economic parameters laid down by the Truman administration (Kolko and Kolko, 1972). During the Eisenhower years (1953–1960) the balance of payments deficits persisted and U.S. dollars accumulated abroad. In 1961 foreign dollar holdings stood at U.S.$22,853 million, almost twice the level they were when Eisenhower took office. Gold reserves, which had been slowly accumulating till 1957, began to drop at a rapid rate. The curves crossed for the first time in 1959 (see Figure VIII.1) and the gold backing of foreign dollars fell bellow 100%. This was not a crisis in itself but signalled the potential for a crisis if the trend continued.

One of the few economists to understand this was R.Triffen.[6] His statement of the problem to the Joint Economic Committee of the 87th Congress on the International Monetary Position and Policy of the United States, in October 1956, subsequently published with a collection of his other essays (Triffen, 1960), turned out to be prophetic. He identified the 'terrifying and disproportionate defence burdens' as the most significant single factor contributing to the revolutionary turnaround in the dollar balance. Triffen also predicted the inevitability of a rise in the price of gold if the balance of payments deficit continued.

Apparently Eisenhower did try to get Germany to pay for some of the U.S. troops stationed there during the dying months of his presidency, but as he was a lame duck president nothing happened (Gilbert, 1980: 128).

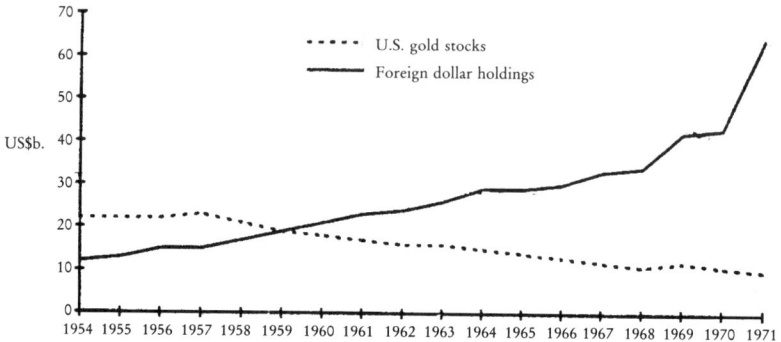

FIGURE VIII.1   *U.S. gold stocks and foreign dollar holdings*

When Kennedy assumed power in January 1961 he drew attention to the balance of payment problems he inherited but, for electoral reasons, refused to implement policies that placed the burden of adjustment on U.S. capital or the U.S. voting public. Consider his first State of the Union message delivered on January 30:

> [The] overall deficit in our balance of payments increased by nearly $11 billion in the last three years—and holders of dollars abroad converted them to gold in such quantity as to cause a total outflow of nearly $5 billion of gold from our reserves ... this country has continued to bear more than its share of the West's military and foreign aid obligations. Under existing policies, another deficit of $2 billion is predicted for 1961—and individuals in those countries whose dollar position once depended on these deficits for improvement now wonder aloud whether our gold reserves will remain sufficient to meet our own obligations (KCA, 1961: 17924).

One of the policy options open to Kennedy was to devalue the dollar by raising the price of gold. He explicitly rejected this. 'This administration will not distort the value of the dollar in any fashion' he asserted. This was the beginning of the policy of so-called 'benign neglect' (Stockman, 1986: 26; and Kolko, 1985: 346). In reality it was a policy of malign aggression in international financial relations and signalled a determination on the part of the U.S. to resort to whatever means possible to pass its dollar problems on to the rest of the world.

Another policy option open to Kennedy was to reduce military expenditure. He did precisely the opposite. Following Vice-President Lyndon Johnson's visit to Saigon in May 1961 the U.S. government made an agreement to 'increase and accelerate' U.S. economic and military aid to South Vietnam. This was the beginning of the costliest war in U.S. history.

The declining gold value of the dollar became a serious problem. Kennedy introduced the first of a series of stop-gap measures that succeeded in delaying the day of reckoning for a decade. In October 1961 the U.S. proposed the establishment of a 'gold pool'. Loss of international faith in the value of the dollar was putting upward pressure on the price of gold and the gold pool was an informal arrangement 'to share the burden of the cost of intervention on the London Gold Market to keep the price within reasonable limits in the event of exceptional and concentrated demand for gold arising either from an international political crisis or from speculative movements of funds' (KCA, 1964: 20057). The European Countries—West Germany, France, Italy, U.K., Belgium, the Netherlands and Switzerland—contributed 50%; the U.S. provided the other 50%. The gold pool worked well until 1965 when uncontrollable upward pressure on the gold price emerged. Heavy selling by gold pool members in 1966 and 1967 exhausted reserves and a new crisis arose. This was solved, in March 1968, by another stop-gap measure, the two-tier gold price system.

The gold pool served U.S. interests first and foremost. Other members participated because disruption to the international financial system served nobody's interests. The question was one of how long they would subordinate national self interest to the U.S.'s national interest and the general good. France was the first to weaken. It withdrew from the pool in June 1967 with a call, the third within six months, for an extra contribution of U.S.$50 billion. The French were the most vocal critics of the U.S. foreign economic policy and, like

Triffen, correctly predicted the inevitability of a rise in the price of gold. In 1965 they moved to protect their own reserves and converted U.S.$300 million dollars into gold reducing the U.S. gold stock to U.S.$14.5 billion, the lowest since 1938. In 1966 they acquired another U.S.$220 million in gold from the U.S., a move that was subsequently to prove of immense financial benefit to them. Meanwhile on 4 February 1965 De Gaulle launched a scathing attack on U.S. financial imperialism and called for a return to the gold standard. Other European countries rejected this plea, held on to their dollars, and lined up behind the U.S., much to their ultimate cost.

While France's financial war with the U.S. was a contributing factor to the March 1968 crisis—'the most serious international financial crisis since the Second World War' (KCA, 1968: 22597)— President Johnson's decision to escalate the American involvement in the Vietnam War was the crucial determinant. At the end of 1964 U.S. troops in Vietnam totalled 23,300 but by December 1965 there were 184,300. This increased to 385,000 twelve months later and 485,600 by December 1967. The bombing of North Vietnam also escalated at a similar rate with 285,000 tons dropped in 1965, 458,000 tons in 1966 and 845,000 tons in 1967. Budget appropriations rose from U.S.$103 million in 1965 to U.S.$19.4 billion in 1967; estimates for 1968 were put at U.S.$21.9 billion (KCA, 1967: 21907).

Apologists for the U.S. government find the war to be 'an economically trivial' event in the macroeconomics statistics (Walker and Vatter, 1982: 605).[7] They note that defence expenditure as a percentage of GNP rose from 7.7 to 8.8 over the period 1964–1967 and fell to 7.5 in 1970.

Opponents of the U.S. government, on the other hand, have tended to exaggerate the absolute cost of the war and use it to explain everything. Estimates of the cost of the war vary greatly, from U.S.$353 billion to U.S.$750 billion (Burns and Leitenberg, 1984: 232). Exercises of this kind are ultimately rather pointless because, apart from the accounting difficulties in arriving at a precise figure, the exact ratios of defence expenditure to GNP for the period 1965–71 are of little consequence in assessing the war's impact. What mattered was the historical timing of the 'blank cheque' approach to Vietnam military expenditures and the issue of who was to pay.

McNamara's decision in March 1965 to unlock unlimited funds for the Vietnam War led to an orgy of wasteful expenditure at the Pentagon as the generals rushed to spend their blank cheque. At the end of 1965 advisers, who saw the looming budget deficit, told Johnson that a tax increase might be necessary to pay for war. Johnson chose to ignore these warnings and devoted his energies to getting his anti-poverty Great Society legislation through Congress by lying about the real estimates for the war. In January 1967 he eventually asked for a 6% surcharge on corporate and individual taxes; in August he raised it to 10%. A hostile Congress did not pass this until mid 1968 and then only after U.S.$2.5 billion were cut from earlier authorisations for social welfare (Kolko, 1985: 196, 287). This tax increase, estimated to produce extra revenue of U.S.$7.4 billion, was too little too late (Halberstam, 1969: Ch.27). The budget deficit blew out from U.S.$1.6 billion in 1965 to U.S.$15.19 billion in 1968.

The timing of this could not have been worse.[8] In 1964 the gold backing of the foreign holdings of dollars was 53% and it declined to 32% in 1968[9] as the balance of payments worsened, foreign liabilities increased and gold drained out (See Figure VIII.2).[10]

Had it not been for the war the economic strength of the U.S. would have been much greater and the international monetary situation much more stable at the beginning of 1968. For example, an

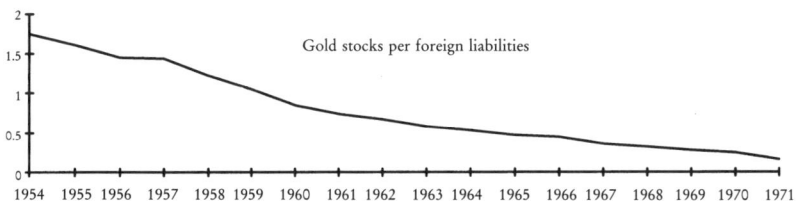

FIGURE VIII.2   *Gold-value of the U.S. dollar*

economic analysis of the impact of the war on the U.S. balance of payments revealed that 'the U.S. would have been in international payments surplus in 1967 in the absence of Vietnam War expenditures (Dudley and Passel, 1968: 442). Johnson was forced to admit much the same thing in a special address to the nation on 1 January 1968.

This was summarised as follows:

> For 17 of the past 18 years, the President said, the United States
> had had balance of payments deficits (the exception being 1957).
> For a time they were needed to help the world recover from the
> ravages of the Second World War and 'could be tolerated by the
> United States and welcomed by the rest of the world,' since they
> distributed more equitably the world's monetary gold reserves
> and supplemented them with dollars.
>
> Once recovery was assured, however, these large deficits were
> no longer needed and began to threaten the strength of the
> dollar. The U.S. government had been working since 1961 (ie.
> the beginning of President Kennedy's term of office) to reduce
> the deficit, which had been cut from $3,900,000,000 in 1960 to
> $1,300,000,000 in 1965; in 1966, however, because of the
> increased burden of the Vietnam war, the improvement had been
> interrupted and the deficit had remained at about the same level
> as in 1965.
>
> In 1967 the progress had been reversed, due principally to a
> further increase in the costs of the Vietnam war, a rise in private
> loans and investment abroad, a smaller rise in the trade surplus
> than expected, and greater expenditure by U.S. tourists abroad.
> There had in addition been 'the uncertainty and unrest
> surrounding the devaluation of the British pound,' which had
> strained the international monetary system and sharply
> increased America's balance of payments deficit and gold sales in
> the last quarter of the year. As a result, preliminary reports
> indicated that the deficit might be 'in the area of $3,500,000,000–
> $4,000,000,000—the highest since 1960' (KCA, 1968: 22467).

If the economic realities of the Vietnam War finally dawned on
Johnson at the end of 1967 then, within 30 days of his special message
to the nation, the political realities became apparent to him and the
rest of the world. On January 30, North Vietnam launched the Tet
offensive and shattered any illusions that the U.S. was winning the
war. The North Vietnamese understood the economic, political, social
and ideological context of the U.S.'s involvement in the war better than
the U.S. did and were able to use this knowledge to their military
advantage. These facts became obvious to the world in April 1975 as
they watched the revolutionary forces smash into the U.S. embassy
grounds in Saigon on their TV screens.

As a crisis of confidence in U.S. power swept the world in the late 1960s, investors everywhere switched from paper currencies to gold, creating a rapid and unprecedented increase in the demand for gold in the first half of March. On Monday 11th March 1967, gold pool losses were U.S.$118 million, on Tuesday U.S.$103 million, Wednesday U.S.$179 million and by lunchtime Thursday 14th U.S.$220 million. In view of the chaotic conditions prevailing, the U.S. Government requested the British Government to close the London Gold Market on the 15th March so that members of the gold pool countries could make new arrangements. The market remained closed until 1st April 1968 during which time the Central Banks agreed to buy and sell gold among themselves at U.S.$35 but not to intervene in the London market. Following the introduction of this two-tier price system the market price of gold rose to U.S.$41 in June and fluctuated slightly below this price until the end of the year.

This was yet another stop-gap measure but of importance in that it signalled an unwillingness of U.S.'s allies to use their gold to save the dollar any longer. By abolishing the pool, and rejecting an American request that they forgo their right to convert their U.S. dollar holdings into gold from the U.S. Treasury, they were putting their own interests above those of the dollar (Kolko, 1985: 314–315). The U.S. was now on its own.

The Nixon administration did nothing to alleviate the dollar's problem and everything possible to make it worse. Henry Kissinger, a self-confessed economic ignoramus, advised Nixon on how to do this (Kolko, 1985: 349).

It is true that under Nixon the number of U.S. troops in Vietnam dropped from its peak of 543,000 in April 1969 to almost nil by June 1973. However, this masks the fact that the U.S. dropped more bombs in the period 1969–73 than any other period during the war. Over 8 millions tons of ground, air and sea munitions were spent in the Nixon years, representing 60% of the total over the period 1965–1973 (Burns and Leitenberg, 1984: 77). In other words, the Nixon Vietnam War years were the most costly. A budget surplus in 1969 of U.S.$5.4 billion became a deficit of U.S.$11.38 billion in 1970 which doubled to U.S.$24.81 billion in 1971. The balance of payments deficit[11] grew in proportion, reaching the record figure of U.S.$29.73

billion in 1971. The effect of this was to widen the gap between foreign
dollar holdings and gold stocks even further. Foreign dollar holdings
almost doubled from 1968 to 1971, gold stocks declined and the gold
value of the U.S. dollar tumbled from 32% to 19%. Yet another crisis
had arrived.

The actions of the U.S. Government had created upward
pressure on the U.S. dollar prices of gold and downward pressure on
the exchange rate of the U.S. dollar vis-a-vis the Deutsche Mark and
other strong currencies. The sticking point in both cases was the fixed
price of gold. If the U.S. had officially increased the price of gold it
could have gone some way to overcoming both problems
simultaneously, for a rise in the dollar price of gold is tantamount to
a devaluation of the dollar. This action would have required the U.S.
to shoulder the burden of adjustment. However, the Nixon
administration refused to do this and shifted the burden of adjustment
to other countries by breaking the pledge to convert foreign holdings
of dollars into gold at the fixed rate of 1:35 (KCA, 1971: 25000). 'The
dollar is our currency,' declared Treasury Secretary John Connally, 'but
your problem' (quoted in Kolko 1985: 350). This took the
international financial community completely by surprise because it
meant that, somehow, they had to realign their exchange rates relative
to the U.S. and to each other. This decision, announced on 15 August
1971, signalled the formal beginning of the decline of U.S. imperialism.
As the Treasury Secretary, John Connally was to remark later:

> The era of American supremacy in international finance that
> began in World War II is finished. The monetary and trading
> system that provided the basis for the postwar era has collapsed.
> There is no point kidding ourselves about it, that it is just shaky,
> that we will reconstruct it. It's gone (quoted in Rolfe and Burtle,
> 1973: 104).

THE ECONOMIC CONSEQUENCES OF
THE VIETNAM WAR

Nixon's announcement of 15 August 1971 immediately led to
the closure of most major financial centres. In the gold market the
fiction of an official price of gold was abandoned and the free market

price increased by two thousand per cent in the space of ten years. In the foreign exchange market, the post war Bretton Woods system of stable exchange rates collapsed. The values of the free market asserted themselves and the value of the dollar began to fall relative to other major currencies.

The combination of these two effects was runaway inflation. The U.S. consumer price index rose dramatically as the following figures show:

1960–64	1.2%
1965–70	4.2%
1971–73	4.6%
1974–75	8.8%
1976–78	6.8%
1979–80	12.6%

Following Nixon's decision foreign dollar liabilities grew at an astronomical rate. In 1970 they were U.S.$43 billion but fifteen years later they were U.S.$606 billion. Gold reserves valued at official prices stayed relatively constant with the result that official gold backing of foreign-held dollars dropped to less than 3%. The rise in the U.S. dollar price of gold was an expression of this debasement. The effect of this price rise has been to maintain the *de facto* gold backing of foreign dollars of around 25%.

The question that now arises concerns the relationship between the rise in the consumer price index, the global redistribution of wealth from poor countries to rich, and Nixon's decision to break the gold pledge. The unifying political factor is the problem that has plagued U.S. foreign policy since the early 1950's: the negative effect of military expenditure on the balance of payments. U.S. Treasury Secretary John Connally correctly identified this factor in 1971.

> I find it an impressive fact, and a depressing fact, that the persistent, underlying balance of payments deficit which causes such concern is more than covered, year in and year out, by our net military expenditures abroad, over and above the amounts received from foreign military purchases in the U.S …We spend 9% of our gross national product on defence—nearly $5 billion of that overseas, much of it in Western Europe and Japan (Quoted in Rolfe and Burtle, 1973: 79).

A feature of post-Nixon U.S. budget policy has been tax cuts without corresponding expenditure cuts. Defence expenditure has been allowed to grow in an almost unconstrained fashion.

In Carter's first budget speech, for example, we find tax cuts coupled with proposals for 'significant increases in our overall defence effort, with special emphasis on those forces and capabilities most directly related to our NATO commitments' (KCA, 1978: 29133). A real growth of 3% in budget outlays was projected, the only constraints being the introduction of 'important efficiencies' and the placing of 'careful priorities' on defence needs.

It was under Reagan that defence expenditures really flourished. A feature of all Reagan's budgets was proposals for large increases in military expenditure and the freezing or reduction in real terms of many categories of domestic expenditure, but mainly on those programs to assist the poor. His tax reforms benefited business and wealthy individuals while increasing the tax burden on the poor. Receipts from corporation income taxes, for example, declined in absolute terms from U.S.$60 billion in 1978 to U.S.$37 billion in 1983; as a percentage of total budget receipts this represents a fall from 15% to 6%. Meanwhile, the tax paid by a family of four on the government determined poverty level rose from 4% of income to 10% over the same period (KCA,1984: 32901–2).

The following figures (in billions of U.S. dollars) on the growth in the size of the U.S. budget deficit under Carter and Reagan reflect their respective philosophies:

1977	U.S.$52
1978	59
1979	36
1980	76
1981	79
1982	127
1983	209
1984	185

Right wing economists were divided over the importance of these deficits. The monetarist position is that the deficits do not matter. This claim was vigorously rejected by the supply-siders (Paul and

Lehrman, 1982: 12). They were united on the question of a big defence budget though. Even Reagan's most hard line cost cutter, budget director and self-styled supply-side revolutionary David Stockman, was a big budget proponent on defence (Stockman, 1986: 106). Reagan's 'defence is not a budget issue' stance made his 1980 election promise to produce a balanced budget by 1983 impossible to achieve.

Reagan's budgets exacerbated the U.S. balance of payments problems and it was only the continued willingness of foreigners to hold U.S. dollars that enabled him to do this. This appeared to be something of a mystery.[12] If U.S. gold reserves were valued at the official price of $42.22 per ounce (used by the U.S. Government) then by this measure the official gold backing of foreign dollars declined to less than 5%. However, foreign holders of U.S. dollars clearly used market price valuations of U.S. gold reserves. The gold backing of the U.S. dollar has fluctuated around an acceptable 27% from this perspective. While the dollars are no longer 'as good as gold' so far as dealings with the U.S. government is concerned, they are convertible into gold on the free market. Furthermore gold holders receive no interest and the fluctuating price of gold makes it a risky asset. This de facto remonetisation of gold, then, has given the U.S. dollar a new lease of life as a reserve currency. How long this lasts remains to be seen. When Clinton won office in December 1992 he inherited the biggest budget deficit in the history of the U.S., $254 billion equivalent to 4.9% of the Gross Domestic Product.

Institutions such as the IMF have tried to stop the remonetisation of gold. They tried to depress the price of gold by selling one-sixth of IMF gold stocks over the period 1976 to 1980, but the price went up instead (Kettle, 1982: 146–150). They tried to promote Special Drawing Rights (SDR) as the principal reserve asset but many countries elected to value their gold reserve at market prices instead, with the result that SDR only accounted for an insignificant 2% of total reserves in 1985 (Brodsky and Sampson, 1980a). They have been successful in changing the monetary rate of gold by amending the IMF's articles. Gold no longer serves as the numeraire for members' exchange rates. They also abolished the official price of gold and eliminated the obligation of members to use gold. The fact remains, however, that gold has re-emerged as the supreme source of international value. IMF officials now reluctantly admit this fact (Wittich, 1982: 234).

Anti-gold economists held sway during the Carter administration and the U.S. sold 4 million ounces in 1978 and 11.75 million ounces in 1979 in an attempt to demonetise gold. The pro-gold Reagan administration discontinued these sales which led to speculation about a return to the gold standard (Business Week, 1981). The report of the Gold Commission (1982) which recommended otherwise put these rumours to rest, although the lengthy minority report of the Commission suggests that there were grounds for the rumours. The most important impact of the Carter gold sales was to improve the country's trade deficit (Kettell, 1982: 146).

HOW THE POOR NATIONS WERE MADE TO PAY FOR THE WAR

Table VIII.1 shows the impact of higher gold prices on the valuation of foreign reserves. Prices for the year 1985 of are taken as the standard. The effect of revaluing reserves at market prices is to create an extra 249 billion in SDR's (1SDR = U.S.$1.10) and to increase the relative share of gold in foreign reserves from 8% to 42%. The figure of 42% is conservative because the 1985 gold price of U.S.$328 per ounce, the equivalent of 298 SDR, was the lowest annual price of gold in the 1980s.

TABLE VIII.1   IMPACT OF HIGHER GOLD PRICES ON THE VALUATION OF FOREIGN RESERVES, 1985

	Gold at 35 SDR (billions)		Gold at 298 SDR (billions)		Increase (billions)
Gold reserves	33	(8%)	282	(42%)	249
Paper reserves	383	(92%)	383	(58%)	
TOTAL	416	(100%)	665	(100%)	249

1 SDR = U.S. $ 1.10

Source: IMF, International Financial Statistics

Table VIII.2 shows the distribution of this windfall gain between the U.S., other industrial countries, and the developing countries. At the official price of 35 SDR the respective shares of total reserves are 9%, 52% and 39%. Revaluation of gold increases the U.S. share to 16%, other industrial countries to 53% and decreases the developing countries share to 31%. In other words the developing countries lost 8% of the value of their foreign reserves, the U.S. gained 7% and the other industrial countries 1%. Thus, the poor countries were the losers in this zero sum game, the U.S. the main winner.

TABLE VIII.2   IMPACT OF HIGHER GOLD PRICES ON
THE DISTRIBUTION OF FOREIGN RESERVES, 1985

Country	Before %	After %	Change %
U.S.	9	16	+ 7
Other Industrial	52	53	+ 1
Developing	39	31	– 8
Total	100	100	0

Source: IMF, International Financial Statistics

Tables VIII.3 and VIII.4, which show the distribution of gold and paper money reserves respectively for the years 1960–1985, helps us understand why this redistribution happened. In 1960 the U.S. held 47% of total gold reserves (Table VIII.3). This declined to 28% in 1971 and has remained stable ever since thanks to Nixon's convertibility announcement. The shares of the other countries have remained relatively stable since then too.

The remarkable fact about this, though, is the small share (17%) of the world's gold reserves that the developing countries have. This is even more striking when compared with the relatively high proportion of reserves developing countries hold in the form of paper currencies (mainly U.S. dollars).[13] As Table VIII.4 shows, this figure stood at 41% in 1984 Also worthy of note is the dramatic climb in

TABLE VIII.3   DISTRIBUTION OF GOLD RESERVES
(PERCENT OF TOTAL)

Country	1960	1971	1985
U.S.	47	28	28
Other Industrial	44	58	55
Developing	9	13	17
Total	100	100	100

Source: IMF, International Financial Statistics.

TABLE VIII.4   DISTRIBUTION OF PAPER RESERVES
(PER CENT OF TOTAL)

Country	1960	1971	1985
U.S.	7	2	7
Other Industrial	62	74	52
Developing	31	24	41
Total	100	100	100

Source: IMF, International Financial Statistics.

this share since 1971. This was the direct result of the oil price boom which saw the proportion rise from 24% in 1971 to 47% by 1975. The oil exporting developing countries gained paper reserves at the expense of the other industrial countries. However, this paper was not convertible into U.S. gold and their short term gains in higher dollar reserves were offset by the long run decline in the value of the dollar.

The rise in the gold price, then, benefited the U.S. most because of its relatively large gold stocks. The decline in the value of the U.S. dollar hit the poor developing countries most because they held relatively more paper money reserves. The other industrial countries ended up slightly in front because gold gains just outweighed dollar losses. The roots of the post-1971 financial crisis are to be found in a militaristic U.S. foreign policy. This has caused a chronic balance of payment deficits since the Korean War and chronic U.S. budget deficits since the Vietnam War. This has flooded the world with U.S. paper dollars which ceased to be as good as gold in 1959. The growing gap between foreign dollar holdings and U.S. gold reserves reached a crisis in 1971 when the gold backing of foreign dollar holdings fell to 19%. This put uncontrollable upward pressure on the price which set the gold price soaring and brought about a de facto remonetisation of gold reserves. The gold price rise, which was simultaneously a debasement of the dollar, caused a massive redistribution of wealth from the dollar-holding developing countries to the gold-holding U.S. The debasement of the dollar also contributed to the world-wide inflation of the 1970s and 1980s. More importantly, Nixon's breaking of the gold pledge marked the beginning of the end of statism and created the conditions for free market anarchism as a value to flourish. Its public face has been the social, economic and political agenda of U.S. President Ronald Reagan and British Prime Minister Margaret Thatcher but its real force is concealed by the 'invisible hand' of the market. An anthropological examination of the workings of one world market, silver, can reveal some of the human owners of this 'invisible hand'.

THE SILVER BUBBLE

One aftermath of the beginning of the era of savage money was the 'silver bubble' which developed in the late 1970s and burst in the 1980s. In 1971 the world price for silver was U.S.$1.55 per ounce. It rose to $4.42 in 1975 and kept on rising to peak at $20.58 in 1980. It fell to half this price in the following year and has kept on falling. In 1990 it was back to $4.82.

Figure VIII.3 converts these U.S. dollar prices per ounce into Rupees per kilogram and plots them against the Bombay price for silver for the period 1971 to 1992. The bubble in the world price of silver contrasts sharply with the steady upward trend in the Bombay price. These two graphs index two quite distinct standards of valuation: the dictatorial values of a free market anarchist family and the aggregated values of millions of Indian households.

The 'invisible hand' in the world market for silver in the late 1970s and early 1980s was revealed to be the Hunt brothers of Dallas who, with the help of Saudi princes and bank credit, accumulated over 200 million ounces in a buying frenzy that almost enabled them to corner the market. Journalist Stephen Fay (1982) tells the fascinating story of this saga in his *The Great Silver Bubble*. A reviewer complained that the book does not answer the most interesting question: what drives unimaginably rich people to behave in such a fashion?

George Marcus (1985), the American cultural anthropologist who has made the study of Texan elites his speciality, has noted this alleged defect of Fay's book and tries to provide an answer. His concern is to see the event as 'one variant expression of behaviour that *generally characterises* the culture of dynastic families and fortunes in

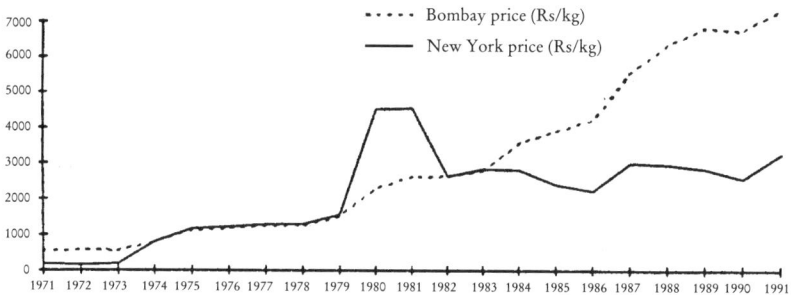

FIGURE VIII.3   *Silver prices in Bombay and New York*

America as a distinctive kind of private corporate organisation' (1985: 227, his emphasis). Building on the work of Bataille and Mauss, he argues that the 'Hunt foray into silver can be seen as a bourgeois analog of potlatch'. The analogy holds, he argues (1985: 228), because 'the level of excessive expenditure among the Hunts, headed for destruction, approximates the intensity of excess in potlatching from which Bataille takes off.' This 'dynastic potlatch', he concludes (1985: 258), 'relocates "the gift" in the basic functions of capitalist economics and demands their understanding, at different points in the system, in appropriately cultural terms'.

This type of analysis is typical of one that is becoming common nowadays as anthropologists reclaim the West as a subject of study using concepts developed for studying the Rest. Thus whereas Marcus sees potlatch at work in the world market, another sees moieties in Berlin[14] and so on. There are many problems with this type of approach and they begin with the adequacy of concepts like 'potlatch' and 'moiety' to explain problems in the 'tribal' societies for which they were first developed. For example, Marcus wants to 'relocate' potlatch into the basic functioning of capitalism but the fact is an historically informed analysis of nineteenth century potlatch among the Kwakiutl shows that capitalism has always been there. The destruction of property for which the Kwakiutl are famous began in earnest after a logging company built a sawmill near them in the late 1800s.[15] The money earned in the sawmill financed the purchase of the blankets and other commodities that were potlatched. Marcus's analogy, then, denies the coevality that gives potlatch its historically informed anthropological meaning. This criticism aside, the analogy fails even in its own terms. Potlatch is an intentional destruction of wealth; successful potlatchers are successful destroyers of wealth. The Hunts had no intention of destroying their wealth and nor did they. The paradox of this case, as Marcus has correctly noted, is that their creditors (the banks and other public authorities) protected their debtor from financial ruin in order to save themselves.

The *cultural terms* that Marcus uses, then, are most inappropriate; they obfuscate rather than clarify. However, Marcus's essay does contain the traces of a more appropriate analysis in *value terms*. The 1970s, he notes (1985: 242), 'was generally an anxious time for the established rich as well as for the affluent middle class, who faced, in quite different spheres, the decline in value of their assets'. 'The move to silver generally reinforces the value of money in uncertain times', notes Marcus (1985: 249). 'Financial analysts argued that there were special opportunities for profits in silver, and Bunker Hunt was persuaded, according to Fay, to purchase large quantities of bullion in 1973' (1985: 252). Fay develops this argument in his book. Missing from Marcus's analysis, but not Fay's, is a treatment of the theory of value (free market anarchism) that informed the actions that 'generally characterise' the behaviour of people like the Hunts.

On the question of why the Hunts got into the silver market, an informant of Fay's said: 'It's all to do with the defence of wealth

versus a deteriorating currency' (1982: 29). Hunt named the source of
the idea when he gave evidence to a congressional committee in 1980:
'I first became interested in silver as an investment, not as speculation,
in 1973 after reading about it in several publications including one
entitled *Silver Profits in the Seventies* by Jerome A[16]. Smith' (Fay,
1982: 30). This book, not mentioned by Marcus, outlines the theory
of value that informed the actions of the Hunt brothers.

Smith is a rhetorician who knows the values of his elite audience
and his opening paragraph gets straight to the heart of the matter:

> If you have the patience to study this report and follow its logic,
> and if you have some money to invest—it could make you rich.
> If you are already rich, it can, at least, provide you a means to
> keep what you have.

He announces that he has developed a 'new theory of money'
and that this tells him that 'silver could become more valuable than
gold' (Smith, 1974: 5).

> Only gold and silver remain widely available as an escape hatch
> for those relatively few individuals who have the fore-sight to
> store their wealth in *real money* (Smith, 1974: 70).

Revolutionary stuff! A new theory of the supreme commodity
and a new vision of the future. Silver, the long time deputy of King
Gold, is 'within our lifetime, and perhaps within this decade' (1974: 5)
to topple the absolute monarch who has ruled the market since the
beginning of commercial time. While he was certain about this fact
he did have a worry. For Smith the 'over-riding social issue of all time'
was Statism. 'Either there will emerge a fundamental change in our
conceptions and actions concerning government in this decade,' he
argued (1974: 66), 'or we'll have our investments confiscated and
become either employees or prisoners of the state before another
decade passes'. He then outlined his political philosophy:

> Democracy, does not require elected or appointed intermediaries;
> pure democracy in fact requires that there not be suchlike.
> Democracy does exist, it does function (greatly hampered by the
> state). Its common name is the free market. The free market, to
> the extent that it is free, is an economic democracy; each bid to
> purchase is a vote for the product or service wanted, a vote that

is weighted by the money amount offered and accepted, to register precisely the transaction price level that will yield a profit for the seller and the buyer (Smith, 1974: 66).

Here it is, then, a dollar a vote and the more dollars you have the more votes you get. What distinguishes Smith's version of free market anarchy is that these votes will be cast with silver, 'real money', not worthless state paper money. As it turned out, Smith's analysis of the principles determining the relative values of gold and silver was faulty and his prediction hopelessly wrong. Gold has consolidated its supremacy and silver's relative status has fallen. The long term trend in the ratio of silver to gold has moved in favour of gold. For hundreds of years prior to the eighteenth century 12 ounces of silver would buy one ounce of gold; by the mid nineteenth century the rate was around 15. In 1975 it was 36. This dropped to 30 in 1980 as a result of the Hunt's attempt to corner the silver market but has risen rapidly since. In 1990 it was 80 and rising. Gold, then, has been recrowned.

The crisis of 1980 in the silver market exposed not only the invisible hand of the Hunt brothers and the invisible mind behind it, it also revealed the identity of a growing political force: free market anarchism and the philosophy of 'tough shit'. Compare Fay (1982: 248):

> 'Tough shit' is not merely invective; the phrase has recently been elevated into a political and economic principle. Although many of its practitioners express it more delicately, the principle is a fundamental principle of libertarianism, a system that has its own political party ... The principle has also deeply tinged the New Conservatism of President Ronald Reagan and Margaret Thatcher. The phrase would, no doubt, never pass the lips of either of them, but their economic policies bear harshly on the least privileged members of society: the poor, the ill-educated, ethnic minorities, and the unemployed. Theoretically, these groups should be grateful for the economic liberty imposed by the New Conservatism and pull themselves up by their bootstraps; if they cannot do so ... well, tough shit.

Tough shitism, however, works one way for the elite and another the for subaltern. This is because Statism and free market anarchism need each other. As creditors the central banks and other financial institutions had to save the Hunts or go down with them. There were many other cases in the 1970s. In 1973 and 1974 the governor of the Bank of England launched a lifeboat operation when the collapse of a number of malfeasant banks (to which the central bank turned a blind eye) endangered the whole British banking system. In the U.S. the Federal Reserve Board bailed out Penn Central, Lockheed, Chrysler, and the Franklin National Bank (Fay, 1982: 254). The traditional role of the central bank is that of 'lender of last resort' but the fallout from the era of savage money is turning them into lenders of first resort as the market place transforms itself into a casino.

THE VANDALS' CROWN

The Hunt Brothers attempt to corner the silver market made it unlikely that regulators would approve new ways of speculating in the world market for gold and silver. This prompted the big money men to look around for new markets to conquer. They found it in currencies, the token monies of the various nation-states.

Prior to 1971 there had been no way to buy and sell token money without going through the central banks. Furthermore, given the fixed link between the U.S. dollar and gold on the one hand, and the fixed rates between the dollar and other currencies on the other, the buying and selling of a currency was tantamount to buying and selling gold. Nixon's act of 15 August 1971 broke the link between the dollar and gold creating the possibility for futures trading in the dollar and other national currencies. The creation of the possibility of buying and selling a currency at a certain price at some point in the future meant that state-created token money itself became a commodity. While forward currency contracts were common before 1971, the contracts were such that commitments were firm: there was no freedom to get out of a forward contract by, for example, selling it to someone else. Here, then, was an unfree market. Why not free it up by inventing a 'currency option' that could be bought and sold at will?

This question occurred to a trader on the Philadelphia Stock Exchange but he faced two obstacles when he tried to realise his new market invention. The first was a complex set of government regulations designed to meets the needs of the pre-1971 era. The second was a reluctance on the part of the makers of token money, the central banks, to participate.

By 10 December 1982 the obstacles were no more and the Philadelphia Stock Exchange began to trade currency options for the first time. The markets grew so big and powerful that the governments of the world proved incapable of controlling them. Not since the invention of paper money, writes Millman (1995) in his *The Vandals' Crown: How Rebel Currency Traders Overthrew the World's Central Banks,* has a financial invention had such impact. The central bankers, he notes, compare it to a nuclear explosion. Millman, for his part, likens the rebel currency traders to the Vandal kings, the Germanic tribe whose name is synonymous for wilful desecration and destruction. This analogy occurred to him as he watched them celebrate the end of a triumphant year in September 1993 in the Musée de Cluny in Paris where the crowns of the old Vandal kings hung suspended over their heads from golden chains. They were celebrating their destruction of the European Monetary System's Exchange Rate Mechanism (ERM). 'They had taken a great risk,' notes Millman (1995: 6), 'and reaped a great reward.' These new traders, he argues, are the most powerful people in the world today. The collapse of the ERM is the latest victory of free market anarchism over statism. 'I'm a free market animal,' one of the new Vandal kings shouted at the celebration, 'Supply and demand. Thats it, that the name of the game!' (Millman, 1995: 189).

These new Vandal kings, then, are the new rulers of the world and savage money is the instrument of their rule. They have converted state money tokens such as the U.S. $, the Japanese ¥, and the British £ into commodities and have assumed control of the their relative prices. However, the other side of the savage coin, the price of precious metals, is not fully under their control. It is here that the values of the subaltern gains its expression.

WOMEN AND GOODS IN INDIA

'Jewelry is the same as money', declared an Indian jewellery vendor to a hesitating customer. The customer, as Jacobson (1976: 167) notes, was well aware of this fact. If my experience is anything to go by, the customer was probably hesitating because she was worried about the source of credit to finance her purchase and not the wisdom of spending large sums of money on jewellery. Typical, I suspect, is the action of the girl we employed to bring us our daily water when we were living in Bastar. Before leaving we made her a gift of some Rs 800 which was equivalent to about 100 days work at the going rate for a labourer. She immediately set off to the jewellers and came back proudly wearing a chunky silver necklace which attracted much favourable comment from people in the neighbourhood. It turned out that she paid Rs 1,000 having received Rs 200 credit from the merchant. She was from a very poor home—her mother was a widow—and the necklace was probably the most valuable possession the family owned. The cumulative actions of millions of people like this girl has created a market for Indian silver (and gold) that has defied world trends for hundreds of years. It is indices like that shown in Figure VIII.3 that have given India (and more generally Asia) its reputation as the 'sink' of the precious metals because when the Bombay price of silver is higher than the world price it means that silver pours into the country. The era of the silver bubble (1979–82) was one of the few times in the history of the country when the sink began to empty a little.

The precious metals, then, are obviously very important standards of value in Asia. The interesting theoretical question is not 'Is silver money?' but 'What kind of standard of value is it?' Is it a standard of *commodity* value, a standard of *good* value, a standard of *gift* value or a standard of some altogether different kind? Clearly, all of these answers contain elements of truth especially at the macro level. However, a comparison with the Hunt case above does enable us to make a few observations of comparative interest concerning the role of silver as a *good* in both elite and subaltern families.

Marcus's research among the Texas elite shows that they are not totally money minded in the sense that standards of commodity value are not the only values they think about. A very important form of property is what he calls 'sacred property'. Some of the personal property of the dead acquires this status as it passes on to descendants. It includes cheap items, such as pocket knives, combs, etc., and expensive items such as paintings, houses, land and furniture. 'The importance of such property,' he argues (1985: 237), 'is not its commodity value, but its domestic exchange value—the powerful sentimental meanings that an object acquires by its possession and transference and in the memories and it evokes among descendants.' He found that value of this kind is created not by the will of the ancestor but by the more or less orderly *grabbing* by the descendants. This grabbing poses absolute restrictions on spending: 'it defines a class of dynastic assets which as long as they carry sacred meanings must not be alienated' (1985: 238). It my terms, these 'domestic values' are *goods*, inalienable keepsakes.

Values of this kind create scarcity. It is clear that the type of scarcity the Hunt Brothers sought to bring about on the world silver market was not scarcity of this type. They were not concerned to convert silver into family *goods* but, rather, to establish *monopoly* control over the market so that they could *dictate* prices. In other words, free market anarchy as a political philosophy means freedom of the super rich to become dictators. But what about the Bombay silver market? Could it be that the prices on this market reflect a generalised tendency to convert commodities into goods?

The thesis is a plausible one. There can be no doubt that precious metals are highly valued as goods throughout Asia. I have given an example from my fieldwork in India above at the beginning of Chapter III. Consider the following case from Nias Island in Indonesia. Here villagers have three types of ornaments for the house ancestors. The first are the original clan relics, distinguished as the 'trunk of the *marapu*' (ancestors) which are stored in a wooden chest at the peak of the clan's ancestral house. These comprise gold and silver jewellery and they secure the ancestral spirit within the house. In other words, these metals have divine associations. It is forbidden to touch these relics. The second type consists of metal ornaments that are added to the oldest relics but are placed in a separate container; these are out of bounds but may be handled by old men. The third category is more general and includes several varieties of clan heirlooms; these may be viewed and handled by women and men (Rodgers, 1985: 174–75).

This example serves to remind us that the 'sacredness' of goods has as much to do with *political theology* as it does with religious belief. It is one thing for a person to believe that a certain object is 'sacred', quite another for elder males to deny younger males and women access to it. A political theology of *goods* is one that locates beliefs like this on the matrix that reveals associations between gold and silver, elite family and subaltern, men and woman, land and jewellery, etc. and analyses the power behind the patterns. A simple pattern found throughout, India, for example, is the correlation between gold and silver and rich and poor. This is cross cut by a correlation between land and jewellery and male and female. As Jacobson (1976: 172) notes in her important essay on this topic, jewellery is owned primarily by women who tend to have less control over other forms of wealth. The most heavily ornamented women in the village usually belong to prosperous joint families where the land is owned and controlled by men. The family purse in these families is kept by the oldest woman who, in concert with the males, often prevails upon a daughter-in-law to pawn her ornaments. The jewellery of this woman falls into three categories: items purchased jointly by a couple after marriage, gifts from the spouse's kin, and gifts from natal kin. It is improper for affines to ask for jewellery of the latter kind and if they do a woman is within her rights to refuse; however, for jewellery in the other categories the woman may find it impossible to resist. Jewellery, then, is at the heart of the gender politics of consanguinity and affinity. Daughters need inalienable keepsakes like jewellery in their struggles to assert their dignity and humanity. The transformation of commodities into goods of this kind may not be able to explain the steady upward trend in the Bombay price of silver but it is certainly one of the contributing factors.

Standards of value are alike in that they are all expressions of power. But as power is never the same everywhere, different standards of value have emerged. Standards of commodity value are the dominant standards in the world today. They are the standards of free market anarchists and the statists. These values are behind the sentiments which label village people as 'backward' and their desire for *goods* as 'unproductive' and 'contrary to the national interest'. They are also the sentiments which have informed government policies to change these values such as regulations designed to limit private holdings of gold and silver. They have failed, evidence that commodity standards of value do not prevail in all parts of the world. Of course, these opposing values are alternate but not necessarily subalternate. The value of gold as a good belongs as much to the elite as it does to the subaltern; the fact that the subalterns tend to hold silver rather than gold is an expression of their relative poverty. Political values cannot be read off the material form of things because that would be to read things upside down. Things are mere instruments of power and their values spring from the relations between people located historically, geographically and anthropologically.

ON THE SYMBOLISM OF MONEY: A SUMMARY STATEMENT

The symbolism of money is as simple as its historical realisation is complex. Symbolic analysis is a matter of grasping a material object in its historically specific concreteness and asking: 'What material object was formerly united to this one?' 'What invisible value relation binds the two parts together today?' 'Who are the valuers behind this relation and what is the political nature of their relationship?' There are as many answers to this question as there are material objects in the world and selection of the starting object depends on the problem being considered. My problem in this chapter has been the paramount money value in the world today and, as such, the money of the paramount power, the U.S. dollar over the period 1934 to 1971 and beyond, was my starting object. The missing part of this material object, I argued, was the gold at Fort Knox; its original undivided form was the gold coin of yesteryear, and its present forms are the independent, but related, free markets for paper money, tokens and precious metals. The value relation that bound the two objects together over the period 1934 to 1971 was the U.S. government pledge to convert foreign holdings of dollars into gold at the fixed rate of 35:1, while the value relation effective after 1971 was the free market price. The power of the U.S. government maintained the former; free market anarchists control the latter and their power grows as they succeed in destroying yet more instruments of state control and in creating yet more new markets for symbolic objects that did not previously have a price. The 'currency options' market they have created is a market for state-created symbols of a type that has never existed before in financial history. An invariable measure of value has become a variable standard that is itself now measured by other formerly invariable standards in the quest for profit. This is commodity fetishism in its highest form. Traders gain not so much by trying to solve the mathematical quandary of finding the variable value of a variable standard by means of a variable standard but by observing the actions of the central banks, decoding their intentions, and doing, in most cases, precisely the opposite so that the aims of the banks are thwarted. This is the politics behind the fetishised meta-values and the traders are winning the battle at the moment. The implications of this struggle affects us all, from the anthropologist in the academy to the people they work amongst in the remotest village of India or Papua New Guinea. These are the forces that lie behind the free market anarchist values that both unify the world by the Market and divide into so many ethnic spaces in the name of this Culture and that Identity. These values have a history and will change over time but always as a result of the actions of people. Values like this are the water we goldfish— the living *homo sapiens* of today—swim in; hopefully, unlike goldfish, this water will not be the last thing we learn about. A culturalist approach to the theory of commodities that persists in dissolving historically specific unifying values into endless cultural diversity by appeal to the notion of 'indigenisation' (Appadurai, 1990) will never understand the symbolism of the money tokens that pass through their hands on countless occasions each and every day. Indigenisation is,

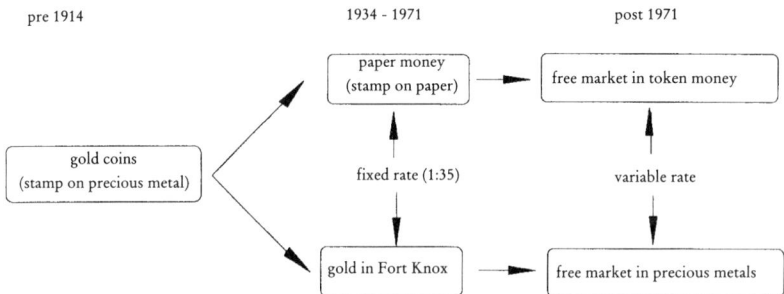

FIGURE VIII.4   *The symbolism of money*

of course, a factor in the world today but so to is 'Americanisation'. These are not opposing tendencies but complementary expressions of the one underlying value: free market anarchism. Modern day leaders like Fiji's Rabuka not only 'indigenise' Fiji by continuing to exchange whale teeth and by expelling the settler Indian population, they also actively embrace the values of high finance.

Figure VIII.1 below summarises of my argument in a schematic form. Those who like to think visually may find it useful device for grasping the essentials of the forgoing argument. It is clear that the free market for precious metals is one that is open to everyone from the subaltern villager in India to the elite families in Texas. The free market for token money, however, is, for the time being at least, in the hands of the elite, the new Vandal kings.

NOTES

[1] Not domestic holders. U.S. citizens were legally prevented from holding gold in 1933. This law was not repealed until 31 December 1974.

[2] Foreign reserves are held by countries to facilitate international trade. They fall when the balance of payments runs a deficit and rise when there is a surplus. They consist of gold and strong foreign currencies (See IMF, 1958: Ch.1). The official gold price of 35 SDR was still being used in the 1990s, although market price valuations are now also included.

[3] The only article on the topic to my knowledge is Brodsky and Sampson (1980b). This received some publicity in the March, April and September editions of *South* (1981).

[4] 'Most Americans were not aware of any serious economic deprivations during the most active phase of the Vietnam War 1966–69' (Stevens 1976: 5).

[5] 'Throughout the post war period the security of Europe has been the centre piece of U.S. foreign policy. In no other region have the two great superpowers deployed so many nuclear weapons' (McNamara, 1986: 20). U.S. warheads (missiles and bombs) grew from 450 in 1950 to 4750 in 1955 and stabilised at this level until 1970. In 1975 they numbered 8,500 and were around 11,200 just prior to the end of the Cold War.

[6] Soviet economists familiar with Marx's theory of gold and money also analysed the problem correctly. See Frumkin (1969).

[7] See Garrison and Mayhew (1983) for an excellent internal critique of this argument.

[8] Stevens (1976: 11) makes the additional point that the extra budget allocations for defence came just as the country was arriving at full employment.

⁹ Defence expenditures accounted for 9% of GNP in this year. In 1945, by way of contrast, defence was 41% of GNP. This did not bring about a dollar crisis because the gold flowed into the U. S. during the Second World War giving the dollar a backing in excess of 300% by 1945.

¹⁰ Source: Gold Commission (1982: 84).

¹¹ More precisely, the official reserves transactions balance.

¹² Triffen (1979: 5) examines this question and considers a number of answers. Incredibly, he overlooks the issue of de facto remonetisation of gold.

¹³ In 1972, 79% of world foreign exchange reserves were in the form of US dollars. By 1982 this had fallen to 60%. The Deutsche Mark has increased by 4.6% to 10.4% over the same period while the European Currency Unit (ECU), first established in 1979, accounted for 14.4% of total foreign exchange in 1982 (IMF, 1983). The ECU'S popularity was clearly related to its gold backing. The major European countries—West Germany, France, United Kingdom, Netherlands, Italy, Belgium—between them held 36% of the world's monetary stock of gold in 1982 . The ECU was backed by gold because all participating members were required to deposit 20% of their gold reserves with the European Monetary Co-operation Fund (Kettell, 1982: 56). The European Monetary Systems Exchange Rate Mechanism of which this was part broke down in 1992–93 (See Millman, 1995).

¹⁴ See Borneman (1992).

¹⁵ See Gregory (1980) for an elaboration of this argument.

¹⁶ This is a mistake. He meant Jerome *F.* Smith.

CHAPTER IX

Toward a Radical Humanist Anthropology

Man is the measure of all things...
Each and every event is for me as it appears to me,
and is for you as it appears for you.

Protagoras[1]

We read the same facts differently. 'Waterloo,' with the same fixed details, spells a 'victory' for an Englishman; for a Frenchman it spells a 'defeat.'

James (1907: 118)

'Its terrible!' [as a description of a peasant rebellion] is obviously a theory of the landlord class; 'Its fine!' is the theory of the peasants.

Mao Tse-tung quoted in Guha (1983a: 89)

AFFIRMING COEVALITY

This book has attempted to deal with the challenge posed by Fabian's *Time and the Other: How Anthropology Makes its Object*. He defined the denial of coevalness as the 'persistent and systematic tendency to place the referent(s) of anthropology in a Time other than the present of the producer of anthropological discourse' (1983: 31) and noted that its affirmation involves 'the problematic simultaneity of different conflicting, and contradictory forms of consciousness' (1983: 146). The implication of his analysis is the need for a radical transformation in the way anthropologists think about the world. The current rash of writing about the Other by anthropologists would suggest that Fabian's work has had the opposite effect to that intended because, far from bringing about the dismantling of the notion of the Other, he has merely provided us with a semantic successor to the Savage, the Primitive, the Tribal and the Traditional. However, there is also evidence of a change in anthropological thinking as the politics of the era of savage money forces anthropologists to confront the moral dilemmas of thinking and working in the world today. The obligation of the anthropologist is no longer to merely represent the native point of view but to critique it. The native point of view has always been a problematic simultaneity of different conflicting and contradictory forms of consciousness even though it is often presented as otherwise. Free market anarchist values are just as much a part of the native point of view as the so-called non-Western values.

In this book I have tried to dismantle the notion of the anthropological Other by beginning with unity rather than difference. Free market anarchist values are dominant today and became ascendant after 1971 when President Nixon broke the forty year old U.S. government pledge to convert foreign dollar holdings into gold at the fixed rate of 35:1. This marked the symbolic fall of statism, the end of the era when the state was able to control the market for gold. I have called this new era of disorganised capitalism the era of 'savage money'. In choosing this title I am not arguing that the economy is determinate in the last instance as certain varieties of Marxism would have it. To the contrary, I see the money form of value as a mere *index* of power analogous to the mercury in a thermometer; power, for its part, is analogous to the heat that moves the mercury. Power is a human relationship that assumes a myriad of historically, geographically and anthropologically specific forms; this is the basis of the economic relations such as wages, prices and profits as Sraffa (1960) showed.

Guha's conception of power as a general relation of domination and subordination is nothing more than an intellectual tool for studying its many contingent manifestations. Whereas Dumont separates status from power and gives primacy to the former, Guha sees the struggle for prestige as an aspect of the manifestation of power. His work has quite literally changed the terms of debate about Indian society and culture and the question arises as to the generality of the paradigm shift that he has sought to bring about. As I see it, his thought can be read as a partial rehabilitation of a radical humanist tradition of anthropological thought. The values, logic, and rhetoric of this school of thought are needed more than ever today by those of us who prefer to take a critical stance on the values that are now paramount in the world, values that affect the thought and actions of the anthropologist as much as the people they study.

Anthropologists, as Fabian reminds us, must come to terms with the fact that the relationship between the West and the Rest is first and foremost an imperialist power relationship. From the perspective of domesticated money, four eras are clearly defined: the three centuries from 1497 when the new Spanish dollar began its reign as the international standard of value; the century from 1825 when the English pound sterling was paramount; the half-century from 1934 when the U.S. dollar reigned supreme; and the era of savage money which began in 1971 when the U.S. dollar went wild. The history of anthropological thought can be read both as an apology for these relations of domination as well as a radical humanist critique of them. This ambivalence is to be found as much within the thought of a single anthropologist as it is between them. It is also necessary to see the paradoxes and contradictions within images of the West and the Rest that scholars in other disciplines have developed. Such images must inform the premises of any anthropological analysis and it is necessary to be constantly questioning them.

Nelson's (1969) idea of the rise of modern capitalism as a journey from Tribal Brotherhood to Universal Otherhood is a seductive one that captures something of the transformations in value that have occurred since Columbus. This argument is a variation on a familiar theme: status to contract, organic solidarity to mechanical solidarity, feudalism to capitalism, the rise of individualism. My fieldwork on markets and merchants in India, along with the comparative work I have done on money as reported in this book, leads me to question not so much the conceptual distinction between Otherhood and Brotherhood as the evolutionary theory that informs dichotomies of this kind. What he calls the 'Deuteronomic double standard' — make a profit from Others[2] but not Brothers — has not been resolved in favour of Otherhood by the elimination of

Brotherhood but, rather, has seen profit making emerge as a paramount value of the Brotherhood. Thus the commonplace contradiction of the double standard has created a situation where the Universal Otherhood of the market has become a dominant value because of the strength, especially in the rural areas of Asia, of Tribal Brotherhood as a value.

Brotherhood, I have tried to show, divides, in the first instance, into superalternate and subalternate varieties. The internal workings of any Brotherhood are informed by the values of patriarchy, its external workings by the values of temporality and territoriality. These create stratified Brotherhoods characterised by discrete boundaries of inclusion and exclusion rather than smooth continuities. The Brotherhood is not only a feature of so-called 'semi-feudal' countries like India. As I have shown in Chapter III, the values of an elite English Brotherhood maintained land as an inalienable keepsake, as a *good*, and this helped capitalist *commodity* production to flourish in that country in an historically unprecedented way.

The Brotherhood is to the House as Otherhood is to the Market and Nationhood is to the State. But whereas the Otherhood found in the Market is a universalising and unifying value, Brotherhood is a particularist and divisive cultural force. As values, Brotherhood, Otherhood and Nationhood can coexist but the form of the coevality is forever changing. If the statism of the era of the U.S. dollar was characterised by the intersection of Otherhood and Nationhood, the free market anarchism of the era of savage money is defined by a new intersection, that of Otherhood and Brotherhood as manifested in the new 'clean' ethnic spaces that are being created in some parts of the world today.

The cultural constructionists of the montage school have identified this post-modern cultural diversity and given it pride of place in their analysis. As such, the historical unity upon which diversity is premised is de-emphasised and the commonplace contradictions between the coeval values often overlooked. Culturalists employ the logic of juxtaposition and the rhetoric of representation to decode the meaning of cultural diversity. But the unmeaningness of the connections that can arise from commonplace contradictions, identified and analysed by Das (1994b), pose insoluble problems for the cultural constructionist school as they struggle to come to terms with the real problems posed by the era of savage money.

Consider the new series, *Late Editions: Cultural Studies for the End of the Century,* the first edition of which appeared as *Perilous States: Conversations on Culture, Politics and Nation* edited by George Marcus (1993a). This is heralded as a new *fin-de-siècle* style of ethnographical research and writing aimed to provide 'unconventional but deep access to emergent cultural formations'; it emphasises 'direct exposure to the quality of other "voices"'(Marcus, 1993b: 1). What 'deep access' means can be seen by examining one of the essays, that by Holmes entitled 'Illicit Discourse'. This essay consists of 24 pages, some 18 of which consists of direct quotation. Most of this is in the form of an interview with Bruno Gollnisch, a Member of the European Parliament and a member of the Technical Group of the European Right led by Jean-Marie Le Pen. The interview is interspersed with quotations from a report on the Committee of Inquiry into Racism and Xenophobia. Here is a sample.

> HOLMES: But the implication of Mr. Le Pen's polices can lead to discriminations based on race?
> GOLLNISCH: Yes, but it depends on the way you take the word *racism*. Our adversaries try to say that it is a racist policy to retain some form of identity. Obviously, it is easier to assimilate if your origins are from the same race, culture, religion, and so on, than for people from a completely different race, culture, and religion from the majority of the people in the country. I don't know if Le Pen told you when you met him but there was an interview when he went to America ... Among the questions put to Le Pen was 'Why are you against immigration, because you see a country like America built entirely on immigration?' Le Pen responded, 'Yes, I know this, but remember in France I am the representative of the aborigines.' American immigration policy may have been good for the melting pot, but certainly not for the Sioux, Navaho, and so on (Holmes, 1993: 266).

What is the reader to make of texts like this? Is this an anthropology of the sort of views that go to make up what I have called free market anarchism or is it an apology for them? Holmes (1993: 257), to his credit, asks himself this question and notes that it 'gets at the heart of what anthropologists owe to their informants'(emphasis added). He decides to err 'on the side of candour, depicting the arresting character of various political aspirations while opening interpretation and scrutiny to the reader'. But is he not abdicating responsibility by doing this? A member of the editorial board, who was concerned 'about the danger of letting Gollnisch's commentary stand unanswered or unengaged by his interviewer', raised this question (Marcus, 1993b: 13). Marcus defends Holmes' position on the grounds that he uses excerpts from the Committee on Racism report 'which effectively *juxtaposes* the simplifications in "social analysis" commentary to the disturbing complexities of well-articulated right-wing positions' (emphasis added). But wherein lies the effectiveness of this juxtaposition? Marcus merely asserts that it is effective; he does not argue the case.

One problem with montage, as its leading theorist Sergei Eisenstein (1943) noted, is that it is a form of logic that relies on *established conventions*; as such, it is possible to draw the wrong conclusions from juxtapositions. When two facts, two phenomena or two objects are juxtaposed, he notes, we are accustomed to make, almost automatically, a deductive generalisation. When we see a woman in mourning weeping beside a grave, notes Eisenstein (1943: 14-15) we tend to jump to the conclusion that the woman is a widow; a writer like Bierce, he adds, exploits this quality of montage for creative effect:

> A Woman in widow's weeds was weeping upon a grave.
> Console yourself, madam,' said a Sympathetic Stranger.
> 'Heaven's mercies are infinite. There is another man somewhere, beside your husband, with whom you can still be happy.'
> 'There was,' she sobbed—'there was, but this is his grave.'
> (Quoted in Eisenstein, 1943: 14–15).

Montage, then, must be handled very carefully to get the effect desired. Representation A juxtaposed with representation B will not necessarily give the desired effect C. As Eisenstein (1943: 19) noted:

> Representation A and representation B must be selected from all the possible features within the theme that is being developed, must be sought for, so that their juxtaposition—that is the juxtaposition of those very elements and not alternative ones— shall evoke in the perception and feelings of the spectator the most complete image of the theme itself.

While 'scissors and paste' montage is obviously the essence of a temporal medium like film, in a written article it becomes a series of sequential collages that evokes confusion in the reader rather than an image of a unifying theme. Marcus implicitly recognises this when he gives us the benefit of his editorial authority. 'Holmes's point,' he (1993b: 13) tells us, 'is that the left-right traditional frame of political discourse in the new Europe is evolving into really different kinds of moral allegories that conventional social science or theory, as yet, fails to grasp.' Such editorial intervention only serves to confuse the issue further. If this is Holmes's antithesis, what is his thesis?

Some members of the editorial board also had worries about another article in collection where the unchallenged views of certain apologists for the Russian government are represented. 'In this case,' Marcus (1993b: 14) argues, 'the staged cross-referencing of the interviews is a reflexive technique of presentation which should reinforce suspiciousness of readers about taking any of the statements at face value.' Authoritative editorial interventions of this kind may stop the reader from taking the statements at face value but how do they help the reader to gain deep access? If *Late Editions* provides no answer to this question, it deserves credit for having raised an extremely important moral issue. Le Pen, after all, is not the only Aborigine who holds such views. One can find Australian Aborigines who think like him on certain issues. What is the anthropologist to do with such values? Is it sufficient to translate and represent them? It seems to me that juxtaposition of views does not amount to the affirmation of coevality and that the problem can only be confronted by going beyond culture theory in whatever form. This includes the Chicago 'historical ethnography' school of global culture whose theories reproduce the same problems as the cultural juxtapositionalists, if in a slightly different way. Sahlins's (1994) 'Goodbye to Tristes Tropes: Ethnography in the Context of Modern World History' serves to illustrate this point.

Sahlins draws our attention to the paradox 'that global modernity is often reproduced as local diversity' (1994: 377). The apparent unity of world capitalism, he argues, is everywhere dissolved by the novel accents it acquires in particular places. 'The first commercial impulse of the [colonised] people is not to become just like us but more like themselves,' he writes (1994: 388). The empire is striking back. We are witnessing, he argues, a 'spontaneous, worldwide movement of cultural defiance, whose full meanings and historic effects are yet to be determined' (1994: 379). What needs to be studied, he says, is the 'indigenization of modernity' (1994: 390). He illustrates this notion with brief discussion of the history of Fiji, a subject on which he has done a great deal of original research. In vintage Sahlins fashion, he inverts the orthodoxy by asserting that 'it was not European muskets that made Fijian chiefs powerful so much as the chiefs that made the muskets historically powerful' (1994: 391). This argument is illustrated by examining the history of whale teeth in Fiji, items that fetch an extraordinarily high price in the pawnshops of Suva today. He notes, too, that Colonel Rabuka, who led a *coup d'état* in 1987, begged forgiveness from traditional authorities by the presentation of whale teeth.

The general thrust of arguments of this kind cannot be denied. Indeed, I noticed similar things happening in PNG. In *Gifts and Commodities*, for example, I argued that there was a 'tendency for the transformation of commodities into gifts'. However, I also argued for the countervailing tendency and for the existence of a contradiction between the two. Sahlins does not give any weight to this countervailing tendency. As Jonathan Friedman (1994: 12) notes, 'while there is surely a tendency towards a local encompassment of the global in cultural terms, there is at the same time an encompassment of the local by the global in material terms.' Sahlins is aware of arguments of this type but he argues against them. Sahlins asserts that 'not everything in the contest is contested' and develops the following argument about the importance of non-contradiction:

> In order for categories to be contested at all, there must be a common system of intelligibility, extending to the grounds, means, modes, and issues of disagreement. It would be difficult to understand how a society could function, let alone how any knowledge of it could be constituted, if there were not some meaningful order in the differences. If in regard to some given event or phenomenon, the women of a community say one thing and the men another, it is not because men and women have different positions in, and experience of, the same social universe of discourse? Are not the differences in what men and women say expressions of the social differences in the construction of gender?

If so, there is a noncontradictory way—may one say, totalizing way?—of describing the contradictions, a system of and in the differences (Sahlins, 1994: 386).

A common system of intelligibility presupposes reciprocal recognition. In such a case, there is a 'noncontradictory way of totalising': hierarchical opposition of non-antagonistic Radcliffe-Brownian, Lévi-Straussian, Dumontian, etc. kind. But there is no common system of intelligibility with asymmetrical recognition. This is what characterises commonplace contradiction. The history of Fiji provides ample illustration of this contradiction if one considers the history of the Indian community in Fiji. Significantly, Sahlins does not mention this history when talking about the indigenisation of modernity in Fiji. Rabuka's conception of Fijian culture cannot be understood without reference to this antagonistic contradiction. His values with respect to the Fijian Indians are, I suggest, of the depressingly familiar free market anarchist variety; he and Le Pen and have much in common on this point. He has other whale-teeth type values too, of course, and he switches between these opportunistically. The events of 1987 suggest that the switching he did then had one common aim: to eliminate the commonplace contradiction between Indians and Fijians through the creation of a 'clean' cultural Aboriginal Fijian space.

Anthropologists should not be like the Sympathetic Stranger in Bierce's tale. Nor should they be Unsympathetic Strangers. Anthropologists need values to cope with the dilemmas of coevalness: we need theories to help us describe what is and we need norms to help us evaluate the facts as we see them. In other words, if coevality is to be affirmed and the dominant unifying values of the world today are to be correctly identified and criticised, then we must move from the reifications of culture theory to a humanist value theory.

TOWARD A RADICAL HUMANIST ANTHROPOLOGY

A sympathetic reading of the history of anthropological thought reveals a long history of critical humanist thought. However, to find it one must sometimes get beyond explicit positions to the implicit assumptions. Many anthropologists of the interwar period concealed a passionate commitment to the values of a humanist anthropology behind an explicit advocacy of a dispassionate, value-free, social scientism. They did not take a dispassionate value free approach to the rise of fascism in the 1930s. This contradiction is apparent in a book such as Firth's (1938) *Human Types.* This has the rhetoric of a dispassionate scientist but the passions of a humanist as anthropological evidence is marshalled to debunk the racist views about Aboriginal peoples. It is interesting to note that in his latest book Firth (1995) actually identifies as a humanist of the scientific realist variety. Radcliffe-Brown's humanism is, paradoxically, most explicit in his most scientific book, *Natural Science of Society* (1957). Here we find culture defined as 'a certain standardization of behavior, inner and outer, in a certain group of human beings' (1957: 92). 'Culture,' he adds, 'continues by the fact that *individuals are subjected to acts of other people on them,* not to acts of culture' (emphasis added). He then proceeds to critique the cultural constructionists of his time for the 'fallacy of reification of culture'. This fallacy, as my discussion of the work of Appadurai in Chapter II revealed, is not only alive and well today, it is championed as a methodological principle of great originality.

Radcliffe-Brown's scientism leads him to erect a barrier between fact and morality and to place an intellectual taboo on the latter. For example, in his discussion of the Principle of Justice, which he calls 'the fundamental principle of human society', he argues that 'such a principle is not to be discussed ethically'. The social scientist, 'is not concerned with what justice ought to be. He is concerned only with finding what actual principles have appeared and in what form in various societies they represent justice' (1957: 131). This taboo, along with the principle of contradiction that informs his theory of society and culture, gives his humanism a non-radical twist. 'One way of standardizing behavior in such a way that there cannot be any dispute or disagreement,' he argues (1957: 138), 'is to standardize value.' Yes, but how to establish the standard? 'Principles,' he answers (1957:140), 'vary only according to the different standards of what is adjudged as just in different social systems. All revert to one fundamental point: to the need for the adjustment of interests between individuals.' But what if there is irreconcilable conflict between individuals? While Radcliffe-Brown (1957: 118-9) has contradiction at the centre of his theory of society, it is contradiction of the non-antagonistic, ying-yang kind. The way to avoid disagreement, then, is to standardise value by imposing the values of the elite onto the society as a whole. If Dumont has described how an ideal Indian hierarchical society functions, then Radcliffe-Brown has described the egalitarian Aboriginal Australian equivalent. He was not blind to the fact, for example, that the Kariara were living as station hands on their dispossessed land, he just denied the coevalness of antagonistic commonplace contradictions of this kind.

The affirmation of the coexistence of contradictory forms of consciousness has implications for a theory of knowledge. The American humanist philosopher, F.C. Schiller, stressed this point in his interpretation of the ancient debate between Plato and Protagoras the humanist.

> Throughout the Theaetetus ... Plato has made the assumption that 'knowledge' is of 'universals' and not concerned or connected with the fleeting and variable judgements of individual men about their personal experience, that thought and sense-perception are antithetical and hostile, that the logical concept is something wholly superior to and independent of the psychical process, and the Protagorean suggestion, to start the theory of knowing from the actual knowing of the individual's perceptions is a proposal for the abolition of truth. No wonder after this that it becomes for him a serious 'contradiction' when A judges to be warm and B judges to be cold, seeing that 'it' cannot be both. But 'it' does not exist in abstraction from the divergent judgements; 'it' stands in this case for the problem of constructing a 'common' perception; if the two 'its' are to be brought together into an objective scheme of temperature, A and B must set to work to construct a thermometer, as to the readings of which they can agree. Plato, therefore, has merely debarred himself from understanding the de facto genesis and development of our common world of subjective intercourse, and by starting with abstraction from the personal character of both judgements, he has manufactured a fallacious contradiction (Schiller, 1907: 109).

Schiller's philosophy was inspired by William James's pragmatism and his work contains many thought provoking ideas. But his humanism, too, is conservative. He was a eugenicist who regarded the offspring of the lower class as less fit than those of the upper class. His ideal eugenical state, his biographer notes (Abel, 1965: 145–46), would encourage superior individuals. Such ideas, I believe, spring from the ahistorical and non-anthropological assumptions that inform his variety of humanism. 'Humanism,' he says (1907: 12), 'is really in itself the simplest of philosophic standpoints: it is merely the perception that the philosophic problem concerns human beings striving to comprehend a world of human experience by the resources of *human mind*' (emphasis added). Psychology, then, was the foundation of Schiller's humanism. He recognised this much and described his position as a form of 'logical psychologism'. In other words, *individual cognition* rather than *reciprocal recognition* was the basis of his humanism. A radical humanist does not deny the importance of individual cognition but assigns it a secondary role behind reciprocal recognition. The latter, as I have tried to show in this book, elevates an historically informed anthropology to pride of place above psychology.

A humanism of this kind has its historical precedents in the logical and rhetorical writings of John Milton, the great English poet and revolutionary of the seventeenth century. Milton (1672 [1982]) was one of the last writers in the Ramist logical tradition. His logic, like most Ramist logics, consisted of two parts. The first part dealt with the 'inventions' of *commonplace*[3] logic, the second part with the 'dispositions' of *axiomatic* logic. Commonplace logic, which has a long history going back to Aristotle, fell by the wayside as the mathematicians in the post-Cartesian world concentrated on developing the formal existential logic of axiomatic thought. By the mid-nineteenth century it was as if the tradition of commonplace logic never existed. Boole's logic, for example, is based solely on the principle of axiomatic contradiction, the idea that nothing is both x and not-x.

Milton makes much of the distinction between commonplace and axiomatic contradiction, one of the few logicians in the English tradition to do so, as far as I can tell. Commonplace logic is of no use to the mathematician because, by definition, it is based on a form of doubt that scepticism cannot transform into a self-evident truth. Whereas Cartesian style scepticism raises questions to *remove* doubt, pre-Cartesian scepticism raises questions to *create* doubt. Commonplace logic, then, is a logic of doubt; a logic where the argument 'A is B' is thrown into doubt by asking 'Is A B?' It questions the logical *commonplace* that is supposed to link the antecedent A with the consequent B. These commonplaces, grounded as they are in history, geography and anthropology, are always open to question. Consider the following example from Cicero's *Topica*. If a wife was bequeathed silver by her husband, is coin found in the house hers? Using the argument *commonplace genus*, notes Cicero (1960: 391), one can argue in the affirmative because coin (A) is silver (B) via the commonplace genus. Arguments like this only hold when and where silver is coined. This particular argument was relevant in Europe from Cicero's time to 1914 when token coinage entered circulation, sending the precious metal content of money underground to places like Fort Knox. In other words, *commonplace* logic has historical and geographical *generality*; unlike *axiomatic* logic, it makes no *eternal* and *universal* truth claims.

What then is a commonplace contradiction for Milton? This is found in his discussion of *negating contraries* which are opposed to *affirming contraries*. The latter include *relatives*, such as father/son or the eaglehawk/crow distinction as understood by the Australian Aborigines, and *adverses* such as pure/impure in the Indian sense. In my language, these affirming contraries presuppose *reciprocal recognition*. Negating contraries are those characterised by asymmetrical recognition and they fall into two types: *contradictories* and *privation*. An example of the former is the Englishman who says 'Waterloo spells victory' and finds himself contradicted by the Frenchman who says 'Waterloo does not spell victory'. An example of privation is the Aristotle who says 'Slavery is natural because slaves have no soul' and finds himself questioned by the slave who claims he has a soul.

This, at least, is my interpretation of the implications of Milton's important logical distinctions. Others, I hasten to add, find little value in Milton's logical work. On this point I part company with Fabian (1982: 178) who, quoting the formidable authority of W.J. Ong,[4] dismisses Milton's logic as philosophy for teenagers. What is more, he finds in the Ramist tradition the philosophical origins of his 'denial of coevality' thesis. I could not disagree more. If coevality is to be affirmed then commonplace contradiction is to be affirmed.

It is beyond the scope of this book to dispute Fabian (and Ong) on the value of Milton's logic. I can merely assert my belief that Guha's 'logic of subaltern consciousness' and Lévi-Strauss's 'logic of concrete quality' develop Book I of Milton's logic in a way that Boole's logic develops Book II. This requires a critical analysis of Milton's logic in the light of Boole, Lévi-Strauss and Guha. Such an analysis, situated in the light of twentieth century anthropological thought on the 'modes of thought' question, would, I believe, reveal that the 'logical scandals' supposedly found in the heads of informants reside in the head of the anthropologist. It would reveal, too, the problems involved in an anthropology that begins with psychology rather than an historically informed conception of anthropological unity. In sum, Marcus and company have moved us in the right direction by rehabilitating a humanist rhetoric; the task is now to rehabilitate humanist logic.

A final word must be said about the concept of *subalternity*. This word has at least two meanings in Guha's work. On the one hand it is a social scientific classification which refers to that segment of the population left after the numbers in the triumvirate of government officials, money lenders, and landlords have been deducted. On the other hand, subalternity as a *value* refers to that form of critical consciousness which, for example, leads slaves to question the values of their masters. When such questioning leads to rebellion the *commonplace contradictions* create sharp social divisions as villagers switch value systems. The result is that actions such as the wrecking, burning, looting and plunder of elite property acquire positive values. Before the rebellion these values are subordinated to others, be they those of a temple priest, day-labourer, vegetable seller, or bank robber. Value switching, then, brings about a qualitative change in the social fabric of society analogous to that of a *rite de passage* as, for example, when the criminal dies and is reborn a rebel. These switches are not always obvious to outsiders and Guha (1983a: 99) cites an instance where a clash between a group's view of themselves as rebels and a policeman's insistence on dealing with them as criminals triggered off an insurrection. Rival cognitions, then, may lead to violence but this is by no means a necessary implication. The working out of the logic of commonplace contradiction is always concrete, always located historically, geographically, and anthropologically. Subalternity as a value, then, is a form of consciousness about human relationships.

Subalternity as the radical questioning of the received doctrine of the elite is not something that only politically subordinated people can do. It is a value that intellectuals can appropriate for themselves if they so desire; for the radical humanist intellectual subalternity is the supreme value.

NOTES

1 See Waterfield (1987: 30) for the context of this famous statement and a commen-tary on Plato reportage of it.
2 Nelson's notion of the Other, as I mentioned in the chapters above, must not be confused with Fabian's notion; Nelson's Otherhood is akin to Marx's notion of alienation.
3 Milton used the term Latin term *topica* which comes from the Greek *topos* for 'place'. Translators of logical texts for this period generally prefer the English 'topic' but the word 'commonplace' is also frequently used.
4 See Ong's introduction to Milton 1982.

Bibliography

Abel, R. (1965). *The Pragmatic Humanism of F.C.S. Schiller*. New York: King's Crown Press.

Alexander, J. (1987). *Trade, Traders and Trading in Rural Java*. Oxford: ASAA Southeast Asia Publication Series No. 15.

Anderson, R. S., & Huber, W. (1988). *The Hour of the Fox*. Seattle: University of Washington Press.

Appadurai, A. (1986). Introduction: Commodities and the Politics of Value. In A. Appadurai (ed.), *The Social Life of Things: Commodities in Cultural Perspective*. Cambridge: Cambridge University Press.

Appadurai, A. (1990). Disjuncture and Difference in the Global Cultural Economy. *Public Culture*, 2(2), 1–24.

Baden-Powell, B. H. (1892). *The Land-Systems of British India*. Oxford: Oxford University Press.

Baijal, P., & Deo, S. M. (1977). Madhya Pradesh (Bastar District). In S. N. Dubey & R. Murdia (eds), *Land Alienation and Restoration in the Tribal Communities of India*. Bombay: Himalaya Publishing House.

Bailey, F. G. (1957). *Caste and the Economic Frontier: A Village in Highland Orissa*. Manchester: Manchester University Press.

Bailey, F. G. (1964). Capital, Saving and Credit in Highland Orissa (India). In R. Firth & B. S. Yamey (eds), *Capital, Saving and Credit in Peasant Societies*. London: George Unwin.

Beals, R. L. (1975). *The Peasant Marketing System of Oaxaca, Mexico*. Berkeley: University of California Press.

Bhaduri, A. (1993). *Unconventional Economic Essays*. Delhi: Oxford University Press.

Blaikie, P., & Brookfield, H. (1978). *Land Degradation and Society*. New York: Methuen.

Boagey, E. (1977). *Poetry Workbook*. Slough: University Tutorial Press.

Bohannan, P. (1959). The Impact of Money on an African Subsistence Economy. In G. Dalton (ed.), *Tribal and Peasant Economies: Readings in Economic Anthropology*. New York: The Natural History Press.

Boole, G. (1854). *An Investigation of The Laws of Thought, on which are founded The Mathematical Theories of Logic and Probabilities.* New York: Dover Publications, Inc., 1951.

Borneman, J. (1992). *Belonging in the Two Berlins: Kin, Nation, State.* Cambridge: Cambridge University Press.

Briggs, G. W. (1953). *The Doms and Their Near Neighbours.* Mysore: Wesley Press.

Brodsky, D. A., & Sampson, G. P. (1980a). The Value of Gold as a Reserve Asset. *World Development,* 8, 175–192.

Brodsky, D. A., & Sampson, G. P. (1980b). Gold, Special Drawing Rights and Developing Countries. *Trade and Development,* Autumn, 49–68.

Burns, R. D., & Leitenberg, M. (1984). *The Wars in Vietnam, Cambodia and Laos 1954–1982: A Bibliographic Guide.* Santa Barbara: ABC-Clio Information Services.

Business Week (1981). A Return to the Gold Standard. *Business Week,* 21 September, pp. 58–64.

Butlin, S. J. (1953). *Foundations of the Australian Monetary System, 1788–1851.* Melbourne: Melbourne University Press.

Carrier, J. G. (1995). *Gifts and Commodities: Exchange and Western Capitalism since 1700.* London: Routledge.

Carrier, J. G., & Carrier, A. H. (1989). *Wage, Trade, and Exchange in Melanesia: A Manus Society in the Modern State.* Berkeley: University of California Press.

Carrithers, M., & Humphrey, C. (1991). Introduction. *The Assembly of Listeners: Jains in Society.* Cambridge: Cambridge University Press.

Chakrabarty, D. (1995). Radical Histories and the Question of Enlightenment Rationalism: Some Recent Critiques of *Subaltern Studies. Economic and Political Weekly,* 30(14), 751–759.

Chalmers, R. (1893). *History of Currency in the British Colonies.* London: Eyre & Spottiswoode.

Chayanov, A. V. (1966). *The Theory of Peasant Economy.* Homewood: Irwin.

Cicero, M. T. (1960). *Topics* (H.M. Hubbell, trans.). London: William Heinemann.

Clay, C. (1968). Marriage, Inheritance, and the Rise of Large Estates in England, 1660–1815. *The Economic History Review,* 21(3), 503–518.

Comaroff, J., & Comaroff, J. L. (1990). Goodly Beasts and Beastly Goods: Cattle and Commodities in a South African Context. *American Ethnologist,* 17(2), 195–216.

Connell, J. (1977). The Bougainville Connection: Changes in the Economic Context of Shell Money Production in Malaita. *Oceania,* 48(1), 81–101.

Connolly, B., & Anderson, R. (1988). *Joe Leahy's Neighbours (video).* Sydney: Arundel Productions.

Cottam Ellis, C. M. (1991). The Jain Merchant Castes of Rajasthan: Some Aspects of the Management of Social Identity in a Market Town. In M. Carrithers & C. Humphrey (eds.), *The Assembly of Listeners: Jains in Society.* Cambridge: Cambridge University Press.

Crooke, W. (1926). *Religion and Folklore in Northern India.* Oxford: Oxford University Press.

DaMatta, R. (1994). Some Biassed Remarks on Interpretivism: A View from Brazil. In R. Borofsky (ed.), *Assessing Cultural Anthropology.* New York: McGraw-Hill.

Das, V. (1989a). Subaltern as Perspective. In R. Guha (ed.), *Subaltern Studies VI: Writings on South Asian History and Society.* Delhi: Oxford.

Das, V. (1989b). Voices of Children. *Daedalus,* 118(4), 263–294.

Das, V. (1990). Our Work to Cry: Your Work to Listen. In V. Das (ed.), *Mirrors of Violence: Communities, Riots and Survivors in South Asia.* Delhi: Oxford University Press.

Das, V. (1994a). The Anthropological Discourse on India. In R. Borofsky (ed.), *Assessing Cultural Anthropology.* New York: McGraw-Hill.

Das, V. (1994b). Moral Orientations to Suffering: Legitimation, Power, and Healing. In L. Chen, A. Kleinman, & N. C. Ware (eds.), *Health and Social Change in International Perspective.* Cambridge, MA: Harvard University Press.

Davis, W. G. (1973). *Social Relations in a Philippine Market: Self-interest and Subjectivity.* Berkeley: University of California Press.

DDRS. (Various). *Declassified Documents Reference System.* Carrollton Press.

De, S. C. (1952a). The Cowry Currency in India. *The Orissa Historical Research Journal,* 1(1), 1–10.

De, S. C. (1952b). Cowry Currency in Orissa. *The Orissa Historical Research Journal,* 1(2), 10–21.

Desjarlais, R., & Kleinman, A. (1994). Violence and Demoralization in the New World Disorder. *Anthropology Today,* 10(5), 9–12.

Dewey, A. (1962a). *Peasant Marketing in Java.* New York: The Free Press.

Dewey, A. (1962b). Trade and Social Control in Java. *Journal of the Royal Anthropological Institute,* 92, 177–190.

DOD (1972). *The Economics of Defense Spending: A Look at the Realities.* Washington: US Department of Defense.

Dorward, D. C. (1976). Precolonial Tiv Trade and Cloth Currency. *The International Journal of African Historical Studies,* 9(4), 576–591.

Douglas, M., & Isherwood, B. (1980). *The World of Goods.* Harmondsworth: Penguin.

Dubbeldam, L. F. B. (1964). The Devaluation of the Kapauku-Cowrie as a Factor of Social Disintegration. *American Anthropologist,* 66(4), 293–303.

Dudley, L., & Passell, P. (1968). The War in Vietnam and the United States Balance of Payments. *Review of Economic and Statistics,* 50, 437–442.

Dumont, L. (1977). *From Mandeville to Marx: The Genesis and Triumph of Economic Ideology.* Chicago: Chicago University Press.

Dumont, L. (1980a). *Homo Hierarchicus: The Caste System and Its Implications.* Chicago: Chicago University Press.

Dumont, L. (1980b). On Value. *Proceedings of the British Academy*, 66, 207–241.

Dumont, L. (1983). *Affinity as a Value: Marriage Alliance in South India, with Comparative Essays on Australia.* Chicago: Chicago University Press.

Duncan, D. (1966). The Whole Thing Was a Lie. *Ramparts,* February, 76–96.

Eisenstein, S. (1943). *Film Sense* (J. Leyda, trans.). London: Faber & Faber.

Elwert, G. (1973). *Wirtschaft und Herrschaft von Daxome (Dahomey) im 18. Jahrhundert.* München: Kommissionsverlag Klaus Renner.

Elwert, G. (1989). *An Intricate Oral Culture: On History, Humour and Social Control Among the Ayizo (Benin).* Berlin: FU Berlin Institut Für Ethnologie, No. 16.

Elwert, G. (1995). Boundaries, Cohesion and Switching: On We-groups in Ethnic and Religious Form. *Unpublished paper.*

Elwin, V. (1942). The Use of Cowries in Bastar State, India. *Man,* 72 (November–December), 121–124.

Elwin, V. (1947). *The Muria and their Ghotul.* Oxford: Oxford University Press.

Emeneau, M. B. (1940). A Classical Indian Folk-tale as a Reported Modern Event: The Brahman and the Mongoose. *Proceedings of the American Philosophical Society,* 83, 503–513.

Etzioni, A. (1991). Socio-Economics: A Budding Challenge. In A. Etizoni & P. R. Lawrence (eds), *Socio-Economics: Towards a New Synthesis.* New York: M.E. Sharpe.

Everett, J., & Savara, M. (1984). Bank Loans to the Poor in Bombay: Do Women Benefit? *Signs,* 10, 272–290.

Fabian, J. (1983). *Time and the Other: How Anthropology Makes its Object.* New York: Columbia University Press.

Fay, S. (1982). *The Great Silver Bubble.* London: Hodder and Stoughton.

Feaveryear, A. (1963). *The Pound Sterling: A History of English Money* (2nd ed.). Oxford: Oxford University Press.

Fenton, R. (1611). *A Treatise of Usurie.* Amsterdam: Theatrum Orbis Terrarum, 1975.

Ferguson, J. (1988). Cultural Exchange: New Developments in the Anthropology of Commodities. *Cultural Anthropology,* 3, 488–513.

Fifi'i, J. (1989). *From Pig-Theft to Parliament: My Life between Two Worlds.* (R. Keesing, trans.). Suva: Solomon Islands College of Higher Education & University of the South Pacific.

Firth, R. (1938). *Human Types.* London: Thomas Nelson.

Firth, R. (1995). *Religion: A Humanist Interpretation.* London: Routledge.

Foster, G. M. (1965). Peasant Society and the Image of Limited Good. *American Anthropologist,* 67(2), 293–315.

Fox, R. G. (1967). Family, Caste, and Commerce in a North Indian Market Town. *Economic Development and Cultural Change,* 15(3), 297–314.

Friedman, J. (1994). *Cultural Identity and Global Process.* London: Sage.

Friedman, M. (1962). *Price Theory: A Provisional Text.* Chicago: Aldine.

Friedman, M. (1987). Quantity Theory of Money. In J. Eatwell, M. Milgate, & P. Newman (eds), *The New Palgrave: A Dictionary of Economics.* London: Macmillan.

Friedman, M., & Schwartz, A. J. S. (1963). *A Monetary History of the United States 1867–1960.* Princeton: Princeton University Press.

Frumkin, A. (1969). *Modern Theories of International Economic Relations.* Moscow: Progress.

Garrison, C. B., & Mayhew, A. (1983). The Alleged War Origins of the Current Inflation: A Comment. *Journal of Economic Issues,* 17, 175–186.

Geertz, C. (1963). *Agricultural Involution: The Process of Ecological Change in Indonesia.* Berkeley: University of California Press.

Geertz, C. (1979). Suq: The Bazaar Economy in Sefrou. In C. Geertz, H. Geertz, & L. Rosen (eds), *Meaning and Order in Moroccan Society.* Cambridge: Cambridge University Press.

Geertz, C. (1983). *Local Knowledge: Further Essays in Interpretive Anthropology.* New York: Basic Books.

Geertz, C. (1994). The Uses of Diversity. In R. Borofsky (ed.), *Assessing Cultural Anthropology.* New York: McGraw-Hill.

Geertz, C. (1995). *After the Fact: Four Decades, Two Countries, One Anthropologist.* Cambridge, Mass.: Harvard University Press.

Gell, A. (1982). The Market Wheel: Symbolic Aspects of an Indian Tribal Market. *Man,* 17, 470–91.

Gell, A. (1986). Newcomers to the World of Goods: Consumption Among the Muria Gonds. In A. Appadurai (ed.), *The Social Life of Things.* Cambridge: Cambridge University Press.

Gell, A. (1992). Inter-tribal Commodity Barter and Reproductive Gift-exchange in Old Melanesia. In C. S. Humphrey & S. Hugh-Jones (eds), *Barter, Exchange and Value.* Cambridge: Cambridge University Press.

Gell, S. M. S. (1992). *The Ghotul in Muria Society.* Reading: Harwood Academic Publishers.

Gilbert, M. (1980). *Quest for World Monetary Order: The Gold-Dollar System and its Aftermath.* New York: John Wiley.

Gold Commission (1982). *Report to the Congress of the Commission on the Role of Gold in the Domestic and International Monetary Systems.* Washington, D.C.: Congress of the United States.

Gouldner, A. W. (1960). The Norm of Reciprocity: A Preliminary Statement. *American Sociological Review,* 25(2), 161–78.

Gregory, C. A. (1980). Gifts to Men and Gifts to God: Gift Exchange and Capital Accumulation in Contemporary Papua. *Man,* 15(4), 626–52.

Gregory, C. A. (1982). *Gifts and Commodities*. London: Academic Press.

Gregory, C. A. (1988). Village Money Lending, the World Bank and Landlessness in Central India. *Journal of Contemporary Asia*, 18, 47–58.

Gregory, C. A. (1989). How the USA Made the Third World Pay for the Vietnam War. In P. Limqueco (ed.), *Partisan Scholarship: Essays in Honour of Renato Constantino*. Manila: JCA Press.

Gregory, C. A. (1992). The Poison in Raheja's Gift: A Review Article. *Social Analysis*, 32, 95–110.

Gregory, C. A. (1996). Cowries and Conquest: Towards a Subalternate Quality Theory of Money. *Comparative Studies in Society and History*, 38(2), 195–216.

Groenewegen, P. (ed.). (1983). *Quesnay: Farmers 1756 & Turgot: Sur la Grande et la Petite Culture*. Sydney: University of Sydney Economics Department Reprints of Economic Classics Series 2, Number 2.

Guha, R. (1982). On Some Aspects of the Historiography of Colonial India. In R. Guha (ed.), *Subalterns Studies I*. Delhi: Oxford University Press.

Guha, R. (1983a). *Elementary Aspects of Peasant Insurgency in Colonial India*. Delhi: Oxford University Press.

Guha, R. (1983b). The Prose of Counter-Insurgency. In R. Guha (ed.), *Subaltern Studies II*. Delhi: Oxford University Press.

Guha, R. (1985). The Career of an Anti-God in Heaven and on Earth. In A. Mitra (ed.), *The Truth Unites: Essays in Tribute to Samar Sen*. Calcutta: Subarnarekha.

Guha, R. (1989). Dominance Without Hegemony and Its Historiography. In R. Guha (ed.), *Subaltern Studies VI: Writings on South Asian History and Society*. Delhi: Oxford University Press.

Habakkuk, H. J. (1939–40). English Landownership, 1680–1740. *The Economic History Review*, 10, 2–17.

Habakkuk, H. J. (1950). Marriage Settlements in the Eighteenth Century. *Transactions of the Royal Historical Society*, 33, 15–30.

Habib, I. (1961). The Currency System of the Mughal Empire (1556–1707). *Medieval India Quarterly*, 4(1), 1–21.

Halberstam, D. (1969). *The Best and the Brightest*. New York: Random House.

Harcourt, G. C. (1982). *The Social Science Imperialists*. London: Routledge & Kegan Paul.

Harriss, J. (1982). *Capitalism and Peasant Farming: Agrarian Structure and Ideology in Northern Tamil Nadu*. Oxford: Oxford University Press.

Hart, K. (1986). Heads or Tails? Two Sides of the Coin. *Man*, 21(4), 637–656.

Hart, K. (1987). Barter. In J. Eatwell, M. Milgate, & P. Newman (eds), *The New Palgrave: A Dictionary of Economics*. London: Macmillan.

Hayden, I. (1987). *Symbol and Privilege: The Ritual Context of British Royalty*. Tuscon: University of Arizona Press.

Hazlehurst, L. W. (1968). Caste and Merchant Communities. In M. Singer & B. Cohen (eds), *Structure and Change in Indian Society*. Chicago: Aldine.

Heesterman, J. C. (1985). *The Inner Conflict of Tradition: Essays in Indian Ritual, Kingship, and Society*. Chicago: The University of Chicago Press.

Heimann, J. (1980). Small Change and Ballast: Cowry Trade and Usage as an Example of Indian Ocean Economic History. *South Asia,* 3(1), 48–69.

Hill, P. (1982). *Dry Grain Farming Families*. Cambridge: Cambridge University Press.

Hill, P. (1986). *Development Economics on Trial: The Anthropological Case for the Prosecution*. Cambridge: Cambridge University Press.

Hobsbawm, E. (1994). *Age of Extremes: The Short Twentieth Century 1914–1991*. London: Michael Joseph.

Hocart, A. M. (1952). *The Life-Giving Myth and Other Essays*. London: Methuen.

Hogendorn, J., & Johnson, M. (1986). *The Shell Money of the Slave Trade*. Cambridge: Cambridge University Press.

Holmes, D. R. (1993). Illicit Discourse. In G. E. Marcus (ed.), *Perilous States: Conversations on Culture, Politics, and Nation*. Chicago: Chicago University Press.

Hughes, I. (1977). *New Guinea Stone Age Trade. Terra Australis 3*. Canberra: Australian National University Press.

Hughes, I. (1978). Good Money and Bad: Inflation and Devaluation in the Colonial Process. *Mankind,* 11(3), 308–318.

Hunter, W. A. (1900). *Introduction to Roman Law*. London: Sweet and Maxwell.

IMF (1958). *International Reserves and Liquidity*. Washington: International Monetary Fund.

IMF (1983). *Supplement on International Reserves*. Washington: International Monetary Fund.

Jacobson, D. (1976). Women and Jewelry in Rural India. In G.R.Gupta (ed.), *Family and Social Change in Modern India*. New Delhi: Vikas.

Jain, L. C. (1929). *Indigenous Banking in India*. London: Macmillan.

James, W. (1907). *Pragmatism*. Cambridge, MA: Harvard University Press, 1975.

Jevons, W. (1871). *Theory of Political Economy*. Harmondsworth: Penguin, 1970.

Jones, I. H. M. (1991). Jain Shopkeepers and Moneylenders: Rural Informal Credit Networks in South Rajasthan. In M. Carrithers & C. Humphrey (eds), *The Assembly of Listeners: Jains in Society*. Cambridge: Cambridge University Press.

Jones, N. (1989). *God and the Moneylenders: Usury and Law in Early Modern England*. Oxford: Basil Blackwell.

KCA (1961–94). *Keesing's Contemporary Archives: Record of World Events.* London: Longman.

Keesing, R. (1994). Theories of Culture Revisited. In R. Borofsky (ed.), *Assessing Cultural Anthropology.* New York: McGraw-Hill.

Kettell, B. (1982). *Gold.* Oxford: Oxford University Press.

Keynes, J. M. (1982). Ancient Currencies. In D.Moggridge (ed.), *The Collected Writing of John Maynard Keynes.* London: Macmillan.

Kipling, R. (1959). *The Jungle Book.* London: Macmillan.

Klinghoffer, A. J. (1983). *The Political Economy of Soviet Gold: Some Implications for American Foreign Policy.* Research Paper No.51, Soviet and East European Research Centre, Hebrew University.

Knudtson, P., & Suzuki, D. (1992). *Wisdom of the Elders.* London: Allen and Unwin.

Kolko, G. (1985). *Anatomy of a War: Vietnam, the United States and the Modern Historical Experience.* New York: Pantheon.

Kolko, J., & Kolko, G. (1972). *The Limits of Power: The World and United States Foreign Policy, 1945–1954.* New York: Harper and Row.

Kottak, C., & Colson, E. (1994). Multilevel Linkages: Longitudinal and Comparative Studies. In R. Borofsky (ed.), *Assessing Cultural Anthropology.* New York: McGraw-Hill.

Kula, W. (1986). *Measures and Men.* Princeton: Princeton University Press.

Lash, S., & Urry, J. (1987). *The End of Organized Capitalism.* Cambridge: Polity.

Law, R. (1991). *The Slave Coast of West Africa 1550–1750: The Impact of the Atlantic Slave Trade on an African Society.* Oxford: Clarendon Press.

Lenin, V. I. (1899). *The Development of Capitalism in Russia.* London: Lawrence and Wishart.

Lévi-Strauss, C. (1984). *Anthropology and Myth: Lectures 1951–1982.* Oxford: Basil Blackwell, 1987.

Lewinski, J. S. (1913). *The Origin of Property and the Formation of the Village Community.* London: Constable.

Loveday, A. (1930). *Gold Supply and Demand.* Geneva: League of Nations.

Lowie, R. H. (1962). *The Origin of the State.* New York: Russell & Russell.

Lynch, J. E. (1976). Regional Impact of the Vietnam War. *Quarterly Review of Economics and Business,* 16, 37–50.

Malinowski, B., & de la Fuente, J. (1957). *Malinowski in Mexico: The Economics of a Mexican Market System* (S. Drucker-Brown, trans.). London: Routledge and Kegan Paul.

Marcus, G. E. (1985). Spending: The Hunts, Silver, and Dynastic Families in America. *Archives Européennes de Sociologie,* 26, 224–259.

Marcus, G. (1990). Once More into the Breach between Economic and Cultural Analysis. In R. Friedland & A.F. Robertson (eds), *Beyond the Marketplace: Rethinking Economy and Society.* New York: Aldine de Gruyter.

Marcus, G. E. (ed.). (1993a). *Perilous States: Conversations on Culture, Politics, and Nation.* Chicago: Chicago University Press.

Marcus, G. E. (1993b). Introduction. In G. E. Marcus (ed.), *Perilous States: Conversations on Culture, Politics, and Nation.* Chicago: Chicago University Press.

Martin, D.-C. (1995). The Choices of Identity. *Social Identities,* 1(1), 5–20.

Marx, K. (1867). *Capital, Vol. I.* Moscow: Progress.

Marx, K. (1894). *Capital, Vol. III.* Moscow: Progress.

Mauss, M. (1925). *The Gift: Forms and Functions of Exchange in Archaic Societies* (I. Cunnison, trans.). London: Routledge and Kegan Paul, 1954.

Maynes, C. W. (1993). Containing Ethnic Conflict. *Foreign Policy,* 90, 3–21.

McFarlane, A. (1976). *Resources and Population: A Study of the Gurungs of Nepal.* Cambridge: Cambridge University Press.

McNamara, R. (1986). *Blundering into Disaster: Surviving the First Century of the Nuclear Age.* New York: Pantheon.

Miller, D. (1995). Consumption and Commodities. *Annual Review of Anthropology,* 24, 141–61.

Millman, G. J. (1995). *The Vandals' Crown: How Rebel Currency Traders Overthrew the Worlds' Central Banks.* New York: The Free Press.

Milton, J. (1982). *A Fuller Course in the Art of Logic Conformed to the Method of Peter Ramus (1672)* (W. J. Ong & C. J. Ermatinger, trans.). New Haven: Yale University Press.

Mintz, S. W. (1961). Pratik: Haitian Personal Economic Relationships. *Proceedings of the 1961 Annual Spring Meeting of the American Ethnological Society.*

Mintz, S. W. (1985). *Sweetness and Power: The Place of Sugar in Modern History.* Harmondsworth: Penguin.

Mitchell, W. E. (1987). *The Bamboo Fire: Field Work with the New Guinea Wape.* Prospect Heights: Waveland Press.

Mueller, F. M. (ed.). (1979). *The Laws of Manu.* Delhi: Motilal Banarsidass.

Mundle, S. (1979). *Backwardness and Bondage: Agrarian Relations in a South Bihar District.* New Delhi: IIPA.

Murray, M. A. (1939). The Meaning of the Cowrie-Shell. *Man,* 165(October), 167.

Nadel, S. F. (1942). *A Black Byzantium: The Kingdom of Nupe in Nigeria.* Oxford: Oxford University Press, 1969.

Nagengast, C. (1994). Violence, Terror, and the Crisis of the State. *Annual Review of Anthropology,* 23, 109–36.

Nash, J. (1979). *We Eat the Mines and the Mines Eat Us: Dependency and Exploitation in Bolivian Tin Mines.* New York: Columbia University Press.

Nelson, B. (1969). *The Idea of Usury: From Tribal Brotherhood to Universal Otherhood* (2nd ed.). Chicago: Chicago University Press.

Netting, R. M. (1993). *Smallholders, Householders: Farm Families and the Ecology of Intensive, Sustainable Agriculture.* Stanford: Stanford Univerity Press.

O'Flaherty, W. D. (1973). *Hindu Myths: A Sourcebook.* Harmondsworth: Penguin.

Ofonagoro, W. I. (1979). From Traditional to British Currency in Southern Nigeria: Analysis of a Currency Revolution, 1880–1948. *The Journal of Economic History,* 39(3), 623–654.

Parry, J. (1980). Ghost, Greed and Sin: The Occupational Identity of the Benares Funeral Priests. *Man,* 15(1), 88–111.

Parry, J. (1986). The Gift, the Indian Gift, and the 'Indian Gift'. *Man,* 21(3), 453–473.

Parry, J. (1989). On the Moral Perils of Exchange. In J. Parry & M. Bloch (eds), *Money and the Morality of Exchange.* Cambridge: Cambridge University Press.

Paul, R., & Lehrman, L. (1982). *The Case for Gold: A Minority Report of the US Gold Commission.* New York: Cato Institute.

Pennington, J. (1848). *The Currency of the British Colonies.* New York: Augustus M. Kelley, 1967.

Perlin, F. (1987). Money-Use in Late Pre-Colonial India and the International Trade in Currency Media. In J.F. Richards (ed.), *The Imperial Monetary System of Mughal India.* Oxford: Oxford University Press.

Phillips, M. J. (1972). Currency. In P. Ryan (ed.), *Encyclopaedia of Papua and New Guinea.* Melbourne: Melbourne University Press.

Polanyi, K. (1966). *Dahomey and the Slave Trade: An Analysis of an Archaic Economy.* Seattle: University of Washington Press.

Prakash, G. (1994). Subaltern Studies and Postcolonial Criticism. *American Historical Review,* 99(5), 1475–1490.

Radcliffe-Brown, A. R. (1957). *A Natural Science of Society.* Glencoe: The Free Press.

Radcliffe-Brown, A. R. (1958). *Method in Social Anthropology.* Chicago: Chicago University Press.

Radin, P. (1933). *The Method and Theory of Ethnology.* New York: Basic Books.

Raheja, G. G. (1988a). *The Poison in the Gift: Ritual, Prestation, and the Dominant Caste in a North Indian Village.* Chicago: Chicago University Press.

Raheja, G. G. (1988b). India: Caste, Kingship, and Dominance Reconsidered. *Annual Review of Anthropology,* 17, 497–522.

Raheja, G. G. (1993). Caste Ideologies, Protest and the Power of the Dominant Caste: A Reply to Gregory and Heesterman. *Social Analysis,* 34, 17–34.

Raheja, G. G., & Gold, A. G. (1994). *Listen to the Heron's Words.* Berkeley: University of California Press.

Ricardo, D. (1817). *On the Principles of Political Economy and Taxation.* Cambridge: Cambridge University Press, 1975.

Richards, J. F. (1987). Introduction. In J.F. Richards (ed.), *The Imperial Monetary System of Mughal India.* Oxford: Oxford University Press.

Rist, C. (1938). *History of Monetary and Credit Theory.* New York: Kelley.

Rodgers, S. (1985). *Power and Gold: Jewelry from Indonesia, Malayasia, and the Philippines.* Geneva: Prestal-Verlag.

Rolfe, S. E., & Burtle, J. (1973). *The Great Wheel: The International Monetary System.* London: Macmillan.

Safer, J. F., & Gill, F. M. (1982). *Spirals from the Sea: An Anthropological Look at Shells.* New York: American Museum of Natural History.

Sahlins, M. (1976). *Culture and Practical Reason.* Chicago: Chicago University Press.

Sahlins, M. (1994). Goodbye to Tristes Tropes: Ethnography in the Context of Modern World History. In R. Borofsky (ed.), *Assessing Cultural Anthropology.* New York: McGraw-Hill.

Schiller, F. C. S. (1907). *Studies in Humanism.* London: Macmillan.

Schmitt, J.-C. (1983). *The Holy Greyhound: Guinefort, Healer of Children since the Thirteenth Century.* Cambridge: Cambridge University Press.

Schrauwers, A. (1995). The Household and Shared Poverty in the Highlands of Central Sulawesi. *The Journal of the Royal Anthropological Institute (Incorporating Man),* 1(2), 337–357.

Schultz, T. W. (1964). *Transforming Traditional Agriculture.* New Haven: Yale University Press.

Schumpeter, J. A. (1954). *History of Economic Analysis.* London: George Allen & Unwin.

Shal, A. M., & Shroff, R. G. (1959). The Vahivanca Barots of Gujarat: A Caste of Genealogists. In M. Singer (ed.), *Traditional India: Structure and Change.* Philadelphia: The American Folklore Society.

Shaw, W. A. (1895). *The History of Currency, 1252–1894.* London: Wilsons and Milne.

Simmel, G. (1982). *The Philosophy of Money.* London: Routledge & Kegan Paul.

Skinner, G. W. (1964). Marketing and Social Structure in Rural China. *Journal of Asian Studies,* 24, 3–43, 195–228, 363–399.

Smith, A. (1776). *An Inquiry into the Nature and Causes of the Wealth of Nations.* London: Everyman's Library, 1970.

Smith, J. F. (1974). *Silver Profits in the Seventies (The Economics of Silver).* West Vancouver: ERC Publishing.

South (1981). *South: The Third World Magazine.* London: South Publications Ltd.

Spiro, M. E. (1992). Cultural Relativism and the Future of Anthropology. In G. E. Marcus (ed.), *Rereading Cultural Anthropology.* Durham: Duke University Press:

Sraffa, P. (1960). *Production of Commodities by Means of Commodities: Prelude to a Critique of Economic Theory.* Cambridge: Cambridge University Press.

Stcherbatsky, F. T. (1962). *Buddhist Logic.* New York: Dover Publications.

Stevens, R. W. (1976). *Vain Hopes, Grim Realities: The Economic Consequences of the Vietnam War.* New York: New Viewpoints.

Stockman, D. A. (1986). *The Triumph of Politics: How the Reagan Revolution Failed.* New York: Harper and Row.

Strathern, A. (1969). Finance and Production: Two Strategies in New Guinea Highlands Exchange Systems. *Oceania,* 40(1), 42–67.

Strathern, M. (1972). *Women in Between: Female Roles in a Male World.* London: Seminar Press.

Strathern, M. (1975). *No Money on our Skins.* Port Moresby: New Guinea Research Unit Bulletin No. 61.

Strathern, M. (1988). *The Gender of the Gift: Problems with Women and Problems with Society in Melanesia.* Berkeley: University of California Press.

Strathern, M. (1992). Qualified Value: The Perspective of Gift Exchange. In C. Humphrey & S. Hugh-Jones (eds), *Barter, Exchange and Value.* Cambridge: Cambridge University Press.

Sundar, N. (1994). *In Search of Gunda Dhur: Colonialism and Contestation in Bastar, Central India, 1854–1993.* Unpublished PhD, Columbia University.

Swedberg, R. M. (1991). 'The Battle of Methods': Toward a Paradigm Shift? In A. Etizoni & P. R. Lawrence (eds), *Socio-Economics: Towards a New Synthesis.* New York: M.E. Sharpe.

Szulc, T. (1978). *The Illusion of Peace: Foreign Policy in the Nixon Years.* New York: Viking.

Taussig, M. (1978). Peasant Economics and the Development of Capitalist Agriculture in the Cauca Valley, Columbia. *Latin American Perspectives,* 5(3), 62–91.

Taussig, M. T. (1980). *The Devil and Commodity Fetishism in South America.* Chapel Hill: University of North Carolina Press.

Taylor, C. (1992). *Milk, Honey, & Money.* Washington: Smithsonian.

Thirsk, J. (1984). *The Rural Economy of England: Collected Essays.* London: Hambledon Press.

Thomas, N. (1991). *Entangled Objects: Exchange, Material Culture and Colonialism in the Pacific.* Cambridge, MA: Harvard University Press.

Timberg, T. A. (1978). *The Marwaris: From Traders to Industrialists.* New Delhi: Vikas.

Triffin, R. (1960). *Gold and the Dollar Crisis: The Future of Convertibility.* New Haven: Yale University Press.

Triffin, R. (1979). *Gold and the Dollar Crisis: Yesterday and Tomorrow.* New Haven: Princeton University Press.

Vansina, J. (1962). Trade and Markets Among the Kuba. In P. Bohannan & G. Dalton (eds), *Markets in Africa.* Evanston: Northwestern University Press.

Vatuk, V., & Vatuk, S. (1971). On a System of Private Savings among North Indian Village Women. *Journal of Asian and African Studies,* 6, 179–190.

Veblen, T. (1899). *The Theory of the Leisure Class.* New York: Macmillan.

von Fürer-Haimendorf, C. (1982). *Tribes of India: The Struggle for Survival.* Berkekey: University of California Press.

von Wright, G. H. (1963). *The Varieties of Goodness.* London: Routledge & Kegan Paul.

Walker, J., & Vatter, H. G. (1982). The Princess and the Pea: or, The Alleged Vietnam War Origins of the Current Inflation. *Journal of Economic Issues,* 16, 597–608.

Wanniski, J. (1978). *The Way the World Works: How Economies Fail — and Succeed.* New York: Basic Books.

Waterfield, R. A. H. (1987). *Plato Theaetetus.* Harmondsworth: Penguin.

Weiner, A. (1992). *Inalienable Possessions.* Berkeley and Los Angeles: University of California Press.

Werbner, P. (1990). *The Migration Process: Capital, Gifts and Offerings among British Pakistanis.* Oxford: Berg.

Williams, A. (1930). *Tales from the Panchatantra.* Oxford: Basil Blackwell.

Wittich, G. (1982). *The Role of Gold in the International Monetary Fund Today.* Oxford: Oxford University Press.

Wolf, E. R. (1982). *Europe and the People without History.* Berkeley: University of California Press.

Wolfe, A. (1989). *Whose Keeper? Social Science and Moral Obligation.* Berkeley: University of California Press.

Yorke, M. (1982). The Situation of the Gonds of Asifabad and Lakshetipet Taluks, Adilabad District. In C. von Fürer–Haimendorf (ed.), *Tribes of India: The Struggle for Survival.* Berkeley: University of California Press.

Zelizer, V. (1994). *The Social Meaning of Money.* New York: Basic Books.

Index

.

Finding
My Way

ALSO BY MALALA YOUSAFZAI

I Am Malala
We Are Displaced

CHILDREN'S BOOKS

I Am Malala (Teen Edition)
Malala: My Story of Standing Up for Girls' Rights
Malala's Magic Pencil
My Name Is Malala

Finding My Way

Malala Yousafzai

W&N

WEIDENFELD & NICOLSON

First published in the United States in 2025 by Atria Books,
an imprint of Simon & Schuster, LLC
First published in Great Britain in 2025 by Weidenfeld & Nicolson,
an imprint of The Orion Publishing Group Ltd
Carmelite House, 50 Victoria Embankment
London EC4Y 0DZ

An Hachette UK Company

The authorised representative in the EEA is Hachette Ireland,
8 Castlecourt Centre, Dublin 15, D15 XTP3, Ireland (email: info@hbgi.ie)

1 3 5 7 9 10 8 6 4 2

A CIP catalogue record for this book is
available from the British Library.

ISBN (Hardback) 978 1 3996 1934 9
ISBN (Export Trade Paperback) 978 1 3996 1935 6
ISBN (Ebook) 978 1 3996 1938 7
ISBN (Audio) 978 1 3996 1939 4

Interior design by Davina Mock-Maniscalco
Printed in Great Britain by Clays Ltd, Elcograf, S.p.A.

MIX
Paper | Supporting
responsible forestry
FSC
www.fsc.org FSC® C104740

www.weidenfeldandnicolson.co.uk
www.orionbooks.co.uk

For Abai, Toor Pekai and all the Shangla girls

Finding
My Way

Introduction

I 'll never know who I was supposed to be. Maybe everyone feels that way, curious about the invisible crossroads in their lives, the wrong turns and chance encounters that change everything. But I am haunted by it, the gulf between how I imagined my life and what it became. I can't escape the feeling that a giant hand plucked me out of one story and dropped me into an entirely new one.

On a mild October afternoon, a bullet changed the trajectory of my life, cutting me off from my home, my friends and everything I loved, spinning me out into an unfamiliar world. At fifteen years old, I hadn't had time to figure out who I wanted to be when, suddenly, everyone wanted to tell me who I was. An inspiration, a hero, an activist. But also a wallflower, a punchbag, a pay cheque. To my parents, I was an obedient daughter. To my friends, a good listener. When I was alone, I unravelled – because the hardest thing to be was myself.

My early twenties were a tangle of anxiety and indecision, reckless nights and foggy mornings, friendship and first love. It was never going to be easy, in this wonder-struck season of life, when the world feels full of possibility, to find the path that was right for me. Still, I tried to shrug off other people's expectations and hear my own voice, to reckon with what I had lost and who I might become. What I wanted, more than anything, was to make sense of my story.

1.

If you get up in five minutes, you'll be on time, I bartered with myself, calculating how long it would take me to brush my teeth and throw on some clothes. Half an hour later, I was still in bed, scrolling on my phone – room décor, virtual campus tours, packing lists. I would start university in just two days, and my brain was buzzing.

New friends! No parents! No rules! I could barely contain my excitement, bouncing on my toes and humming to myself as I got dressed and took the lift down to a windowless conference room in a midtown Manhattan hotel.

'You're late,' the PR woman sighed, 'and I'm not even going to ask if you reviewed your talking points.'

I smiled and shrugged. Over the summer I'd travelled to four continents, met with nine prime ministers and spoken at multiple events. Now I was in New York to promote *Malala's Magic*

Pencil, a new children's book – six hours of back-to-back interviews and then an overnight flight home to Birmingham, England. It was my last day of work for a while, but my mind was already out-of-office.

The PR rep left the room and, a few moments later, a child entered. I was about to ask if she was lost when I noticed her polo shirt was embroidered with a magazine logo and *Kid Reporter* underneath it.

'When you were little, what did you want to be when you grew up?' she asked.

'A car mechanic!' I replied, adding that I'd always loved puzzles and figuring out how to put things together.

The next journalist was far less charming. He didn't want to hear about my children's book and tried to shift the focus to hot topics, hoping I'd say something controversial enough to spice up a slow news day. Most of his questions were about the American president: 'As the youngest Nobel Peace Prize laureate, what is your message to him on women's rights?' and 'You visited the White House to meet with Obama. If the new administration invites you, will you go?' I knew how to avoid having my name plastered across headlines and didn't take the bait.

The last interview was for a morning TV show. The host asked thoughtful questions about my work and day-to-day life. We were close to wrapping up when she leant towards me, her face full of concern.

'Five years after the attack, do you think about it every day?' she asked.

Inevitable, I thought. *No way I was leaving this room without talking about it.* I wasn't bothered or surprised by questions like this, only by how often people asked them. That part of my life felt so long ago and far away in my mind, yet it always seemed to push past me and fill the air every time I stepped into a room.

FINDING MY WAY

I GREW UP in a remote region of Pakistan, in a place called Mingora. My hometown ran alongside the Swat River, surrounded by forests, wildflower meadows and colossal, snowcapped mountains. Life in our valley wasn't perfect – most families were poor and strict social norms held back progress, especially for women. But it was a stunningly beautiful and peaceful place.

That changed when I was ten years old. Strange men with long beards and assault rifles came down from the mountains and took over our town. The Taliban began bombing hospitals and hotels; executing musicians, teachers and policemen in the streets; and issuing new rules over the radio several times a day: no TVs or music allowed, no entertainment at all, not even board games for children. Men must not shave their beards. Women must not leave their homes.

As the bombs and gunfire got louder, our lives got smaller. We lived in constant dread of breaking some new rule that we had not yet learnt. A man in a nearby neighbourhood was killed because the Taliban said the hem of his trousers was too long. One day I saw my five-year-old brother Atal digging a big hole in the garden and asked what he was doing. 'Making a grave,' he replied.

When I was eleven, the Taliban announced that, in three weeks' time, girls would be banned from going to school. Fear gripped my heart. If I kept going to school after the deadline, they might kill me. If I didn't, my life was over anyway. Even at that age, I knew the fate of uneducated girls in my community: marriage in your early teens, several children before you turned twenty, the rest of your life spent behind the walls of your husband's house. It was a future I could not bear to face.

I started writing an anonymous blog for the BBC, chronicling life under the terrorists' rule. *Our school told the girls not to wear our uniforms*, I wrote, *because it might make us targets. We all showed up in our favourite pink and purple dresses. Then they told us not to wear colourful clothes because the Taliban don't like that either.*

As the deadline for girls to leave school drew closer, I went public, declaring to anyone who would listen that education was my right. The Taliban could not keep me from learning, I vowed, no matter how many schools they destroyed. On national TV, I demanded that our leaders stand up and defend us. The fear I had felt over the last two years was replaced by outrage and indignation. I could not let these men take away my future.

Eventually the Pakistani army launched a large-scale military operation against the extremists. My parents, two little brothers and I, along with thousands of others, fled Mingora when the fighting began. After a few months, the army prevailed, and we returned to our homes and life went back to normal. But the Taliban were not gone for good, and they had not forgotten my defiance. When I was fifteen, a gunman boarded my school bus and asked, 'Who is Malala?' Before I could answer, he shot me in the head at point-blank range.

In an instant, my entire world changed.

I came out of a coma a week later, waking up to find myself in Birmingham at a trauma centre that specialised in complex brain injuries. Before the shooting, I'd never left Pakistan; now I was surrounded by strangers. I spent the next several months there, undergoing multiple surgeries and learning how to walk and talk again.

As my story travelled around the world, people began to describe someone I didn't recognise – a serious and shy girl, a wallflower forced to speak out when the Taliban took away her books. They made me into a mythical heroine, virtuous and dutiful, predestined for greatness.

Sometimes the absurdity of it made me laugh. Growing up in

Mingora, I was a troublemaker. At school, I ferried bits of gossip back and forth between groups of girls and cracked jokes that made my friends laugh and scold me in the same breath. If a classmate did better than me in exams, I cried bitter, undignified tears at the injustice of it. At home, I was messy, rambunctious. I'd watch John Cena – my favourite wrestler – on TV and try out his moves on my little brothers, then tell tales to my father when they fought back. Even on my best day, I was not the reticent saint that everyone now claimed I was.

I was still in the hospital when people came with offers to turn my story into books and films. Journalists jockeyed to land my first interview. Talent agents wanted to represent me, though I wasn't sure what talents they thought I possessed. 'Why are you famous now?' Atal asked. I told him I didn't know.

Before I understood what was happening, I was thrust into an unfamiliar, unbidden life – crossing the globe to give speeches and pose for photos, spending most of my time with adults. Backstage at big events, one of them would spin me around by the shoulders and cry, 'High energy, Malala! Give them everything!' To these grown-ups, I was a public figure and a product to be marketed; they were blind to the awkward teenager sitting next to them, trying to do her homework. In their orbit I withdrew, becoming the quiet girl they assumed I'd always been.

Everywhere I went people asked the same question: 'What do you remember about the shooting?' When I said that I couldn't remember anything about it, they seemed almost disappointed, as if it was impolite of me not to recall my fear and suffering. As if the worst thing that ever happened to me was the most interesting part of my life. It made me feel like a butterfly with a straight pin through its heart, forever trapped under dusty glass. The living girl in front of them was not as captivating as the one on the school bus, a young dreamer about to die.

'DO YOU THINK about it every day?'

I blinked at the morning-show host. It would be easy to say what she and her audience wanted to hear – that, at times, I felt afraid or that I might never fully recover from my injuries. Why complicate the tidy, tragic narrative that people seemed so drawn to?

But something was changing inside me – I didn't want to play the part any more. I was ready to be young and free, to go on adventures and make mistakes, to have a life that happened somewhere other than airports and conference rooms. The future was wide open and waiting for me.

'I don't think about it at all,' I said. 'My life is moving forward.'

2.

The night before I left for Oxford University, I sat on the floor, wishing my bedroom door had a lock. It was broken when we moved in, and no matter how many times I'd asked my parents to fix it over the years, they never got around to it. I reached under the bed, pulled out the contraband items I'd been hiding there, and stuffed everything into my suitcase as fast as I could.

My mum and I had been locked in a cold war all summer, ever since she assigned herself the job of assembling my university wardrobe. This wasn't a new dynamic for us: for years, she hung what she wanted me to wear on the front of my wardrobe before I went to bed. When I tried to exert some independence, emerging the next morning in something other than what she'd assigned, she would say, 'Do you think Allah approves of daughters disobeying their mothers?' It seemed unwise to try to answer that, so back to my room I'd go.

Wherever I went, my mum insisted that I wear the traditional clothes of Pashtun people, the ethnic group to which my family belongs. That meant only one outfit, the *shalwar kameez* – billowy trousers, a tentlike tunic and a headscarf. In our deeply conservative culture, a woman's clothes must cover all skin above the wrist or ankle; garments are shapeless, giving no hint of the female form.

All summer, my mum assembled her 'university collection' of shalwar kameez for me. There were hot-pink paisley trousers and a top with matching pom-poms on the cuffs. A lime-green number with heavy silver beading. Delirious floral patterns that could make you dizzy if you stared at them too long. Black, ivory and tan were out of the question because, according to her, neutrals were a waste of good fabric.

I can't say I had a clear personal style at the time, but I knew I absolutely could not go to Oxford dressed like a set of neon highlighters. So, while my mum was out shopping, I googled 'what to wear to university 2017' and ordered what I saw in the pictures – jeans, striped tees, a quilted bomber jacket. A search for 'Selena Gomez casual' led me to oversize cardigans and Adidas Superstars. Chunky knit scarves, embroidered sweatshirts, a black dress with bell sleeves and several pairs of ankle boots were all squirrelled away, awaiting their debut.

I stuffed everything I'd purchased in my suitcase and threw a couple of kameezes on top in case my mum decided on a last-minute inspection. I knew she would find out about my new look eventually and wouldn't be happy, but that was a risk I was willing to take.

To me, they weren't just clothes – they were camouflage. The Malala everyone recognised, who stood on stages, signed autographs and shook hands with world leaders, wore shalwar kameez. At Oxford, I wanted to blend in, just another student in trainers and jeans. I had to make sure that university was nothing like high school.

〜

WHEN I WAS released from the hospital and started Year 10 at an all-girls' academy in Birmingham, I assumed I would quickly acquire a gang of friends, Brummie versions of my classmates in Mingora. I imagined us walking home every afternoon, arm in arm, laughing over inside jokes. They would bring me up to speed on all the gossip and tell me which teachers could be sweet-talked and which were strict.

Things didn't turn out exactly as I planned. Most of the girls in my new school had known each other since they were young and, years ago, had formed tight circles of two or three – not un- kind, but not welcoming either. At lunch, I'd take my tray and find the nearest seat, furtively glancing around for friendly faces. If no one spoke to me, I'd take out a book and pretend to read. One day I worked up the courage to ask the other girls a ques- tion. Leaning across the table, I pointed to my plate, and said, 'Sorry, but could you tell me the meaning of "fish fingers"?' They all looked confused, then one of them said, 'It's just fish, yeah?' – before returning to their conversation.

If someone told a joke in class, I laughed along with the other girls, pretending I got it too. I couldn't understand any of their references. In Mingora, where almost no one had internet access, we'd only heard echoes of American or British pop cul- ture, those loud enough to ring around the world and land in our valley – *Titanic*, World Wrestling Entertainment, Taylor Swift. What little I knew about life in England came from reading one Jane Austen novel. After my first day at school, I gathered that the book was slightly out of date.

11

Sometimes photographers turned up at the front gates, trying to snap photos of me going in or out of school. I hated it, and worried the other girls would think I was either full of myself or fake. But no one cared that I was famous, it quickly became clear, because I simply wasn't cool. We all wore uniforms, but the hem of my pleated skirt fell to my ankles, double the standard length. On top of that, my mum insisted that I wear opaque black tights, even in spring, to avoid showing any part of my legs.

My injuries made it worse. I was fifteen years old and wore a hearing aid. The bullet had destroyed my left eardrum and severed my facial nerve, leaving one side of my face paralysed. My mouth could no longer form a smile, so an uneasy grimace was all I had to offer my new classmates. Despite months of relearning how to walk in rehab, I moved slowly through the riot of teen girls – a hopeful little ghost, trying to rejoin the land of the living.

You're not here to socialise anyway, I told myself after weeks of trying and failing to make friends. *School is for getting good marks, so you can get into university.* Then I saw the scores on my first few tests: 41 per cent in English, 57 per cent in biology, 63 per cent in geography. Having always been a top student, I was stunned and embarrassed.

In Pakistan, teachers focused on memorisation. You didn't need to grasp the underlying concepts as long as you could parrot the textbook. My new school expected critical thinking and analysis, a way of learning that I didn't understand. For a while, my only solid marks were in algebra, as maths seemed to have the same set of answers everywhere in the world.

Eager to restore my academic standing, I studied for hours every night. I read the books my teachers assigned and supplemental reading I assigned myself. When I came across a word I didn't recognise, I looked it up and wrote the definition on a Post-it note. Soon the walls of my bedroom were covered in little yellow squares, scrawled with the meanings of 'cat burglar', 'crepuscule' and 'pensive' in my loopy handwriting.

While my marks steadily improved, my social life did not, and I often found myself watching the clock throughout the day. It was noon in Mingora when I arrived at school in the morning. My old friends were eating lunch, pooling their rupees to buy samosas and mango juice. A few hours later, while I pushed cold peas around a cafeteria tray, they were in front of the TV, catching up on *Shararat*, an Indian knockoff of *Sabrina the Teenage Witch*. Maybe if any of the Birmingham girls thought about approaching me they were put off by the haunted look in my eyes, the way I always seemed to be somewhere else in my mind.

Every few weeks, I called my best friend, Moniba, and quizzed her on the latest news and gossip. *What Bollywood song is everyone singing on the bus these days? Who got in trouble at school? What are the older girls up to?* I did my famous impressions of our teachers just to hear her laugh. But she always knew when something was wrong. 'Why do you never talk about yourself?' she asked.

'Pfft, because everything at my school is boring,' I'd demur. 'Trust me, you'd fall asleep on the phone.' I didn't want to tell her that I was no longer the fun, talkative girl she remembered.

After six lonely months, I decided to take action, trying everything I could to restart my life. On Sports Day, I signed up for the fifty-yard sprint and came in last place. I ran for student council and lost the election. When the popular girls insisted everyone participate in a flash mob, I did as they commanded, standing on top of my desk and clapping off-beat to a song I'd never heard. It was all as awkward as it sounds.

Then, finally, I made a friend. Alice had fallen out with her best mate, and I was available to fill the role. I clung to her in the hallways and at lunch tables, whispering questions in her ear when I couldn't follow the other girls' conversation. Sometimes she came over for dinner. She liked my mum's pakoras, and I liked feeling normal for an hour or two. When Alice went to parties that I wasn't allowed or invited to attend, she sent pictures so I didn't feel left out.

As grateful as I was for her, I yearned to belong to a group of girls again, to be surrounded by people who understood me and shared my memories. My childhood friends had shaped me in ways I couldn't explain to Alice or anyone else. In primary school, we survived a massive earthquake, huddling together in our classroom as the room began to shake and the floor cracked beneath us. A few years later, the river swelled and flooded our classroom, covering everything in chest-high mud. The odour was awful, but we cleaned the floors and walls together. The school was our world, a place where we could be ourselves, and we wanted to take care of it. On the last day of class before the Taliban's deadline, we stayed in the courtyard long after the final bell rang, playing freeze tag and singing songs. When the teachers told us we needed to leave, we hugged each other and cried. Whatever disasters or dangers we encountered, I always felt safe when we were together.

When the army saw off the Taliban and we went back to school, we were euphoric, unshakeable. On a field trip to the mountains, Moniba and I stood under a waterfall, singing 'Love Story' by Taylor Swift at the top of our lungs. Later that year, our class travelled to Islamabad, the capital city, where we watched a play, tried duck pancakes at a Chinese restaurant and marvelled at women walking down the street without headscarves. It was our first glimpse of the world beyond our remote mountain town, and we came home with wild dreams for the future.

I thought we would go to university together. At fifteen, I hadn't thought much past that, but I'd never imagined a life without my friends. Now I was heading to Oxford alone, carrying a bag of trendy clothes and dreams for a less lonely life.

3.

On the first day of orientation week, I woke up and surveyed my shabby kingdom. The carpet had frayed edges and burn marks left by former students ironing their clothes on the floor. Sickly yellow paint was flaking off the walls, and the sink in the en-suite bathroom was no bigger than a soup bowl. But all of it was mine – a place where no one could tell me when to go to bed or what to eat – and I immediately fell in love with it.

I opened my phone and scrolled through Instagram, where other students were already posting about their morning runs, breakfast in the dining hall or trips to the bookshop. Not wanting to miss any of the action, I hopped out of bed, got dressed, and was halfway down the hall when a voice behind me called, 'Wait for us, please!'

'Sorry, guys,' I said, spinning around and walking back. In the room next to mine were two Metropolitan Police officers, members of the Specialist Protection unit who provide security to high-profile people. After I came to the UK, the government informed me that they were monitoring threats to my life and offered their services. I was thousands of miles away from Pakistan, but my life was still in danger, as the Taliban periodically renewed their pledge to kill me. Since then, the security team had become part of my everyday life: dropping me off at school, picking me up at the end of the day, and watching over my parents' house at night.

A few weeks before I went to Oxford, the officers laid out their plan: they would bunk in the halls and walk with me to all my classes. Anywhere I couldn't walk, they would drive me in a bulletproof car. If I went out to dinner or a party, a few middle-aged dads in blazers and earpieces would be there too. *Just what every university girl wants*, I thought. I was grateful for their protection and understood it was necessary, but I hoped they wouldn't create a barrier between me and the other students.

With security following discreetly behind, I walked to the registration centre to complete my first task of the day: taking a photo for my Oxford ID. *Smile, make eye contact, be approachable!* Since arriving the day before, I had exchanged hellos with a few students on my floor, but hadn't really talked to anyone yet. Now was the time to get serious about meeting people. *It's everyone's first day. This isn't high school. I don't need to hang around waiting for someone to talk to me.*

After picking up a map and a schedule for the week, I spotted another girl standing on her own and walked towards her. She was short like me, with strawberry blonde hair, tortoiseshell glasses and a reassuring smile.

'Hey, I'm Malala,' I said, trying my best to sound casual but friendly.

The other girl took a step back and didn't speak. *Not this again.*

'Sorry, sorry! Brain freeze,' she blurted out. 'I'm Cora – nice to meet you.'

'What do you study, Cora?'

'PPE.'

'Me too!' I beamed, delighted that I'd met someone else in my major – Philosophy, Politics and Economics – on my first try.

Cora and I walked together to the Freshers' Fair, a carnival-like event showcasing Oxford's extracurricular activities. The cavernous Examination Hall was transformed into a maze of hundreds of stalls, jam-packed with enthusiastic older students pitching their clubs and wide-eyed newbies trying to take it all in. We followed the flow of bodies in a daze, not sure where to start.

'Do you play any instruments?' Cora asked, as we walked past booths for heavy-metal fans, Irish folk musicians and a jazz ensemble called the Oxford Gargoyles.

'No,' I said. 'I like to sing, but I'd be *terrified* to do it in front of other people.'

We turned a corner to see a boy in an Oxford Cheese Society T-shirt passing out samples of brie and Gruyère. 'A cheese-tasting club? That's a thing that people do?'

Cora laughed. 'A thing that posh people do, yeah. Not my idea of a night out, but whatever makes them happy.'

In the sports section, I made a beeline to sign up for cricket and badminton, games I had loved to play on the streets and rooftops of Mingora. Then, on a whim, I joined the rowing club too. On the walk to the fair, I'd seen students in little wooden boats meandering down the river that ran through campus, and thought it looked like a dreamy way to spend an afternoon.

The women at the Islamic Society stall called me 'sister' and invited me for mocktails later in the week. Next I joined the Christian Union and the Hindu Society, hoping to learn more about the faiths practised by religious minorities in Pakistan.

I may have also heard a rumour that the Christians brought baked goods to your room and the Hindus threw the best parties.

We hadn't been at the fair for a full hour when the complimentary tote bag I'd received at the entrance was bulging with new-member packs, event flyers and free pens. I handed over my contact information and money for membership dues to anything that caught my interest – a philosophy reading group, a film club, the Pakistan and South Asia societies. Cora, by contrast, had signed up for only two organisations – the Conservative Association and the pub quiz team. 'I definitely want to socialise,' she explained. 'I'm just not particularly sporty or musical or into whatever speedcubing is.'

We both agreed that joining the Oxford Union, one of the oldest debating societies in the world, was essential. As a member, you could attend events and hear well-known politicians, writers and artists argue over statements like 'Celebrity icons have corrupted the feminist movement' or 'Democracies should never ally with authoritarian regimes'. You even got access to the Union's secret library.

The sign-up queue snaked around the room and out into the corridor. It was so densely packed that I couldn't even see the stall. As Cora and I approached the front of the line, a banner featuring the Union's famous former speakers came into view. I scanned each face: Albert Einstein, Malcolm X, Queen Elizabeth II, Ronald Reagan and . . . me.

Oh no. My stomach dropped. I had nearly forgotten my first visit to the Union four years earlier. The details of my speech were long gone, but I remembered looking out at the students in their seats, wishing to fast-forward to a time when I could be in the audience and not at the podium. Now I was finally here, and I had to resist the urge to run away. How was I going to be a normal student with my spotty teenage face blazed across the Freshers' Fair?

If Cora noticed that my cheeks had turned bright red, she didn't let on, though I was sure she'd seen the banner too. I kept my head down while I filled out my membership paperwork, trying not to make eye contact with my younger self.

As we walked away from the table, I noticed a group of girls staring at me and whispering. One of them rushed over. 'Can we take selfies with you?' she asked. I was mortified, but declining felt rude, so I smiled and said yes. As soon as they snapped the first picture, I realised my mistake. Other students had noticed what was happening and began to form a line. When they started handing their phones to Cora to take group pictures, my chest tightened, certain that this would be our first and last outing together. Why would she want to be my friend if other students were pushing past her to get to me? But Cora just smiled as the line grew longer. 'Maybe I should sign up for photography club,' she joked, handing back the last selfie-seeker's phone.

'I'm so sorry,' I said, and I meant it. I didn't want Cora to think that I was some sort of diva, the type of person who expects her friends to stay in the shadows while she takes the spotlight.

'Oh, it's completely fine,' she said. 'Though it must be pretty weird for you, no? Having people stop you like that?'

I gave her a surprised smile – it was rare for anyone to acknowledge the strange conditions of my life. 'I mean, I'm used to it,' I replied. 'But I don't want people to treat me differently at university. I just want to blend in, be a normal student, you know?'

'Yeah, of course. Though I have to tell you . . . when my mum saw the news that you would be studying PPE in my year, she was so obnoxious. She said I should read all about your life in case we met!'

'Oh . . .' I paused. 'Did you?'

'No! I told her it would be weird to go into uni knowing

everything about you, like a stalker,' Cora said, rolling her eyes. 'I figured if we got on, I could just ask you questions.'

But Cora never asked about the shooting or the Taliban, meeting celebrities or being famous. In our first days on campus together, we talked about the dining-hall food, her life growing up in Wales, the fact that we both had little brothers, what music we liked, whether we'd met any other nice people at Oxford so far. Sometimes we sat in my room, drinking tea and scrolling social media, not talking at all. The more time I spent with her, the more relaxed I felt.

My habit of curating myself and thinking before I spoke – shaped by years of being onstage and in front of cameras – started to fade in her presence. I must have seemed years younger to Cora, who, like most other students, came to Oxford with her first hangovers and heartbreaks already under her belt. But she didn't mock my outsize enthusiasm for every part of student life, from getting my own pigeonhole to seeing shirtless boys run past us in the park. Whatever I wanted to try, she was ready and willing to be my wingwoman. I even dragged her to Quran Club at one point.

As much as I wanted to get swept up in all the activity on campus, I found I was equally happy taking a long walk or sitting quietly with my new friend. In those early days, Cora gave me what I needed most – a blank page to write whatever story I chose.

4.

On Friday of Freshers' Week, I tumbled into a small, rectangular office two floors above the dining hall. 'I got lost – I'm sorry,' I stammered. Arriving twenty-five minutes late to our first meeting was not the way I had hoped to meet my academic advisor, the professor assigned to monitor my progress for the next three years.

Lara had short brown hair and wore a simple navy frock, no make-up. I guessed she was in her mid-thirties. 'First appointments are for finding your way,' she said, gesturing for me to sit down.

I suspected I would need a lot more than one appointment to navigate this new world. Oxford is made up of forty-three different colleges – each with its own history, character and campus – all under the banner of one university. I was studying at Lady Margaret Hall, otherwise known as LMH, a college set in a quiet corner of the city on twelve acres that are mostly riverbank, woods and gardens. I'd had a week to learn LMH's four main buildings, and was still taking wrong turns anytime I ventured out on my own.

In the remaining half-hour of our meeting, Lara sped through Oxford's academic mechanics. PPE is a three-year degree. A year at Oxford comprises three eight-week terms, starting in October and ending in June. Around Christmas and Easter, undergraduates have five-week breaks, but are expected to dedicate no less than twenty hours a week to their studies while they're away from campus.

'Oxford is very different from high school or college as it's depicted in American movies,' she said. 'We teach through tutorials, not classes, and students are expected to manage their own learning process.'

Lara said I would take two courses per term. For each course, I would be expected to do the following every week: read three or four books, plus academic journal articles and case studies; write a two-thousand-word essay on an assigned topic; for economics, complete a mathematical problem set and mini-essay; attend a tutorial – a one-hour meeting with my professor and one or two other students on the course.

'In tutorials, you will demonstrate what you've learnt during the week,' she said. 'You should arrive prepared to participate in rigorous discussion and defend the ideas in your essays. Think of it as education through interrogation.' I nodded energetically, like I couldn't wait to be questioned for my intellectual crimes.

'You also have the option of attending lectures on your subject matter,' she continued. 'These are open to all students in your discipline, from every college at Oxford. Not required, but strongly encouraged.'

Lara informed me that undergraduates take exams at the end of their first and third years. The first-year exams, or prelims, determine whether a student is allowed to continue with their degree, whereas final exams determine your academic marks. Prelims, essays, tutorials – none of it counts towards your end result. But if you fail finals, you leave Oxford without a degree.

'Students are not allowed to have jobs during term time,' Lara continued. 'They must be present on campus and attend all tutorials.' She folded her hands and looked at me with concern. 'I know you have a lot of competing pressures and requests for your time, Malala. But I hope you will give yourself the space you need to succeed at Oxford.'

She sat back and put her palms flat on the desk. 'Okay, now that the basics are out of the way, did you bring your first problem set for economics? I would love to take a look at it to see where your maths skills are at the starting point.'

I felt an electric shock go through my body, followed by a prickling sensation in my scalp, feet and armpits. *What problem set?*

Lara saw the look on my face. 'In June, we sent all PPE students a reading list and mathematical exercises to complete before the start of term. Did you miss them?'

I had nothing to say but 'I'm sorry.' I'd spent the summer months travelling, giving speeches and attending meetings. In what little downtime I had, I'd hung out with Alice and shopped for my new university wardrobe, totally unaware that I had homework to complete.

'All right,' she said, logging on to her computer and emailing the documents to me. 'Do the maths assignment and drop it in the box outside my office. And you might want to dedicate the weekend to catching up on some of the pre-course reading.'

On the stairs outside Lara's office, I reflexively bit my nails, a nervous habit I'd worked hard to curb in high school. University hadn't officially started and I was already behind.

BEFORE WE LEFT Pakistan, I had read only a handful of books, maybe seven or eight. My small collection made its way to me in haphazard fashion – a friend of my father's brought me *A Brief History of Time*; tourists at a local guesthouse had left behind a worn-out paperback of *Pride and Prejudice*. Journalists from the United States and Europe contributed *Oliver Twist* and *Sophie's World*. I can't remember where Moniba and I found copies of the *Twilight* series, only that we read them together and spent many afternoons pretending we were vampires. Until I came to England, I'd never been inside a bookshop or a public library. To me, books were like fireflies – delighting with their unexpected arrival but not something you could see whenever you wished.

My younger self would've been overwhelmed by the library at Lady Margaret Hall, both a cosy refuge from busy student life and a fantasy world of more than eighty-five thousand books. Inside, it looks a bit like an old ship, with bookshelves surrounding the upper and lower decks and a long, open galley in the middle to let in the sunlight. Between every two rows of shelves, the architect placed study nooks that feature built-in desks centred on windows overlooking the gardens and river. When I first saw the library during my prospective student tour, I'd imagined spending hours and hours there, trying to read as many books as possible.

After my meeting with Lara, I was determined to plant myself at a desk in the library until I was caught up on my summer homework. I swung open the heavy wooden door and an eerie stillness hit me immediately. There were no other students or even staff in the room, just the brindle-coated library cat stretching out in the sun. *Quiet is good for concentration,* I reminded myself.

The first few problems weren't difficult – I'd always been decent at maths. But further down the page they got more complicated, and I realised this was going to take longer than I'd expected. I put down my pencil and stared out the window at the autumn sunset flushing through the trees. On the other side of the glass, students were walking to dinner and riding bikes along the riverbank. A group of friends drifted across the lawn, chatting like they'd known each other for years. Suddenly the library felt claustrophobic and airless. *It's only Friday. Plenty of time to catch up over the weekend.* I tossed the books and papers into my bag and abandoned the ship.

5.

'So, Club Night – you interested?' Cora asked me at dinner that evening.

I was definitely interested. Not because I intended to drink or go wild – I just wanted to see what it was like. In high school, a few of the girls went clubbing on weekends. They always described it the same way – 'soooo crazy' – as if the rest of us couldn't possibly understand. Club Night was the closing event of Freshers' Week, an off-campus dance party at a place called Emporium. From the RSVPs on Facebook, it looked like everyone would be there.

My curiosity was outweighed by my fear of being photographed. British tabloids and Pakistani journalists had been hanging around LMH all week, taking pictures as I walked around campus and asking other students if they'd met me. I figured they would give up when they saw that I was just doing boring things

27

like going to the library and the dining hall. Dancing at a night-club, though – that would be newsworthy.

If I said this to Cora, she would feel sorry for me and stay behind to keep me company. 'Ugh, I wish I could, but I promised my academic advisor that I would finish this problem set,' I sighed. 'I want to hear all about it in the morning, though!'

After half an hour trying to make a dent in the maths home-work, I gave up and wandered down to the LMH bar, where the Freshers' Week schedule said there would be a pizza party for those who weren't attending Club Night. I arrived to an empty room and checked to make sure I was in the right place. When I confirmed that I was, I didn't know what to do, so I sat down at a table by myself, cringing every time I made eye contact with my security officers across the room.

I was debating leaving when another student arrived and marched over to my table. She had a wide smile and wore a denim dress over a white T-shirt and trainers. To me, she looked like the cheery older girl they put on advertisements for things children don't want to do, like going to the dentist or summer school.

'Not clubbing tonight?' she asked, continuing before I could answer. 'Me neither. I'm Hen. Henrica, but only to my mother.'

'Hi, I'm Malala,' I said, almost laughing in astonishment at her social confidence.

'Nice to meet ya. You shoot pool, or are you more of a Trivial Pursuit person?' We settled on Scrabble and, as we clicked our tiles around the board, Hen talked nonstop – about her favourite YouTubers, why she'd chosen history for her major, the boy she'd met earlier in the day who didn't know how to use the washing machine. She barely seemed to take a breath, and I nod-ded along, a willing audience for her thoughts. At heart, I'm an extroverted introvert; someone who knows how to be 'on', but prefers not to take the lead in social situations. With Hen, I didn't have to say a word, and that alone moved her to the top of my potential friends list.

'Do you want to come up to my room and have some tea?' I asked when we were both full of pizza and bored with Scrabble.

'Lead the way,' Hen replied.

We talked for hours that night. I learnt about her life growing up in Zimbabwe, how she moved to the UK at age seven and worked the night shift at McDonald's in high school to help support her family. My jaw dropped when she recited her list of life goals: 'Graduate from Oxford. Get master's degree at Harvard. Become a TV host. Create my own talk show.' Hen was only nineteen, but I was fully convinced she would make her dreams come true. I also knew we were destined to be friends. Her openness and energy made me feel included without being overwhelmed – like I could blurt out anything that popped into my head or say nothing at all, and she would understand me either way.

WHEN I INTRODUCED Cora and Hen, they hit it off and we formed a trio. I spent every minute I could with one or both of them – not in the way I'd clung to Alice in high school, like she was a human life-raft, but because I loved every new thing I learnt about them. Cora liked to blast movie soundtracks at top volume while she studied, and Hen had an elaborate seventeen-step night-time ritual that could not, under any circumstances, be interrupted. They teased me for eating food past its sell-by date and only cleaning my room when my mum was coming to visit. We borrowed clothes from each other's wardrobes and ate dinner together every night. After a lifetime of brothers, sisterhood felt like going to a foreign country and discovering I somehow already knew the language.

The effortlessness of my first two friendships gave me the courage to add to their number. I met Yasmin early one morning, while I was taking a walk by the river. In the first few weeks of university, I'd picked up the habit of starting my weekly essays the night before they were due and drinking tons of tea to stay awake, desperate to make the 8 a.m. deadline. If I finished early, I'd reward myself with a stroll down to the water to watch the sunrise in my pyjamas.

One day I found a girl sitting cross-legged on my favourite bench in her bathrobe. 'Did you have an essay crisis too?' I asked her. Yasmin and I kept meeting there once a week, watching the dawn light catch and swirl in the currents, then grabbing hot hash browns from the dining hall before going back to our rooms to catch up on sleep. As we talked, I learnt her life story: she was born in Iran, but had fled an abusive father, immigrating to the UK as a teenager. At high school, she'd faced the same hardships as many refugees – the language barrier, poverty, paperwork – but she'd thrived in London, falling in love with indie bands, noodle shops and detective shows. Now she was studying English literature and hoped to become a writer.

Anisa studied finance, and we were paired as tutorial partners for an economics course. I hadn't even introduced myself when she told me I was stirring my tea the wrong way. 'Side to side, without touching the spoon to the mug,' she said. 'If you swirl it like that, you'll splash it on your shirt.'

Anisa's parents were from India, and had sent her to a British boarding school where she learnt to play polo and shoot clay pigeons. Almost every time I saw her, she was laughing – often at someone else's expense, sometimes at mine. I had lived in the UK for five years at that point, but there were still a lot of things I didn't know. When I asked questions like 'What's a bagel?' she called me 'categorically thick' or 'an absolute broomstick'. My

Topshop jeans were 'naff' and my taste in music was 'mouldy'. Most of the time, I had no idea what she was saying. I only knew it wasn't nice.

At high school, I stayed as far away as possible from girls like Anisa. But by the time we met, I felt like I could handle the challenge of a mean friend. Sometimes her natural bossiness was an asset. On weekend days when I wanted to be lazy and sleep until 2 p.m., Anisa barged into my room and said, 'Get up, we're leaving in ten minutes.' She planned itineraries with military precision – brunch at the Jericho Café, browsing the stalls at the covered market, exploring the colleges we hadn't visited yet. And I was always glad I followed her orders.

For the first time in five years, I belonged to a gang of friends again. On my way back from lectures and tutorials, I would stop by each of their rooms to check in, chat, make plans. On week-nights, two or three of them would pile into my room under the pretence of studying together. That usually ended with our text-books stacked on the floor and used as makeshift tables to hold nail polish or takeaway food. The day after essays were due, when no one felt like working, we would go out to a pub or the college bar to chat with other students, or cram ourselves into a twin bed to watch a movie on someone's laptop.

I never went anywhere by myself. Even a routine trip to the supermarket felt more exciting with friends, getting their thoughts on shampoo brands and recommendations on frozen meals. When Yasmin needed new bras, we all tagged along and couldn't stop laughing at the middle-aged dads on my security team trying to figure out where to stand in the tiny lingerie shop. They were supposed to keep eyes on me at all times, but eventu-ally decided it was acceptable, in this particular case, to wait out-side on the street.

We were hanging out in Anisa's room one night when I

opened my email to see a message from the Hindu Society. 'Oh my god! The members-only pre-sale for the Diwali Ball is open,' I announced. 'We should all go together! Say yes and I'll get the tickets right now.'

'You're in the Hindu Society?' Yasmin asked.

Cora laughed. 'Remember when I told you she went wild at the Freshers' Fair? It would be easier to list the clubs she didn't sign up for.'

Most Oxford societies and colleges host balls every year. They begin with a fancy dinner, then live music and dancing until the following morning. I was dying to go to one, and the Diwali Ball, with its promises of an Indian food buffet and Bollywood music, sounded perfect.

Three weeks later, everyone gathered in my room to touch up their hair and make-up before we left for the ball. Anisa, Cora and Hen opted for elegant strapless gowns in satin or crêpe. I'd spent a lot of time perfecting my look: a black dress covered in sparkly beaded flowers and a headscarf with little pearls around the hem.

When Yasmin arrived in a sari, I thought she looked beautiful, but Anisa was not impressed. 'Your pleating is all wrong,' she said.

'It can't be!' Yasmin moaned. 'I followed every step of the You-Tube tutorial!'

'Yaz, I'm literally Indian. Let me fix it.'

Re-draping the sari – and a mad scramble for safety pins – took an hour, which meant the party was in full swing by the time we arrived. I felt lightheaded and giddy as soon as I stepped into the ballroom. Spotlights had turned the cream-coloured walls of Oxford Town Hall into a pink and purple fever dream and the ceiling was covered in twinkly stars. Everywhere I looked, there were women in electric-blue lehengas and cherry-red Anarkali suits; gold bangles cascaded up and down their forearms, rattling as they danced. Onstage, a DJ was spinning Bollywood and bhangra hits with occasional Western pop interludes. The music was so loud I could feel it in my chest like a second heartbeat.

'Let's dance!' Hen shouted.

'We just got here, and there's a whole other room to see. With food!' I replied.

'You can eat anywhere – I'm hitting the floor!' And then she disappeared into the pulsing crowd.

The second room had a live band playing Indian folk and classical music, henna stations where guests were getting their hands painted, and a large buffet. As we picked up our plates, I realised we'd lost Yasmin. I scanned the room and saw a tall guy in a suit hovering over her, talking a mile a minute. 'Poor Yaz, that guy won't let her leave,' I said. 'I'll go and save her.'

Cora put her hand on my arm to stop me. 'Check out her face,' she said. 'Not sure she wants to be rescued at the moment.' I put on my glasses and saw that Yasmin was smiling and running a hand through her hair. *We've been here five minutes! How did she already find someone to flirt with?*

After dinner, Anisa and Cora joined Hen on the dance floor. I wandered around the room, taking it all in. After a few minutes of eavesdropping on a group of women discussing South Asian soap operas, I took a step closer and said, 'Mind if I join you?' We spent almost an hour cracking up over the ridiculous plotlines – vengeful daughters-in-law, reincarnated husbands who come back as six-year-old boys, random nuclear bombs in corner shops. 'It's like, I fully realise how absurd a show is, but then I'm also crying?' one of the women exclaimed.

A little after midnight, my friends finally got tired of dancing and were ready to go. Anisa went to find Yasmin, returning to report that she was at the bar, chatting with some boys, but would find us soon. Twenty minutes later, Anisa stomped off again and came back with an apologetic Yaz in tow.

In the line for the cloakroom, Hen suggested we stop by Mc-Donald's on our way back to halls. 'Oh, *now* you're hungry?' the rest of us squawked, before eventually acquiescing to her plan.

The place was packed with students ordering burgers and fries to sober up or fuel their late-night study sessions. As we stood in the back of the line, I asked, 'So, what's good here?'

Hen whipped around to face me. 'Wait, wait, wait . . . have you *never* been to McDonald's?'

'Only once. It was in Pakistan and I got something called a "McArabia", which is basically just a shawarma. So . . . not too exciting, I guess.'

The four of them were completely silent for a moment, then erupted in laughter.

'All right, here's what we're doing,' Hen said. 'Everybody pick their favourite thing on the menu and order it for Malala.' I ended up with two boxes of chicken nuggets, a Big Mac and a caramel frappé. We took our trays up to the first floor and sat by the window, where we could watch the other students drifting in and out. When Yasmin started showing off her henna to the boy at the next booth, Anisa insisted we call it a night.

The old bell tower on the quad chimed twice just as we reached the gates of Lady Margaret Hall. *Two a.m.!* I had never stayed out this late in my life. After my last day at high school, I'd gone to dinner at Pizza Express with Alice and got home at eight thirty. At the time, even that small taste of freedom was thrilling for me. Now here I was, roaming around a city with my friends in the early morning hours.

After the Diwali Ball, my excitement for university life bordered on mania – I wanted to try everything. I combed through upcoming campus events, adding as many as possible to my calendar. There's a saying that every Oxford student knows: 'University is study, sleep and social life – but you can only pick two.' It didn't take long to decide that one was enough for me.

6.

Rowing club met at sunrise. As I dressed in the dark for our first practice, I already regretted signing up for it in my Freshers' Fair haze. The full extent of my error hit me as soon as I reached the docks. These were not the charming wooden rowing boats I'd seen lazing along the river – they were racing shells, long and narrow aluminum tubes with a heavy, twenty-foot oar at each seat.

'First thing you need to know, if you want to be a rower: you can't just step into the boat,' the instructor announced. 'If you put all your weight in at once, you'll sink. You place one foot on the side furthest from the dock and then squat, lowering yourself down and hovering your other leg over the boat until you're fully seated.' I was now sure I did not want to be a rower, but it was too late to run away. Everyone had seen me.

With eight of us inside, the top of the boat was almost level with the water. One wrong move and I would go overboard, drowning in the river in my first month at Oxford. I had neglected to tell anyone that I didn't know how to swim. Just a small, unimportant detail.

The instructor pushed the boat off the dock with her oar. I rowed as hard as I could but did little more than splash the water's surface, alternating between saying prayers and holding my breath for the entire practice. Afterwards I went back to my room, collapsed on the bed and slept for a few hours.

When I woke up, my phone was buzzing with Twitter notifications and WhatsApp messages. Someone had snapped a picture of me walking back to my halls after rowing practice and sent it to a popular Pakistani Facebook group. From there it spread to other social media platforms, then to Urdu-language news sites and TV channels. In the photo, I'm wearing jeans, a T-shirt and a nylon bomber jacket. The faint morning light is falling on my headscarf.

Hundreds of people, mostly Pakistani men, voiced their shock that I was wearing jeans instead of a shalwar kameez. There were comments calling me a traitor or a porn star; others claimed my clothes were a sign that I had abandoned my country and religion. A few wrote that it was shameful that I had walked down the street on my own without a father or brother to monitor me. *This is absurd*, I thought. *Because of jeans?* I'd expected some sort of uproar about my university life, but not this soon, or over something so stupid.

My phone rang and I knew who it was without looking at the screen. 'Why did you wear those clothes?' my mum demanded. 'Our relatives are calling! Everyone at home is talking about you.'

My mum's anger always shook me, but I knew I had to stand up for myself. If I gave in now, I'd have to do it again and again for all three years of university. I might as well move back home and let my parents run my life.

'I was going to rowing club, not on a religious pilgrimage, Mum. I'm not a diplomat representing my country or culture. I'm just a student! And I want to have a normal life, at least while I'm at Oxford.'

'You are not *just a student*,' she hissed, then changed tack. 'Zia, you speak to her.'

My shoulders relaxed – I'd always had an easier relationship with my dad. 'Hello, Malala,' he said in a weary voice. 'So what will we do about this? People are very upset.' Criticism from Pakistan always unnerved him. He desperately wanted to go back home someday, and didn't want to find himself an outcast when he got there.

'Dad, this is so unfair. Look at my brothers, *your* sons – they wear jeans and hoodies every day and no one says they're less Muslim or Pakistani or Pashtun. Men and boys can wear whatever they please, so why can't I?'

I could hear the resignation – and a hint of pride – in his voice. 'I suppose you're right about that, Malala,' he said. 'You are right.'

I hung up the phone feeling justified but still frustrated. Jeans are not a crime against Islam and not wearing a shalwar kameez didn't make me any less Pakistani. But too often in my home country, women's bodies are used to measure the strength of our religious beliefs and national identity. Challenge the social norms created and enforced by men, and you disgrace your family and community. That morning, it meant that the patriarchy had grown so fragile that it could be threatened by a pair of jeans. On darker days, it meant a woman could be killed for rejecting a suitor or posting pictures of herself on Instagram. When a man's honour lies in a woman's body, he will take her life to reclaim it.

I was only eight years old when I learnt what would happen if I broke these rules. One afternoon my little brother Khushal and

I followed some neighbourhood kids to a nearby stream. On hot days, we liked to splash around and throw water on each other, soaking our hair and clothes until we cooled off. Walking home, we ran into our teenage cousin. 'Where have you been?' he demanded.

'Playing with my friends,' I answered, unsure what I had done wrong.

'You bring dishonour on your family,' he seethed, 'parading around with your clothes tight and sticking to your body for everyone to see.' Then he raised his hand above his head and slapped me hard across the cheek.

The shame lingered much longer than the physical pain. For a while, I stopped going outside and kept to my room when we had guests. I felt nauseated when I thought about the slap, yet I couldn't stop replaying it in my mind. It was a brutal introduction to the way some men police women's bodies, protecting their power under the guise of 'honour' and 'tradition'.

My phone kept buzzing; when I picked it up again, I found that the online conversation was spreading beyond Pakistan. Tabloid websites had compiled the most hateful tweets and rushed to publish their clickbait. Thousands of people shared the *Daily Mail*'s story: 'Nobel Prize Winner Malala Yousafzai Is Targeted by Vile Trolls for Wearing Skinny Jeans'.

Most of the comments were a mix of 'her body, her choice' and 'leave her alone'. I paused at a reply from a reader in the Czech Republic: *It is not the UK or the Western world she needs to impress. They, for the most part, respect a woman's right to education. But her own people expect her to dress the part. No matter what she does or where she is, she will always be an object of interest as well as ridicule. By adhering to a dress code acceptable to her critics, she will get more positive attention for her cause.*

It surprised me that someone who didn't know me or live in

my country could understand the impasse so well. It was true: if I wanted to promote education and equality for girls and women in Pakistan, I had to be inoffensive in every way. I felt responsible for proving that an educated girl is not a threat. As long as I conformed to my culture's rules and dress code, no one in my community could say, 'Look how Malala turned out. We are right to keep a tight leash on our daughters.'

Every time I gave a speech and mentioned the millions of girls around the world who weren't in school, the same faces ran through my mind: my cousin who came home one day to learn she would never go back to the classroom because her father had arranged her marriage. A friend who had had two babies by the time she was fifteen. The child labourers I saw everywhere in Mingora – girls who cleaned houses, sold oranges by the side of the road, sifted through rubbish dumps for scrap metal.

To help girls like them, I had tried, for a long time, to obey all the rules – to wear the clothes my mum picked out, to be the deferential daughter that Pakistani parents expect. But maintaining that balance was starting to feel like a trap. I could stand behind a podium all day, calling out the worst abuses perpetrated by men, and it would never stir up the level of media attention that wearing jeans did. So why should I even try to placate my critics?

Choosing what I wore was a small rebellion, but clothes symbolised freedom and anonymity to me. They gave me confidence, especially at Oxford. I couldn't live a normal life if I was always looking over my shoulder, trying not to cause a scandal.

I knew I should turn off my phone for the rest of the day, but morbid curiosity made me open the *Daily Mail* story again. A few commenters were taking issue with my headscarf, claiming it was a symbol of oppression and arguing that I could not be fully emancipated until I erased all traces of my ethnicity and my faith. Those opinions were as unwelcome as the others – I wouldn't justify my choices to the secular mob any more than I would to the denim police.

My scarves reminded me of home and helped me connect to a world I had lost. No matter what the misogynists or Islamophobes said, I wanted girls in Pakistan to know that I had not forgotten them. If I was going to be photographed without my consent, at least they would see that a girl in a scarf could walk down the street on her own, go to university – or even row a boat.

7.

One night in the dining hall, shortly before the winter break, Cora and I chatted with a third-year student. I've since forgotten his name, but I remember the question he asked us: 'Have you been to the bell tower?' When we said no, he insisted it was an experience that every Lady Margaret Hall student must try once. 'If you're up for it,' he said, 'meet me in the quad at midnight.'

Something about the way he said it told me this would be a covert mission. I informed my security guards that I was staying on campus for the night. If they assumed I meant in halls, that was their mistake. Cora and I slipped outside and stared up at the cupola housing an old iron bell that rang every hour. 'How do we get up there?' I asked.

'Quietly,' our guide whispered. 'If the college catches us . . . well, I don't want to say we'd be kicked out. No one has ever been caught, so I'm not really sure what the punishment is, but it likely won't be good.' He put a finger to his lips, and we followed him into the building.

On the third floor, he opened the door to the student prayer room – a cramped and carpeted rectangle with a small window on the opposite wall. 'First step, climb out this window and walk to the corner of the building.' I looked below the windowsill to see a narrow ledge, not more than seven inches wide. Below the ledge was a multi-storey drop to the cobblestone courtyard.

'When you get to the end, there's a short jump to the next section of roof, only about three feet. You can easily make it – just don't look down.'

I stuck my head out to watch as he balanced along the ledge, made the jump, and threw his arms in the air to show us how easy it was. Then I looked back at Cora. 'I can't,' she said, shaking her head.

'That's all right,' I replied. 'But . . . do you mind if I do?'

Whatever her answer, I knew I would go anyway. People had been watching me my entire life, making sure I followed the rules, obeyed orders, stuck to the script. Since arriving at Oxford, I felt high on independence. Every choice, even the bad ones, belonged to me.

Cora's face shifted from concerned to supportive and back again. 'If you're sure. I'll wait for you here and . . . pray, I guess?' She gave a weak laugh, and I went out of the window.

A blast of cold December air hit my face. Keeping my eyes straight ahead, I teetered down the narrow ledge and jumped as quickly as I could. As soon as my shoes hit the flat, square section of roof, blood poured through my heart like a whirlpool. I tossed my head back and inhaled, putting a hand on my chest to mark the spot where I needed the air to travel to. A few seconds later, I was full of energy and ready to climb higher.

'Good job, you've done the hard part,' my guide said. 'But the next bit is dangerous in its own way.' He pointed to a steel stair-case leading up to the bell tower, built for maintenance workers who needed to access the cupola. 'We climb up this little slant of roof, lob ourselves over the railing and then scramble up those stairs. The challenge is those floodlights. Until we make it to the top, we'll be in full view of the whole college, so be quick and si-lent, okay?' I nodded, and off we went, racing across the roof tiles, up the stairs and finally into the bell tower.

This rooftop path, I later learnt, was likely discovered by the Night Climbers, a secretive student society dedicated to scaling tall buildings and walking high above the sleeping city. Founded in the 1930s, the group has climbed every university landmark, in-cluding Radcliffe Camera (140 feet) and Tom Tower (150 feet) at Christ Church College. At roughly 50 feet, the bell tower was a beginner course, though just as punishing if you happened to fall.

All Night Climbers are thrill-seekers, but they have different reasons for taking risks. Some enjoy working out the puzzle of an old building with its jumble of parapets, cornices and crenellations. There are pranksters who steal weather vanes, and protestors who hang banners against homelessness and war. Others simply love to climb, using libraries and cathedrals in place of mountains. I sus-pected a few of them were like me, chasing the wonder and end-less possibility in the world. Most of my peers couldn't imagine growing old, but I understood how quickly youth escapes, how you could lose it even as a child. I'd seen enough of the adult world to trade my safety for freedom and adventure.

I smiled to myself, imagining what my parents, high-school teachers and all the adults I knew assumed about my Oxford life. In their minds, I was studying day and night, certain to earn aca-demic honours. They probably pictured my friends and me having heady debates about global politics in our free time. *That girl, the one I'm supposed to be, wouldn't take any risks*, I thought. *She wouldn't know what her college looks like from the rooftops. She would never see any of this!*

As I stood in the bell tower, I scanned the horizon, looking out at the halls of residence, the yellow light shining back at me from almost every window. Behind those walls, my friends were laughing, reading, brushing their teeth before bed or putting on their coats to go out again. Crossing to the other side of the tower to see the gardens, I watched a group of students huddled together on the grass. I smiled, wondering what secret they were sharing. Beyond them, the River Cherwell lay still and quiet in the moonlight, like a silver ribbon dropped at the edge of the woods.

I want to stay here forever, I thought.

My first term at university felt like living in a constant state of amazement, new wonders and revelations unfolding all around me. I had rowed a boat, stayed out past midnight and now scaled a rooftop! But the best part was waking up every morning and remembering that I had friends – four friends who were always there, saving me a seat at breakfast or waiting for me to get ready so we could walk together to the lecture halls. For the first time in years, I felt like myself again.

The 1 a.m. bell was about to strike, and my guide said it was time to go. On the way up, I hadn't thought at all about the reverse trip. Instead of hurling my body onto a flat surface, now I had to make the leap and touch down toes-first on the narrow ledge with nothing to grab on to, no way to steady myself. A shudder ran through me as I looked down, searching for ground beneath four storeys of shadows. But the moment I jumped, I knew I would do it again and again.

8.

My parents' doorbell must have rung a thousand times over the Christmas break. Every afternoon guests came for tea; as soon as they left, another group arrived for dinner. My dad, who had always thrived on socialising, loved it. I was less enthusiastic.

When I was in Birmingham, my dad treated our house like an art museum and me like the signature piece in the collection. In his mind, no one would go to the Louvre without seeing the *Mona Lisa*; the least I could do was give our visitors an autograph, a selfie and a couple of hours of polite conversation. I half expected to come home one day and find our small vestibule converted to a gift shop featuring key chains and postcards with my face on them, maybe a Malala-themed umbrella or snow globe. It was my first break from university, and I wanted to lounge around the house, watch TV and eat my mum's food. But it's impossible to relax when you're always on display.

With all the commotion, I couldn't devote twenty hours per week to studying over the break as Oxford recommended. I needed time to prepare for 'collections', a series of mini-exams undergraduate students take at the start of every new term. They don't count towards your final marks, but professors and academic advisors use the tests to monitor your progress. As I wasn't the most diligent student in my first term, I had hoped to spend the holidays catching up. But between the parade of visitors and finally getting some proper sleep, that seemed impossible.

I went back to Oxford a couple of days early, hoping to somehow master eight weeks of material in forty-eight hours. The dining hall was closed, so I ate dry cereal in my room, not wanting to spend the fifteen minutes it would take to run out for milk. My philosophy study session went pretty well, but I couldn't bring myself to open the economics textbook. If I did, it would only remind me of all the things I didn't understand and couldn't possibly learn before collections.

The next day, I shuffled into the econ test a sleep-deprived wreck. When the professor called time after three hours, my hands were shaking. I had only answered half of the questions, and the finished half was subpar at best. On the walk back to my room, I was filled with regret – angry at myself for not staying on top of my coursework, angry at my dad for making it so difficult to study at home.

Hen was waiting at my door. 'Yay! You're done with first collections! Mine are tomorrow – tell me everything. How did it go?' she said. I shook my head, went into my room and cried for the first time at university. Two days later, Lara sent an email asking to meet with me about the results. When I opened her message, I was at the airport boarding a plane for Beirut.

BEFORE GOING TO Oxford, I didn't think about how being a university student would affect my work for girls' education. At high school, I'd spent my free time on calls or in meetings, dedicating weekends and summer breaks to travelling around the world to advocate for every child's right to learn. But now I had friends, a packed social calendar, a much fuller life. When I was binge-watching TV shows or gossiping with my girlfriends, I sometimes felt guilty for having fun, telling myself that I was wasting time and ignoring my mission. I thought of girls I knew in Pakistan or those I'd met in refugee camps on my travels: *Why should I be here when they are not?* Socialising, and even studying, could make me question my value as an activist, as if having any sort of life while other young women suffered was a betrayal.

In the months after I was shot, thousands of people reached out to ask how they could support me. From my hospital bed, I signed the paperwork to set up Malala Fund, an organisation that could redirect all the attention I received into helping other girls go to school. Once I'd recovered, my dad and the staff at Malala Fund encouraged me to take advantage of interest in my story – to speak at events, give interviews, meet politicians. If I really wanted to help girls, they said, I needed to leverage my public profile and advocate for education in every possible forum.

The pressure – of knowing I could make an impact, yet always feeling like I wasn't doing enough – built inside me, until I started to believe that I was personally responsible for delaying progress. If I wanted to sleep in on a Saturday instead of practising for an upcoming speech, out-of-school girls would suffer. If I skipped a meeting and went to the movies with my brothers, new schools wouldn't be built for children in need. *God saved my life for a reason*, I reminded myself. *And I must spend it helping others.* I felt compelled to say yes to every invitation, to go wherever people told me I was needed.

I assumed Oxford would offer a mandatory break from work, as students weren't permitted to travel during term time. But the requests kept coming. 'Could you miss just a couple of days?' people asked. 'If you come to this event, it will really make a difference for girls' education.' I couldn't say no. That's how I found myself, in the first week of my second term at university, blowing off essays and skipping tutorials to fly to three countries in eight days.

First I went to Lebanon to give Apple CEO Tim Cook a tour of Malala Fund's alternative education programmes for Syrian girls, refugees of their country's civil war. I came back to Oxford for one afternoon to repack my bag. Then I flew to Switzerland to speak on a panel with Canadian Prime Minister Justin Trudeau. In truth, the panel was just a ruse; the team at Malala Fund wanted me to corner Trudeau in the green room and press him to make education aid a priority when Canada hosted the G7 Summit later that year.

Both efforts paid off: Apple's support helped fund education programmes in countries like Brazil, Nigeria and Pakistan; and G7 leaders pledged $3.8 billion to girls' and women's initiatives when Trudeau hosted the summit that year. But I returned to Oxford exhausted and stressed out over missing a few days of coursework.

My friends could sense my anxiety and tried to help. Cora shared her lecture notes and essays with me; Anisa spent a few hours walking me through the week's economics problem set. I studied all weekend, but still hadn't caught up.

On Monday morning, Lara sent a note asking me to come to her office later that afternoon. I watched the hours tick by all day, and felt like a big rock had settled in my stomach as I opened her door. 'Well, I would ask why you missed your tutorials last week, but I don't have to because you were on the news twice from two different continents!' she said with a cheeriness that slightly scared me.

'I'm sorry I had to skip them, but I felt like it was important for my work,' I replied solemnly.

'Malala, your professors and I realise you have responsibilities that your peers do not. But it is our duty to prioritise your education, and we can't do that if you're not physically here.'

'I understand,' I said, slumping in my chair.

'I know that your work is not a job in the traditional sense, but the end result is the same. You are not focused on your studies.'

I shifted uncomfortably in my seat and waited for Lara to continue.

'Your collections results show that your proficiency is not where it should be and, after last week, you've fallen further behind. I can help you regain your footing, but can we agree that you won't travel again during term time?'

The stone in my stomach rolled over. 'I, um . . . I have to go to Monaco tomorrow.' Lara's face reminded me of a Pashtun idiom I'd heard as a child – she looked like she was 'sitting on a sack of pepper'.

'I'm going to speak to business leaders about the economic importance of girls' education,' I added, as if it were an extra credit project.

It was true, but not the whole truth. I didn't tell Lara that, unlike my trips to Lebanon and Switzerland, the conference organisers in Monaco were paying me for my appearance. When she'd mentioned the 'no job' rule during Freshers' Week, I'd pictured working in a bookshop or coffee shop. Getting paid to give speeches didn't seem the same to me. I wasn't sure Lara would agree.

The truth was, I couldn't stop working, even when I wanted to. After my family settled in Birmingham, I became our only source of income. My dad had been a teacher in Mingora, but he wasn't licensed in the UK. My mum couldn't speak English, and my brothers were too young to take jobs. My speaking engagements paid for my parents' mortgage, my brothers' school fees, my take-away dinners – everything we needed to live.

Like Hen and many other first- and second-generation immigrant kids, I was expected to share everything I earned – not just with my immediate family, but with those in our home country as well. We sent thousands of dollars a year to people in Pakistan to buy medicine, food, air conditioners for the sweltering summer months. We paid for cars, livestock, even entire homes. My dad had promised to cover the costs for two daughters of a family friend to study abroad, as their lives were in danger at home. One girl was accepted into university in the United States and one in Canada. When my brother Khushal graduated high school the following year, I would need to make enough money for four university tuitions on top of all the other expenses.

At twenty years old, I was earning more than my family ever had in Pakistan. But we gave so much away that we lived pay cheque to pay cheque, and I worried about our household bills. I couldn't cancel my speaking engagement in Monaco, and I didn't know how to explain this to Lara.

'So counting last week and this week, you will miss a quarter of the tutorials this term,' she said with a heavy sigh. 'I will speak to your professors about scheduling some replacement sessions. And you will need to work very hard to catch up.'

Lara continued talking, her voice fading in and out in my mind. I could only focus on one thing: for the first time in my life, I was a bad student. Not just struggling, like I had at high school, but unfocused and irresponsible. As I walked away from her office, my legs felt unsteady as if gravity, and everything else I thought I understood, had vanished.

9.

Cora, Anisa and I were working on our econ problem sets in my room when Hen and Yasmin burst through the door. 'Yaz is bailing on me! At the very last minute!' Hen wailed.

Yasmin gave a look that was half frightened, half amused. 'I told you I'd go next time,' she said.

'There won't be a "next time"! Malala, you have a Nobel Peace Prize – mediate,' Hen demanded.

'Not sure that qualifies me for interpersonal conflicts, but what's the problem?' I asked.

Hen explained that, weeks ago, Yasmin had agreed to go with her to a cooking class with a visiting American chef, an expert in soul food. 'You have to have a partner to participate, and now she's saying she can't because some guy said he *might* be free to hang out tonight.'

'I could go with you,' I offered.

Without looking up from her calculations, Anisa overruled me: 'No – you need to study. Also there will probably be ham involved.'

'Fair points,' I said, looking back at Hen with sympathy. 'Yaz, what's the story with this boy?'

She handed me her phone and I scanned her texts with the potential love interest. Over the last week, Yasmin had been trying to keep the conversation alive with jokes, invitations, questions that required more than a yes or no response. She'd send five or six messages in a row. A day or two later, he'd respond with 'nice', 'sorry, can't make it. essay deadline' or 'maybe this weekend if I have time'.

It seemed obvious to me that he was signalling disinterest, but Yasmin refused to take the hint. 'If you met him, you'd understand why he's perfect for me,' she said. 'I just need us to hang out more so I can show him that I'd make a great girlfriend.' Out of the corner of my eye, I saw Cora wince.

'Yaz, maybe don't get off the train at the first stop,' I said gently. 'There are lots of boys at Oxford; try meeting as many as you can.'

'But I have tried – you've all seen me trying!' Yasmin replied, as the rest of us cackled in agreement. 'This guy, though . . . he's different. You're telling me to just give up on him?'

'Give up on *waiting* for him. Make your own plans; keep the plans you've already made. You're at university and you have more exciting things to do than audition for his attention.'

All four of them gawked at me like they'd just discovered I had a secret superpower. After that night, everyone started asking me for advice. Cora couldn't figure out why her relationship with her high-school boyfriend wasn't working any more. He hadn't done anything wrong, but she'd felt so bored and restless when they hung out over the Christmas break.

'It's because you've changed,' I said. 'Your life is here now, and you want to be free to explore, but you feel guilty about it.' They broke up a week later. (He had a new girlfriend within a month, and Cora tried to follow her private account on Instagram. When the girl blocked her, we tried again from my verified profile with more than a million followers. She blocked me too, which both Cora and I had to admit was pretty cool on her part.)

Hen preferred dating apps to meeting a man at university. At night we would sit on my bed and scroll through the latest crop of profiles. '*Looking to meet new people and see where things go,*' I read aloud, rolling my eyes. 'Why doesn't he just say he only wants to hook up?' I acted as Hen's unofficial security consultant, weeding out the bad prospects – mainly those who mentioned crypto or posed in front of their car. One time I sensed a guy was trouble and she ignored me; he ended up stealing her debit card and emptying her bank account.

I had somehow become the resident advisor on romance, examining carefully cropped photos, cryptic text messages and astrological charts with much more intensity than I brought to my textbooks. 'How are you so good at spotting red flags when you've never been on a date?' Hen asked me.

I shrugged it off. 'I guess I'm a better coach than a player.'

It was a quippy line that hid the truth: getting a boyfriend would be pushing my independent streak much too far. In Pashtun culture, dating doesn't exist. Most men in my community forbid their wives, daughters and sisters to have any contact with the opposite sex. If a girl was seen talking to a boy, she disgraced her family and put her own life at risk. Even looking could cause trouble. People liked to remind young women of the rules with old sayings like 'The most honourable girl will always keep her eyes on the ground, even when her village is on fire.' And if a man ogled her? That was also her fault, as she must have done something to draw attention to herself.

Most Pashtun fathers decide when their daughters will marry, often at around fourteen or fifteen years old. Marriages are arranged and negotiated, a routine transfer of property between men. Defying their authority – and following your heart – can be dangerous. Growing up, I knew of several young women who were poisoned by their families for crimes of 'dishonour' – from looking too long at a boy in the street to having a secret mobile phone to exchange messages with their crush. The parents always claimed it was suicide, but everyone knew the truth.

I was now living five thousand miles away in a place with very different social norms, but people in my home country were still monitoring me. On a flight home from a trip to New York, I saw David Beckham on the plane, and we took a quick photo together. When a Pakistani newspaper published the image, friends and family called my dad to say the Pashtun community was outraged that I had stood so close to a man. 'Did you tell them it was *David Beckham* and that he smells amazing?' I wanted to say to my parents, but I knew better and held my tongue.

On another occasion, Prince Harry and I were invited to speak at the same event. When he put his arm around my shoulders for a photo, my mum stepped in front of the cameras and swatted his hand away, to the dismay of everyone in the room. 'No touch!' she boomed, wagging her finger in his face. Harry apologised profusely, and I was mortified. But my mum couldn't concern herself with royal protocol or publicly embarrassing her daughter in front of a prince; she was much more worried about what would happen if her neighbours in Mingora saw the picture.

Wearing jeans was one thing, but a university romance would make me a pariah in the eyes of my people. If I had explained all this to my friends, I knew what they would say: *Those views are archaic and antifeminist! You are an adult woman in a free country with the power to make your own decisions!* They would be right – but that didn't mean I could live as I pleased. Dating wasn't worth the potential damage to me, my family and my work.

Besides, boys were a huge distraction. How else to explain my brilliant, accomplished friends making such poor decisions in their love lives? Not me, I was above all of that. I would have some fun at university, graduate and then go straight back to work, dedicating the rest of my life to the good cause of girls' education. *I'll be like a nun*, I thought. *But Muslim.*

At least, that's the story I told myself. Sometimes late at night when I couldn't sleep and took to writing in my journal, another truth emerged: I didn't believe that anyone would want me. No matter how much confidence I projected onstage and in speeches, I felt too ugly to love.

It was a harsh truth, and one I hated admitting to myself because it felt so vain and trivial. Once upon a time, I would spend hours in the bathroom styling my hair, imagining myself in a Bollywood movie with Shah Rukh Khan. That teenage girl was puckishly pretty, quick to smile. But ever since the shooting, I was something different – my face and body were now meant for service, not romance. *You don't need to be attractive to be an activist*, I told myself.

When I was in hospital, doctors said that my facial paralysis would decrease and the ability to move my face would return over time. After five years, the improvements were minor at best. My left eye still drooped. When I smiled, my mouth only moved on one side. Online trolls created memes comparing my laughing face to a braying donkey. I started covering my mouth with both hands whenever someone told a joke.

Every few months I saw a nurse for Botox injections; they

froze the muscles on the working side of my face to make the paralysis less noticeable. It seemed the best I could hope for was a flattening of all expression, a face locked in permanent solemnity like a statue in a cemetery.

Between the strict social norms I grew up with and the damage to my face, it was easier to tell myself that dating wasn't an option and put it out of my mind. Why spend time being sad about things you can't change?

Instead, I channelled all my energy into my friends' love lives, living vicariously through their dating dramas and laughing at their aspirational swooning. It seemed like every girl I knew was obsessed with Timothée Chalamet that winter, and could spend a full hour discussing his hair or playing clips of him speaking in French. I didn't get the infatuation, as I'd always been immune to the appeal of pretty boys. The man of my dreams was brown-skinned, rough and hairy. My knees went weak at the sight of a dark beard, wooly forearms and tufts of chest hair poking out of a shirt. Telling myself that I'd never have a boyfriend wasn't enough to stop me from secretly wanting one.

But that was all a fantasy, something to smile about as I fell asleep at night. Even if I woke up with a normal face and no cultural baggage, I wouldn't find a guy like that among the gawky Oxford undergrads.

And then I met Tarik.

10.

The first time I saw him, I was sitting on a bench outside my halls, enjoying a fleeting moment of January sunshine. I looked across the quad to see a tall, broad-shouldered stranger walking towards me. As he got closer, I could make out his loose black curls and broody eyes.

He sat down on the opposite end of my bench; I froze. He didn't speak or even look at me, just curved his perfect lips around a cigarette, took out a book and started to read.

'Um, hi,' I said. My voice sounded like someone was squeezing it out of a tube. 'I don't mind at all, but I think you're not allowed to smoke here?' I pointed to the space between us where a brass NO SMOKING sign was tacked to the back of the bench.

'Can't read that,' he replied, still looking at his book. 'Dys-lexic.'

'Oh, of course, I'm sorry. Well . . . enjoy!'

I hopped off the bench and scurried back to my room. 'Of course' you're dyslexic? 'Enjoy' smoking? Was there a type of dyslexia that meant you could read books but not signs? Had he made a joke and I missed it? For all the advice I gave to other people, I was disastrously bad at talking to boys.

The cold weather was back when I saw him again. Yasmin and I were standing in a hallway outside the library, warming our legs on the radiators and drinking low-grade hot chocolate from the vending machine. He walked past me and mumbled, 'All right, mate.'

As soon as he was gone, Yasmin grabbed my arm. 'How do you know Tarik?'

'I don't even know his name! I've only seen him once before. Though I wouldn't mind seeing him again . . .'

'Eh, I don't know, Malz,' she said. 'Gorgeous for sure, but he hasn't got the best reputation.'

She told me Tarik's family had immigrated from Morocco to a rough neighbourhood in North London. At high school, he'd been an academic sensation, earning some of the best scores in the country on his entrance exams. When he enrolled in the business course at Lady Margaret Hall, he was one of the brightest students in his year. 'But that was three years ago,' Yasmin continued.

Since then, the college had put Tarik on academic probation multiple times for blowing off essays, skipping tutorials and getting into fistfights. 'I've heard a rumour he sells drugs,' she said. I assumed Yasmin was exaggerating. And if she wasn't, then all the more reason to befriend this mystery man. *I could help him get back on the right path . . .*

Tarik was twenty-four and starting from scratch in first-year classes. Oxford was giving him one last chance to deliver on his academic promise. 'So he'll graduate with us?' I asked.

'Don't hold your breath,' she replied.

A week later, he drifted past the library around 11 p.m., looking so mysterious with the collar of his black coat pulled up around his ears to block the wind. I was on my way to pick up a book I needed for an essay due the next morning. I thought he might walk right by me, but he stopped about a foot away, looked at his phone, and said, 'Ah, I guess I missed dinner.'

'Yes, by about . . . four hours?'

'Shit, I'm so hungry now.'

I saw my opening and took it. 'I have some snacks in my room if you want to come up.'

He shoved his hands deep in his pockets. 'Sure.'

We crossed the quad to my halls. 'You're in my building. That's me. Room 205,' he said, pointing to a second-floor window.

'Really? How are you one floor below me and I've never seen you on the stairs?' I asked. Tarik shrugged.

'Would you like some tea?' I offered when we reached my room. He nodded.

'There's a bowl of fruit and some snacks on the bookshelf,' I said. He took a banana. When he finished that, he ate an orange. Then he polished off a whole packet of biscuits and two flapjacks with his tea. Neither of us said a word until he was finished.

'Well, thanks for that,' he said, standing up to leave. 'Appreciate it.'

'Stop by anytime!'

He was gone, but my room still smelt like him. As long as I can remember, I've been attracted to strong scents. Petrol. Fresh paint and felt-tip pens. Chlorine fumes at an indoor pool. Tarik's sharp mix of cigarettes and cheap cologne made me collapse on my bed and laugh into my pillow.

IN ANTICIPATION OF another encounter, I restocked my snacks, adding Pot Noodles and heartier fare I thought Tarik might enjoy. He stopped by again and didn't ask for food but ate everything I offered him. Given his background, I assumed he was on scholarship and receiving a living expenses stipend from the university. Most of my friends got financial assistance, so I knew it was enough to cover books, meals and more. But I had never seen him at the dining hall, the halal cart or any of the restaurants in town. It seemed like the only time he ate was in my room.

'Maybe his family needs help, and he gives them his stipend to make ends meet,' I suggested to Yasmin.

'Or maybe you just want to see the best in him,' she replied. My shoulders slightly tensed at the thought that she was now the sensible one and I was the fantasist. I shook it off.

It must have been my snack selection, because Tarik certainly wasn't in it for the conversation. I tried my best to seem interesting and bright, but our chats usually went like this:

Me: 'Are you going to the bop this week?'
Him: 'Nah, I hate that stuff.'
Me: 'Do you like studying business?'
Him: 'It's all right.'
Me: 'Well, it must be harder than my courses because you can't make things up like we do in politics and philosophy! Ha-ha!'
Him: 'Ha. Yeah.'

After a few lacklustre visits, I had an idea to liven things up. 'Do you want to see my favourite place in the whole college?' I asked. He looked mildly intrigued. 'But it has to be our secret,' I said mysteriously. 'You can't tell anyone.'

61

'I'll take it to my grave,' he replied.

Climbing up to the bell tower, I was thrilled by how many rules I was breaking: Oxford's restrictions against night climbing, my parents' prohibition on boys, the law of gravity. Tarik might've been the bad boy of Lady Margaret Hall, but tonight we were partners in crime.

When we reached the top, I looked up and saw a canopy of stars. Usually I preferred looking down at the campus – but tonight it felt like I was floating in the sky, like I could reach out and touch things that were light years away. Tarik sat with his legs stretched out, looking more relaxed than I'd ever seen him.

'If you could go anywhere right now, where would it be?' he asked.

I put a hand to my mouth to hide a smile. It was the first real question he'd ever asked me – and the same thought I'd had the first time I stood in the bell tower. My answer hadn't changed: I wanted to stay here forever.

'I would go and find my dad and bring him home,' he continued. 'He's in Marrakesh or maybe Algiers. I don't know where, but I think I could find him.'

'When was the last time you saw him?' I asked.

'Years ago,' he replied.

I understood what it was like to miss someone you hadn't seen in a long time. You worry that the other person might change in your absence, that you won't be able to connect in the same way when you see them again. As time goes on, you think of them less and feel guilty when you do. *I should call Moniba soon*, I thought. Tarik looked back up at the sky and we sat in silence for a while.

On the descent, I went ahead of him, deftly manoeuvring over the balustrade and down the roof tiles. As Tarik made the big jump onto the ledge, one of his shoes came loose. I heard a loud *thwack* as it hit the ground and then watched with mounting panic as a campus security guard appeared on the ground below, shining his torch into the space between the buildings. Tarik and I scrambled through the window and then ran out of the prayer room in opposite directions.

My heart was still pumping when I reached my halls and bumped into Cora. 'Where were you?' she asked.

'On the roof. With Tarik.'

'Yikes.' Her face became a human emoji, mouth pulled into an exaggerated grimace.

She doesn't understand him like I do, I thought.

Tarik was always away on the weekends, and I lay in bed wondering where he went. To see his family? Or maybe Yasmin was right and he was wherever drug dealers go – I imagined a shadowy lair filled with men counting money and fixing motorcycles.

He turned up again after midnight on a Wednesday. I was still awake, sitting at my desk and working on an essay. 'Hey! Where have you been?' I asked.

'Had to take care of some business. And see some friends.'

'Am I your friend?' I said. My heart thumped hard in my chest, caught off guard by the flirtation in my voice.

'Of course you are,' he replied without smiling.

I sat down on the floor next to him and tried to subtly play detective. 'So you were . . . in London?'

'Yeah, and it made me wish I'd never left.'

'Why is that?'

''Cause there's real people in London, right? These university kids act like we're all in it together, but they only think about themselves. Everyone says they love Oxford, but they secretly hate it and hate each other. I'm just honest enough to admit it.'

Everything in me wanted to shout, *That's not true!* and tell him all the reasons he was wrong – how amazing it was to make friends at university, how it felt to explore the world with them, how they could bring out the best in you. But I felt like I was finally making progress in getting him to open up, so I nodded coolly, like I understood what he meant.

He went silent again and I stared at the array of large silver rings he wore on his fingers. Before I could stop myself, I took his right hand and brought it up to my face. 'Can I try this on?' I asked, pointing to a giant ring with a black stone in the middle and skulls engraved on either side.

'Sure,' he said.

I slid it down my index finger and held out my hand to examine it. 'I think it suits me. Can I keep it?' I asked, my stomach full of butterflies.

'Yeah,' Tarik replied.

When he was gone, I felt relieved, like I could finally exhale. Flirting was a rush, but also terrifying, like it could careen out of control at any moment and take you in a direction you weren't ready to go.

Tarik's ring was too big for me, but I wore it all the time, turning it over and over around my finger. Sometimes I took it off, placed it in the centre of my palm, closed my hand around it and then opened it again like a present. My friends didn't ask where I got the ring. They all knew about Tarik by now, and had made their uneasy peace with it.

It felt like we'd seen each other enough times now for me to invite him out. Not on a date, but something more interesting than tea in my room. Having already played my night-climbing card, I needed another idea. The opportunity came a few days later when Hen texted Cora and me:

> Dinner out tonight? Then back to campus and hang out in the bar?

> I'm in. Do you mind if I invite Tarik?

Hen replied 😐. Then 👍.

As I walked down the stairs to his floor, I clutched a note in my hand. I assumed he'd be out and planned to slip the invite under his door, then scurry back up to my room. When I arrived, though, the door was open and he was sitting in his desk chair, facing the hall. Too late to run. I shoved the note in my pocket and looked around the room, trying to take it all in. A toothbrush and a couple of bath products sat on the edge of his sink. His bed had a thin blanket that didn't look warm enough for winter. Next to the door, an open dresser drawer held six or seven identical flip phones, but no clothes. There were no snacks or school supplies, no fairy lights or family photos. It felt more like a safe house than a student's room.

After a few moments, I realised he was waiting for me to speak. 'I thought I'd stop by your place for a change,' I said, hoping he remembered telling me his room number a few weeks prior. 'I'm going out with some friends for dinner tonight. Care to join us?'

He rubbed the back of his neck and looked at the floor. 'Yeah, uh, thanks. It's just . . . my professors are being mental about my essays. And there's stuff outside Oxford I need to do . . .' He paused for a moment. When he spoke again, it was more to himself than to me. 'If I could undo it, I would. But it's too late now.'

I tried to lighten the mood. 'Maybe getting out of your room would help?'

'You're a good one, Malala. Sure, I'll stop by if I can.' We exchanged numbers and I dropped a pin from the restaurant. Throughout dinner, my eyes darted to the door every time it opened. The evening came and went without him. I wasn't surprised, but it still hurt.

When nearly two weeks passed with no word from Tarik, I started to worry. If he missed this many days at Oxford, he could get put on academic probation again – or worse. My mind played out excuses: maybe he was hurt somewhere and needed help. Maybe he wasn't texting me back because he'd lost his phone. I made myself frantic thinking of potential scenarios. I needed to know he was all right, and I wanted to be the one to rescue him if he wasn't.

One afternoon I went to Yasmin's room to ask if she knew anything. 'You're not the only one looking for him,' she said. 'This girl was ranting in the laundry room a couple of nights ago. Apparently she let him borrow her textbooks for a few hours and he never brought them back. She's tried calling and he doesn't pick up.'

Another weekend went by with no sight of him, but on Monday evening I found him pacing outside the dining hall. 'Hey, you're here! Is everything all right? I was worried.'

'Hey,' he replied without looking at me. Then he started pacing again. 'I went to my tutorial and the professor threw my essay in the bin without even looking at it!'

'Why would he do that?'

'He says I'm two essays behind. The one I turned in today was from last week, when I wasn't on campus. So now he refuses to read it. He gave me until tomorrow morning to turn in the current one. I missed the lectures, and no one will let me borrow their notes. The business course is full of assholes.'

'Okay, but you have all night. I've started essays at three a.m. and still made it by the deadline! You're so clever, you can do this.'

'Nah, 'cause it's useless, right? They promised I could stay at Oxford as long as I pass collections every term. But my professor said today I might as well leave now and save everyone the trouble. Like they've already decided.'

'Don't leave! If your professor won't help you get back on track, we can take your case to the student welfare advisor. Just get started on your essay. Come to my room and work on it. I'll make some tea.'

He stopped pacing and looked at the ground. When he spoke, his voice was calm and quiet. 'No. No, thanks. I'll be all right. See ya around.'

I wasn't ready to accept defeat, but the best person to help Tarik was the last person I wanted to ask. When I got to Anisa's room, she was sitting at her desk, deep in a problem set.

'Sorry to bother you, but I really need a favour. You know Tarik in your course? He's about to get kicked out of Oxford.'

'Worse things happen at sea,' she replied, turning away from me and flipping open her textbook.

'It's just that . . . you really helped me with econ when I got behind. I was wondering if you might share your last essay with him, just so he can get some ideas for his. It's due in the morning and he hasn't started yet.'

'I help you because you're my friend, not some druggy git with no interest in university. If he rips off my essay, I could get into trouble too. Think about what you're asking here.'

'Please, Ani, he might lose his place.'

'Malala! Chicks before dicks!'

'I don't know what that means.'

'It means you're obsessed with this guy, and you need to pull yourself together.'

Walking away from her room, I felt strange, like the spell that had brought me there was broken. I'd failed in my mission to help Tarik, and Anisa thought I was a fool for trying. She was right – he had not asked for my help and didn't accept it when I offered. So why was I doing this?

Because I *enjoyed* crafting elaborate narratives around our brief interactions. I could have snapped myself out of the delusion at any time, but I didn't want to.

When Tarik disappeared for days, I would sit on my bed and listen to Bollywood duets, imagining the two of us embroiled in an epic love story. Then he'd show up again without explanation, eat my food and leave. He didn't want to be close to me, didn't ask about my friends or weekend plans. And that never bothered me because I preferred the fantasy in my head, where everything was both thrilling and safe.

Obsessing over an unapproachable boy was just another way of avoiding rejection and staying single, filling my need for connection with a one-sided romance. When I realised I'd tricked myself into thinking it was real, I wanted to stamp out both the infatuation and the longing that created it.

A few days later, I walked to the pharmacy on a mission to buy a bottle of Axe Body Spray like the one I'd spotted in Tarik's room. I purchased a fragrance called Anarchy XL, went back to my room and sprayed it all over my body.

When Yasmin came over that night, she stopped dead in her tracks at the door. 'Ugh, why does your room smell like the patriarchy?' I showed her the can.

'I'm using it on myself, so I won't get distracted by Tarik or any other guy,' I explained. 'I know I am attracted to this smell, and now I have removed the temptation and claimed the power for myself.' I looked at her smugly, satisfied by my genius solution.

'Well, I guess you solved it, Malz. There's nothing left that could attract you to a man,' she said with a smirk.

The last time Tarik stopped by my room, I was at badminton practice. He sent a text saying he was sorry he had missed me, and he'd come back later, but I never saw him again. My friends spotted him in town a few times after that. Eventually he disappeared altogether. I don't know if Oxford kicked him out or if he just gave up. Maybe he was far away, looking for his father.

Over the next year, I sent occasional texts to check on him. One night I sat in my room alone, listening to thunder rattle the old windowpanes.

Do you like storms? I wrote. I want to go outside right now and dance in the rain. He never replied.

11.

People often associate the scent of pine trees with winter, but it's actually strongest in the spring. I know this because, in Mingora, blue and longleaf pines grow on both sides of the Swat River; our valley smells like a Christmas candle when the temperatures rise and the snow melts.

One sunny afternoon at Oxford, I opened my window to find the air smelt like home. In a rush of nostalgia, I grabbed my laptop and opened Google Maps. A few clicks and I was there again, on the streets where I grew up.

Starting at my old house, I traced the route I used to walk to school. *There's the mulberry tree in our neighbour's yard.* When it dropped its fruit on the street in the summer, I would mash it until the soles of my shoes turned purple, leaving a trail of inky footprints behind me. I clicked past the ruins of a two-thousand-year-old Buddhist monastery where my brothers and I liked to play hide-and-seek. Turning the corner, I zoomed in to read a banner hanging on a restaurant: *Ramadan Iftar Dinner for Orphan Children.*

The porch light was on at Moniba's house. I stared at the image on the screen and then closed my eyes, picturing myself standing on her street, my hand on the garden gate, a moment away from seeing my oldest friend again.

Suddenly I missed everything at once – mangoes that tasted like butterscotch, the way the sun made the river sparkle, sleeping outside under the stars with my grandmother. The stillness of my room began to agitate me. In Mingora, there was always noise – cars honking, people shouting out of windows, the crack of cricket bats, the local mosque's call to prayer. Instead of soothing my homesickness, taking a digital walk through my hometown had dredged up a dormant bitterness in me, grief at being ripped away from my old life.

When you haven't seen your home in years, it can become a mythical place in your mind. For days after I arrived at the hospital in Birmingham, I gazed out the window expecting to see the mountains that greeted me every morning when I woke up in Mingora, only to be startled by skyscrapers and traffic lights. In the years since, I'd travelled the world, seen the Colorado Rockies and the Sierra Nevada, flown over Qurnat as Sawdā' and Mount Kenya. And I always said the same thing: 'The mountains in Swat Valley are taller than these.' I felt honour-bound to defend the place where I grew up, to never be impressed by another mountain range as long as I lived.

When I realised my family would be staying in the UK, I promised myself that I wouldn't change – I'd be the same Pakistani girl I'd always been. But as the years went by, I felt like I was splitting into two different people. The new Malala understood the basics of football, the difference between Harry Potter and Harry Styles, what Brexit was and why everyone had an opinion about it. At the same time, the old Malala was still inside me, compiling years of thoughts on Pakistan's cricket team, TV shows, politics, even little things like why chicken biryani didn't taste the same in Birmingham. I kept all of these reflections in my head because I had no one to share them with. It made me feel like I could never be true to myself, like I didn't belong anywhere.

With eighty-five Pakistani students enrolled at Oxford in my first year, university should have been the perfect place to finally connect with people from my homeland. Instead, I kept my distance, sitting in the back row at Pakistan Society meetings and skipping their social events. If I walked past people having a conversation in Urdu, my ears perked up, but I didn't stop. Being alone, I decided, was better than being rejected or, worse, attacked.

~

LESS THAN A week after I was shot, people in Pakistan started claiming that the attack was staged. When I eventually heard about the conspiracy theories, I thought they were silly and pathetic, that no one would actually believe such a thing. Then thousands of people – even some politicians and journalists – began saying that my family had faked the whole thing for money and British passports. The Taliban issued a statement claiming credit for the attack. Doctors who'd treated me in Pakistan and the UK were interviewed on TV. But none of that evidence made a dent in the growing masses who believed it was all a set-up. When my mum heard the lies people were spreading, she would cry and say, 'I wish they were right. I wish it never happened.'

The constant, widespread denial of what had happened to me was a second assault, leaving wounds that wouldn't heal. In one of my first interviews after being released from hospital, the journalist asked me what I would say to the man who attacked me. I said that I forgave him – and that was true. But what I wrote in my diary that night, at fifteen years old, was also true: *What would I say to him? I only ask that next time you aim for the middle of my forehead. Make sure everyone sees it. Then they won't say I wasn't shot.*

While the conspiracy theorists maintained the shooting was staged, other people believed the attack was real, but loathed the attention I received after it. 'Why does the world love Malala so much?' they asked over and over in comments on news sites and social media. Western countries had colonised our land, used our people as pawns in decades-long proxy wars, killed children and civilians in drone strikes. After all this, many Pakistanis resented that the United States and Europe now wanted to heap praise on a teenage girl from a mountain town. If the West loved me, that was reason enough for my fellow citizens to hate me. It felt like I had to live my life as if I were on trial, trying to prove myself to people who had already judged me guilty.

One afternoon, during a high school free period, I was scrolling on my phone and saw a picture of myself that a Pakistani news outlet had posted on Instagram. I paused to read the comments; as usual, they were full of words like 'bitch', 'whore', 'traitor'. Then I read: *I want to kill her.* I gasped and shrank down in my chair, feeling exposed and vulnerable. *Is he really planning to attack me? Is he part of the Taliban?* I clicked on his profile, but it didn't give any clues about who he was. Just some grainy pictures and stupid memes on his grid. If that was actually him in the photos, he wasn't much older than me.

I needed to understand why he hated me so much. *Did I say something in an interview that made him feel this way? Could I talk to him and change his mind?* Before I had time to think it over,

I was creating an Instagram profile with a fake name and filling it with pictures of male bodybuilders, virtual bodyguards for me to hide behind. Then I messaged the man who'd written that he wanted to murder me.

Why? I don't understand. Why do people from her own country think this way?

He replied quickly: Where you from?

I'm Pakistani. But I live in England, I answered truthfully.

Then you can't understand, he wrote. Those of us in Pakistan know she is a liar and a traitor. Don't worry, we will send her to hell.

My hands were still shaking when I found Alice in the student common room. 'Malala! What were you thinking? Block him right now and don't ever do that again,' she said, her eyes flashing with alarm. I promised her, and myself, that I wouldn't talk to trolls any more.

For my own survival, I had to become immune to seeing hundreds of hateful comments about me every time I opened my phone, try to numb the pain and build a wall around my heart. But it always hurt when people said I had done nothing to help girls in Pakistan. It wasn't only that they ignored the physical price I'd paid for standing up to the Taliban, or the years of my life I'd spent advocating for education – what upset me was the implication that I didn't care, that I had voluntarily walked away from my home, forgetting about the millions of girls still fighting to go to school. That couldn't have been further from the truth.

No matter how many times people claimed that I'd done nothing to help, I kept quiet about my biggest project in Pakistan – it was so close to my heart that I couldn't bear to see it torn apart by my critics. When I won the Nobel at seventeen, I used the prize money to purchase land in Shangla, a remote cluster of villages high in the mountains, where my parents grew up. As a child, I spent every Eid holiday there, at my grandmother's house. And when my family fled the Taliban in Mingora, we took refuge in Shangla's rocky hills.

83 per cent of the women from these villages, including my mum and aunts, were illiterate. Most parents took their daughters out of school in Year 3, when they were old enough to help with cooking, cleaning and caring for younger children. There wasn't a single high school for girls in the entire region – so I decided to build one.

Getting the school up and running was urgent to me: I had many cousins in Shangla; some were almost thirteen and fourteen, the age when fathers start to negotiate marriages for their daughters. If we opened a school, I thought, we could buy them some time, convince my relatives and other parents in the community that girls should finish their education before becoming wives. At the very least, they wouldn't grow up like their mothers and grandmothers, unable to read or write. I dreamt that some might even go to university.

For years, people claimed it was impossible to start a school in Shangla. They said it was too difficult to build anything on the craggy shoulders of the Hindu Kush mountain range. Most homes in the area consist of one or two rooms, are made of mud and stones, and can't be reached by car. Even if you somehow managed to construct a building, the parents would never allow their daughters to go to school, people warned. Tilting at windmills. Fool's errand. Lost cause, they said. But I was determined to pull it off. *If I can make this school successful*, I thought, *it will prove that girls' education is possible anywhere in the world.*

By the time I started at Oxford, construction was nearly complete – a four-storey feat of engineering and determination. Soon we would throw open the doors and welcome the first students, from primary to middle school. Our plan was to add a school year every year until the oldest girls graduated. I pored over every scrap of information that came in from the architects, building foreman and school administrators in Shangla – budgets, blueprints, photos, text messages – impatiently dreaming of the day when I could see it for myself.

If I didn't care about girls in Pakistan, I would have chosen a quieter life, one away from cameras, spotlights and endless criticism. But I wanted to see my community thrive, so I ignored the haters and kept working. At night before I went to sleep, I told myself that someday this torment would end. Someday I would be able to speak freely about my homeland without labouring over every word, trying not to say anything that could be used against me. Someday there would be a place for me in Pakistan again.

All of this ran through my mind one winter afternoon when I received a message from Parveen, a computer science student at Oxford:

Hey hey Malala! Hope your first year at Oxford has been great so far! A group of Pak students will be hanging out and ordering food at my friend Raja's house tonight. We'd all love to meet you, so I was wondering if you want to join?? It's a really good group of people, a safe place to have fun and relax. The address is 24 Observatory Street.

I read the invite again and again, searching for subtext. Did Parveen and her friends have a good opinion of me? It was one thing to be mocked online, where I knew a good portion of the posts came from trolls who found it fun to start fights and spread misinformation; I didn't know how to handle someone saying those things to my face. Did 'safe' mean I could trust them? Would our conversations stay between us? Would they post a picture of me standing too close to a boy or not wearing my headscarf? The last thing I wanted was another angry call from my mum saying that people were up in arms over something they'd seen on WhatsApp.

I could stay in my room and think about these questions all night, telling myself there would be another chance, another party, another invitation. But I wanted people from my country to believe the best about me and thought I owed them the same.

I typed Thanks, Parveen, I'd love to come and hit send before I had time to change my mind.

12.

As the car turned down Observatory Street, I told my security officers that it wouldn't be a late night – just a quick hello, then back to campus. My stomach fluttered with a mix of anticipation and dread. I'd never even been to a birthday party at high school, and now I was going to a student house party where I didn't know a single person.

Thoughts tumbled over each other in my mind: *Will they think I'm less Pakistani than they are? Will they be conservative or open-minded? If they're open-minded, will there be dancing? And if I dance, will it end up on social media and cause a scandal? Be careful with everything you say and do, Malala . . .*

I stood on the pavement and smoothed down the creases in my carefully chosen outfit. Back in my room, almost every item of clothing I owned was on the floor, as I'd changed ten times before leaving. I still wasn't sure if I'd got it right, but it was too late now. I took a deep breath and knocked on the door.

'Come in!' someone shouted from the other side. As soon as I stepped over the threshold, Parveen jumped off the couch to greet me. 'Malala! You came! I'll give you a tour,' she said. I tried to take it all in as she showed me round, stealthily clocking every person's face to see if they were smiling or scowling at me. A few glanced up and nodded warmly, but most were too wrapped up in their own conversations.

In the kitchen, Parveen introduced me to Raja, our host. 'Great place,' I said. The living and dining spaces were small, but much nicer than my dingy room.

'Welcome to 24 Obs! And thanks. I lived on campus my first year and then my parents rented this house for me. I told them it would help me study, but it's turned into a bit of a party spot.' As he was speaking, the front door swung open and five more people arrived. All the guests seemed to know each other, greeting one another by name and fetching food and drinks for the new arrivals.

As the house filled up with people, everyone was talking loudly in a mix of Urdu and English, huddled around biryani and shish kebabs on the dining-room table. They all seemed nice, but whenever one of them spoke to me, I braced myself, wondering if this was the person who was going to ask me if I'd really been shot or why I no longer lived in Pakistan.

I'm going backwards, I thought. Since coming to Oxford, I'd had no trouble making friends. I had not lurked on the edges of the Diwali Ball or pub outings. *These people seem fun. Why can't I just be myself?*

I gathered up my courage and walked over to the dining room where Raja was hanging out. 'So, if you weren't here tonight, what would you be doing?' he asked. 'Let me guess . . . studying?' He had confident, happy eyes and a black pompadour that bobbled when he talked.

I chuckled. 'Uh, less than you might expect.'

'Same,' Raja replied. 'I'm in the engineering postgraduate programme and I get by, but just barely. Technical reports, simulations, lab work . . . who has the time? Too easy to get sidetracked by all the great people at Oxford.'

As we talked, I learnt that his first love was cricket. After attending high school in Dubai, he'd gone back to Pakistan for a year to try to make it as a professional athlete. 'I'm obsessed with cricket!' I said, proceeding to pepper him with questions about up-and-coming players, the advantages of left-handed bowlers and recent ball-tampering scandals.

'Do you play, Malala?'

'I did when I was little and I *loved* it. I joined the cricket club here, but I haven't been to any of their events yet. I'm a bit too rusty, I guess.'

'How about next weekend I get out my gear and we'll have a practice session in University Park? You'll be back in shape in no time.' I smiled, feeling looser and more at ease.

Parveen walked over with a few friends she wanted me to meet. One of the girls handed me a little red box. 'Cocomos!' I squealed. The cookies were a staple of Pakistani childhood. In Mingora, I used to buy them from street vendors after school. 'I haven't had these in so long.'

'My mum sent them in a care package,' the girl replied. 'She sends the same thing every month – Cocomos and two bottles of Fair & Lovely.' All of us doubled over with laughter and joked about the aunties we knew who swore by the popular skin-lightening cream. 'Light skin opens doors!' Parveen shrilled, repeating a saying we'd all heard over and over growing up.

Around 10 p.m., the party guests stacked the dining chairs in a corner and wedged the coffee table into the hall to make room for dancing. I noticed Zayan right away. Unlike the other guys, he didn't have a beard or hi-top haircut, instead sporting a shoulder-length style with feathered layers. And he *owned* the dance floor. I watched in baffled amazement as he effortlessly transitioned from a bhangra step to a pop-and-lock, all while carrying on a conversation with the person next to him.

We bumped into each other in the kitchen when he took a break. 'You're here!' Zayan roared, tossing a sweaty arm around my shoulders. 'I'm glad you came 'cause there's something I've always wanted to ask you . . .'

I mentally prepared myself for whatever he was about to say. *Here it comes . . .*

'What name do you give the barista when you go to Starbucks?' he asked.

I made a loud honking sound, a mixture of laughter and relief. 'Sorry to disappoint you,' I said, 'but I don't drink coffee. So that's never happened.'

'Ugh, lame. Okay, what about restaurant reservations then?'

I leant against the kitchen cabinets and smirked at him, not sure if I wanted to give up my alias. But I was having too much fun so I decided to go for it. *'Jane Lewis,'* I whispered.

'Shut up! Whaaaat?'

'Yep, it's the name on my university ID too.'

'I mean, why? Like, no offence, but you don't really look like a Jane.'

'Because my security team wanted me to pick a pseudonym to make it harder for people to find me on campus. They gave me a month to decide, but I couldn't choose one. So at the last minute, I looked around my room and saw this shopping bag from John Lewis, the department store. Changed John to Jane and now I'm stuck being Ms Lewis for three years. On paper, at least.'

We moved to a settee in the alcove under the stairs to keep chatting – that's when I learnt that Zayan gossiped as well as he danced. Though only a fresher like me, he seemed to know everything about everyone. 'There's a guy who just walked in, light-blue shirt. No, don't look! Okay, so he's *in love* with Parveen, seriously crazy for her. Like he's studying law, right? But *for some reason*, he does all his reading in the science library where she hangs out. And Parveen keeps getting mystery gifts from a secret admirer in her pigeonhole! She's really into calligraphy, so, like, a nice set of pens or whatever, stuff like that.'

'Does she know they're from him?'

'No! She can't figure it out!'

'Shouldn't you tell her?'

'Well, it seems obvious to me, but I don't know *for sure*. And anyway, I want to see where this goes! Philosophical question: do you think this is stalker behaviour or is it sweet?'

'I think it's sweet,' I said, and then paused, reconsidering. 'I *hope* it's sweet. Tonight I'm choosing to believe in the good in people.'

A moment later, the first notes of 'Billo De Ghar', a Punjabi hit from 1995, erupted from the speakers and the room went electric. People abandoned their conversations mid-sentence and leapt off the couch. 'I love this song!' I shouted.

'Come dance with us!' Zayan shouted back.

I motioned for him to go on without me and took it all in from my perch on the settee, nodding along as the crowd sang and jumped around Raja's living room. I couldn't stop smiling, amazed that I could be feeling the same unfiltered joy as everyone else at the party.

Around midnight, as I stood at the front door putting on my jacket to leave, Raja dropped his voice low and said, 'Look, I know you deal with a lot of criticism. I've seen what's out there on the internet and heard what people say. But please believe that you're welcome here. Ask anyone and they will tell you I've always been a Malala fan.'

I put a hand to my chin and cocked my head. 'Malala?' I repeated. 'Never heard of her.'

~

SOON I WAS stopping by 24 Obs two or three times a week. It was our shared clubhouse, the place I wanted to go for everyday activities and special occasions. My new friends and I piled in front of the TV to watch Bollywood movies or cricket matches. During Ramadan, we gathered for iftar dinners and pre-dawn doughnuts. We threw surprise birthday parties so often that the guest of honour was rarely caught off guard but played along anyway. Around Raja's dining table one night, I picked up a new hobby when a couple of postgraduate students introduced me to poker. An enthusiastic and reckless beginner, I hated to fold and sometimes went all-in without even glancing at my cards. I was intrigued with the game as a way to test how well people could read my face and body language. At first the more experienced players felt bad taking ten pounds off me, but I kept showing up and they got over it.

My new friends were very different from anyone I knew growing up in Mingora. They were city dwellers born in Karachi, Lahore or Islamabad; some had homes there but had grown up in Dubai, Kuala Lumpur or London. Worldly and well travelled, they knew how to shoot pool and find their shoe size in multiple countries. They would visit family and friends in Pakistan once or twice a year, and come back with the latest news, fashions and music. I slightly envied their sophistication, the way they moved through different cultures yet never felt scared of breaking some invisible rules. Wherever they roamed in the world, they seemed like themselves – comfortable and free.

The 24 Obs crew also represented a range of religious and cultural practices. About half only ate in halal restaurants; the rest were fine with any food except pork. The more devout students never missed morning prayers. Others drank whisky and smoked weed. A few split the difference and partied until it was time to pray.

I was fascinated by their varied approaches to relationships as well. Some observed the 'halal gap', standing a foot away from members of the opposite sex and keeping their hands in front of their bodies where everyone could see them. Others gave indiscriminate bear hugs to everyone in their path. There were guys with white American girlfriends, women who wanted to stay single forever, and those who planned to let their parents arrange a marriage after university. There were gay students too – though even in this liberal-by-Pakistani-standards group, no one talked about that. What I loved most was that none of these differences kept us apart – everyone was welcome and treated like family, no matter their background or beliefs.

That heaviness inside me, the fear of engaging with people from my home country, started to fade away. I began to think of the last five years not as a lonely era of my life, but as a time when I stored up friendship and love, waiting to bestow it on these exact people. It was nothing like the Pakistan where I grew up, but inside the walls of 24 Obs, every version of myself felt at home.

⌒

THAT SPRING, PARVEEN and I, along with a few other friends, decided to go to the Pakistan Society's *qawwali* concert, a celebration of Sufi devotional music popular across South Asia, held in a small park on campus. On my way to the event, I remembered that I'd promised to bring mango juice to share and hurried to the nearest supermarket. I arrived late to find eight musicians sitting on a Persian rug on the grass, already playing their first song.

Qawwali is often described as 'mystical' but it's far from the soothing, ambient sound popular at spas and health-food shops. The frenetic, maximalist music combines percussion from a tabla and handclaps, the atonal drone of a harmonium and a lead vocalist who sings or chants religious poems while the other musicians form a dissonant chorus in the background. A single song can run from fifteen minutes to an hour. The music is intended to induce a trancelike state, bringing listeners and performers closer to God.

From the edge of the park, I noticed the other students sitting still and silent, politely observing the artists at work. But qawwali should be a communal fever dream, not a performance. The musicians and audience should provoke each other, escalating the volume of their voices, while the tabla mimics a heart attack. Across South Asia, it's not unusual to see people dancing wildly or spinning in circles with their arms above their heads. The best qawwali sessions feel like getting caught outside in a sudden storm. You surrender to the rain, shivering and shaking, damp and delirious long after the sun returns.

At the back of the crowd, I noticed a group of elderly men from the local mosque, crowded together on a blanket. They sang along and clapped, their limbs flailing as they rocked and lurched to the music. The old men understood the art in a way that my peers did not. As I watched them, I wondered how ancient traditions could be lost over one generation or a few thousand miles.

My friends at 24 Obs helped me feel closer to my culture, but homesickness still gripped me in unexpected moments. It had been five years since I'd had to leave Pakistan. How long would it be before I could see my country again? What would I lose in the meantime?

To me, leaving home felt like entering a hedge maze. At the

start, you believe you can always find your way back. You hold tight to memories, retrace each step – take a right, another right, then a left at the birdbath and you've returned to your original self. But the deeper inside the labyrinth you travel, the more you change. You forget the scent of your best friend's hair and the Urdu word for 'rain'. You develop a taste for expensive cheese and an ear for English irony.

When we emerge at the end of the maze, our best hope is to find people like the old men at the qawwali, those who remember who we were at home. At least we are together in this new place. At least someone here knows the songs we used to sing.

13.

When I arrived in Birmingham for the spring holidays, I told my dad we needed to go to Pakistan. If my university friends could visit the country on their holidays, I should have that right as well. It felt like if it didn't happen now, it never would. I had waited long enough.

'Let's put it off until summer,' he said.

'If you want to wait, that's fine. I'll go on my own,' I shot back, with a dare in my voice. 'I will book my own flight, leave this house in a cab and call Moniba when I land to pick me up.' Deep down, I knew I wasn't that bold, but I wasn't sure my dad knew it – and that might give me some leverage.

We'd had this conversation dozens of times over the years. Whenever I asked my dad to book the trip, he reached out to the Pakistani government, who had to give their permission for me to visit. They wanted to be sure they could protect me – and that my presence wouldn't disrupt the country or stir up controversy.

Every time, the same answer came back to us: 'It's not the right moment for Malala's return.' My dad had heard it so often that I worried he was giving up. 'It will *never* be the "right" moment!' I railed, trying to infect him with my indignation. 'I am a Pakistani citizen with a valid passport. I have committed no crime. And they have no grounds to stop me.'

I sounded angry, but inside, my heart was breaking. At 24 Obs, I'd had more experiences that reminded me of home – food, music, sports, language – in a few weeks than I'd had in the past five years. And now that reawakening felt painful, like blood rushing back into numbed limbs. I was done with stalking my old friends on Facebook, done with walking the streets on Google Maps. I couldn't keep dreaming of home at night and waking up disoriented every morning.

I don't know what my dad said, or if he channelled the righteous outrage that I felt, but the prime minister and the army chief agreed to a visit. Their approval came with some conditions: the trip would last four days, and they would oversee the itinerary. But we were going home.

I could barely believe it. My heart, so accustomed to yearning, struggled to catch up. I tried to temper my excitement in case the trip got cancelled, filling pages of my diary with *Let's see what happens! Stay positive! Fingers crossed!*

My parents threw themselves into preparations – Mum selected my clothes for the trip, and Dad made plans to see his many friends and family members. My seventeen-year-old brother Khushal was apprehensive, though. In the two weeks leading up to our trip, he had terrible dreams. Some nights he didn't sleep at all, just paced around the house, checking and rechecking the locks on the ground-floor doors and windows. 'I already have bodyguards,' I told him gently. 'Just be my brother, that's enough.'

On the flight, my excitement unexpectedly curdled into anxiety. I fell asleep and dreamt of standing on the side of a dusty road, waving as my family boarded a bus and rode away. Then I watched the bus speed into a turn and career over the side of a cliff. One nightmare rolled into another. I was in a wheelchair, surrounded by men in dark suits. They pushed me onto a stage and told me to make a speech. A man in the audience stood up, took out a gun and shot me. My subconscious was scrambling my worst fears – losing my family, being attacked, never feeling safe in the world.

I woke up sweating as the plane descended into Islamabad. In the seat across the aisle, my dad closed his eyes and cupped his hands in front of his face in prayer. Was he thanking God for returning him to his homeland or asking for protection? Probably both.

In the airport, I didn't feel the exhilaration I had imagined I would. Instead, I examined every face for signs of trouble – the woman who inspected our passports, the men pushing carts of luggage, families of the other passengers waiting in the lobby. *What do they think of me? Have they seen the conspiracy theories on the internet? Are they happy I'm here or wishing I'd stayed away?* My legs were unsteady as we walked through the airport, like they wanted to break free and run.

Military personnel showed us to our cars, one for me and my parents, another for my brothers. As I sat in the back seat, waiting for the convoy to pull away, a dark thought overcame me: *If someone tries to kill me again, am I going to freeze? Will I know how to save myself?* My fears were not unfounded: as he started the car, our driver turned around and said, 'If we suddenly stop, duck down as low as you can.' I texted his instructions to Khushal and told him to look out for Atal. *Duck down*, I whispered to myself over and over.

The sky turned from black to pale blue on the thirty-minute drive. We reached the hotel just before dawn. As news of my arrival was already spreading across TV and social media, the hotel managers wanted to hurry us into our rooms. They worried about journalists swarming the lobby, disturbing the guests and creating a security risk.

As they whisked us towards the lift, I caught a glimpse of the hotel's walled garden. 'I'd like to go out there for a moment,' I said. My parents started to protest, but I held up my hands. 'Please,' I said. 'I promise not to wander too far or stay too long. I just want to watch the sunrise on my own.'

Outside, I stepped onto a stone path lined with Madagascar periwinkles. Thick clusters of jasmine sat atop the garden walls, spilling their vines towards the ground below. There were apple blossom trees, spiky silver palms and shades of green I had not seen in years. I took off my shoes, sat down and sank my hands into the grass. *You are one of us*, the flowers and trees seemed to whisper. *Your skin was made to sit under this sun, your lungs were made to breathe the warm air.* As the sky changed from pink to gold, I felt at peace, grateful. When I stood up, my legs were strong again. I was determined not to waste another moment of the trip in fear.

That afternoon we piled back in the cars for a visit to the prime minister's office. My mum wore a dusty-rose shalwar kameez in a traditional print, like her grandmothers and great-grandmothers before here. Mine was more modern: a solid column of canary yellow topped with a colour-blocked headscarf in purple, hot pink, green and orange. Alarmingly bright in person, but perfect for television.

I was mortified by Khushal's and Atal's outfits – both wearing jeans, both a complete mess. Khushal's long-sleeved button-down shirt was wrinkled and untucked. But that was nothing compared to Atal, who had dressed to meet the leader of our country in an Air Jordan T-shirt and trainers. 'What is wrong with you?' I hissed. We sent him to change, and he came back in a tie-dye hoodie, the only other shirt he'd packed.

I could barely contain my annoyance. To prepare for the trip, my mum had spent two full days buying and tailoring outfits for herself and me. No one had bothered to think at all about my brothers' clothes. My outfit, my hair, my shoes, my scarf would all be described and dissected in newspapers and Facebook posts across Pakistan. But they were boys – it didn't matter what they wore because their bodies would never be a cause for scandal or shame.

We met Prime Minister Shahid Khaqan Abbasi in his office and took a few photos. I thanked him for providing security for me and my family and told him how happy we were to be back in Pakistan. Not one to waste an advocacy opportunity, I asked about initiatives aimed at promoting school enrolment for girls and pressed the prime minister to increase the budget for education.

After the meeting, we walked to an auditorium packed with scores of dignitaries and about as many TV news cameras. I had not been expecting to give a speech and had nothing prepared. *You only need to speak from your heart*, I told myself.

I stepped to the podium and began by thanking the government, the army and everyone who had made the trip possible. With the pleasantries out of the way, I took a breath and continued: 'For more than five years, I have dreamt of being able to set foot in my country. I have travelled around the world and, on every plane, I looked down to catch a glimpse of the city below. I always told myself, "It is not New York, it is not Dubai or Rio or London.

91

When I land, I will be in Karachi, in Lahore, in Islamabad." But it was never true.'

My voice cracked. I covered my face with my hands and wiped away the tears. 'I don't cry often. But I am only twenty years old, and I have seen so much in my life. When I was attacked, everything was out of my control. It wasn't my choice to leave Pakistan, but it was always my dream to return. Today, I am so happy to be home.' Walking back to my seat in the auditorium, I felt the same contented buzz that I had experienced when I climbed the roof at Oxford. Yes, I was scared and nervous; there were certainly risks for me in travelling to Pakistan. But I was becoming a person who was willing to take chances to have the life I wanted, and that included being able to visit my home country.

We left the prime minister's residence and went straight to a ballroom back at the hotel, where my dad had arranged a lunch for our extended family. He had ordered flowers, table settings and a buffet for 150 people. When we arrived to greet the guests, we quickly realised there weren't enough seats. More than 300 people had made the five-hour drive from Khyber Pakhtunkhwa province to the capital.

The hotel staff scrambled to bring in more chairs and prepare more food. Wide-eyed children watched as waiters paraded through the hall with platters of chicken, saffron rice and roti. I smiled at the women sitting and enjoying their meal without having to worry about cooking, serving and cleaning up like they did at home. Familiar and unfamiliar voices layered on top of one another – an uncle's booming laugh, a baby's cry, my brothers yelling back and forth to their cousins across the room. It was overwhelming to see generations of my family reunited, to be surrounded by faces I remembered from my childhood.

As the guests took their plates and settled in their seats, I walked from table to table, taking care to speak to each person and pose for as many pictures as they liked. My favourite cousin, Nazneen, rushed up to hug me, and a dozen girls followed in her wake, swarming me and touching my hands and my hair.

'Hold on, hold on!' I said. 'Not all at once, let me hug each of you individually.'

They looked shocked at hearing my voice. 'You remember Pashto?' one of them asked.

'Of course I do,' I replied. *What a strange question*, I thought. Did they think I'd been away for so long that I'd forgotten my first language, or that the attack had injured my brain so badly that my life before it was erased?

Then they all took a shot at testing my memory. 'Do you remember the time we ducked down in a field and hid from a farmer because we picked some fruit from his orchard?'

'Yes!' I said, laughing. 'And then we ran all the way to the river with our stolen plums.'

'Do you remember when we used to take our mums' jewellery and pretend we were getting married?'

'Yes, and you were always the bride because you're so pretty.'

'Do you remember when you were mean to me?'

'Hmmm, I might have forgotten that one.'

While we talked, I kept one eye on the door for my personal guest of honour, my grandmother Abai. About an hour after the gathering began, I saw my dad push her wheelchair into the room. Her head bent forward a bit and her frail hands trembled as she clutched a bouquet of flowers in her lap.

Abai was as beautiful as I remembered her. In a photo of her when she was about my age, she is pretty, but not remarkable. By the time I was born, though, age had revealed her exquisite features – bright eyes, high cheekbones, a playful smile. Almost all the women I knew as a child avoided the outdoors, careful to keep their complexions as pale as possible. But Abai's love of sitting in the sun gave her deep-brown skin and aristocratic creases around her eyes and mouth. Now in her seventies, she was the most stunning woman in the room.

After my grandfather's death, Abai lived with my uncle in Shangla and came to visit us in Mingora several times a year when I was young. I loved to sit in her lap and hear all the news from my cousins. She often spoke in Pashto proverbs or *tappa*, couplets of folk poetry passed down through oral tradition. When I felt slighted by some minor quarrel at school or left out of my brothers' games, she was ready with one of her favourites: 'I have ridden on horses, so I cannot be jealous of your donkey.' If I whined when she told me to stop watching cartoons and turn off the TV, she said, 'Malala, you are playing the flute to a buffalo.' Usually I resented our nonstop stream of house guests, having to share my food and getting less time in the bathroom to style my hair. But I always wanted Abai to sleep in my room, to have her all to myself and spend the evening hours showing her my drawings and papers from school. When she had to leave, I begged her to stay. Every time, she would pat my head and whisper, 'Love grows by coming and going.'

Abai prayed all the time, raising her hands to Allah to ask for happiness and good health for her family and friends. If a stranger passed her on the street, she would pray for him too. The day I was shot, she was visiting my family. I had eaten a few bites of breakfast and rushed through my goodbyes, excited to get to school. Abai told me to stop, then put her hand on my head and said, 'May God give her a long life.' For years, I wished I hadn't been so impatient to leave the house that day, that I'd spent another moment with her. Once we were in Birmingham, I worried that it would be my last memory of her, that she might pass away before I saw her again.

Now, in the ballroom, she looked just the same as she had that day. I walked over and knelt in front of her wheelchair. 'Abai, I'm so happy to see you,' I said. She looked down at me, then up at the women around her as if to ask them who I was. I took one of her hands in mine and she started to cry. Through her tears, she began to pray, like I'd watched her do so many times when I was young. When she opened her eyes, she asked, 'What are you doing here?'

My parents had known for a while that something was wrong with Abai. When they called to speak with her, she said strange things. Sometimes she was like a child again, talking about her mother and father as if they were still alive. At other moments, she couldn't remember what she'd done that day. Shangla had no hospital or doctors who could diagnose her with dementia or Alzheimer's disease. Everyone just called it 'old age'. I sat on my knees in front of her wheelchair for a long time, trying to memorise her face. She didn't speak, but never let go of my hand. I hoped she knew that I loved her, even if she didn't know me.

A few hours into the gathering, my dad stood on a small platform at one end of the room and asked me to join him. *Time for more speeches*, I thought. Pakistanis love to talk in front of a crowd. In the old days, people sat around sharing wild folk tales and poetry. Now every school holds oratory competitions and every event features competing monologues. A gathering of almost any size will usually include a few men taking turns to gesture and pontificate for twenty or thirty minutes each, sometimes more.

After my dad spoke about what an honour it was to have so many guests, he handed the microphone to me. I tried not to glare at him. I gave speeches for a living – why did I have to perform for our family and friends, especially when I'd already given individual greetings to all three hundred people? I thanked everyone for coming, said how happy I was to be reunited with them and especially to see Abai and meet all the new babies. When I finished, one of my many uncles stepped up to the platform.

'We are happy to welcome our family back to their country,' he said, 'and hope it will not be too long before they are living among us again. We are grateful that the daughter has survived, though she will never be the same. Look at her face – she has sacrificed her beauty to give a good image to Pashtuns and Pakistan.'

He continued with this particular point for the next few minutes, as I shrank to the back of the stage, embarrassed that hundreds of people I hadn't seen in years were now staring at me. Before the event, I had been nervous about how our friends and family would react to my facial paralysis. I knew they had a different picture of me in their minds. But my cousins hadn't seemed to notice at all; they only wanted to reminisce and be together again. The one reference they'd made to my appearance was gloating that I hadn't grown any taller. Now I felt exposed and reduced, as I had been so many times before, to my injuries and scars.

My uncle's comments also implied a worldview I could not endorse – that a woman's beauty was worth more than her mind or spirit, and that martyrdom was something to celebrate. I did not endure multiple surgeries and years of pain for 'the glory of Pakistan'. I didn't 'sacrifice' my hearing, the ability to move the left side of my face, or the large piece of my skull that had to be removed. Those things and more were taken from me by men who didn't believe I had the right to go to school, who thought killing a child would make them stronger. I was seething by the time he finally finished and another man reached for the mic. But my dad stepped in and said we were done with speeches for the day.

Most of the guests left the hotel before dark, departing for their long journeys home. A few families stayed overnight, and I spent the evening playing with my little nieces and nephews, talking with their mothers and shaking off any lingering annoyance from my uncle's speech. By the time I went to bed, I was full of excitement again – when I woke up the next morning, I would finally see the mountains.

14.

The helicopter ride from Islamabad to Mingora was one of the most thrilling hours of my life. My heart soared as we flew out of the city, over farmland and forests, between the peaks of the Hindu Kush mountain range. On the approach to Mingora, we glided over the Swat River, following the path the water had cut through the mountains thousands of years ago.

I pressed my face against the window and stared down at the valley, trying to spot the landmarks I remembered from my childhood. The icy-blue waters of Saifullah Danda, an alpine glacial lake where people catch trout and build campfires on the shore, frying their fresh fish in mustard oil and chilli flakes. The dense Ushu Forest, home to Himalayan black bears, golden eagles and a three-hundred-foot waterfall. I looked for all the unnamed places too – wildflower meadows, hidden ravines, mountain caves – the rambling beauty and splendour of Swat Valley.

As we hovered over the helipad and prepared to disembark, my mum and dad looked at each other, then at me, and started to cry. It had not occurred to any of us that we would be landing in the exact same spot where another helicopter had taken me away five years ago. On that flight, I lay on a stretcher, semi-conscious and vomiting blood, as the pilot prayed I would live long enough to reach the hospital. I could see the grief on my parents' ashen faces, how that moment had marked them forever – but I didn't want them to dwell on it. Today was sunny and gorgeous. I was alive and strong, in no mood for tears. When we stepped outside, I inhaled the mountain air, trying to fill up every inch of my lungs. 'Come on,' I said, grinning back at them. 'Let's go home.'

On the short drive to our old house, I expected to see the narrow streets crowded and bustling with activity as I remembered them. Instead, they were quiet and empty, no children playing, no fruit vendors jockeying for the best position, no brightly coloured buses chugging along. The driver said the roads were closed for our arrival. I missed the noisy street life and imagined little kids stuck in their homes, grumbling that I had ruined their day.

The family who now lived in our house ushered us straight to my childhood bedroom, proud to show me how they had kept everything exactly as I had left it: my trophy case, stuffed with academic awards and textbooks. The spot on the wall where I used to measure myself every morning, making a pencil mark to see if I'd grown overnight, stubbornly stuck at five feet since I was twelve years old. The scratchy bedspread my mum had bought at the bazaar. In the bedside table, I found drawings of ducks and kittens, and a small stuffed animal with a hidden zip where I used to keep all the notes my friends and I passed during school. The scraps of paper were still inside, scrawled with petty feuds and rumours of field trips.

I put the fragments of my former life back where I'd found them and went to sit on the bed with my mum. 'I never set foot in this room again after the helicopter took you away,' she said. 'I could have brought more of your things, you could have had them with you all this time, but . . .' She stared down at her hands and began to cry again.

'Mum, I want you to be happy today,' I said, placing my arm around her shoulders. 'Be *glad* you didn't bring anything – because I never got to take a last look at this room. And now everything is here just as I left it and I can say a proper goodbye.'

We left the room to find my dad and Khushal speeding through the house, giddy with nostalgia. 'Do you remember . . . ?' one of them would say; the other would finish his sentence and then they would both laugh. Atal followed with an artificial light in his eyes. When we left Mingora, he was only seven years old. He was a British boy now, unable to share our memories or match our enthusiasm.

We'd been in Mingora for less than an hour when we were herded back into the cars. There was so much to see; we needed more time. Maybe a trip to the bazaar would put a smile on my mum's face. Khushal might want to chat with his friends who lived down the street. If I could persuade the pilot, it would take less than thirty minutes by helicopter to get to Shangla. The school I'd built had just opened its doors to the first two hundred girls – I could meet the students!

But I knew the security officials would never agree to that, nor would they turn my family loose in Mingora for our individual nostalgia tours. If I wanted to stay a little longer, I needed to ask for something simple, a nearby place that we could all enjoy.

My mind immediately went to the river, where I'd spent my happiest afternoons as a child. When Abai came to visit, we would load a rickshaw with pots of chicken and rice and enjoy a picnic on its banks. My dad would dunk a bag of mangoes in the water until they were cold, then scoop them out like ice cream for us kids. Khushal and Atal would dig up worms to tie to the ends of sticks with string, trying to catch a fish without a hook, as my mum sat in the shadow of the pine trees, watching me run back and forth through the wildflowers.

I only wanted a moment to feel the water run over my feet, to hear the river rumble through the valley and echo off the mountains. 'Not possible,' the security officials said when I asked. 'It is too public and open a space to ensure your protection.' My heart sank. I thanked them for doing their job, even as I silently mourned that I might never be able to roam freely along the riverbank again.

Everyone was quiet on the flight back to Islamabad. My mind drifted to a bit of philosophy I'd recently read, attributed to the ancient Greek thinker Heraclitus: 'No man can step in the same river twice, for it is not the same river and he is not the same man.' The idea, as I understood it, is that people and places are always changing, and that these changes are vital to our existence. Without the constant flow of water, the river cannot survive.

As a child, I was impatient for change – to be older, to grow taller, for the snow to melt, for the guests to leave. Then suddenly the changes would not stop: thousands of girls kicked out of school. Millions of people afraid of the Taliban and fleeing their homes. And me waking up in a faraway land, not yet realising I had left my world behind. I needed to see Mingora again, even if I knew things would never be the same. My life had changed forever, but the river in my heart would always flow towards home.

∽

WE ARRIVED BACK in Islamabad just after lunchtime, in time to receive one final guest – my best friend, Moniba. Her mum had agreed to bring her to the hotel for an hour or so, as long as we could meet in private. Her father and brothers didn't want her to be photographed with me.

I paced around the hotel room waiting for her to arrive. Growing up, I couldn't have imagined a life without Moniba. Even though I am half a year older, she always felt like my confident, slightly bossy big sister. In primary school, I wanted to emulate her, coveting her straight, silky hair and elegant penmanship. As we got older, we competed for top marks and awards. I signed up for every contest – public speaking, drawing, essay writing, whatever gave me a shot at adding to my trophy case. Moniba tried to get me to focus my efforts. 'Don't stretch your feet beyond the sheet, Malala,' she said. My mischief-making and rivalries went too far on occasion, and she could be a bit of a wet blanket sometimes – but together, we found our centre.

I hoped things would be the same between us. *Will I still be able to make her laugh? Will her memories be the same as mine? What if she thinks I've changed too much?* Finally I heard a soft knock on the door; I ran over and threw it open. As soon as she stepped inside, we fell into each other's arms and Moniba started to cry. I felt like crying too, but I wanted her to see me smiling and happy, the fun-loving girl she remembered.

'Until this moment, I don't think I really believed you were alive,' Moniba said through her tears. We had talked on the phone often over the past five years. She'd seen pictures of me travelling around the world. But I understood what she meant. When an ordinary day is ripped apart by violence, your sense of certainty is shaken. For the rest of your life, it can be hard to know what's real and what's not.

The last thing I remembered on the day I was shot was sitting in the back of the school bus, chatting with my best friend. After that, everything was blank until I woke up in hospital in

Birmingham. Over the last five years, when Moniba and I talked, I'd sometimes ask her to tell me what had happened, what she saw that day. I trusted her – and no one else – to fill in the gaps for me.

Moniba always said the same thing: *The gunman asked, 'Who is Malala?' You stared straight ahead and didn't speak. As he came closer, you gripped my hand so tight it hurt for days afterwards. Then the gun went off and you slumped into my lap. I screamed when I saw the blood. The bus driver raced to the local medical centre. Your injuries were too severe, so they flew you to a better hospital in a bigger city. I didn't get a chance to say goodbye.*

In the hotel room, I asked her to tell me again. She ran through the familiar beats, but then she said something I hadn't heard before: 'When I got home that evening, I saw myself in the mirror. There was blood all over my school uniform, and I thought I'd been shot too. For days after that, I kept checking my body for bullets. Sometimes, even now, I wake up in the middle of the night and think that I've heard gunshots.'

In that moment, I realised that Moniba was not the girl I remembered. How could she be? The attack on my life had changed everyone who witnessed it, everyone who loved me. So many people had talked about the pain I went through, the severity of my injuries, my difficult recovery. But they rarely asked about the other girls on that bus or the trauma they suffered from seeing blood run down the walls and hearing each other scream. Talking with Moniba, I came to believe that we were equally affected, just in different ways. My body carried the scars, but I had no memory of that day. Five years later, my best friend still had nightmares.

The hotel room was dark and heavy, and I couldn't stay there any longer. 'Could we go outside to the garden?' I asked her mother. 'All the journalists know I'm leaving tomorrow, and they've gone home now. Do you think we could walk around for just a few minutes?' She reluctantly agreed to my plan. We could go outside for a moment, then they would leave.

In the garden, Moniba and I made several laps around the perimeter, happy to stretch our legs and feel the sun on our faces. 'You look amazing,' I said to her. She was as beautiful and glamorous as always – shiny hair, perfect complexion, stud earrings and a trendy handbag slung over her shoulder. When we were young, she dreamt of becoming a fashion designer. Even then, she knew her family would never allow it; now she studied medicine.

'Thanks,' she replied. 'So do you.'

'Stop lying, Moniba!' I laughed. 'I am like a middle-aged auntie, always trying to figure out what's cool to wear and never getting it right.'

I told her about my attempts to put together a new wardrobe last summer and the rowing club controversy. 'Oh, I wish I could have seen your mum's face when she found out about the jeans,' she snickered.

'How are you enjoying university?' I asked.

'I love it, but my brothers are making it difficult,' she sighed. They insisted on accompanying her to campus to make sure she didn't speak to men. If she became a doctor, they would only allow her to treat women. 'It considerably narrows my options.'

Moniba had never been interested in marriage, but now she was considering it. 'If I happened to get a husband who was a nice man, maybe he would interfere less in my education and let me have a job in a hospital someday.'

I took her hand, and she changed the subject. 'Do you remember, when we were in primary school, you used to say that the only way we would ever get married was to a man who was willing to take both of us? You said we would marry as a set and that way we would always stay together!'

She broke into cascading giggles, each burst of laughter lasting until another one rose to take its place. I joined in and soon we were both struggling to compose ourselves. Everyone in the garden turned their heads to see what was so funny, but I didn't care. *Look if you like*, I thought. *We're just two girls, two best friends, reunited.*

Moniba's mum hurried to catch up with us and told her it was time to go. As I watched them walk away, I was glad that my last memory of this trip would be with her, just as it was five years ago.

15.

The trip helped to heal the disorientation that I had experienced over the previous five years. Pakistan was not 'before' and England was not 'after', but parts of an ongoing story. My country, family and friends were no longer memories that I had to look backwards to see; now they were the future too – people and places I could return to again and again.

When I got back to campus, I felt unstoppable, like my life could finally move forward. I wanted to have fun and push the boundaries of my independence – and it started with College Club Night.

As long as I can remember, I've loved to dance. In Mingora, dancing was forbidden for girls and women – 'It's a sin,' my mum would say. But at school, my friends and I would wait until the teacher left the classroom, race over to the tape player, and put on a mix of our favourite Bollywood hits. We didn't know any formal steps or technique; we just let our bodies find the rhythm and tried to outdo each other with increasingly dramatic moves. In those moments I felt weightless and free, like nothing outside those walls mattered.

When we moved to Birmingham, I would dance alone in my room and watch tutorials to try to improve my skills, even picking up a few hip-hop routines. By the time I got to university, I thought I was pretty good and wanted to show off my moves. 'Damn, girl! Where did you learn to body-roll like that?' Hen asked one night while we were blasting Cardi B's 'Bodak Yellow' in my room. I loved our dance sessions, but now I was ready to go public.

The invite popped up in my Instagram feed: CLUB NIGHT // 1980s AEROBICS THEME // AT FEVER ON MAY 17. I had no idea what any of it meant, but I immediately sent it to Cora and Hen and wrote, Guyzzz, I think I want to go! Come with me! No excuses!

I wasn't sure what to wear, so I put on a chic grey sweater, black trousers and high-heeled patent leather boots. When my friends arrived to pick me up, they were not impressed. 'No, no, this is all wrong,' Hen said, pointing at my outfit and then throwing open the doors of my wardrobe.

Cora was dressed in what appeared to be a bright-orange bathing suit over pink and yellow nylon leggings. 'What's up with your headband?' I asked, gesturing at her forehead.

'It's a sweatband! For workouts. In the eighties?' When she saw I wasn't getting it, she pulled up a video on her phone of women with big hair doing some sort of choreographed dance in a gym. I'd never seen moves like these, a mix of exaggerated marching, jumping jacks and hip thrusts. The woman in the front of the group yelled, 'Feel the burn! Feel the burn!'

'Oh, I can't do this. I've changed my mind,' I said, backing away from both of them.

'*Relax*,' Hen replied. 'One step at a time, let's get your look sorted first.' She pulled out a neon-yellow silk shirt from my wardrobe. The price tag was still dangling off a sleeve.

'I don't even know why I bought that,' I said. 'It's too low-cut – it would get me in trouble.'

But my friends were not having it and fired off a raft of instructions: 'Add a black tank top underneath for coverage. Put the yellow shirt on over it, but leave the last few buttons undone and tie it at the waist. You can keep the black pants but swap out the boots for heels.'

Cora ran to get her make-up kit and painted a lightning bolt in gold glitter on my right cheek. Hen found a pair of oversize hoop earrings in my dresser and handed them to me. They spun me around to face the mirror. I looked unrecognisable. *But maybe cool?* I thought. In a last-minute surge of caution, I added a baseball cap and sunglasses for anonymity.

Having only seen clubs on TV shows and social media, I assumed we would arrive to long lines, velvet ropes and paparazzi jostling for position. I was relieved, if a little confused, when the car stopped in front of what looked like an office building. The club entrance was sandwiched between a dermatology clinic and a vacuum repair shop, and the only people outside were a few students smoking cigarettes.

We walked through the door, downstairs to the basement, and into a sea of undergrads dressed in neon and spandex. A few people were buying drinks at the bar, but most were on the dance floor – a giant chessboard with lights under each square that changed colour in time with the song. There were overhead lights as well, spinning blues, reds and yellows. I'd never seen a disco ball in real life and marvelled at the fleet of glittering fireflies it sent whirling around the room.

A synth-y beat dropped and Cora pulled me onto the dance

floor. I didn't know the song, but I liked the soaring vocals and how everything sounded happy, even when the words were sad. In the packed crowd of students, dancing seemed the same as it had with my school friends in Mingora – everyone doing their own thing, making it up as they went along. Except that, back then, I couldn't have imagined how electric it would feel to be encompassed in sound, light and the collective energy of dozens of people losing themselves in the music. I loved it.

A few mutual acquaintances came over to talk and dance with Cora and Hen. At first I wondered why they were ignoring me, then realised they didn't recognise me in my clubbing disguise. 'Hey, guys,' I shouted, taking off my sunglasses. 'It's me – Malz!' Their eyes widened dramatically and they looked at each other to make sure they were all seeing the same thing. 'Malala Yousafzai at Club Night,' one of them said. 'I'm literally deceased right now.'

Around 4 a.m., we tumbled through the LMH gates. 'Ugh, these shoes are trying to take me out,' Hen groaned. Cora looked pale and exhausted.

'What's wrong?' I asked. 'You two go clubbing all the time.'

They looked at each other, then back at me. 'Malala, you're a legend,' Hen explained, 'but no one who isn't doing heavy drugs stays until the *very end* of Club Night. Like, they were packing up the bar by the time we dragged you out!'

'Usually we dance for an hour or two and then head to a pub to wind down,' Cora added. 'And, you know, *eat something*. God, I'm starving.'

The corners of my mouth twitched as I tried not to laugh, then burst into giggles and snorts. It might be a long time before they went dancing with me again, but that was fine. I couldn't imagine a more magical night anyway.

AT HIGH SCHOOL, I would have prepared for weeks and stayed up all night reviewing my notes before a big test, but I wasn't worried going into my first-year prelims. They don't count towards your degree; as long as you pass, you get to stay at Oxford for two more years. Lara, though, remained concerned about my grasp of economics, and recommended I attend a couple of pre-exam study sessions with the tutor. I missed them both, too tired to make the 9 a.m. start time after late nights at 24 Obs.

Lara's job was to make sure I maximised my academic potential and performed at the highest possible level. I didn't want to disappoint her, but I had been a hardworking student at the top of the class since childhood – and now my goals had changed. I wanted to learn the fundamentals: how to seek knowledge, evaluate it, use it to make decisions. If I actually read the hundreds of pages my professors assigned every week, though, I'd never leave my desk. At any point in the rest of my life, I could go to the library, check out the same books and pick up the finer points of price elasticity. But dancing all night with my friends? Hanging out at 24 Obs? Those moments were more precious to me than academic honours.

On the morning of my econ prelim, Cora and Hen barged into my room to wake me up and make sure I made it to the Examination Halls on time. I took my seat and waited for the test to begin, said a little prayer and hoped I wouldn't bomb too badly. Whatever marks I received at the end of term didn't matter, I told myself. I had already passed my own test, the one I'd set at the start of the year: to find a group of friends who understood me.

At Oxford, I could be myself, free from the expectations of the outside world. My friends didn't care about my thoughts on global events or what I wore. They accepted my quirks and contradictions, my bad days and chronic tardiness. Sometimes when they saved me a seat at dinner or laughed at my jokes, I tried to hide the swell of gratitude in my heart. I knew it wasn't normal to show so much intensity or say out loud how much I loved them. Though I never told them, their friendship made me feel that I'd finally come back to life. I couldn't imagine wanting anything more than what I had right now.

16.

I was loading my bags into the car when I got a text from Sofia, a music student I knew from 24 Obs: Hey you still around? Feel like going to the track to race go-karts?

I didn't think twice, happy to stay at university a little longer and delay my return to Birmingham, to work and the real world. In the car park outside the race track, I waved to Sofia, who was standing with two guys. I recognised Jamal, a part-time MBA with a good sense of humour and a trendy haircut. The other man was tall and seemed younger than Jamal, wearing a cherry-red spring jacket that looked out of place amid Oxford's ubiquitous olive-toned Barbour coats. I was curious as to why I'd never bumped into him before.

'Hi, I'm Asser,' he said, sticking out his hand to shake mine.

'Thanks for coming out today,' Jamal chimed in. 'My friend

just arrived from Lahore and doesn't know anyone, so we have to show him a good time.'

'What brings you here, Asser?' I asked.

'Just visiting,' he replied. 'I run an amateur cricket franchise back home and our team is playing in an international tournament in August. Until then, I'm visiting my sister, seeing some friends and hopefully enjoying a warm English summer.'

I laughed. 'Well, good luck with that.'

We went inside and the staff at the raceway said it didn't matter that Sofia and I didn't know how to drive a car, that go-karts were easy. A group of eleven-year-old birthday party guests were speeding around the track – how hard could it be?

On my first lap, I took a turn too fast, slammed on the brakes and skidded into a nearby wall. The impact of it shocked me, and I immediately felt dizzy. Asser pulled up behind me and I asked him to get my security team, who took me inside to lie down on a couch in the manager's office.

One of the guards checked my vital signs, and asked me to follow his finger with my eyes and wiggle my fingers and toes. He said I was fine, but advised me to rest for a bit and let them know if anything changed. As they stepped out of the office, Asser poked his head in and said, 'Feeling better? Want to get back out there?'

'In a minute,' I replied, keeping my eyes closed, annoyed by his presence. *Is this grown man so excited by go-karts that he can't wait to see if I develop a concussion? What is he doing here? Where is Sofia?*

Asser sat down on the arm of the couch, unfazed by my grumpy tone. After a few moments, I propped myself up on my elbows. 'All right, I think I'm okay now.'

'That's good,' he said. 'I'm sure it was just a shock. I mean, you hit a bank of rubber tyres at less than twenty miles an hour. Not exactly Formula One-level damage, is it?'

He smiled at me, and we both started to laugh. We'd only just met, but I liked that he didn't regard me as a breakable object, someone who couldn't cope with a minor accident or joke at her expense.

For the first time that day, I noticed how handsome he was. His hair was just ruffled enough to make you want to run your hands through it and change its shapes. A deep scar above his left eyebrow suggested competitive sports or youthful misadventure – an active, unpredictable life. His smile wasn't flashy or overly charming, but warm and sincere. Even under the fluorescent office lights, I thought he was gorgeous. For the rest of the afternoon, I found myself sitting up straight and posing anytime I felt he might be watching me.

By the time we got to dinner, my body felt possessed – an instinct to flirt with this good-looking stranger took over and I was powerless to stop it. I fidgeted, twirled my hair and laughed too loudly at everything he said. When he asked me how I liked university, I tried to make myself sound cool and rebellious. 'My favourite thing is climbing on the rooftop of this four-storey building,' I said. 'I'd definitely get thrown out if anyone knew, but I only go late at night and I'm too good at it now to get caught. And I also go clubbing.'

Sofia, who knew I'd only been out dancing once in my life, kicked me under the table. When I looked at her, her eyebrows shot up. *Okay, cool it*, I told myself. I kept it together for a few minutes until, while trying to maintain eye contact with Asser as he told a story, I reached for my glass and spilt water all over the table.

At the end of the night, Jamal suggested we take a group photo. He handed the waiter his phone and we all huddled together. As we were moving into position, Asser's arm brushed mine and a shiver raced through my entire body. *I'm dead*, I thought.

As soon as my car pulled out of the car park, I got a text from Sofia.

> WHAT WAS THAT?!? You were flipping your hair so hard, it fell in your food a couple times.

> Do you think he's single? Do you think he liked me?

> I have no idea, but the entire restaurant absolutely knows that you like him.

On the drive back to Birmingham that night, I scanned his social media profiles. It felt a little subversive checking out a grown man, one with lines around his eyes that crinkled when he laughed, and who probably did a lot of things I hadn't tried yet like yoga or skincare. Everything I could find on him seemed nice and normal. And, most importantly, I saw no sign of a girlfriend. *Don't lose your head*, a voice in the back of my mind said, but I ignored it.

When I arrived home that night, I asked my mum to book laser hair removal for my unibrow. She had been badgering me to do it for over a year, and I was relieved she didn't ask why I'd changed my mind. I knew shapely eyebrows wouldn't fix all the flaws I saw in my face. But maybe, I thought, I should put a little more effort into my appearance – brush my hair, a dab of lip gloss, some concealer. Just in case I ever saw him again.

Two weeks later I had to travel to Brazil for Malala Fund work, and found myself with a free afternoon and evening in London before the early-morning flight to Rio. I pulled out my phone and composed a message to Jamal, asking if he and Asser wanted to meet up. As my finger hovered above the send button, I felt like I was standing on the edge of a cliff, nervous that I might actually jump.

We met for tea at the Ham Yard Hotel, where Jamal was staying for a few weeks. Asser looked better than I remembered – his long arms a deeper shade of brown than before, his face ruddy from days in the sun. He had just returned from visiting a friend in Scotland, where they went hiking and ate fish and chips by the sea. I had been to Scotland once myself, but only saw the inside of SUVs and conference rooms, the sterile cocoon of my working life.

'And the friend you were visiting . . . a man? A woman? Someone from university?' I asked.

'A man, a friend from high school,' he replied.

'Asser has sworn off women,' Jamal interjected. 'He's been cursed by . . .'

'. . . the circumstances!' they shouted in unison, and laughed.

'Sorry for the inside joke,' Asser said. 'Please ignore us.'

'Unfortunately for you, I have a couple of free hours and enjoy nothing more than prying into other people's love lives. So I will require an explanation.'

'Oh, I'm happy to bore you with my stories, as long as you remember that you asked for this.'

He began in high school, at age sixteen, when he met his first girlfriend. 'She was a punk girl, black clothes, black leather boots – not something you see a lot in Lahore and that's why I liked her. We would talk online every night, and she would send me songs by the Ramones and the Sex Pistols.'

They went on their first – and last – date at Pizza Hut. 'I could claim it "fizzled out", but the truth is, I wasn't cool enough for her.'

It always made my head spin to hear stories like these from

people who grew up around the same time as me, in the same country. When I was a child in Mingora, there were no Pizza Hut dates or punk records or online chats. I'd never imagined that the teenage world was so different just a few hundred miles away in Lahore.

Asser met his second girlfriend at university. 'She was sweet and very smart. I could listen to her talk for hours. And I loved her parents and her siblings.'

They had been dating for almost a year when she was accepted to an exchange programme at a prestigious university in the United States. He was proud and happy for her – and crushed that the relationship was over. He told her she should be free, to focus on her studies and enjoy her new surroundings without being tied to him.

'But she wouldn't accept it. She kept saying, "It's only a year. Then I'll come back, and everything will be exactly as it is now." I still felt uneasy about staying together, but I wanted to make her happy.' While she was away, he worked odd jobs, texted her every day and called most nights. He kept in touch with her family, visiting them for occasional dinners and delivering gifts on Eid.

As the academic year was coming to an end, the woman called Asser to say that an investment firm had offered her a great job. 'I see my future in America,' she told him. 'And I don't think this will work any more.'

'I'm so sorry,' I said, feeling genuinely bad for him.

'Thank you, it's really fine now. She's a good person and we're still friends. And I know how hard things are for women in Pakistan, so I couldn't blame her for taking the opportunity to build the life that she wanted.'

Once he'd recovered from the heartbreak, he started dating again and found many women who were interested in seeing him. For a while, at least. 'Everyone loved me in December,' he said. 'That's wedding season in Lahore – the best weather, the best parties, it's magical.' Asser was a popular date for the festivities; his mum and older sisters had taught him to be punctual, respectful and a good conversationalist.

'But things would always change by January, February at the latest. Girls who seemed really into me suddenly broke it off. It's like one of those signs for cancelled events, businesses closing, the internet going down, whatever it is. And they always say, "Due to the circumstances, we can no longer provide service." But you never find out what the circumstances are! You're just supposed to accept that unseen forces will wreck your plans. That was my love life, essentially.'

'So girls just broke up with you . . . for no reason?' I asked, sceptical.

'I had my suspicions,' he answered. 'Then finally one of the women spelt it out . . . and I really wished she hadn't.'

He decided he was done with casual relationships, done with feeling like an accessory tossed in a closet after the party. That's when he met his third girlfriend. At first he thought it wasn't that serious. When he told her he was looking for a long-term relationship, he thought she'd move on. But she surprised him by saying she wanted the same thing.

Asser knew her parents were status-conscious, high-society types. He'd gone to a fancy private high school on scholarship and worked his way through university. Would her mum and dad approve of a mid-level cricket manager without a family fortune?

They spent the next few months eating street food, taking long walks and watching movies. 'She was going for it, trying to prove how down to earth she could be, sitting on the floor of my friends' living rooms, rolling joints and cracking jokes.'

Asser thought things were going well when she asked him to lunch one day and said she couldn't see him any more. 'It's just that . . . my sister got engaged last week. Her fiancé's family is quite wealthy. As you know, I've never cared about any of that, but . . .' She hesitated and then looked up at him with big tears in her eyes. 'What if my sister's husband buys her a designer bag and you can't afford one? It's not about the money – it just wouldn't be fair to me.'

My mouth dropped open, and I covered my face with my hands.

'Yeah, that was my reaction too,' Asser said with a laugh. 'I was kind of disgusted with the Lahore scene after that, and have been really looking forward to these summer months out of the city. And now you know my story.'

I sat staring into my tea, considering what advice I should give him.

'The worst is when everyone tries to give you advice,' he said. 'A friend who thinks he's a therapist told me, "Maybe deep down you really want to be alone – that's why you're always chasing unavailable women." That wasn't true, though. I don't *want* to be alone.

'And then some other friends took me to a psychic – a big, burly man named Kitty – who stared into my eyes and said, "Buy a journal and start writing every day because when you find true love, your romance will be remembered for ages."'

'Did you do it?' I asked.

'No. I don't believe in palm reading, divination, any of that stuff. I'd be happy to be wrong, though!'

When I got back to my room that night, I sank into the bank of pillows on the hotel bed, pulled out my phone and sent him a message.

> I think I should help you find a girlfriend. What are your requirements?

> Hahaha

How do you have time to
care about my love life??

I'm sure you have waaaaaay
more important things to do

I care about a lot of
things.

My heart is so big that the
entire city of London could
live inside it.

This was a lie. In what I believed to be the most clever and
subtle way possible, I was doing reconnaissance for myself – trying
to determine if I had a shot with this handsome and charming
man. If Asser said he was hoping for a statuesque girl with a perfect face who played tennis and wanted to bear him seven children,
then I could put him out of my mind and move on without embarrassment.

My 'requirements'
(your word) are pretty
simple

–Honesty

–Sense of humour

–Not obsessed with money
and status

Okay, what about
nationality, religion,
profession, etc?

MALALA YOUSAFZAI

None of those are
deal-breakers to me.
I'm open to anyone.

Age range?

No preference

Height? Eye colour?
Straight hair or wavy hair?
Athletic or curvy?

The world is full of beauties.
I am looking for a friend.

17.

I spent my twenty-first birthday in Rio, talking with teenage street artists who used graffiti to bring attention to violence against women. Over lunch, the young women told me about frequent school closures due to clashes between police and gangs, discrimination against Afro-Brazilian students, the different styles of their art and their individual passions for chemistry, rap music and football. They even gave me a can of spray paint and let me contribute a small doodle to one of their walls.

Back at the hotel that evening, I opened my messages to a flood of birthday texts from friends and family. I skipped past all of them to read two from Asser:

> Happy Birthday! Hope you have fun plans today. Inshallah this will be your best year yet!

Also – I'm staying with my sister in Birmingham, starting next week. Don't have any friends there. Will you show me around the city?

My stomach did backflips as I fumbled to open my calendar app. On Tuesday, I would arrive back in London, head straight to a breakfast meeting, then make the two-hour drive back to Birmingham to toss my dirty clothes in the laundry and pack for Wednesday's flight to Dubai. I didn't want to miss my chance to see him again – so we made plans to meet for dinner on Tuesday night and I promised to give him a tour of the city later in the month when I had more time.

I booked a table at a quiet neighbourhood pub called the High Field. The food was organic and the atmosphere was cosy, but the best thing about it was that I'd never seen anyone from Birmingham's sizeable Pakistani community there. I didn't want to be spotted alone with a handsome young man on anything re-sembling a date.

But was it a date? I had no way to know. Maybe he was just being friendly or thought I was a good contact to cultivate. I hoped he wouldn't ask me if I'd made any progress in finding him a girlfriend.

'So last time,' I began as soon as we sat down, 'you told me about your recent past, but nothing about your family—'

'No, no, absolutely not. Tonight it's your turn.'

'Nah, my life is boring.'

Asser rolled his eyes. 'I know for a fact that's not true.'

'Come on, start at the beginning,' I pressed on. 'You were born in . . . what, the eighties?'

He feigned offence and then laughed. 'For an Oxford student, your maths is pretty bad. I was born in 1990.'

'Close enough. What happened next?'

He rubbed his trim black beard and smirked at me. 'If I tell you all my remaining secrets tonight, you'd have no reason to see me when you're back from Dubai.'

I felt the heat rise in my cheeks and hid my face behind the menu. 'Fine. You win,' I said.

Over dinner, I told him about Oxford – my friends, parties at 24 Obs, the parks and sunrise walks – and how it felt strange to be back at home after months living on my own. My family had changed a bit, particularly Khushal. Last year he couldn't wait for his chance to go to college. Now he woke up at 2 p.m. every day and played video games until late at night. My parents kept pushing me to give him a motivational speech, to try to get him to do his summer reading in the hopes he could bring up his marks next year, but I didn't know what to say.

'That's pretty normal behaviour for teenage boys in the UK, right?' Asser said.

'It makes me feel like I've failed. I'm supposed to be an advocate for education, and I can't even convince my own brother to care about school.'

'It's not you. As a former adolescent boy myself, I can say they are often terrible, truly some of the worst people on the planet. And then they grow up!' He spread his palms and flashed a wide, reassuring smile.

When he asked about my work, I chatted excitedly about the Shangla school. 'Right now, it's open to girls from primary to middle school. Because they've never had a high school for girls in the area, we are adding a school year every year until they complete high school. It's so exciting to know that tomorrow morning a child is going to wake up, put on her uniform and go to school. And in a few years, she will be the very first girl ever to graduate from a high school in these villages. Can you imagine it?' I beamed, so proud to tell him about my work. If I accomplished nothing else in my life except helping these girls to graduate from high school, I would be happy.

'That's amazing! I'm so thrilled for you and for the community. How many students do you have?'

'Two hundred at the moment, but we're building more space every day.'

'And what about sports facilities for the girls?'

'There's a playground and a basketball court.'

'No cricket? You have to have cricket!'

'I would *love* to build a cricket facility for girls, but it wouldn't be in this area. There isn't enough ground for a pitch.'

'What do you mean?'

'Well, these villages are jammed into the space between mountains and so narrow that a car can't fit on most of the roads. People use motorbikes or donkeys for transport. Or they walk. An "ambulance" is just four guys and a wooden stretcher! But being so isolated is part of what makes it beautiful.'

Before I realised what I was saying, I added, 'I'll take you there someday.'

⌒

A WEEK LATER, we met for the tour of Birmingham that I'd promised him. Because I hadn't spent much time out in the city, even when I lived there, I had trouble planning a day's worth of sights to see. When I tried to think of my best days there, I kept picturing the time Alice took me to Victoria's Secret and helped me buy my first underwire bra. Not appropriate for Asser and likely not on the Birmingham Tourism and Hospitality Board's top ten either.

Then I remembered an afternoon while I was still in the hospital, when the nurses drove me to the Birmingham Botanical Gardens. It was my first time outdoors in months. As they pushed my wheelchair beneath a canopy of trees, I felt like I could finally breathe again.

I decided we'd meet there in the afternoon and then have dinner. When I arrived, Asser was waiting outside, looking handsome in a pale-pink button-down shirt, freshly ironed and tucked into jeans. We walked along the path past dogwood trees, Irish irises and foxtail ferns while he filled me in on his cricket league and their upcoming tournament.

At the southern border of the gardens, we entered a small greenhouse with glass walls. Inside, hundreds of butterflies drifted and hovered around tropical flowers, a kaleidoscope of colours in motion. 'Can we live here?' Asser whispered. I bit my lip and looked away, suddenly feeling very shy.

Just before sunset, we headed to a rooftop steakhouse with panoramic views of the city. 'What are "French beans"? Do you know?' Asser asked, browsing the menu.

'Maybe like chickpeas . . . but fancy?'

'Let's find out!' He ordered a small steak and two sides, and I got the roast chicken.

While we waited for the food, he kept his promise to tell me about his family and childhood. Asser's mum was forty years old when he was born; his sisters were nineteen and fifteen. 'No one will admit that I was an accident, but it seems pretty obvious to me,' he said.

The family lived in a nice Lahori neighbourhood across the street from a public park. His father worked in a bank and wasn't around much. During the day, his mum packed curries, flatbread and fruit into a bag and took him on picnics or to the zoo. In the evenings, Ambreena and Afsa, his sisters, spent hours on the living-room floor playing his favourite game, casting tiny rods into a battery-powered pool of plastic fish. Before bed, they would read to him from Roald Dahl books. When he was old enough, his parents enrolled him in a private boys' academy, one of the best schools in the country.

'Sounds like a lovely childhood,' I said.

'It was . . . until the afternoon when Mum and I came back from visiting my cousins and the house was empty.' Asser was eight years old when everything they owned disappeared in a weekend – the car, the furniture, the TV, even the little radio that sang him to sleep every night. That's when he learnt that his father was not just a banker, but a gambling addict and an alcoholic. 'In some ways, it's impressive. You have to work hard to be a drunk in a dry country.'

Growing up, I'd never even seen a bottle of beer and had no clue about the underground alcohol trade in Pakistan or the rise in alcohol-related diseases and deaths. Gambling was also illegal. I was glad I had not mentioned my poker games to Asser.

His father fled the country to escape his debtors and left the family with nothing. Like most women in Pakistan, Asser's mum, Farida, had never had a job. But she knew how to sew, so she went to work as a seamstress. His middle sister, Afsa, a graduate student in business, took a low-level position in a finance firm. Ambreena, now married and living in the UK, sent whatever money she could spare.

They rented out the bulk of their house to tenants while the family entered through the back door and kept to the small utility rooms behind the kitchen. For years, Asser slept on the floor in Farida's cramped workroom, surrounded by dress forms, poked by errant sewing needles in his sleep.

'My mum and sisters gave up a lot to make my life as normal as possible, but I could still feel the change. I was really young when I started to worry about where we would live if we lost the house and if we would be able to afford food the next day.'

This revelation surprised me. When I first met Asser, I'd assumed he was like a lot of my Pakistani friends at Oxford – from a middle- or upper-class family, elite education, living an easy, urban lifestyle untouched by the struggles of the poor. I didn't blame these friends for their good fortune or for the decades of poverty, illiteracy and conflict that people in my community suffered, but I couldn't fully relate to them either.

Now I realised Asser and I shared a deeper connection. Loss had shaped our childhood, dislodged our sense of security and changed the meaning of home. We both understood the damage that men could do, either through guns and bombs or through abandonment and neglect.

The waiter returned with a tray and dramatically raised each silver cloche to reveal our meals – my chicken, Asser's steak, roast potatoes and . . . green beans. The same green beans that mothers all over the world force their children to eat. We looked at each other and burst out laughing.

'Well, that is the most disappointing thing the French have ever done,' Asser said.

I let him eat for a few minutes, then asked, 'So how was high school for you?'

He told me his classmates became obsessed with physical fights as they got older, brawling in the streets almost every afternoon. If the altercation escalated, their fathers or older brothers would rush in and break it up before anyone was seriously hurt.

Asser actively avoided conflict with the other boys. 'I had no backup, no older man who could step in before things got bad,' he said.

'So you were a pacifist out of necessity, not principle,' I reasoned.

He laughed. 'In a way, I guess.'

One afternoon, a boy he thought was a friend led him to a park where a group of guys ambushed him, knocked him to the ground and took turns kicking and punching him. 'I remember this one kid yelling, "He thinks he's such a pretty boy and I'm going to ruin his face!" And I lay there getting killed and thinking, "But I'm not pretty! I'm skinny, my teeth are crooked, my facial hair is wispy and pathetic!"'

For the first time that evening, I wondered if he was telling the truth. I couldn't imagine that he'd ever been less than beautiful.

18.

O ver the next few days, I felt a mixture of giddiness and confusion. The thrill of possibility, imagining waking up in the
morning and seeing his face on the pillow next to mine, and the
fear of rejection – *You don't even know if he feels the same way about
you*, I reminded myself. Maybe this was a waste of time, a distraction from all the things I should be doing, like summer reading or
working. Or maybe it was worse than that: I'd seen what happened
to my friends when they staked their emotional equilibrium on
someone else's moods and actions. But by that point, it didn't matter. I was too deep into my crush to pull back from the brink.

The following week, Asser and I met at a bowling alley. Halfway through the game, I had a thought: *If our combined score equals
150, then we're meant to be together.* Some part of me understood
this was ridiculous, but I was desperate for a sign. I had no idea
how to ask if he liked me. *What if I'm reading him all wrong?*

We chatted and shared chips as I watched the numbers tick up – 75, 91, 129. Asser got a spare, and then it was my turn to roll the last ball of the game. When it was over, I held my breath and looked up at the scoreboard: 148 points.

That night I lay awake in bed wondering how to interpret the number. I'd picked a random score, so it meant nothing. On the other hand, I'd asked the universe a question and it had returned the wrong answer. Unsatisfied, I grabbed my phone and texted Asser.

> What's your birthday?

> September 15

I wasn't sure how fully I believed in astrology, but it had to be better than bowling scores. According to Google, 'Cancer [me] and Virgo [him] are highly compatible, making a relationship between the two destined for success.' I fell asleep grateful for the good omen.

When I wasn't seeing Asser or working that summer, I hung out with my friends as much as possible: shopping with Alice, a weekend trip to the Lake District with Cora, lunch in London with Raja. I tried to keep doing normal things, tried to remind myself that Asser was just a new friend in my life and not the centre of it. But no matter where I was or who I was with, his smile kept floating to the surface of my mind.

I started to have new worries as well. *If he actually does like me, then what?* Dating was forbidden, so would I have to keep our relationship a secret indefinitely? Was I falling in love? Or was I about to ruin my reputation? Both?

Since Sofia already knew about him and understood all the pressures on single young women in Pakistan, I decided to text her for advice. She was sceptical.

I can't believe you've seen him five times. Just feels like a lot of your summer to waste on a maindak.

Maindak means 'frog' in Urdu. It's city kid slang for a guy who dates a lot, like a toad jumping from lily pad to lily pad.

That's really not Asser, though. He seems genuine.

I guess he didn't strike me as a serious person.

What do you mean?

Like shouldn't you be with someone more on your level, a guy who could become the head of the UN or IMF one day?

I couldn't think of anything I wanted less. I'd been in rooms with those types of men for years and never fancied any of them. And Asser *was* serious about his work in the sports world. I hadn't asked Sofia's opinion on whom I should date, but if I was dating at all.

How do I find out how he feels about me?

Want me to casually ask Jamal if he's heard anything?

I said yes and hoped for good news.

IN MID-AUGUST, I had to go to the US for six weeks, a combination of work travel and seeing a new doctor about my facial paralysis. When I returned, Asser would be back in Pakistan. He invited me for one last outing before I left – a visit to a cricket club in Chester where his amateur team from Pakistan was playing a match against New Zealand.

When I checked myself in the mirror before I left the house, I was surprised to find that I liked what I saw – two distinct and well-shaped eyebrows (thanks to my mum) and clear skin (thanks to my new skincare routine). Make-up still seemed too much for me, but I had started wearing tinted lip balm. I'd learnt how to part and style my hair in a way that made the left side of my face less noticeable. Aiming for an outfit that was casual enough for cricket but sophisticated enough for a date, I settled on a gauzy white shirt, slim black jeans and a chiffon headscarf. Pretty might be a stretch, but I thought I looked elegant and almost cool.

The afternoon sun cast long shadows on the pitch where the players were warming up. Pakistan threw out the first ball, and my eyes were fixed on the game. For the first time since we met, I wasn't taking every opportunity to steal glances at Asser.

'Bowl him out!' I yelled, gripping the handrail in the front row of the stands. 'Did you catch that seam position? Perfection!'

Asser looked at me, eyes wide, mouth slightly open.

'What?' I said. 'I told you I love cricket!'

'Yeah, you did,' he replied, grinning and shaking his head. 'I guess I just wasn't expecting so much fist-pumping and . . . growling!' I punched him on the arm and returned my focus to the pitch.

After the match, I posed for photos with the team. Normally I would have hung out with cricket players as long as they'd have me, but Asser and I only had ninety minutes left together, just as long as it took to get back to Birmingham. I said a silent prayer for heavy traffic.

When we got in the car, I gestured to the middle seat and asked, 'Will you sit here, closer to me?' I spoke to Asser in Urdu so the security guards in the front couldn't eavesdrop. He smiled and slid towards me.

When the sun set and everything was dark, he pulled me closer and I laid my head on his shoulder. It was so quiet that I worried he would hear how fast my heart was beating.

The car stopped in front of his sister's house, and I sat straight up in a panic, unclear how to say goodbye or ask when I might see him again. He turned to me and said, 'Will you keep in touch on your trip? Thank you for spending time with me this summer. I really loved getting to know you.'

⌐‿⌐

I WAS IN San Francisco when Sofia called. Anxious to hear what intel she'd gathered, I excused myself from a meeting and stepped into the hall to talk to her.

'Asser knows you like him,' she said. 'He had the best time with you, and he values your friendship, but . . . he thinks you're in different places in your life. I'm really sorry, Malala.'

I felt the hot sting of shock and embarrassment spread across my face. Why had he kept asking me out if he knew it wasn't going to work? Did I say or do the wrong thing? I pulled up his number and almost called, but stopped myself. *He isn't your boyfriend and he doesn't owe you an explanation. Don't humiliate yourself.*

It was all my fault, in the end, for hoping he might fall in love with me.

Standing in the beige corridor of a California office block, I blinked back tears. *Pull yourself together. You're supposed to be working.* I wiped my eyes, walked back into the meeting, and tried to avoid speaking until I was sure my voice wouldn't break.

19.

More bad news was waiting for me back in Birmingham –
a letter from Lara:

> *While I am pleased to share that you passed your*
> *preliminary examinations, your marks correspond to a*
> *Lower Second Class degree, near the bottom for Philosophy,*
> *Politics and Economics students in your year. For context,*
> *in a typical year, approximately 22 per cent of students attain*
> *First Class, 73 per cent attain Upper Second Class and 5 per*
> *cent attain Lower Second Class.*
>
> *This is substantially below the level at which I believe you*
> *are capable of performing. Given your passionate commitment*
> *to education, I feel it would be a great pity if you do not fulfil*
> *your academic potential while studying at Oxford.*

The letter continued, itemising my sins: essays submitted after the deadline, failure to complete my weekly reading assignments and skipped tutorial sessions meant to help struggling students catch up before exams. *You did not appear to be doing sufficient independent work.* I had passed my first year at university, but I wouldn't continue to scrape by as classes got more difficult, Lara warned.

I didn't care where I ranked among the other students, but Lara's line about my 'passionate commitment to education' stung. Would people think I was a fraud or a hypocrite for giving speeches about the importance of girls going to school if they saw my prelim exam marks? My critics would love it: the world's most famous education advocate, the poster girl for bookish children and perennial teacher's pet, unmasked as a student delinquent.

When I received Lara's letter, I called her and asked if she could write another one for me – the same dire language about my academic performance, but in this version reiterating that she forbade me to travel during term time and that I needed to study over breaks as well. Then I put on a grave face and showed her letter to my dad, my speaking agent and the staff at Malala Fund. If I didn't have the nerve to decline an important event or tell my family not to pack the house with guests while I was home, I knew Lara did. The plan worked: my team agreed not to schedule events while I was at Oxford, and my dad promised to try to contain his hospitality when I was at home.

This year will be different, I thought. I'd had a lot of fun as a fresher, but now it was time to hunker down and focus on my studies. I promised myself I'd spend more time in the library, do my reading and turn in my essays on time. It was for the best that I wouldn't have a boyfriend to distract me.

But first: one last hurrah.

I didn't bother knocking at 24 Obs, where a welcome-back

party was in full swing on the eve of the new academic term. As soon as I stepped inside, I saw a sea of unfamiliar faces. If it weren't for the fact that most of them were speaking Urdu, I might have checked that I'd come through the right door.

I found Raja refilling drinks in the dining room. 'Want to introduce me to your new friends?' I asked.

'I would if I knew who they were! First-years who somehow found their way here, I guess? I expect we'll get to know them by the end of the evening!'

The living-room armchairs had been replaced by floor cushions and the coffee table removed to make way for a giant, four-hose hookah. Zayan was exhaling perfect rings of smoke and entertaining a crowd of newbies with his summer adventures in Karachi.

Parveen was not smoking, but continually shuffling coconut coals between the kitchen stove and the hookah. 'Take a break,' I told her. 'Let the boys handle that and come and chat with me.'

We went out to the patio and commandeered chairs from two of Raja's mystery guests. Shortly after we sat down, her phone started pinging over and over. 'Hmmm, something you want to tell me?' I pried. 'Did you get a *boyfriend* since I saw you last?'

Parveen cackled and held the phone up for me to see a series of WhatsApp messages from her mum, recipes for aloo gosht, chicken jalfrezi and kheer. 'She does this at the start of every year. As if I have any time to cook as a postgrad.'

I had planned to get to bed at a reasonable hour, but stayed longer than I intended – long enough to see the hookah cleared away, the 10 p.m. dance party kick off, and almost all of the guests depart. When the clock struck midnight, I was curled into a corner of the couch, deep in conversation with Zayan and two girls who had been strangers when the night began. *It's fine*, I told myself. *The term doesn't start until tomorrow.*

The next morning, I jolted awake and grabbed my phone to

check the time: 11:03 a.m. *No, no, no!* I'd missed the first lecture of the year. Lara's admonishments ran through my head, and I buried my face in the pillow in shame. This was more than a minor backslide – I hadn't managed to be a responsible student for *a single day*. Then, a week later, I was asking for an extension on my first essay. My complete inability to manage my time felt more like defeat than a setback. Why was my life such a mess?

Lara's letter had warned that the workload would be harder in my second year, and it was. Leonard, the professor for my political sociology course, assigned a weekly average of four hundred pages of reading from academic journal articles. I couldn't manage a fraction of it. After the sixth or seventh article, I was using my yellow highlighter not to mark important passages, but to keep my eyes focused on the page. I looked up information on how to speed-read, which suggested that humming while you read could help. It didn't.

Cora was my tutorial partner again, and at our Thursday meetings, Leonard assessed our analysis of the material in the Oxford tradition of 'education through interrogation'. Whenever he asked a question about one of the articles I'd failed to read, my eyes darted to Cora, and she jumped in to do the talking for both of us. Leonard wasn't fooled. 'It seems that the empirical literature, of which there is a lot in this course, poses a challenge for you,' he said to me with a smirk.

Determined to get on top of my work, I googled study tips. The suggestions included tidying your room ('physical clutter leads to mental clutter'), ten minutes of meditation before studying ('calm your mind') and drinking a full bottle of water ('brains need hydration too'). I tried all the suggestions except the ones I'd already mastered – 'take breaks to see friends' or 'reward yourself with ice cream or your favourite TV show'.

I vowed to go to sleep early, get up by 6 a.m., and take an invigorating walk before beginning my studies. That strategy lasted forty-eight hours. Then I tried positive thinking. Before bed, I left motivational notes to myself for the following morning: *If you wake up late, that's fine. Don't worry, just go to the library and start your work.* These affirmations were worth less than the Post-its on which they were written. No matter what tricks and techniques I took up, my essays and tutorial contributions were mediocre at best.

This was all the more frustrating because, after slogging through political theory and economic models in my first year, I'd finally found a course that captivated me. In ethics, we studied the forces that shape our personal morals and the practical applications of value systems. In tutorials, I participated with enthusiasm, debating various points with the professor, but I still couldn't articulate my thoughts in an essay.

Lara advised me, as she had several times in the previous year, to visit the Study Skills Centre, where specially trained teachers could help me improve my writing and analytical skills. Billed as a place for students to unlock their 'latent potential', it sounded like remedial education to me.

I had never been embarrassed to ask for help. At high school, I would stay after class to get extra support from my teachers when I needed it. At Oxford, though, I didn't want the other students to know I was struggling. I worried that they suspected I wasn't as smart as them and didn't deserve to be there, having jumped the queue because I was famous.

At first I didn't believe that was true. I'd scored high marks on my A levels, the tests that determine university placement. I didn't mention the Nobel or any of my awards in my application essay, against the advice of my guidance counsellor. But now I was putting real effort into my work and still falling short. *Maybe I'm not cut out for Oxford*, I thought as I struggled to put words on the page for an essay or complete a problem set. When I couldn't grasp a concept or keep up with the reading, I thought about my dad, Malala Fund and the Shangla school – how embarrassed everyone would be if I had to drop out, how it would hurt my work. I felt like I was standing in quicksand, scrambling to stay on top of my studies and only sinking further and further below the surface.

After the ethics professor tactfully described my essay on Kant as 'not so good, I'm afraid', I swallowed my pride and made an appointment at the Study Skills Centre. My legs felt slow as I walked towards the building, defeated and sheepish. A woman named Valerie greeted me and showed me to her office. I expected to see a desk and a whiteboard, but this small, sunny space felt more like a Victorian drawing room. There were cookies and fruit on the coffee table, sunlight pouring through the window. She gestured for me to sit down on the sofa, then sat down next to me and asked how she could help.

'I have to ask for an essay extension almost every week. But extra time doesn't seem to help because my professors' comments aren't usually . . . complimentary.'

'All right, we can work on time management and writing skills together. When are your essays due?'

'Ethics at nine a.m. on Monday, political sociology at nine a.m. on Thursday.'

'And when do you start them?'

'I try to work on them over the weekends.' I hesitated for a moment, and realised that wasn't entirely true. 'It takes me *a lot* of time to get through the reading, so I usually don't start writing until the night before they're due. Like, sometimes I'll begin an essay at five a.m. and turn it in four hours later.' As the words came out of my mouth, I started to wonder if maybe I needed the pressure, if my brain simply refused to engage until I was in crisis.

'That sounds quite stressful!' Valerie commented without judgement. 'The good news is that there's a much easier way. What is missing from your writing process is the planning stage.'

She told me to start my essay as soon as my professor assigned it. Before I dived into reading, I should analyse the question, think about my argument and draft an outline. This would help me focus my reading on supporting my case, not on trying to form one. If something in the journal articles or philosophy texts changed my thinking, I would already have come up with the counterpoints.

I tried her approach and felt more confident in that week's essays, so I went back again and again, working with Valerie on how to structure my arguments and make a study plan that allowed me time to see my friends and fulfil my duties to the various clubs I had joined. The reading still took me a long time; I fell behind and sometimes missed deadlines, but the quality of my papers inched up. Over the eight weeks of the term, the feedback on my essays went from 'a pile of unconnected thoughts' to 'under-developed but improving'.

One of the biggest things I learnt was how to say no to my friends. In the past, I'd accepted every invitation, not wanting to miss a moment of social time. People still invited me out, but it quickly became a running joke that my reply to every offer was 'Essay, mate.' *Dinner in town? Poker tonight? Want to watch the world's sexiest Bollywood actors feeding ice cream to kittens on the quad?* Whatever the question, if my work wasn't finished, the answer was, 'Can't. Essay, mate.'

I wish I could say that the rest of the year ran like a movie montage – scenes of me clacking away on my laptop morning and night, professors beaming as they returned my near-perfect essays, sprinting through campus to tell Valerie the good news, the look of surprise on Lara's face when I moved up to First Class Honours. None of that happened. Studying was always a struggle for me at university. But I made progress and proved to myself that I deserved my place.

20.

Going into the spring term, I felt self-assured and steady. As long as I stuck with my study plan, I could have it all – nights out with friends, extracurricular activities and good academic standing. The weather was getting warmer and everything in my life was going well.

On Friday night before the official start of term, Zayan and I went for an early dinner at 24 Obs. In eight weeks, so many of our friends from this group would be graduating and leaving Oxford to start their adult lives. Raja would complete his engineering degree and give up the lease. Next year, our clubhouse would belong to someone else.

I would particularly miss Raja, who had become like a big brother to me, giving me tips on everything from surviving the dreary Oxford winter to changing the settings on my phone so my parents couldn't read my texts from the lock screen. I wanted to spend as much time with him and Parveen as possible – and that meant sticking to a schedule, so that I wasn't constantly stressed about falling behind.

'What next?' Zayan asked as we left 24 Obs. 'Ooh, let's climb on the roof!'

'I think I might get a jump on my econ reading for next week, actually.'

'On a Friday night? Get this girl in some yoga pants because she is *balanced*!'

'Shut up,' I said, laughing and rolling my eyes.

Back in my room, I opened a textbook, uncapped a highlighter and reviewed the first essay question before beginning my reading, as Valerie had taught me to do.

Explain how the time inconsistency of optimal monetary policy can lead to a stabilization bias. How would the introduction of a price path target help to address it?

After reading the question three times, I still couldn't make sense of it. I groaned, went back to the textbook, tried to read, made a cup of tea and tried again. Nothing improved my focus. Then my phone lit up with a message from Anisa: a picture of my name spelt out in Scrabble letters.

On my way. Stay there, I replied.

Perhaps a little break was what I needed. It was only 10:30 p.m., early by my standards. And maybe, if I asked nicely and she was in a good mood, Anisa would come back to my room and explain the essay question to me. I left the textbook on my desk and grabbed my coat.

Outside, the moon lit up rows of daffodils, and the fresh cut grass stuck to my shoes as I crossed the playing fields. At the furthermost edge of Lady Margaret Hall's gardens sat my destination –

an old potting shed that the college calls 'the summerhouse' and students call 'the shack'. It had three walls clad in clapboard, small rectangular windows and a wood-shingled roof covered in moss. The builders, whoever and whenever they were, had left the fourth wall open to nature. Sometimes I sat in the shack alone and listened to the rain splashing off the roof or watched otters play on the riverbank. It was one of my favourite places on campus, like something out of a storybook.

The interior was furnished with a wooden bench, chairs and two small tables. On one wall, shelves held broken plates, green and blue glass bottles and a bowl of old keys – treasures the gardeners dug up during their daily maintenance. On the opposite wall, three old mirrors hung above a bookshelf containing weatherbeaten board games, pillar candles and the occasional book. Dozens of loose Scrabble letters were scattered around the shack; students used them to spell out their names, an impermanent version of writing *X was here* on a bathroom wall.

Anisa was sitting with two boys I recognised from the business course, hovering around an unusual object on the table between them. The clear glass container had a smaller glass tube poking out at the base and looked like something nicked from the chemistry lab.

'Hi, guys,' I said, nodding to the room. 'What's that?'

Without answering, one of the boys picked it up and hovered a lighter over the smaller tube. I heard a bubbling sound and he disappeared behind a cloud of smoke. The smell answered my question.

It wasn't the first time I'd been around people smoking weed. I'd even tried it myself at 24 Obs; my friends shouted confusing instructions like 'You have to inhale! Swallow and then breathe out at the same time! No, breathe with your mouth, not your nose!' As far as I knew, I'd never actually been high, but it felt cool and grown-up to blow smoke in the air and lazily pass the joint to the next person.

'Your turn,' the boy said.

'Nah, I've done it before and it doesn't work on me,' I replied. The beaker-thing looked complicated, plus I still had econ reading to do.

'Chalk and cheese,' Anisa said. I gave her an exasperated look; she knew very well by now that I never understood her British-isms. 'What I mean is,' she continued, 'a bong is totally different from a joint. Much more effective, fit for purpose.'

I easily talked myself into it. *Fine, why not? I'm already out here, might as well have a new university experience.* The boy to my right held the lighter while I lifted the bong to my face. Then my face filled with smoke and I doubled over, coughing. Anisa laughed. Everyone took a turn while we chatted about our holiday travels.

Eventually it came back around to me. 'Okay, one more, but this is it,' I said. I held the lighter myself this time, brought the mouthpiece slowly up to my face, and didn't cough. I sat back in my chair and zoned out while the others continued their conversation.

At some point, I looked at my phone and saw it was past 1 a.m., hours later than I expected. *How is that possible? I've only been here for a few minutes.* My mind tried to fill in the gaps, to find a logical explanation for where all the time had gone, but everything was blank. *How did I just erase two hours of my life without realising it?* 'I have to go,' I said.

'I'll walk with you,' Anisa offered.

The short path back to the halls seemed to stretch out for miles. My legs felt heavy and rooted to the ground. *What's wrong with me?* I thought. Walking required a conscious effort, and it seemed like another hour had passed before I managed a single, stumbling step. 'Sorry,' I said to Anisa. 'Just . . . feeling wobbly.'

My leg muscles started to twitch and then my knees locked up. I couldn't move. *Just take a step. One foot in front of the other.* My brain was sending signals into a void. Again and again, no response, no movement. I balled up my fists, dug my nails into my palms and tried again, more forcefully this time: *Keep walking, Malala!* When nothing happened, a cold, sharp fear climbed up from my stomach and settled in my shoulders.

Then everything went black. As I started to pass out, the truth hit me: I knew this feeling, the terror of being trapped inside my body. This had happened before.

SUDDENLY I WAS fifteen years old again, lying on my back under a white sheet, a tube running down my throat, eyes closed. For seven days, as doctors tended to my wounds, I was in a coma. From the outside, I looked to be in a deep sleep. But inside, my mind was awake, and it played a slideshow of recent events:

My school bus.

A man with a gun.

Blood everywhere.

My body carried through a crowded street.

Strangers hunched over me, yelling things I didn't understand.

My father rushing towards the stretcher to take my hand.

As the images repeated in the same sequence over and over, I raged against them, trying to beat them away. *This isn't true!* I told myself. *The real Malala is the one trapped in this nightmare, not the girl on the stretcher. Just wake up and it will stop. Wake up!*

I had tried to force my eyes open, to see something other than this carousel of horrors. Inside, I screamed; outside, my lips stayed closed, motionless. I was awake and buried alive in the coffin of my body.

And now, on a garden path in Oxford, it was happening again: my mind telling my body to move, my body turned to stone. 'I can't walk!' I finally cried out to Anisa. 'Please help me!'

'Shhhh, I'm here, you're okay,' Anisa answered, her voice strained with alarm. Strong from years of competitive sport, she lifted me up and carried me back to her room. I crumpled to the floor, exhausted and dizzy, struggling to catch my breath.

Everything was still for a moment. I felt relieved to be inside, in the comfort of my friend's room. Then, out of nowhere, the images I had seen in the coma flashed before my eyes again: *Bus. Man. Gun. Blood.* It was like seeing it all for the first time, fresh waves of panic coursing through my body. I was not in a coma, but fully awake – and still, the memories found a way to reach me. There was no escape, no place to hide from my own mind.

'I need to go to hospital,' I gasped, barely able to get the words out.

Anisa sat down next to me. 'You're having a bad reaction, but this will be over soon – thirty minutes, an hour at most. If you go to a doctor, they might run tests. It stays in your blood.'

Seconds later I felt something caught in my throat, cutting off my air supply. I instantly remembered the pressure of the intubation tube, the sensation of choking every time I tried to swallow or speak. *Get it out now!* I thought, my memories of that time colliding into the present. Gathering all my strength, I lunged into Anisa's bathroom, leant over the toilet and vomited.

After a few minutes lying on the cold floor, I grabbed the sink and pulled myself up, catching sight of my pale, terrified face in the mirror. *What is happening to me?*

'Did that help?' Anisa asked. 'Sit back down and let me get you some water.'

I took a deep breath and tried to calm down. *It's over, lean back, just relax.* As soon as I closed my eyes, the slideshow began again. The images came faster now, relentlessly attacking me. My mind was free-falling deep inside my body. I opened my eyes and screamed.

'Malala, snap out of it!' Anisa yelled, shaking me by the shoulders. She ran down the hall and woke up a friend. They sat on either side of me, bracing my body upright. Anisa gave me a pillow to muffle the screams and wiped the sweat off my face with a damp cloth.

We stayed on the floor for what seemed like hours, until the screaming and shaking had stopped. 'Let's get some sleep,' Anisa said. 'You take the bed, I'll pass out here. In the morning you'll feel better, okay?'

I got into bed, but I didn't sleep. I could still see a familiar world around me – her books on the desk, a polo mallet in the corner, the waning moon shining through the window. If I closed my eyes, it would all be gone forever. The nightmares would trap me, hold me hostage in an endless loop of terror. I drifted off only to jerk myself back to consciousness, jolting my body upright and slapping my own face. *Wake up, Malala! If you fall asleep, you will die!*

I was still awake in the morning when Anisa got up from the floor and stood over me. 'I'm so relieved you're okay now,' she said, tousling my hair. She stepped into the bathroom and turned on the shower. I slipped out the door, hoping I wouldn't run into anyone on the walk to my building.

Attempting to wrest control of my thoughts made me seasick. I sat at my desk all morning, trying to distract myself – social media, news sites, Candy Crush – but the replay of the previous night, the helplessness I felt collapsed on Anisa's floor, kept creeping to the front of my mind and overwhelming me. I was nauseated, unable to stand up without feeling dizzy or sit down and be calm without shaking.

In hospital, when I finally came out of the coma, I had no

memory of what had happened to me or how I'd got there. Later I saw news footage of myself from the day of the shooting, bandaged and bleeding, carried through the street on a stretcher. In the video, the sun hits my face and my eyelashes flutter. Over the years, I'd seen that clip hundreds of times, but it never felt like part of my life. Those moments were a glitch in my timeline, the 'and' in 'before and after'.

People always asked me what I remembered of the shooting. 'My brain just erased it,' I told them. 'One moment I was at school and the next I woke up in Birmingham.' I told myself that same story over and over – but now, I knew it wasn't true. I had seen it all, and the memories were still lurking in my brain, years later.

What had Anisa said?

It stays in your blood.

It stays in your blood.

It stays in your blood.

⌒

I CALLED MY assistant and asked her to come to Oxford. Maria was nine years older than me, a Pakistani immigrant to the UK. She lived on her own as a single woman in London, and felt more like an older sister than an employee. She heard my shaky voice on the phone and left right away to make the two-hour drive from the city. When she got to my room, I told her everything. 'Right,' she said. 'Take me to Anisa.'

'Come to get your jacket?' Anisa asked. 'You left it on the bed. Hey, Maria, what are you doing here?'

Maria closed the door behind us. 'Tell me what happened last night.' Anisa broke into nervous laughter, but Maria wasn't having it. 'What did you give her?' she demanded. 'Was it acid?

Mushrooms?' I steadied myself against the wall. I hadn't even thought of the questions Maria was asking.

'It was just weed!' Anisa shot back. 'And then she started acting *insane*. She wouldn't stop screaming. It really freaked me out.' I looked at the floor, Maria scowled and Anisa's voice softened. 'Look, I don't know what happened. She did a couple of bong hits. It was honestly nothing.'

'But my head is still spinning,' I said. 'It's been hours and I can barely breathe.'

'Then it can't be the weed,' Anisa replied. 'It's something else.'

From the look on Maria's face, I knew she was right.

21.

I staggered through the next few days, dragging myself to lectures and tutorials, but otherwise hiding out in my room. At night I was still afraid that when I closed my eyes I'd see those horrifying images on repeat, so I stayed awake and watched for the sun to rise. The best feeling I could manage was hollowness – a blank space was better than one filled with nightmares.

When Lara gave me the good news that I had done well in collections – 'Upper Second Class marks. I knew you could do it!' – I was ashamed instead of relieved. Since the night in Anisa's room, I hadn't done any of my reading. My first essays of the term would be late. After trying so hard to stay on top of my coursework, I felt lost. It wasn't a matter of will, priorities or study skills any more. I couldn't focus my mind long enough to read and write.

One of my courses that term focused on Plato's *Republic*. In the allegory of the cave, prisoners who have lived their whole lives in darkness believe that the shadows they see are the real world. When a prisoner is freed and walks into the sunlight, he realises what he thought was reality was only an illusion. *Now I'm in the cave*, I thought. I desperately wanted to see things clearly again, to shake off the shadows and return to the light.

A week after that night in the shack, Lady Margaret Hall held its triennial Commemoration Ball, meant to be the social highlight of our college years. For months I had been beside myself with excitement for the big night – planning my outfit, checking every update from the ball committee on Instagram, making plans with my friends. Now I worried that it would be too much, too taxing for my fragile mental state.

On the afternoon before the ball, I went to the salon for an appointment I'd booked months earlier. The menacing rattle of the hairdryer frayed my nerves, and I couldn't wait to leave. Back at halls, everyone was getting ready in Cora's room, helping each other zip up their gowns and make last-minute decisions on jewellery and eyeliner. I wished I had another week to recover, or some sort of emotional decompression chamber that would help me switch from brutal flashbacks to this giggly, festive mood. But I didn't want to be the sad girl at the party, so I tried to mirror their energy and match the excitement in their voices.

We made the short walk to the gardens together, my friends' contagious laughter and exuberance pulling me along like a gentle current. By the time we arrived, I felt almost normal. Lady Margaret Hall had been transformed into an elaborate dreamscape of music, revelry and romance. Even the plants were putting on a show – the purple wisteria in full bloom, the magnolia tree bursting with giant, glossy leaves.

Throughout the evening, anxiety loosened its grip on me. I watched a troupe of drag queens warm up the crowd before the musical acts, ate churros and marvelled at the midnight fireworks. At 3 a.m., I sat on the ground in the corner of the silent disco tent, smiling as my friends donned headphones and danced to whatever beats were in their ears. At sunrise, we stood in line for breakfast sandwiches, then joined the crowd for the traditional 'survivors' photo', a group picture of those who had made it through the ball from start to finish.

It was the first time in days that I didn't have to stay vigilant all night, trying not to fall asleep. Everyone I loved was awake with me, filling the hours with laughter and movement. I wondered if the people who partied all the time, the ones I rarely saw sober, were also running away from nightmares.

The night after the ball, though, I went back to staying awake until dawn, afraid that if I closed my eyes the flashbacks would start again. During the day, I tried to rest, missing lectures and essay deadlines. I didn't want to alarm my friends, but Anisa and Cora saw me stumbling, ragged and bleary-eyed, and started to worry anyway. As Cora finished her reading for the week, she sent me her notes and outlines, hoping to kick-start me into doing my work. Anisa appointed herself the homework police, checking on my progress before she went to bed at night.

Have you handed in your econ problem set?

no

It was due at 9 pm! How much do you have left?

haven't started yet

What about your philosophy essay?

Nothing

nothing is done

My friends were trying their best to help me stay on top of the academic work, but sleep deprivation made it impossible to study. Falling behind made me feel even more panicked and depressed, like I'd never be able to dig myself out of the hole. When I got overwhelmed, my heart would race. If I lay on my bed to try to slow it down, it felt like a stack of bricks was sitting on my chest. Standing up again made me dizzy. All of it made me want to scream and cry in frustration, but most days I was too tired to do more than sit and stare at the wall.

One evening, I asked Anisa if she would stay in my room for the night. If I tried to sleep and something went wrong, she could call for help. We set up her mattress on the floor next to my bed, changed into our pyjamas and talked for a while. At midnight, she turned out the light and dozed off. I lay awake and stared out the window for a long time. Eventually I took a deep breath, rolled over, closed my eyes and prayed for rest.

And it worked – I slept through the whole night. I was so relieved that I got over my hesitation in telling my other friends about the flashbacks and asked them to sleep over in my room. Hen stayed the following night; Yasmin took the next shift. They seemed to know exactly what I needed – never pushing me to go into detail about my problems but merrily chatting about boys or showing me funny memes and videos. As much as their presence comforted me at night, I knew I couldn't keep doing this. My friends needed their space and time to study, and my problems were disrupting their schedules. I felt very old and way too young at the same time.

Could we maybe have a phone call? If you're busy, no worries.

Asser and I had continued to text each other, going from a few times a month at the start of the year to several times a week by the spring. At first it had been challenging. I felt a flicker of embarrassment and sadness when his name lit up my phone in our group chats with Jamal and Sofia; I would purposely respond to everyone but him. Eventually, though, Asser and I started texting on the side about cricket or music, and fell back into the easy banter we'd had over the summer. I knew it was a risk to ask for more, but he rang me as soon as he saw my message asking him to call.

I told him everything – the bong, the flashbacks, the sleepless nights. It all tumbled out of me, and I wasn't nervous or worried about what he would think. Like Maria, Asser was older than me, and I felt like I could share my experience without judgement. From some of the stories he'd told me about his high-school and university experiences, I knew he'd experimented with drugs himself; a bad trip wasn't going to shock him. We were friends, I was a mess, and he might have good advice.

'Have you been to the doctor?' he asked.

'I can't. They could find the drugs in my blood and send me to jail.'

On his end of the phone, I heard what was either a sigh or a muffled laugh. 'Please, please listen to me: you are not going to jail. There is no law against smoking marijuana.'

'Yes, there is, in the UK. You're thinking of America—'

'No, I'm not. The laws in the UK are against possession and only possession of large amounts. They are aimed at dealers, not people who touched a bong once in their life.'

'Are you sure?'

'And if the doctor does a blood test, they will not be looking for drugs. Doctors and nurses don't report users, even for harder drugs like heroin.'

'How do you know so much about this . . . possession and stuff?'

'Malala, I'm not a drug mule, if that's what you're wondering! It's just common knowledge. But I am worried about you. Please make an appointment and see a doctor.'

I promised I would and thanked him for the advice. As soon as we said goodbye, I opened a message and wrote:

I miss you.

Go to the doctor.
I miss you too.

With time, the fear subsided, and I was able to sleep through the night on my own. I waited for the burst of energy that comes after you've been sick, when you wake up one morning and realise you're no longer vomiting or clammy, and you want to run out and greet the day, grateful to be alive and well. That feeling never came, but slowly I started to slip back into the routines of Oxford life.

In May I went to my doctor's appointment and told her about my insomnia, exhaustion and breathing difficulties. I left out the weed and flashbacks. She did a blood test and, a few days later, called to say I was anaemic. 'It's common for South Asian women and nothing to worry about. Take an iron supplement every day, and try to eat meat, leafy green vegetables and fruit.'

I knew anaemia wasn't the source of my recent troubles, but I picked up the pills and informed Asser that I had completed the mission. A few days later, a package from him arrived in the post.

Inside was an Iron Man toy and a note that said, *Put this on your desk to remind you to take your vitamins every morning.*

As spring turned to summer, I counted the days until I could leave Oxford; university wasn't a safe, happy place for me any more. The flashbacks were gone, but I no longer felt free. Now I had to steady myself on an endless tightrope, worried that a loud noise or a sudden movement could knock me off-balance or shake loose a bad memory. The parties I'd once loved now made me unsteady and hypervigilant. I went to the 24 Obs graduation celebration but left before 10 p.m. Most nights I swapped dinners out for takeaway and TV in my room. I was cautious with myself, careful not to disturb the enemy in my brain.

Every night I prayed, *Ya Allah, heal me quickly.*

22.

I looked to the summertime as a reset, a chance to put the night-mares behind me and start over – and Asser was a big part of that. When he told me he was coming back to the UK in July, I was delighted if not completely surprised. His niece was graduating from med school and England was hosting the Cricket World Cup, a great opportunity to broaden his professional network. But the main reason was me. He didn't need to say it – I knew I wasn't wrong about his feelings this time.

After that first phone call when I told him what I was going through, he called almost every day. At first he mostly checked on my health, making sure I took my iron pills and gently lecturing me when I admitted to eating nothing but chips for two days in a row. Then our conversations got longer, stretching to include topics like celebrity crushes, our childhood dreams, the existence of God. Asser kept up with all the gossip about my friends' love lives; I learnt that he loved to DJ but gave it up after he witnessed a murder at an illegal rave in Lahore. Like most people my age, I preferred texting over phone calls, but with Asser, I could talk for hours.

We had become more than friends and we both acknowledged it – he called me 'babe' and said I looked beautiful in the pictures I sent him. My lack of dating experience sometimes meant I was trying to court a twenty-nine-year-old man with the romantic tool kit of a twelve-year-old girl. If he sent a text saying he had a busy day and couldn't call at our usual time, I sulked and replied, u don't even have time for me. must not be that important to u. Sometimes I picked fights just to get his attention. He laughed off these antics, calling me 'president of the drama club' and promising that he missed me.

'How much time will we have together in your busy summer schedule?' he asked one night, a couple of weeks before he was set to arrive in London.

'Short trips to Ethiopia and France, a longer stay in the US in August. But my calendar has a lot of open spots and they're all yours! I'm actually more worried about . . .'

'Your parents?'

'Yeah. Last year they didn't pry too much, but the more we see each other, the more questions they'll ask. Could get tricky.'

'Okay, what if I write your dad a letter? It will say, "Dear Mr Yousafzai, Hope you are doing well. As you are aware, you have a daughter who has grown up to be a wonderful and beautiful woman. And . . ."'

At this point, he broke into song, warbling, '*Le jayenge, Le jayenge, Dilwale Dulhania le jayenge!*' The song, 'The Brave-Hearted Will Take the Bride', was an old Bollywood hit about a man making his case to the father of the woman he loved.

I had two thoughts at once:

FINDING MY WAY

I can't wait to see him again.
That is possibly the worst singing voice I've ever heard.

❧

FROM THE MOMENT Asser arrived in England, all our experiences – last summer's fumbling around feelings and our recent four-hour phone calls – blended to create the thrill of a new relationship with the worn-in ease of an older one. We would spend all day together, then call each other the minute we got home, staying on the phone for hours. On long drives to London, we sat in comfortable silence, content to simply exist next to each other while watching the countryside roll by and listening to my security guards' nineties playlists.

One evening we went to a restaurant at an old manor in the English countryside. 'Excuse me for just one minute,' I said to Asser after the host had shown us to a table by the window. I'd left my parents' house in a shalwar kameez that met my mum's approval but stuffed a change of clothes in my bag: a sleeveless, form-fitting dress in pale pink lace and my highest heels.

When I returned to the table, Asser stood up and his mouth broke into a smile I hadn't seen before. He pulled out my chair and whispered, 'You're a sex bomb!' in my ear. I hid my face behind my dinner napkin, both delighted and bashful.

Asser's arrival vanquished the dark clouds that had hung over my third term at Oxford, but it wasn't exactly the carefree summer romance of rom-coms, as I worried a lot about getting caught. When we were together, it was hard for me to turn off premonitions of being publicly shamed in Pakistan for having a boyfriend. I agonised over what would happen to the Shangla girls, imagining their parents pulling them out of our school over my carelessness.

On a walk through London's Chiswick Gardens one afternoon, I was showing off for Asser, climbing up a tree and daring him to race me to the top. When I jumped down, I grabbed his hand and pulled him close to me. That's when I caught the eye of a woman on a park bench staring at us. She broke into a wide smile of recognition and pulled out her phone to take a picture. I freaked out and ran behind a hedge to hide, alarming both Asser and my security team. It was exhausting to constantly worry about being observed or photographed, to spend so much energy being aware of my surroundings that I could never fully be myself.

The next day I travelled to the airport with my dad to catch a plane to Addis Ababa. I couldn't put it off any more – I had to tell him about Asser. As he read the morning news on his phone, I stared out the window, rehearsing what I would say and bracing myself for his response. I wanted to stay in my secret world a little longer, free of people's opinions and reminders about what I was risking. But that couldn't last. My dad needed to hear it from me before someone snapped a picture of Asser and me together.

My dad and I loved to debate each other about politics, world events, feminism, anything at all. I would try to convince him to my side, and most of the time, I succeeded. My whole life, I felt like I could tell him anything – but I'd never been in love before.

'Dad, you know . . . it's hard to meet good people . . . like, people who have a good sense of humour but also find me funny,' I began. He looked attentive, like he was trying to understand me. *Ugh, you're making this worse*, I thought. *Just spit it out!*

'It's just, like . . . when you meet someone and want to spend more time with them? Well, I guess . . . I guess, basically, I have met someone like that. He's, uh, twenty-nine . . . he lives in Lahore, but comes to England in the summer to see his sister. And he works in cricket, which is great for me.'

My dad nodded slowly, as if everything I'd said up to this point was fine. 'We . . . Asser and I . . .' I continued. 'I like him, Dad. I like him . . . romantically.' A wave of nausea rolled through me as I choked the word out, but my dad just stared back at me without even blinking.

'I wanted you to know,' I continued, 'but please, *please* don't tell Mum. I'm begging you – I am not ready to have this fight with her yet.'

At first it seemed like he was about to ask a question. But he stopped himself, looked straight ahead and said nothing. Then I watched in disbelief as my dad, my lifelong confidant, pulled out his phone and called home.

On the other end of the line, I heard my mum say, 'Absolutely not! Does he even speak Pashto? She must marry a Pashtun man!'

'If he's here for the summer, we should meet him,' my dad said crisply after he hung up. 'But we won't announce the engagement until after your graduation.' I glared out of the window, fuming at myself for bringing it up, at my dad for calling my mum, at my mum for being so small-minded, and at them both for jumping to engagements and husbands.

Why are you even thinking about marriage? I wanted to scream. *Can I not just live my life like all the other twenty-one-year-olds at university?* But I knew the answer: while my parents wouldn't force me to get married against my will, they would never accept me having a boyfriend. No looking, no touching, no dating. Any conversations you had with a man before marriage had to be supervised by the parents. Those were the Pashtun rules, and I'd already broken all of them.

Asser, on the other hand, was thrilled that I'd told my dad. 'What did he say? When can I meet your family? I am ready!' I hated the thought of him and my family in the same room, but I agreed to a visit, as I didn't want Asser or my parents to think I had something to hide.

It felt like things were moving too fast, like I'd been caught in the undertow and dragged out to sea against my will. The family introductions weren't Asser's idea; my dad was the first to suggest it. Still, I was irritable and withdrawn over the next few days, even feigning illness and cancelling a lunch date with Asser.

Though we hadn't discussed it, I worried that someday he might want to get married – and I knew I didn't want that, with Asser or anyone else. In my culture, everything revolves around the man. After marriage, a woman is supposed to follow orders and do everything she can to please him. I would never submit to that sort of control, of course – but I wasn't keen on Western images of marriage either. The thought of meal planning on the weekend or loading the dishwasher together honestly gave me the ick. I even hated the word 'wife'. In my ideal world, my relationship with Asser could go on forever, free of expectations, existing without context or formal commitment.

I suppose some part of me considered falling in love not as a path to marriage, but simply part of my student experience – in the basket of risky behaviours like clubbing or night climbing. In my second summer with Asser, I was only beginning to understand that I could not control my feelings, or stop my dreams and desires from changing. Whatever fixed idea I had of myself, however rigid my future plans – to stay single and dedicate my life to my work – my humanity kept breaking through, kept leading me to connection, friendship and love.

We waited until the day before my three-week trip to the United States for his visit with my family. I planned everything to the minute: Asser would arrive by train into Birmingham at 11:45 a.m., get to my parents' house for a 12 p.m. lunch, and leave by 1 p.m. to return to London. Not much could go wrong in an hour, I figured.

He turned up bearing flowers and seemed a little bit nervous. I was flustered too, and could barely look him in the eye as I showed him into the living room where Khushal and Atal were blaring drill rap and playing video games. My dad, who had double-booked by mistake and invited seven guests of his own, was in the garden trying to man the barbecue, serve tea and carry on multiple conversations. My mum sat under a tree in a garden chair, evaluating everyone, particularly Asser. She asked him if he knew any Pashto and he gamely stumbled through the few phrases he knew. My mum wasn't impressed, but she seemed at least to credit him for making an effort. The whole situation was making me increasingly anxious, while Asser loosened up, chatting with my dad and his guests about his grilling techniques, encouraging Khushal to keep up with his studies and even beatboxing with Atal.

At 1 p.m. sharp, I called a car for him and whispered, 'I'm sorry,' as he left. When he was gone, a weight lifted from my shoulders. I was relieved to have my identities – the chaste Pashtun daughter my parents expected me to be, and the fun-loving girlfriend Asser knew – separated again, back in their own boxes. But the reprieve was short-lived, quickly replaced by the desire to run after his car, hop in and escape together. I didn't know how I would survive the next few weeks without him.

23.

Before sunrise the next day, my parents and I travelled to Heathrow and boarded a plane for Boston. They were taking me to Massachusetts Eye and Ear to see Dr Tessa Hadlock, a Harvard Medical School professor and pioneer in treating facial paralysis.

Under Dr Hadlock's supervision, I was undergoing a complex series of surgeries called a cross-facial nerve graft. If it worked, I would have more movement on the left side of my face. A year earlier, in the first procedure, doctors had removed a long nerve from my left calf. Then they'd made a series of discreet cuts – at my right ear, inside my right cheek, under my upper lip, inside my left cheek – and positioned the nerve to run across my face. In order to achieve 'facial reanimation', both halves of the face had to be 'talking' to one another via the nerve.

The doctors had warned me I wouldn't see any improvement after the first surgery – and I didn't. The left half of the nerve couldn't connect to the facial muscles until they added fresh tissue. On our current visit, they would remove part of my upper left thigh and deposit it inside my cheek. With any luck, the nerve from my calf would attach to the tissue from my thigh and begin sending signals to the muscles in my face.

Initially I did not want to do the cross-facial nerve graft; it meant spending weeks of time in hospitals and recovery rooms for three consecutive summers. My parents, however, kept pushing for a cure. They wanted to erase the memory of seeing me for the first time in the Birmingham hospital with sunken eyes and a paralysed mouth – to silence the comments, from relatives and online trolls, about how pretty I 'used to be' before the shooting. My parents and the doctors had convinced me it would be worth the effort in the end, so off we went to Boston.

On the plane, I got a message from Asser: Have your mum and dad said anything about us? I told him the truth. They were worried. Someone could take a photo, they said, or word could get out through one of our friends. They anticipated a scandal and said I should stop seeing him. I wasn't going to do that, but I hated the tension my relationship created with my parents. Wasn't it their *job* to be happy for me? I normally would have sat next to my dad on the flight and chatted with him for hours. This time, I put a blanket over my head and went to sleep.

The morning of the surgery, Dr Hadlock and her team stood over my hospital bed giving a matter-of-fact overview of the five-hour procedure, as if I were a car in the garage coming in for a routine tune-up. At this point, I'd had seven surgeries in my life and never felt scared of hospitals, doctors, the beeping machines or bright lights. But now I was full of dread. What if something went wrong, and the doctors put me back in a coma? What if I didn't wake up this time? I would rather live the rest of my life with facial paralysis than be held hostage by the abyss in my brain.

I kept my fears to myself; it wasn't something I wanted to share with my parents or the doctors. Luckily, the procedure went as planned. When I woke up, I saw the sunshine coming through the hospital-room window and my whole body relaxed. *You made it*, I thought. Even the overcooked porridge and jelly the nurse brought the next morning tasted good to me.

After two days in the recovery ward, I transferred to a nearby hotel. That evening I took oxycodone prescribed for the searing pain in my thigh and cheek. Half an hour later, my head was reeling. The dizziness and nausea transported me back to that night in Anisa's room, and I began to panic. What if it happened again? I stayed awake all night, praying that the flashbacks would stay away, making bargains with the universe: *I won't go to another party as long as I live; I'll study and turn in all my work on time as long as I never have to experience that again.* In the early-morning hours, I finally drifted off. When I woke up, I was resolute: no more pain pills. It wasn't worth the risk. Better to tough it out than open the door to my nightmares.

⌒

WHEN I GOT back to England, I met Asser at a Cantonese restaurant in London's Dorchester Hotel for one last dinner before he returned to Lahore. My face was still heavily swollen from the surgery, but he smiled at me the same way he had at the start of the summer when I wore my 'sex bomb' dress.

For months we'd avoided defining our relationship, enjoying each other's company as if nothing would ever need to change. I had preferred it that way, but being away from him the past few weeks had intensified my feelings. Now I needed to know what he was thinking. Throughout dinner, I fumbled around the question, never quite asking it. But he must have known what I was after.

'I'm going to miss you a lot when I leave,' he said. 'I feel kind of . . . hollowed out at the thought of not seeing you every week. You know – because I told you the second time we saw each other – that I'm looking for a long-term relationship . . .' He paused in thought and my heart sped up, unsure where the conversation was going next. Was he proposing or dumping me? They were both unfavourable outcomes in my mind.

'The truth is, I would marry you tomorrow, and I *hate* myself for saying that. It's not a fair thing to put on you. Because you're too young. You're still changing as a person, still trying to figure out what you want in life.'

In the moment, his words seemed so condescending that I didn't pause long enough to admit to myself that they were true. 'You think because I'm young I can't know how I feel? How do you, at the advanced age of twenty-nine, know if you love someone?'

'I ask myself questions. Do you have the best time with her? Enjoy talking to her for hours? Do you trust her? Do you want to kiss her in the cloakroom at the Dorchester Hotel?'

My face flushed and I tripped over my words. 'What about . . . just for now . . . let's call it an open relationship . . . except that it's closed at your end,' I ventured.

Asser laughed so loud that people at nearby tables turned to look at us. 'Okay, that was funny . . . but it's also part of the problem. You won't even call me your boyfriend. Being someone's secret doesn't feel great, especially when I want to tell the world how amazing you are. I would love to go on beach holidays with you and have a phone full of pictures of us. And I don't know when, or if, that will happen.'

'The secrecy is to keep my parents calm. They're scared of creating a scandal.'

He leant over and took my hand. 'I will always protect your privacy. Always. But if I'm honest, Malala, I also think you're keeping it a secret because you're not sure what you want in life, or with me. And that's fine! But that feeling doesn't really change as you get older; there are no signs pointing us in the right direction. None of us are ever certain – there's always the possibility of making the wrong choice or getting your heart broken. It never goes away.'

I pulled at the sleeve of my dress, suddenly nervous around him for the first time all summer. 'Could we maybe pause our feelings for now, just until I finish my last year at Oxford? We can pick up right here next June and figure things out.'

'I'm not sure feelings work that way,' he said. 'But, for you, I'm willing to try.'

We found a low-lit corner of the hotel lobby to say goodbye. When he put his arms around me, I whispered, 'I love you.' Then he was gone, and the summer was over.

24.

I have heard of people snapping or breaking, seeming to shift in an instant from a sister or friend into a stranger. But I lost my mind in pieces.

My grasp on reality. Hope for the future. My faith in my friends. The sense of peace I felt watching the sun rise over the river or hearing Asser's voice on the phone. The ability to control my own body. That autumn, I lost them all.

❦

IT WAS SUPPOSED to be my best year of university. Sure, there were exams at the end, but also balls, picnics and graduation parties to look forward to. I felt like I'd shaken off the fear and anguish that the flashbacks had brought into my life. Asser and I had had a great time over the summer and left things in a good place. I was ready to be the diligent student I knew I could be, and, of course, have some fun.

My friends and I had decided to leave the halls on the main quad and move to a smaller residence hall on the edge of campus. In the new building, we would have a kitchen, a little balcony and the top floor all to ourselves – me, Cora, Hen, Yasmin and Anisa. As usual, my security team would take the room next to mine. There was one space left over, and the college assigned it to a sweet and, in terms of the housing lottery, unlucky guy named Alan.

On moving-in day, we discovered the flat was hardly the oasis we imagined. The building's lift rarely worked and the walls between our rooms were as thin as hospital gowns. The kitchen was no bigger than a walk-in wardrobe, so we had to maximise every inch of space. Most of us were, in theory, willing to share our stuff, but you couldn't put meat in a vegetarian's frying pan, milk in a vegan's mug or pork in a Muslim's pot. All of which added up to six kitchens' worth of cookware and pantry items crammed into four tiny cabinets.

Hen's neat-freakery and need for order meant she was often sending scolding messages to the rest of us. In previous years, our group chat had always been full of dinner plans, inside jokes and requests to borrow clothes. Now it was: Someone forgot to turn off the stove. Be responsible! or Who left raw chicken on the worktop?? or If you use my dishes, wash them. It's common courtesy!

When you live with your friends, you see another side of them – and sometimes you don't like what you see. I thought our last year was going to be one big slumber party, but there were near-constant arguments instead. Someone was always forgetting it was her turn to replace the milk, borrowing things without asking or sleeping through her morning alarm, leaving the rest of us to suffer through *beep! beep! beep!* until someone else finally got up and banged on the door.

The constant noise set everyone on edge. We couldn't have a conversation at normal volume without disturbing the adjacent rooms. When I had a few 24 Obs friends over or Yasmin hosted study group, it sounded like the entire college had gathered in the kitchen. In the past, we might have just rolled our eyes, put on our headphones and ignored it, but this was our final year. In May and June, we would all go to the Examination Halls and spend hours writing essays and solving equations. Eight gruelling exams over four weeks, designed to test everything we'd learnt at Oxford. Underperform and you'd hurt your career prospects. Fail a test and you left without a degree, as if the last three years of your life had never happened. All the third-year students were stressed, shuffling quickly from the library to the lecture hall and back again – and in our case, shouting at each other to be quiet in the kitchen.

The collective stress level was higher than ever as my friends were all working towards ambitious post-Oxford goals. Anisa already had a conditional offer from a top consulting firm, and Cora was interviewing for jobs in finance. Hen and Yasmin were applying for master's programmes at Harvard and Cambridge. Yasmin wanted to study law at Cambridge. Unlike them, I pitched from plan to plan: I decided to go to grad school. Then I changed my mind, thinking I should take a job and learn about the working world. No, I resolved, I'd travel and get a better understanding of girls' education in other countries. Sometimes I daydreamt about running away to a sunny beach with Asser. Then I'd cycle back to grad school and repeat my thought processes again. The longer my indecisiveness wore on, the more nervous and insecure I felt about not having a road map for my future.

I was working hard, but the study skills I'd learnt from Valerie had got rusty over the summer. My professors gave sobering comments on my first few essays of the term – *little mention of extant literature / empirical examples were weak / argument lacked structure.* My friends would drop by my room in the evenings, as they always had, but I no longer looked forward to their interruptions. When I asked them to come back later, after I'd finished my reading, Hen and Anisa would make snide comments like 'Wow, can't believe even *you* are feeling the pressure now' or 'Well, well, the girl who advocates for education has finally picked up a book!' In the past, I'd laughed off these jokes; now my responses were clipped and annoyed.

Everywhere I went – tutorials, library, dining hall – felt stressful, and my equilibrium started sliding away. I stayed up all night writing essays, often missing the deadlines. The instructions the doctor had given me last spring – 'eat meat, leafy green vegetables and fruit' – were long forgotten, and my diet was reduced to digestive biscuits or cereal, if I bothered to eat at all. My friends snarked and sniped at each other. I felt disoriented, like all of Oxford was a video game and I was a coding error.

⌒

ON MY WAY to a lecture one morning, I got a text message from a cousin in Pakistan: Please call. I rang him right away, but no one answered. When I hung up the phone, I had a terrible premonition: my grandmother Abai was dead.

The panic welled up inside me, and I tightened my throat, fighting off the urge to cry or vomit. I couldn't focus on the lecture, lost in dark thoughts, eyes fixed on my phone in case my cousin called back. The second the professor finished speaking, I raced out of the room. A girl from the PPE study group called my name, but I pretended not to hear her. *Just get to your room. Just get to your room.* As soon as I closed the door, my eyes filled with tears. I always hated to cry, hated the way that it made me feel weak. But my body was acting without my permission now, throwing itself into grief.

Lying on my bed, I shut my swollen eyes and tried to remember everything I could about Abai: how she built a campfire in front of her house in the mountains every time I came to visit because she knew I'd be cold when I arrived. The way she smelt like woodsmoke and roses. How, unlike a lot of older women in Pakistan, she never treated her daughter-in-law like a servant, and always gave my mum the best cut of meat at dinnertime. The day I was attacked, when she put her hand on me and asked God to give me a long life. I cried over all the things I didn't know about her as well. Who was her best friend? What were her dreams when she was a child? Had she ever seen the ocean?

I should have realised that none of this made sense. If anything happened to Abai, our relatives in Pakistan would notify my father, not me. I would hear the news from him. But I was incapable of rational thought, disconnected from reality. *Who will pray for me now that Abai is gone?* The hours ticked by. I was supposed to be working on a problem set, but I couldn't focus on anything but my sorrow and fear.

My cousin finally called back that afternoon. I answered the phone breathlessly – 'Hello, what happened? Why did you call?' – and steeled myself for the news I knew was coming.

'Wanted to tell you I stopped in at the girls' school in Shangla,' he said. 'Construction on the new building is going well and we should be able to double enrolment next year.' He mentioned a few other things about plumbing and playground equipment, but I cut him off.

'Is Abai okay?'

'Yes, she's fine. Stopped by to see her this evening and she was sitting outside, watching the sunset, like always. She forgets a lot of things these days, but her health seems good.'

Those words should have been a huge relief to me; they should have lifted the curse that had possessed my heart and mind all day. But I was still staggering, trying to understand what had just happened. Why wasn't I able to control my thoughts, calm myself, wait to find out why he was calling before falling apart? I didn't have an answer, and that frightened and unnerved me.

My friends' voices drifted down the hallway and I locked my door from the inside. I couldn't see them right now – though I felt scared to be alone too, like I couldn't trust myself. I splashed cold water on my face, and looked around my room, trying to find comfort in familiar things – family photos, my favourite scarf, the cricket bat Raja gave me when he graduated. But it felt like I was seeing it all through someone else's eyes.

A WEEK OR so later, I was working on an essay when Hen barged into my room. It was after 1 a.m., and she was a bit drunk. I needed to study and thought about telling her so; but it had been a while since we hung out, and I figured I could spare a few minutes.

'Where have you been?' I asked.

'Oh, just out with Brandon,' she replied.

'Brandon who?'

'You know . . . the American one.' She twirled her hair with her fingers and blinked slowly at me.

'Brandon from PPE? What were you doing with him?' I saw Hen every day and Brandon almost as often at lectures and study groups. In the last two years, I'd never seen them together.

'I mean . . . well, we've been seeing each other for a few months.'

I rolled my eyes at her and turned back to my textbook. My friends had this annoying prank where they would make up stories and convince me to believe them – a rolling game of Two Truths and a Lie, except they were always fibbing, and I fell for it over and over. The joke had been played out long ago, and I wasn't in the mood for it tonight.

'No, I'm serious!' Hen said. I tapped my pen on my notebook, hoping she would get the hint and leave me alone.

'Really, I don't know how you haven't noticed,' she continued. 'Remember last term, the "Dress Like a London Tube Station" bop at the college bar?'

'Yeah, what about it? Brandon wasn't there.'

'He was, though. You even talked to him on your way to the loo! And then he came and sat by me and we were, like, making out in front of everyone. I can't believe you missed it!'

I whipped back around, studying her face for the truth. For the next twenty minutes, I grilled her on the details of their relationship and she told me everything – the initial spark between them, first kiss, late-night phone calls over the summer. 'No,' I protested at various points, 'I don't believe any of this.' How could one of my best friends have a boyfriend that I didn't know about? She mentioned specific events and places we'd been together; I had no recollection of Brandon being there. If this was reality, what world had I been living in? How could I trust my own memory if all this had been happening and I didn't realise or remember it?

My left eye started to pulse in time with my heartbeat. It seemed to speed up with every disorienting revelation. *How long have we been talking?* I asked myself, realising I was no longer sure if it was morning or night. Sweat rolled down my back and my hands went numb.

'Hen, I don't feel well,' I mumbled.

'What's wrong, babe? Did you forget to eat today?'

'I don't know, I just . . . please tell me the truth. Is this real?'

She looked hurt for a moment, then broke out laughing. 'Of course not! I've never even talked to that guy. I *cannot believe* you thought I was serious.'

If I'd had the strength, I might have thrown a book or a mug at her. 'Get out!' I growled. She froze for a moment, then started apologising, repeating that it was only a joke. 'Please,' I said, my voice deflated, 'just leave.'

When she was gone, a fever seemed to grip me; even the roots of my hair felt like they were on fire. The pulsing migrated from my eye to my ears, getting louder and louder with every second. It sounded like a stampede, like I had a thousand hearts, all running for their lives.

I flew out of the room and banged on my security team's door. Liam, one of the older bodyguards, answered, his grey hair sticking out at wild angles, eyes squinting at the hall lights. I'd never woken them up before and felt bad about it, but I was too scared to be polite.

'Something is wrong with me,' I choked out, struggling for air. 'I think I'm having a heart attack.'

He quickly helped me to my bed and checked my vital signs. 'Your heart rate is high,' he said. 'But you're conscious and breathing.' His voice sounded like an announcement in a busy airport. I heard the sound and recognised some of the words, but I couldn't process their meaning.

For the next hour, Liam kept checking my temperature, pulse, respiratory rate. Eventually my heart went back to normal and he went back to bed. My body felt heavy with exhaustion, and I fell into a deep sleep.

When I woke up the next day, I was afraid to leave my room,

convinced that the real world – the one I recognised, the one where I felt safe – wouldn't be on the other side of my door when I opened it. Whatever I encountered out there might send me spiralling again, so I stayed inside, alone and afraid. *What is happening to me?*

25.

W hen you search my name, the word you see over and over is 'brave'. I always thought it was true, thought I had a strong heart and a tough chest, that I could handle anything. When I started breaking down at university, I felt powerless. It made me angry that I couldn't conquer my fears or control my thoughts. Being afraid made me feel like I'd lost an essential part of myself.

My isolation grew more severe every day. After that night on Anisa's floor, I'd told my close friends about the flashbacks, but this new reality – the constant state of fear, the physical reactions, the endless bottoming out – was too much to share. They had already helped out so much the year before, checking on me, sharing their lecture notes and essays, staying in my room at night. How could I lean on them again, especially when they were so stressed about exams and post-Oxford life? I didn't want to be the needy friend. I had to handle this on my own.

Suspecting that I'd been having panic attacks, I consulted Google for advice. *Dissociation or derealisation can be triggered by schizophrenia, temporal lobe epilepsy, migraines, sleep disorders, head injury . . .* The list went on and on, and reading it only made me more frantic. I put down my phone and shuddered.

Going about my daily life and having to be 'on' felt excruciating. In tutorials, I told the professors I was sick, so they'd go easy on me. When my friends bickered over who made a mess in the kitchen, I quietly walked away. Every interaction with other people felt dangerous, like it might cause my mind to fracture even further.

In my journal, I inventoried my mental state.

Something is wrong with me and I'm worried that I can't stop it from happening again.

My recent problems
- *flashbacks last spring*
- *final year of university and exams coming up*
- *trouble with friends*
- *relationship with Asser / uncertainty*

Feelings and physical issues
- *heart racing, hard to breathe*
- *fear of someone I love dying*
- *unable to sleep*
- *constantly thinking 'What am I thinking?'*
- *head feels heavy and body feels weak*

Seeing it on paper, in my own handwriting, was jarring. *Normal people don't have lists like this,* I thought.

> Malz, you've left me on
> read so long i'm growing
> grey hairs

> u alive or what?

> so we just don't talk
> any more or ???

I'd been ghosting Sofia for weeks, ignoring her texts and DMs. Finally I agreed to meet her in town for dessert one night in early November. On the walk over, I was already planning my exit – just say a quick hello, and then make an excuse and go back to my room. From across the street, I watched groups of friends filter in and out, smiling and laughing, hot chocolate in hand. *They don't even know how happy they are*, I thought. I had once been among these cheery students, and Oxford had been my favourite place in the world. But I couldn't make myself feel that way again, and I didn't think that feeling would ever return. The realisation crushed me.

'Hey there,' I said to Sofia as soon as I walked up. 'Really sorry to do this, but I need to leave, not feeling well. You stay, though. I'll be okay.' She heard the cracks in my voice and looked concerned.

'At least let me walk with you,' she replied.

I wanted to be alone, but I didn't have the energy to argue with her. After walking in silence for a while, Sofia turned and faced me. 'What's wrong, Malz?' she asked. 'You haven't been yourself lately. Is it Asser?'

'I'm . . . uh . . .' I stammered. 'It's not Asser.' Sofia looked at me expectantly. 'I don't know, Sof, I don't want to bother you with this.'

'You don't have to pretend to be okay around me,' she said. 'I'm not going to push you, but I will worry about it whether you tell me or not.'

'I mean . . . part of the problem is that I don't know what's wrong.' I paused for a moment, still reluctant to say it out loud. 'I think I'm having panic attacks. Really bad ones. For no reason, out of nowhere . . . It's scary.'

She put her arm around my shoulders. 'I'm so sorry, that sounds really intense. Have you thought about seeing a therapist?'

'No, not sure it would help.'

'They can't solve every problem in your life, but you might get some answers, you know? You could at least make sure your self-diagnosis is correct.'

'I feel like fixating on it won't really help,' I said. 'It will probably resolve itself on its own, right?' After all, the flashbacks had gone away on their own last spring, I reasoned. I just needed to wait this out, I told her.

Sofia looked at me cautiously and said, 'I mean . . . maybe? But there's no harm in asking for help.'

I wish I had listened to Sofia. Four days later, I was studying alone in the kitchen on a grey, rainy morning. I tried to focus on my textbooks, hoping I could absorb enough to prevent another lecture from Lara. But I couldn't concentrate, no matter how hard I tried. *This is pointless,* I thought. *You're never going to make it through exams. Why can't you get it together?*

When I got up to rinse my mug and make a new cup of tea, my eyes settled on a large knife at the bottom of the sink. A cold dread spread over me, the same sensation as watching the sky turn a sickly, unnatural green before a cyclone. For a moment, you stand still, uneasy but awestruck by the sight of it. Then you remember to be afraid.

My hands trembled, and violent thoughts took over my brain.

What would happen if I picked up the knife? Would I hurt someone with it? Would I hurt myself? What if I leave the knife alone and someone comes into the room and uses it on me? Overwhelmed, I dropped my mug and sank to my knees, gasping wildly to catch my breath.

When I had the strength to stand, I went back to my room. *It's over, it's over*, I repeated. I was supposed to be strong, someone who looked fear in the eye and kept walking. But I could not make myself believe that everything was fine. I can't remember how long I sat there screaming into a pillow, pulling my hair, pounding my fists on the floor – only that, when it was over, I knew I needed help.

26.

In Pashto, my mother tongue, we have no word for 'anxiety'.

Where I grew up, people didn't speak about their mental health – I hadn't heard the words or the concept before we came to England. In Pakistan, psychological concerns are often ignored or seen as 'a curse from God'. When I finally worked up the courage to ask Maria to book an appointment with a counsellor for me, she understood why I asked her not to mention it to my parents. 'I've been there too,' she said. 'When I had a long period of depression at seventeen, my mother said to make *duas* and ask Allah for forgiveness. According to her, I had strayed from God and the devil was controlling me.'

In communities like Maria's and mine, mental illness leads to social isolation. It's better to suffer in silence, people believe, than to give your neighbours something to gossip about. The stigma against mental illness is so strong that, until 2022, suicide was considered a criminal act. If you attempted it and lived, you could be thrown in jail for a year or more. Those brave enough to ask for help are not likely to find it. The country has fewer than five hundred psychiatrists to serve a population of 235 million.

My only experience with therapy had been in hospital in Birmingham. A month into my recovery, a counsellor had started coming to my room every week and asking me questions: *How are you feeling about what happened to you? Do you feel afraid on a regular basis? What is causing you the most distress today?*

I hated these visits. At fifteen, I was learning how to walk and talk again, like a baby. Doctors had just put a metal plate in my head where a large piece of my skull used to be. Everyone had to stand on my right side to speak to me because the bullet had shattered my left eardrum. *What is causing me distress? Look around, ma'am!* My physical problems seemed so much bigger than my feelings.

When doctors suggested I continue to see a counsellor after leaving hospital, my dad declined. 'Only a completely nonfunctioning person needs a therapist,' he said. 'Malala is fine.' My parents were raised to ask 'What will people say?' in every situation and choose the option least likely to embarrass or shame their families. He thought he was protecting me.

But was I a functioning person now? A kitchen knife had brought me to my knees.

⌒

MY DRIVER STOPPED in front of a small pebbledash house on the outskirts of Oxford. We were a few miles from campus, but I looked out the window before opening the car door, checking to make sure there were no students or photographers nearby. As I walked past the rows of cheery flowers that lined the path to the house, I wondered if I was making a bad choice.

I was considering turning around and going back to the car when the door opened. A tall, middle-aged woman with hair pulled into a tidy French braid said, 'Hello, Malala. I'm Evelyn. Nice to meet you.' She led me back to her office, a cosy space with a fireplace and lots of lamps – a much more welcoming environment than the hospital's clinical setting. 'How can I help?' she asked with a smile.

Earlier that day, I'd done a little research online about what to expect at my first appointment. The main advice was: *Tell your therapist why you're there. Don't be vague.* Part of me was nervous to trust a complete stranger with things I kept secret from my family and friends. But I desperately wanted to get better, so I pushed my doubts aside and began.

'I'm worried about failing my exams,' I said. That was definitely true, but far from the only reason I was sitting in Evelyn's office. *Okay*, I thought, *maybe not quite ready yet.*

'Anything else?' she asked in a gentle, even tone.

I took a deep breath and looked up. My eyes stayed on the ceiling as I spoke, as if not seeing the room I was sitting in, or the world around me, made my problems less real. For a moment, I wondered if Evelyn thought it was rude of me not to look at her while I was speaking. But focusing on the ceiling was working, so I kept going.

I started with what I considered the beginning – when I got high last spring. I described the flashbacks of the shooting and that night in Anisa's room. Then I told her about my relationship with Asser, that summer's surgery, the conflict with my parents. I moved on to the recent panic attacks – Abai and Hen, chest pains, intrusive thoughts, the overwhelming dread that hung over me most days. My list of worries was long: that I couldn't trust my friends. That Asser would move on with someone else. That I had no plan beyond university.

When I was finished, I lowered my eyes and looked at Evelyn, scared of what I would see. But she was calm and still, and did not seem overwhelmed or alarmed by my confessions. 'Let's start with last spring,' she said. 'The flashbacks began after you took marijuana – do I have that right?'

'Yes, but those aren't happening any more. Now it's something different,' I replied.

'Can you describe a bit more about what you experienced during the flashbacks?' she asked.

I tugged at the sleeves of my sweater and looked back at Evelyn, hoping she'd see that I was uncomfortable and tell me I didn't have to answer. When she said nothing, I began softly, 'It felt like I had nowhere to hide. Even if I closed my eyes, those images were there.' I looked up at the ceiling again before continuing. 'I always thought my brain had erased the shooting. That my mind just . . . shut off. But I had seen things. And now I want to forget again.'

'Malala, I believe what you experienced was post-traumatic stress disorder.'

It wasn't the first time I'd heard of PTSD or considered that I might have it. But I didn't like the term or how overused it was. People at university claimed they 'got PTSD' from group projects or waiting in line too long for food. This experience was so awful and different that I couldn't imagine the same four letters capturing what I felt.

'Intrusive memories and flashbacks are common symptoms,' Evelyn explained. 'And stress can exacerbate PTSD. For instance, your concerns about your academic performance and the pressures of your work, your family, your relationship – they aren't directly related to the shooting, but they can trigger the same trauma response. Think of it like your body's alarm system getting stuck in the "on" position.'

'That's interesting,' I said. 'But, again, the flashbacks went away and haven't come back. The panic attacks happening now are different.'

Evelyn nodded and leant towards me a bit. 'I understand. At some point, though, when you're ready, I'd like to talk about PTSD again, as we can't separate it from your overall mental health just because you're not having flashbacks at the moment.'

I looked away. It had been hard enough to show up for this first appointment. I didn't want to think about having to come back.

'Now, when it comes to your more recent experiences,' Evelyn continued, 'the first thing you should know is that feeling panicked or unable to control your thoughts can be very frightening, but it is not unusual. Many of your fellow students are going through similar struggles, especially in their last year of university. For you, this might be heightened by PTSD, and the fact that you're a well-known person who is always in the spotlight. There is no blood test for mental illness, but I believe most of what you are describing is anxiety. And we can work on strategies to help you manage these episodes.'

'Anxiety' didn't sound so bad. I knew it was something a lot of people experienced, as common as allergies or paper cuts. Maybe I had a particularly bad case – but when Evelyn said she could teach me to control it, I started to relax. That was what I had hoped to find today: a way out.

She went on to explain the concept of 'the window of tolerance'. If a person is functioning day to day, navigating stressful situations and regulating their emotions, they are 'within their window'. Some windows are wider and some smaller – but everyone can be pushed outside the frame if the stress piles up too high. Beyond the window lie all the things I had been experiencing – panic, fear, disorientation.

As Evelyn spoke, the patterns became clearer. With everything going on in my life, I had been constantly climbing in and out of my window. Sleepless nights, poor nutrition and stress narrowed my margins, making my window smaller. Getting back to safety grew more difficult each time – and that was part of the reason I was having these extreme reactions.

It was helpful to get this context – how the pieces fitted together, how the hard parts of my life sparked off each other and started a fire. I wouldn't say that I felt good, necessarily, but for the first time in weeks, I had hope that I might get better.

Evelyn ended our first session by asking me to keep a log of when I felt panicked, overwhelmed, 'outside the window'. The last thing I wanted was more homework, but if it would help, I was willing to try.

27.

It didn't take me too long to start noticing the ups and downs. A visit from my parents raised my anxiety level, and listening to music lowered it. Throughout the week, I also identified a sensitivity to certain words – 'killed', 'murdered', 'dead' – the violent words we reappropriate all the time, but that had never set me on edge before. The same thing happened when people touched me; hugs made me feel trapped. One day I was gripped with fear for no clear reason. I could hear my heartbeat ringing in my ears again. *Weird thoughts remain,* I wrote in my journal.

'Did you know we are the only species who can think about our thoughts?' Evelyn asked in our next session. She told me to look at unwanted thoughts like waves on a beach. They come and they go. You can observe them. You can be curious about them. But they are not, in themselves, something to fear. Everyone has thoughts that are strange, unnerving, unkind. We all have feelings that take us by surprise. But we are judged on our actions, not what creeps around our brains.

'When we're anxious, we sometimes generate "what if" scenarios in our heads – the brain might show us its version of the worst that could happen to prepare and protect us. That may be why you felt you'd go back into a coma if you went to sleep or why you were afraid when you saw the kitchen knife.'

It gave me comfort to think of my brain as overprotective instead of addled or broken. Next time it happened, I would tell myself, 'That's just a thought. It's not something I am going to do.' If that didn't work, if the feelings still triggered my body to respond, Evelyn taught me to 'take manual control of my limbic system'. When my heart sped up and I felt dizzy, I would try 7/11 breathing – breathe in for a count of seven and out for a count of eleven – for at least five minutes. The long exhale calms the body.

A few days after our session, I was tense and scared again, overwhelmed by exam prep. *It's coming back*, I thought, my pulse quickening. I sat on the edge of my bed and tried the breathing exercise Evelyn had taught me. After a few minutes, I realised I was feeling more lucid, my pulse steady and strong.

I was grateful that it hadn't turned into a full panic attack, but another part of me was frustrated that I had not conquered my anxiety yet. All of my health issues took so long to fix – months in recovery after the shooting, years of surgeries to restore my facial symmetry. This was my last year of university, and I wanted to feel better already, to return to my fun, independent life before the responsibilities of the real world took over.

A few sessions later, Evelyn and I talked about my inclination to divide the world into good and bad people, why Hen's joke had shocked and disoriented me. She told me that this binary way of thinking was causing me more anxiety and paranoia, narrowing my window of tolerance. Everyone is capable of kindness. Everyone, including me, has hurt people we love.

I had been avoiding Hen since the Brandon incident, declining her dinner invites and studying in the library instead of my room. I took Evelyn's words into consideration. Hen had had a bad moment, but she wasn't a bad person. It felt like Evelyn was giving me permission to trust my friends again.

'That night, the prank about Brandon really messed me up, made me feel so disoriented,' I told Hen the next time she stopped by my room.

'Aw, babe! Why didn't you tell me?' she said.

'I was *trying* to tell you.'

She looked at the floor and I continued, 'After you left, I had a panic attack. It was scary, Hen, like I thought I would die. But that wasn't the first time or the last. It's been happening a lot, so I finally decided to see a therapist.'

'I'm so sorry, Malz. I had no idea.'

'It's okay. Normally what you did would just *really* annoy me,' I joked. 'It's not your fault that I had such a bad reaction. I just wanted you to know I'm not upset. But also I'm still working on this, and I feel pretty delicate right now. So maybe don't try to test my gullibility for a while?'

'No more fake boyfriends – I promise!' she said. 'The truth is, I haven't been on a date in forever. My love life is in its flop era. I'll open the apps and be like, "Is this phone on airplane mode?" What is happening?! Just tumbleweeds in the DMs . . .'

Hen went on and on, and I laughed for the first time in weeks, feeling happy that I could enjoy the simple pleasure of chatting with a friend again. Little by little, I was finding my way back to myself.

LATER THAT WEEK I had a long call with Asser. He knew I was going to therapy – and that I didn't want to talk about it every time we spoke. It was nice to hear his voice and catch up on his latest news. But after we hung up, I found myself thinking about the state of our relationship. The next day I wrote in my emotional log: *Preoccupied with thoughts about my boyfriend. How do I know whether my feelings for him are real or not? I am looking for an answer . . .*

'What do I do about him?' I asked in my final therapy session before the Christmas break. 'How can I be sure we're meant to be together? And if we can't be, how do I stop feeling in love with him?'

Evelyn smiled. 'Well, Malala, you might be better off asking a poet or musician that question. Therapy can only go so far.

'I can tell you this, not just about relationships, but every big decision you face – there are different paths through this wonderful journey of life, and whichever one you pick will bring different problems and different rewards. When you make a choice, don't look back and imagine that there were other better options. Make the best decision you can with what you happen to know at the time and then explore, enjoy, meet the challenges.'

That evening, I took a walk to the river and thought of Abai. Whenever she came to visit our home in Mingora, she would sleep in my room. As she grew older, she didn't like sleeping indoors, so my parents made up cots for us to sleep on the porch. Abai would fall asleep quickly, but I would stay awake looking up at the stars and imagining myself one day studying physics, even going to space. I pictured the many places on earth I wanted to see as well, imagining all the possibilities for my future, my own ever-expanding universe.

Tonight I thought of constellations closer to home – and how quickly they could change. At fifteen, I had almost died. Survival and recovery didn't mean reclaiming everything I had lost. Abai and I might never sleep under the stars together again. I would never know the person I could have been in Pakistan. And if the shooting hadn't happened, I would not have gone to Oxford and had wild adventures with my friends. Girls in Shangla would not have a high school. *Different paths through life, each with its own challenges and joys.*

Who knew what would happen next? Maybe Asser and I would end up together, maybe not. I might pass my exams and come up with the perfect post-Oxford plan, or move back home with my parents. Perhaps the panic attacks would never completely go away, and I would have to fight them off each time. But I felt stronger now, able to face all I had lost and all the uncertainties ahead.

28.

On January 1, 2020, I sat on my bed in Birmingham making a list of things I wanted to do before graduation. I hadn't had a panic attack in weeks. The relief I experienced was not a manic high, but that of a breaking fever – serene at first, then followed by excitement and impatience to rejoin the world.

Now, going into the second term of my third and final year of university, I was determined to make up for lost time. I wanted to drink tea in my favourite café, spend lazy afternoons by the river and have all the classic Oxford adventures I'd yet to experience in my first two years – crossing the Bridge of Sighs, taking in the view from the top of Radcliffe Camera, watching horses roam across Port Meadow. Instead of saying yes to every invitation, I would guard my time and reserve it for my closest friends, the people I missed when they weren't around. But I wouldn't let my social life get so busy that I fell behind in my studies and stayed up all night trying to catch up. I planned to keep writing in my journal and practising the breathing exercises Evelyn had taught me. After three years of university, I finally felt like I had the tools to keep my life in balance.

When I returned to my flat at the end of the holidays, everyone on our floor seemed to be getting along better. There were no shouting matches, and about half as many kitchen and noise complaints on the group chat. I smiled when I heard them laughing in the kitchen together or when we all gathered for dinner. The initial growing pains of going from friends to roommates were behind us, and I was overjoyed to have my girl gang back together again.

I was also thankful we'd all made up in time for our annual Galentines' Day brunch, an event I looked forward to every February. The tradition had started in our first year, as an attempt to cheer up Cora after a break-up. From there it morphed into a general celebration and an excuse to bring everyone together.

I wouldn't get out of bed early for anything other than morning lectures, but on Galentines' Day, I was up with the sun. After sending a brunch reminder to the group chat, I popped into Yasmin's room to work on a playlist, adding a couple of songs from each of our friends' favourite artists – a peculiar jumble of Stevie Wonder, M83, Stormzy, Billie Eilish and more.

Thump, thump. Back in my room getting dressed, I opened the door to find Cora gently kicking it, both her hands around a large flower arrangement. 'For you,' she said, winking. I opened the card – from Asser, of course. He never forgot a holiday or a special occasion. I sent him a thank-you message, then tucked his card in my desk. *A perfect centrepiece for brunch!* I thought. I appreciated Asser's thoughtful gesture, but today was for the girls.

In the kitchen, Hen blew up balloons, and I hung them on the wall alongside some multicoloured bunting I'd bought. 'What do you think?' I asked her halfway through.

'Well . . .' she said, trying to contain the giggle in her voice. 'You've put everything at eye level. Like, *your* eye level. There's a lot of empty wall above your head, shorty. Let me help.'

'Yeah, that's better,' I said when she'd rehung the decorations. 'It still looks a bit sad, though, and I don't have anything else to add. Unless . . .' I grabbed the tape and stuck a heart-shaped red paper plate on the wall.

Hen cracked up. 'Nobody's gonna put it on Pinterest, but . . . sure, that works!'

I'd planned to serve heart-shaped waffles as well, but the novelty waffle maker I'd ordered had not arrived by the morning of the brunch. Anisa, who had volunteered to cook, found me standing in the kitchen, furiously scrolling my phone to order takeaway. She riffled through my bag of supplies and said, 'Okay, relax. We've got waffle mix, which is basically the same thing as pancake mix. Step aside, please.' Then she pulled her hair into a ponytail, took out a frying pan and cooking oil, and went to work churning out batches of perfectly fluffy pancakes.

After everyone had arrived, we took our seats and clinked our mismatched mugs in a toast to friendship. 'To our last Galentines' Day!' Hen said.

'Ugh, no, don't remind me,' Yasmin grumbled. 'That means it's only four months to exams.'

'How about some rules of order for this brunch?' Anisa said. 'No discussion of exams, essays or tutorials.'

'And no mention of love interests,' Hen added. 'Or lack of love interests.'

When I turned on my playlist, Cora rolled her eyes. 'Please tell me you've spared us that Future song that Hen played on repeat all of our first year!'

I laughed. 'Oh, it's on here! It wouldn't be our last Galentines' Day if we didn't relive our questionable choices.'

That set my friends off, listing all the embarrassing things they'd done: *Waking up alone at a desk in the library at 2 a.m. Trying to make a cheese toastie with an iron. Getting mono from making out with too many people during Freshers' Week.*

'Jelly shots,' Hen volunteered.

'Oh, I remember jelly shots!' I said. 'You and Cora busted into my room singing One Direction songs. Or slurring them actually. I'd never seen a drunk person before!'

'Your face!' Cora snorted.

'Yeah, well, we had only just met a week earlier, and that night Hen kept telling me she loved me,' I added. 'It was extremely confusing! Like, should I say, "I love you too"? Was it rude not to? I had no idea!'

'Not the first or last time she's put one of us to bed after a night out,' Yasmin said.

Anisa covered her face with her hands and said, 'I just remembered the time I sent her to get me bagels the next morning. Oof, sorry, Malz.'

'A toast to our Hangover Helper!' Hen cheered.

The kitchen door swung open and a startled face stared back at us. 'ALAN!' everyone roared.

'Sorry, guys, didn't mean to interrupt the party,' he replied. 'Just got back from the library and grabbing a snack before econometrics study group.'

'Isn't that later this afternoon?' Anisa asked.

'Uh, it's two-thirty now, so in half an hour.'

Everyone grabbed their phones to check the time, surprised to learn we'd been chatting for so long. 'Wait, Alan,' I said. 'Can you take a picture of us before you go?' The photo he snapped that afternoon remains one of my favourites from Oxford – half-eaten pancakes, plates on the wall and all my friends smiling from ear to ear.

As I cleaned up the kitchen afterwards, my brain ticked through the list of philosophy texts I needed to reread for exams. That night I opened Aristotle's *Nicomachean Ethics*, much of which is dedicated to his thoughts on friendship. Three years prior, when I'd read 'The wish to be friends can come about quickly, but friendship cannot,' it had made me sad. I didn't like the idea of waiting so long to feel close to someone, as if it was a skill you had to master over many years.

I understood it better now. It took effort to see past differences in someone's background, beliefs or personality. It took courage to be vulnerable, to share the embarrassing and scary parts of yourself – the parts you don't even understand – with friends. It took humility to repair your connections, to forgive and be forgiven.

Friendship is the only type of love available to all of us, at any point in our lives; it is common, often overlooked, unmarked by major holidays. To me, friends should be embraced with the same magnitude of wonder and care that we feel for lovers and family members. When I started university, I just wanted to be less lonely. Three years later, I felt like I belonged – not simply included, but loved.

I kept my promise to myself to enjoy as much of Oxford as possible that term. My memories from those three months are some of the happiest of my university years – dancing with Zayan at the Bollywood Bop, binge-watching *Sex Education* with Hen, gossiping in the kitchen until 4 a.m. with Cora and Yasmin. At the Polo Club Ball, I stood outdoors under a space heater and laughed as Anisa arrived on her horse – a cowboy in an evening gown.

On the last night before the spring holidays, Sofia threw herself a birthday party at a high-street bar. She and I sat side by side in a demilune booth like queens granting an audience to the public. A stream of friends drifted in and out, dropping by between stops on the end-of-term party circuit or on their way to catch a night train out of town. 'Have a good holiday! See you in April!' we said.

The next day I loaded my bag into the car and settled in for the drive to Birmingham, ready to relax before exam season. As we pulled away, I looked back at Lady Margaret Hall, feeling grateful for the bounty of experiences I'd had that winter – completely unaware that they were a farewell tour, that my days as an Oxford student were already over.

29.

I sat on my bed reading and rereading the email: *All teaching and assessment next term will take place remotely.* Then I texted all my friends to make sure I wasn't misinterpreting the words. They confirmed the bad news: Oxford was closed for the spring term; tutorials, exams and likely graduation would be online.

Covid was new and scary – they had no other choice. But I couldn't help but feel stunned and heartbroken at the loss. I would miss the warm weather months with my friends, walking down to the river in my pyjamas at sunrise, climbing up to the bell tower at night, post-exam parties and tearful goodbyes. For the third time in my twenty-two years, I'd been forced out of a place I loved and a life I was building for myself.

But graduation is months away, I thought. *Surely it will be over by then and we'll go back.* So many students had travelled to their home countries for the five-week break. Now we were all stuck as borders closed and flights were cancelled. I didn't want to believe I might never see them again, so I told myself that wouldn't happen, that this would get sorted out and we'd be back after a few weeks, a month at most.

While I tried to maintain hope for a return to Oxford, my mum couldn't hide her happiness at having all her children under the same roof again with nowhere to go and no one to see but each other. She spent the afternoons cooking – chicken pilau, curried okra, paratha – and insisted my brothers and I sit at the table and eat together every night.

I noticed my dad watching me at dinner. 'You should have more chicken,' he'd say, heaping food on my plate before I could protest. During the day, he barged into my room with bowls of fruit cut into neat squares. 'Please eat it,' he'd insist, then stand over me to make sure I did.

After a couple weeks of this, I was done. 'Enough, Dad! You are not allowed to stare at my plate or monitor my diet. I eat what and when I want to. Sometimes I like to have extra chicken. Sometimes I don't. But the moment you interfere, I feel like a child who can't make a choice for herself. If your goal is to get me to eat more, then leave me alone.'

He switched up his tactics. When I sat down in the living room, a bowl of fruit would magically appear on the coffee table. 'I am not asking anyone to eat this,' he'd announce, even though we were the only two in the room. 'I'm just pointing out that it's here should someone want it.' Or he would sit on the sofa by himself, peeling an orange: 'Wow, this is the best orange I've ever had in my life! If you don't taste it, you're really missing out.' Most of the time, I rolled my eyes and went about my business, but on occasion I sat down and ate the orange to keep him from backsliding into more aggressive fruit-marketing efforts.

My mum, on the other hand, kept trying to give me a makeover.

'Why do you have to wear these grey clothes, Malala?' she asked, pointing at my leggings and cosy jumper. 'Go and change into something more colourful. Put on some earrings for once.'

'It makes no sense to dress up only to sit at home all day. No one is looking at me.'

'I don't understand – you wear sad clothes, have no interest in fashion, never want to go shopping. You are too young to stop enjoying your life.' If her favourite Pakistani dress shops weren't closed because of lockdown, I had no doubt she would have taken me shopping and forced me to 'enjoy my life' for hours a day. I thumped upstairs and came back in a pink shalwar kameez just so she would stop complaining.

Being at home felt like going in reverse. As soon as I stepped through their door, my parents saw me as a child again, a daughter in need of supervision and direction. Did they not realise I'd been managing my life for the last two and a half years? At Oxford, I'd overcome so much – nerves over making friends, poor study skills, heartbreak, mental health challenges – and I'd done it on my own. Part of me wanted to tell them everything, to show them I could handle myself, but a bigger part wanted to retain what little privacy I had at home.

While they still thought of me as a little girl, I noticed how much my parents had changed while I was at university. Since my dad no longer travelled with me for speaking engagements or advocacy work, they had settled into a new domestic routine: he picked up some chores and looked after my brothers, while my mum had more time for leisure and her English language classes. In years past, I rarely saw my dad in the kitchen; now he fried eggs for breakfast and vacuumed under the table after dinner. The entire house knew when he was doing dishes because he clanged the pots and pans around like a one-man marching band, leaving behind a trail of sudsy water on the floor and a shaky tower of cookware piled high on the drying mat. My mum found the transformation amusing. 'When guests come over and see him standing at the sink in his apron, they say, "How impressive, what a good man,"' she snickered. 'I did these things my whole life and nobody gave me a parade!'

During lockdown, Dad did all the shopping as well. It gave him an excuse to get out of the house and talk to strangers, one of his favourite pastimes. He was bewildered and sad at the start of the pandemic, when people crossed to the other side of the street to avoid coming too close to him. Social distancing was a concept he could never quite grasp.

My mother tried and failed to get him to stay at home. One afternoon she sat on the couch lamenting the grey hair cropping up around her temples and wishing she could go to the salon. 'Toor Pekai, do you remember the Pashtun legend about the woman who had no food for dinner and the man who went on an epic hunt through the forest to prove his love?' my dad asked. 'I will take up this quest for your hair dye!'

'You may bring the hunt, Ziauddin, but you will also bring coronavirus!' she yelled after him, but he was already halfway out the door. Three days later, he sequestered himself in the guest bedroom, suffering joint pains and a fever.

As the weeks wore on, both my irritation at being stuck at home and my hope that things would change blanded out into a spiritless monotony. Every time I left my room to make tea, it seemed smaller when I came back. I tried to break up the days with computer games like *Among Us*, Netflix binges and awkward birthday parties on Zoom. When I ran out of ideas, I picked up a dull pair of desk scissors and gave myself a fringe.

Right before the pandemic, Asser had taken a prestigious job as a performance manager for the Pakistan Cricket Board. Our country is so obsessed with cricket that his office never went remote during lockdowns and his team was among the first to get the vaccine. He worked all day and I tried to keep him on the phone all night. After a few hours of talking to me, he would yawn and say, 'All right, I need to do my prayers and get to bed.'

'Pray for my exams!' I said.

'I will, but maybe you should also study for them?'

'Pray that this will be over soon so we can see each other again.'

'*Inshallah.*'

'And pray for all the people who are ill, of course.'

'I always do. *Goodnight*, Malala.'

My brothers might have provided some distraction were they not lost in their own worlds. Atal, the youngest, had always been able to turn my mood around. In my lonely high-school years, he'd provided hours of entertainment. I cracked up at his rising exasperation as he tried to explain the foreign concept of a sleepover to my parents or teach them new words like 'burrito'.

But he was a teenager now, and I saw less and less of him. During lockdown, he spent all day in his room, writing rap lyrics or computer code. More than once, he faked a cough to get out of Mum's mandatory dinners. And sometimes, when my parents went to sleep, he'd slip out the back door and vanish for hours. He became a hologram in the house, only a blurry version of himself appearing here, while the real Atal existed somewhere I couldn't see.

Meanwhile, my middle brother, Khushal, was having his own academic crisis. At high school, he'd spent more time playing video games and smoking weed than studying. To no one's surprise but his own, he had failed his A levels and couldn't get into university.

When he made the decision to retake the tests during the pandemic, Khushal threw himself into his studies. He commandeered our living room, piling up books, flash cards and practice essays on every available surface. My dad rejoiced, believing his wayward son had finally become a serious student. As the only one in the house who understood the level of concentration that A levels required, I was more sceptical. But either way, Khushal was too preoccupied saving himself to spend time with me.

The group chat pinged less and less as the weeks went by. Maybe my Oxford friends were focused on exam prep or enjoying their time at home, having socially distanced get-togethers with their high-school pals. Or maybe they were feeling the same as me – stripped of the life I'd created for myself at university and realising that, without my friends, without our inside jokes and midnight snack runs, without our favourite restaurants and hidden corners of campus, without Club Nights and essay deadlines, I had little to say.

30.

In my parents' house, I turned nocturnal, drawing the curtains and climbing into bed at the first hint of daylight. *The days don't count if you can't see them*, I decided. I felt hollow and listless, a bit depressed. If I had been able to laugh, I would have found it funny that Evelyn and I had never covered this type of mental illness. My anxiety at university was unpredictable, explosive and violent. I had learnt to interrupt a panic attack, but not how to stop this slow-creeping void.

From the day I came home, my mum and dad had been badgering me to join them on their nightly stroll through the neighbourhood. After reading an article on 'low mood' that suggested that exercise, particularly walking outside, could help, I relented and agreed to go with them. Just one time.

My mum ambled out of our house and down the street where

the pavement deposited us at the top of a steep concrete stairway. 'Where are we going?' I asked.

'To the canals!' she replied. Though I'd lived here for four years of high school, I had not set foot alongside any part of Birmingham's extensive waterway system. Built during the Industrial Revolution to haul iron and coal to London, the canals were eventually repurposed for leisure activities like running and kayaking. My mum led us along the pebble footpath by the water, under tree canopies and old bridges. Why had I spent so much time cooped up in my room when this sanctuary existed two streets from our house? I should have realised, by that point, that the outdoors always brightened my spirits.

We exited the canals via another long flight of stairs. When we reached the top, we were standing near a football pitch. My mum pointed to a brick building across the field. 'See where the grass ends?' she asked. 'That's my gym.'

'Your . . . gym?' I was struggling to keep up with all this new information. The mum I knew had never shown a hint of interest in sport or fitness. I looked over at my dad, who was smiling proudly at her.

'I had just started weight-lifting right before everything shut down,' she sighed.

My eyes bugged out and I felt almost lightheaded for a moment. The mum I remembered was decidedly not a gym rat. Before we came to the UK, she had not travelled far beyond Mingora and never outside of Pakistan. At first, Birmingham's lifts and escalators terrified her. She startled at everything from street musicians to skyscrapers. After I was released from hospital, she rarely left the house.

My dad, my brothers and I could all speak in Pashto, Urdu and English. Because my mum had not gone to school, she could only speak Pashto, the language she'd heard as a child. In Mingora, she chatted all day with neighbours as they cooked over wood fires and hung their laundry to dry in the yard. In Birmingham, she could not, as my father put it, 'convey to anyone but us the thoughts in her head or the emotions in her heart'. As her oldest child lay hovering between life and death in hospital, she had no friend with whom she could pray.

For the first three years we lived in Birmingham, my mum cried every single day. She would call our relatives in Pakistan and talk for seven or eight hours at a time. The first phrase she learnt in English was 'top up' so she could refill the minutes on her mobile phone card at the corner shop.

Eventually she started settling into her new home. She made a few friends. She learnt the bus route to Ladypool Road, where you can find shops selling shalwar kameez and halal meat. When she didn't feel like cooking, she sent my dad to pick up roti and kebabs from a restaurant. She didn't cry as much, but I always had the sense that she was treading water, waiting for her 'real life' to start again in Pakistan.

On our first evening walk, my mum revealed how much she had moved on. She talked about Janet, her former English teacher and now a close friend. 'We have movie nights because she thinks that watching will help me learn the language,' she said. 'But her choices are so boring, I always fall asleep!' My mum preferred films featuring Mr Bean, whose physical comedy needed no translation. I overheard her on the phone with Janet some nights while she made dinner and was shocked at how much her English had improved. My mum had clearly put more effort into her studies than I'd put into mine over the last three years.

The following night we walked in the opposite direction, towards Queen Elizabeth Hospital, where my mum had spent every day during the months of my recovery. Before the pandemic, she visited patients there a few times a week. My parents quietly helped cover the costs for other Pakistani children, victims of violence like me, to come to Birmingham for surgeries to repair their limbs, faces and teeth. When their families couldn't accompany them, she brought them home-cooked meals and used the knowledge she'd gained from my time in hospital to make sure they received the best care.

She was even planning to travel alone, to take her sisters on a girls' trip to Dubai once it was safe to fly again. In Mingora, she wouldn't leave the house without my dad or one of my brothers; few Pashtun women would face the scrutiny and shame of breaking our society's rules. I was happy to see her building a life for herself now. And, as she claimed her independence, I hoped she might extend some of it to me.

My mum and I had never enjoyed the easy, warm relationship I had with my dad. As a child, I was scared of drawing her ire, which I seemed to do every day. She was strict and didn't hesitate to punish me, often physically, when I fell short of her standards. I didn't feel like I could talk to her at all. When I got my first period at eleven years old, I told my dad and asked him to buy menstrual pads for me.

She refused to relax the social norms I'd known growing up when we moved to the UK. My brothers could do whatever they liked, but I was forbidden to wear Western clothes or go to high-school parties. She shouted at me if I let my scarf slip off my head in public or stood too close to a man in a photo. I was an adult now, but her rebukes still stung, and I gave in to almost all her demands.

When I'd spent time with Asser the previous summer, she admonished me every time I left the house: we were not allowed to be alone, we were not to take photos together, we had to stay ten feet apart at all times. Of course, I broke all of these rules – but

I didn't feel great about deceiving my mum. I knew she was only trying to protect me.

She understood how dangerous a bad reputation could be to a Pashtun woman. My mum mourned women and girls we knew – a fifteen-year-old poisoned by her family for looking too long at a boy on the street, a woman strangled to death for running away from her abusive husband. She heard the news of a student hanged for speaking to a man at her university, a woman shot because her father saw a picture of her on Facebook, four women murdered for dancing at a wedding. We were thousands of miles away now, but my mum still lived in fear of me losing my 'honour'. I could trace each of her concerns back to those we had buried.

When I was thirteen years old, my mum brought a girl named Apana to live with us. She was my age, and her father had died when she was a baby, leaving her mother to clean homes for a few rupees a week to support the children. My mum decided that Apana would share my bedroom and go to my dad's school for free. He and I had no say in the matter.

Shortly after she arrived, I noticed Apana was sick all the time. She would go pale and run outside to vomit. 'You're always ill, you must be pregnant!' I joked. The only thing I knew about how a girl got pregnant was what I'd seen on Indian soap operas. A man and a woman looked longingly at each other; in the next scene, she was throwing up. Then came a big belly and, finally, a baby.

One day my mum took Apana out of the house without mentioning where they were headed. When they returned, Apana slept for hours. After that day, she wasn't sick any more. Years later I heard the story: the girl had been in a park on her own one afternoon when a man approached her. He said he was visiting from Dubai and seemed friendly, even inviting Apana to see his hotel room. She'd never been inside a hotel, so she said yes. As soon as the door closed, he raped her.

Abortion is illegal in Pakistan, except to save the life of the mother, and is punishable by three to ten years in prison, depending on how far the foetus has developed. If I had asked my mum whether she supported reproductive rights, she would have said no. She might have added that none of this would have happened if Apana had followed the rules, stayed inside her house and never talked to men. But she knew the fate of an unmarried, pregnant thirteen-year-old in our society. And she risked what little freedom she had to save a girl's life.

My mum was a hero, brave and generous. She was also judgemental, unsparing and strict, especially with me. I longed for a day when I could tell her all my secrets and call her my friend. In the meantime, I laced up my trainers and joined her evening stroll every night.

31.

In the month before exams, I never needed to set an early-morning alarm; I woke up at dawn, my mind already racing with practice essays and problem sets. During the day, I combed through my notes and participated in Zoom study groups with Cora and the other PPE students. I was pleased to discover that I'd retained more than I had realised, and started to feel a bit of excitement about the approaching finish line.

'You're working so hard that I'm concerned about study burn-out,' Valerie said in one of our remote study skills sessions. 'You don't have the same fun distractions as you did at Oxford, but try to take a break and reward yourself once in a while.'

As soon as she said that, I realised how much I missed take-away dinner nights, the times when my friends and I would all order from a different place and then sit on the floor in my room sampling each other's meals. I told my mum to take the night off from cooking and ordered hamburgers from Five Guys and mango mochi from Kyoto Grill for dessert. The next night, I ordered us falafel and salads from Shawarma City. A few days later, we compared the spicy chicken dishes at Nando's and Pepe's Piri Piri.

Hen told me she and her sister liked a place called TGI Fridays. I had never heard of it, but when I scrolled through the menu, I saw that the barbecue ribs were the most popular item and had them delivered. My family was obsessed with the meal, and asked me to order the exact same thing almost every night for two weeks. The next time I spoke to Hen, I thanked her for the tip. 'We can't get enough!'

'Um, before I say what I'm about to say, I want you to remember that I recommended the *restaurant*, not the *ribs*,' she replied. 'Malala . . . you've been eating pork!'

I gasped and immediately googled it to make sure she wasn't pranking me again. Pork is haram, forbidden to Muslims by multiple verses of scripture. It wasn't technically a sin if you did it unwittingly, but what God might forgive, I suspected my mum would not. When I confessed the mistake to my family, though, no one got mad or said I'd been careless. They were too caught up in the disappointment of learning that our rib-eating days were done.

Asser was my other 'reward' at the end of every day. Around 1:30 a.m., when my brain was tired from studying, I would sit in the window seat in my room, look up at the stars, and call him. 'I've been reading a little bit of astronomy at night to clear my head,' I told him one night. 'Supposedly Jupiter and Saturn are having some sort of big conjunction. They're the two brightest planets so I thought I'd be able to see them. But maybe you need a telescope for that because all I see is the moon.'

For a couple of weeks, our calls included my nightly astronomy report. He listened to my bleary-eyed rambling about stars and planets, how I wished I could get a better view. Meanwhile, it was 5 a.m. in Lahore and he was just waking up before getting dressed and heading to his office at the Cricket Board. I suspected he was only half listening to me, and I couldn't blame him. Still, I loved that he was the last person I spoke to before going to bed.

⌒

ON THE MORNING of my first exam – macroeconomics, my most challenging subject – I woke up early and dressed in my black academic robes. The clothes weren't required at home, as they would have been if I were taking the test at Oxford, but I wanted to honour the tradition, to give the moment the weight it deserved.

My dad made me eggs and toast, but I was too nervous to eat more than a couple of bites. 'Don't worry,' he said. 'I have every confidence that you will get the highest possible marks!' He had been exaggerating my academic abilities since the day I was born, but I didn't have time to manage his expectations this morning.

'Promise me you'll keep the house quiet. Don't let *anyone* knock on my door.' He gave me a solemn nod, like a knight turning his horse towards the battle.

The exam began at 9:30 a.m. I had four hours to solve three complex maths problems, write two essays and upload my answers. I used up fifty minutes on the first question. As I was reading over the second problem, my bedroom door swung open. My dad stood there, wide-eyed and smiling with a cup of tea and a plate of biscuits in his hand. Before he could speak, I glared at him and went back to my work. He set the mug on my desk and tiptoed out of the room.

When it was over, I stomped downstairs. 'What did I tell you? No interruptions! I don't have time for a single sip of tea during an exam.'

'You said "don't knock"!' he replied, bewildered.

There wasn't much time to feel relieved that I was done with macroeconomics for the rest of my life, as it was only the first of eight exams spread over three weeks. As soon as I finished a test, I would jump on a group call with the other PPE students for a debrief. I was glad when we all found the same questions difficult, as it meant I hadn't been the only one ill-prepared for a particular topic or problem. After we hung up, I'd dive into preparing for the next exam. I would study in five-hour blocks, take a short break to eat, and plunge back into my books.

In the middle of all this, people kept contacting me to participate in TV programmes and online events meant to encourage other students who were missing their last month of high school or university because of Covid. I was exhausted and didn't want to do any of it. 'Doesn't anyone realise that I'm also trying to graduate right now?' I snapped at Maria. But I still had not learnt to say no, especially not when LeBron James, who was organising a star-studded virtual graduation ceremony, made the request. In the middle of my second week of exams, producers and camera operators were lugging equipment through my parents' house and setting up in the backyard. I spent an afternoon shivering in the rain while they filmed me smiling and congratulating the class of 2020. The whole time I could only worry about how much exam prep I was missing. *Failing to graduate because I was busy doing virtual graduations for other people will be my villain origin story*, I thought.

When I remembered all the third-year traditions I was missing at Oxford, my sense of disappointment was intense. If I were still on campus, I would exit the Examination Halls after my last-ever exam, step into the sunshine and participate in the hallowed Oxford tradition of 'trashing', where friends gather around a newly liberated scholar and cover her in shaving foam, confetti, custard pies, canned beans – anything sticky and messy. The chaos ends with everyone jumping in the River Cherwell together to wash off the mess.

It was a trivial thing to obsess over, but I had been looking forward to that moment ever since I'd watched my first trashing two years ago. Determined to salvage what I could, I ordered all the typical trashing supplies and gave them to my dad to distribute on the big day. It wouldn't be the same without my friends, but any celebration was better than the anticlimax of closing my laptop and announcing 'I'm done with university!' to an empty bedroom.

If my first exam was the hardest, my last, Politics in South Asia, was a breeze. When it was over, I bounced out of my chair, and headed downstairs to find my family in the living room, holding cans of whipped cream and bags of glitter. They looked uneasily at each other, waiting for someone to make the first move.

'No, not here! You'll ruin the furniture!' I cried. 'Go outside!'

My brothers unleashed their inner vandals in the backyard, emptying cans of Silly String directly into my hair. I covered my face with my hands to protect my eyes and alternated between screaming, laughing and shouting curses in Pashto. *We should have warned the neighbours*, I thought. They chased me around the garden with packets of Holi powder and confetti until everything I'd bought was used up.

In a picture of that day, I look like something from a children's book – a more silly than scary monster with a patchy white foam beard and brightly coloured paper feathers poking out of my head. The boys are in T-shirts, their forearms netted with Silly String and their hair sparkling like cartoon fairies. My mum, who was hit with a cloud of neon-yellow powder, looks like someone dragged a giant highlighter over her face. Somehow my dad, in his smart navy blazer and leather lace-ups, emerged unscathed.

In the years since I left Oxford and students returned to in-person classes, university officials have tried to crack down on trashing, claiming it's wasteful and expensive to clean up. But I think they're unlikely to kill the tradition. To me, it seemed that only something so ridiculous, something with no purpose other than to joyfully make the biggest possible mess, could carry us from the underworld of exams back to normal life. I was happy to join the long line of students who took one last moment to be care-free before stepping into adulthood.

⌒

EXAMS WERE OVER, but I couldn't fully relax until Oxford released my results and I was certain that I'd earned a degree. While I waited, my family learnt that Atal had done well in his GCSEs. Even better, Khushal had brought his A-level marks up enough to get into university.

My dad was thrilled with the boys. I tried to manage his expectations and warn him that my results might be disappointing. Over the years, Lara had informed me several times that I was on track for Lower Second Class Honours – the stamp of mediocrity assigned to those whose work was, on the whole, without effort or excellence – and I wasn't confident that I had done enough in the past year to bring myself up a level.

'Look, I'm not a genius,' I explained to my dad. He opened his mouth to argue, but I kept going. 'I would have had to work really hard to get a First Class degree. You can't have a good life and good grades at Oxford. So even if I get a 2:2, wouldn't you rather I was happy at university?' He said, 'Of course, Malala,' and I hoped he meant it.

My friends in other disciplines started receiving their results – a First for Zayan! Upper Second for Sofia, Yasmin and Hen! Since

Anisa already had a job lined up, she'd taken predicted marks and skipped exams.

Then I got a text from Cora: 2:1! Have you checked yet?

I typed my name and password into the portal, closed my eyes and hit enter. *All you need to do is pass*, I said to myself, as if I could change the result at this point. When I finally looked at the screen, I saw:

Malala Yousafzai
BA in Philosophy, Politics and Economics
Final Award: Second Class, Division One

I blinked. It took me a minute to realise that I'd also scored a 2:1. Upon further inspection, I saw that I'd made the cut-off by a single percentage point. But who cares about that? I'd made it! I sprinted downstairs to tell my parents, then ran back upstairs to text my friends and call Asser.

After sharing the good news with everyone I knew, I collapsed backwards on my bed, still buzzing with happiness. That's when I realised: I won. From the time I was a girl, I had carried this dream of graduating from university, even when I didn't know a single woman who had done it. *I won't be a teenage bride and spend my life wondering what I could have contributed to the world*, I had told myself. *I will go to university*. The Taliban had forced me out of school when I was eleven years old and tried to kill me when I was fifteen. With bombs and guns, they'd fought against little girls who only wanted to learn, to understand the world around them. There were long periods of my childhood and teen years when even finishing high school seemed impossible.

I am not someone who believes everyone should go to university; I know plenty of brilliant people who don't have a degree.

But, for me, education was my guiding light, the only way I could save myself from a life I didn't want.

Now, no matter where my life went next, I was a university graduate, and I always would be. It didn't mean the end of misogyny or an enduring triumph for the right to education, of course. This was a personal victory. Between me and the men who'd tried to stop me, the fight was over. I had won.

32.

Two weeks after I received my exam results, the security team drove me back to Lady Margaret Hall to collect everything I'd left in my room before the spring holidays.

As I stood at the front gate waiting for the porter to buzz me in, the quiet unsettled me – no students calling to each other across the lawn, no music drifting from open windows or food delivery bikers ringing their bells at passing cars. The normally pristine hedges were overgrown, and weeds sprouted in the flower beds. It felt like someone had cast an evil spell on Lady Margaret Hall, stopping time and turning it into a haunted place.

It looked so different from the first time I saw this beautiful campus as a high-school student on a prospective college tour. After visiting the library, dining hall and accommodation that day, I had hung back and let my guidance counsellor chat with our guide; I was hoping for a quiet moment to get a sense of the place. We followed a winding path past formal gardens, woods and meadows full of wildflowers. The landscape felt so familiar to me, even though I'd never been there. When the trail ended at a riverbank dotted with daffodils, I stood watching the late-afternoon sun glint off the surface of the River Cherwell. It was all so dreamy; I envisioned myself spending hours in that very spot, sitting by the water until the stars came out.

Some people assume that I chose Lady Margaret Hall because it was the first women's college at Oxford. Or because Benazir Bhutto, Pakistan's first female prime minister, studied PPE there. They imagine I had some master plan to follow in her footsteps and one day lead my country.

The truth is: the flowers on campus reminded me of Swat Valley in the springtime, and the lazy swirls of the Cherwell brought back memories of the streams and rivers in Mingora. For the first time since moving to the UK, I had found a place that felt like home.

And now it was time to say goodbye.

⌒

PACKING ANYTHING, EVEN an overnight bag, always makes me melancholy. I tend to wait until the last possible minute, throw some things into my luggage, and, without fail, arrive at my destination missing a toothbrush or socks. Lingering too long in the flat – to neatly fold my Diwali ball gown or consider why I'd dog-eared the page of a book – would only dredge up memories of all the homes and people I've had to leave behind.

As I entered my room, I found it precisely as I left it, albeit dustier. I loaded my belongings as quickly as possible, not even stopping to label the boxes. When I was finished, I drifted down the long hall towards the common space, running my hands along the door frames of each friend's empty room. The kitchen was dark, quiet and cleaner than I'd ever seen it, scoured of the literal and emotional messes we'd made while learning to be adults.

I stepped out onto the little balcony off the kitchen and scanned the horizon, my eyes landing on the bell tower. I'd climbed it so many times, but I couldn't recall the very last one. *It must have been in February or March*, I thought. *Who was with me?* It bothered me that I couldn't remember – because I knew I'd never do it again, never be the person I was when I flew across the rooftops.

Something moved and caught my eye on the ground below – *Yasmin!* She was there, reading a book on the bench where I'd first met Tarik. My heart leapt, but I didn't call out to her – somewhere inside I knew that this must be some sort of waking dream, that she wasn't really there. Then I heard laughter and saw Hen rounding the corner, talking a mile a minute on her phone. In the distance, Cora and Anisa lugged their backpacks into University Park and towards the lecture halls.

The quad filled up with friends and acquaintances, professors and librarians. Raja, Parveen and everyone from 24 Obs were playing music and dancing. Zayan bounced from foot to foot excitedly as Sofia laughed. I spotted Lara, Valerie and the professor who always gave me a permissive smirk when he knew I hadn't done the reading. There was the guy who wore his pyjamas to breakfast every morning and the girl who coached the rowing club. I saw faces I couldn't place too – groups of friends picnicking and chatting, people I'd never met. At some point, I realised that these strangers were our inheritors, the next batch of students who would fill this place with curiosity, laughter and longing. My college would be theirs soon.

Some religions believe in the concept of the 'astral plane', a space between heaven and earth where the souls of those who have passed away mingle with those yet to be born. That's the closest description I can find for what I experienced that day, seeing backwards and forward, past and future, at the same time. It only lasted a few moments. The sun emerged from behind a cloud, I blinked, and everyone was gone.

I stepped off the balcony and back into the kitchen, my heart full of love and gratitude. I thought I understood what the vision was meant to teach me, the last lesson of Lady Margaret Hall: I wasn't here to grasp at ghosts, to stop time or even mourn its loss. At university, I was surrounded by friends, free to explore, happy. Of course, I never wanted it to end. But this was not another home I was forced to leave – it was a gate I passed through to become something new.

33.

Asser sent me a telescope for my birthday. *What an odd gift,* I thought, staring at the long, narrow box in the middle of the living-room floor. Then I remembered my brief exam-season obsession with astronomy, how I'd mentioned in passing that I would like to have a telescope one day. Every night that month I'd called Asser and rambled, delirious from exam prep and half asleep. He had been listening after all. He'd collected my transient thoughts, the things I'd already forgotten I said, and held on to them.

I knew how much he loved me – and that felt heavy at times, like a countdown clock always ticking in my mind. I'd made him a promise almost a year ago, that we would figure out our future after I finished university. He wasn't pressuring me for an answer, but I felt a kind of fog between us, a distance that hadn't been there before.

I loved Asser, but I did not want to get married. When I told him this in the month after exams, he said that was fine. He didn't care what we called it – marriage, partnership, cohabitation – as long as we were together. For a few weeks, I let myself live in that fantasy, looking up London apartments and researching visa options that would allow him to live in the UK. When my friends asked how things were going with him, I told them we were moving in together. They all seemed excited for me, but I could tell they knew it would never happen.

Asser knew it too, though I think he hoped I would find the courage to follow my heart. But I couldn't do it. If we lived together without getting married, my parents would stop speaking to me, at least for a while. People would inevitably find out about us, and all my work in Pakistan would go up in flames. It was too big a risk.

There were only two options – get married or let him go. I hated them both.

✑

I HAD ALWAYS known marriage was not for me. When I was nine years old, I made a vow never to learn to cook because I figured that no man in Mingora would take a wife who was useless in the kitchen. As I got older, I started saying, 'I'll consider marriage when I'm thirty-five,' but that was just a placeholder, something to placate my mum and keep her from launching into a lecture. 'You will get married,' she always said. 'You must. Marriage is beautiful.'

For my mum and most women in Pakistan, I suppose it was self-preservation to believe marriage was 'beautiful', as it was also mandatory. Growing up, I spent hours in my aunts' kitchens as they prepared meal after meal, caring for eight or nine children at a time, waiting hand and foot on husbands they hadn't chosen and,

I suspected, would never love. Their sons, barely old enough to talk, would amble in and order their mothers to bring more tea for their fathers' guests. And marriage could be dangerous as well. I remembered walking down the street as a child, hearing a woman being beaten behind the walls of her home. None of it was beautiful to me.

As a girl, I believed that things would be different for me and my friends. We were an unstoppable force who would fight for our right to be educated, to have careers as airline pilots and engineers. My cousin Nazneen planned to be a doctor and also a poet. She and I would talk for hours about the changes we wanted to see in our community, how things would be better when we were adults. While I was in hospital in Birmingham, she sent me a package containing page after page of handwritten poems. As I read them, I learnt her father had forced her to marry. She was sixteen and devastated.

When we talk on the phone now, she tells me she's fine. Her husband is nice enough. She loves her children. But I can't forget the girl she was, the aspirations she had, and how she lost them all when she got married. I thought of her often at Oxford – how she would have thrived at university, how unfair it was that I was the only one living the life we both dreamt of when we were young.

My friends at university, of course, lived in a very different world, one where they would be allowed to choose their partners. Still, most of them weren't sure they wanted to marry. When they had a crush, they swooned like romance novel heroines. But they talked about marriage as an abstract, political concept, in terms of compromise and how much women stood to lose – the expectation to prioritise a husband's needs over your own, putting your professional life on hold to have children, the emotional labour and unequal division of domestic duties, the cost of divorce if it doesn't work out. It seemed to me that, in a society where you could choose whether to marry or not, a lot of women preferred to stay single.

The only argument for marrying Asser was how I felt inside. I loved him and loved the prospect of having his companionship for the rest of my life. I couldn't imagine him ever hurting me or imposing harsh rules after we were married, but I knew women who never expected it to happen to them either. If I was going to change my mind, I needed some guarantees.

'Would you try to tell me what I can and can't wear?' I asked Asser over FaceTime early in the summer. I was thinking of a Pakistani student at Oxford, who had got engaged to a supposedly educated and 'feminist' man. He ended up barring her from attending parties and balls, and made her remove any photos from Instagram that he hadn't approved, including a perfectly normal picture of her in a tank top.

'Well, last summer when we planned to go hiking, you showed up in heels,' Asser replied. 'I would prefer you not do that again. Otherwise, dress however you like.'

I swatted away his joke and moved on. 'Fine, what about kids? I don't want any. I may change my mind in the future, but you should not assume that I will. Can you live with that?'

He was quiet for a moment. 'To be honest, I haven't thought a lot about having children.' In my mind, this was the heart of the problem. Women have to contemplate every aspect of a relationship, how it will affect them, what they might lose – while men can afford to consider only themselves and their desires.

'I guess not thinking about it is a kind of an answer in itself, though,' Asser continued. 'Kids aren't as important to me as being with the woman I love. When I picture my future, you are the person I see. And if you do change your mind at some point, we can talk about it then, right?'

That response seemed good enough for now, so I pressed on. 'Would you ever want to take another wife?'

Some people interpret the Quran as allowing a man to have up to four wives, as long as he can care for them all equally. From my perspective, it's impossible to treat multiple partners with parity, and hard enough to have a happy marriage with only one spouse.

Asser rolled his eyes and said, 'You are all four wives in one, Malala.'

'This isn't a joke!' I shot back. 'I need some assurances. I need to know your answers to all my questions before I could even think about getting married. Will you be faithful to me? Will you get angry and yell? Would you ever lie to me?'

'I can only tell you that I love you and would never intentionally hurt you,' he replied. 'There are no promises or magic words to take away all your doubts. No one can guarantee the future.'

I ignored that nonanswer and kept ploughing through my list of questions like an interrogator one query away from nailing the suspect. 'You know my work for girls' education is the most important thing to me. It always will be. Would you try to stop me from working?'

'And you know I was raised by three women who work.' His voice had changed from upbeat to annoyed. 'If I'm honest, Malala, it feels like we've known each other too long for you to still wonder what kind of man I am. You're looking for certainty, a sign that will give you a definitive yes-or-no answer. But anything can be a sign if you want it to be. So my question to you is, what do you want?'

That night I wrote him a letter.

Asser,

I have a huge fear of marriage. I don't want a ceremony, and I don't want to sign legal papers. I don't want to take any man's last name (though I'll happily offer mine).

I just want a partner who I trust. I want to support your dreams and for you to support me in my work. I want a friend who will listen to my thoughts no matter how stupid or silly they are. I want a man who looks sexy playing cricket!

You should be sure about me too. There are things I have accepted about myself, but I understand if other people can't accept the asymmetry of my face and smile, my hearing problems, my scars. I would rather die alone than think you took pity on me because no one else would have me.

My life hasn't been and won't be easy. I have already lived through the worst things, so gossip and lies, the cruel things people say online, and even the death threats don't bother me. But you might not want that in your life. Are you sure you can live like this?

I am trying to push myself to consider what it would mean to marry. Right now I feel like I'm still learning who I am. Our brains don't fully develop until twenty-five years old! I have to wonder if I can trust my own judgement at twenty-three. I need more time.

In all of this, I love you and don't want to lose you. But I don't want to hurt you either. Is it wrong to continue our relationship when there is so much uncertainty within me?

I didn't send the letter, but getting my thoughts out on paper brought some temporary solace. I stopped grilling Asser over the phone. These types of conversations were better in person, when I could look in his eyes and search for the truth. I hoped that could happen again soon, though it seemed like I might be waiting a long time. Asser had applied for a UK visitor's visa, but, five months into the pandemic, he was still waiting on approval to travel. I tried not to dwell on the fact that we hadn't seen each other in almost a year.

⁓

WHILE I WAS contemplating marriage with Asser, Sofia was going through her own relationship drama. We spent hours talking about our problems and getting nowhere. Then she came up with the idea that we should read our way to clarity – to consult the experts on matters of love and feminism. I joked that Oxford had taught us well how to analyse a text and form an argument, so it was worth a shot.

That summer we developed our reading list, everyone from bell hooks to Dolly Alderton, books by American psychologists, Lebanese poets, Victorian-era novelists. Soon we were talking about Amia Srinivasan's *The Right to Sex* as much as we talked about our boyfriends, and that alone felt like progress. The list kept growing – Chimamanda Ngozi Adichie, Virginia Woolf, magazine articles with titles like 'The Five Red Flags to Look Out for in Men'. As she was in Islamabad and I was in Birmingham, we mostly conducted our book club via text, both waking up in different time zones to messages full of quotes and pictures of highlighted passages.

Several books gave strong evidence for how marriage supports patriarchy. I filed away the stats and arguments, always eager to add more nuance to my understanding of gender and power dynamics. But I was also moved by stories of marriage that matched Adichie's description – 'a source of joy and love and mutual support'. The passage seemed to describe what I already had with Asser, though not what I'd seen in most married couples. And as much as I enjoyed the reading, I couldn't find an answer to my specific question: how to choose between an institution I didn't believe in and a life without the person I loved.

I decided to poll a few of my older married friends, on the assumption that people who knew my situation might be better able to guide me. The British and American women said things like 'You *cannot* marry your first boyfriend!' and 'Think of it as a corporate procurement policy: you need to review at least three quotes from vendors before you sign a contract.' I wondered if Tarik or my teenage crushes on Bollywood stars and cricket players qualified as romantic experience. How did other women face going through this crucible – having a crush, flirting, worrying about your ambiguous relationship status, falling in love, deciding your future – multiple times?

When I spoke to married women from Pakistan, they were focused on certainty. One of them said I should take a long time to decide because 'being single isn't good, but it's better than a bad marriage'. I knew she was right about the last part at least.

These conversations made me think about my mum. When she got married, she knew a lot less about her future husband than I did about Asser. Though they came from neighbouring villages in Shangla, my parents had never been alone together or exchanged more than a few words until their wedding day. I felt embarrassed that I'd never thought about my mum as a young woman, how scared she must have been, what dreams she might have given up after becoming a wife.

One night, while we were alone in the living room, I decided to ask her. 'How did you know you could trust Dad? I mean, before you got married, were you scared to go and live with him?'

She let out a long sigh and closed her eyes. 'Malala, listen, you *must* marry a Pashtun man, and he *must* speak Pashto and come from our culture. Your father and I will come up with a list of options and you can pick from those.'

In the weary way she answered me, I glimpsed the exhaustion of a life spent trying to be a mother in a restrictive patriarchal society; the constant scrutiny and blame placed on you if your children, particularly daughters, stepped out of line. I wasn't sure if she really believed what she said or if she was only repeating the admonitions she would hear from extended family members if they learnt about Asser. 'Mum, can we just forget about my life right now?' I pleaded. 'I really want to know how you felt when you got married. You've never told me.'

She cocked an eyebrow at me as if to say, *I know exactly why you're asking these questions. But, fine, I'll play along.* 'Your dad was one of the only men in the nearby villages who had been to university. I thought I was very fortunate to be marrying him. Because he was educated, I imagined we might go away someday. It was an opportunity to make my dream come true.'

'What was your dream?' I asked, a bit shocked. My mum had never admitted to these sorts of things, and my mind ran through images of her as a scientist, a businesswoman, a diplomat.

'Well, as you know, there are hardly any roads or cars in Shangla. And no restaurants. So I hoped for a faster pace of life. My biggest wish was to sit in the back seat of a car as it drove through the rain, eating a takeaway kebab.'

Hearing that was shocking, funny and heartbreaking all at the same time. My mum deserved more than such a small, achievable dream. But she and the women she grew up with weren't allowed to have lofty aspirations. They looked at marriage as a bet, a gamble that their lives might slightly improve if they ended up with a decent man. My mum got lucky; many of her sisters and friends did not.

'If you ask me what's my biggest blessing,' she added, 'I will always say my husband.' I was happy for my mum that she felt safe and content in her marriage; but it was deeply unjust and depressing that her life's fortunes had always been bound to men.

At that point, I'd asked dozens of people for advice; sought revelation everywhere from social science to astrology. And I still hadn't landed on a decision that felt right. Maybe what Asser said was true – no one can guarantee the future. But I still clung to the myth of certainty, to the idea that someday I would find a definitive answer.

The one person I wished I could talk to – my beloved grandmother, Abai – was no longer with me. She'd passed away on a quiet afternoon, early in the pandemic. My grief over her loss was very different from the uncontrollable sorrow I'd felt at Oxford, when I had convinced myself that she was dead. I was sad, of course, but spent more time reflecting on how grateful I was for the time we'd spent together and her influence on my life. My parents, brothers and I sat around the kitchen table for hours and shared our favourite Abai stories. We mourned her with the gifts she gave us – family, laughter and prayer.

In the weeks after she died, I kept coming back to one particular memory – a visit to Shangla when I was nine or ten years old. Abai called me in from playing with my cousins and led me to the backyard where she had built a fire under her clay oven. 'Sit here and chop this tomato,' she said. 'Today I am going to teach you to make chicken karahi.'

'I'll help,' I replied. 'But I'm not learning to cook.'

Abai smirked. 'Lots of girls your age can already prepare this dish on their own.'

If she thought she could use my competitive nature against me, she was wrong. 'That's why I'm not going to learn – because then I'll get stuck doing it all the time!'

'No, you learn because one day you'll want to get married.'

'I will *never* want that,' I vowed.

Abai looked at me appraisingly for a moment, smiled, and handed me another tomato. She didn't scold me for disrespecting my culture or try to tell me that marriage was beautiful – she didn't say anything at all. Thinking about this memory now, I wondered about that look she gave me. I'll never know exactly, but I believe what I saw in her eyes was a grandmother's knowledge that the dreams we have when we're young will reshape themselves as we grow. As I agonised over the decision to marry or not, I wished that Abai and I could talk again, that I could have one more chance to ask her everything she knew about love.

34.

'The . . . what? Doesn't ring a bell for me, sorry . . .'

'*The Cotswolds*, Malala! Storybook England? Charming villages? Rolling green hills?'

I knew exactly what Zayan was describing, but played dumb because I wanted to hear his over-the-top sales pitch for the weekend getaway he was planning.

'Look, I'm sending you the details,' he said. 'It's you, me and Parveen. I've made a full itinerary – hiking, shopping, dinner in a fifteenth-century pub. All you have to do is show up next Thursday.'

'I'll be there,' I promised.

By midsummer, the UK had lifted lockdown restrictions, and I fled my parents' house to be with friends as often as possible – Yasmin's birthday party in London, sleepovers with Hen, spa days with Alice. It was overwhelming to see a face you knew so well, no longer trapped in a tiny digital square on Zoom but attached to a body and walking around in the real world. I loved hearing my friends' laughter again, so much more alive and contagious in person than over the phone. Typically I'm not much of a hugger, but I couldn't stop myself at these happy reunions.

When I arrived at the stone cottage Zayan had rented, he and Parveen tumbled out to meet me. 'Hurry up!' he said. 'We've been waiting till you got here to start movie night.' I tossed my bag in the bedroom assigned to me and settled in on the couch to watch a nineties film called *The Bodyguard*.

'So, how accurate was it?' Zayan asked me as the credits rolled.

'Uh, let's see . . . I've never been picked up and carried out of a crowd. Never fallen in love with anyone from the Met Police. But the scene where the bodyguard is annoyed because she wants to go shopping? That's definitely accurate in my experience.'

After the movie, we stood around in the kitchen, snacking on chocolate and crisps. 'We should do this for all our breaks,' Parveen said to Zayan. 'Maybe the Lake District or Scotland after autumn term?' They were both heading back into academia soon – an MBA for him, a PhD for her.

'What about you, Malz? What's next?' she asked.

'I wish I knew,' I said, biting a hangnail. 'I need to get back to work. I feel so useless stuck in my parents' house while all these schools are closing because of Covid. Like I should be doing something about that. And I want to travel, but it's impossible right now with all the border closures.'

'And what about . . .' I knew what was coming and shot her a look to say *Stop talking right now*. I'd told Parveen a bit about Asser, but Zayan was too much of a gossip to handle sensitive information. At least, that's what I thought at the time. I later learnt that he knew all along, but somehow managed to keep the secret.

The next day, Zayan donned a bright-yellow raincoat and led Parveen and me on a soggy hike through the countryside. 'English weather builds character!' he shouted over loudly bleating sheep.

'I'm standing in half a foot of mud, bro,' Parveen snarked. 'Please spare us your life lessons.'

My phone buzzed and I tried to read a text from Asser through my rain-speckled screen.

> I got the visa!!!

After shrieking and nearly dropping my phone in a puddle, I told my friends to go ahead of me while I made a quick call. Asser picked up right away and gave me the details: he would visit for fifteen days in mid-September, and was bringing his mother, who wanted to see her daughter and grandchildren.

'Cannot wait to see you,' he gushed. 'I love you, Malala! And I love you too, Lahore Visa Office!'

I doubled over laughing. 'Please tell me you're not standing in a government building and shouting my name.'

'No, no, I'm in the car,' he replied. 'Sorry, I'm just really excited.'

Later that evening, I sent him a message:

> I would love to meet your mother. Bring her to my parents' house for lunch.

I watched as Asser's text bubble appeared and disappeared several times.

I don't know. She's 70 years old and I don't want to get her hopes up. With my last two girlfriends, she thought I would get married each time. I can't disappoint her again.

The next time he called, we talked it over and agreed to manage both our parents' expectations, firmly establishing that this was a meal between friends, nothing more. When I got home from the Cotswolds, I informed my parents of the plan. '*Don't* be awkward,' I instructed them. 'Don't ask any questions about marriage. Don't ask if Asser will move to the UK or what his mother's expectations are for a daughter-in-law. Don't ask . . . anything!' They seemed momentarily cowed by my hectoring, but I knew better than to assume that they would behave and reminded them several times in the days leading up to Asser's arrival.

FARIDA LOOKED LIKE a film star standing in my driveway – brown hair with golden highlights, big sunglasses, lip gloss. She wore a perfectly pressed shalwar and taupe kitten heels, waving hello to my family and me.

My mum and dad greeted her first. Then Farida gave me a hug and thanked us for inviting her. I hugged Asser's sister Ambreena next, and gave him a circumspect nod. He laughed.

By the time we got from the front door to the living room, my dad and Asser's mum were deep in conversation, discussing all the latest headlines from Pakistan. When my dad went off to fetch tea, Farida sat down next to my mum. English was the only language they had in common, and neither was fluent, but their shared interest in fashion carried them through. For an hour, Farida held court, the chat bouncing between Pakistani politics and shopping tips. To my relief, no one even glanced at Asser and me sitting quietly nearby.

We moved outside to the garden where my parents had prepared lunch. As everyone took a seat, my dad turned to Farida and said, 'So what can you tell us about your son?'

My stomach lurched. *What is he doing?* This was supposed to be a visit among friends with no expectations or serious talk. I didn't want anyone, on Asser's side or mine, to think this gathering meant that a wedding was coming. To stay out of the spotlight, I assigned myself the job of sitting next to my mum and translating the conversation into Pashto.

'I was forty when Asser was born,' Farida said. 'He's much younger than his sisters, but I was so excited to have him. He was due in November, but he came two months early.' I made a mental note: *Asser was supposed to be a Scorpio. Recheck astrological compatibility.*

'As soon as he was out, the nurses told me, "This baby is not going to survive." I refused to believe it and began handing out the box of pastries I'd brought to the hospital to celebrate his birth. He was so tiny and weak, and stayed in the incubator for many days. All I could do was to pray for him.'

She looked at Asser and said, 'He is very precious to me.'

My mum quietly wiped away tears, and I wondered if she was remembering the baby she'd lost before I was born. Farida patted her hand and said, 'You'd think, after all that, he could have at least become a doctor.' Everyone laughed and she shot me a conspiratorial wink. I had not changed my mind on marriage, but if I were ever to have a mother-in-law, Farida would be my first choice.

ASSER AND I packed as much as we could into his fifteen-day trip. The evening after Farida's visit, we fled to the city for the weekend. We ate sushi and shopped for shoes; I made him ride the London Eye with me. In the remaining days, we watched a match at the Newbury Cricket Club, played badminton in the backyard with my dad and brothers, and went back to the botanical gardens for long walks. I didn't initiate discussions about our relationship as I had planned, preferring to enjoy his company without thinking of the future.

But two nights before he had to go back to Lahore, I felt so depressed that he was leaving, unable to hold in my sadness and confusion. 'When we're together, I forget all the worries that I have about getting married,' I told him. 'I'm just so happy and want to be with you forever. And when you leave, I start over-thinking again.'

'I want to make it easy for you to be with me,' he said. 'I hate to see you under so much pressure when my goal is to add joy to your life. I wish I had the resources to take a year off and stay here with you until we figure it out, but I can't do that.'

He reached for my hand and added, 'Sometimes it's stressful for me too. My job is full-on, all the time. Trying to keep my mum safe during a pandemic. Trying to impress your parents. Trying to figure out how to show you that I will make a good partner. I wouldn't put you or myself through this if I didn't think we were right for each other.'

'You're already a good partner, Asser. Things are great between us, but I still don't know how I feel about being a wife.'

'So . . . you're saying that I just need to find a way to reverse about five thousand years of patriarchy and social norms around marriage . . . and then we can be together?'

I rolled my eyes at him.

'For you, I'll try anything,' he said.

35.

Asser didn't need to start an international debate about marriage. I did that all on my own.

In January 2021, *British Vogue* asked if I could do a photo shoot and interview for their July issue. I'd never done a fashion magazine cover before and didn't understand why they would want to feature someone who was five feet tall and couldn't form a proper smile. But my team said the interview was a chance to 're-introduce myself to the world', and that got my attention.

After Asser left in September, the UK government issued new lockdown orders. I was stuck in the house again, unable to travel or see friends, and wondering why my life seemed to be going in reverse. At age eleven, I was on TV, telling the world about life under Taliban control. By fifteen, I'd gained so much influence that the extremists tried to kill me. At seventeen, I won the Nobel Peace Prize. And now I was an adult living with my parents.

Even though I was still working as much as I could, I sometimes felt like I was drifting from my purpose in life – to help girls who were denied their right to education. Schools around the world were closed because of Covid, and millions of students, mostly girls, might never return to the classroom. Some had been married off, some aged out. Others were working as street vendors and factory labourers to try to support their families.

The Shangla school provided all students with tablets so they could join online lessons and stay on top of their studies during the lockdowns. This caused a major issue with many of the parents, as giving girls access to technology went against their social norms. They wanted complete control and surveillance of their daughters' lives, and the internet made that impossible. The principal and school administrators stood their ground, saying that the girls were required to attend remote classes and do their homework during the pandemic. Still, it wasn't a perfect option. Hardly any of the families had internet access and cellular service was often too spotty for the girls to get online. I hoped that the girls wouldn't give up and would try to keep learning from home however they could.

I wanted to be out in the world, advocating for young women. Every night I lay awake wondering how to prove myself worthy of this calling. Maybe *British Vogue* wasn't the perfect match for my message, but it was definitely high-profile and a big microphone I could use to remind people what was at stake for millions of girls.

In early April, I travelled to London for the photo shoot and interview. The first day was fittings, making sure the clothes were precisely hemmed, gathered and darted to my body. I woke up at 6 a.m. the following morning to make my call time at the studio. For the next ten hours, the creative team plucked my eyebrows, curled my hair, painted my nails, dressed me in multiple outfits, told me where to stand and what to do with my hands while the photographer's camera snapped away. Halfway through the shoot, the make-up artist suggested we try a bright-red lipstick. It was much more dramatic than the tinted lip balm I usually wore, but I was in the mood to try something new, so I said, 'Let's do it!' When I got back to the hotel that night, I collapsed on the bed. Everyone at the shoot had treated me so well, but it was strangely exhausting to be photographed for an entire day.

The next morning I woke up, ate breakfast in my room and walked down to the hotel lobby to meet Sirin Kale, the writer doing my interview. As it was a cover story, I expected to find a middle-aged journalist with stately streaks of grey hair, wearing a business suit. But Sirin wasn't that much older than me; she had a nose ring, dark wavy hair that fell to her waist, and black eyeliner drawn in an impressive cat-eye shape.

We left the hotel and went for a walk in St James's Park, chatting easily about Oxford and my student life. She wanted to hear about my trip to Pakistan, and I told her how it felt to breathe the air of my home country again. We talked about online activism and how outrage so often gets in the way of real change.

She asked what I would do with my life now that I'd finished university. I said that was the question keeping me up at night, and that my biggest fear was failing girls like the one I used to be – girls who were full of dreams, but living at the mercy of a patriarchal society that doesn't value them. Millions of girls watch their brothers go to school in the morning, while they stay at home to cook and clean. I talked about the girls I'd met who were married off to old men, and those in refugee camps who felt their aspirations and hopes slipping away day by day. 'I care a lot about my work and I worry about how long it will take to reach the goals we have set,' I said.

Sirin was so disarming that I sometimes forgot our talk was a magazine interview and not an overdue catch-up with a friend.

I snapped back to reality when she asked if I'd met someone, a romantic partner, at Oxford. *How does she know?* I wondered.

My eyes went wide at this unexpectedly personal question. If I said no, that would be a lie. If I said yes, it would cause a controversy. I finally mumbled something about hoping to find a person who understands and respects me. Sirin saw how uncomfortable I was and, to her credit, quickly moved on. But I spent the rest of the interview trying to rephrase my answer in my mind. I worried Asser would read it and feel like he didn't exist, that I was writing him out of my story.

The middle of an interview is not the time to plunge yourself into an existential debate about marriage – but that's exactly what I did. The books Sofia and I had read, the chat with my mum and the pro/con lists in my journal were all circling around in my brain as I answered other questions. When it was clear that Sirin was winding down the conversation, I wanted to try to restate my views on love. I told her that I'd seen a few of my friends get more serious about their relationships since graduation and start coupling up. What I didn't understand, I explained, was how you could ever trust someone enough to make that commitment. Even if you thought the other person was wonderful, how could you be sure?

With a nervous laugh, I blurted out, 'I still don't understand why people have to get married. If you want to have a person in your life, why do you have to sign marriage papers, why can't it just be a partnership?' It wasn't meant to be a statement on the institution of marriage or any sort of call to action – just venting my personal frustrations to an affable stranger. Sirin smiled and nodded, as if she understood exactly what I meant.

That went well, I thought, as we took a selfie and said goodbye. I got in the car for the long ride back to Birmingham, feeling glad that I'd agreed to the cover story and relieved that it was over.

FINDING MY WAY

WHEN MY ISSUE of *British Vogue* was published and the photos went online, I paused for a moment before looking at them. I've sat for hundreds of professional portraits in my life, and when I see the final images, I often feel like there's a stranger looking back at me. Sometimes she's dressed in lavender parachute pants that I would never wear in real life, the choice of an overambitious stylist. Or her face is suspiciously flawless, the imperfections I see in the mirror airbrushed away. But I loved the woman facing the world from the cover of *British Vogue* in a red headscarf and matching lipstick.

Within minutes, my phone was buzzing nonstop. Friends sent hyperactive, barely coherent texts with lots of emojis. My parents huddled around their iPad, my dad reading the interview while my mum examined the photos. 'Did you get to keep the jewellery? Where is it?' she asked, looking disappointed when I told her that everything goes back to the designers after the shoot.

I padded up to my room to read the interview in peace and scanned the page for things that might cause a controversy. The article revealed that I played poker and went to pubs at university, but made sure to include that I don't drink. I thought I'd probably get some sermons about that from pious Pakistanis, but nothing too damaging. Sirin had done a beautiful job with the piece, and I most appreciated that my work for girls' education was the heart of the article.

Asser called to say I looked stunning and that he thought the interview was great. If he was uncomfortable about the way I'd stumbled over the question about whether I had a romantic partner, he didn't mention it. I picked up my phone to share the story on Instagram and found that my dad had already posted an enthusiastic review on his Twitter account. That night I read glowing

247

comments from people all over the world who connected with the words and images.

When I woke up the next day, though, no one was celebrating. #ShameOnMalala was trending in Pakistan, as people had decided that my comments on marriage were 'lewd', 'un-Islamic' and an 'assault on the foundations of society'. They claimed I was encouraging adultery, and seized on the word 'partnership', as if equality between men and women was unnatural and profane. Thousands upon thousands of tweets were calling me an atheist, a prostitute, a foreign agent intent on destroying the country, everything but what I really was – a twenty-three-year-old asking questions about love and relationships.

The attacks ranged from commentary on my appearance – 'too ugly to get a husband anyway' – to saying I should be raped, burnt or strangled. One man wrote that the Taliban's 'poor aim' had shamed the entire country. A popular meme showed two dogs having sex, with my name written under the female dog. I scrolled through page after page of replies with only one word: *bitch*.

They wanted me to feel shame, but I was angry. The attack seemed coordinated – like people were deliberately misreading my words to cause a scandal. And in the process of tearing me down, they were sending a message to every young woman in Pakistan: marriage is not optional.

Over the next few days, the hysteria grew every time I opened my phone. A coalition of independent schools announced that their students would wear black armbands on my birthday. Lawmakers in Khyber Pakhtunkhwa, my home province, debated issuing a resolution against me and demanded a government probe into the interview. They called on my father to offer an explanation, as if I was not worthy of speaking for myself. A cleric gave a sermon promising a suicide attack on me the next time I set foot in the country.

I saw many versions of 'She is supposed to be an education activist, not give her opinions on marriage.' But what was the point of sending girls to school if they did not become women who could choose their own futures? These people, some of whom claimed to be feminists or liberals, were revealing the limits of their commitment to women's rights: you can go to school, but you can't choose your husband. You can go to university, but you can only have children, not a career. You can use your voice, so long as you never criticise the system.

My parents were assailed with calls and text messages. Our relatives gave breathless reports of the damage, what their neighbours were saying, every stupid meme or WhatsApp message they received. 'Why does Malala reject marriage? It's against our religion!' they gasped. An imam from Shangla phoned to lecture them for over an hour.

My dad pressured me to make a statement clarifying my comments. 'It's harming our reputation. You need to do it now before the situation gets worse,' he said.

I wanted to laugh. How could it get worse? 'If I give in to this,' I countered, 'what will people ask me to explain tomorrow? Every time I speak, they'll come back with their notes.' And he had been the first one to share the interview, I pointed out. He was proud of it until the backlash began.

For years, when people asked my dad about how he raised me, he'd always replied, 'Don't ask what I did. Ask what I did not do. I did not clip her wings.' He often spoke of me as a bird, but sometimes I felt more like a kite – flying high when it served him, pulled back to earth by a string when it did not.

Meanwhile, my mum sobbed and walked around the house like she'd been physically wounded. When she finally spoke to me, it was with an anger that bordered on contempt: 'How could you do this, Malala? I wish you'd never opened your mouth.'

I knew better than to talk back, so I went to my room and messaged Asser.

> My parents are receiving calls from relatives saying I'm 'anti-Islam'.

> My mum won't stop crying.

Please tell her not to be sad.

This is just the 'outrage of the week' in Pakistan. It's really not that serious.

> I'm 23. Why am I supposed to have all the answers? I should be allowed to be confused.

Can I talk to them? Would that help?

> Up to you.

He called and I walked downstairs with the phone on speaker. 'It's Asser. He wants to talk to you.'

My parents looked stricken. 'Is he upset?' my dad asked.

'Ask him yourself,' I said, holding out the phone to them.

'No, of course not – I am not upset,' Asser told them calmly. 'There's nothing wrong with the interview or with an open discussion on marriage.'

'What about your family?' my mum said. 'Your mother must be *very* disappointed.'

'Oh, my family is fine! My mum loves the photos. Her only comment was how beautiful Malala looked. Please don't even think of it.'

Asser paused for a moment and added, 'I think the social media reaction is making this seem bigger than it is, especially from afar. The people who won't let it go – the trolls, politicians, radicals – are just using this to build their own profiles. They don't speak for everyone in Pakistan. But even if the whole world was saying this rubbish, Malala is not alone. I will always support her.'

They talked for a few more minutes, and I watched my mum and dad relax. With Asser's reassurance, they stopped their scolding and prodding for me to make a statement. I could walk around the house again without feeling like a monster.

In the early evening, I called my high-school friend Alice. 'Let's have dinner,' I said. 'I need a change of scenery, and I want to go somewhere expensive.' We booked a table at one of Birmingham's better restaurants and ordered everything that sounded good to us. Alice kept me distracted and entertained with wild stories about her job as a paramedic. When I got home, I felt more like myself again. But the night out with my friend only reinforced my desire to go further away, to be with the person I most wanted to see.

I waited until 3 a.m., when it was morning in Lahore, to send the message.

> Let's take a trip, just the two of us, and talk about everything.

> Tell me where and I'll leave now. When I hold you again, I will never let go.

36.

My childhood made me feel so much older than I was, forcing me to contend with violence and physical pain, to provide financial support for my family, and to stand in a spotlight I had not sought out. Then university made me feel like I had plenty of time to grow up, that I should enjoy being young and free. During the pandemic, I was relearning time as a finite thing. The days I slept away passed just the same; I couldn't get them back. Brooding about marriage in the pages of *British Vogue* wouldn't buy me another two years to see if my feelings changed. If I wanted my life to move forward, I needed to make some adult decisions, starting with my relationship.

Due to Covid travel restrictions in July 2021, Asser couldn't come to the UK and I couldn't go to Pakistan. The US would allow us both to visit, so we decided to meet there at the end of the month. On the plane from London, I wrote down all my remaining relationship questions in my notebook. I'd told Asser to think of everything he wanted to ask me as well. This was not a philosophy tutorial that prized the depth of enquiry over conclusions. I was determined to come home with an answer about our future, one way or another.

Asser's flight from Lahore to New York landed hours before mine. He sat outside international baggage claim most of the day, watching people reunite with their loved ones. Nine months had passed since his last visit; when I saw him, my legs wobbled and I almost cried. He wrapped his arms around me, and I pressed my head into his chest. I couldn't hear the luggage carousel rumbling to life or the people shouting all around us, just the sound of his heartbeat, steady as a clock.

After finding our driver, we headed to a resort in Lake Placid, New York. The five-hour drive was a perfect opportunity to kick off the conversation, but I only wanted to look at Asser and hold his hand. We spent most of the ride entertaining each other by trying to pronounce town names like 'Poughkeepsie' and 'Schroeppel' in terrible New York accents.

Tucked between tree-covered mountains and a sparkling lake, the resort was cosy and quiet. It looked like a good place to contemplate the future. Asser stopped at the front desk and signed us up for a few activities – yoga, tennis lessons, a falconry demonstration from a local bird expert. He also picked up a trail map. 'Don't worry,' he said, 'if we need more time to talk, we can cancel whatever you like. I know we're here for a serious reason, but we should try to have some fun too.' I am usually a person who prefers to lounge around all day on holiday, and yoga did not sound at all 'fun' to me. But, either because I'd been climbing the walls at my parents' house for more than a year, or because I was just so happy to see him, I smiled and said, 'Sounds great!'

It rained from sunrise to sunset on our first full day. I might have seen it as a sign, the universe scrapping our outdoor plans, forcing us to sit inside and address our issues. Instead, I challenged Asser to a game of poker and won three straight hands. Then we played table tennis on a covered porch. Just as I felt like I was getting the hang of it, Asser said, 'Should we find a place to sit and talk?'

'Eh, not yet. Can we watch a movie instead? You pick,' I replied.

'As you wish.'

He chose *Zoolander*, a comedy about male models unwittingly entangled in an international assassination plot. I'd never seen the film – released in 2001 when I was four years old – or even heard of it. Asser spent most of the movie watching me nearly laugh myself off the sofa. As the credits rolled, I asked him how he knew I would love it.

'I didn't, but I hoped you would. I just really wanted to see you laugh,' he said.

Whatever I'd imagined when I daydreamt about running away with him at university, this was better. Asser had an infectious enthusiasm to try new things, and over the next two days I found myself waking up in the mornings excited for our next adventure. We watched a falconer send hawks and eagles soaring over the water and return to his arm. In the Adirondack Mountains, we hiked up an out-and-back trail. I walked behind Asser on the narrow path, running my hand along the tree trunks, leaves and rock outcrops, remembering similar trails outside Mingora. The lookout point felt like standing inside a painting, shades of green, blue and purple in every direction. In the evenings, we lay on a blanket in the grass watching the sun set over the water and the stars appear in the sky.

On the fourth day, I woke up feeling the heavy burden of time. In a little more than twenty-four hours, we'd be heading back to the airport. We still needed to talk, so I proposed a fool-proof plan: 'Let's get a canoe and some lunch and paddle out on the lake. We won't come back to shore until we have an answer about the future. And, whatever happens out there, we'll return as friends.' Asser agreed and went off to find a boat.

After an hour or so on the water, we pulled in our paddles for a rest. I opened a Coke and Asser unwrapped a sandwich. Gusts of wind blew across the lake and we drifted through the water as we ate.

'Ready to talk?' he asked when we finished lunch.

'Asser . . .'

'Yes?'

'Where is the hotel?'

We spun around in all directions and could see nothing but water and trees – no trace of the resort, swimmers or other boats. The shoreline was a bank of massive black rocks. We were lost in the middle of a miles-long lake.

He caught a flash of panic in my eyes. 'Just hang on,' he said. 'We can figure this out. If we pick a direction and paddle, we'll eventually see something, right?'

We headed in the same direction as the wind. About fifteen minutes later, we saw a weathered dock jutting out into the water. We rowed as hard as we could to reach it and clung to the splintery pilings.

Just as we were catching our breath, three enormous dogs came rushing down the planks, barking wildly at us. In the years since, I've learnt to love dogs, but at the time they terrified me. I had to make a quick decision – be eaten alive by animals or perish at sea. I let go of the dock.

'Malala, no!' Asser cried, still holding on to the piling as the bow drifted away.

'I'm sorry,' shouted a woman running up behind the dogs. 'Do you need help?' We explained what had happened, and she told us the wind always kicked up in the afternoon. 'It's easy to get lost out here. Happens all the time. They'll swing by in a motorboat and pick up your canoe later.' She corralled the dogs, helped us tie down the canoe and drove us back to the hotel. 'I need a nap,' I said when we got inside.

In the evening, I sat outside by myself, watching the sunset and wondering if it had been a mistake to set an artificial deadline to determine our future. The intention was right – it wasn't good for either of us to keep agonising about it. But something was keeping me from the actual conversation. *Maybe it's just happiness,* I thought. *I don't want to break the spell in the little time we have together.*

And maybe I already had the answers I needed. Asser made me happier than anyone else. When I was down, he lifted my spirits. He was patient and respectful with my parents. Ambitious but not self-serious. And so ridiculously hot; after three years, I still felt dizzy when he smiled at me. Most of all, I loved his kind and gentle heart. When he said he would never intentionally hurt me, I believed him.

As for marriage, I wasn't sure what to believe. Somewhere along the way personal decisions about our future had got wrapped up in the patriarchal history and practice of matrimony. That wasn't the point when I'd first considered spending my life with Asser. I only wanted to know that I'd be safe with him.

The next morning, we packed our bags, ate pancakes and walked down to the lake. I put my feet in the sand and watched the water lap at my toes. Asser sat down next to me. We had twenty minutes until the car arrived to take us back to the airport.

I took a deep breath and looked at him. 'Okay, I think I'm ready.'

'To talk? You've really left it to the last possible minute,' he replied, laughing and shaking his head. 'But that's all right, let's—'

I held up my hand to stop him. 'Asser, I'm ready to marry you.'

37.

Two weeks later, Asser, his sister Ambreena and his brother-in-law Atif came to Birmingham for the *haan*, a formal visit where the groom's father asks the bride's father for her hand in marriage on behalf of his son. I didn't love the tradition, but I thought it was important for both of our families to know that we were serious. The formal rituals are helpful in legitimising 'love marriages', still rare and frowned upon in most parts of Pakistan.

I suspected my mum would be upset or angry about me getting engaged, as she had shown no signs of relenting in her insistence on me marrying a Pashtun man. When I played out the situation in my head, I guessed that my dad would try to pacify my mum and find a middle ground. 'You can marry Asser, if you wish,' I imagined him saying. 'Just wait a year or two.' But I had made my choice, and now I was ready to get on with my life. I decided, perhaps immaturely, that it would be better to rip the plaster off with my parents, rather than preparing them for what was about to happen. So I casually mentioned that Asser and his sister were popping by without revealing the true purpose for the visit.

When Asser's family arrived and my dad saw Atif, he caught on immediately and looked at me with bulging eyes. He showed our guests to the living room and made small talk in Urdu and English, while my mum sat on the sofa looking confused and increasingly agitated, unable to follow the conversation. Then Atif, standing in for Asser's father, turned to my dad and said, 'We're so lucky to know Malala. She and Asser make each other very happy, and we would like to extend our formal proposal.'

My dad looked down at his lap. For a few frantic seconds, I wondered what he would say. He looked up again with tears in his eyes and raised his eyebrows at me. I nodded. 'I am happy for them,' he said, and wrapped Atif in an enormous hug. Ambreena presented me with a gold bracelet, a traditional engagement gift.

'What is happening?' my mum snapped in Pashto.

'It's fine, Mum, it's okay,' I replied, my hands patting the air, the universal gesture for *please calm down.*

She stood up and tugged at my father's elbow. 'Did you just give her away? What have you done? You're here crying and hugging them, congratulating everyone, saying "Take her! She's yours!"'

Asser and his family didn't understand her words, but they heard the rising panic in her voice. My throat closed with embarrassment and I looked at her with pleading eyes. Then my dad took her hand and, in his most gentle voice, said, 'Toor Pekai, I am only the messenger. Malala gave herself away.'

⸎

BEFORE WE COULD plan a wedding, I had to complete the final procedure in facial paralysis treatment – the unpleasantly named 'debulking surgery'. Dr Hadlock would again cut into my face through my cheek and reshape the muscle and tissue she'd implanted two years ago. This would correct the bulge on my left side and, at last, allow me to see the new nerve at work in my smile. I was relieved to finally complete the reconstructive work on my face; with luck, this would be my last summer of hospital visits.

Covid restrictions limited me to one companion on this trip to Boston. Since my dad spoke English, he was the obvious choice. We boarded the plane in early August and, though we didn't say it out loud, I think we were both relieved to escape my mum's simmering ire over the engagement.

The day before the surgery, the two of us sat on a couch in my hotel room to take a conference call with Malala Fund's partners in Afghanistan. On the line were lawyers, journalists and educators who used their varied backgrounds to help more Afghan girls access education. There were tech specialists who developed digital lessons and distributed tablets to girls who couldn't go to school in person; researchers who studied the issues contributing to high drop-out rates. Others served as the Afghan equivalent of social workers, advocating on an individual and community level, persuading parents and religious leaders of the importance of education for all children.

My dad and I were concerned about their safety. Since the United States military had begun their withdrawal from the country that spring, the Taliban and Afghan military engaged in firefights almost every day. At first these conflicts were limited to border towns, but the insurgents seemed to be gaining momentum, launching attacks in twenty-six of the thirty-four provinces.

Malala Fund worked in eight countries, and while I cared about each of them, Afghanistan had a special place in my heart. My family's ancestors came from Afghanistan, and Pashtuns like us are the predominant ethnic group in the country. When we

lived in Mingora, my dad used to cross the border, only eight minutes' drive from some parts of our province, to attend poetry festi-
vals there. Through Malala Fund, we had invested millions of
dollars in girls' education efforts across the country. Now I worried
that all our work would be reversed if the Taliban took power.

The Afghan activists on the phone were worried too, but most
of them seemed determined to stay in the country. Since the major
cities – Herat, Mazar, Kandahar, Kunduz and Kabul – were still
under government control, they believed the Afghan army would
prevail. We all prayed it would happen soon, before more civilians
were killed. As we said goodbye, my dad told them to keep in
touch. 'Don't even look at the clock,' he said. 'If you need help
in the middle of the night, call us.'

If our Afghan partners did come into contact with Taliban
fighters, any connection to me could put them in more danger.
Later that night, the team at Malala Fund took their names and
photos off our website, and I removed all references to them from
my social media accounts.

Before I went to bed, I got out my laptop and opened my old
university files. Reading through the notes from my International
Security and Conflict course, I searched for a law or treaty or
emergency panic button we could push to stop violent extremists
from taking over an entire country. When I couldn't find one, it
took me back to being a child in Mingora and watching as our city
was overtaken by the Taliban, wondering why no one was coming
to save us. I played out the worst-case scenarios in my mind, which
all seemed increasingly plausible the longer I went without sleep.
It will only get worse, I thought. *If the Taliban win, people around the
world will be shocked. But they have no idea of the barbarity that will
follow their victory.*

At five the next morning, we drove to the hospital. The nurses
ran through their pre-op checklists, administered injections and

tried to make me comfortable. Dr Hadlock came in and drew on my face with a Magic Marker, outlining the spots where she would work. I kept my phone with me as long as I could, constantly checking for updates on the conflict. When the doctors injected the anaesthesia, I wasn't thinking about the surgery at all; my mind was consumed with worry for Afghanistan. As they rolled me into the operating room, the Taliban held four provincial capitals; when I woke up in the recovery ward a few hours later, they had six.

According to Afghan human rights groups, the Taliban were approaching local imams after taking control of a city or town, instructing them to make a list of all unmarried women between fourteen and forty-five years old. Fathers began arranging hasty marriages for girls as young as ten, telling them a cousin or family friend would be a better husband than a Taliban fighter.

Lying in the hospital bed, I saw a clip of an activist we supported speaking to a British broadcaster from her home in Kandahar. Like me, she was twenty-four and not married. 'What will you do if there's a knock on your door?' the journalist asked. 'Pray,' she answered. I put down my phone and shuddered.

The next day Afghan forces in Kunduz surrendered to the Taliban. Then Herat, Kandahar and Mazar fell, and everything turned into chaos. Taliban fighters raided the office of a Malala Fund partner who trained female teachers, taking laptops and staff lists. Several of our contacts in rural provinces fled to Iran, Uzbekistan and Pakistan. But those in the cities were trapped, as the Taliban set up checkpoints along the major roads. Our team in the US and UK began arranging for them to move to safe houses and working on evacuation plans. Just a few days earlier, our partners had planned to stay in their country – now we needed to get them out fast.

I returned to the hotel where I would stay for the following week until the doctors removed my stitches and told me it was safe to fly home. My dad, who has Pakistani contacts in every city in the world, had already filled the fridge in my room with containers of homemade mutton korma and dowdo soup. 'My friends have brought us this food, Malala,' he said. 'Come and eat. I will make a plate for you.'

I couldn't even think about food; all I wanted to do was lie in bed and scroll through the latest news. But I could always read my dad's face, and I saw that he was also feeling helpless and scared, exhausted from worrying about my surgery and waiting by the phone at night in case someone called from Afghanistan. 'Just soup, please,' I said. He smiled and seemed to relax a little as he fiddled with the hotel microwave and set the small tea table with a napkin, spoon and glass of water.

In response to the Taliban's offensive, the United States sped up its withdrawal plans, pulling out not just military personnel but the embassy staff who were processing visas for their Afghan translators, drivers and other allies – all in danger and desperate to leave. The Afghan army was running out of ammunition and the will to fight. That night I got into bed and prayed, saying the names of every Afghan man, woman and child I knew, pleading with God to keep them safe.

When we woke up the next day, the Taliban had control of all land border crossings in and out of the country. Thousands of people gathered on the tarmac at Kabul Airport, pleading to be evacuated. A video from the scene showed a teenage boy holding on to the wing of a US military aircraft at take-off. As the plane gained altitude, he lost his grip and fell to his death. The camera captured his descent, back down into the city he'd tried to escape. I had experienced violence in my life, but I had never watched someone die. My dad began to pray, his voice shaking; but the shock of it left me speechless and sickened.

Every day the paths for getting Malala Fund's Afghan partners out seemed to narrow. We needed to find a country willing to waive the entry visa requirements, and then get them seats on one of the scarce evacuation planes. With millions of people trying to leave through a single operating airport, it felt like we needed a miracle.

I requested calls and sent urgent emails to presidents and prime ministers in various countries to ask for help, nervously fiddling with the stitches around my ear while I waited for an answer. For years, I'd smiled in pictures with these leaders, shaken their hands and stood next to them at podiums – but not one of them picked up the phone or replied to my messages now. To the men who ran the world, I was just a photo op, not someone worthy of their time and attention, even when I needed it most.

Women, on the other hand, responded immediately, answering my calls and jumping into action as soon as we hung up. Norwegian Prime Minister Erna Solberg, former US Secretary of State Hillary Clinton, and their teams helped our Afghan partners get seats on the planes leaving Kabul. Lolwah Al-Khater, the assistant foreign minister of Qatar, allowed them to enter the country without paperwork, or even passports in some cases, and provided housing until we could sort out their relocation plans. Lisa Cheskes and Elizabeth Snow, resettlement managers in the Canadian government, guided us through the process of securing refugee visas. I may not personally agree with every opinion these women hold or every decision they made as leaders – but I will forever be grateful to them for helping save so many lives. With their support, Malala Fund helped evacuate 263 people from Afghanistan.

All week, journalists requested interviews with me. I declined, hoping things would change and not wanting to speculate about what the Taliban would inflict on the country in the middle of the fight. But the day Kabul fell, we knew it was over. 'Complete

Collapse in Afghanistan,' the headlines said. I unwrapped the surgical bandage around my head and went on TV from the hotel room.

CNN's Christiane Amanpour mentioned the promises coming from the Taliban, vague statements about ensuring 'no discrimination against women within the framework of Islamic law'. 'Does that give you hope?' she asked.

What I wanted to say: *If they stopped subjugating women and banning girls from school, they wouldn't be the Taliban any more. Hating us is fundamental to who they are – and only fools believe they will change.*

What I actually said: 'It's too early for hope.'

When a crisis arises in the world, people often chastise me for not speaking out as early or often as they expect, and not sounding angry enough when I do. It happened the week of my surgery; commenters flooded social media to claim I didn't care about Afghanistan, that I had sold out, that I wasn't 'a real activist'.

These keyboard warriors didn't have to worry about our Afghan partners hiding in safe houses across Kabul and Kandahar, about the men and women who had publicly associated with Malala Fund, now trapped in their country as insurgents roamed the streets arresting and executing dissenters. They didn't live with the constant dread that their words could put people in even greater danger.

I might have looked calm on TV, but I was outraged. It made me angry that, after decades of using Afghanistan in their proxy wars and killing tens of thousands of civilians, the United States and its allies were leaving millions of women and girls at the mercy of the Taliban. In the early 2000s, President George W. Bush used girls' education to make the case for America's presence in Afghanistan. 'In helping the Afghan people rebuild their country, we have placed a central focus on education,' he said.

'Education is the pathway to progress, particularly for women.' Twenty years later, when President Donald Trump began negotiating with the Afghan government and the Taliban on the US withdrawal from the country, women – who had the most to lose – were not even allowed in the room. Now, under President Joe Biden, the US was leaving Afghanistan with no guarantees on women's rights or girls' education.

Was the US government unable to predict this outcome? Or did they just not care enough to stop it? In my eyes, they exploited Afghan girls when they needed good PR and tossed them aside when the cost of staying in the country got too high.

I also seethed at Pakistani politicians who hailed the Taliban as liberators, using the conflict to hype their one-sided rivalry with America – and at the Afghan leaders who were reportedly fleeing their country for fancy houses in foreign cities, leaving civilians to be slaughtered.

Cowards, all of them.

And I was angry at myself for feeling blindsided and betrayed. All those years that had I stood on stages while people clapped and told me, through tears, how my story moved them – I had thought it meant that they wouldn't let this happen to other girls. I believed they would rise up to defend us. Only now, as the world sat back and watched while an entire country was handed over to the men who'd tried to kill me, did I realise I was wrong. While I will always be grateful for the support I received after the Taliban's attack on my life, it was wrenching to know that such an outpouring of sympathy was possible, and then watch as it failed to materialise for other girls.

When I was a child, I thought that if I spoke out, things would get better. Surely, once world leaders understood our problems, they would fix them. As a teenager and young adult, I learnt that the issues were far more complex. You had to advocate for every policy change and budget increase, sit through hours of negotiations to take a small step forward. Change was slow but steady.

Afghanistan shattered the promise of progress for me. For the first time, I realised the world was not committed to fighting for the rights of women and girls. The worst moment of my life had been not a turning point, but a pause – an opportunity for leaders to act appalled that the Taliban would dare to shoot a child, throw some money into girls' education, and then return to the business of growing economies and winning elections.

Later in the week, I went back to the hospital. Dr Hadlock took the stitches out and said I should start to see the improvements in my facial mobility as soon as the swelling went down. A few weeks at most. 'Congratulations, it's finally over!' she said. It should have been cause for celebration – nine years and dozens of procedures trying to fix my face were now behind me. But it felt meaningless in that moment. So we had repaired some of the damage from one Taliban bullet – what was that compared to the thousands of bullets raining down on Afghanistan, to the suffering of girls whose names we'll never know, whose cries will go unanswered?

On my last night in Boston, I climbed into bed and wept for the first time that week. My chest heaved at the thought of ten-year-olds learning they would soon become wives. I'd spent the last year deliberating over whether to marry a man I loved. Even now, I knew I had the power to walk away if I changed my mind before or after the wedding. I shuddered, picturing little girls held captive by their husbands.

I remembered the long, listless days of the pandemic when I'd yearned to be back at Oxford with my friends. How foolish that seemed in light of the lifetime lockdown facing young Afghan women, years upon years confined to kitchens and bedrooms, their dreams dying in slow motion.

When I was eleven years old, the Taliban began bombing schools in Mingora and throughout Swat Valley. Of the 1,600 schools that existed when they arrived, some 400 were destroyed and many more damaged; 70 per cent were girls' schools. They attacked teachers by splashing acid on their faces or gunning them down in the street – now they had a laptop with the names of hundreds of female teachers in Afghanistan. I cried harder, realising that we couldn't save all of them.

Between sobs, I struggled to breathe and my lungs burnt. A sharp, stabbing pain radiated through my ribcage. When the room began to reel, I saw images of bearded men carrying automatic rifles. *These are just thoughts,* I told myself. *They aren't real. They are just waves on a beach.* But they were real – I'd seen them on TV that day. My nightmares were alive and walking around in the world.

⤴

LESS THAN A month after taking control of Kabul, the Taliban prohibited girls from attending school past Year 7. Today, Afghan women are not allowed to attend university or hold a job. They are banned from public parks, gyms and swimming pools. If they leave their homes, they must cover their faces and bodies from head to toe and be accompanied at all times by a male chaperone. They must also remain completely silent, as they are forbidden to speak or sing in public. Afghanistan is now one of the only countries in the world where the suicide rate is higher for women than for men.

For months after the fall of Afghanistan, I thought about long nights in the Birmingham hospital, when I would lie awake imagining a conversation with the Taliban. If they would just sit down with me, I had thought, I could reason with them and convince them to end their reign of misogyny and violence. With the pen and notebook I kept by my bed, I wrote down the names of journalists I knew who might be able to broker a meeting and scribbled down talking points. Because the Taliban claimed that their rules and doctrine were 'true Islam', I planned to recite all the verses from the Quran that prove girls have a right to education. Then I would show them what a good Muslim I was by listing all ninety-nine names for Allah from memory. I thought they would be impressed by my arguments and moved by my commitment to God. Back then, I didn't understand that their ideology wasn't about faith, but about power and control. I didn't realise that they would never respond to openness and dialogue, especially with a fifteen-year-old girl.

As an adult, reflecting on those nights I spent planning for a meeting that would never happen made me wince a bit. But they also revealed how much I had grown – I could see the Taliban for what they were now, and I knew that we would not defeat them with reason or compromise. The women risking their lives to protest on the streets in Kabul knew it too – and I wanted to stand with them, to amplify their voices, to follow where they led.

I thought back to my last year of university, when all my friends were lining up jobs and applying to grad school, while I waffled about what to do with my life, which path to pursue. At times, these thoughts were egocentric and self-obsessed. Becoming so famous so young left me feeling washed up at twenty-four, searching for ways to prove that I was still worthy of attention, still capable of commanding a room. The fall of Afghanistan clarified all of that for me. I had choices that millions of young women had just lost. To agonise over my place in the world seemed immaterial.

My purpose is the same today as it has always been – I will continue to advocate for girls, to do everything in my power to ensure they can choose their own futures. For me, there is no career path, no ladder to climb. I can only keep trying to make progress.

When I was young and full of hope, I used to say that I wanted to see every girl in school in my lifetime. I don't know if that will happen – most of the time, I feel it won't. But for every day that God gives me, you will find me working in service of that dream.

38.

Neither Asser nor I wanted a grand, expensive wedding; we'd both seen those events that seemed more about proving how much money the couple's families had than celebrating the relationship. So we decided to hold a small *nikah* at my parents' home in Birmingham – a simple ceremony where the bride and groom confirm their wish to wed in front of an imam, then sign the marriage contract. It takes less than five minutes; after that, the union is legal under Islamic law. We settled on mid-September, but the day after Asser landed in the UK, my mother's eldest brother died of Covid. She booked a one-way ticket to Shangla and packed a suitcase big enough for the forty-day mourning period. The wedding would have to wait.

While my mum was in Shangla for my uncle's funeral, Asser stayed at his sister's house, waiting for the wedding to be rescheduled and trying to appease his bosses at the Pakistan Cricket Board.

Once we'd announced the marriage, he planned to resign his position and move to England. To keep our relationship confidential until then, he had asked for ten days off work, telling his managers he needed to see his family in the UK. After he'd been away for three weeks, they were understandably getting impatient, asking why he had overstayed his leave period and when he would return. With a big match against India approaching, the team needed his help to analyse data and develop the best batting line-up against their rival's dangerous bowling line. He spent a lot of time calling in to meetings and working remotely, but he felt the chill from his bosses on the other end of the line.

Forty, forty-five, then fifty days passed since my mum had left. Sometimes I wondered if she was still unhappy about the marriage and planned to stay in Shangla until we gave up and called off the wedding. I still wasn't sure about her true feelings towards Asser, and I didn't know how to ask. During lockdown, I'd felt like I was getting close to my mum for the first time, but our progress had stalled in the year since. The benchmarks of adulthood, like graduating from university and getting engaged, had not reshaped our relationship as I'd imagined they would. All I wanted was for her to be happy for me.

On the fifty-third day, we got good news: my mum was coming home in a week. Asser and I decided that we would be married a few days after her return and jumped into action. We booked the imam, a photographer and a flight from Lahore for Farida, but I told my mum I would wait for her to help me pick out a dress. She said she would buy my outfit in Pakistan and bring it with her. I knew better than to argue.

She arrived bearing a dusty-pink shalwar kameez with gold embroidery at the sleeves and neck, and a matching dupatta. *It's perfect. I love it. Thank you, Mum.* I had pictured myself in something more modern, a simple silk dress with no embellishment.

But her selection was pretty, and the colour complemented my skin tone and hair. As I hung it up in my wardrobe, I thought, *This might be the last time she picks out my clothes. Maybe after the wedding, we'll be friends, two married ladies sharing a laugh.*

The day before the nikah, Asser and I went shopping to pick up a few final touches – a new pair of heels for me, a tie and pocket square for him. That evening my mum insisted on a dress rehearsal to inspect our clothes. She fussed with my headscarf and studied the jewellery – drop earrings and matching *maang tikka* headpiece – gifts from my soon-to-be mother-in-law. I also wore the custom wedding ring Asser had given me, a Swat Valley emerald set in a simple, delicate gold band. Every time I looked at it, I was amazed that he knew exactly what I wanted to wear on my hand for the rest of my life.

'You're fine,' she said, dismissing me and turning her attention to Asser.

In the time we had spent together, I'd mostly seen Asser in casual clothes. Now he stood before me in a midnight-blue three-piece suit, such a handsome and elegant man. I was proud of him and proud of myself for being someone he could love. He winked at me, and I smiled dreamily back at him. We were so lost in our own world that we didn't notice my mum staring at his shoes.

'His shoes are not new,' she snapped at me in Pashto.

'You can go and change – looking good!' I said to Asser, sensing what was coming and trying to spare him.

'Everyone knows you must have new clothes for a wedding,' my mum continued. 'What did he buy? Not shoes. Shirt? Suit?'

'Mum, it's fine. He looks nice.'

'What is new?' she demanded.

'Only the tie, I think. He already owned everything he needed. But why does it matter?'

'Oh, it doesn't matter? Why doesn't he wear pyjamas on the most important day of your life?' I held my tongue and looked at the floor, which only made her angrier. 'Does this guy not care about anything? Does he even care about you?'

I felt the tears forming and ran upstairs, already rationalising her reaction before I reached the first-floor landing. She grew up in a culture where even the poorest farmers were expected to spend several times their annual income on weddings; she was worried that people would criticise our low-key ceremony. She was tired after her long journey home from the funeral. She was frustrated by the language barrier that kept her from having a real conversation with Asser and his family. She was emotional about letting go of a child, and her sadness came out the wrong way.

I reminded myself that my mum meant well, that she only wanted to protect me. Over the years, I had learnt to let go of the things she forbade, to forget I'd ever wanted them – jeans, the high-school parties where I might have made friends, the freedom to smile for a photograph without thinking how it could be used against me. I loved her, so I tried not to love things that made her angry or scared. Whatever her reasons, she was not happy about the wedding – and I needed to fix it.

My hands trembled as I changed clothes, then went back downstairs and out to the garden where I knew Asser would follow me.

'Is everything okay?' he asked.

'I'm just curious why you didn't buy new shoes.'

He cocked his head, confused. 'Those are my special occasion shoes. I've had them for a few years, but only worn them two or three times and kept them polished. No reason to let them go to waste when they're practically new.'

'That's not the point – my mum says you're supposed to wear new things. She's an expert in—'

'—in men's shoes? Come on, Malala.'

When he laughed, my upper lip curled in disgust. 'It's not just the shoes. You should have got a new suit as well! New everything! People expect it *at a fucking wedding, Asser.*'

I sometimes used curse words in text messages for emphasis, but rarely in speech. Asser looked stunned. Then I dug deeper, kicking up enough dirt to fill the crater of pain my mum had created. 'I guess I'm just really surprised that your own family didn't bother to check your outfit. Was it too much trouble for them to make sure you are properly dressed?' As soon as I said it, I wanted to take it back. I loved Farida and Ambreena – but it was too late.

'I don't know what to say. I feel good in those clothes and they look nice, so I didn't see a reason to replace them. But I made that decision, so please don't blame my family.'

'Explain that to my mum. She thinks you don't care about me.'

His shoulders crumpled and his head fell. After a few moments, he drew himself back up with a deep breath. 'I can't really afford a whole new look right now,' he said on the exhale. 'The cricket board stopped paying me when I didn't go back to Lahore.'

. . . *What?* I scanned through his recent expenses in my mind – multiple round-trip flights, mandatory Covid tests, dinners out with my family, train fares to London, the wedding ring. My stab at sympathy came out as condescension. 'Why didn't you tell me? I would have paid for everything you need.'

'I think "need" is what we're debating right now. I would never ask you – or anyone – to buy things for me. It makes me uncomfortable, brings up memories of my dad and all the debts he never repaid. Also, it's . . . embarrassing?

'I have money in a savings account, but it's set aside to support my mum and help us buy a house someday. I don't use it to splurge on unnecessary things. And that's because I *do* care about you.'

Now I didn't know what to say. I wanted him to fight back, to justify my cruelty with his own. Or to beg for forgiveness, to promise he would secure suitable wedding attire by morning and never make my mum angry again for as long as he lived.

'Can I ask you something?' he said. 'Do you really care about the shoes? When you first saw my outfit, you were smiling and said I looked great.'

'I don't care, but it's not about what I think. People will notice and they will talk. Not just the people in the room but everyone who will see the photos online.'

'If people talk, I hope they will say how happy we are and how much I love you.' He walked back inside, said goodbye to my family and left. I didn't look up to watch him go.

That night I lay awake for hours, doubts circling above my bed, taking turns to dive-bomb into my brain. *Why didn't Asser tell me he was running out of money? What other secrets is he keeping? Will I ever make my mum happy? Is it too soon to get married?*

The advice Evelyn had given me, which once seemed soothing and optimistic, now felt like a curse. *Make the best choice you can with what you happen to know at the time. Don't look back and imagine that there were other better options.* It meant that I had to question everything before it was too late. Until the nikah was over, the decision to marry was open – I could make and unmake it a million times before morning. I could hold my own head underwater and drown myself in a sea of uncertainty.

I believed the problem was with Asser or with marriage itself, that my hesitation signalled danger. That night, I was only beginning to understand the truth: for my entire life, people had told me who I was and how I should act. They would not allow me to grow beyond their reach. They taught me not to trust my own choices. Now I felt paralysed anytime I tried to make one.

39.

At university, I was fascinated by hangovers and the way my friends woke up from them in various emotional states – confused and irritable, sheepish and self-loathing. The most compelling were those who got out of bed with a manic drive to redeem themselves. As soon as they could stand, they were deep-cleaning their rooms, taking five-mile runs with a pounding headache, planting themselves in the library and finishing a week's worth of essays.

On the morning of the wedding, I finally understood that reaction. As soon as I opened my eyes, I was overwhelmed with shame and disgust that I'd fallen asleep doubting Asser's love and my own mind. I came back to my senses, and they all seemed to tremble at the narrow escape. Normally I would wallow in an emotional assault like this, staying in bed for hours replaying my sins. But today I had a mission: I was determined to get married, if Asser would still have me.

I hesitantly picked up my phone, praying not to see a message saying that he'd changed his mind.

7:08 am

Asser

Morning!

7:09 am

Asser

I am soooooo excited!

7:32 am

Asser

Missing you! Can't wait to see you SOON!

7:56 am

Asser

Remember that I love you

Reading his messages filled me with joy at how much he cared about me and fresh remorse over the way I'd treated him the previous night. I replied:

Love you too. I'm sorry for the things I said. I pray to Allah to make this the happiest day of our lives.

8:14 a.m.

Asser

Let's get married

Maria was on her way over to help with the preparations and I texted her next: Bring the hair and make-up crew up to me. To

278

avoid potential distractions and derailments, I decided to stay hunkered in my room as long as possible, not realising I already had the house to myself. My brothers were still asleep, and my dad was out for a walk. My mum had gone shopping for new dress shoes for Asser – part peace offering, part chokehold.

'What do you think?' the make-up artist asked me an hour later.

I glanced at my reflection and said, 'Looks great, thanks.' I've never wanted to be vain or self-absorbed. After the shooting, I had spent so many years telling myself that it didn't matter how I looked that it was hard to admit, even to myself, when I felt beautiful. That day, I looked into the mirror and saw a young woman staring back who was glowing, confident, gorgeous. And more important than anything else: she was happy.

At noon I left to meet Asser and the photographer for wedding portraits at the Winterbourne House and Garden, a nearby arboretum. The first time the world saw us as a couple, we wanted to be surrounded by nature – trees and grass, not glitter and gold.

As soon as our eyes met, I knew I was forgiven for the things I'd said the night before. He took my hand and said, 'You're stunning, Malala.' I blushed.

We were both so relieved about the fight being over and giddy for our wedding day that we could not stop laughing during the shoot. We snickered at his new shoes slipping on the slick stone path, giggled at the security guards turning into bridesmaids as they tried to keep my dupatta from dragging on the ground. We laughed when the photographer asked us to stop laughing so she could get the shot.

I am sure the handful of people at our wedding could give more expansive descriptions of that afternoon, but the day was a blur to me. Here's what I remember: the imam said a few words. We signed the marriage contract. My dad cried. Farida beamed.

My mum smiled for the family portrait. Khushal and Atal brought out a supermarket sheet cake with *Malala & Asser* chicken-scratched in icing across the top. Everything was perfect.

Towards the end of the evening, the photographer pulled me aside to review 'selects', three dozen of her best photos from the day, the ones I might want to share when announcing the wedding.

The portraits took my breath away. There we were, tucked in a tall thicket of gemmy reds and quiet greens, looking like fairy-tale lovers on the last page of a picture book. In the next photo, we stood arm in arm under an arch of twisted hazel. We'd just been told to pull ourselves together, but the remnants of laughter lingered in our open-mouthed smiles. Then the two of us were glowing against a backdrop of autumnal-gold ginkgo leaves. The otherworldliness of the images somehow made them feel more real, as if they revealed a beauty you couldn't create with anything less than true love. The indisputable proof I'd sought for so long was right here in high-resolution.

I sat with the laptop, flicking through the photos until they became a choppy little film, the two of us turning in to face each other, out to face the world, and back in again. Then I stopped. 'This one. This is my favourite,' I said.

Asser and my parents drifted over to the couch where I sat next to the photographer. They peered down at the laptop to see the two of us standing on a wide swathe of lawn. A bright-orange maple tree appears in the background, framed like a flame between our bodies. I am looking up at Asser as he holds my left hand to his lips and kisses it.

'No, no, no!' my mum exclaimed. 'You cannot use it.'

She'd never seen a wedding portrait like this. In our culture, weddings are segregated – the men sit in the garden or the largest room of the house, eating a feast that their wives spent all day preparing. The women and girls pile into a smaller space with smaller plates of food. Photos are usually limited to the groom and his male relatives. On rare occasions when there is a picture of the new couple, they will be sitting side by side, several feet apart, not touching or even smiling. A photo showing any physical contact between a man and a woman, even a husband and wife, is prohibited. Where we come from, my parents are considered liberals, yet you will never see a picture of them holding hands or hugging.

I had said the photo of Asser and me was my favourite, not that I intended to make it public. But my mum's reaction made me wonder if it could, in its own way, announce my marriage as the true partnership that it was. After all, these rules weren't handed down by God. If people create culture, they can also change it. I wanted my community to see that men can show affection for their wives, that devotion and love are the highest forms of honour.

My mum shook her head, and my dad frowned. I looked at Asser. 'It's your decision,' he said.

With apologies to my parents, I shared the photo with the world.

40.

My world today is nothing like what I imagined as a child or even at university, when I pictured my adult self as a nun, dedicating all my time to good works. Nor is it what I feared when I worried about losing my autonomy if I got married. I still have reservations about marriage as an institution – and I probably always will. But my life with Asser is one of freedom and joy.

After the wedding, Asser resigned his job at the cricket board and started working freelance, which meant he could accompany me for speaking engagements and advocacy trips. As we travelled the world together, I found the grind of airports and living out of my luggage more enjoyable in his company. Everywhere we went, Asser insisted that we take time to check out local scenery or restaurants, something I'd rarely done in the past. He scheduled lessons in a sport I'd never tried, like pickleball, skiing or archery. To my surprise, I learnt that I'm a decent athlete. I particularly took to golf, and after six months of lessons, my husband couldn't take a round off me. These outings weren't just aimed at having fun; Asser showed me that taking a break, eating well, moving my body and getting enough sleep were critical to taking care of myself.

For a while, I worried that, as happy as I was travelling the world with Asser, I would lose touch with my friends. I didn't want to be a person who only hung out with her husband and other couples after marriage. Staying close to them wasn't easy, though, because we all had adult lives and responsibilities now. Many of my friends had moved away and taken jobs in other countries. So whenever they were back in town or in between flats in London, I invited them to crash at our place. In the first few years after our wedding, Asser often came home from a meeting or a workout to find me on the couch with one of my Oxford pals, eating take-away pad thai, binge-watching *Love Is Blind* and howling with laughter. I know he sometimes felt like a thirty-two-year-old man living in student accommodation, sharing a bathroom with a re-volving cast of my friends, but he rarely complained, remaining as patient with me as he had always been.

He needed an equal amount of patience to deal with my fam-ily. One afternoon he and I arrived home after several weeks away. Our flat in London overlooks the Thames, and I couldn't wait to plant myself on the couch with a cup of tea and watch the sun set on the water. As I stood in the kitchen flipping through the post, suitcase still at my side, Asser called my name from the bedroom. I walked down the hall and gasped at the sight: our tasteful, neutral-toned bed linens had been replaced by a teal-and-gold duvet set. There were tassels, beadwork, fringe trim, even velvet throw pil-lows featuring long, wispy peacock feathers. If you have seen Prin-cess Jasmine's room in the animated version of *Aladdin*, you have an idea of what we encountered that day.

It wasn't the first time this had happened. My mum frequently came over to our flat with a new rug or lamp and attempted to redecorate our space. 'You have to tell her not to do this any more,' Asser sighed. But he knew I wouldn't do it. As of this writing, I am twenty-eight years old and I still can't say no to my mum.

Of all our adventures in the first three years of marriage, my favourite was visiting Lahore, Asser's hometown. I'd only been there once before, when I was fourteen years old. It was a quick trip to give a speech and accept an award for standing up to the Taliban, and I didn't get to see the city. Through my friends at university, I had come to understand Lahore as the country's cultural capital, with thriving art and food scenes. But I was most excited about seeing the streets where Asser grew up and imagining the boy he used to be.

At Farida's house, I flipped through old photo albums, delighted by pictures of Asser as a fat, angry-looking toddler. A few of his extended family members stopped by to welcome us. When I heard a child refer to me as 'Auntie' for the first time, I nearly jumped out of my skin, surprised at the thought that anyone could see me the way I saw my own aunts. It took me a moment to comprehend that, to Asser's littlest relatives, I was just another grown-up, their favourite uncle's new wife.

Towards the end of our visit to Lahore, I was scheduled to give a speech at an event promoting the Oxford Pakistan Programme, a scholarship fund created by a few members of the old 24 Obs crew. I was so proud of my friends for starting this initiative and happy to give my time to help disadvantaged Pakistani students study at Oxford. On the day of the event, though, I looked in the mirror and noticed that my hair was a mess; the blunt fringe I'd given myself during lockdown two years ago was longer now and stuck out at odd angles. We had been on the road so much that I couldn't remember the last time I'd had a proper haircut. *Was it before Covid?* I wondered in dismay.

Maria, who was travelling with us, tracked down a local stylist who could come to our hotel, as security wouldn't allow an un-scheduled visit to a salon. As I sat listening to the quiet snip of the scissors on my wet hair, I couldn't stop smiling to myself, surprised by the contentment and joy I felt at doing something as ordinary as getting a haircut in my homeland.

When we were back in London, I shared pictures from the trip on social media. In addition to many kind responses, my post triggered the usual round of hateful comments – 'traitor', 'bitch', conspiracy theories, insults about my clothing and appearance. One person wrote, 'Go away. This is not your home.'

That taunt would have hurt me a few years earlier, sending me into a spiral of trying to prove to myself and others that there was still a place for me in Pakistan. Now, though, I knew what home meant to me, what it feels like, how to recognise it. It is the first sip of chai at Farida's house in Lahore, and walks along the Bir-mingham canals with my mum. The mountains in Mingora, the rooftops of Oxford, the gardens of Islamabad, boats gliding along the Thames in London. It is sitting on the couch, laughing with my friends. It is falling asleep in my husband's arms, anywhere in the world. And no one can take that away from me.

41.

Whenever I experience a period of profound happiness, like my first months at university or first years of marriage, I know it won't last. It's not that I'm a pessimist – but after so much upheaval in my life, I never assume that things will stay as they are. When the change comes, I try not to be afraid and hope I can learn from it.

In December 2023, I was invited to deliver the 21st Annual Nelson Mandela Lecture in Johannesburg. Since I was a girl, Mandela had been a hero to me, and I wanted to honour his legacy by speaking out for women and girls in Afghanistan.

The Taliban had issued more than eighty edicts against the female population in the two and a half years since they had taken control of the country. Where women and girls had once been university students, government ministers, dentists and shop owners, now they were erased from public life and confined to their homes. The punishments for those who broke the rules ran from indefinite detention to forced marriage to being stoned to death.

In the months before I travelled to Johannesburg, Afghan activists had been pushing for gender apartheid to be included in the United Nations' new Crimes Against Humanity Treaty. It was, by no means, a perfect solution. Even if they were successful, the treaty would not put an immediate stop to the daily horrors facing Afghans. It did mean, though, that the Taliban and others who commit crimes against women and girls might someday face justice. South Africa was an important player at the UN, and I hoped my remarks would rally their leaders to our cause and bolster the treaty.

The speech went well. At a reception afterwards, politicians and influential women pledged their support, promising to use whatever means they had to help bring an end to the Taliban's reign. Their solidarity lifted my spirits, and I left the event feeling hopeful that together we might make some progress for Afghanistan.

At the hotel that night, Asser sat next to me in bed, looking up things to do on the second half of our trip – a short holiday in Cape Town. He suggested we take surfing lessons and visit a wildlife sanctuary called World of Birds. 'Can we not just sit on the beach for once?' I said, laughing. 'We're back in London in four days, and I need to store up some sunshine to survive the winter.'

'The things I'm suggesting are also outside,' he countered. 'You'll get sun either way. I think what you really want is to be lazy.'

'You know what? You're right. I *do* want to be lazy . . . starting now.' I kissed him goodnight, tucked myself into the sheets and closed my eyes.

I woke up a few hours later, my body soaked with sweat and my heart racing. When I sat upright, the room began to spin.

Breathe, I told myself. *Inhale seven, exhale eleven. Repeat.* I thought the breathing exercise had calmed me down – *You're fine, you just sat up too fast* – and went to use the bathroom. But as soon as my feet hit the ground, I felt like I was falling, like being trapped in a broken lift and plunging to my death. I dropped to my knees, crawled to the sink and reached for the tap, but couldn't stand up long enough to turn it on.

'Asser!' I shouted. He jumped out of bed and found me on the floor. He must have asked 'What's wrong?' but his voice sounded distorted, unrecognisable. Not being able to understand him, the person I loved most in the world, shocked and terrified me. I didn't even realise I was crying until Asser reached for a tissue and wiped my tears away.

The air pressure in the hotel room kept getting lower, as if I were climbing a mountain. 'Balcony!' I gasped, struggling to breathe. Asser ran to open the sliding door, then carried me outside. A warm, thick breeze wrapped around me. I could see the treetops and stars; the night was quiet and still. *It's okay, you're fine.* Then a threatening tightness crept across my chest. I assumed it was from being held, from my body compressed and folded up in Asser's arms. 'Inside,' I pleaded.

He laid me on the bed and my legs began to shake uncontrollably. Asser tried to hold them still, but then my arms trembled and flailed. That's when he grabbed the phone and called for paramedics. As he spoke, I watched all the colour drain from his face.

The medical team arrived quickly, checked my vital signs and gave me water with electrolytes. The shaking eventually stopped, and I lay on the bed depleted and self-conscious. 'We can't find the problem,' the paramedics said. They asked Asser questions about potential food poisoning, medications I was taking, allergies and pregnancy.

But I knew what it was. The only panic attacks I've had since university have involved Afghanistan. Not a day goes by when I don't read something about the horrors that women and girls there are living through. I never scroll past them, no matter how painful it is. If I can do nothing else, I will be a witness to their suffering and their courage.

When I see images of women being beaten in the streets or read about girls who are confined to their homes and losing hope, my own violent memories come crashing through the barriers again, the walls that my mind built to keep them out. It was easier for me when my story was in the past, a thing that happened once years ago, a tale of uncommon brutality by evil men. Sometimes, when I think about it happening today to millions of Afghan women and girls, my body tears itself apart with grief.

42.

The first time I went to therapy, I imagined it would be like tightening a screw – a quick fix for the bad thoughts rattling in my brain. When I started to feel better, I put the flashbacks and panic attacks behind me, not wanting to dwell on terrible times when there was so much happiness in my life.

After Johannesburg, though, I called Evelyn and made an appointment. I didn't want to wait like I had at Oxford, hoping it would resolve itself on its own. I knew I needed to face the problem before it got worse.

When I stepped into her office, I felt at peace in the familiar setting. There was the same sofa, the side table with a glass of water waiting for me, the soft lighting. I remembered the first time I saw this room – how I was desperate for help, but sceptical and nervous about therapy; how much I eventually learnt from it.

'Malala, it's good to see you again,' Evelyn began. 'I'm glad you called. How can I help?'

I recounted my recent panic attack, the way it caught me off guard, the intensity of it. The breathing exercises hadn't worked, and I didn't understand how I could've gone to sleep feeling content, only to wake up in such overwhelming terror. 'It's like I've lost control again,' I said. 'I mean, I feel fine now, but I don't like knowing that this could happen at any moment.'

'I'm very sorry to hear this, but not surprised,' Evelyn said. 'Mental health is a journey – certain times are easy and others more challenging, just like the rest of our lives. Were you feeling a lot of stress on the trip to Johannesburg?'

'I wasn't stressed at all. My speech went well, and Asser and I were going on a beach holiday the next day. I was happy.'

'Can you think of any other triggers that might have been present for you at that time?'

My stomach lurched, and I realised I'd have to say it out loud: 'It's Afghanistan. And it's the shooting. My shooting.'

Evelyn folded her hands and leant towards me. 'Do you remember several years ago when we spoke about PTSD?' I nodded. 'In this case, we have to treat the source, not the symptoms. Breathing exercises and learning to recognise triggers can help manage anxiety and, sometimes, interrupt panic attacks. But those are symptoms of PTSD, not the cause.

'Trauma lives in our bodies, and it stays there until we process it,' she continued. 'Our brains work hard to keep us from reliving a difficult experience, using disassociation and repression to try to protect us. Unfortunately, that gets in the way of healing. We have to acknowledge and understand our pain before we can move past it.

'The good news is that there are several types of treatment. Before you leave today, I'm going to give you some information to read on EMDR, somatic therapy and trauma-focused cognitive therapy. We can talk about the options in our next session.'

'Will I ever get rid of PTSD? Will I be "cured" at some point?' I asked. My old resistance to therapy welled up in me. Maybe I'd prefer to take my chances with an occasional panic attack than spend an hour every week talking about my past.

'That's a great question, but not one I can answer, I'm afraid,' Evelyn replied. 'Recovery is certainly possible, but the timeline can vary from person to person. And some people will have symptoms throughout their lives, though treatment can help to reduce them.'

'My life is so happy now – and it's hard to look back.'

'Processing does not mean constantly dwelling on painful memories. But when we acknowledge trauma in a safe environment, it helps us to regulate our nervous system and stress responses, leading to better physical and mental health. The goal is to build resilience and give you more freedom to fully experience all the wonderful things in your life.'

I thought of Asser and how frightened we had both been in that hotel room. If there was something I could do to get better, I knew I had to try.

～

TALKING WITH EVELYN became part of my weekly routine, no matter where I was in the world. We didn't always discuss trauma, as I learnt that therapy is for more than healing old wounds, more than a fire alarm to be pulled in emergencies. Evelyn also helped me with the day-to-day stresses that piled up in my life. Through our sessions, I got better at setting boundaries with my family, recognising when I needed some alone time and communicating my needs to the people in my life.

A few years earlier, I'd rolled my eyes anytime someone mentioned self-care. To me, it seemed self-indulgent and silly, a hobby for people who didn't have any real problems. But the longer I spent in therapy, the more I realised how my physical and emotional well-being affected my mental health and ability to function in my daily life.

Evelyn might say I became 'proactive' about taking care of myself; my friends would call it 'nerdy'. I started tracking my sleep every night – not just total hours, but efficiency, heart rate and body temperature. A nutritionist helped me balance my diet, swapping out chips and pad thai for fresh fish and vegetables. I'll admit, I was pouty at mealtimes for a while, but noticed I felt less sluggish and irritable throughout the day. When I looked in the mirror one morning and saw that my skin was clear and glowing, I knew I could learn to love salmon.

In January last year, I set a secret goal of running on the treadmill for an hour without stopping. At first I could only make it two or three minutes. But I kept showing up at the gym, trying to increase my stamina a little bit each time. One morning in September, I got on the treadmill and just kept going – fifty minutes, one hour, an hour and five minutes. *This is incredible! How far can I go?* I wondered. Starting out, running was just about not giving up. Then I wanted to achieve more and more. When I ran, my body was no longer something I feared, but my teacher, revealing all the possibility and strength inside me.

⌒

I HAD LESS success in learning to swim. My muscles tensed up every time I got in the pool and my hands slapped wildly at the water instead of gliding through it. My mind was calm – I just couldn't figure out how to tell my body not to fight. Even in the shallow end, some part of me imagined I would drown.

In a similar way, the panic attacks can feel like a betrayal. After all I've lived through – displacement, violence, physical pain, loneliness, hate – why must I continue to suffer? No matter how much therapy I do or how well I take care of myself, I know someday I might feel the tightness in my chest or the pulse in my ears again. But I've come to understand these episodes as a beacon, a reminder to be gentle with myself, to protect my heart and mind, to resist the urge to shoulder so many burdens alone. To trust that I will continue to change and grow.

At my third swimming lesson, my instructor stood next to me as I tried to float. My legs were stiff, teeth clenched, toes curled. 'Allow yourself to relax,' she said. 'You won't be able to float until you believe that the water will hold you.'

43.

I looked down from the helicopter as it hovered above the landing site, a white circle chalked in the dirt. This was the moment I had been imagining for years, the dream I carried wherever I went, the prayer I whispered at night before bed: Shangla.

Finally I was going to see the school I'd built, meet the students and teachers, and talk with the first girls about to graduate – the first young women to complete high school in these villages. As Asser reached for my hand to help me out of the helicopter, I remembered what I'd said to him about Shangla on our very first date: *I'll take you there someday.* I could hardly believe that we were now here.

The dirt road that led to the school was bounded by mountains on one side and a steep drop into the valley on the other. Deep potholes could send the car tumbling down into the river if we drove too fast. Several times a year, classes were suspended when rainy-season landslides or winter snow made driving too dangerous.

Above and below the road, mud houses were built into the mountainside like mushrooms growing up a tree trunk. My dad grew up in a house like this, without electricity or plumbing, nine people in two rooms. I tried to picture him walking this road as a teenager, going to school, out to the fields to tend the buffalo, to the mud mosque to pray with his father. At night he hovered over his books with a kerosene lamp, determined to make it to university. Forty years later, many children here did the same.

In the distance, I could see the walls around the school, twelve feet high and topped with barbed wire, an ugly necessity in a place too familiar with terrorists and thieves. Driving through the metal gates, though, was like entering another world. For years I had pored over photographs of this place. My heart fluttered to finally see it for myself, bigger and more beautiful than I ever imagined. It was a sprawling three-storey complex, with white stucco walls and a bright-blue metal roof – a miracle of construction in such a remote and challenging landscape.

In every corner of the campus, girls in their green gingham uniforms were walking to classes, shouting to their friends, playing basketball or reading quietly on the lawn. After seven years in operation, the school now had seven hundred students and forty teachers. When I set out to build the school, people told me that parents in the region wouldn't support education for their daughters. Now our applications exceeded the number of desks available. I've never been prouder of anything in my life.

'Welcome!' the principal said with a big smile. She seemed so proud that we were visiting, as if we were doing them a favour when this day had lived in my imagination for years. As we followed her across the courtyard to the main entrance, I was eager to step inside, but anxiety pecked at the corners of my mind. I had built up so many expectations for what this place could be, and I worried that the reality couldn't possibly match my vision.

I wanted the school to be a place where students didn't feel the limitations of the outside world, where they could dream about the future and believe in themselves. I also wanted to see that the deficiencies in my own education, the things lacking for most Pakistani girls, were remedied here. In schools across Pakistan, biology textbooks often come with the pages on human reproduction glued together so students cannot read them. The boys pry them apart with rulers, but girls wouldn't dare. Were the teachers here covering reproductive health? Did they talk about emotional well-being? Were the students encouraged to play sport and be physically active?

It wasn't acceptable for this place to be equivalent to the local boys' schools or 'good enough' for a forgotten, largely illiterate community. I wanted it to be a palace of learning, worthy of the girls' wildest dreams. *Your standards aren't realistic*, I told myself, trying to reset my hopes to 'low' and my facial expression to 'neutral'. As we stepped inside and began to look around, my eyes filled with surprised and happy tears. The school was everything I'd imagined and more.

The principal showed us a sunny library full of books and separate science labs for biology, chemistry and physics. From the corridors, we heard teachers giving lessons in Pashto, Urdu and English. We peeked in the art studio, where Year 5 girls in matching blue aprons were learning to sculpt, covered up to their elbows in clay. The middle-school girls were holding a chess tournament; I stopped to play for a minute and quickly lost the game to a twelve-year-old.

In my work, I visit schools around the world. They all look different, but every time I walk the halls, I feel like a child again. In Shangla, I wanted to put on goggles in the chemistry lab, sing with the choir, join the basketball team and gossip with the older girls at lunch. I thought of my friends when we were young, how Moniba would have been thrilled to take an art class, how my cousin Nazneen would have checked out every book of poetry in the library. Some of my tears were for us, imagining how we would have thrived in these gleaming halls.

The principal showed us the back garden, where the girls were planting and raising trees, a programme aimed at combating rampant deforestation in the region. Then we saw the daycare, which the school provided for the teachers' younger children; it helped in recruiting top educators from all over Pakistan, especially women. We toured the large assembly hall, where all students start the day with free breakfast – eggs, toast and milky tea – to ensure they have a full stomach before going to class.

When we passed a room labelled COUNSELLOR'S OFFICE, I poked my head in to see a woman with a heart-shaped face and big brown eyes. She had the look of a sympathetic older sister or young aunt, and told me she'd moved to Shangla from Lahore to be part of the faculty. I asked a few questions about the mental health services she offered to students. 'It is the first, and so far only, counselling programme of its kind in the entire province of Khyber Pakhtunkhwa,' she told me. I knew that was true; when I was a child, having a therapist in a school would have been considered absurd.

The final stop on my visit was a meeting with the 'pioneer batch', the twenty-five girls who would graduate in the spring. We sat in a circle outside on the lawn, and I looked at each of their faces, so bright and eager. I began by asking them to tell me what they loved best and least about the school, and how we could improve it for the girls who came after them. They all said they loved their teachers. About a third ranked mental health training as the best part of their high-school education. 'We can talk to the counsellor about anything we want,' said Hira, the top student in the class. Then she got a conspiratorial glint in her eye and confessed, 'Sometimes she even takes us outside into the woods and tells us to scream as loud as we can!' I could imagine how profound that release must be for girls who lived in a society that disapproved of women expressing their emotions.

'If you're accepted into university next year, what do you hope to study? What are your dreams for the future?' I asked.

The answers worried me: doctor, doctor, cardiac specialist, army doctor, neurosurgeon, programmer. So many Pakistani parents push their children towards medicine or engineering, unable to imagine or accept other professional paths. I thought of Moniba's dream to be a fashion designer and how she'd set it aside for medical school. I wanted these girls to know that no matter what path they chose, their education would have value.

A girl named Eman fiddled with her fingernails and brushed her hair out of her eyes. 'Honestly, I don't know,' she said. 'I'm so moody and I change my mind all the time.' I swallowed a laugh and gestured for her to continue. 'I just want to be a good person, and I'm not too concerned about my profession.'

'Well, university is the perfect place to learn all you can and see what sparks your interest,' I told her. 'You don't have to have all the answers right now. Just be open to new experiences and ideas when you leave this school.'

I looked at each of them as I continued, 'I know how hard it is to go against thousands of years of tradition and believe that your life can be different. Because of you, other girls in Shangla will see what is possible for their own lives.

'But that can also lead to a lot of stress. You might find yourself thinking, "My parents allowed me to study, so now I have to perform at the highest level." But you don't need to get the best marks or be a perfect person to prove yourself worthy of your rights – they belonged to you from the moment you were born.'

The principal walked over and said it was time to go, as the school day was almost over, but I wasn't ready. There was so much I wanted to ask the girls, more I wanted to say. Were they hurt when their mothers were overbearing or unkind? *Remember that your world is new and unknown to them – and they're afraid of losing you.* What did they think of love and marriage? *If you choose to marry, I hope you find someone who tells you jokes as you drift to sleep at night and clears the dinner plates, a partner who will love you and support your dreams.* Were they worried about losing touch with their friends when they went to university? *Keep them close, as they will always carry a piece of you and help you find your way when you feel lost.*

I wanted to tell them that I understood how easy it is, especially when you're young, to get caught up in an idea of yourself. You might inherit an identity and feel obliged to carry it, even as it crushes you. You may be certain of your path and have every step planned out. It's hard to imagine your allegiances, ambitions and desires will ever change.

But someday when you don't expect it, the river may rise and carry you away to a new place. You can try to fight it, swim upstream, cling to the rocks on the shore. *It's safer to stay here*, you think. *To hold on to what I know and who I'm supposed to be.* I had those thoughts too, before I understood we are always changing, always growing into an uncertain future.

Let go, I wanted to say. *Trust the water to hold you, trust yourself to float.*

OVER THE LAST decade, people have often asked me if I would give up my current life to go back to a time before I was attacked. If I could wave my hand and erase the shooting from history, would I want to be the old Malala, knowing what I know now? Would I exchange fame and relative wealth, all my awards and achievements, for the anonymity of life in rural Pakistan?

It's an odd question, and I don't really understand why people ask it. Are they trying to test my goodness and humility? Or do they want to prove that their lives of airports and washing machines are so enviable that I would choose being shot in the head to gain what they have?

For years, I answered yes – I would give up everything to go back. To see my parents surrounded by their lifelong friends. To finish high school with Moniba. To hold my grandmother's hand as she grew old. Who knows what my life would've been like, in that parallel universe? I might've had a job and my own apartment in a city like Lahore, spent my weekends watching cricket matches and meeting my friends for tea. But more likely, my life would be difficult – a never-ending effort to mollify men who felt entitled to determine my future.

As Asser and I walked back to the car to leave, I contemplated these phantom timelines, and what remains when your world is turned upside down. I stopped for a moment to wave goodbye to the school, breathe in the pine-scented air and look up at the massive White Mountain, covered in snow all year long.

A few minutes into our drive, I spotted the narrow path to Abai's house. 'Please stop,' I said to the driver. He hesitated, eager to get further down the road before it filled up with buses taking the schoolgirls back to their villages. 'I just need a moment,' I promised.

Cut around the rocks and through the forest, the trail led to a sunny clearing in the foothills. As a child, I leapt off the bus that carried my family from Mingora to Shangla, and ran up the path as fast as I could. But on this trip, I took my time, observing the light breaking through the branches and listening to the muffled crack of pine needles under my feet.

On the right side of the clearing, I found her burial site, a small mound of soil surrounded by wildflowers. Seeing her name on the headstone made it real: Abai was no longer here. Yet I felt her spirit all around me, in the warmth of the sun on my face and the memory of her sleeping under the stars.

Kneeling by the grave, I spoke to her. 'Thank you for all your prayers and for everything you taught me. You won't be surprised to hear that I still haven't learnt to cook . . . but I did get married! You were right about that, and I think you would like him. Today I visited the school, and it was incredible. I wish you had been there with me. The girls would make you laugh – they're a lot like me at that age. Please watch over them and keep them safe. I love you, Abai.'

I sat there for a little while, watching the flowers tilt in the warm breeze. When I stood up, I could see the school off in the distance. Girls were spilling out of the gates, singing and laughing, walking arm in arm or racing each other to the bus. Their voices echoed around the mountains and down to the valley. I smiled at how loud they were, unafraid to fill the air with their high-spirited songs, bursting with determination and joy.

Walking back down the trail, I was grateful for the mountains and Abai's meadow, comforted that the places I loved in my child-hood remained the same. But I didn't feel sad that I couldn't stay in Shangla. Listening to the chorus of girls in the distance, I changed my answer to the question people always asked me: no, I wouldn't go back to my old life. I would not trade this life for anything. Whatever I have lost or gained, the path that led me here is the one where I belong.

Acknowledgements

I love to read. Sometimes, when I come to the last page of a book, I linger for a while, trying to avoid the head rush that comes with leaving the author's world and returning to my own. If you've just finished *Finding My Way*, can we have one more moment together? I want to thank you for spending time with me, for letting me tell you my story and introduce you to all the people and places I love. If we meet someday, I hope I can return the favour.

Writing this book was a journey of healing in itself. I could not have done it, especially the tough parts, without Taylor Royle being there with me. You have helped me write for many years, and have been beside me on my journey since I was seventeen. When I decided to write this book, you were the only person I felt comfortable with to help me share my story, and I feel so lucky for our friendship.

To my editors – Jenny Lord at Weidenfeld & Nicolson and

ACKNOWLEDGEMENTS

Kate Napolitano at Atria Books – thank you for your kindness, enthusiasm and patience throughout the writing process, and for believing in me and my story. Getting a book from an idea in your head to readers' hands requires the dedicated work and talents of many people. To the team at Weidenfeld & Nicolson in London – Susie Bertinshaw, Aoife Datta, Steve Marking, Lily McIlwain, Francesca Pearce, Hennah Sandhu, Nick Shah, Lynsey Sutherland and Virginia Woolstencroft – I'm so grateful to each of you.

To my literary agents, Albert Lee and Meredith Miller, who made this process so fun and exciting from start to finish. Thank you for each emoji and gif, for the last-minute phone calls and long lunches. I love working with you. To everyone at United Talent Agency who helped with this book: Margaret Alisberg, Sophie Baker, Brittany Balbo, Melissa Chinchillo, Eddie Clemens, Edwin Garcia, Katie Harrison, Charlotte Perman, Zoe Neely, Ethan Schlatter, Sam Solomons, Isaiah Telewoda, David Zedeck, and my longtime agent and friend, Darnell Strom.

I know that there are memoirists who write only from their own memory, photographs, diaries – but I forget things too easily and needed a lot of support to fill in the details in this book. My friends and family spent hours going through text messages, Snapchat videos, file cabinets and notebooks to help me find the answers. I can't thank them enough for giving so much of their time throughout the writing process.

I would also like to thank current and former colleagues at Malala Fund, the Shangla school and my personal team who pitched in: Lena Alfi, Amanda Cosby, Mubashir Hassan, Hannah Orenstein, Leila Seradj, Tess Thomas and Danielle Wivell-Wagner. Maria Qanita – few things in my life are possible without you, including this book.

My friends brought laughter, youth and a sense of home back into my life. I wish I had enough space in this book to share what each and every one of them mean to me, but, at the very least, I would like to tell you their names: Bilal, Ellen, Gabriella, Haroon, Jess, Kia, Maahnoor, Maham, Mehroz, Minahil, Munirah, Nina, Saad, Sarah, Shazil, Talha, Vee, Zahra. Thanks as well to the understanding adults who guided me in and out of Oxford: Mrs Coley, Margaret Coombe, Natalie Quinn, Fiona Spensly, my tutors and my therapist.

To Moniba and the Mingora girls who were my first friends – you knew me before I knew myself, and I carry you with me wherever I go.

To my mum and dad – thank you for loving and protecting me. I am so glad to have parents who keep trying to understand me as I change and grow. To my brothers – I am proud of the men you are becoming . . . but I could always be prouder, so keep trying!

Thank you to my husband Asser, my cheerleader and the first reader of this book. Everything in my life changed when I met you.

To Afghan girls, Shangla girls and every child around the world struggling to go to school and follow their dreams: you are never alone. People you may never meet believe in you, in your right to education, in your future. Do not lose hope.

About the Author

Malala Yousafzai is an education activist, the youngest-ever Nobel laureate, bestselling author and an investor in women's sports. She was born in Mingora, Pakistan, in 1997 and graduated from Oxford University in 2020.

RAISING READERS
Books Build Bright Futures

Dear Reader,

We'd love your attention for one more page to tell you about the crisis in children's reading, and what we can all do.

Studies have shown that reading for fun is the **single biggest predictor of a child's future life chances** – more than family circumstance, parents' educational background or income. It improves academic results, mental health, wealth, communication skills, ambition and happiness.[1]

The number of children reading for fun is in rapid decline. Young people have a lot of competition for their time. In 2024, 1 in 10 children and young people in the UK aged 5 to 18 did not own a single book at home.[2]

Hachette works extensively with schools, libraries and literacy charities, but here are some ways we can all raise more readers:

- Reading to children for just 10 minutes a day makes a difference
- Don't give up if children aren't regular readers – there will be books for them!
- Visit bookshops and libraries to get recommendations
- Encourage them to listen to audiobooks
- Support school libraries
- Give books as gifts

There's a lot more information about how to encourage children to read on our website: **www.RaisingReaders.co.uk**

Thank you for reading.

hachette
UK

---

[1] National Literacy Trust, Book Ownership in 2024, November 2024
https://nlt.cdn.ngo/media/documents/Book_ownership_in_2024

[2] OECD. 2021. 21st-century readers: developing literacy skills in a digital world. Paris, France: OECD Publishing.
https://www.oecd.org/en/publications/21st-century-readers_a83d84cb-en.html

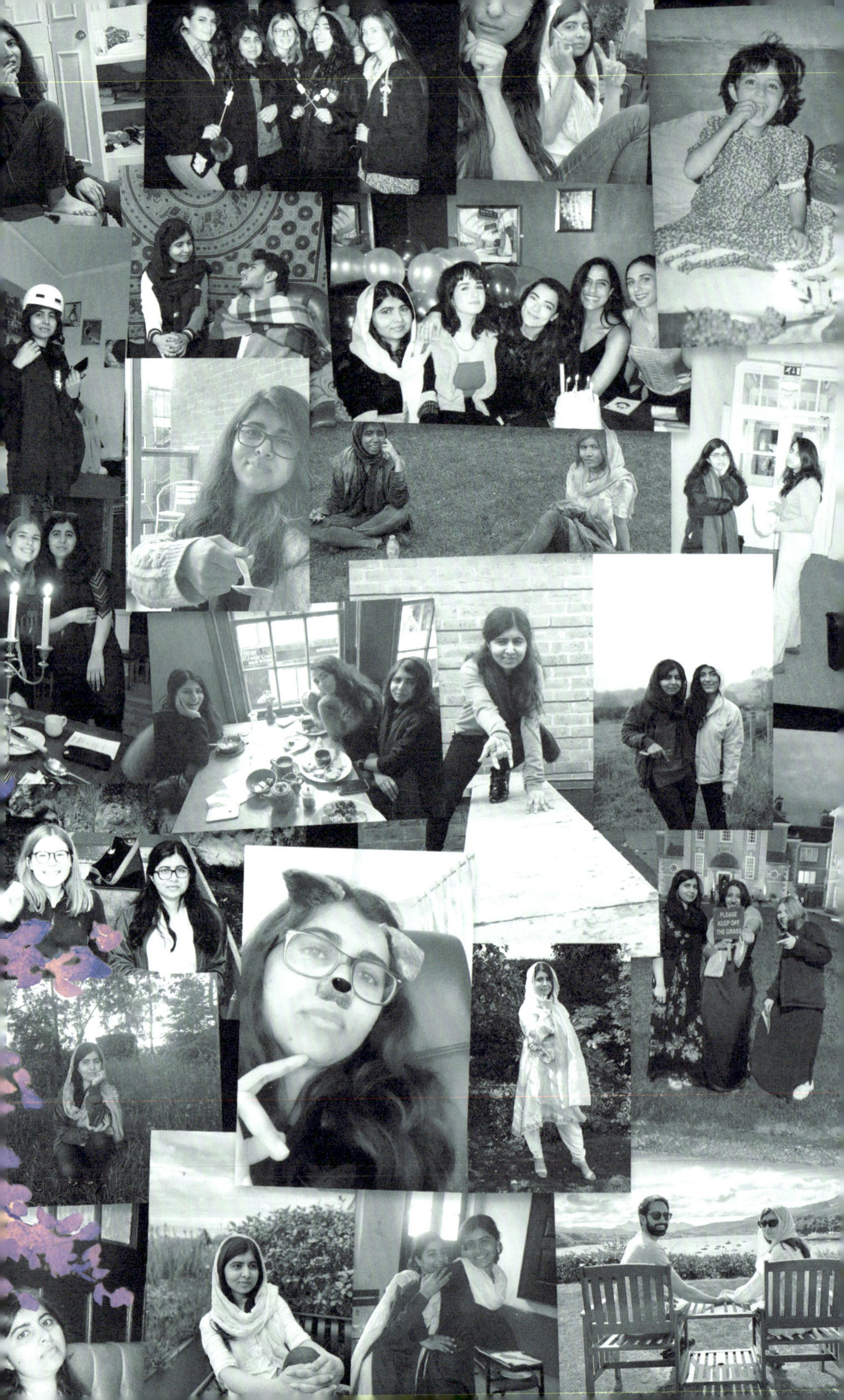
PLEASE
KEEP OFF
THE GRASS